Windows 7 Annoyances

Windows 7 Annoyances

David A. Karp

O'REILLY®

Beijing · Cambridge · Farnham · Köln · Sebastopol · Tokyo

Windows 7 Annoyances
by David A. Karp

Copyright © 2010 David A. Karp. All rights reserved.
Printed in the United States of America.

Published by O'Reilly Media, Inc., 1005 Gravenstein Highway North, Sebastopol, CA 95472.

O'Reilly books may be purchased for educational, business, or sales promotional use. Online editions are also available for most titles (*http://my.safaribookson line.com*). For more information, contact our corporate/institutional sales department: 800-998-9938 or *corporate@oreilly.com*.

Editors: Laurel Ruma and Julie Steele
Production Editor: Kristen Borg
Proofreader: Kristen Borg

Indexer: Lucie Haskins
Cover Designer: Karen Montgomery
Interior Designer: David Futato
Illustrator: Robert Romano

Printing History:

May 2010:   First Edition.

ISBN: 978-0-596-15762-3

[LSI]   [2010-11-10]

1289268696

Table of Contents

Preface

Why Am I Annoyed?

They say no one should see how sausage or laws get made, and I feel the same is true for software.

Imagine a windowless room in a nondescript office building. Inoffensive tan carpet lines the floors, fluorescent lights hum softly overhead, and 20 seated Microsoft employees flank a rectangular folding table in the center of the room. On the table rests a Windows PC, and at its helm, a slack-jawed cipher punches blindly at the controls in a vain attempt to carry out a task requested by the team leader.

"OK, here's the next exercise: transfer a photo from this digital camera to the PC and then upload it to the Internet," says the leader.

The observers—members of Microsoft's User Research Group—diligently note each click, key press, and hesitation, hoping they'll learn the answer to the industry's big secret: why do so many people find computers difficult to use?

With this system, Microsoft has uncovered many startling facts about PC users over the years, and the software you use has been changed accordingly. For instance, people new to computers apparently have a hard time with the concept of overlapping windows. (Did I say "startling?" I meant "idiotic.") So now we have the Glass interface with translucent borders that sort of show stuff underneath, AeroSnap, which pulls windows to the edges of your screen as you drag them around, and a new Alt-Tab window which makes all your windows vanish if you hesitate too long. Of course, most people new to PCs figure out the concept of stacking windows after about 10 minutes of fiddling, so are these gizmos effective solutions to a genuine usability problem, or just glitzy affectations included to give those still using XP a compelling reason to upgrade?

Another common problem is that people have a hard time finding their stuff, which is why every Windows Explorer window has a search box in the upper-right. But the search tool in Windows 7 doesn't work particularly well—it's slow, the search results are often incomplete, and the interface is clumsy—so what exactly have we gained here?

Here's another one: lots of people seem to get lost searching through long menus for the tools they need, so once again, Microsoft snapped into action. The team's first attempt was "personalized menus"—a user-interface disaster included in earlier versions of Windows (including XP) and Microsoft Office—which caused about half the items in a menu to vanish so *nobody* could find them. Subsequently, Microsoft took a different tack and removed the menus altogether. At least you'll no longer get lost in menus; of course, you won't be able to find anything, either.

Hundreds of design decisions are made this way, and if that's all we had to worry about, Windows would be annoying enough. Now consider the "Strategy Tax," the concept that a company like Microsoft has so many strategies to juggle that its products suffer as a result. For instance, the Strategy Tax is why Windows still doesn't include an antivirus program, why Internet Explorer is still unsafe at any speed, and why there are six different editions of Windows 7.

Take *content protection*, Windows 7's copy-protection initiative for so-called premium content like high-definition movies from Blu-Ray and HD DVD discs. According to Microsoft's standards, software and hardware manufacturers are supposed to disable "premium content" across all *interfaces* that don't provide copy protection. One such interface is the S/PDIF digital audio port—usually in the form of a TOSlink optical plug—that comes on most high-end audio cards. Since S/PDIF doesn't support copy protection—meaning that you could theoretically plug it into another PC and rip the soundtrack off an HD movie—Windows 7 requires that your TOSlink plug be disabled whenever you play back that HD movie on your PC. As a result, you'll only be able to use your analog audio outputs when watching HD content, and that expensive sound card you just bought is now trash. Why would Microsoft hobble an important feature? For you, the consumer? Of course not. Windows 7's content-protection feature is intended to appease piracy-wary movie studios, so Microsoft won't be left behind as the home theater industry finds new ways to rake in cash. And ironically, Microsoft boasts content protection as a feature of Windows 7.

Would Microsoft be making decisions like these if it weren't so beholden to its corporate strategy? After Europe's second-highest court upheld a ruling that Microsoft had abused its market power and stifled innovation, Neelie Kroes, the European Union competition commissioner, stated that "the court has confirmed the commission's view that consumers are suffering at the hands of Microsoft."

So that leaves us lowly Windows 7 users with a choice: do we continue to suffer with the shortcomings of Windows, or take matters into our own hands?

Of Bugs and Features

The point of this book is to help you solve problems. Sometimes those problems are the result of bad design, such as the aforementioned shortcomings of Windows 7's search tool, and sometimes the problems are caused by bugs.

Take the *Blue Screen of Death*, a Windows mainstay for more than a decade. Yes, it's still alive and well in Windows 7, but now it has a cousin: the *Green Ribbon of Death*. As explained in Chapter 2, the Green Ribbon of Death—capable of bringing Windows Explorer to its knees—comes from a combination of poor design and bugs in its code. And thus the reason for distinguishing where an annoyance becomes clear: you need to know what you're dealing with in order to fix it.

The User Account Control (UAC) feature in Windows 7 is a perfect example of a feature gone awry. Most of the time, UAC does precisely what it was designed to do—prevent programs from doing harm to your PC, occasionally asking your permission when it deems it appropriate to do so—but the result is a system that frequently bothers you with UAC prompts (although mercifully less than Vista) while intermittently breaking older applications without telling you why. Because this behavior isn't caused by a bug per se, fixing the problem is instead just a matter of tweaking a few features to better suit your needs.

This inevitably leads to an important conclusion: one person's annoyance is another's feature. Although Microsoft may be motivated more by profit than excellence, often leading to products designed for the lowest common denominator, you're not bound to that fate. In other words, you should *not* be required to adjust the way you think in order to complete a task on your computer; rather, you should learn how to adjust the computer to work in a way that makes sense to you.

But I prattle on. Feel free to dive into any part of the book and start eliminating annoyances.

How To Use This Book

Windows 7 Annoyances is not documentation; you can get that anywhere. Rather, it's a unique and thorough collection of solutions, hacks, and time-saving tips to help you get the most from your PC.

Although you certainly don't need to read the chapters in order, the solutions and chapters are arranged so that you can progress easily from one topic to the next, expanding your knowledge and experience as you go. You should be able to jump to any topic as you need it, but if you find that you don't have the proficiency required by a particular solution, such as familiarity with the Registry, you can always jump to the appropriate section (Chapter 3, in the case of the Registry).

There are nine chapters and two appendixes, as follows:

Chapter 1, *Get Started with Windows 7*
> Get the low-down on what's special about Windows 7 and what's annoying. Learn how to install (or reinstall) the operating system in a variety of scenarios, how to set up a virtual machine, and how to get the Ultimate edition goodies if you're stuck with a lesser version.

Chapter 2, *Shell Tweaks*
> Customize Windows Explorer, the desktop, the Start menu, and the Search tool to be less annoying and more useful. Then, uncover a host of window management tricks and shortcuts, improve the Search tool, improve your experience with multiple monitors, and put the kibosh on the green ribbon of death.

Chapter 3, *The Registry*
> Dive inside Windows' giant database of settings and system configuration data, and learn about the various tools you can use to explore, hack, and manage this valuable resource. Protect your file types, export settings to other PCs, and back up your registry.

Chapter 4, *Video, Audio, and Media*
> Make Windows better at playing videos, displaying color, recording TV, organizing photos, and burning CDs and DVDs.

Chapter 5, *Performance*
> Speed up your PC and get it to work better. Get Glass on older PCs, start your computer in less time, make your laptop battery last longer, and manage your hard disk space.

Chapter 6, *Troubleshooting*
> Learn what to do when Windows won't start, when applications crash, and when Windows can't set up your new hardware. Deal with the Blue Screen of Death, get shadow copies to work, and finally fix that nagging printer problem.

Chapter 7, *Networking and Internet*

Get your local network up and running, get your wireless working (safely), and connect to the Internet. Once you've connected, close all of Windows 7's backdoors, and then improve your experience with the Web and email.

Chapter 8, *Users and Security*

Protect your privacy and your data with permissions, encryptions, and user account management. Tame the User Account Control (UAC) prompt, customize your login, share your files and printers with others on your network, and find out why easier is not always better with Homegroups.

Chapter 9, *Command Prompt and Automation*

Automate Windows, Command Prompt Batch files, Task Scheduler, and the Windows PowerShell. Explore the good ol' DOS commands still used in the Command Prompt, not to mention the times when Windows won't start.

Appendix A, *BIOS Settings*

This is a brief glossary of the often-neglected motherboard settings that can significantly affect the stability and performance of your PC.

Appendix B, *TCP/IP Ports*

Look up common network port numbers, used to identify data traveling on a network (or over the Internet), and essential for configuring and securing your network.

Conventions Used in This Book

The following typographical conventions are used in this book:

`Constant width`

Indicates text you're supposed to type, output from a command-line program, code examples, Registry keys, and paths to Registry keys.

`Constant width italic`

Indicates user-defined elements within constant-width text (such as filenames or command-line parameters). For example, Chapter 8 discusses a file encryption utility, *cipher.exe*, which has a variety of command-line options. A particular solution might instruct you to type:

```
cipher /r:filename
```

The italicized portion of this code, *filename*, signifies the element you'll need to replace with whatever is applicable to your system or needs. The rest—the non-italicized portion—should be typed exactly as shown.

Bold

Identifies captions, menus, buttons, checkboxes, tabs, clickable links, keyboard keys, drop-down lists and list options, and other interface elements. Bolding interface elements makes it easy to distinguish them from the rest of the text. For example, you may wish to turn off the **Force Windows to crash** option. Window/dialog titles are typically not bolded, nor are OK buttons or error messages.

Italic

Introduces new terms, indicates website URLs, and sets apart file and folder names.

Italic is also used to highlight Chapter titles and, in some instances, to visually separate the topic of a list entry.

{Curly braces}

Denote user-defined elements in paths or filenames, e.g., *C:\Users\{username}\AppData\Roaming\Microsoft\Windows\Start Menu*.

"Quotation marks"

Are used sparingly in this book, and are typically used to set apart topic headings and emphasize new concepts. Note that if you see quotation marks around something you're supposed to type, you should type the quotation marks as well (unless otherwise specified).

Path Notation

The following shorthand path notation is used sparingly to show you how to reach a given user-interface element or option. The path notation is always presented relative to a well-known location. For example, the following path:

Control Panel→Date and Time→ Internet Time tab

means "Open Control Panel, then open **Date and Time**, and then choose the **Internet Time** tab."

Keyboard shortcuts

When keyboard shortcuts are shown, a hyphen (such as **Ctrl-Alt-Del**) or a plus sign (Winkey+**R**) means that you should press the keys simultaneously.

 This is an example of a tip, often used to highlight a particularly useful hint or time-saving shortcut. Tips often point to related information elsewhere in the book.

This is an example of a warning, which alerts you to a potential pitfall of the solution or application being discussed. Warnings can also refer to a procedure that might be dangerous if not carried out in a specific way (or if not carried out at all).

Using Code Examples

This book is here to help you get your job done. In general, you may use the code in this book in your programs and documentation. You do not need to contact us for permission unless you're reproducing a significant portion of the code. For example, writing a program that uses several chunks of code from this book does not require permission. Selling or distributing a CD-ROM of examples from O'Reilly books does require permission. Answering a question by citing this book and quoting example code does not require permission. Incorporating a significant amount of example code from this book into your product's documentation does require permission.

We appreciate, but do not require, attribution. An attribution usually includes the title, author, publisher, and ISBN. For example: "*Windows 7 Annoyances*, by David A. Karp. Copyright 2010 David A. Karp, 978-0-596-15762-3."

If you feel your use of code examples falls outside fair use or the permission given here, feel free to contact us at *permissions@oreilly.com*.

Request for Comments

Please address comments and questions concerning this book to the publisher:

O'Reilly Media, Inc.
1005 Gravenstein Highway North
Sebastopol, CA 95472
800-998-9938 (in the United States or Canada)
707-829-0515 (international/local)
707-829-0104 (fax)

You can also send messages electronically. To comment or ask technical questions about this book, send email to:

bookquestions@oreilly.com

The O'Reilly website has a section devoted especially to this book, on which can be found errata, sample chapters, reader reviews, and related information:

http://oreilly.com/catalog/9780596157623/

For extra tips, additional software, and user-to-user discussion forums, visit:

http://www.annoyances.org/

For more information about books, conferences, software, Resource Centers, and the O'Reilly Network, see the O'Reilly website at:

http://www.oreilly.com/

Safari® Books Online

Safari Books Online is an on-demand digital library that lets you easily search over 7,500 technology and creative reference books and videos to find the answers you need quickly.

With a subscription, you can read any page and watch any video from our library online. Read books on your cell phone and mobile devices. Access new titles before they are available for print, and get exclusive access to manuscripts in development and post feedback for the authors. Copy and paste code samples, organize your favorites, download chapters, bookmark key sections, create notes, print out pages, and benefit from tons of other time-saving features.

O'Reilly Media has uploaded this book to the Safari Books Online service. To have full digital access to this book and others on similar topics from O'Reilly and other publishers, sign up for free at *http://my.safaribooksonline.com*.

Acknowledgments

I'd like to start by thanking the folks at O'Reilly Media, Inc. It's a supreme pleasure to work with people who are dedicated to quality and are passionate about their work. Special thanks to Tim O'Reilly for his enthusiasm, support, and commitment to quality. Thanks to Julie Steele, Laurel Ruma, and Kristen Borg for helping me get this edition together.

Thanks also to Aaron Junod, Tony Northrup, and Chris Williams for their comments, and thanks to everyone on the team who worked on this book.

I'd like to thank my family, friends, and well-wishers—in that they didn't wish me any specific harm—all of whom put up with my deadlines and late-night writing binges.

Finally, all my love to Torey and our beautiful son, Asher.

CHAPTER 1

Get Started with Windows 7

Windows 7 is like a pumpkin: handsome and plump on the outside, but a big mess on the inside. So get out your knife and start carving.

Now, there was a lot in 7's predecessor, Windows Vista, that Microsoft got right, or almost right. But face it: Windows 7 exists because of everything that was wrong with Vista.

First and foremost, Windows 7 is faster than Vista, and by some accounts, faster than XP on the same hardware. The staggeringly annoying User Account Control (UAC) system is still around, but is slightly smarter, in that it doesn't interrupt you quite as often, and more customizable than when it debuted in Vista. And beginner-level networking is theoretically easier with Homegroups, provided everyone in your house, condo, office, commune, or wikiup drinks the Kool-Aid and upgrades to Windows 7 (and doesn't care much about security).

The new taskbar holds icons for open applications and those not yet running side by side, much like the dock in Mac OS X (which is itself an adaptation of the NeXTstep dock from the 1980s). Better yet are the "jump lists," handy shortcut menus that appear when you right-click taskbar icons, replacing the useless 25-year-old system menus found in every preceding version. Windows 7 also throws in a bunch of crowd-pleasing window management shortcuts, like Aero Peek, Aero Snap, and Aero Shake, as well as some nifty features for those using multiple displays.

But it's not all lollipops and rainbows. For starters, upgrading from XP or an earlier version of Windows can be a chore if you don't know a few tricks. Microsoft made some stupid decisions when it came to security which you'll need to rectify to keep your data safe and your OS malware-free. Windows Explorer needs tweaking before it'll work reliably, and the Search feature is too slow and its results incomplete.

Windows 7 doesn't provide any convenient tools to associate more than one application with a file type or even customize file icons. The backup tool doesn't let you restore individual files from a complete PC backup, meaning that you have to back up your data *twice* in order to get complete protection. Sharing files with older PCs, non-Windows machines, and in some cases, even Windows 7 PCs can be needlessly frustrating. And the list goes on and on.

Fortunately, Windows 7 is pliable. UAC can be tamed. The Green Ribbon of Death found in Windows Explorer can be dealt with. The Backup and Search tools can be reconfigured to be more useful. You can hack up the Registry to protect Windows from itself and customize the interface in ways Microsoft never intended. And Windows 7's networking can do everything you need if you know where to look.

Think of it like carving a jack-o'-lantern: a little planning, hacking, and cleaning, and your face will light up!

Editions of Windows 7

Ironically, the internal version number of Windows 7 is version 6.1,* which implies that Microsoft considers its newest operating system to be a (relatively) minor revision of Windows Vista (version 6.0). This relationship is more or less accurate as it turns out, and is akin to that between Windows XP (internally, Windows 5.1) and its predecessor, Windows 2000 (Windows 5.0).

Windows 7 is available in six different editions, all targeted for different markets and carefully designed to give customers the illusion of choice. They're all the same version of Windows—effectively, the same software—differing only in some of the toys included in the box. Only three editions, *Ultimate*, *Professional*, and *Home Premium*, are available to the general public.

Home Premium lacks some of the data security, management, and networking features found in the *Professional* and *Ultimate* editions, but comes with the "premium" games (Chess Titans, Mahjong Titans, Purble Place) missing in *Professional*. Of course, *Ultimate* has it all; the only thing you lose with *Ultimate* is a little hard disk space (not to mention a large sum of cash).

On the fringe, you'll find the *Starter* and *Home Basic* editions, intended for so-called emerging markets, and the *Enterprise* edition, which has more or less the same feature set as *Ultimate* (minus the games and Media Player) but with volume-licensing for large corporations.

---

* Open a Command Prompt window (*cmd.exe*) and type **ver** at the prompt to see Windows' internal version number.

The specific differences between the three primary editions are outlined in Table 1-1. See the next section for ways you can make up the difference if you're not lucky enough to have the Ultimate edition.

Table 1-1. What you get (and what you don't) with the primary editions of Windows 7

	Home Premium	Professional	Ultimate
Aero Glass interface	✓	✓	✓
Backup and Restore	✓	✓	✓
Backup and Restore – Create a system image	✓	✓	✓
Backup and Restore – Network storage support		✓	✓
Create a Home Group	✓	✓	✓
Corporate tools (AppLocker, BranchCache, DirectAccess)			✓
Encryption – BitLocker drive encryption			✓
Encryption – file and folder encryption (EFS)		✓	✓
Fax and Scan	✓	✓	✓
Group Policy Editor (*gpedit.msc*)		✓	✓
Join a corporate network domain		✓	✓
Local Security Policy Editor (*secpol.msc*)		✓	✓
Local Users and Groups Manager (*lusrmgr.msc*)	✓	✓	✓
Location Aware Printing		✓	✓
Maximum physical memory (64-bit edition)	16 GB	192 GB	192 GB
Multilingual User Interface Pack			✓
Offline files and folders (sync with network folders)		✓	✓
Pen and Touch (Multi-Touch)	✓	✓	✓
Premium Games	✓		✓
Presentation Mode (Winkey + X)		✓	✓
Previous Versions (Shadow Copies)	✓	✓	✓
Remote Desktop Client	✓	✓	✓
Remote Desktop Host		✓	✓
Subsystem for Unix-based Applications			✓
Virtual Hard Disk Booting			✓
Windows Media Center	✓	✓	✓
Windows Media Player Remote Media Experience	✓	✓	✓
Windows XP Mode for Windows Virtual PC		✓	✓

Got Ultimate Edition Envy?

Got the Home Premium or Professional editions of Windows 7, and are considering forking over more cash to Microsoft for a "better" version? Not so fast! Here are most of the goodies included with Ultimate but missing in lesser editions, and how you can get them for free:

Back up to a network location
See "Preventative Maintenance and Data Recovery" on page 404 for information on using network storage with Windows Backup on the Home Premium edition.

BitLocker Drive Encryption, and the Encrypting File System (EFS)
The NTFS file system used by all editions of Windows 7 supports compression and encryption for individual files and folders, but the encryption feature is made unavailable in the Home Premium edition. If you want to encrypt files in Home Premium, try SafeHouse Explorer Encryption (*http://www.safehousesoftware.com/*) or Cryptainer LE (*http://www.cypherix.co.uk/*), both free.

BitLocker, included only with the Ultimate and Enterprise editions, is a method by which you can encrypt an entire drive (as opposed to the aforementioned folder and file-level encryption). Freeware alternatives for Professional and Home Premium include FreeOTFE (*http://www.freeotfe.org/*) and TrueCrypt (*http://www.truecrypt.org/*).

See Chapter 8 for the skinny on encryption.

Corporate tools
These tools are only available on the Ultimate and Enterprise editions of Windows 7, and are mostly of use to PCs in a corporate environment that uses Windows Server 2008 R2. Anyone who doesn't need to be constantly connected to a central server at a large company to do his or her work will likely be bored to tears by these tools.

AppLocker allows you to control which users can run certain applications; for instance, you can restrict a group of less-privileged users to only running apps by certain publishers (like Microsoft). You can download AppLocker for free from *http://www.smart-x.com/*. You can also accomplish this in a much more limited fashion with file permissions, discussed in Chapter 8.

BranchCache caches files and web content from central servers to improve performance when working on large-scale team projects on low-bandwidth connections. (There's no direct replacement at the time of this writing, aside from upgrading your Internet connection.)

DirectAccess allows you to connect a Windows 7 PC to a corporate network running a DirectAccess server. If you have a lesser edition of Windows, you can still set up a Virtual Private Network (VPN) connection, as explained in Chapter 7, to do something similar, albeit with more fuss.

Group Policy Object Editor

Several solutions in this book use the Group Policy Object Editor (*gpedit.msc*) to change a few esoteric settings, but this tool isn't included in the Home Premium edition. If the *gpedit.msc* file isn't on your system, you can access most of these settings with the net command-line tool (provided you open the Command Prompt in administrator mode), as explained in Chapter 8.

Local Security Policy Editor

The Local Security Policy tool (*secpol.msc*) provides access to advanced settings, the useful ones relating mostly to UAC; see "Control User Account Control" on page 569 for details and alternatives.

Offline files and folders

Offline Files is a caching feature, allowing you to work with files stored on remote network drives even when you're not connected. When you're reconnected, the files are synchronized invisibly. A free alternative for those using Home Premium is Microsoft's own Windows Live Sync, formerly FolderShare (*https://www.foldershare.com/*). There's also Microsoft SyncToy (*http://www.microsoft.com/prophoto/downloads/synctoybeta .aspx*) and SyncBack Freeware (*http://www.2brightsparks.com/*).

Presentation Mode

In the Professional and Ultimate editions, you can press the Windows Logo key (Winkey) and **X** to quickly disable the screensaver, set the volume level, and change your desktop wallpaper, all to make your PC more suitable for hooking up to a projector and giving a PowerPoint-ish presentation. (It's worth noting that this feature is only available on laptops through the Windows Mobility Center page in Control Panel, and it's disabled by default.) In other words, Presentation Mode is nothing more than a shortcut, and one that may indeed duplicate similar features in presentation software you're already using. Users of Home Premium can easily accomplish the same thing through more traditional means (e.g., Control Panel). See Chapter 2 for more nifty Winkey shortcuts that work for everyone.

Remote Desktop

All editions of Windows 7 can control another PC remotely with Remote Desktop, but you'll need the Professional edition or better if you want your PC to be *controlled* remotely (act as the *host*) with Remote Desktop.

UltraVNC (*http://www.uvnc.com/*) is a free remote control package that works with any version/edition of Windows, or for that matter, Mac OS X, Linux, and even Apple's iPhone. See the section "Control a PC Remotely" on page 488 for details.

Subsystem for Unix-based Applications
Also known as Interix, this is basically a Unix and POSIX layer that allows you to run Unix software on your Windows 7 PC. Don't have the Subsystem for Unix-based Applications? Cygwin (*http://www.cygwin.com/*) does more or less the same thing, and is free for all versions of Windows.

Virtual Hard Disk Booting
If you use the Windows Backup tool to create an image of your hard disk as described in Chapter 6, you'll end up with a VHD (Virtual Hard Disk) file. VHD files are also used by Windows Virtual PC (see "Virtualize Whirled Peas" on page 30). In the Ultimate and Enterprise editions of Windows 7, you can boot your PC off a VHD file *without* using a virtual environment, effectively offering another means of multiple booting. If you have a lesser edition of Windows, you can do the same thing with multiple hard disk partitions, as described in "Set Up a Dual-Boot System" on page 26. See Chapter 6 for more on virtual hard disks.

Windows XP Mode
See the sidebar "Windows XP Mode" on page 33 for details on this feature, and how you can get basically the same thing in Home Premium.

64-Bit Windows

More bits gets you access to more memory, and more memory means a faster, smoother-running OS. The processor inside your PC communicates with your system memory (RAM) with numeric *addressing*. Thus the maximum amount of memory a 32-bit processor can address is 2^{32} bytes, or 4 gigabytes. Newer 64-bit processors—not to mention the 64-bit operating systems that run on them—can address up to 2^{64} bytes of memory, or 17,179,869,184 gigabytes (16 exabytes) of RAM. (17 million gigabytes may sound like a lot of space now, but it won't be long before you'll be taking baby pictures with a 9-exapixel digital camera.)

In reality, 32-bit Windows can only make use of about 3 GB of RAM before hitting a wall; see Chapter 5 for details.

Windows NT, released in 1993, was Microsoft's first fully 32-bit operating system. But it took eight years before the platform, which had since evolved into Windows 2000 and then XP, became mainstream. (For those keeping track, Windows 9x doesn't count because it was a hybrid OS that ran 32-bit applications on a 16-bit DOS foundation, which was one of the reasons it was so terribly unstable.) 64-bit Windows became a reality in XP, but Vista—and, by extension, Windows 7—was Microsoft's first serious attempt to take 64-bit computing mainstream. But the question is, how mainstream is it?

When Vista first hit store shelves in 2007, x64 computing was a hobbyist niche, barely registering on any radar. By the middle of 2008, Microsoft reported that 20% of new PCs connecting to Windows Update—mind you, that's *new* PCs, not *total* PCs—were using 64-bit Windows. Many of those machines were likely sold with 4 GB of RAM or more, necessitating Windows x64 to be pre-installed. But why isn't everyone using x64?

While 64-bit (x64) Windows can run nearly all 32-bit applications without a problem, it's not compatible with 32-bit hardware drivers or 32-bit utilities like Windows Explorer extensions (e.g., context menu add-ons). This means that you need native, signed 64-bit drivers for every device on your PC, which only recently have become commonplace. (In fact, for a product to be marked "Certified for Windows 7," it must be compatible with both 32-bit and 64-bit editions of the OS.) Of course, you still may have trouble finding support for older hardware, but isn't that always the case when you upgrade the operating system?

Now, native 64-bit software running on 64-bit Windows has been known to run as much as 10% faster, which illustrates the other reason—apart from memory addressing—that people find 64-bits alluring. But fully native x64 applications are still rare; even Microsoft Office is still natively 32-bits, with only a handful of x64 DLLs thrown in to make everything work smoothly on a 64-bit system.

 All 64-bit editions of Windows 7 require a 64-bit (x64) processor (both Intel and AMD make x64 CPUs). If you're not sure if your PC has an x64 CPU and you're already using Windows 7 or Vista, open the Performance Information and Tools page in Control Panel and click the **View and print details** link (available only after you've run a performance check). Otherwise, the free Securable (*http://www.grc.com/securable.htm*) utility works on any version of Windows. If you haven't yet installed any OS on your PC, use the "Processor Check for 64-Bit Compatibility (*http://www.vmware.com/*)" tool.

So, if you're on the fence about x64, let's make it simple. Unless you have fewer than 2 GB of RAM, a non-x64 processor, or some software or hardware product that won't work on 64-bit Windows, there's no reason to stick with a 32-bit OS.

All editions of Windows 7 (except Starter) are available in both the 32-bit or 64-bit varieties; the retail Ultimate edition even includes both 32-bit and 64-bit DVDs right in the box. If you have a 32-bit edition (other than Ultimate), you can get the 64-bit version of your edition (in the US, call 1-800-360-7561), and assuming your license key checks out, you only pay shipping. But beware: once you "convert" your license key to work with the 64-bit version, you won't be able to use it to reinstall the 32-bit version, should you decide to go back. (Thus you may want to try a virtual install first, as described in "Virtualize Whirled Peas" on page 30.)

Once you've got your 64-bit OS installed and functioning, it'll look and feel just like its 32-bit (x86) counterpart, with only a few minor quirks. See Chapter 2 for Windows Explorer considerations on 64-bit Windows, Chapter 3 for 64-bit registry issues, and Chapter 6 for troubleshooting 64-bit hardware and software.

Unless otherwise noted, all of the solutions in this book apply to both the 32-bit and 64-bit versions of Windows.

Install Windows 7

It used to be that installing an operating system was a dreadful experience. More specifically, it should be said that it was *always* a dreadful experience. Fortunately, things have improved to the point where installing Windows 7 is only occasionally dreadful. In fact, it's usually fairly painless, provided you have a relatively new PC, a true installation disc, and no data you care about on the target drive.

But what if you're upgrading and you don't want to ruin a functioning system? Or what if upgrading isn't an option, and you have to perform a clean install? Or what if setup halts halfway through with nothing more than a blue screen to show for your trouble? Or worst of all, what if setup is completely successful, and now all that awaits you is a bloated, buggy OS that you need to spend time optimizing and configuring? (OK, that last scenario is what the *rest* of this book is about.)

Microsoft took a somewhat odd approach with Windows 7's setup tool. Previously, you could install the latest Windows OS on top of just about any recent version, and the installer would perform an "upgrade." The process was convenient, in that anyone could upgrade Windows by simply popping in a disc, but the resulting system never worked very well because of all the detritus left behind by the previous OS. "Perhaps this was why everyone hated Vista," Microsoft reasoned, "so we'll just disable the upgrade feature in Windows 7." (Or maybe building an installer that actually worked was just too much trouble.)

Whether you're allowed to install Windows 7 over an older version or you're forced to perform a "clean install" is unrelated to the special pricing or licensing you may've gotten when you purchased Windows 7. In other words, just because you got an "upgrade" version of Windows 7 doesn't mean you can do an in-place upgrade over Windows XP.

So, can you do an in-place upgrade? If you have Windows Vista or a lesser edition of Windows 7 (e.g., Home Premium to Ultimate), see Table 1-2 to find out. If you have any other operating system, then the answer is no. Frustrating to be sure, but trust me: Microsoft is doing you a favor.

Table 1-2. Allowed Windows 7 in-place upgrade paths; no checkmark (✓) means you must perform a clean install

	Windows 7 Home Basic	Windows 7 Home Premium	Windows 7 Professional	Windows 7 Enterprise	Windows 7 Ultimate
Vista Home Basic	✓	✓			✓
Vista Home Premium		✓			✓
Vista Business			✓	✓	✓
Vista Enterprise				✓	
Vista Ultimate					✓
XP or earlier					

Furthermore, if you want to switch from 32-bit to 64-bit or vice versa, you must do a clean install. You'll also need to install clean if you're changing the core language, installing a hobbled version of Windows 7 (e.g., Windows N, Windows KN, etc.), or are upgrading from any beta or release candidate.

Install Windows on an Empty Hard Disk

Use this method to set up Windows on a brand-new, empty hard disk; if your PC already has a Windows installation, even if it doesn't support an in-place upgrade, skip to the section "Upgrade from a Previous Version of Windows" on page 18.

The Windows 7 installation disc is bootable, which means that you can pop it in your drive, turn on the computer, and the installation process will start automatically.

If your PC doesn't boot off your setup disc, you'll need to do one of the following:

BIOS setup
> Enter your BIOS setup utility (see Appendix A), navigate to the **Boot** section, and change the **boot device priority** or **boot sequence** so that your DVD drive appears *before* your hard disk. Save your changes and exit BIOS setup when you're finished.

Boot menu
> Alternatively, some PCs provide a "boot menu" that lets you choose the boot drive on the fly. Look for a message above or below the boot screen right after you power on your PC; usually, all you do is press the **F12** key—before the beep; don't dawdle—select your CD/DVD drive from a list, and hit **Enter**.

When your PC detects a bootable disc, you'll usually see this message for three to four seconds:

```
Press any key to boot from CD or DVD . . .
```

Press a key on the keyboard, and in a few moments, setup should load normally and display its Welcome screen. (See the section "Boot Without a Boot Disc" on page 15 if you can't boot off the Windows setup disc.)

On the first screen, click **Next** to display the Install Windows screen shown Figure 1-1. From here, click **Install now** to proceed.

On the next page, setup asks for your product key, which you can read off the DVD sleeve or the sticker on your PC case. Mercifully, Microsoft allows you to skip this step—leave the field blank, click **Next**, and then answer **No**—so you don't have to waste time fishing around for the sticker and typing the excruciating 25-digit key, only to have setup laugh at your propensity for typos. This is a particularly useful time-saver if you're only setting up a temporary installation for software testing or data recovery.

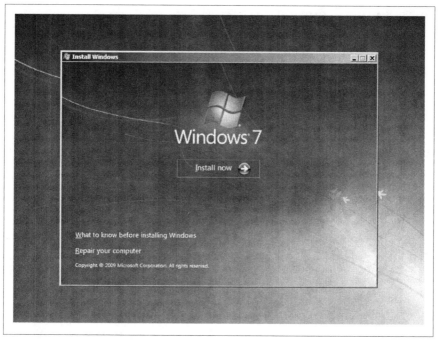

*Figure 1-1. From this page, click **Install now** to begin setup, or **Repair your computer** to use the repair tools explained in Chapter 6*

 If you complete setup without typing your key, make sure you choose the edition of Windows 7 for which you actually own a license. If you choose the wrong edition, you won't be able to change it later without reinstalling from scratch. When Windows boots, it'll operate in a fully functional "evaluation mode" you can use normally for 30 days. If you don't enter a valid product key for the edition you chose during setup in time—through the System page in Control Panel—Windows goes into a lockdown mode. (See "Install clean with only an upgrade disc" on page 13 for a way to extend this evaluation period.) So, if this installation ends up being a keeper, don't put this step off, lest you risk giving yourself a nice big headache.

A few pages later, you'll be asked "Which type of installation do you want?", at which point you can select **Upgrade** or **Custom (advanced)**. The **Upgrade** option is only for performing an in-place upgrade from Windows Vista; try it with an earlier version like XP, and setup will display an error and then start over.

So click **Custom (advanced)** to advance to the "Where do you want to install Windows?" page, and then click the **Drive options** link to reveal the partition editor shown in Figure 1-2. See Chapter 5 for more information on partitions and the tools included with Windows to manage them.

If the hard disk is clean and you want to use the entire hard disk for your installation, just click **Next** to proceed. Otherwise, use **Delete** to wipe out any existing partitions—as well as the data on them (*warning:* there's absolutely no undo here)—and **New** to create new partitions on the drive. See Chapter 5 for more on partitions and the reasons you might want more than one.

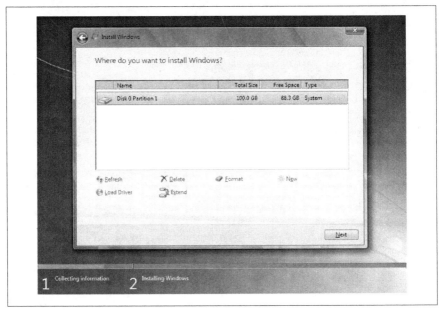

*Figure 1-2. Click the **Drive options** link to show these drive preparation and partition editing tools*

 Windows 7 setup creates a 100 MB "System Reserved" partition when you install on a blank hard disk (Professional edition or better). To keep this from happening and use your *entire* hard disk for the Windows installation, see "Prevent extra partitions during setup" on page 14.

Follow the screens to complete setup. If setup crashes along the way, or Windows won't boot after you're done, see the section "Fix Problems with Windows Setup" on page 25.

Install clean with only an upgrade disc

So you thought you'd save a little money by purchasing the "upgrade" version of Windows, but now you find yourself in a bit of a jam. Your hard disk crashed, and without a full backup (see Chapter 6), you need to rebuild your system. Or perhaps you've decided against an in-place Vista upgrade to avoid passing on two years of accumulated junk to your new operating system. Either way, you've undoubtedly discovered that your upgrade disc won't install if it can't find an eligible Windows installation to upgrade.

In this scenario, Microsoft suggests that you install Vista and then install Windows 7 over it. Not bloody likely.

Instead, just follow these steps to get a fresh Windows 7 installation from an upgrade disc:

1. Use your Windows 7 disc to boot your PC, as described in "Install Windows on an Empty Hard Disk" on page 10.

2. When setup loads, click **Install now** and proceed normally.

3. When prompted for the product key, leave the field blank, and just click **Next**. Without the key, setup will ask you which edition of 7 you'd like to install; make sure you choose the edition you actually own.

4. When setup is complete, you'll be operating in the 30-day evaluation period, but you won't be able to activate 7 until you enter your product key.

    To enter the product key, open a Command Prompt window in administrator mode, as explained in the section "Control User Account Control" on page 569, and then type this at the prompt:

    ```
    cscript \windows\system32\slmgr.vbs -ipkxxxxx-xxxxx-xxxxx-xxxxx-xxxxx
    ```

    where *xxxxx-xxxxx-xxxxx-xxxxx-xxxxx* is your Windows 7 product key, taken from the DVD sleeve or the sticker on your PC case. Press **Enter** to proceed.

     If this doesn't work, you may need to temporarily deactivate the UAC feature as described in Chapter 8, and then try again. Then, reactivate UAC when you're done (should you so desire).

5. Next, activate Windows with this command:

    ```
    cscript \windows\system32\slmgr.vbs -ato
    ```

    and press **Enter**. To verify that activation was successful, type this:

    ```
    cscript \windows\system32\slmgr.vbs -dlv
    ```

6. Type `exit` or close the Command Prompt window when you're done.

 Using a process known as *rearming*, you can extend the evaluation period up to two or three times, for a total of 120 days. Just execute the *slmgr.vbs* script with the `-rearm` parameter. It will take 15–30 seconds to make the change, at which point you'll need to restart Windows.

Prevent extra partitions during setup

When you install Windows 7 (Professional, Ultimate, or Enterprise editions) on an empty hard disk, setup creates an extra, hidden 100 MB partition. It's used for BitLocker drive encryption (see Chapter 8), although BitLocker works fine without it. It also holds a copy of the Windows Recovery Environment so you can repair Windows without having to fish out the setup DVD, as described in "What to Do When Windows Won't Start" on page 355.

 If you're installing on a hard disk that already has partitions with data, if you have the Home Premium edition, or you don't mind the extra partition—admittedly, 100 MB isn't much by today's standards—then you can skip these steps.

Since this is space you can never use for your own data, you can use the following procedure to keep this partition from ever being created:

1. On the "Where do you want to install Windows?" page (Figure 1-2) partition screen of Windows 7 Setup, click **Drive options (advanced)**. Delete any existing partitions (if applicable) and then create a new partition to fill the drive. See Chapter 5 for more information on partition management.

2. When Windows warns you, "To ensure that all Windows features work correctly, Windows might create additional partitions for system files," click OK.

3. At this point, you'll see two partitions:
   - **Disk 0 Partition 1**: System Reserved (System)
   - **Disk 0 Partition 2** (Primary)

   Highlight the **Primary** partition and then click **Delete**.

4. Next, select the **System Reserved** partition and click **Extend**. Type the maximum size available for the partition and then click **Apply**.

5. Again highlight the newly extended **System Reserved** partition and click **Format**.

6. When the format is complete, proceed to install Windows on the lone partition.

See Chapter 5 if you've already installed Windows and you wish to remove this partition.

Boot Without a Boot Disc

I still have a box of floppy disks in my closet, most of which are boot disks for old operating systems (Windows Me, Windows 95, DOS 6.2, DOS 4.0, etc.). Not a single one of my PCs still has a floppy drive, but each was such a hassle to create or obtain, I can't bear to part with them lest someone knock on my door one day with a 25-year-old IBM XT that won't start up.

Suffice it to say, it can be a real pain to boot a PC before any operating system is installed. Windows 7 comes on a bootable DVD, but if you have an older drive that doesn't support bootable DVDs, or if you don't have a working optical drive at all, what do you do? One method is to pull the hard drive from the PC and then use another PC to copy files from the Windows setup disc to a temporary folder on the drive. But that still leaves the question: how do you boot the PC so you can get to those files?

Or, what if Windows is already installed, but you need to accomplish a task you can't do from within Windows, such as updating/flashing your PC's BIOS, your video card BIOS, or your hard drive BIOS?

 If you're unlucky enough to be stuck with one of those BIOS update utilities that insists on writing files to a floppy drive, you can use the free Virtual Floppy Drive tool from *http://chit chat.at.infoseek.co.jp/vmware/vfd.html* to add a fake drive letter. Run your tool, and then use Windows Explorer to retrieve the files.

Fortunately, there are several "alternate" ways to boot a PC if, for whatever reason, you can't boot the conventional way: a network (PXE) boot, a bootable USB flash drive, and a bootable CD.

Set up a network (PXE) boot

Using your PC's built-in support for Preboot Execution Environment (PXE), you can place boot files on a shared folder on another PC on your network, and then boot the PC off of those files. Setting this up is a bit involved, but it's often simpler than using a boot disk.

To get started, you'll need a working PC with an Internet connection. Install the Windows Automated Installation Kit (WAIK), available for free at *http://go.microsoft.com/fwlink/?LinkId=136976*. Open the **Windows PE Tools Command Prompt** from the Start menu, and if you're installing the 32-bit edition of Windows 7, type:

```
copype.cmd x86 c:\output
```

or if you're installing the 64-bit (x64) edition, type:

```
copype.cmd amd64 c:\output
```

and press **Enter**. The batch file will create the *c:\output* folder automatically. When the files have been copied, issue this command to mount the Windows Preinstallation Environment (PE) image:

```
imagex /mountrw C:\output\winpe.wim 1 C:\output\mount
```

Next, open Windows Explorer and create a subfolder inside of *c:\output* named *boot*. Copy all the files from *c:\output\mount\Windows\Boot\PXE* to the new *c:\output\boot* folder. When that's done, unmount the Windows PE image:

```
imagex /unmount C:\output\mount
```

Back in Windows Explorer, copy the *boot.sdi* file from the WAIK installation folder to the *c:\output\boot* folder. If you're installing the 32-bit edition of Windows 7, get *boot.sdi* from *C:\Program Files\Windows AIK\Tools\PETools\x86\boot*, or if you're installing the 64-bit (x64) edition, get it from *C:\Program Files\Windows AIK\Tools\PETools\amd64\boot*.

Return to the command prompt window and copy the *winpe.wim* file to the *boot* folder and rename it to *boot.wim*, like this:

```
copy c:\output\winpe.wim c:\output\boot\boot.wim
```

After all that, there are a bunch of other tedious commands required to create a Boot Configuration Data (BCD) file using *bcdedit.exe*, the same tool used in "Set Up a Dual-Boot System" on page 26. For a shortcut, just download *makebcd.bat* from *http://files.creativelement.com/annoyances/makebcd.bat*, and run it on your PC. When prompted to cut and paste the GUID, right-click any part of the command prompt window, select **Mark**, select the text in curly braces just above the prompt, and press **Enter** to copy the text. Right-click again, select **Paste** to paste the text, and press **Enter** to continue execution. If all goes well, you'll only see a series of messages stating that "The operation completed successfully."

The last step is to install Trivial File Transfer Protocol (TFTP) server software, such as Tftp32 (free from *http://tftpd32.jounin.net/*) so the target PC can connect to the working PC to retrieve the boot files. Install Tftp32 and start *tftpd32.exe*. Click **Browse**, select the *c:\Output* folder and click OK to set it as the **Current Directory**. Next, choose the **DHCP server** tab, click **Help**, and fill out the fields as instructed. In the **Boot File** field, type boot.sdi. When you're done, click the **Save** button.

Now that the PXE server is set up, you need to enable PXE Network boot in your new PC's BIOS setup screen, as explained in Appendix A. You'll need the host name or IP address of the PC acting as the PXE server; see Chapter 7 for more on IP addresses, general networking tips, and troubleshooting.

Create a bootable CD

There are many ways to make a bootable CD, but to make a bootable Windows 7 CD, follow these steps.

1. First, install the WAIK, as described in the previous section. Open the **Windows PE Tools Command Prompt** from the Start menu, and if you're installing the 32-bit edition of Windows 7, type:

   ```
   copype.cmd x86 c:\bootcd
   ```

   or if you're installing the 64-bit (x64) edition, type:

   ```
   copype.cmd amd64 c:\bootcd
   ```

   and press **Enter**. The batch file will create the *c:\output* folder automatically.

2. Next, copy the Windows PE image file like this:

   ```
   copy c:\bootcd\winpe.wim c:\bootcd\ISO\sources\boot.wim
   ```

   and copy the imagex.exe tool as well:

   ```
   copy "C:\program files\Windows AIK\Tools\x86\imagex.exe" C:\bootcd\iso\
   ```

3. Finally, create the ISO (disc image) by issuing this command:

   ```
   oscdimg -n -bC:\bootcd\etfsboot.com C:\bootcd\ISO C:\bootcd\bootcd.iso
   ```

When the ISO file is ready, use Windows' own Disc Image Burner (*iso-burn.exe*) or a program like ISO Recorder (free from *http://isorecorder.alexfein man.com/*) to burn the ISO to a blank CD. Insert the CD and turn on your computer to boot. See the section "Install Windows on an Empty Hard Disk" on page 10 for tips on booting off a CD.

Create a bootable USB flash drive

A flash drive is the modern day floppy, so why not use it like one?

You'll be wiping the flash drive clean, so back up any data on the drive before you continue. With the flash drive inserted into a USB port, and your Windows setup disc in your DVD drive, make note of each of these drive letters.

 You'll need a flash drive of at least 4 GB, and one that plugs directly into a USB port. (In most cases, flash cards used for cameras are not suitable.) Also, only newer PCs can boot from flash drives; to see if yours can, check the documentation or snoop around your PC's BIOS for settings to enable this feature, as explained in Appendix A.

Next, open a Command Prompt window in administrator mode (see Chapters 9 and 8, respectively), and type diskpart to open command-line disk partitioning tool (discussed in "Work with Partitions" on page 328). At the *diskpart* prompt, type:

```
list disk
```

Look through the list and find the number assigned to your USB flash drive. Then type:

```
select disk n
```

where *n* is the number of your flash drive. Then type these commands in order:

```
clean
create partition primary
select partition 1
active
format fs=ntfs
assign
exit
```

to prepare the flash drive. When that's done, type:

```
d:\boot\bootsect.exe /nt60 u:
```

where *d:* is the letter of your DVD drive and *u:* is the letter of your USB flash drive. Finally, copy all of the files from the Windows DVD to the flash drive root (top-level) folder.

When all the files are in place, plug it into one of the target PC's free USB ports and use it to start your computer.

Upgrade from a Previous Version of Windows

In a departure from earlier versions, Microsoft has made it impossible to perform an in-place upgrade on any Windows older than Vista. (And XP users thought they were unhappy when *Vista* came out!)

This means you've got some work to do before you can install Windows 7 on a hard disk that already has an earlier version of Windows on it. (If you don't have anything of value on the drive and don't mind wiping it clean, check out "Install Windows on an Empty Hard Disk" on page 10 for instructions.) The good news is that there isn't much to do, despite what Microsoft would lead you to believe.

Reinstall Windows 7

You may find yourself in a position where you'll need to reinstall Windows 7, usually in an effort to solve a nasty problem or to repair a damaged installation. The procedure you choose depends on the state of your computer.

If Windows won't start, see the section "What to Do When Windows Won't Start" on page 355. In most cases, you'll need your original Windows setup disc, but you won't need to reinstall.

If you're able to start Windows and it's working well enough to reliably access your DVD drive, but poorly enough that you're considering reinstalling, then you'll need to decide whether to reinstall ("upgrade" as Microsoft setup puts it) or install a clean copy on your PC.

An in-place reinstallation is the easiest way to go, and despite the warnings in the previous section, probably won't make things any worse. Just pop the DVD in your drive and follow the prompts. When asked what type of installation you want, select **Upgrade** and then follow the prompts. But if your Windows installation is sufficiently munged, you may choose to install fresh without harming your existing installation, as described later in this section.

 Before you get started, it's a good idea to collect a few things that might be harder to get once you've begun setup. For one, put a Windows 7-compatible driver for your network adapter on a USB flash drive or CD, just in case Windows doesn't support your hardware and thus won't allow you to download the files you need. Also, since you're essentially doing a fresh install, make sure you have the installers for your most important applications. And if there's anything you absolutely can't live without, use Microsoft's Compatibility Wizard to see if you'll need to put off a Windows 7 upgrade until there's an update for your must-have application or device driver.

Now, if you're upgrading from Vista, you can technically use the **Upgrade** feature shown in Figure 1-3, but don't be fooled: it's not all it's cracked up to be. Sure, you won't have to reinstall all your applications—although many will need to be updated anyway to work with Windows 7—and you won't have to do any real prep work, but what you'll end up with may be slower and more buggy than it needs to be, all because of the junk left behind by the old installation. Now's your chance to start over with a clean slate—take it!

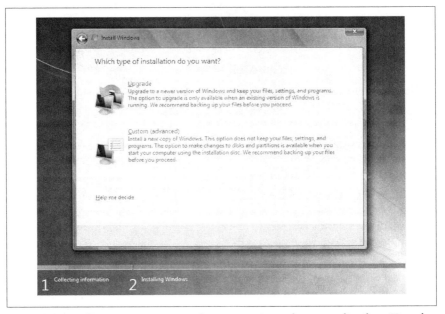

*Figure 1-3. Windows 7 setup gives you these two options when upgrading from Vista, but be warned: the **Upgrade** option is for suckers*

 One of the upgrade scenarios that Microsoft doesn't support—regardless of the version of Windows you're upgrading—is upgrading from 32-bit Windows to 64-bit (even from Windows 7 to Windows 7). So if you're considering taking the x64 plunge, right now is your best chance if you don't want to bother with yet another clean install in a few months. See "64-Bit Windows" on page 6 for details.

Microsoft's answer is to use the Windows Easy Transfer (WET) tool (formerly known as the Migration Wizard) to copy your personal files to an external hard disk, USB flash drive, or network drive, wipe your hard disk, and then install Windows 7. To do this, pop in your Windows 7 install disc and open Windows Explorer. Navigate to the *\support\migwiz* folder on the DVD, double-click *migsetup.exe*, and follow the prompts.

What gets transferred? By default, Windows Easy Transfer grabs most—but not all—of the stuff in your user account folder (*c:\users\{your user name}*), which includes your desktop, your *Documents* folder, your Internet Explorer Favorites, and a handful of application saved settings (e.g., iTunes library, Firefox bookmarks). It also collects most of the stuff in the *All Users* folder, which it calls **Shared Items**. To customize what is saved, click the **Customize** link next to any item in the **Choose what to transfer from this computer** list, and then click **Advanced**. On this Windows Explorer-like window shown in Figure 1-4, place a checkmark next to any folder or individual file you want to keep.

When you're done choosing files, Windows Easy Transfer compresses your files into a single *.mig* file, which you can save anywhere you like, presumably on a removable or network drive.

Figure 1-4. Microsoft suggests using the Windows Easy Transfer tool to save your personal files before wiping your hard disk clean in preparation for Windows 7

Once your data is safe, go ahead and install Windows 7, following the instructions in the previous section. When setup asks "Where do you want to install Windows?" (see Figure 1-2, shown earlier), you can delete the existing partition on your hard disk and then recreate it to ensure a totally clean install. (Keep in mind that any data not backed up with Windows Easy Transfer will be lost for good if you do so.) Or, just leave the partition intact, as described later in this section. As soon as Windows 7 is installed and running, just connect the drive and double-click the *.mig* file to restore your stuff.

So what's wrong with the WET approach? For one, it doesn't save all your files, only those in standard locations (like the *Documents*, *Music*, and *Pictures* folders) plus the ones you explicitly check off. Miss something and you might lose it. WET also doesn't save registry settings for your installed applications (e.g., settings, toolbars) or any of your custom file types (see Chapter 3). Don't be surprised if you lose your file encryption (Chapter 8) and shadow copies (Chapter 6). WET also doesn't transfer installed applications, but even if it did, you'd have to reinstall them anyway.

> To move registry data (including file types) from your old Windows to the new one, use registry patches, as described in Chapter 3.

Another problem with WET is that it requires that you move all the data you want to keep—which might be sizable—to another medium. Say you've got 675 GB of home movies and photos, another 60 GB of music, and 12 GB of business documents. You'll have to wait while WET tries to compress and consolidate all 747 GB of data, and then try to find a place to put the resulting 746 GB file. Don't have a 750 GB drive handy, and don't want to go buy one just for 3 hours use? Or maybe you just don't feel comfortable relying on a single piece of hardware and a potentially buggy program to safeguard your data?

But the biggest problem with WET is that it is largely unnecessary. Instead, why not do some Drive Reorganizing Yourself, or DRY? By going DRY, you simply take charge of migrating your own data so you can be sure that you've got everything and that it all ends up where you want it.

> Whether you do a WET or DRY upgrade to Windows 7, it's an awfully good idea to back up your entire hard disk first. That way, if there's some catastrophic problem with the upgrade—or you decide this PC isn't ready for Windows 7—you can restore the previous Windows installation and all your data in one step. But make sure your backup software is compatible with Windows 7, or you may not be able to get at any of your files.
>
> If you're upgrading from Vista (Business edition or better), you can use the Complete PC Backup and Restore feature in Control Panel to image the hard disk, allowing a full restore to the pre-upgrade state, or quick restore of individual files from within Windows 7 (see Chapter 6). Other editions and versions may require third-party backup software.

The **Custom (advanced)** installation type shown in Figure 1-3 is a workable choice for upgrading Windows XP and older machines, despite the explanation beneath it. In fact, the bit that reads, "This option does not keep your files, settings, and programs" is a flat-out lie. (It really means that it won't *migrate* your stuff.)

When you perform a **Custom** installation on, say, Windows XP, setup moves your old *Windows*, *Program Files*, and *Documents and Settings* folders into a new folder called *Windows.old* so it can install Windows 7 on the drive unhindered. Other folders (e.g., *c:\Dave's Personal Stash*) are left alone. None of your data is deleted, and provided you have enough free disk space (at least 11 GB), setup performs what's called a "parallel installation," where Windows 7 is placed alongside your old operating system.

A parallel installation isn't the same as a dual-boot setup. After installing Windows 7 in this way, the old version will no longer be bootable. If you want to keep both versions of Windows bootable, you'll need more than one hard disk or hard disk partition, as described in the section "Set Up a Dual-Boot System" on page 26.

The end result is effectively the same as installing on an empty hard disk as described in the previous section, except that all your old data stays on the drive. It's not quite as convenient as WET, but it potentially takes less time, and you don't have to worry about missing any files because nothing from the old installation is deleted. Here's how you do it:

1. Boot your PC into the old version of Windows, and insert your Windows 7 DVD.

If your old Windows installation won't start, boot off the DVD as described in the previous section. But doing so will permit setup to make changes to your partitions, making it possible to delete your primary partition and lose all your data.

2. When the Install Windows page appears, click **Install now**.

3. If you have a working Internet connection and wish to do so, click **Go online to get the latest update for installation**. Or, if you prefer, click **Do not get the latest updates**.

4. Choose your Windows 7 edition from the list and click **Next**; make sure to pick the one for which you have a valid license key, or you'll have to do this all over again.

5. Accept the license terms and click **Next**. You're not going to read all that, are you?

6. When setup asks "Which type of installation do you want?" (Figure 1-3), choose **Custom (advanced)**.

7. On the "Where do you want to install Windows?" page (Figure 1-2), click the drive with the previous version (usually drive C:) and click **Next**. Don't delete or reformat any partitions here, or you'll lose data with no hope of recovery.

8. At this point, you'll get a warning about files from a previous installation; click OK.

9. Go get yourself a nice cup of tea while Windows copies half a million files to your hard disk and reboots a few times.

10. When Windows 7 finally loads, it's time for the DRY step: reorganize the old folders so the new Windows installation can find all your data. Fire up Windows Explorer (Chapter 2) and navigate to your *c:\Windows.old \Documents and Settings* folder (or, if upgrading Vista, *c:\Windows.old \Users*).

11. Next, open the subfolder of your user account, and then open the *Desktop* folder. Press **Ctrl-A** to select all files and then drag them to your new Desktop folder at the top of the tree. (Or, create a new folder called *Old Desktop* if you don't want to clutter up your new desktop with all that old junk.)

 If you want to keep the old files in the old locations, hold the Ctrl key while dragging and dropping (see Chapter 2 for subtleties) to copy the files instead of moving them.

12. Repeat the previous step for *Pictures* (or *My Pictures* in XP), *Music* (or *My Music*), etc., copying each collection of files to the appropriate new location.

13. Next comes *Application Data*, which houses the various personalized data files created by Windows and most of your applications. By default, both the old folder and its new Windows 7 counterpart are hidden, but if you show hidden files in Windows Explorer (explained in Chapter 2), you'll see them.

    In Windows XP, the old files are in *C:\Windows.old\Documents and Settings\{your_user_name}\Application Data*. For Vista, they're divided in both *C:\Windows.old\Users\{your_user_name}\AppData\Roaming* and *C:\Windows.old\Users\{your_user_name}\AppData\Local*.

You don't have to copy all the files in these folders. In fact, you may prefer to only copy certain branches as you discover you need them; that way, you won't put anything in your new installation you don't actually need. For instance, your Mozilla Firefox profile—complete with your old bookmarks, cookies, and saved passwords—from your old Vista installation can be found in *C:\Windows.old\Users\{your_user_name}\AppData \Roaming\Mozilla\Firefox\Profiles*. But inside the *Profiles* folder is also your Firefox cache, which is better left behind. In this case, you'd copy or move everything except the *Cache* subfolder to *C:\ Users\ {your_user_name}\AppData\Roaming\Mozilla\Firefox\Profiles*.

14. When you're done, leave the *Windows.old* folder intact and close Windows Explorer. Once you're sure you've got everything from the old folder—perhaps weeks or months from now—you can go back and delete the defunct *Windows.old* folder.

Another use for the DRY method is to repair a seriously munged Windows 7 installation. If Windows 7 won't boot, you can perform a parallel installation to place a new copy of Windows 7 on your PC without harming the existing data on your hard disk.

One downside to the DRY method—apart from the need to do some manual shuffling of files—is that your hard disk never gets formatted. If it's an old drive with a long history of upgrades, a clean format may improve reliability.

Fix Problems with Windows Setup

The most common cause of a failed installation of Windows 7 is an out-of-date system BIOS. If setup crashes, or if Windows won't boot after you finish installing, check with the manufacturer of your system or motherboard for any BIOS updates, and update your BIOS if needed. Better yet, make sure you have the latest BIOS before you begin installation, particularly if your PC is more than a year old. See Appendix A for details.

Another common stumbling block to a successful Windows 7 setup is your video card (display adapter). If setup stops with an unintelligible error message, reboots unexpectedly during setup, or just hangs at a blank screen, your video card may be at fault. Unfortunately, setup will rarely, if ever, warn you about such an incompatibility before you begin. Of course, updating the driver won't help, since you'd either be installing the driver software on an older version of Windows that will soon be replaced, or installing it on the new OS that won't boot. Your best bet is to replace the video card and try again.

Installing on a desktop PC and suspect your video adapter is sabotaging your installation? If your motherboard has built-in video that you're currently not using because of an add-on card, just re-enable the on-board video through the system BIOS (if necessary), and then remove the troublesome card. Or if the on-board video is to blame, try assigning it more video memory (again, see Appendix A) or replacing it with an add-on video card.

Next, if you see an error that says something like "failed to open the Windows image file," this is an indictment of your DVD drive. Setup installs Windows 7 from a single, huge hard-disk image file, and some older drives can't handle files larger than 3 gigabytes in size. The solution is to replace the drive, or, if you're particularly attached to the drive *and* you're not in a hurry, purchase a copy of Windows setup on a stack of CDs (which Microsoft calls "alternate media") and try again.

Lastly, if it's an older disc, the culprit might be nothing more than a little dust; wipe the disk against your shirt and try again.

Set Up a Dual-Boot System

Dual-boot (or multiboot) installations used to be all the rage, and even though virtualization (discussed in the next section) has stolen a lot of their thunder, there are still times when having two or more operating systems installed side by side on the same PC can be useful.

For instance, you can have both Windows 7 and Windows XP—or Windows 7 and Linux, for that matter—installed on the same PC, and choose which to boot each time you power on the machine. Now, virtualization does this one better by allowing you to run both platforms simultaneously, but it has its limitations. Most notably, a virtualized Windows won't run nearly as fast as a non-virtualized installation; if speed matters for every OS you use, a dual-boot setup is the way to go.

Also, virtualized operating systems don't have full access to your PC's hardware—particularly non-USB devices—while each OS on a multiboot system can use everything for which drivers are available. Games are a great example; without unfettered communication with your 3D video hardware, many games won't run, and that rules out virtualization.

Windows 7 comes with built-in support for a multiboot setup called the *Windows Boot Manager*, which is installed automatically whether you want a dual-boot system or not. If, at the end of the installation, Windows 7 is the only operating system on your computer, it boots automatically without giving you a choice. Otherwise, you'll see a menu of installed operating systems, from which you can choose the OS you wish to use.

To set up a dual-boot system, you'll need at least two partitions or two physical drives: one for each operating system. Install the first OS on any drive you like. Then, during Windows 7 setup, when you see the "Where do you want to install Windows?" page (Figure 1-2, shown earlier), just select the empty drive, and setup will do the rest.

> See Chapter 5 for more information on partitions, including a way to divide your current single-partition drive into two partitions *without* having to reformat.

In most cases, the boot manager of the most-recently installed operating system is the one that will be used for all your operating systems, so the sequence in which you install your operating systems is very important. Most of the time, you'll need to install older operating systems *before* newer ones. For instance, on a PC already running Windows 98, just install 7 on a different drive, and voilà: you'll have a functional dual-boot system.

> Some other operating systems, such as FreeBSD and Windows 2000, have boot managers of their own, and can therefore be installed either before or after 7 is installed with little additional fuss. However, those operating systems *without* their own boot managers, such as Windows 9x/Me, will break the Windows 7 boot manager if installed subsequently. For another consideration, see the sidebar "Of Operating Systems and Filesystems" on page 29.

Modify the Boot Manager configuration

The Windows Boot Manager is responsible for loading Windows 7, and, optionally, booting any other operating systems you may have installed.

The Boot Manager in both Windows XP and 2000 stored its configuration in a tiny, easily editable file called *boot.ini* in the root folder of your C: drive, but in Windows 7, this file is no longer used. If you install 7 on an XP system, and then open the *boot.ini* file left behind, you'll see this message:

```
;Warning: Boot.ini is used on Windows XP and earlier operating systems.
;Warning: Use BCDEDIT.exe to modify Windows 7 boot options.
```

The BCDEdit (*bcdedit.exe*) tool that comes with Windows 7 is a command-line tool, and isn't exactly user-friendly. Open a Command Prompt window

(in administrator mode, as described in Chapter 8), type bcdedit and press
Enter, and you'll see output that looks something like this:

```
Windows Boot Manager
--------------------
identifier {bootmgr}
device partition=C:
description Windows Boot Manager
locale en-US
inherit {globalsettings}
default {default}
displayorder {ntldr}
 {default}
toolsdisplayorder {memdiag}
timeout 3

Windows Legacy OS Loader
------------------------
identifier {ntldr}
device partition=C:
path \ntldr
description Earlier version of Windows

Windows Boot Loader
-------------------
identifier {default}
device partition=D:
path \Windows\system32\winload.exe
description Microsoft Windows 7
locale en-US
inherit {bootloadersettings}
osdevice partition=D:
systemroot \Windows
resumeobject {70c7d34d-b6b4-12db-cc71-d30cdb1ce261}
nx OptIn
detecthal Yes
```

What a mess. In short, the first section describes the menu you see when you
first boot; the second section here—Windows Legacy OS Loader—describes the
older version of Windows (XP); and finally, the third section—Windows Boot
Loader—describes your new Windows 7 installation.

If you type bcdedit /? at the prompt, you'll see a bunch of command-line
parameters you can use to add or remove entries, choose a new default (the
OS that's loaded if you don't choose one before the timer runs out), or run a
variety of debugging tools.

But if all you want to do is choose a default and maybe change the timeout,
there's a better tool. Open your Start menu, type msconfig in the **Search** box
and press **Enter** to open the System Configuration window, and choose the
Boot tab as shown in Figure 1-5.

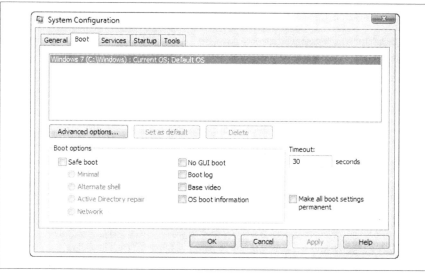

*Figure 1-5. The **Boot** tab of the System Configuration tool provides most of the features of BCDEdit in a much more pleasant interface*

Here, the easy options are truly self-evident, and the advanced options are at least available. On the right, you can adjust the **Timeout** from its default of 30 seconds; type 5 here, and you'll instantly shave off 25 seconds from your unattended boot time. (Don't use a value so small that you won't have time to change it, lest you set an inoperable installation as the default and have no way to get around it.)

To choose the default OS, select it in the list and click **Set as default**. When you're done, click OK, and then restart Windows to see your new settings.

Of Operating Systems and Filesystems

When setting up a dual-boot system for day-to-day use, you'll need to consider the matter of sharing files between your operating systems.

In order to share files between operating systems, both partitions must use filesystems supported by at least one OS. For instance, if you have a dual-boot setup with both Windows 7 and Windows 98, you'll be able to see both drives while you're in 7, but you'll only be able to see the 98 drive while 98 is running. (Although 7 can read drives formatted with the FAT32 filesystem, it can't be installed on one.) See Chapter 5 for details.

Now, if both your partitions use the NTFS filesystem—which is what you'd likely get if you set up a dual-boot system with Windows 7 and XP—you also may have ownership problems to contend with. As explained in Chapter 8, every file and folder on your PC has an "owner," a user tied to a specific account on your PC. If, for instance, you create a file in XP and then attempt to modify it in Windows 7, you may be denied permission until you "take ownership," as explained in the section "Protect Your Files with Encryption" on page 558.

And in regards to protecting your data, encryption is also effective at preventing an intruder from reading your files by installing a second operating system on your PC.

Virtualize Whirled Peas

A *Gedanken experiment*—also called a "thought" experiment—is a means of testing a hypothesis without actually conducting any physical experiment. ("Maxwell's demon" and "Schrödinger's cat" are both Gedanken experiments.) And as luck would have it, there's a way to conduct a Gedanken experiment of sorts with Windows 7.

Say you're using Vista or XP, and you're considering upgrading (or rather, "transitioning") to Windows 7. How do you find out if the new OS works with all your software without actually completing a painful, laborious, and possibly one-way operating system upgrade? Virtualize!

Virtualization has been around for years, but thanks to processor-level optimizations and recent improvements in virtualization software, it's easy, quick, practical, and, for the most part, free. The idea is that you can run a second copy of Windows—or any other operating system, for that matter—in a window. The new OS behaves as though it was installed on its very own PC, and even shows up on the network; the experience is not unlike remote control software discussed in Chapter 7, except you don't need to buy any more hardware. In most cases, you can copy and paste data between the "host" OS and the OS running in the window (the "guest"), and even drag-drop files onto the virtualized desktop.

 For best performance for your virtualized operating system, make sure support for virtualization is enabled in your PC's BIOS; see Appendix A for details. Not sure if your CPU supports this? Try Securable (*http://www.grc.com/securable.htm*).

Also, you'll need at least 3 GB of physical RAM (4 or 8 is better) and more than enough free hard disk space for a virtual hard disk (20 GB minimum).

With virtualization, you can test Windows 7 right on your Vista or XP desktop before you commit. Or, if you're already running Windows 7, you can set up a virtual Vista or XP desktop to allow you to run older software that isn't yet 7-friendly (see "Windows XP Mode" on page 33 for a special case).

The process itself is quite easy. All you need is virtualization software (see Table 1-3) and an original installation disc for the operating system you wish to install in a window.

Table 1-3. Virtualization software comparison chart

	Microsoft Virtual PC 6.0	Windows Virtual PC 6.1	VMware Workstation 6.5	VirtualBox
Windows 7 as host OS		✓	✓	✓
Windows Vista or XP as host OS	✓		✓	✓
Runs Windows 7 in a window	✓	✓	✓	✓
Runs Vista or XP in a window	✓	✓	✓	✓
Includes Windows XP for free		✓[a]		
Supports 64-bit host OS	✓	✓	✓	✓
Runs 64-bit OS in a window			✓	✓
Supports direct file drag-drop	✓	✓		
Clipboard sharing	✓	✓	✓	✓
Dynamic desktop resize	✓	✓		
Non-network folder sharing				✓
Virtualized windows alongside host windows		✓		✓
Supports multiple virtual processors			✓	✓
Supports multiple virtual monitors			✓	✓
USB devices recognized by guest system		✓	✓	✓
Snapshots[b]			✓	✓
Record movies			✓	
Runs Linux/Unix in a window	✓ (unofficially)	✓ (unofficially)	✓	✓
Runs Mac OS X in a window			✓ (unofficially)	
Cost	Free	Free	Free 30-day trial	Free
Available from	http://microsoft.com/virtualpc		http://vmware.com/	http://www.virtualbox.org/

[a] *Windows XP Mode* is included in the Professional and Ultimate Editions of Windows 7 only; see the upcoming sidebar "Windows XP Mode" on page 33 for details.

[b] See the sidebar "Virtual Time Machine" on page 36.

In order to run a 64-bit operating system in a window, the host PC must also be running a 64-bit operating system. And 64-bit Windows requires a 64-bit processor, as described in "64-Bit Windows" on page 6. At the time of this writing, running a 64-bit guest OS is only supported in VMware and VirtualBox.

Setting up a new virtual machine is a snap. Here are a few sample scenarios:

Run a virtualized Windows 7 in Vista

Want to test Windows 7 in a virtual environment on your Vista PC before you commit? Here's how.

Start by installing Microsoft Virtual PC 6.0 on your Vista PC, and then start Virtual PC. On the Virtual PC Console window, click **New** and then follow the prompts in the New Virtual Machine Wizard.

When it asks you to choose an operating system, select **Windows Vista** and click **Next**.

Next it'll ask you to allocate memory; this is the amount of physical RAM the guest OS sees, so give it enough to run (at least 1.0–1.5 GB). Whatever you allocate for the virtual machine will be sucked out of your host PC's memory, so don't give it more than you can spare. Click **Adjusting the RAM** and move the slider or type a value (1536 MB for 1.5 GB) and then click **Next**.

Next comes the virtual hard disk, the *.vhd* file your virtual machine uses for storage. Select the **A new virtual hard disk** option, click **Next**, and then specify a filename (and folder). Thankfully, the virtual hard disk works differently than the RAM: the file starts off small and grows as needed. The value you specify for **Virtual hard disk size** is only a cap, so type a sufficiently large number (like 100000 for 100 GB) and then click **Next**. Click **Finish** to close the wizard.

You can change the virtual hardware assigned to your new virtual PC at any time—unless the virtual machine is running or paused—by clicking the **Settings** button in the Virtual PC Console.

When you're returned to the Virtual PC Console window, select the new virtual machine and click **Start**. Immediately a black window will appear, and you'll see Virtual PC attempt to boot off the network. Since that's not likely to work, open the CD menu, select **Use Physical Drive D:** (or whatever drive letter is assigned to your DVD drive), and pop in your Windows 7 disc. Or, if you're installing off an ISO, select **Capture ISO Image** and select the *.iso* file. When you're ready, open the **Action** menu and select **Reset** to boot off the disc (or image).

From this point, install Windows 7 as described earlier in this chapter.

Windows XP Mode

One of Vista's biggest failings was its incompatibility—or rather, its perceived incompatibility—with a broad range of applications and devices during its early days. Microsoft was so concerned that the same thing might happen with Vista's successor that the Professional, Enterprise, and Ultimate editions of Windows 7 include a free licensed copy of Windows XP for use with the Windows Virtual PC software.

But rather than running Windows XP in a window, thereby confining XP applications to a smaller, isolated desktop, *XP Mode* applications run alongside Windows 7 applications. Windows 7 and the virtualized XP share the same desktop, Start menu, and even file type associations. (XP Mode uses a Terminal Services session for its hosted applications via the same protocol—RDP—as the Remote Desktop feature covered in Chapter 7.)

The result is a fully functional, licensed copy of Windows XP running more or less as a layer on top of Windows 7, not altogether different from the 32-bit layer on 64-bit Windows. And this means, at least in theory, no compatibility problems, and thus no barrier to the inevitable upgrade to Windows 7. (The big exception here is non-USB hardware; if you don't have a Windows 7-ready driver for one of your devices, the virtualized XP system won't be able to talk to it.)

But what if you have the Home Premium edition of Windows 7? Although you won't have access to Windows XP Mode per se, you can install XP in Windows Virtual PC, provided you own an XP license and have an XP install disc. Or, if that's overkill, you can try running that cranky application in "compatibility mode," as described in Chapter 6.

Virtual Machine Additions is a sort of link between the guest and host sessions; it makes the guest OS aware that it's running in a virtualized environment. First and foremost, VMA lets you move your mouse in and out of the Virtual PC window freely; otherwise it'll get stuck whenever you click in the window. (Without VMA, press the right **Alt** key to release the mouse pointer.) It also lets you drag-drop files directly onto— and out of—the windowed OS, and it even resizes the virtual desktop when you resize the Virtual PC window.

When Windows 7 first loads, open Virtual PC's **Action** menu and select **Install or Update Virtual Machine Additions**. In a few moments, the guest Windows 7 session will detect a new virtual CD and ask if you want to run *setup.exe*. Follow the prompts to install the software and then answer **Yes** to restart Windows.

Run a virtualized XP in Windows 7

Need to run an application that won't work on anything newer than Windows XP? Here's one way to do it in Windows 7.

First, install Windows Virtual PC 6.1 (or later). If you're using the Professional, Enterprise, or Ultimate editions of Windows 7, you can also install the optional Windows XP Mode software, also available at *http://www.microsoft.com/virtualpc*; see the sidebar "Windows XP Mode" on page 33 for an introduction. Otherwise, you'll need an original Windows XP install disc and appropriate license code.

Now, Windows Virtual PC doesn't have a central control panel like the one found in earlier versions; click the Windows Virtual PC icon in your Start menu, and it'll just open the *Virtual Machines* folder in your home folder. "Now what?" you may ask. Good question.

Don't waste time looking for instructions or a way to create a new virtual machine here; you won't find it. Instead, just open the Start menu, and in the **Search** box, type *VPCWizard.exe* and press **Enter**.

When prompted, choose a name for the new virtual machine configuration (e.g., "Windows XP in a box") and click **Next**. Specify how much memory (RAM) you'd like to allocate—give it at least 1024 MB (1 GB) if you have it to spare—and click **Next**. On the next page, choose **Create a dynamically expanding virtual hard disk** and then click **Create**.

Back in the *Virtual Machines* folder, you'll see your new *Windows XP in a box.vmcx* file; double-click it to start your virtual machine. When it first starts, your virtual PC will attempt a PXE network boot (described in "Boot Without a Boot Disc" on page 15), which will almost certainly fail.

Next, from the **Tools** drop-down, select **Settings**, and then highlight **DVD Drive** in the list on the left. Select **Access a physical drive** and choose the drive letter where your Windows setup disc can be found. (Or, if you're installing from an ISO disc image, select **Open an ISO image** and click **Browse** to locate it.) Click OK when you're done, and then click the **Ctrl+Alt +Del** button on the Virtual PC toolbar to restart the virtual machine and boot off the CD.

At this point, you can install Windows normally; when setup is complete, you should get something like the setup shown in Figure 1-6.

Figure 1-6. Run an older operating system in a window to provide absolute compatibility for applications that aren't yet 7-friendly

Virtual Time Machine

One of the advantages of virtualization is that it lets you test applications (and in some cases, hardware devices) in an isolated environment. But once you soil that environment with software or drivers, it's no longer the "clean room" it once was. Rather than delete the virtual machine and start over, there are ways to revert back to earlier stages—an undo, if you will—to save you time and trouble.

If you're using VMware Workstation, just open the **VM** menu, select **Snapshot** and then **Take Snapshot**. Name the snapshot and click OK to save the current state to your hard disk. Thereafter, changes you make to your virtual hard disk (software you install, files you delete, etc.) are saved in a separate file on your real hard disk.

You can revert to a saved state at any time; from the **VM** menu, select **Snapshot→Snapshot Manager**, select the snapshot you wish to use and click **Go To**.

Microsoft Virtual PC doesn't have a snapshot feature, but you can get a crude approximation, provided you have enough free disk space. When the virtual machine is in a state you'd like to save—like right after you've installed Windows and VMA—shut down the virtual session. Then, open Windows Explorer on the host and navigate to the folder containing your *.vhd* virtual hard disk (usually *Documents\My Virtual Machines*). Using the right mouse button, drag your *.vhd* file to another part of the same folder and select **Copy Here**, creating a duplicate copy (e.g., *Windows 7 - copy.vhd*); that's your snapshot.

To revert to a saved state, make sure your Virtual PC session is shut down, and then reopen Windows Explorer on the host. Delete or rename the *.vhd* file in use, and then rename the backup (e.g., *Windows 7 - copy.vhd* to *Windows 7.vhd*).

Run a virtualized Windows 7 x64 in Windows 7

Here's a handy way to create a clean Windows 7 install for testing purposes. For this you'll need the VMWare Workstation software and the 64-bit edition of Windows 7 running on the host PC. (The same procedure also works if the host is running Vista x64 or XP x64.)

Start VMWare, and from the **File** menu, select **New** and then **Virtual Machine** (or press **Ctrl-N**). On the first page of the New Virtual Machine Wizard, select **Custom (advanced)** and click **Next**. From the **Hardware compatibility** list, select **Workstation 6.5** and click **Next**.

Next, specify the location of your installer disc—either a physical drive on your PC or an *.iso* image file if applicable—and click **Next**. On the Easy Install Information page, VMware lets you enter the license key, user account name to create, and associated password, all of which are optional; type them in, and VMware will pre-enter them for a (nearly) unattended setup.

When asked to allocate memory, you'll need to specify at least 2048 MB (2 GB); more is better, if you can spare it. (Whatever you allocate for the virtual machine will be sucked out of your host PC's memory, so don't give it everything you've got.)

On the Network Type page, select **Use bridged networking** and then click **Next**. What follows is the selection of a SCSI adapter, which doesn't matter. (In fact, for some other operating systems, you'll need to disable the SCSI support altogether.)

Just like with Microsoft Virtual PC, you'll need to set up a virtual hard disk, so on the Select a Disk page, choose **Create a new virtual disk** and click **Next**. For the virtual disk type, select IDE. On the Specify Disk Capacity page, choose a large **Maximum disk size**—at least 100 GB, since you can't easily enlarge it later—and make sure the **Allocate all disk space now** option is *not checked*.

Complete the wizard and then click **Finish**. If all is well, VMware will automatically start the virtual machine, load the Windows 7 installer, and get to work.

Akin to Microsoft's Virtual Machine Additions described earlier in this section, VMware offers *VMware Tools*, which allow you to easily move your mouse pointer in and out of the VMware session window. From VMware's VM menu, select **Install VMware Tools**, and then follow the prompts to install.

Virtual Glass

Neither Virtual PC nor VMware gives the guest operating system low-level access to your PC's hardware. This means it can't play with your 3D video card, and thus can't display Aero Glass. But there is a nifty workaround if you want Glass on your Virtual Windows 7 or Vista: use Remote Desktop!

If your host OS is Windows 7, you're using Windows Virtual PC, and you have Aero Glass enabled on the host, just fire up Virtual PC and from the **Tools** menu, select **Enable Integration Features**.

But what if your host OS is Vista or an earlier version? You can do it, provided your guest OS is the Professional edition or better.

On the guest OS, open the System page in Control Panel and click the **Remote settings** link on the left side. In the **Remote Desktop** section, select either

---

Allow connections only from computers running Remote Desktop with Network Level Authentication (assuming your host OS is either Windows 7 or Vista) or **Allow connections from computers running any version of Remote Desktop** (for XP and earlier). When you're done, minimize the Virtual PC session.

Then on the host OS, start Remote Desktop (see Chapter 7) by typing mstsc into the Start menu Search box and pressing **Enter**. Before you connect, click **Options**, choose the **Display** tab, and make sure the **Colors** setting is set to **Highest Quality (32 bit)**. Then choose the **Experience** tab and turn on all the options here (or just choose **LAN** from the drop-down list).

When you're done, choose the **General** tab, type the computer name of the virtualized PC into the **Computer** field, and click **Connect**. Type in your login credentials when prompted, and then enjoy Glass in a window!

See "Get Glass" on page 286 for more on Aero Glass, and "Control a PC Remotely" on page 488 for more on Remote Desktop.

Migration to Windows 7

Migration isn't just for the birds. It's the process you go through to make all of your day-to-day tasks—the ones you're accustomed to doing on Windows Vista or XP—function on a new Windows 7 installation.

If you haven't yet installed Windows 7, one way to determine what will work and what won't is to use the free Windows 7 Upgrade Advisor (UA) (*http:// microsoft.com/windows7*). UA does nothing more than construct a laundry list of warnings, each pointing out a potential problem with products it knows Windows 7 doesn't like. In many cases, you can remedy such issues by installing free updates from the respective manufacturers. But don't expect anything more; UA is useless for products not on its compatibility list.

For instance, UA might bring to your attention that your printer, antivirus software, backup software, CD burning software, and perhaps your Bluetooth adapter are all unsupported on Windows 7. So, this means you'll definitely need new versions of your antivirus and backup software (see Chapter 6) and your CD burning software (Chapter 4). You'll also need to check with the manufacturers of your printer and Bluetooth adapter to see whether they've released native Windows 7 drivers (in nearly all cases, native Vista drivers will do). If there aren't yet compatible drivers and you don't want to wait, you'll need to replace those devices.

Beyond that, you'll need to actually try any mission-critical software or hardware with Windows 7 to see if it'll work. To make sure you've covered all your bases before you commit to the new OS, you can either set up a dual-boot system or install Windows 7 in a virtualized environment, both explained earlier in this chapter.

What follows is a brief roadmap and some tips to help you get up to speed with Windows 7 quickly.

Coming from Windows XP?

Disorientation is probably the prevailing sensation among those users coming to Window 7 from XP or earlier versions of Windows. Here's where you can find some of the more elusive entities you may have grown accustomed to:

Add or Remove Programs
> This is still in Control Panel, but now it's called **Programs and Features**.

Aero Glass interface
> Windows 7 features the same see-through Glass interface introduced in Vista, although the Desktop Window Manager (DWM) has been improved in this latest version to be more memory-efficient. See Chapter 5 if you're having trouble getting Glass to work.

Address Bar
> The path box in Windows Explorer doubles as an address bar, so if you want to type a path or copy the current path to the clipboard, click just to the right of the text, and Explorer will show you a familiar, backslash-equipped folder path in an editable text field. See Chapter 2 for a complete tour of the new Windows Explorer.

Display Properties
> Right-click an empty area of the desktop and select **Screen resolution**. Or, in Control Panel, open the Display page, and on the left side, click **Adjust resolution**.

File Types window
> Sorry, you don't get one of these in Windows 7. The best Microsoft could do is the nearly useless **Default Programs** page in Control Panel. If you want to edit your context menus, you'll need File Type Doctor, explained in Chapter 3.

Menus in Windows and Internet Explorer
> Microsoft took the menus out of both Windows Explorer and Internet Explorer, and replaced them with tool ribbons and drop-down buttons that do pretty much the same thing. But you can always press the **Alt** key on the keyboard to temporarily show the old, familiar menu bars in either application. See Chapter 2 if you want to make it permanent in Windows Explorer.

Network Connections

As explained in Chapter 7, the Network Connections window has been subjugated and buried in Windows 7. In Control Panel, open the Network and Sharing Center page. On the left side, click **Change adapter settings**.

Start Menu→Run

You can use the **Search** box at the bottom of the Start menu to run any program; just type the filename (e.g., `control.exe`) and press Enter.

System

The familiar System Properties window that has been around since Windows 2000, and the only way to change your PC's name on your network, is now buried under the **Advanced system settings** link on the new System page in Control Panel. Alternatively, you can type `SystemProper tiesAdvanced.exe` in the Start menu's **Search** box and press **Enter** to open this window.

And there's more; see the next section for some goodies that are unfamiliar even to Vista users.

Coming from Windows Vista?

Since Windows 7 is a incremental update to Vista, your transition should be pretty easy. Aside from some minor changes to the way the registry is handled on 64-bit systems (see Chapter 3), most of the changes are skin-deep:

Action Center

It's taken too long, but Microsoft has finally acknowledged that people hate the barrage of pop ups, reminders, warnings, and confirmation windows that has been thrown at them all these years. But instead of simply eliminating them, Microsoft has consolidated them into the Action Center. So you now know where to go if you want to be reminded to activate Windows, find and install antivirus software (that should've come preinstalled, mind you), and download a gigabyte of updates to fix all the bugs that have been found so far.

Device Manager

Device Manager (*devmgmt.msc*) is still present in Windows 7, but there's a new icon-based tool in Control Panel called Devices and Printers. Right-click any device in the Devices and Printers window to access features and tasks specific to that device. See Chapter 6 for more information.

Homegroups

The Homegroups feature doesn't replace traditional file and printer sharing, it only augments it, and then only when everyone on your network is running Windows 7. See Chapter 7 for details.

Libraries & improved search

At first glance, Libraries aren't much different than the specialized folders found in earlier versions of Windows: *Documents, Music, Pictures,* and *Videos.* (Although the cutesy "*My*" prefix is absent here, it's still used for the folder names, like *My Pictures.*) But these folders are now accompanied by a background database that improves searches and connects to the Homegroups feature for improved media sharing. See Chapter 2 for ways to improve searches and customize your Libraries, as well as a way to get rid of the Libraries entry in Windows Explorer if you don't like the clutter.

Nifty window management shortcuts

Microsoft has added a bunch of keyboard and mouse shortcuts to improve window management in Windows 7. For instance, grab a window title bar and shake vigorously from side to side, and Windows will minimize all windows but the one you're holding. Or if you're using multiple monitors, hold the Windows logo key and the **Shift** key while pressing the left or right arrows to move the active window to a different screen. (Without holding **Shift**, one press only docks a window to the side of the active screen—you'd need three presses to do the same thing.) For more shortcuts, see Chapter 2.

Sidebar

The Vista Sidebar is gone, at least on the surface. Sidebar gadgets are now simply called *Gadgets,* and they can be placed anywhere on the desktop. It's unsettlingly similar to the horrible Active Desktop that was lumped into Windows 98, but greatly improved.

Taskbar & Jump Lists

The taskbar in Windows 7 now holds icons for running applications and shortcuts to start new applications, side by side. (Previously, shortcuts were confined to tiny, annoying dockable toolbars.) Right-click a running task to *pin* it to the taskbar so it sticks around even after you exit the program.

Right-click a taskbar icon (representing a running application) in a previous version of Windows, and you'll see the same boring *system menu* that appears when you click the top-left corner of any open window. In Windows 7, you'll see a customized *jump list* with a list of open windows (if there's more than one), as well as frequently used locations—folders, if it's Windows Explorer, or websites if it's Internet Explorer—and tasks, like opening a new window.

Shell Tweaks

Programmers like to draw pictures of how their software is structured, and more often than not, those drawings make an operating system look a lot like a cantaloupe. There are invariably concentric circles of different colors or shades of gray, each with an impressive-sounding label, like *kernel* and *abstraction layer*. (I never found those diagrams terribly helpful either.) But on the outside, like an old friend, you'll always find the *shell*.

The term *shell* conjures up images of a snail or hermit crab, using its hard shell for protection from the outside world. But an operating system shell works more like that of an egg, which is just as effective at protecting the rest of the world from the goo inside.

Windows Explorer is the shell that comes with Windows 7, and along for the ride comes the Windows desktop, the Start menu, the taskbar, and those windows that turn your data into cute little icons you can kick around with your mouse. In short, the shell is what you see when you first boot Windows, and what responds to your clicks and drags until you start an application. Its job is to protect you from the goo inside Windows 7.

Figure 2-1 shows Windows Explorer as it appears right out of the box.

You can open an Explorer window by double-clicking any folder icon on the desktop or selecting one of the locations on the righthand column of the Start menu (e.g., **Documents**, **Pictures**, **Computer**). There's also the "pinned" Explorer icon on the taskbar. Or quicker still, hold the Windows logo key (which we'll call *Winkey*, just to be cute) and press **E**.

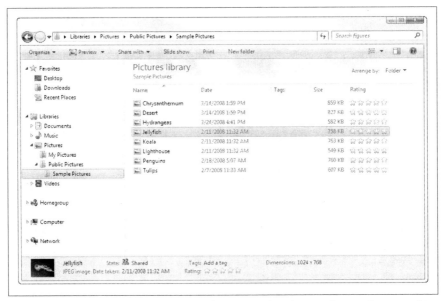

Figure 2-1. Windows Explorer may have been gussied up for Windows 7, but everything you need is still within reach

Disappointingly, the cloying "My" prefix that was mercifully absent in Vista has returned in Windows 7. But it's only used on the four folders for which there are matching libraries: *My Documents*, *My Music*, *My Pictures*, and *My Videos*. In Windows 7, when you see one of these locations without the dreaded *My* label (such as the aforementioned Start menu entries), it usually means the library, not the folder. The upshot is that there's nothing stopping you from renaming the *My Documents* folder to simply *Documents*.

While the basic layout is more or less the same as versions of Explorer dating back to 1995, the menu and the title bar are both gone, replaced with many subtle—almost hidden—controls that do most of what you'll need to accomplish while working with your files. But that's only the beginning.

The right side of the window more closely resembles a restaurant menu than a list of files, which, while friendly in appearance, does little to make day-to-day file management any easier or faster.

And to the left, where you might expect to find a straightforward folder tree, resides *Favorites* (how does it know?) and *Libraries*. Microsoft *really* wants you to organize your stuff into these rigidly defined categories, although it's often more efficient to organize files by project rather than data type.

Luckily, a lot of what seems hardcoded in Windows Explorer can be changed to suit your needs, or, as the case may be, your obsessive-compulsive disorder (e.g., me).

Your actual files—all of 'em—are in the *Computer* entry, buried near the bottom of the Navigation pane (that's what Microsoft calls the lefthand part of Windows Explorer). Fortunately, the basic premise of the Explorer window remains the same as it has for years: click a location (e.g., folder) on the left side to see the folder's contents on the right.

 If you're looking for those little plus [+] and minus [–] boxes you might be accustomed to from earlier versions of Windows, forget it. Instead, you navigate the tree with tiny triangles (arrows) the size of bacteria that fade in and out as you move your mouse around. An arrow pointing to the left indicates a collapsed branch; an arrow pointing down (or rather, southeast) indicates an expanded branch.

Across the bottom of the Explorer window is the Details pane; it's resizable, so you can enlarge it to show more information, or shrink it out of the way. If you lose the preview pane and want to get it back, open the **Organize** drop-down and select **Layout→ Details Pane**.

See Figure 2-2 for a visual rundown of everything you can do in Windows Explorer.

Want to make Explorer look more like an earlier version? You sentimental fool, you. Start by collapsing the *Favorites* and *Libraries* branches by clicking those tiny arrows to the left. (Or get rid of them for good with a Registry hack as described later in this chapter). Right-click an empty area of the right pane, select **View**, and then choose **Details** (actually, any view is better than the default, **Tiles**). And if you want your menu bar back, just press the **Alt** key, or open the **Organize** drop-down and select **Layout→Menu Bar** to make it permanent.

Customize Windows Explorer

The Folder Options window—used to control a lot of the way Windows Explorer displays and handles files—is a mess. Like many other Control Panel windows, it's a remnant of earlier times, having not changed very much in the 14 years since its debut in Windows 95.

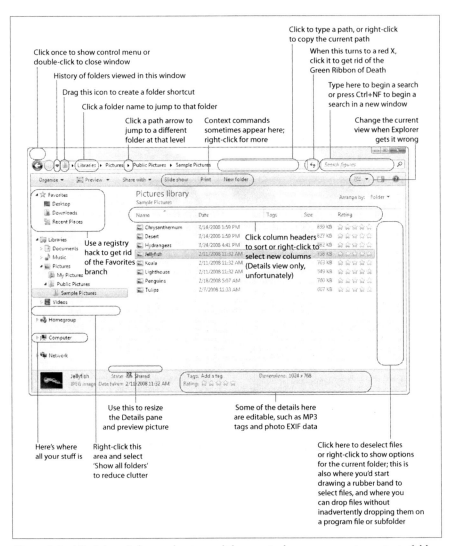

Click to type a path, or right-click
to copy the current path

When this turns to a red X,
click it to get rid of the
Green Ribbon of Death

Click once to show control menu or
double-click to close window

History of folders viewed in this window

Drag this icon to create a folder shortcut

Type here to begin a search
or press Ctrl+NF to begin a
search in a new window

Click a folder name to jump to that folder

Click a path arrow to
jump to a different
folder at that level

Context commands
sometimes appear here;
right-click for more

Change the current
view when Explorer
gets it wrong

Use a registry
hack to get rid
of the Favorites
branch

Click column headers
to sort or right-click to
select new columns
(Details view only,
unfortunately)

Use this to resize
the Details pane
and preview picture

Some of the details here
are editable, such as MP3
tags and photo EXIF data

Here's where
all your stuff is

Right-click this
area and select
'Show all folders'
to reduce clutter

Click here to deselect files
or right-click to show options
for the current folder; this is
also where you'd start
drawing a rubber band to
select files, and where you
can drop files without
inadvertently dropping them on
a program file or subfolder

*Figure 2-2. All of the subtle—and not so subtle—controls you can use to navigate folders
and manage your files in Windows Explorer*

Because so many annoyances can be caused by—or solved with—settings in
Folder Options, it's only fitting to begin this section with an explanation of
what these options do.

In Explorer, open the **Organize** drop-down and select **Folder and Search
Options** (or open **Folder Options** in Control Panel). First up is the **General** tab, which essentially has only four options.

The first, **Browse folders**, is a throwback to the way folder windows worked in Windows 95. In Windows 7, if you select **Open each folder in its own window**, you'll get a new Windows Explorer window when you double-click a folder icon in the righthand pane only, whether or not the Navigation pane (folder tree) is shown. Regardless of this setting, Explorer opens a new window whenever you double-click a folder icon on the desktop, click a shortcut for Explorer, or **Shift**+click the Explorer taskbar button.

 Use the **Ctrl** key when double-clicking a folder icon to override your choice here: open a new window when it would otherwise use the same window, or vice versa. (It only works if the folder isn't already highlighted.) And you can always right-click any folder icon and select **Open in new window** to do just that.

The **Click items as follows** option lets you choose between traditional mode (**Double-click to open an item**) and a web browser-like mode (**Single-click to open an item**). Now, the point of double-clicking is to prevent you from accidentally opening a program or folder when you're just trying to select, delete, move, copy, or rename a file, but it can also be a pain. Here's how to live with either setting:

Living with the double-click interface

If you don't like double-clicking, but you like Explorer's single-click interface even less, most pointing devices (mice, styli, trackballs) with more than two buttons allow you to program additional buttons to handle double-click duty. Make your middle mouse button (or stylus barrel button) your double-clicker, and you'll have the best of both worlds.

Living with the single-click interface

If you choose the single-click interface, you'll no longer be able to rename an item by slowly clicking it twice. Instead, you either need to right-click and select **Rename** or carefully move the mouse pointer so that it hovers over the icon and press the **F2** key.

In the Navigation pane section, the **Show all folders** option doesn't really do what it says. All your folders are shown whether this option is turned on or off. Instead, it only controls where in the tree some of the special folders (like *Homegroup* and *Libraries*) are shown, and displays your account folder under *Desktop*. See "Clean Up the Navigation Pane" on page 53 for details.

Finally, the **Automatically expand to current folder** option is turned off by default, but it's handier to have it turned on. When enabled, it navigates the tree and highlights the active folder being displayed on the right. (Apparently, the Microsoft committee that designed this page thought your brain was too small to comprehend the sight of so many folders appearing in a hierarchical tree when you first open the window.)

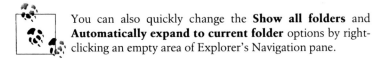 You can also quickly change the **Show all folders** and **Automatically expand to current folder** options by right-clicking an empty area of Explorer's Navigation pane.

Next, the **View** tab (Figure 2-3) houses settings that affect how much information Explorer shows you, arranged in alphabetical order.

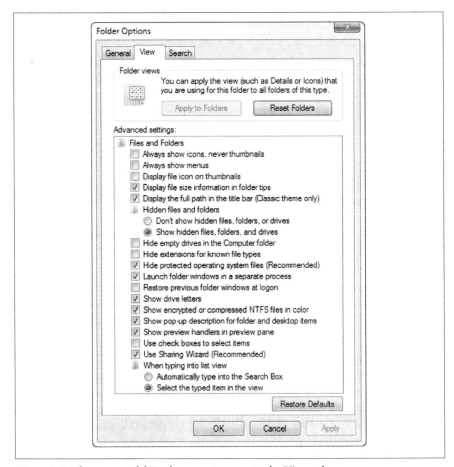

*Figure 2-3. The most useful Explorer settings are in the **View** tab*

Unfortunately, the defaults are set in favor of a "simpler" (read *dumbed-down*) interface, which has the unfortunate and ironic side effect of making many everyday tasks—like organizing files, sharing folders over a network, or even opening certain folders—more difficult. Here are some quick ways to make Explorer more useful:

Always show icons, never thumbnails
This is a setting Windows has been lacking for years. By default, Explorer automatically shows large thumbnails when a folder (or search results window) contains mostly image files. Turn on this option to disable thumbnails except when you specifically select **Thumbnails** from the **Views** drop-down. See "Green Ribbon of Death" on page 380 for another reason to use this setting.

Always show menus
You can display Windows Explorer's menu bar at any time by pressing the **Alt** key; turn on this option to make it permanent.

Display file icon on thumbnails
This option displays a file's generic file icon superimposed over its dynamically generated preview. Turn this off for cleaner-looking thumbnails, or turn it on if you want to more easily distinguish a *.jpg* image from a Photoshop document. Better yet, turn off the **Hide extensions for known file types** option, described later in this section.

Display file size information in folder tips
This name of this option is a little misleading. If it's turned off, the pop-up that appears when you hover your mouse over a folder on the desktop or the right pane of Windows Explorer (but not the left) shows only the date and time the folder was created. Turn on the **Display file size information in folder tips** option, and the pop-up also contains the total size of all the folder's contents, as well as the names of the first few files contained therein. The only reason to turn this off is to make the pop-up appear slightly sooner on slower PCs (it takes time to add up all the files and subfolders of large branches). To turn off folder tips altogether, use the **Show pop-up description for folder and desktop items** option, described later in this section.

Display the full path in the title bar (Classic theme only)
This poorly worded setting does more than its name suggests. True, when using the "Classic" theme (open Personalization in Control Panel), you can turn on this option to display the full path of the current folder (e.g., *C:\Program Files\Windows Journal\Templates* instead of simply *Templates*).

But when used with any modern Aero theme, enabling this option causes the full path to appear in the Task Bar, in Jump Lists, and in the **Alt +Tab** window.

 Regardless of this setting, Explorer's title bar never contains any text at all when used with Aero, and the full path of the current folder is *always* shown in the path box at the top of the window in any theme. See "Navigating files and folders" on page 76 for more information on the path box.

Hidden files and folders

Windows doesn't show hidden files by default in Explorer. If you set this option to **Show hidden files and folders**, any files with the *hidden* or *system* file attribute will appear in Explorer, but their icons will still appear semitransparent.

 To hide or unhide a file or folder, right-click it, select **Properties**, and change the **Hidden** option. For quicker access to a file's attributes, try the **Change file attributes** tool, part of Creative Element Power Tools (*http:// www.creativelement.com/powertools/*).

Hide empty drives in the Computer folder

This is one of the more stupid options in this window—particularly in light of the numerous unused items that *can't* be removed—and this one is turned on by default. The idea is to reduce confusion for those users overwhelmed by the breadth of the English alphabet, and hide drives that don't have data on them. Never mind that those same mythical users will be even more baffled by the disappearance of empty USB drives, new backup hard disks, and blank DVDs.

 To hide a drive you don't use, just unassign its drive letter with the Disk Management tool covered in Chapter 5.

Hide extensions for known file types

Filename extensions—the last few letters after the dot in a file's name— are hidden by default in Windows, and have been in every Windows release since '95. Filename extensions (e.g., *.txt*, *.jpg*, *.doc*) determine how

Windows interacts with your documents, and hiding this information only makes it harder for you to tell your files apart and predict what will happen when you open them. For instance, the files *tardis.jpg*, *tardis.xls*, and *tardis.pdf* will appear by default as *tardis*, *tardis*, and *tardis* in Explorer, with only their tiny icons to distinguish them. See "File Type Associations" on page 166 for a further examination of why you'll probably want to turn this option off and leave it off.

Hide protected operating system files

When this option is turned on (the default), files with the *system* file attribute are hidden in Explorer, regardless of the **Hidden files and folders** option discussed earlier. So-called *system* files include most of the boot loader files discussed in Chapter 1, the *$RECYCLE.BIN* and *System Volume Information* folders found on every hard drive, the *hiberfil.sys* hibernation file (see Chapter 5), and a handful of other files. Normally, I don't like it when Windows hides anything from me, but most of the time, such files are of limited utility to the hacker. Leave this option turned on to protect these important files from accidental damage, or turn it off temporarily if you want to see and mess around with them.

Launch folder windows in a separate process

By default, the desktop, Start menu, and all open Explorer and single-folder windows are handled by the same instance of Windows Explorer. That is, only one copy of the *Explorer.exe* application is ever in memory at a time. Turn on this option if you'd prefer your Explorer windows to operate in a separate instance of the program from the desktop. Although this takes slightly more memory and may slightly increase the time it takes to open the first new Explorer window, it means that if one Explorer window crashes—see "Green Ribbon of Death" on page 380—it won't bring down your desktop and Start menu.

 To see this feature in action, open Task Manager (Ctrl+Shift+Esc), choose the **Processes** tab, and click the **Image Name** column header to sort the list alphabetically. At first, you'll see only one instance of *Explorer.exe* in the **Image Name** column. As you open a few Explorer windows, you'll see a second *Explorer.exe* instance appear.

If you want each Explorer window to open in a separate instance, meaning that three or more *Explorer.exe* entries may appear in Task Manager, See "Start Explorer with Any Folder" on page 60. See Chapter 6 for more on Task Manager and what to do when an application crashes.

Restore previous folder windows at logon

Turn this option on if you want Windows to remember which folders are open when you shut down or log out and then reopen them the next time you log in. Another way to do this is to not shut down at all, but rather put your PC to sleep as explained in "Start Windows Instantly (Almost)" on page 274.

Show drive letters

Turn this off to hide drive letters (e.g., *C:, D:, N:*) from Explorer's folder tree.

Show encrypted or compressed NTFS files in color

Among the additional services provided by the NTFS filesystem (see Chapter 5) are support for on-the-fly encryption and compression. Turn on this option to visually distinguish encrypted and compressed files and folders by displaying their names in blue. See "Protect Your Files with Encryption" on page 558 for a way to customize the colors used for these files.

Show pop-up description for folder and desktop items

Commonly referred to as "tool tips," pop-up descriptions show additional details about the file or folder underneath the mouse pointer (except for folders in the Navigation pane). Turn off this option to hide these tool tips. See also the **Display file size information in folder tips** option, earlier in this section, for a related setting.

Show preview handlers in preview pane

Preview handlers are the DLLs used to generate thumbnail preview icons for some of your files (like *.jpg* images). Turn this option off to disable resizable previews in the Preview pane (open the **Organize** drop-down and select **Layout→Preview Pane**), which you'd probably only do if thumbnails were causing problems (see "Green Ribbon of Death" on page 380) *and* you wanted to keep the Preview pane visible.

Use check boxes to select items

If you enable this option, you'll be able to select multiple files without having to drag a *rubber band* or use the keyboard. See "Slicker Ways to Select Files" on page 94 for tips involving this feature.

Use Sharing Wizard

Disable this option to use the Advanced Sharing window instead of the feeble Sharing Wizard each time you right-click a folder or drive and select **Share**. Despite the fact that Microsoft apparently recommends that you use this feature, only the Advanced Sharing window lets you specify sharing permissions to properly protect your data. See Chapter 8 for details.

When typing into list view
See "Keyboard Is My Friend" on page 76 for tips involving this setting.

What it comes down to, of course, is that you should use what works best for you. Don't blindly accept the defaults just because they came out of the box that way. (By the way, you can add your own settings to this list, as described in "Create an Interface for a Registry Setting" on page 143.)

The **Search** tab in this window is dissected in excruciating detail in "Fix Windows Search" on page 111.

Shell Tweaks

Clean Up the Navigation Pane

Every so often, Microsoft builds a baffling amount of rigidity into a feature, something that's usually unwarranted—not to mention unwanted—given that so many other aspects of Windows are pleasantly flexible and customizable. Case in point: the Navigation pane in Windows Explorer.

Out of the box, the Navigation pane shows five main branches: *Favorites, Libraries, Homegroup, Computer,* and *Network* (all shown in Figure 2-1). Don't use *Libraries*? Sorry, it's there to stay. *Homegroup* of no use to you? Too bad; you've got to scroll past it every time you want to get to your drives and files. *Computer* is where all your drives are, but it's near the bottom of the list.

 There's another way to skip the clutter at the top of the Navigation pane (see "Start Explorer with Any Folder" on page 60). Although it won't get rid of any of these items, it will jump right to a folder in Explorer, and the unwanted special folders will likely be scrolled out of view.

First, right-click an empty area of the Navigation pane and turn on the badly named **Show all folders** option. This doesn't hide anything yet, but it does create a new *Desktop* branch and then tosses everything except *Favorites* into it (see Figure 2-4). Already a little tidier, no?

Next, here's how to clean up the major players in the Navigation pane:

Some of the following solutions require editing of the Registry, which is covered extensively in Chapter 3. Proceed carefully and make frequent backups with Registry patches (also Chapter 3), lest you mess up something with no hope of undo.

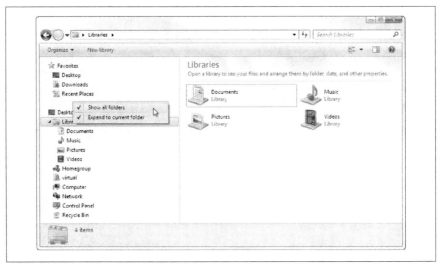

*Figure 2-4. The **Show all folders** option is the first step to tidying up Explorer's Navigation pane*

Favorites

Favorites won't go away without a Registry hack, but you can delete individual favorites to shrink down this section to something manageable. (Collapsing the branch does no good because it'll automatically appear expanded the next time you open an Explorer window.) You can easily recover the default Favorites items by right-clicking *Favorites* and selecting **Restore favorite links**.

 The Favorites in Windows Explorer are unrelated to Internet Explorer Favorites, so all the deleting in the world won't harm your browser bookmarks. Windows Explorer Favorites are stored in the *Links* subfolder of your user account folder (*c:\Users\{your_user_name}\Links*), while Internet Explorer favorites are stored in *c:\Users\{your_user_name}\Favorites*.

To remove the *Favorites* branch altogether, open the Registry Editor (see Chapter 3) and navigate to `HKEY_CLASSES_ROOT\CLSID\{323CA680-C24D-4099-B94D-446DD2D7249E}\ShellFolder`. Double-click the `Attrib utes` value and in the **Value data** field, type `a9400100`. Click OK when you're done; the change takes effect for the next Windows Explorer window you open. To get *Favorites* back, change the `Attributes` value data back to its default of `a0900100`.

Libraries

Like *Favorites*, you can't hide the *Libraries* branch without a Registry hack, but you can remove libraries you don't need. Just right-click *Video*, for instance, and select **Delete**. You won't lose any files, only the associated Video library database. You can get back your default libraries at any time by right-clicking *Libraries* and selecting **Restore default libraries**.

 You may've seen a **Don't show in navigation pane** option, but it's only available for libraries if the aforementioned **Show all folders** option isn't being used.

To remove the entire *Libraries* branch from Windows Explorer without disabling the Libraries feature or deleting any of your personal libraries, open Registry Editor (see Chapter 3 for more on the Registry). Navigate to `HKEY_LOCAL_MACHINE\SOFTWARE\Microsoft\Windows\CurrentVersion\Explorer\Desktop\NameSpace` and delete the `{031E4825-7B94-4dc3-B131-E946B44C8DD5}` key. (Or, to put *Libraries* back, recreate the key.) Close the Registry Editor when you're done, and the change will take effect in the next Explorer window you open. (Though keep in mind that removing the branch will somewhat hinder your access to your libraries.)

Homegroup

To get rid of *Homegroup*, you'll need to disable the Homegroups feature. Open the Homegroup page in Control Panel, click the **Leave the homegroup** link, and then click **Leave the homegroup** on the next page.

Next, open the Services window (in the Start menu **Search** box, type `services.msc` and press **Enter**). Double-click the **HomeGroup Listener** service to open its Properties window, and from the **Startup type** list, select **Disabled**. Click **Stop** and when the service has stopped, click OK. Repeat this for the **HomeGroup Provider** service as well. See Chapter 8 for more on Homegroups.

Computer

This one you can't lose, sorry. (If you could, you'd lose access to all your files; how annoying!)

Network

Even if you use homegroups exclusively, you can't hide the Network branch without some Registry work (see Chapter 3). But you can hide individual PCs from the Network enumerator, as described in Chapter 7.

Close all Explorer windows and then open a new Windows Explorer to see your changes.

Choose Folder View Defaults

Why does the *Taming of the Shrew* line, "There's small choice in rotten apples," come to mind so often when using Windows? It's not so much the choice of operating system (that's another story), as much as the little choices we're asked to make every day.

For instance, Windows Explorer offers eight different ways to look at your files—more than any previous version—yet few are actually useful. Problem is, Windows chooses the view for you based on the location and type of files in the folder, and it doesn't always get it right.

If you're tired of constantly having to go back to the **View** menu (either by right-clicking or using the unnamed drop-down on the top-right) to change the icon size, or having to click the column headers to sort file listings, you can change the default to match your whims. But Explorer's use of your defaults won't make much sense until you figure out the clandestine template system.

A *template* is a collection of folder display settings that includes the view (e.g., Large Icons, Details, Tiles, etc.), the sorting method, and the column arrangement. Each time you open a folder, Explorer automatically picks one of the five preset templates, and uses those settings to configure the view. And herein lies the source of the problem: Windows is no good at picking the default template. You might open a folder full of HTML web page documents, and Explorer will choose the template for music files (see Figure 2-5). Or, a folder with nothing but photos will show up in the **Details** view, rather than thumbnails (Large Icons).

Figure 2-5. Windows 7 doesn't always choose the best view for your files

Now it's easy enough to click the view button to cycle through the various display modes or click the arrow to choose a view from the list, but it's more effective to change Windows Explorer's *perception* of the folder so it uses the appropriate template. Right-click the folder, choose the **Customize** tab (Figure 2-6), and from the **Optimize this folder for** list, choose one of the five available templates.

You'll notice there's no way to edit any of these templates here, nor can you add or remove templates or change the rules Windows uses when it picks a template automatically. All you can do is pick one of these five categories:

General Items
Basically the default view, Explorer uses this template when there's no specific reason to use one of the others. The columns shown by default are **Name**, **Date Modified**, **Type**, and **Size**.

Documents
Used for the *Documents* folder and all of its subfolders, this template is identical to the **General Items** template, except for the addition of the **Tags** column.

Pictures
A thumbnail display by default, this template is shown for folders containing photo and video files. The columns shown are predominantly for photos, though: **Name**, **Date Taken**, **Tags**, **Size**, and **Rating**. (If you want columns useful for video files, such as **Duration** and **Frame rate**, you'll have to add them yourself.)

Music
Shown by default for music tracks (e.g., MP3 and WMA files), this shows files in **Details** view, making Explorer look vaguely like iTunes' music library. The default columns are **Name**, **Artists**, **Album**, **#**, **Genre**, and **Rating**. (Most of the columns get their information from the tags embedded in the music files, as described in the section "Fix Music Tags" on page 229.)

Videos
Similar to **Pictures**, this template uses the **Large Icons** view to show single-frame previews of video files.

Figure 2-6. Use the **Customize** tab to choose a display template for the selected folder, but don't forget to customize the template

Here's how to customize one of these templates:

1. Find a folder with files that are uniquely representative of a certain kind of content, like a bunch of photos or a collection of music files, and open it in a new Explorer window.

2. Right-click the folder in the tree to your left, select **Properties**, and then choose the **Customize** tab. (See the next sidebar, "Missing the Customize Tab?" on page 60, if this tab isn't there.)

3. Choose a template that most closely matches the contents of the selected folder (i.e., **Pictures and Videos** for a folder containing *.jpg* files).

 The **Also apply this template to all subfolders** option here is particularly handy in that it allows you to customize an entire branch of folders in one step. For instance, you might store all your digital photos in various subfolders of the special *Pictures* folder, but this option ensures that they're all shown as thumbnails while preserving the more useful **Details** view for other types of content.

4. Click OK to close the Properties window.

5. Use the view drop-down to set a view you find suitable for the files in this folder (e.g., **Large Icons** for photos).

6. Right-click the column headers in the right pane, select **More**, and then place checkmarks next to all the columns you'd like shown. When you're done, click OK, and then use your mouse to rearrange and resize the columns to taste.

7. Sort the listing by clicking the appropriate column; click a second time to reverse the sort order.

8. When the folder looks the way you want all folders of this kind to look, click **Organize** and then select **Folder and Search Options**.

9. Choose the **View** tab, click **Apply to Folders**, answer **Yes**, and then click OK.

This will save your changes to the active template so that the next folder you view with similar content (at least in theory) will be displayed with the same view settings. This change won't affect any other templates.

So how do you get Explorer to choose the appropriate template automatically, say when you insert a DVD full of pictures or a USB drive full of ZIP files?

One solution is to duplicate the same view settings for each template, so that no matter which template Explorer picks, it'll look the way you want. This is fine if you don't care about large icons for pictures, but would prefer everything to appear in the **Details** view.

Another approach is to use the following Registry hack to reinforce one template as the default, increasing the odds that Explorer will use it above all others unless you specify otherwise with the **Customize** tab.

Now, the hack itself is a bit laborious if performed manually. So why not just download a registry patch that does all the work for you? Just go to *http://www .annoyances.org/exec/show/choosetemplate* and download *ResetExplorer.exe* and *ChooseTemplate.reg*, both free. Right-click *ResetExplorer.exe*, select **Run as administrator**, and answer **Yes** to clear Windows Explorer's cached folder data.

Then double-click *ChooseTemplate.reg* and click **Yes** to apply the patch. This patch adds some new options to the Folder Options window described earlier in this chapter (using the method outlined in "Create an Interface for a Registry Setting" on page 143). To use the new settings, open Explorer's Organize drop-down, select **Folder and search options**, and then choose the **View** tab. From the **Default Folder Template** branch in **Advanced settings**, choose how you'd like all folders to be viewed by default and click OK.

Thereafter, Explorer should use your preferred template rather than guessing. Of course, you can still use the **Customize** tab to manually choose a template for a folder, as described earlier in this section.

Missing the Customize Tab?

If you don't see the **Customize** tab in the Properties window for a folder, all you need is a quick Registry hack to fix the problem. (The **Customize** tab only appears in the Properties window for folders; don't look for it when right-clicking *Drives*, *Libraries*, or special folders like *Desktop*.)

Open the Registry Editor (See Chapter 3) and expand the branches to `HKEY_CLASSES_ROOT\Directory\shellex\PropertySheetHandlers`. Look for a subkey named `{ef43ecfe-2ab9-4632-bf21-58909dd177f0}`; if it isn't there, create a new key with that name by going to **Edit→New→Key**.

Navigate to `HKEY_CURRENT_USER\Software\Microsoft\Windows\CurrentVersion\Policies\Explorer`. Double-click the `NoCustomizeThisFolder` value in the right pane, type 0 (zero) in the **Value data** field, and click OK. Do the same for the `NoCustomizeWebView` and `ClassicShell` values. (If any of these values are absent, skip 'em.)

And finally, navigate to `HKEY_LOCAL_MACHINE\Software\Microsoft\Windows\CurrentVersion\policies\Explorer`, and if the `Explorer` key is present, set the same three values to 0 (zero). Close the Registry Editor when you're done, restart Windows, and try again.

Start Explorer with Any Folder

Tired of *Libraries* when you really want *\Documents\Invoices\My Richest Clients* 90% of the time?

The only difference between the window you get when you click the **Windows Explorer** icon on the taskbar and when you double-click a folder on your desktop is the folder it opens. So why not customize your shortcuts so they send you where you want to go?

Start by making a new shortcut to Explorer. Open your Start menu and type `explorer` in the **Search** box; Windows Explorer should appear in the search results after just `expl`; when it does, use the right mouse button to right-drag Windows Explorer from the search results onto an empty area of your desktop, and then select **Create shortcuts here** from the menu that appears.

Right-click on the new shortcut, select **Properties**, and choose the **Shortcut** tab. Change the text in the **Target** field so that it reads:

```
%windir%\explorer.exe d:\myfolder
```

where *d:\myfolder* is the full path of the folder you want Explorer to open. (You don't have to type it; just open it by hand in Explorer, right-click the path box, and select **Copy address as text**.) Click OK when you're done, and then double-click the new shortcut to try it out.

 By default, when Windows Explorer opens a specific folder, it does *not* show the current folder in the tree. To fix this, right-click a blank space in the Navigation pane (near the tree) and turn on the **Expand to current folder** option.

Want to put this new shortcut on your taskbar? Right-click your customized shortcut and select **Unpin from Taskbar**. Then right-click again and select **Pin to Taskbar**. Close any open Explorer windows and then click your new taskbar button to confirm it takes you to your chosen folder.

Jump lists and Favorites

Got several favorite folders? Of course, you can just drag them into your *Favorites* folder in any open Explorer window, where they're just one more click away. Or, you can take advantage of Windows 7's jump lists.

Open Explorer and navigate to a folder you'd like to make more accessible. Drag the folder icon onto the Windows Explorer taskbar button and when it says **Pin to Windows Explorer**, let go. Then, click the Explorer taskbar button and hold down the mouse button while dragging upward (or just right-click); your new folder is now in the **Pinned** section at the top of the jump list, as shown in Figure 2-7.

Figure 2-7. Drag a folder onto the Windows Explorer taskbar button to add it to its jump list, and then click-slide to open the folder

More Explorer command-line options

There are actually a bunch of different command-line parameters you can use to further customize the shortcut from the beginning of this section. In its simplest form, you just specify a location by itself, like this:

```
explorer.exe location
```

where *location* can be the full path of some folder or a virtual folder (videos for *My Videos*).

Here's the full syntax for *explorer.exe*:

```
explorer.exe [/separate] [/e][[,/select,]location]
```

The square brackets ([...]) indicate an optional parameter, which they all are (you don't ever type the brackets). Note the odd syntax (commas around the /select switch) and the fact that these parameters must appear in this sequence.

/separate

> This starts a separate instance of the *explorer.exe* application for each Explorer window you open.

> This is different than the **Launch folder windows in a separate process** option described in "Customize Windows Explorer" on page 45, wherein only a single separate instance is started for all Explorer windows. See "Open 32-bit Windows Explorer on x64" on page 73 for another use for this switch.

/e

> This ensures that the Navigation pane (folder tree) appears, just in case you turned it off.

,/select,

> This option instructs Explorer to select the folder or file specified immediately afterwards. You'd use it to select a single file, but if you actually want to *open* the path you specify, you'd likely omit /select (otherwise, Explorer would only open the folder's *parent*).

location

> As explained previously, this can be the full path of an actual folder or the name of a special folder. It can also be a filename (when used with the /select switch) or a registry class ID (see upcoming example).

Note that the /n and /root, *object* parameters used in some earlier versions, are ignored in Windows 7.

For instance, to open Windows Explorer to the *Computer* folder so that no drive branches are initially expanded—which is handy if you have several drives and you want to see them all on equal footing—type:

```
%windir%\explorer.exe /e,::{20d04fe0-3aea-1069-a2d8-08002b30309d}
```

The long string of characters in curly braces is a registry class ID, explained in Chapter 3. Another way to do more or less the same thing is with this:

```
explorer.exe /e,/select,c:\
```

Or, to show the folder containing the file *c:\Windows\Cursors\aero_busy.cur*, you'd type:

```
explorer.exe /e,/select,c:\Windows\Cursors\aero_busy.cur
```

This last example is what Windows does when you right-click a file in search results and select **Open file location**. Similarly, you can right-click most things in Windows and select **Explore** to open a new Explorer window at that location.

Get to the Desktop

The problem with the desktop metaphor is that, like a real desk top, it's always covered with stuff. But in Windows, there are things on the desktop, like files, shortcuts, and Gadgets, that you need to get to. Fortunately, Windows offers several ways to do it:

Taskbar
> Click the small, blank button on the far right of the taskbar (next to the clock) to hide all open windows and display the desktop. If you have Aero Glass (Chapter 5) enabled, you'll see ghosted outlines of your Windows when you hover your mouse over the button as part of a nifty feature called "Aero Peek."

Keyboard
> Hold the Windows logo key (Winkey) and press **D** to quickly show the desktop. Press Winkey+**D** again to restore your windows (although not necessarily in the same sequence). Do this many times to give yourself a headache. (If your keyboard has no Winkey, see "Keyboard Is My Friend" on page 76.) You can also press Winkey+**M** to minimize all windows (the same end result), but you can't get them all back quite so easily. And, of course, the desktop is shown alongside your running applications when you press **Alt+Tab** or Winkey+**Tab**.

Custom icon
> Like the show desktop feature, but don't like the placement of the **Show Desktop** button on the taskbar? To make your own **Show Desktop** icon

you can put anywhere, open your favorite plain-text editor (or Notepad), and type the following five lines:

```
[Shell]
Command=2
IconFile=explorer.exe,3
[Taskbar]
Command=ToggleDesktop
```

Save the file as *Show Desktop.scf* (or any other name, provided that you include the *.scf* filename extension) anywhere you like, including your desktop. Just double-click the icon to show the desktop.

Windows Explorer

Another approach is to simply open a Windows Explorer window and navigate to the *Desktop* folder near the top of the tree. That way, you can leave your open programs intact, making it easier to drag files onto them from the desktop.

 You can also drag files onto a minimized application, provided you have a steady hand and some patience. Just drag down to the taskbar and hover the file over the minimized application button you want to restore for a good five seconds. Although you can't drop files on the taskbar button itself, if you wait long enough, Windows will restore the application window, at which point you can drag the file over to the window and drop it.

Icons on the taskbar

Need to get to your desktop icons all the time? Right-click an empty area of the taskbar, select **Toolbars**, and then select **Desktop**. By default, the toolbar will probably be smushed up against the notification area (tray) and the clock, so right-click the taskbar again and turn off the **Lock the Taskbar** option so you can move the **Desktop** toolbar around. Next, right-click the **Desktop** title and select the **Show Text** option to fit more icons on the bar. It's not the most convenient interface, especially if you have a lot on your desktop, but it's there if you need it.

Quick Access to Control Panel

A lot of the clicking and scrounging in this book takes place in Control Panel, a window that provides links to many settings that affect the way Windows looks, sounds, and behaves. It's a hodge-podge of modern web-like pages and older tabbed dialog windows. Some of the dialog windows date back more than a decade to Windows 95, and are still present either to maintain compatibility with add-ons (like extra tabs in the Mouse Properties window) or merely because Microsoft doesn't want to invest the resources to update or replace all their dialogs. As a result, it can be hard to find specific settings in Control Panel.

Many windows are buried several levels deep in Control Panel, so it can be a bit of a pain to make your way around the program, particularly if you need to return to the same spot often.

Want to make a quick and dirty shortcut to a Control Panel window? Just open Control Panel and Windows Explorer side-by-side, and drag any green link from Control Panel into your *Favorites* folder. (Note that blue-colored links on most Control Panel pages can't be dragged.)

Or, drag any green link from Control Panel onto the Control Panel taskbar button and when it says **Pin to Control Panel**, let go. Then, click the Control Panel taskbar button and hold down the mouse button while dragging upwards (or just right-click), and then select your location from the **Pinned** section at the top of the jump list (see Figure 2-7).

Unfortunately, Control Panel only lets you create shortcuts by dragging the green-colored links. To provide quick access to almost any page or window in Control Panel, you'll need to use the old-school command-line syntax (around since the days of Windows 3.x in the early 1990s, if you can believe it):

```
\windows\system32\control.exe sysdm.cpl, 3
```

which opens the **Advanced** tab in the Advanced System Properties window, normally found on the System page. Note that, unlike previous versions, you need to specify the full path of *control.exe*. Or, for some windows, you can use this standalone executable to accomplish the same thing:

```
SystemPropertiesAdvanced.exe
```

For a list of these shortcuts, see Table 2-1.

Not all Control Panel pages can be opened from the command line. For those tools not listed in Table 2-1, you can make a Windows shortcut by typing the name of the tool in the Start menu **Search** box, and then dragging the icon from the search results to a folder somewhere. Thereafter you can run the shortcut from the command line.

Table 2-1. Command-line access to Control Panel pages and tools

Control Panel page	Command line
Action Center	`wscui.cpl`
Administrative Tools	`explorer.exe\ProgramData\Microsoft` `\Windows\Start Menu\Programs\Adminis` `trative Tools`
Advanced System Properties→Advanced tab	`SystemPropertiesAdvanced.exe`
Advanced System Properties→Computer Name tab	`sysdm.cpl` or `SystemPropertiesComputer` `Name.exe`
Advanced System Properties→Advanced tab→Performance Options→Data Execution Prevention tab	`SystemProper` `tiesDataExecutionPrevention.exe`
Advanced System Properties→Hardware tab	`SystemPropertiesHardware.exe`
Advanced System Properties→Advanced tab→Performance Options	`SystemPropertiesPerformance.exe`
Advanced System Properties→System Protection tab	`SystemPropertiesProtection.exe`
Advanced System Properties→Remote tab	`SystemPropertiesRemote.exe`
Backup and Restore	`sdclt.exe`
Bluetooth Devices	`bthprops.cpl`
Color Management	`colorcpl.exe`
Color Management→Advanced→Calibrate Display	`dccw.exe`
Date and Time	`timedate.cpl` or `control date/time`
Device Manager	`devmgmt.msc` or `hdwwiz.cpl`
Devices and Printers	`control network` or `control printers`
Disk Management	`diskmgmt.msc`
Display	`DpiScaling.exe`
Display→Screen Resolution	`desk.cpl`
Ease of Access Center	`Utilman.exe`
Ease of Access Center→Use the computer without a mouse or keyboard	`control keyboard` or `control mouse`
Fonts	`control fonts`
Game Controllers	`joy.cpl`
Internet Options	`inetcpl.cpl`
Mouse Properties	`main.cpl` or `control mouse`
Network Connections	`ncpa.cpl`
Pen and Touch	`TabletPC.cpl`

Control Panel page	Command line
People Near Me	`collab.cpl`
Personalization	`control desktop`
Phone and Modem	`telephon.cpl`
Power Options	`powercfg.cpl`
Programs and Features	`appwiz.cpl`
Programs and Features→Turn Windows features on or off	`OptionalFeatures.exe`
Region and Language	`intl.cpl`
Set Program Access and Computer Defaults	`ComputerDefaults.exe`
Sound	`mmsys.cpl`
Sync Center	`mobsync.exe`
Task Scheduler	`taskschd.msc`
User Accounts	`control userpasswords`
User Accounts (advanced)	`control userpasswords2` or `Netplwiz.exe`
Volume Mixer	`SndVol.exe`
Windows Firewall	`Firewall.cpl`

Shell Tweaks

Does it take an inordinately long time to show Control Panel in the **Small icons** or **Large icons** view? It's possible that an application you've installed made use of a specific "legacy" feature that lets you hide certain Control Panel icons; see the "Hide Unwanted Control Panel Icons" sidebar, next, for details.

Hide Unwanted Control Panel Icons

You can hide certain types of icons in Control Panel's Classic View with a quick Registry hack. Just open the Registry Editor (explained in Chapter 3), and expand the branches to HKEY_CURRENT_USER\Control Panel\don't load.

Then, create a new string value for each icon you want to hide. For the name, type the filename of the *.cpl* file responsible for the icon (see "Quick Access to Control Panel" on page 64). Then, double-click the new value, type No for its data, and click OK.

Refresh the Control Panel window by pressing the **F5** key to see the change. Unfortunately, Control Panel may crash—or at least take a long time to load all its icons—if there's an errant entry in the don't load Registry key. If you see the Green Ribbon of Death (see Chapter 6) whenever you open Control Panel, delete all the values in the don't load key and then try again.

Setting Finder

Wouldn't it just be easier if you could list all the pages and subpages and windows and settings in Control Panel in one alphabetized list? There would be no hunting for settings, clicking from one page to the next, and no guesswork. Strange as it sounds, such a list is built into Windows 7, but it's nowhere to be found in Control Panel.

In any folder or on the desktop, create a new folder and type the following for its name:

```
All Settings.{ED7BA470-8E54-465E-825C-99712043E01C}
```

press **Enter**, and the name will shorten to *All Settings*. Open the new folder to show an alphabetical list of all Control Panel settings, like the one shown in Figure 2-8.

Figure 2-8. This alphabetical list of Control Panel settings is hidden by default

Prune the Start Menu

There's no more "classic" Start menu in Windows 7. Never mind that the single column Start menu that went more or less unchanged since Windows 95 was a user-interface disaster; it had its plusses. Among other things, it was simple,

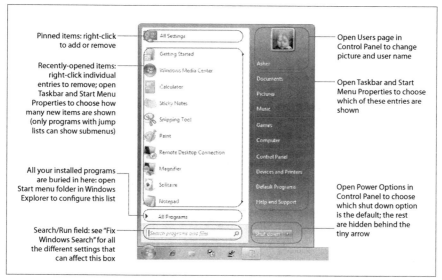

Pinned items: right-click to add or remove

Recently-opened items: right-click individual entries to remove; open Taskbar and Start Menu Properties to choose how many new items are shown (only programs with jump lists can show submenus)

All your installed programs are buried in here: open Start menu folder in Windows Explorer to configure this list

Search/Run field: see "Fix Windows Search" for all the different settings that can affect this box

Open Users page in Control Panel to change picture and user name

Open Taskbar and Start Menu Properties to choose which of these entries are shown

Open Power Options in Control Panel to choose which shut down option is the default; the rest are hidden behind the tiny arrow

Shell Tweaks

Figure 2-9. Each region of the Start menu gets configured in a different place

short, and almost completely customizable—three things you can't necessarily say about the "modern" Start menu.

> Miss the old "classic" Start menu that Microsoft kept around until Windows Vista? Get the free CSMenu (*http://www .csmenu.com/*) add-on to get it back. Or if you like the look of Aero Glass, but the layout of the classic Start menu, check out Classic Start Menu with Aero (*http://www.classicstartmenu .com/*).

But there are some things you can do to trim down the new Start menu so the only clutter is *your* clutter.

Each element—or rather, elements in each region—are configured in slightly different ways, as shown in Figure 2-9.

The contents of the standard Windows Start menu are divided into seven sections:

Pinned items

> At the top of the lefthand column, above the horizontal line, is the list of "pinned" items, and is the only fully-customizable portion of the top level Start menu.
>
> Right-click any application executable (*.exe* file) and select **Pin to Start Menu** to add it to the list, or drag any item (application, folder, Control

Panel page, etc.) onto the Start button, hover for just a moment, and when it says **Pin to Start menu**, let go. Or, if you hover for just a second or two longer, the Start menu pops open, and you can drop the item anywhere you like.

 The pinned items list is peculiar because, unlike the **All Programs** folders, pinned items aren't shortcuts on your hard disk. Rather, the pinned items are stored in the Registry (see Chapter 3) in a format that makes them impractical to edit by hand. This means that application installers can't litter your pinned items list with unwanted icons, but it also means you can't easily rename an item.

For example, pin *diskmgmt.msc* onto your Start menu, and the new entry is titled **diskmgmt**. The workaround is to create a standard shortcut to *diskmgmt.msc* elsewhere—perhaps a subfolder of *All Programs*—and then pin the shortcut instead.

Recently used applications

Below the pinned items on the left side is a dynamic list of recently used programs. The problem with this list is that it is always changing, making it a poor choice to store shortcuts to programs you need to use frequently.

To remove the list entirely, right-click an empty area of the Start menu, select **Properties**, and turn off the **Store and display a list of recently opened programs in the Start menu** option. The space will immediately become available for more pinned items (above).

Or, to change the size of the list, click the **Customize** button here, and in the **Start menu size** section at the bottom, adjust the **Number of recent programs to display** value. (If the section is grayed out, it's because the aforementioned **Store and display** option is turned off.)

All Programs

At the very bottom of the left column is a single entry, **All Programs**, which contains the folders and icons for most of your applications. The items herein are shortcuts on your hard disk, compiled from two sources. First, there are your personal shortcuts here:

C:\Users\{username}\AppData\Roaming\Microsoft\Windows\Start Menu\Programs

and then there's the shared "All users" folder here:

C:\ProgramData\Microsoft\Windows\Start Menu\Programs

Although you can drag and drop shortcuts in this list, it's usually a whole lot easier to work with the folders directly in Windows Explorer, especially if you have a lot of things to change.

 Resist the temptation to consolidate your personal Start menu shortcuts and the All Users shortcuts. Doing so can incidentally change the registered locations of those folders in the registry (see Chapter 3), which can cause problems as applications create new icons (particularly in the *Startup* folder). Instead, just delete unwanted items from both places, and add new items only to your personal Programs folder.

To remove the **All Programs** item from the Start menu, open the Group Policy Object Editor (*gpedit.msc*, which is not present in the Home Premium edition), and expand the branches to User Configuration \Administrative Templates\Start Menu and Taskbar. Double-click **Remove All Programs list from the Start menu**, select **Enabled**, and click OK. You'll have to log out and then log back in for this change to take effect.

You can customize some of the aspects of this menu by right-clicking an empty area of the Start menu, selecting **Properties**, and then clicking **Customize**. If you turn on the **Enable context menus and dragging and dropping** option, you'll be able to drag shortcuts and even right-click them to customize them; turn off this option if you want them to stay put. Next, turn on the **Sort All Programs menu by name** option to keep the list sorted; or, if you turn it off, you can sort a single folder on the fly by right-clicking any entry and selecting **Sort by Name**.

Search box

This is more than just a **Search** box; it's also a quick and dirty replacement for the Run window. You can type any program here—either the application name or the executable filename—and press **Enter** to run the program. Or, type the first few letters of the program to launch, and then click the desired entry in the search results above.

 If you've started a search you want to cancel, click the blue × button to the right of the search text field (or press **Esc**) to get your Start menu back.

By default, search results here are limited to your personal documents, items in your **All Programs** menu, and special locations like Control

Panel. To broaden your searches to include the entire index, right-click an empty area of the Start menu, select **Properties**, and then click **Customize**. Scroll down the list to the **Search other files and libraries** branch, and select **Search with public folders**. See "Fix Windows Search" on page 111, for ways to improve the speed and breadth of the index.

The Picture Box

To change the picture, open the User Accounts page in Control Panel (or just click the picture), and then click **Change your picture**. There's no way to remove the picture box; it's also used to provide visual feedback as you hover over other items in the righthand column. Probably the best you can do is pick a solid color square box for your picture and then pretend it's not there.

You can, however, remove your name from beneath the picture by right-clicking an empty area of the Start menu, selecting **Properties**, and then clicking **Customize**. In the **Personal folder** branch, select **Don't display this item**, and then click OK.

Righthand column

You can have control over every entry in the right column, but not directly with drag-and-drop.

Instead, to get rid of any unwanted entries, or add some old favorites like **Run**, right-click an empty area of the Start menu, select **Properties**, and then click **Customize**. In the list you'll find each of these items—there are twenty in all—interspersed with settings that affect other aspects of the Start menu. To get rid of an item, just clear the checkbox or, if applicable, select **Don't display this item**.

To open the Run box—whether or not it appears on the Start menu—hold the Windows logo key and press **R** (Winkey+**R**). Of course, the aforementioned **Search** box also doubles (mostly) as a "Run" command, except it's lacking the convenient drop-down list of recently run items. The **Search** box also opens a search window when it can't find what you've typed, as opposed to the unfriendly (yet occasionally helpful) error message you get from the Run window.

Shut Down button

Last but not least is the simple **Shut Down** button, which appears at the bottom of the right column, next to a tiny arrow for more shut down options: **Switch user**, **Log off**, **Lock**, **Restart**, and **Sleep**.

By default, the Shut Down button puts your PC to sleep, but you can set it to shut down instead, as described in "Start Windows Instantly (Almost)" on page 274.

Shell Tweaks

To remove the **Shut Down** button et al., open the Group Policy editor (*gpedit.msc*, which is not present on the Home Premium edition), and expand the branches to `User Configuration\Administrative Templates \Start Menu and Taskbar`. Double-click **Remove and prevent access to the Shut Down, Restart, Sleep, and Hibernate commands**, select **Enabled**, and click OK. You'll have to log out and then log back in for this change to take effect. Of course, once that's done, the only way to shut down or restart (necessary to undo the change) is to use the `shutdown` command-line tool described in the section "Control a PC Remotely" on page 488, or press the physical power switch on your PC.

Start button

Yes, you can even remove the Start button from the taskbar, but you'll need a special tool for that. See "Tweak the Taskbar" on page 75 for details.

Open 32-bit Windows Explorer on x64

If you've got 64-bit Windows, then you're using 64-bit Windows Explorer. This means that any Explorer extensions—context menu add-ons, image preview codecs, Property sheet extensions, or drag-drop handlers—must be native 64-bit as well, or they won't work.

So what if you have a 32-bit Explorer extension for which there is no native 64-bit version yet? In previous versions of Windows, you could fire up the 32-bit Windows Explorer (*c:\Windows\SysWOW64\explorer.exe*). But in Windows 7, this doesn't work. Yes, the 32-bit *explorer.exe* is sitting on your hard disk, but if you try to open it, Windows just runs the native 64-bit version.

But that's not where the story ends. In almost every application that works with files, there's a **File→Open** and a corresponding **File→Save As** window, and these windows are basically lightweight instances of Windows Explorer. (Newer apps use the handy two-pane window with the folder tree, while older apps use the more limited single-pane version.) This means that most native 32-bit applications can be used as makeshift 32-bit instances of Windows Explorer.

So how do you know which applications are native 32-bit? Just open Task Manager (**Ctrl+Shift+Esc**) and choose the **Processes** tab. In the **Image Name** column, 32-bit programs are marked with a *32, while native x64 programs are not. For instance, Microsoft Word 2007 appears as

---

WINWORD.EXE *32. And the active window is highlighted in gray, so there's no guesswork.

So the next time you need access to 32-bit Windows Explorer, just fire up a 32-bit application, and from the **File** menu, select **Open**. From there, you can right-click files and folders to your heart's content, as well as drag-drop, rename, delete, and just about anything else you can do with a standard Explorer window.

When all is said and done, you'll have a leaner, cleaner Start menu that contains only the items you actually want and use. If you like, you can basically wipe the Start menu completely clean so that it looks like the one in Figure 2-10, adorned only with the **Search** box and your custom picture.

Figure 2-10. Minimalists may appreciate a clean, uncluttered Start menu like this one

Secrets of Window Management

One of the perks you get with Windows 7 is a whole bunch of window management shortcuts and nifty eye candy to happily accompany the drudgery of generating soils reports. Here are some of the ways you can make working with Windows just a little more enjoyable.

 Aero Snap is the name given to the feature that automatically helps you position windows as you drag them around. Drag a window to the top of the screen to maximize, or to the left or right to *half-maximize*. Or, drag a window so its edge mates with the edge of another window or the edge of the screen, and it'll snap snugly into position.

Don't like it? You can turn it off by opening the Ease of Access Center page in Control Panel. Click the **Change how your mouse works** link, and then turn on the **Prevent windows from being automatically arranged when moved to the edge of the screen** option.

Tweak the Taskbar

Windows window management takes place mostly on the taskbar, which got a big facelift in Windows 7. Gone is the piddly QuickLaunch toolbar; now you can use taskbar buttons to launch programs as well as manage them when they're already open. Jump lists, covered in "Start Explorer with Any Folder" on page 60, help merge these two functions nicely. You can even rearrange taskbar icons now by simply dragging and dropping.

But one thing you still can't do is hide several icons inside of a single icon on the taskbar. As it is now, a program shortcut can either be on the taskbar or desktop, or buried several layers deep in the Start menu. If you're itching for some middle ground, try 7stacks (*http://www.alastria.com/?*) or Standalone-Stack (*http://www.chrisnsoft.com/*), both free, to add submenus of sorts to the taskbar. The term "stacks" is taken from the similar feature in Mac OS X; if you want the Windows 7 taskbar to be more like the Mac OS X dock, check out RocketDock (*http://rocketdock.com/*), also free.

Want a little more room for buttons on the taskbar? Confuse your friends with Start Killer, free from *http://www.tordex.com/startkiller/*, which hides the Start button completely. You can still open the Start menu with the Windows logo key or **Ctrl+Esc**, or you can disable Start Killer by pressing **Ctrl+Alt+Shift +F12**.

If you have a multiple monitor setup, see "Stretch Out on Multiple Monitors" on page 85 for a way to extend the taskbar to all your screens.

Keyboard Is My Friend

Despite the fact that Microsoft has excised those little underlined letters—the ones that show you which letter you have to press while holding the **Alt** key to jump to that control—the keyboard is alive and well in Windows 7. In fact, there are tons of useful keyboard shortcuts that can be real time-savers in Windows, some even used in conjunction with the mouse.

Navigating files and folders

Properties
> Hold the **Alt** key while double-clicking on a file or folder to view the Properties sheet for that object. Or, press **Alt+Enter** to open the Properties window for the selected item without using the mouse at all.

History
> Press **Backspace** in an open Explorer window to go back to the last folder you looked at (which may or may not be the active folder's parent folder).

> You can also hold **Alt** while pressing the left or right arrow keys to go back and forth through the folder history, akin to the two round arrow buttons to the left of the path box.

Parent folder
> Press **Alt**+up arrow to jump to the active folder's parent folder.

Refresh/Reload
> Press **F5** in almost any window (including web browsers and even Device Manager) to refresh the current view.

Folder tree
> With the focus on Explorer's folder tree, press **Enter** to view the contents of the highlighted folder in the right pane. Also, use the left and right arrow keys (or + and -) to collapse and expand folders, respectively, or press the asterisk key (*) to expand all the folders and their subfolders in the current branch.

> Press **Ctrl+Shift+E** to scroll the folder tree so that the active folder is at the bottom of the Navigation pane.

Jump to an item
> With the focus on the right pane, press a letter key to quickly jump to the first file or folder starting with that letter. Continue typing to jump further. For example, pressing the **T** key in your *Windows* folder will jump to the

Tasks folder. Press **T** again to jump to the next object that starts with T. Or, press **T** and then quickly press **A** to skip the first few Ts and jump to *taskman.exe*. If there's enough of a delay between the **T** and the **A** keys, Explorer will forget about the T, and you'll jump to the first entry that starts with A.

 If you prefer, you can have Windows Explorer begin a formal search as soon as you start typing. Open the **Organize** drop-down, select **Folder and Search Options**, and then choose the **View** tab. Scroll to the bottom of the **Advanced settings** list, and under the **When typing into list view** branch, click **Automatically type into the Search Box**.

New Explorer window

Press **Ctrl+N** to open another Explorer window at the same folder. Or press Winkey+**E** to open a new Windows Explorer window, even when you're not currently in Explorer.

Search

In Windows Explorer or on the desktop, press **Ctrl+F** or **F3** to open a separate search window so you can search without losing the current view. To search in the current Explorer window, press Ctrl+E to jump to the search box and start typing. (Or, if you've selected the **Automatically type into the Search Box** option explained earlier in this section, just start typing to immediately jump to the search box.) Press Winkey+**F** to open a search window no matter where you are. See "Fix Windows Search" on page 111 for other ways to improve search.

Show hidden context menu items

Hold the **Shift** key while right-clicking a *file* to show two new items in the file's context menu: **Pin to Start Menu** (normally shown only for programs) and **Copy as Path** (used to copy the full path of the item to the clipboard).

Or, hold **Shift** while right-clicking a *folder* to show three new items: **Open in new process** (discussed earlier in this chapter), **Open command window here** (see Chapter 9), and the aforementioned **Copy as Path**.

Finally, hold **Shift** while right-clicking an empty area of the desktop or open folder window to show the **Open command window here** command.

See "File Type Associations" on page 166 for instructions to customize the context menus for files, folders, and many Windows objects.

Path box

Press **Alt+D** or **F4** to jump to the path box so you can type or flip through recently visited folders. Once you're there, press **Esc** to close the drop-down history and select the text. Press **Esc** once more to revert to the modern "breadcrumbs" path box so you can navigate parent folders with only the arrow keys.

Cycle through all the controls

Press the **Tab** key to jump between the file pane, the file pane column headers, the address bar, the **Search** box, the tool ribbon, and the folder tree. The **F6** key does the same thing as Tab, but it skips the **Search** box.

Preview pane

Press **Alt+P** to toggle the Preview pane on and off.

View / Icon size

Hold **Ctrl** while rolling the mouse wheel to cycle through the various view settings (**Details**, **List**). Roll up past **Small icons**, and further rolling will progressively enlarge the icons.

Selecting and managing files

Select all

Press **Ctrl+A** to quickly select all of the contents of a folder, both files and folders.

Select range

Select one icon, then hold the **Shift** key while clicking on another icon in the same folder to select it and all the items in between. To do this only with the keyboard, hold the **Shift** key while moving up or down with the arrow keys.

 You can select a range of files without using the keyboard by dragging a *rubber band* around them. Start by holding down the left mouse button in a blank portion of a folder window, then drag the mouse to the opposite corner to select everything that appears in the rectangle you just drew.

Select multiple items

Hold the **Ctrl** key and click multiple files or folders to select or deselect them one by one. (Note that you can't select more than one folder in the Navigation pane (folder tree), but you can in the right pane.) To do this only with the keyboard, hold **Ctrl** while moving up or down with the arrow keys, and then press the spacebar to select or deselect the active item.

You can also use the **Ctrl** key to modify your selection. For example, if you've used the **Shift** key or a rubber band to select the first five objects in a folder, you can hold **Ctrl** while dragging a second rubber band to highlight additional files *without* losing your original selection.

Delete files

Select a file or folder and press **Del** to delete it. Or, press **Shift+Del** to delete it permanently without sending it to the Recycle Bin.

Rename

Press **F2** to rename the currently selected item.

Create a new folder

Press **Ctrl+Shift+N** in any folder window or on the desktop to create a new, empty folder.

Automatically resize all Windows Explorer columns

Press **Ctrl+plus** (that's + on the numeric keypad) while in the **Details** view of Windows Explorer to resize all visible columns to fit their contents. You can also double-click column header separators to size-to-fit individual columns (just like in Microsoft Excel).

Starting programs

Start menu

Press the Windows logo key (Winkey) to open the Start menu, and then navigate with your arrow keys. You can also open the Start menu by pressing **Ctrl+Esc**. See the "Hack the Windows Logo Key" sidebar if you don't have a Windows logo key.

Hack the Windows Logo Key

What if your keyboard has no Winkey? Strictly speaking, you don't really need it, but there are a bunch of nifty keyboard shortcuts you can only do with the Winkey, such as Winkey+**D** to show the desktop, Winkey+**R** to run a program, and Winkey+**Tab** to use the corny Flip 3D task switcher.

To give your keyboard a Winkey, or any other key it doesn't have, you need a keyboard remapping tool. Most tools use an obscure feature already built

---

in to Windows, such as Sharpkeys (free, *http://www.randyrants.com/sharp keys/*), KeyTweak (free, *http://webpages.charter.net/krumsick/*), and Microsoft's own Microsoft Keyboard Layout Creator (*http://www.annoyances.org/exec/software/mklc*).

First, pick a key on your keyboard you don't use—the right-hand **Alt** or **Ctrl** keys are usually good candidates for the Windows Logo Key—and remap it to the key you want Windows to think you pressed. In SharpKeys, for instance, click **Add**, select **Special: Right Alt** from the **Map this key** list, select **Special: Left Windows** from the **To this key** list, and click OK. Back in the main window, click **Write to Registry**, and then log out and back in again for the change to take effect.

Of course, the Winkey isn't for everyone. On most keyboards, it's right next to the Space bar, which means it's easy to hit by accident. And since it's one of the few keys that takes the focus *away* from the active window, it can be decidedly inconvenient if you press it while you're typing.

To disable Winkey, all you do is use one of the aforementioned keyboard remapping tools to remap Winkey to something innocuous, like **Ctrl** or spacebar (or **Pause**/**Break** if you want it to do nothing at all). Or, if you have the MyExpose task switcher installed (see "Get Glass" on page 286), you can remap the Winkey to activate MyExpose instead.

While you're at it, you can likewise disable some other nuisance keys like **Insert** (**Ins**), so you'll never again inadvertently delete text as you type.

If you want to keep your Windows logo key, but you don't like the Winkey hotkey combinations (e.g., Winkey+**R**), you can turn those off with a quick Registry hack. Open the Registry Editor (see Chapter 3) and expand the branches to `HKEY_CURRENT_USER\Software\Microsoft\Windows\CurrentVersion\Policies\Explorer`. Create a new DWord value by selecting **Edit→New→ DWord Value (32-bit)**, and then name the new value `NoWinKeys`. Double-click the new value, type `1` for its data, and click OK. You'll need to log out and then back in again for the change to take effect.

Taskbar and jump lists

Hold Winkey while pressing a number key to open the taskbar item at that location; for instance Winkey+**1** opens the taskbar button closest to the Start button, Winkey+**2** opens the next one over, and so on. Or, press Winkey+**T** to cycle through taskbar buttons, and then press Enter to open the one selected. If the program is already running, Winkey+*number* switches to that program.

Hold **Shift** while clicking a taskbar button to open a new window rather than switching to one already open. Similarly, press **Shift**+Winkey and a number to open a new window of the application at that location on the taskbar.

Hold **Shift** while *right*-clicking a taskbar button to show the Properties window for the target file. Or, if the program is already running, hold **Shift** to show the old-school System menu for that window.

Hold **Ctrl+Shift** while clicking a taskbar button (or **Ctrl+Shift**+Winkey +*number*) to open the application as an administrator (see Chapter 8).

Press **Alt**+Winkey and a number to open the jump list for the application at that location on the taskbar, and then use the arrow keys and **Enter** to select an item. Or, when using the mouse, right-click the button or click down and drag (slide) up.

Run
Press Winkey+**R** to open the Start menu **Run** box.

Windows Explorer
Press Winkey+**E** to open a new Windows Explorer window.

Task Manager
Press **Ctrl+Shift+Esc** to open Task Manager (see Chapter 6).

View System Information
Press Winkey+**Pause/Break** to open the System page in Control Panel.

Presentation Mode
Press Winkey+**P** to activate Presentation Mode, provided you have the Professional edition of Windows 7 or better. To customize Presentation Mode, open the Windows Mobility Center (available on laptop PCs only).

Windows Mobility Center
Press Winkey+**X** to open the Windows Mobility Center page in Control Panel.

Ease of Access Center
Press Winkey+**U** to open the Ease of Access Center page in Control Panel.

Press **Shift** five times to toggle *StickyKeys* on and off. Hold **Shift** for eight seconds to toggle *FilterKeys* on and off. Hold **Num Lock** for five seconds to toggle *ToggleKeys* on and off. Press **Alt+LeftShift+Num Lock** to toggle *MouseKeys* on and off. Press **Alt+LeftShift+Print Screen** to toggle *high contrast mode* on and off.

Get Windows Help
Press Winkey+**F1** to open Windows Help and Support, or **F1** by itself (usually) to open Help for the active application or window.

Managing running programs

Switch to a different window

Press Winkey+**Tab** to show the silly Flip 3D Rolodex-style task switcher, or **Alt+Tab** to show the simple "classic" task switcher. See "Get Glass" on page 286 for another alternative. Hold **Shift** (**Shift**+Winkey +**Tab** or **Shift+Alt+Tab**) to go backward.

If you're using an application with more than one document, press **Ctrl** +**Tab** to switch among the open documents. Likewise, press **Ctrl+Tab** to cycle through tabs in a tabbed window. And again, hold **Shift** to go in reverse.

Taskbar and jump lists

Hold Winkey while pressing a number key to switch to the taskbar item at that location, as described earlier in this section.

Hold **Ctrl** while clicking a grouped taskbar button to cycle through the windows in that group.

Drop the current window to the bottom of the pile

Press **Alt+Esc** to move the active window to the bottom of the stack and activate the one underneath it. Hold **Shift** to go backward.

View the desktop

Press Winkey+**D** to show or hide the desktop, Winkey+**M** to minimize all open windows, or **Shift**+Winkey+**M** to restore minimized windows. See "Get to the Desktop" on page 63 for more.

Show only the active window

Press Winkey+**Home** to minimize all windows except the active one. To do this with the mouse, grab the title bar and shake vigorously for at least a second. Do this again to restore the windows.

Resize the active window

Press Winkey+up arrow to maximize a window. Press Winkey+down arrow to restore a maximized window or minimize a standard window.

Once you've minimized a window with Winkey+down, it loses focus, so pressing Winkey+up immediately afterward won't work. Instead, use **Alt+Tab**, Winkey+**Tab**, or Winkey+**T** (all covered previously) to switch to a minimized window.

Press **Shift**+Winkey+up arrow to maximize the current window only vertically; its horizontal size and position won't change.

Press Winkey+right arrow to shove the active window to the right side of the screen (sort of a half-maximize); same thing goes for Winkey+left arrow.

Move a window to another monitor

Got a multiple monitor setup? Hit either **Shift**+Winkey+right arrow or **Shift**+Winkey+left arrow to move the window to a different screen. Or, hit Winkey+left arrow or Winkey+right arrow three times to accomplish the same thing.

Gadgets

Press Winkey+**G** to cycle through active desktop gadgets.

Close a window

Press **Alt+F4** to close the current application, or **Ctrl+F4** to close the current document (if it's the type of program that can hold multiple documents). Press **Alt+F4** while the keyboard focus is on the desktop or taskbar to shut down windows.

Notification area (Tray)

Press Winkey+**B** to send the focus to the notification area (tray).

Menus

Press **Alt** or **F10** to jump to the menu bar (or show the menu if it's hidden).

Zoom in, zoom out

Press Winkey+plus (+ on the numeric keypad) to zoom in where the mouse is pointing (using the Magnifier tool), or Winkey+minus (– on the numeric keypad) to zoom out. Then, just drag your mouse past the edges of the screen to pan to the extents of the desktop.

Log off

Press Winkey+**L** to lock your computer, at which point you unlock it by typing your password or switch users.

Editing text

Clipboard

Press **Ctrl+C** to copy the selected item to the clipboard, **Ctrl+X** to cut (copy and then delete), and **Ctrl+V** to paste the item anywhere else.

Undo

Press **Ctrl+Z** to undo the last text edit, file operation, deletion, etc.

Drop-down listboxes

Use the up and down arrow keys to flip through items in a drop-down box, or press **Alt**+down arrow to open the listbox.

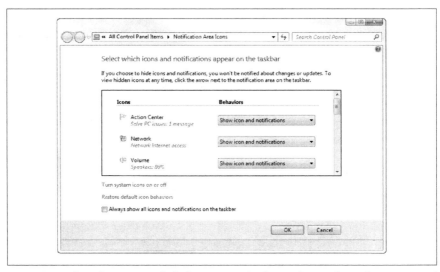

Figure 2-11. If you don't want to hide the tray completely, use this window to bury unwanted clutter under a collapsible panel

Clean Up the Tray

The *notification area* as Microsoft calls it—or *tray*, as it's called on the street—is the box full of tiny icons on the far right side of your taskbar, next to the clock.

It made its first appearance in Windows 95, but it didn't take long for most trays to get cluttered with junk from every program installed on your PC. And since Microsoft wasn't too careful about establishing standards for the icons put there, applications weren't too careful about giving their customers control over those icons. As a result, many applications won't let you remove their icons, and of those that do, the process is a little different for each one.

Microsoft snapped into action to solve the problem, and five years later came up with a system to automatically hide unused/unwanted tray icons. In Windows 7, open the Notification Area Icons page in Control Panel, shown in Figure 2-11, to choose what's shown and what isn't.

Tired of dealing with tray icons on a one-by-one basis? If you're using the Business or Ultimate edition, you can turn off the tray completely. Open the Group Policy Object Editor (*gpedit.msc*, which is not present on Home Premium), and expand the branches to User Configuration\Administrative Templates\Start Menu and Taskbar. Double-click **Hide the notification area**, select **Enabled**, and click OK.

In Windows 7 Home Premium, you'll need a registry hack to do the same thing. Open the Registry Editor (see Chapter 3) and navigate to `HKEY_CUR RENT_USER\Software\Microsoft\Windows\CurrentVersion\Policies\Explorer`. From the **Edit** menu, select **New** and then **DWORD (32-bit) Value**, and type `NoTrayItemsDisplay` for the value name. Double-click the new value, type `1` for the value data, and click OK.

Either way you do it, you'll have to log out and then log back in for this change to take effect.

Problem is, hiding a tray icon doesn't accomplish anything except dealing with the clutter. Those programs are still running, eating up processor cycles and memory. You can turn on the **Always show all icons and notifications on the taskbar** option (Figure 2-11) to make sure there's nothing hidden—with the glaring exception of programs that want to be hidden—but a better approach is to simply stop loading programs automatically that you don't really need. See Chapter 6 for more on Startup programs and malware, and Chapter 5 for more on background processes.

Stretch Out on Multiple Monitors

Add another monitor to double your desktop space, easily view two documents side by side, or work on one screen while watching a movie on the other. It's a relatively cheap way to make your computer considerably more useful.

On most desktop PCs, you can add a second video card to support a second monitor, or better yet, replace your current video card with a high-end model that sports two DVI connectors. And nearly all laptops include a port for a second monitor, although typically only more expensive models have the necessary DVI or HDMI port for a digital connection. If you have none of these luxuries, you can use a program like MaxiVista (*http://www.maxivista.com/*) to use that spare laptop as a second monitor.

While Windows has supported multiple monitors for years, it wasn't until Windows 7 that Microsoft started including some handy tools to make it easier to live with a spanned desktop. For instance, you can hold the **Shift** and Windows logo keys while pressing the left or right arrow keys to move the active window from one screen to the next. (See the section "Keyboard Is My Friend" on page 76 for more shortcuts.) You can also drag a window to the edge of the screen to dock it to the left or right side.

Unfortunately, there's a lot of ground Microsoft still hasn't covered: the taskbar and Alt-Tab window only appear on the primary screen, maximized applications can't span more than one screen, full-screen games can't use more than one monitor, and support for multiscreen wallpaper and screensavers is weak at best. These seem trivial enough until you spend a few hours with a two-monitor PC, at which point you wonder why Windows 7's multimonitor support is so lousy.

 Can't get the colors to match on two otherwise identical monitors? See "Get More Accurate Color" on page 241 to make things right.

In the following sections, learn how to improve your experience with multiple monitors on Windows 7.

Make your background wallpaper span all your screens

This is actually something you can do without any third-party software, but it's not necessarily obvious. First, determine your total desktop resolution: right-click an empty area of the desktop, select **Screen resolution**, and look at the **Resolution** setting. If you have two 1920×1200 screens side-by-side, then your total resolution is 3840×1200.

 You'll need a single image at least as big as your total resolution: this means a photo taken with a 12-megapixel camera for a desktop 3840 pixels wide. If it's too small, it won't look right. If it's too big, you'll need to crop or resize it with your favorite image editor so that it doesn't run off the screen.

Open the Personalization page in Control Panel and click **Desktop Background**. From the **Picture location** listbox, choose **Pictures library** to browse all the photos in your *Photos* folder, or click **Browse** to pick another folder. (Unfortunately, the Browse window only lets you select a folder; to look through your non-*Photos* folders for a single image, open a separate Windows Explorer window.) You can also manually copy your custom image to the *C:\Windows\Web\Wallpaper* folder to make it easier to find (it'll be under **Windows Desktop Backgrounds**).

Highlight your custom wallpaper, and from the **Picture position** list, select **Tile**. (None of the other options here—**Fill**, **Fit**, **Stretch**, and **Center**—work on a desktop spanned across multiple monitors.)

With the **Tile** option, the upper lefthand corner of the image is placed at the upper lefthand corner of the primary monitor. This means that if your primary monitor—the one with your Start menu and taskbar—is not at the upper left of your monitor array, the image tiles will be out of order. (Windows isn't smart enough to pick the correct display in a multimonitor setup.) To get around this without choosing a new primary display, you must open your photo in your favorite image editor, cut it into pieces, and then reconstitute accordingly.

When you're happy with the results, click **Save changes**.

Use different wallpaper on each screen

Windows lets you select more than one desktop wallpaper at a time, but not for the purposes of filling multiple screens. Rather, Windows creates a slideshow with your selected images and changes your background at regular intervals. (Use the **Change picture every** and **Shuffle** controls at the bottom of the "Choose your desktop background" page to customize this feature.)

The quick and dirty way to get a different background on each screen is to piece together your different background images into a single large image, and then use it to span your monitor array as described in the previous topic.

Several third-party tools can do this for you, including DisplayFusion (*http:// www.binaryfortress.com/displayfusion/*) and Desktop Wallpaper Tool (*http:// www.wallpapertool.com/*).

Make a screensaver multiscreen friendly

A screensaver is basically just an application that runs full screen and quits when you move your mouse. Some screensavers work fine with multiple monitors, such as Bubbles (which comes with Windows 7). But a screensaver not written to take advantage of multiple screens will only fill a single screen, forcing Windows to pitch in and replicate the screensaver on all your screens.

To make a screensaver span all your screens, even if it wasn't designed to do so, use Actual Tools Multiple Monitors (*http://www.actualtools.com/multiple monitors/*).

To run a different screensaver on each screen, use Desktop Tools (*http://dru software.com/drusoftware/*).

If you're in the mood for change, get a new screensaver written specifically for multiple monitors from *http://www.reallyslick.com/*.

Put a taskbar on every screen

It can get awfully tiresome to instinctually move your mouse to the bottom of the screen to switch windows, only to find no taskbar at all. Instead, you've got to sweep across two or three desktops to get to your taskbar on the primary screen.

Several third-party tools attempt to solve this problem, but one of the best is UltraMon 3.0 (free trial at *http://www.realtimesoft.com/*).

When you enable UltraMon's **Smart Taskbar** feature, a taskbar appears on every screen. What's more, only those windows open on any particular screen appear in that screen's taskbar so you can further take advantage of your increased real estate and reduce taskbar clutter. Move an application from one screen to another, and its taskbar button follows. (The downside is that you may spend a little more time hunting for minimized applications.)

 Any tool that adds a taskbar to your secondary and tertiary monitors must recreate the additional taskbars from scratch. This means that if you're particularly detail-oriented, you may notice some imperfections. For instance, you don't get Jump Lists on additional taskbars, nor can you pin programs or drag-drop taskbar buttons to reorder them. What sets Ultra-Mon apart is how close it gets: UltraMon automatically adopts your primary taskbar's settings, like **Auto-Hide** and **Locked**, but lets you override them if you want.

Actual Tools Multiple Monitors (free trial available at *http://www.actualtools .com/multiplemonitors/*) also gives you a taskbar on every screen, and adds an optional Start button (and Start menu) and notification area (tray) on each additional taskbar. You also get an **Alt+Tab** window on every screen, but not the Flip3D task switcher (Winkey+**Tab**). The software comes with handy tools to force new windows to appear on a particular monitor, and even extra keyboard shortcuts for added control.

Other taskbar replicators include MultiMonitor TaskBar (*http://www.media chance.com/free/multimon.htm*) and DisplayFusion (*http://www.binaryfortress .com/displayfusion/*).

Force applications to remember which screen to use

Windows has never taken much of an active role in choosing where new windows appear, instead leaving to the applications themselves the job of remembering their window positions. Problem is, many applications—including some Windows components—do a poor job of remembering where they were when they were last closed, and multiple screens just make matters worse.

There's a little trick that's been around for a few Windows versions, and it works much of the time. Begin by starting an application and watch where it opens its window. Drag the window to the screen you'd like to use from now on, and then while holding the **Shift** key, click the close [×] button. The next time you open the program, it should appear on that same screen.

Shift-close not doing it for you? As long as there have been forgetful applications, there have also been utilities to force them to open in the same place every time. For instance, Actual Tools Multiple Monitors, described in the previous section, lets you choose whether new windows should open on a specific screen, whichever screen has the mouse pointer, or the screen of the parent window. You can also make specific rules for specific programs.

 Buggy video drivers have also been known to cause this problem; check the website of your video card manufacturer for a driver update, and try again.

Ultimately, though, it's the application developer's job to make sure a program remembers on which screen it last appeared. If a program won't behave on your multimonitor setup, don't be afraid to contact the developer and request a fix.

Fill multiple screens with a single application or game

Probably the strangest limitation on a multi-monitor PC is that Windows won't maximize a window beyond the extents of a single screen. Sure, you can manually stretch most application windows to span your entire desktop, but that's a lot of fuss for something that should only take a single click of a title bar button.

DisplayFusion, mentioned earlier in this section, allows you to maximize windows to span the entire desktop, and adds hotkey support for convenience.

 Ever run a full-screen, single monitor game, only to have things go awry when you accidentally move the mouse past the screen boundary? Use ComroeStudios Multi-Monitor Tool (CSMMT), available at *http://www.comroestudios.com/*, to solve this problem.

Where most folks run into trouble is with games and video playback software. Any programs that use your video card's 3D processor or video overlay might not work properly when a single window spans more than one screen.

To test how well your PC handles video spanning, open a simple video clip (.mpg, .avi, or .wmv) in Windows Media Player and then drag the (non-maximized) window so that it's split between monitors: half of the video plays on one screen and half on the other. If it works, then your video hardware should support something called *Hybrid Span mode*. If not, check with your video card manufacturer for a driver update.

Obviously, the driver is a big factor in how well your PC handles multimonitor 3D. If both your displays are driven by the same video adapter—a setup called "dual view"—or if you have two video cards with the same graphics chip that can be controlled by a single driver—a setup called "Homogeneous Multi-adapter"—then you'll likely be able to span a 3D game across monitors. In theory, though, Windows 7 also supports a "Heterogeneous Multi-adapter" setup, in which you have two different video cards and two different video drivers; for this to work, both drivers must play nicely.

Working with Files and Folders

What is Windows Explorer if not a file manager at heart? Sure, the Start menu and taskbar form a homebase of sorts, but the desktop and your folders are basically there to provide access to your data. When it comes to copying, moving, renaming, deleting, and opening files, Explorer is where it's at. The rest of this chapter includes topics on tweaking Windows' file management features so you can work with your stuff without getting so annoyed.

The 17 File Context Menu Bug

For years, you've been able to select any number of files in Windows Explorer—hundreds or even thousands—and right-click the lot of 'em. Up pops a context menu with actions you can take on all the selected files and folders.

The items that appear in the menu depend on the types of objects you've selected: right-click a *.jpg* image file, and you'll see a different menu than if you right-clicked a *.txt* file or a folder. These menus are assembled on the fly by various programs called *context menu handlers*—discussed at length in Chapter 3—which is why there might be a slight delay before a menu opens, particularly if you selected a lot of files.

But Microsoft made a change for Windows 7 that looks and feels like a bug. Now, when you right-click 17 or more files, each of those context menu handlers only knows about the first 16 of them. The good news is that when you select an item in the menu, the target program gets all the files you selected, not just those 16. But since the handlers don't have all the facts—like the fact that you selected 43 .*doc* files, 71 .*avi* files, and 3 folders—you may not get the context menu you're supposed to. Instead, the handler thinks you've selected only 16 .*doc* files and builds its menu accordingly.

Of course, Microsoft provides no warnings or explanations, and offers no workaround or way to disable this limit. So you're left with a context menu system that sometimes seems broken.

So the next time you see an incorrect context menu, try again with 16 or fewer files selected. You can also mitigate the problem by selecting files of only a single type (e.g., only .*txt* files or only .*xlsx* files).

Why It Takes So Long to Copy Files

Most people first realize that something is wrong with Windows when they try to copy or move files, and they see the little green progress window shown in Figure 2-12. It'd be understandable to see this window on screen for a minute or two if you're copying a lot of data, but should it really take three full minutes to move one small file, or eight minutes to delete another?

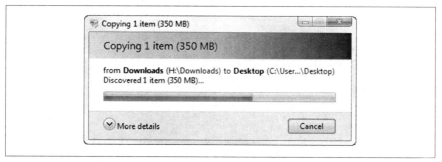

Figure 2-12. Seen this window a lot lately? The tiny "Green Ribbon of Death" could be the harbinger of a crashed Explorer window

This is one of two "Green Ribbons of Death" in Windows 7, the other being the larger progress bar—the one dissected in Chapter 6—that appears at the top of the Windows Explorer window in the address bar/path box. So, what's going on?

It turns out that several things can cause Windows Explorer to take a long time copying, moving, or deleting files, and some of them are actually legitimate. (This problem was much worse in Vista, but still remains in Windows 7.)

Figure 2-13. This handy confirmation window lets you deal with all the conflicts at once, but it can lead to other problems

First, Windows Explorer takes time to examine the files and folders you're copying, moving, etc., and checks—ahead of time—to see whether there are any conflicts, such as existing files in the destination folder or security issues that need your attention. That's why you'll see Explorer's nifty confirmation window (Figure 2-13) *just once* for 34 conflicts, rather than the 34 individual confirmations you'd have to endure in XP and earlier versions of Windows.

The confirmation window in Figure 2-13 is actually quite nice because of all the choices you get. If you're copying media files (e.g., photos, videos, PDF documents), you'll see thumbnail previews to aid your decision; you can even right-click the thumbnails directly in this window if you want to work with the files without interrupting the file operation. What's more, you can choose to copy or move the file *without* replacing the original, renaming it instead to avoid the conflict.

The downside is that Explorer must delay your file operation while it prepares the confirmation window; depending on what it encounters along the way, this can take *forever*.

One of the main reasons for the delay is a side effect of User Account Control, the same security "feature" that turns the screen black for a moment before asking your permission to make a change to your system. Naturally, Explorer has to examine each file you're copying to make sure you have permission to copy it, and then examine the destination to make sure you have permission to put the file there. See the section "Control User Account Control" on page 569 for some ways to ease up the restrictions.

Likewise, if you're copying files over a network, Windows has to do some security reconnaissance, and depending on the speed of your network connection, this can take even longer.

But security checks alone aren't responsible for poor performance in this area; there's also the matter of thumbnails. As described in "Green Ribbon of Death" on page 380, there are a few common problems that can cause Windows Explorer to hang or even crash, and if one of these things hobbles the instance of Explorer you're using, the progress dialog (shown previously in Figure 2-12) can just sit there for what seems like an eternity. Once you've fixed the problems outlined in Chapter 6, the copying, moving, or deleting should go much faster.

Turn off auto-tuning

One of the things that can slow file copying to a network folder is that Windows requests constant updates from the other side to keep its view up to date. To turn this off, open a Command Prompt window in Administrator mode (see Chapters 9 and 8, respectively), type this command:

```
netsh int tcp set global autotuninglevel=disabled
```

and press **Enter**. You'll have to restart Windows for the change to take effect, but thereafter, copying files over the network should be much faster. Of course, you might have to press the **F5** key more frequently to refresh the remote folder, but you can do that when the file copying is done.

To undo the change (re-enable auto-tuning), type this command:

```
netsh int tcp set global autotuninglevel=normal
```

and press **Enter**.

Slicker Ways to Select Files

Why drag 17 files individually when you can select and drag them all at once? For one, it's tremendously aggravating to select the first 16 files, and then lose the selection with an errant click in the wrong place.

Selecting files is an art form, or at least it would be in a much more boring world than ours. Here are some slick ways to select multiple files in Windows Explorer:

Rubber bands

> Need to select a cluster of files? Click in an empty area near the first file and then draw a box around the others to select them all in a single swoop, as shown in Figure 2-14.

Keyboard and mouse

> As described in "Keyboard Is My Friend" on page 76, you can hold the **Ctrl** key to select files one-by-one, or hold the **Shift** key to select a range of files. Just be careful not to drag the files while holding **Ctrl**, lest you inadvertently create copies of them all.

Keyboard alone

> While holding the **Ctrl** key, move through a list of files with the up and down arrow keys. When the dotted rectangle surrounds a file you want, press the **Space bar** to select it.

> Or, to select a range of files, use the arrow keys to find the first file; then, hold **Shift** while you expand the selection with the arrow keys. Thereafter, you can even use the **Ctrl** key to select and deselect individual items.

Filespec

> In the **Search** box in the top-right of the Explorer window, type a *filespec*—a pattern you choose—to filter the list and show only the matching files. Filespecs typically contain ordinary characters (letters and numbers) along with *wildcards*, like the question mark (?) and the asterisk (*), which represent any single character or any number of characters, respectively.

> For instance, type *.txt to show only files with the .txt filename extension, or v??.* to show files of any type that start with v and have only three letters in the filename.

> In a moment or two, Windows Explorer will show only the files that match your filespec, at which point you can press **Ctrl+A** to select them all. Most of the time, this is a whole lot faster—not to mention more accurate—than trying to select the files by hand. See the section "Fix Windows Search" on page 111, for more information.

Figure 2-14. It's dead simple, but rubber bands—or "selection rectangles," as they like to be called—allow you to select a cluster of files in one quick step

Checkboxes

You like clicking checkboxes? In Windows Explorer, click the **Organize** drop-down, select **Folder and Search Options**, and then turn on the **Use check boxes to select items** option. Click OK, and your folder now looks like Figure 2-15; then, click the checkbox next to any file to select it without holding down any keys or worrying about clicking in the wrong place.

Figure 2-15. Windows Explorer lets you use checkboxes to select items

Take Charge of Drag-Drop

The "desktop metaphor" used as the basis for the interface in Windows 7 revolves around a handful of concepts, one of the most basic being that you can drag an item with the mouse to move it from one place to another.

Depending on where the item currently lives and where you're trying to put it, a variety of things can happen. The good news is that with an understanding of what's happening, combined with the visual cues you get from Windows Explorer, you can predict what will happen every single time you drag and drop. What's more, you can use some basic tricks to change what happens.

Here are the basic drag-drop rules by which Windows Explorer lives:

- If you drag an object from one place to another on the same physical drive (*C:\docs* to *C:\files*), Windows moves the object.
- If you drag an object from one physical drive to another physical drive (*C:\docs* to *D:\files*), Windows copies the object, resulting in two identical files on your PC.
- If you drag an object from one place to another in the same folder, Windows does nothing.
- If you drag an object into the **Recycle Bin**, Windows moves the file into the *Recycle Bin* folder, where it is eventually deleted.
- If you drag an object into a Zip folder anywhere, Windows copies the file. (See "Zip It Up" on page 107.)
- If you drag certain system objects, such as Control Panel icons, anywhere else, Windows makes shortcuts to those items.
- If you drag any file onto an application executable (*.exe*) file, Windows opens the target application and then sends a signal to the application to open the dropped document. See "File Type Associations" on page 166 for details.

It used to be that Windows did different things with different types of files, such as creating a shortcut any time you dragged an *.exe* file, but thankfully, those days are long over. Here's how to override those rules:

Always copy.
> To *copy* an object, hold the **Ctrl** key while dragging. If you press **Ctrl** *before* you click, Windows assumes you're still selecting files (covered in the previous section), so make sure to press it only *after* you've started dragging but before you let go of the mouse button. (The exceptions are system objects, like Libraries, that can't be copied.)

Stop Copying Files When You're Trying to Select

Ever accidentally make duplicate copies of 28 files when you were really only trying to select the 29th? The problem is that the **Ctrl** key is used both to select multiple files and copy files when dragging. And if your timing is a little off, you'll get a bunch of duplicate files that you then have to delete.

To fix the problem, you can make Windows a little less sensitive to dragging with a quick Registry hack.

Open the Registry Editor (see Chapter 3) and expand the branches to `HKEY_CUR` `RENT_USER\Control Panel\Desktop`. Double-click the `DragWidth` value, and in the **Value data** field, replace the default value of `4` with a higher value, say `16`, and click OK.

Then try selecting files as well as dragging. A higher value makes it so you have to move your mouse further before Windows acknowledges you're dragging; lower the value to say, `12`, if it's too hard to drag files, or raise it to `20` if it's still too easy. Experiment with different values until you strike a compromise with which you're comfortable.

Duplicate an object.
> Hold the **Ctrl** key while dragging an object from one part of a folder to another part of the same folder.

Always move.
> To *move* an object, hold the **Shift** key while dragging. Likewise, if you press **Shift** before you click, Windows assumes you're still selecting files, so make sure to press it only after you've started dragging but before you let go. (Of course, system objects and read-only files, like those on a CD, cannot be moved.)

Always create a shortcut.
> To create a shortcut to an object under any situation, hold the **Alt** key while dragging.

Choose on the fly.
> To choose what happens to dragged files each time *without* having to press any keys, drag your files with the *right* mouse button, and a special menu like the one in Figure 2-16 will appear when you drop the files. This context menu is especially helpful, because it will display only options appropriate to the type of object you're dragging and the place where you've dropped it.

To help you predict what will happen, even if you haven't memorized the rules, Windows changes the mouse cursor to indicate what it intends to do. While dragging an item, press and release the **Ctrl**, **Shift**, and **Alt** keys and watch

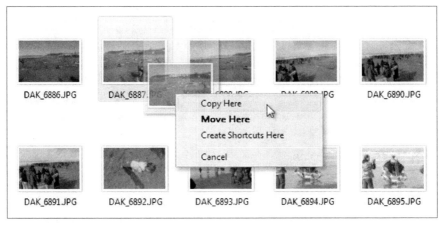

Figure 2-16. Drag files with the right mouse button for more control

Windows change the cursors in real time. As illustrated in Figure 2-17, you'll see a small plus sign whenever you're copying, a straight arrow when moving, or a curved arrow when creating a shortcut. This visual feedback is very important; it can eliminate a lot of stupid mistakes if you pay attention to it.

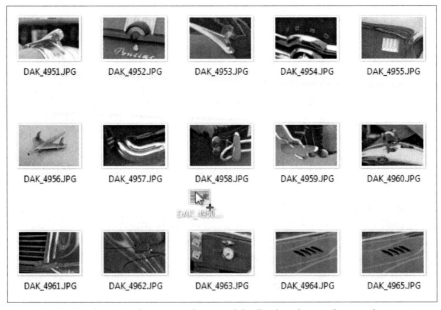

Figure 2-17. Windows Explorer provides visual feedback to let you know what's going to happen when you drop a file

There's no way to set the default action for dragging and therefore no way to avoid using keystrokes or the right mouse button to achieve the desired results. Even if there were a way to change the default behavior, you probably wouldn't want to do it; imagine if someone else sat down at your computer and started dragging icons: oh, the horror.

Make a mistake? Press **Ctrl+Z** to undo most types of file operations.

 Not sure what you're undoing? First, open Windows Explorer, press the **Alt** key to show the menu, and then select **View→Status bar** to turn on the old-school Status bar. Next, right-click an empty area of the righthand pane and hover your mouse over the **Undo** context menu item. Right in the Status bar, beneath the Details pane at the bottom of the window, you'll see something like **Undo Rename of 'My Pictures' to 'Pictures'**.

Copy or Move to a Specified Path

Dragging and dropping is generally the quickest and easiest way to copy or move files and folders from one place to another. Typically, though, it helps if the source and destination folders are both visible at the same time. (And if you have a large enough screen, opening multiple Explorer windows is a must.) But what if the target folder isn't visible when you start dragging?

Solution 1: Drag patiently

In Windows Explorer, navigate to the source folder. Next, drag one or more items over the tree pane on the left, then hover the mouse cursor over the visible branch of the destination folder, and Explorer will automatically expand the branch. You can also hover near the top or bottom of the Navigation pane to scroll up or down, respectively.

If the destination folder you're looking for is buried several layers deep, you'll have to wait for Explorer to expand each level. This requires a steady hand and a lot of patience.

Solution 2: Use cut, copy, and paste

Select the file(s) you want to copy, right-click, and select **Copy** to copy the items or **Cut** to move them. (Or, to use the keyboard, press **Ctrl+C** or **Ctrl+X**, respectively, as described in "Keyboard Is My Friend" on page 76.)

When you *cut* a file, its icon appears faded (as though it were a hidden file) until you paste it somewhere, or abandon the operation. (Abandoning a *cut* operation does not delete the file, by the way.) Explorer makes no visual distinction for files you *copy*.

Next, open the destination folder, right-click an empty area of the righthand pane, and select **Paste** (or press **Ctrl+V**).

Solution 3: Add some hidden entries to Explorer's context menus

Windows 7 actually comes with a couple of handy context menu items—**Copy To Folder** and **Move To Folder**—but they're hidden by default. To show them when you right-click any file or folder, follow these instructions.

Open the Registry Editor (see Chapter 3) and expand the folders to `HKEY_CLASSES_ROOT\AllFilesystemObjects\shellex\ContextMenuHandlers`.

Highlight the `ContextMenuHandlers` key, and then from the **Edit** menu, select **New** and then **Key**. Type `{C2FBB630-2971-11D1-A18C-00C04FD75D13}` for the name of the new key.

Next, create a second key and name it `{C2FBB631-2971-11D1-A18C-00C04FD75D13}`. (Hint: this class ID is identical to the first, except for the `1` in the eighth position.)

(The first key adds the **Copy To Folder** command, and the second adds **Move To Folder**.)

Close the Registry Editor when you're done, and then right-click any file, folder, or drive. If you select either **Copy To Folder** and **Move To Folder**, you should see a window that looks like the one in Figure 2-18.

More Ways to Rename Files

Renaming files is just as common as copying or moving, but it can end up being a much more tedious task in Windows Explorer, particularly if you have 40 files to rename.

In its simplest form, Explorer's rename feature works like this: highlight a file, wait a fraction of a second to avoid double-clicking, then click the filename. When the text field appears, type a new name and then press **Enter** to rename the file. You can also right-click and select **Rename**, or highlight the object and press the **F2** key.

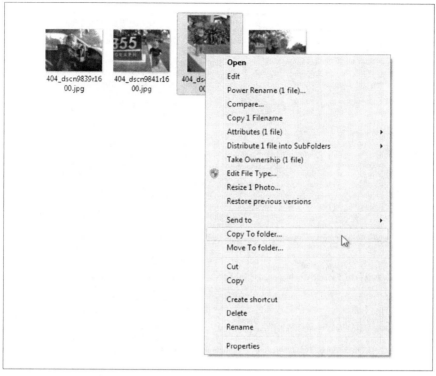

*Figure 2-18. A quick registry hack will add a hidden feature to Windows Explorer; you'll see this window when you right-click any file or folder and select **Copy To Folder***

Then, do it 39 more times to rename all 40 files. Fortunately, there are better ways.

Solution 1: Select multiple files in Explorer

If you press **F2** when more than one file is selected in Windows Explorer, only one file—the active file—gets a text field for you to type in. Nothing will happen to the other selected files, at least not yet.

> The active file is important, since its name is used as a template to rename the other selected files. If the file marked as active is not the one you want to use, hit **Esc**, and then hold the **Ctrl** key while clicking another file. If the new file was highlighted, it will become deselected—in this case, just **Ctrl**+click the file once more to reselect it. Then, press **F2** again to show the text field.

Rename the active file as desired, and press **Enter** when you're done. The active file keeps its new name, and then Explorer assigns the same name—plus a number, in parentheses—to all the other files. Table 2-2 shows what happens when you rename files this way.

Table 2-2. What happens when you try to rename multiple files in Explorer

Old filename	New filename
My file.doc (the active file)	*The Penske File.rtf*
Grandma.jpg	*The Penske File (1).jpg*
Readme.1st	*The Penske File (2).1st*
Purchases.mdb	*The Penske File (3).mdb*
Chapter 2 (a folder)	*The Penske File (4)*

Although Explorer doesn't show you a preview of your new filenames, you can undo a multiple rename operation as easily as a single rename operation by pressing **Ctrl+Z** once for each file that was renamed. Want to undo a single rename of 17 files? You'll need to press **Ctrl+Z** 17 times.

Solution 2: Use the Command Prompt

An alternative is to use the `ren` command (see Chapter 9), either directly from the Command Prompt (*cmd.exe*), or from a batch file or PowerShell script.

First, use the `cd` command, also explained in Chapter 9, to change the working directory to the folder containing the files you wish to rename. For example, type:

```
cd c:\stuff
```

to change to the *C:\stuff* folder. If the folder name contains a space, enclose it in quotation marks, like this:

```
cd "c:\Progam Files\stuff"
```

Next, use the `ren` command to rename the file; the general syntax is:

```
ren source destination
```

where both *source* and *destination* can be any combination of permissible characters and wildcards. Two wildcards are allowed: an asterisk (*), which is used to match any number of characters, and a question mark (?), which is used to match only a single character. For example:

Rename a single file

```
ren oldfile.txt newfile.txt
```

Change the extension of all .txt files to .doc

```
ren *.txt *.doc
```

Rename the first part of a filename without changing the extension

```
ren document.* documentation.*
```

Remove the extensions of all files in the folder

```
ren *.* *.
```

Change the first letter of all files in a folder to "b"

```
ren *.* b*.*
```

Add a zero in front of numbered Chapter files (note the quotation marks)

```
ren "Chapter ??.wpd" "chapter0??.wpd"
```

Rename all files with an "s" in the fourth position so that a "t" appears there instead

```
ren ???s*.* ???t*.*
```

Truncate the filenames of all files in the folder so that only the first four characters are used

```
ren *.* ????.*
```

Now, using wildcards takes a bit of practice and patience. The more you do it, the better intuitive sense you'll have of how to phrase a rename operation. To make things simpler, try issuing several successive `ren` commands instead of trying to squeeze all your changes into a single step.

If a naming conflict occurs, the `ren` command never overwrites a file. For example, if you try to rename *Lisa.txt* to *Bart.txt*, and there's already another file called *Bart.txt*, `ren` just displays an error.

Solution 3: Use a third-party add-on

Got a lot of files to rename? Use Power Rename, part of Creative Element Power Tools (*http://www.creativelement.com/powertools*). To use the tool, open the Creative Element Power Tools Control Panel, turn on the **Rename files with ease** option, and click **Accept**.

Then, highlight any number of files to rename, right-click, and select **Power Rename**. Or, open the Power Rename utility (Figure 2-19) and drag-drop the files onto the window.

Select the renaming criteria to your right. The first option, **As Specified**, allows you to type a file specification with wildcards, as described previously, but the real power lies in **With Operation**, and the operations that follow. For

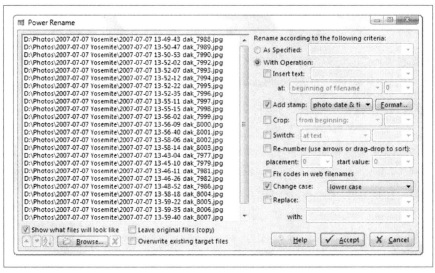

Figure 2-19. Power Rename makes it much easier to rename many files at once

instance, you can insert text anywhere, remove text (crop), search and replace text, add numbering, and even fix numbered codes in files downloaded from the Web.

Turn on the **Show what files will look like** option to see a live preview of the filenames as you adjust the options. When you're done, click **Accept** to rename the files.

Delete In-Use Files

Sometimes Windows won't let you delete a file, which is stupid because it's your PC and you should be able to delete anything you want. So there.

Of course, there are times when Windows does know something you don't, and prevents you from deleting files that are currently *in use* to avoid causing crashes or data loss. An in-use file could be a document that's currently open, a program executable that's currently running, or a folder *locked* by a running application. See the sidebar "Copy In-Use Files" on page 106 for a related tip.

Most of the time, you can get around this by closing the application or restarting Windows, but it's not always that easy.

For instance, if the program has crashed, you'll need to use Task Manager to end the process; see "What to Do When a Program Crashes" on page 371 for details. Or, if the program is actually a Windows *service*, you'll need to use the

Services window (*services.msc*) to stop the service before you'll be allowed to delete the file.

 There are times when Windows won't let you delete a file, not because it's in use, but because you don't have *permission* or you're not the *owner* of the file. See "Permissions and Security" on page 549 for help setting permission and taking ownership, steps you may need to take before you can delete that stubborn file.

Shell Tweaks

But what if the file you're trying to delete is a virus or other form of malware? Or what if you're certain the file isn't open, but Windows still won't let you delete it?

Solution 1: Context menu add-on

Install Creative Element Power Tools (*http://creativelement.com/powertools/*) and turn on the **Delete in-use files** tool. Then, right-click the file you'd like to exterminate, and select **Delete In-Use File**. The tool then prompts you to restart Windows, after which the file will be gone.

Solution 2: Unlocker

Get free Unlocker tool from *http://ccollomb.free.fr/unlocker/* (or *http://cedrick .collomb.perso.sfr.fr/unlocker/*). Right-click the file or folder to delete and select Unlocker to show a list of all the processes that have claimed a lock on the file. Click the **Unlock All** button, and you should be able to safely delete the file. (Note that at the time of this writing, there was no native x64 version, which means it will only work on 32-bit Windows.)

Solution 3: Wininit.ini

You can use this little-known trick that takes advantage of a feature used by application installers to replace program files.

First, open Windows Explorer and navigate to your *C:\Windows* folder. Double-click the *Wininit.ini* file to open it in Notepad (or any other standard plain-text editor). If the file isn't there, just create a new empty text file, name it *Wininit.ini*, and type the following line at the top:

```
[rename]
```

(In most cases, the *Wininit.ini* file will exist but will be empty, with the exception of the [rename] line; any other lines you see here would've been added by a recent application installation.)

Under the [rename] section header, type the following line:

```
NUL=c:\folder\filename.ext
```

where *c:\folder\filename.ext* is the full path and filename of the file you wish to delete. You can specify as many files here as you want, one on each line.

To *replace* a file rather than simply deleting it, the syntax is a little different:

```
c:\folder\existing.ext=c:\folder\replacement.ext
```

where *c:\folder\existing.ext* is the full path and filename of the file you're trying to replace, and *c:\folder\replacement.ext* is the full path and filename of the new file to take its place. If the file specified on the right side of the equals sign doesn't exist, then the *existing.ext* file will be moved/renamed to *c:\folder\replacement.ext*.

When you're done, save the file, close Notepad, and restart Windows. The files will be deleted or replaced as you've specified during the startup procedure.

Solution 4: Safe Mode with Command Prompt

Windows 7 has a special way to get to the Command Prompt without loading most of the rest of the operating system, not to mention any applications or services (or viruses) that can come along for the ride. This method is the one to use when none of the others work.

See "What to Do When Windows Won't Start" on page 355 for details on getting to the **Safe Mode with Command Prompt**, one of the options in the Windows **F8** menu. Once you're there, use the del command (see Chapter 9) to delete the file.

When that's done, close the Command Prompt window, or type exit and press **Enter** to restart your PC and load Windows.

Copy In-Use Files

Windows doesn't let you delete locked and in-use files, nor does it let you even copy them in most cases. But what if you need to back up an in-use file without closing it, or perhaps copy an in-use file before deleting it?

For that, you'll need the free HoboCopy tool, available at *http://sourceforge .net/projects/wangdera/files/HoboCopy/*. (There are native 32-bit and 64-bit versions of HoboCopy, both intended for Vista, but they work fine on Windows 7.) You'll also need to make sure the Shadow Copies service is enabled, as described in Chapter 6.

HoboCopy is a command-line tool, so you'll need to open a Command Prompt window in administrator mode (see Chapter 8) to use it. Then, use cd to change to the folder containing *HoboCopy.exe* (see Chapter 9).

To make a copy of, say, *c:\windows\system32\nastyspyware.exe* and place it in the *c:\archive* folder, you'd type:

```
hobocopy c:\windows\system32\ c:\archive\ nastyspyware.exe
```

Note that the folder containing the file to copy comes first, followed by the destination folder, and then finally the filename, each separated by spaces.

Zip It Up

The late Phil Katz conceived of the *Zip* file format at his mother's kitchen table in 1986, and soon thereafter wrote a little program called PKZip. Although his program, capable of encapsulating and compressing any number of ordinary files and folders into a single archive file, was not the first of its type, it quickly became a standard and ended up revolutionizing the transfer and storage of computer data.

Zip files work somewhat like folders in that they "contain" files, so it's not surprising that they're represented as folders in Windows Explorer. But a Zip file is typically smaller than the sum of its contents, thanks to the Zip compression scheme. Of course, other standards, like RAR, offer much better compression, but Windows 7 doesn't support *.rar* files without a third-party utility like WinRAR (*http://www.rarlab.com/*) or 7-Zip (*http://www.7-zip.org/*).

For example, a folder with 10 spreadsheet documents might consume 8 MB of disk space, but when zipped, might only consume 2 MB (or even less). The level of compression varies with the type of data being compressed; zipped text documents can be as small as 4 or 5% of the size of the original source files, but since movies and images are already compressed, they'll only compress to 95 to 98% of their original size, if that.

This compression makes Zip files great for sending over the Internet, since smaller files can be sent faster. The Zip archive format also has built-in error checking, so if you find that certain files are getting corrupted when you email them or send them through a website, try zipping them up to "protect" them.

To open a Zip file, just double-click it. You can extract files from Zip archives by dragging them out of the Zip folder window. You can also right-click a Zip file and select **Extract All**, but you'll have to deal with a more cumbersome wizard interface.

Create a new Zip file by right-clicking on an empty portion of the desktop or any open folder, and selecting **New** and then **Compressed (zipped) Folder**. (The name here is actually misleading, since Zip archives are actually files and not folders.) Then, add files or folders to the Zip by simply dragging them onto the icon or the open Zip window.

Another way to do this is to right-click a folder or a group of files, select **Send To**, and then select **Compressed (zipped) Folder**. This is especially convenient, as there's no wizard or other interface to get in the way: if you send the *CompuGlobalHyperMegaNet* folder to a Zip file, Windows compresses the folder's contents into a new *CompuGlobalHyperMegaNet.zip* file, stored alongside the source folder.

All of this is possible because Windows 7 supports the Zip format right out of the box. (For years, this wasn't the case because Katz reportedly despised Windows, which may explain why Windows XP, released a year after his death, was the first version of Windows to support Zip files without a third-party program.)

Unfortunately, there are drawbacks to Windows Explorer's built-in support for Zip files. For example, it can interfere with searches, as described in "Fix Windows Search" on page 111. It's also inferior to third-party Zip tools like ZipGenius (*http://www.zipgenius.com/*), WinZip (*http://www.winzip.com/*) , and the aforementioned (and free) 7-Zip, all of which add more features and, ironically, better integration with Explorer's own context menus. But the biggest problem is that, by default, Windows Explorer displays each Zip file like a folder, which can make a big mess if you have a folder full of 'em.

Turn off Zip support

Unfortunately, there's no way to get Windows Explorer to treat Zip files like files without disabling the Zip feature altogether. But if you want to do it, here's how:

1. Open the Registry Editor (see Chapter 3), and expand the branches to `HKEY_CLASSES_ROOT\CLSID`.
2. Highlight the `{E88DCCE0-B7B3-11d1-A9F0-00AA0060FA31}` key and from the **File** menu, select **Export** to create a registry patch backup (also described in Chapter 3).
3. Take ownership of the `{E88DCCE0-B7B3-11d1-A9F0-00AA0060FA31}` key, as described in Chapter 3 and Chapter 8, and then delete the key entirely.

4. Repeat steps 2 and 3 for the {0CD7A5C0-9F37-11CE-AE65-08002B2E1262} key as well.

5. When you're done, close Registry Editor and then restart Windows for the change to take effect.

Once you've disabled Windows built-in Zip file support, you'll need to install a third-party Zip tool, discussed previously.

If you lose the registry patches, or neglect to create the backups in the first place, you can download the *win7zip.reg* file at *http://www.annoyances.org/ exec/download/win7zip.reg* and then double-click it to restore built-in Zip support back to Windows Explorer. Again, restart Windows for the change to take effect.

Shell Tweaks

Customize Drive and Folder Icons

There may come a time when you get a little sick of the generic icons used for drives and folders in Windows Explorer. Now, you've probably figured out that you can create a shortcut to any drive or folder, choose a pretty icon, and place it on the desktop or in another convenient location. Unfortunately, the icon you choose is just for the shortcut; the target object always looks the same.

Here are some ways to give your folders and drives a more custom look.

Solution 1: Choose an icon for a drive

Using the functionality built into Windows' CD auto-insert notification feature—functionality that allows Windows to determine the name and icon of a CD as soon as it's inserted in the reader (see "Fix Windows Search" on page 111)—there's a simple way to customize the icons of all your drives, including flash drives and USB hard disks (but not mapped network drives):

1. Open a plain-text editor, such as Notepad.

2. Type the following:

   ```
   [autorun]
   icon=filename, number
   ```

   where *filename* is the name of the file containing the icon, and *number* is the index of the icon to use (leave *number* blank or specify 0 [zero] to use the first icon in the file, 1 for the second, and so on).

3. Save the file as *Autorun.inf* and place it in the root directory of the hard disk, flash drive, or CD/DVD you wish to customize.

4. This change will take effect the next time you view it in Windows Explorer; press the **F5** key to refresh the display and read the new icons.

Solution 2: Chose an icon for a folder

You can customize the icon for an individual folder with this procedure:

1. Open a plain-text editor, such as Notepad.

2. Type the following:

   ```
   [.ShellClassInfo]
   IconFile=filename
   IconIndex=number
   ```

   where *filename* is the name of the file containing the icon, and *number* is the index of the icon to use; leave the `IconIndex` line out or specify 0 (zero) to use the first icon in the file, 1 for the second, and so on. Note the dot (.) in [.ShellClassInfo].

3. Save the file as *desktop.ini* and place it directly in the folder you wish to customize.

 If there's already a file by that name, you can replace it with your version, but it's better to open the existing file and add the [.ShellClassInfo] text to it.

4. Next, open a Command Prompt window (*cmd.exe*), and type the following at the prompt:

   ```
   attrib +s foldername
   ```

   where *foldername* is the full path of the folder containing the *desktop.ini* file (i.e., *C:\docs*). This command turns on the System attribute for the folder (not the *desktop.ini* file), something you can't do in Explorer; see Chapter 9 for details.

5. Close the Command Prompt window when you're done. You'll have to close and reopen the Explorer or single-folder window to see the change (pressing **F5** usually won't do it).

Solution 3: Choose the default icon for all folders

The more global and far-reaching a change is, the more likely it is to be difficult or impossible to accomplish without some serious tinkering in the Registry. For example, the icons used by some of the seemingly hardcoded objects in

Windows, such as the icons used for ordinary, generic folders, can be changed with this quick hack:

1. Open the Registry Editor (see Chapter 3).

2. Expand the branches to `HKEY_CLASSES_ROOT\Folder\DefaultIcon` (you can also choose a generic drive icon by going to `HKEY_CLASSES_ROOT\Drive\DefaultIcon`).

3. Double-click the (`Default`) value in the right pane. This value contains the full path and filename of the file containing the icon, followed by a comma, and then a number specifying the index of the icon to use (0 being the first icon, 1 being the second, and so on). The file you use can be an icon file (*.ico*), a bitmap (*.bmp*), a *.dll* file, an application executable (*.exe*), or any other file containing a valid icon.

 The default icon for folders is `%SystemRoot%\Sys tem32\shell32.dll,3`, and the default for drives is `%Sys temRoot%\System32\shell32.dll,8`.

4. When you're done, close the Registry Editor. You may have to log out and then log back in for this change to take effect.

Fix Windows Search

I will not be pushed, filed, stamped, indexed,
briefed, debriefed or numbered.

—Number Six

Think you have a hard time finding your keys in the morning? Try finding a paper you wrote seven years ago, buried somewhere on your terabyte hard disk amid thousands of music files, photos, and shortcuts to YouTube videos of cats falling off furniture.

Vista introduced the new search feature to Windows users, but it was somewhat of a failure. Although miles ahead of the Search tool in XP and earlier versions, it was very slow and its search results were unreliable and incomplete. The Libraries feature improves search speed somewhat in Windows 7, but searches outside the libraries are still hopelessly slow. I suppose we can't expect Google speeds—5,120,000 results in 0.39 seconds—but given that Windows uses your PC's idle time to keep an index of all your personal files, it shouldn't take a half a minute to search through a few thousand files.

But if speed were the only problem, there would be no problem. Try changing the sort order during or after a search, and Windows clears your search results and starts over. Switch to a different folder momentarily and then back to the search results, and again, the search starts over.

Unfortunately, many of these problems aren't solvable without replacing Windows Search altogether, but there's quite a bit you can do to make it a much better tool than the one that comes out of the box.

Open search in a new window

One of the biggest search tool annoyances in Windows 7 has actually been around in one form or another since Windows Me/2000. Type text into the **Search** box in Windows Explorer, and all the files you were looking at disappear. Click the Back button on the toolbar (or press the **Backspace** key), and you lose your search results.

If you want to keep your current view, you need to open a separate window and search from there. To start a search from the current folder in a new window, press **Ctrl+N** to open a new Explorer window and then **Ctrl+F** to jump to the **Search** field. (**Ctrl+NF** is also a good way to get a Search window from the Desktop.)

Perform an advanced search

In the early days of Internet search, Google was praised for its minimalistic approach to search: just a single text field and a **Search** button was all you were supposed to need. Since then, many companies, Microsoft and Apple included, have been playing the me-too game.

Problem is, Google never provided enough search options, and now, neither does Windows. (It wasn't until late 2009 that Google added the ability to filter searches by date and, to some degree, by type...although you *still* can't sort search results.) Instead, there's a lone **Search** box at the top-right of every Windows Explorer window: just type something to look for, and press **Enter** to begin.

Often this is enough. Windows looks at your filenames and—for some file types—inside the files for the text you typed. But to search for files with certain dates, certain sizes, or in certain locations takes patience.

At first, your only option is to add a search filter to narrow results. Click the awkwardly-named **Kind:** filter to tell Windows only to look in certain types of files (e.g., music, photos, e-mail) or **Type:** to look for specific filename extensions (e.g., *.txt*, *.avi*, *.xlsx*). Of course, **Date modified**, **Size**, and **Name** are more self-explanatory.

The filters that appear depend on the *template* being used by the current folder. In the *Pictures* library (or any folder using the **Pictures** template), for instance, you'll see the **Date taken** filter. And in the *Music* library, you'll see **Album**, **Artists**, and **Genre**. See the section "Choose Folder View Defaults" on page 56 for more on folder templates.

But usually it's a whole lot easier to type the following filters directly into the **Search** field rather than use those fiddly controls, and with Boolean tools at your disposal, more powerful as well.

To accomplish this:	Type this in the Search box:
Find files containing multiple terms in any order	bottomless peanut bag
Find files containing an exact phrase	"bottomless peanut bag"
Find files with at least one of the search terms	peanuts OR pecans OR pistachios
Exclude a search term	peanuts NOT filberts
Combine operators	(peanuts OR pistachios) AND (almonds OR hazelnuts) NOT cashews
Look only in filenames, not file contents	name: shiny
Search by filename extension	*.jpg
Show all files in all subfolders	*.*
Find files newer than a certain date	modified: >01/12/1997
Find files in a date range	(modified: >09/20/2002) AND (modified: <12/20/2002)
Find files matching a general date	modified: 2007
Find files of a certain size	(size: >10 MB) AND (size: <20 MB)
Search metadata	author: "Hoban Washburne"
Search music by tag	kind: music artist: ("Carbon Leaf" OR "Nerf Herder")

 Note that Boolean operators AND, OR, and NOT must appear in uppercase. Also, as you can see, the AND operator is more or less optional; it's used here mostly for clarity.

Now, if you've come from Windows Vista, you've probably noticed the clumsy **Advanced search** pane is gone. In its place is the aforementioned filter controls and the elusive Choose Search Location window shown in Figure 2-20. Only after you've conducted a search can you scroll all the way to the bottom of the search results and click the tiny, almost-hidden **Custom** icon (also shown in Figure 2-20).

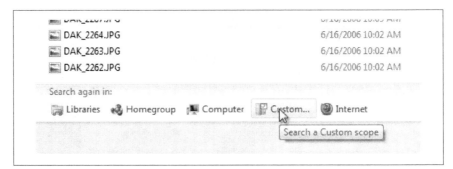

*Figure 2-20. Only after you've begun a search can you click the **Custom** icon to open the Choose Search Location window*

Strictly speaking, the easiest way to choose a search location is to navigate to that folder in Windows Explorer before you search. But the handy Choose Search Location window is the only way to select multiple, disparate folders and drives simply by placing checkmarks next to them; too bad you have to initiate a search before you can get to it.

Find the location of a folder

So once you've completed a search, what do you do with the search results? Clearly the primary intent is to help you find a document or three to open. You can also drag items out of the search window to copy or move them elsewhere, or right-click them to perform other tasks.

But what if you're after a file's location rather then its contents? In the default **Content** view, each object's full path is shown below the filename.

 In the more-useful **Details** view, however, the backward **Folder** column appears, in which the object's parent folder is separated from the rest of the path: *c:\Windows\winsxs\Backup* becomes *Backup (c:\Windows\winsxs)*. To show the complete path, right-click any column header and select **More**. Turn off the **Folder** column, turn on the **Folder path** column, and click OK.

If, among the files in your search results is a folder, you might be tempted to open it to jump to that folder. But wait, it's a trap!

Double-click a folder named *Olive* in search results, and all you'll see in the address bar is **Search Results→Olive**. Click in the address bar to reveal the actual path:

```
search-ms:displayname=Search%20Results%20in%20Windows&crumb=
                location:C%3A%5CSnook\Olive
```

Useless. Even if you've turned on the **Automatically expand to current folder** option in Folder Options (described at the beginning of this chapter), the original search folder (here, *c:\Snook*) remains highlighted in the folder tree rather than the folder you just opened. So how do you get to the actual folder on your hard disk?

First, return to the search results by clicking the **Back** button on the toolbar; you'll probably have to wait while Windows rebuilds your search since Windows never remembers search results once you jump to a different folder. (One wonders why Explorer bothers to keep the Search Results context if it doesn't cache the results.)

Right-click the folder in the search results and select **Open file location** to open the folder's parent folder *for real*. As a bonus, if you hold the **Shift** key while clicking **Open file location**, Windows Explorer opens a new window so you don't lose your search results. (Too bad this isn't the default.) When the parent folder appears, just press **Enter** to open the target folder, and you're there.

Improve search performance

As you work, Windows indexes your files in the background. In theory, this should happen only when the computer is idle, but in practice, it's not unusual to hear the hard disk thrashing while seeing *SearchIndexer.exe* consuming more than a trivial percentage of processor cycles in Task Manager (covered in Chapter 5).

 If you need to complete a processor-intensive task as quickly as possible, or if you just want better performance in a game, you can temporarily stop the search indexer task *without* disabling the search index altogether. Just open the Services window (*services.msc*), find **Windows Search** in the list, right-click and select **Stop**. It will start up again automatically the next time you load Windows, or you can start it manually by right-clicking the service again and selecting **Start**.

But if the search indexer is doing all that work, why aren't searches any faster?

The problem is a matter of expectations. When you do a search with Google or Microsoft's own Bing service, you expect the results to be a little out of date; it would be impractical for a web search engine to query 53 billion live websites each time you do a search. But in Windows, the search tool needs to show the

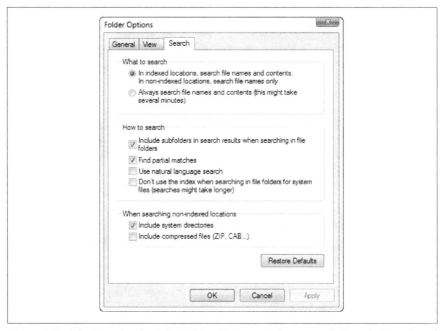

*Figure 2-21. The **Search** tab of the Folder Options window controls how the Search tool uses the index*

letter you saved 90 seconds ago alongside the college paper you wrote 18 years ago. The college paper is undoubtedly already indexed, but Windows doesn't necessarily index new documents the instant you write them to the hard disk (although it *could* and probably *should*).

Realistically, the best way to improve searches is to be selective about what you index, and careful where you search. The more focused your search, the quicker you'll get your search results. And while it may be tempting to index the whole hard disk—and necessary if you're writing a computer book—your search results will appear faster if you just index a few subfolders of your *My Documents* folder.

Inexplicably, there are three separate windows in Control Panel where you can customize the Windows Search tool. The first, shown in Figure 2-21, is the **Search** tab of the Folder Options window in Control Panel: here, you can choose whether or not to search the contents of files in non-indexed folders, search subfolders, and search system files and folders.

But if you want to choose which folders Windows includes in the search index, you'll need to open the Indexing Options window in Control Panel, shown in Figure 2-22. This window is simple enough; just include those folders you're

Figure 2-22. The Indexing Options window controls which folders on your hard disks are indexed, and the Advanced Options window controls how the index is built

likely to search, and exclude those you're not. Note that you should exclude folders with sensitive data, folders on removable drives, and folders in which you absolutely, positively never want to see out-of-date search results.

On the Indexing Options window, click **Advanced** to open the Advanced Options window, also shown in Figure 2-22. Here, you choose how the index gets built: whether to include encrypted files, where the index files are stored, and when you throw away the index and start over.

But the real fun is in the **File Types** tab. Place a checkmark next to files you want to index, or clear the checkmark for files to leave out. Keep in mind that unchecking a file type won't stop those files from appearing in search results, only from appearing *quickly*.

Want to search inside your files too? Highlight a file type and then click the **Index Properties and File Contents** option below to index the contents of the file. Of course, you can instruct Windows to always search file contents—whether the files are indexed or not—with the **What to search** option in the Folder Options window (Figure 2-21). But beware, searching inside files only works if Windows understands the file type *and* a *PersistentHandler* is associated with that file type in the registry, explained in Chapter 3. (You can also choose whether a given file type is indexed with File Type Doctor, also covered in Chapter 3.) In some cases, you can add search support for new file types by installing a free search add-in from *http://gallery.live.com/default.aspx?pl=6*, or for media files, by installing an appropriate codec as described in Chapter 4. But for file types without a *PersistentHandler*, Windows can't search inside; worse yet, it won't tell you when this is the case.

Ultimately, the key to faster searches is to realize that you don't have to wait for a search to complete—for the green ribbon of death to make its way across the address bar—before you can start working with your search results. Whether you include more or fewer file types and folders in your index affects only what shows up *quickly* and what shows up *eventually* during each search. In other words, a larger index is a little slower, but increases the odds that what you're looking for appears faster.

Not happy with the Windows Search tool? Check out Copernic Desktop Search (*http://www.copernic.com/*), Google Desktop Search (*http://desktop.goo gle.com/*), and Locate32 (*http://www.locate32.net/*), all free.

CHAPTER 3

The Registry

The Windows registry is a bit like high school detention: nobody wants to go, but most of us end up there for one reason or another. And a few outcasts even prefer it.

The registry essentially does two things for Windows: it's a database of settings for most of your applications and Windows itself, and it's a repository of technical data for installed hardware devices and software components.

For instance, all of your file type associations—the links between your documents and the applications that created them—are built from registry data. Your network settings, your hardware settings, each of your applications' customizable toolbars, and even Windows' own Control Panel settings are all stored in the registry. The checkboxes you check or uncheck in most Options windows are saved in the registry. And the various software building blocks used by nearly every programs—including those that come with Windows—are "registered" in your registry.

But why is the storage mechanism for all these settings the least bit important?

Because software is imperfect. Windows 7 only lets you make the most basic of customizations to your file types; for more control, you've got to edit the registry. Not all application settings can be changed in the applications themselves; some changes can only be made in the registry. When something goes wrong with software or hardware, sometimes the only remedy is to fix a registry key. And if you want to hack Windows beyond Microsoft's intentions—whether to improve performance, reduce clutter, or eliminate annoyances—the registry is the key.

Indeed, much of what seems hardcoded in Windows 7 is actually governed by data in the registry: delete a certain key, and an icon disappears from the *Computer* folder. Change a certain 0 to a 1, and you disable a user's ability to shut down Windows. Sometimes this is precisely what you're after, but as you can imagine, it's also potentially a recipe for disaster, which brings us to the obligatory warning. You can irreversibly disable certain components of Windows 7—or even prevent Windows from loading altogether—by changing certain settings in the registry. Sure, most modern software is designed to repair broken settings, but you can bet that very few software developers have taken the time to anticipate all the stupid things you'll undoubtedly do to your PC. I'm certainly not suggesting that you cower in the corner, but rather that you employ some of the safeguards described on these pages—such as backing up—before you start hacking the registry to bits. Even taking a few moments to create a registry patch (explained later in this chapter) *before* you change a setting can save you hours of work later on.

The Registry Editor

Most of the changes to the registry are performed behind the scenes by the applications that you run, as well as by Windows; settings and other information are read from and written to the registry constantly. But the primary means of editing registry keys and values *directly* is the Registry Editor (open the Start menu, type `regedit`, and then press **Enter**), included with all editions of Windows 7.

Although the registry is stored in multiple files on your hard disk, it is represented by a single logical hierarchical structure, similar to the folders on your hard disk. When you open the Registry Editor, you'll see a window divided into two panes (as shown in Figure 3-1). The left side shows a tree with folders, and the right side shows the contents of the currently selected folder. Now, these aren't really folders—this is just a convenient and familiar method of organizing and displaying the information stored in your registry.

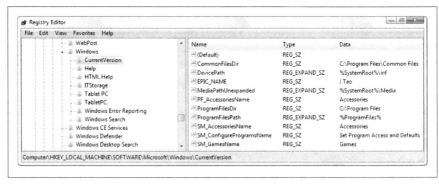

Figure 3-1. The Registry Editor lets you view and change the contents of the registry

Each folder-like object is called a *key*. Each key can contain other keys, as well as *values*. Values contain the actual information stored in the registry, while keys are used only to organize the values. Keys are shown only in the left pane and values are shown only in the right pane (unlike Windows Explorer, where folders are shown in both panes).

To display the contents of a key (folder), just click the key name on the left, and the values contained therein are listed in alphabetical order on the right side. To expand a certain branch to show its subkeys, click the tiny arrow to the left of any key or double-click the key name.

Editing the registry generally involves navigating down through branches to a particular key and then modifying an existing value or creating a new key or value. For instance, this registry path:

    HKEY_CURRENT_USER\Software\Microsoft\Windows

points to the location of the Windows key, which you navigate to by expanding the HKEY_CURRENT_USER branch, then Software, then Microsoft, and then finally clicking Windows to show its contents on the right.

> If you find yourself returning to the same registry location over and over, use the **Favorites** menu to bookmark the item. You can also start a second instance of Registry Editor to view two different registry locations simultaneously by typing regedit /m in the Start menu **Search** box and pressing **Enter**.

Once the key is open, you can modify the contents of a value by double-clicking it. See "The Meat of the Registry: Values" on page 125 for the skinny on editing different types of values.

You can also rename any key or value just like you'd rename a file in Windows Explorer: click twice slowly, right-click and select **Rename**, or highlight and press **F2**. Likewise, you can delete a key or value by highlighting it and pressing the **Del** key or by right-clicking it and selecting **Delete**. (Note that deleting a key will also delete all the values and subkeys it contains.)

You can't drag-drop values or keys here as you can with files or folders in Windows Explorer. Of course, there's very little reason to move a key or value from one place to another in the registry, as the settings are totally location-dependent. (A value in one key will almost always have a different meaning than the same value in a different key.) Thus, renaming or moving a key is often tantamount to deleting it.

There are times, however, when you'll want to duplicate a key and all its contents (such as a file type key), which is something you can do with registry patches, described later in this chapter.

To add a new key or value, select **New** from the **Edit** menu, select what type of object you want to add (Figure 3-2), type a name, and press **Enter**.

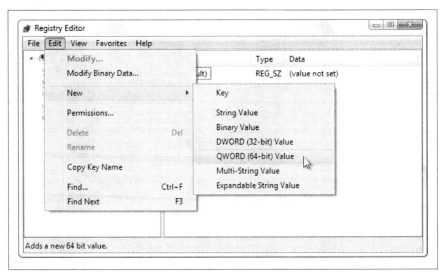

Figure 3-2. Select **New** from the **Edit** menu to add a new key or value to any part of the registry

You can create a value (or key) almost anywhere in the registry and by any name and type that suits your whim. However, unless Windows or an application is specifically designed to look for the value, it will be ignored, and your addition will have absolutely no effect.

So far, the Registry Editor should seem pretty straightforward. But you'll find that the trick isn't so much *how* to change something in the registry as *what* to change, and that's what the rest of this chapter is about.

One way to locate settings is to use the Registry Editor's Search feature (**Edit→Find** or press **Ctrl-F**), but it won't take you long to realize that this tool pretty much sucks. See "Search the Registry" on page 132 for search tips, as well as better search tools you can use. There's also "Locate the Registry Key For a Setting" on page 137, which is useful if you don't know what to search for. But since the stuff in the registry is largely location-dependent, you'll need to be acquainted with the structure of the registry before you know where to go to make a specific change.

The Structure of the Registry

There are five primary, or "root," branches, each containing a specific portion of the information stored in the registry. These root keys can't be deleted, renamed, or moved, because they are the basis for the organization of the registry. They are:

HKEY_CLASSES_ROOT

> This branch contains the information that comprises your file type associations and the registered software components (called *classes*) used by Windows and many of your applications.

> This entire branch is a symbolic link, or "mirror," of HKEY_LOCAL_MACHINE \SOFTWARE\Classes, but is displayed separately here for convenience and, of course, to confuse you.

 A symbolic link is different from a Windows shortcut you'd find on your hard disk. Information in a linked branch appears twice and can be accessed at two different locations, even though it's stored only once. This means that the Find tool may stop in both places if they contain something you're looking for and, as you might expect, changes in one place will be immediately reflected in the mirrored location.

HKEY_CURRENT_USER

> This branch simply points to a portion of the HKEY_USERS root key (later in this section) representing the currently logged-in user. This way, any application can read and write settings for the current user without having to know which user is currently logged in.

In each user's branch are the settings for that user, such as Control Panel settings and Explorer preferences. Most applications store user-specific information here as well, such as toolbars, high scores for games, and other personal settings.

The settings for the current user are divided into several categories, such as AppEvents, Control Panel, Identities, Software, and System. The most useful of these branches, Software, contains a branch for almost every application installed on your computer, arranged by manufacturer. Here and in HKEY_LOCAL_MACHINE\SOFTWARE (discussed later) can be found all of your application settings. As though Windows was just another application on your system, you'll find most user-specific Windows settings in HKEY_CURRENT_USER\Software\Microsoft\Windows.

HKEY_LOCAL_MACHINE

This branch contains information about all of the hardware and software installed on your computer that *isn't* specific to the currently logged-in user. The settings in this branch are the same for all users on your system.

Just like HKEY_CURRENT_USER, the sub-branch of most interest here is the SOFTWARE branch, which contains all of the information specific to the applications installed on your computer. Those settings that are specific to each user (even if your computer has only one user), such as toolbar configurations, are stored in the aforementioned HKEY_CURRENT_USER branch; those settings that are not user-dependent, such as installation folders and lists of installed components, are stored in the HKEY_LOCAL_MACHINE branch. You'll want to look in both places if you're trying to find a particular application setting, because most manufacturers (even Microsoft) aren't especially careful about which branch is used for any given setting.

HKEY_USERS

This branch contains a sub-branch for the currently logged-in user, the name of which is a long string of numbers that looks something like this:

    S-1-5-21-1727987266-1036259444-725315541-500

This number is the SID (security identifier), a unique ID for each user on your system (yours will be different than this one), and is explored in Chapter 8.

While it may sound like a good idea to edit the contents of this branch, you should instead use the HKEY_CURRENT_USER branch described earlier, which is a symbolic link (mirror) of this branch:

    HKEY_USERS\S-1-5-21-1727987266-1036259444-725315541-500

No matter which user is logged in, HKEY_CURRENT_USER will point to the appropriate portion of HKEY_USERS.

Because Windows only loads the profile (this portion of the registry) of the currently logged-in user, only one user branch will ever be shown here. However, there will be a few other branches here, such as *.default* (used when nobody is logged in), and a few other branches that are of little interest to most users.

HKEY_CURRENT_CONFIG

This branch typically contains a small amount of information, most of which is simply symbolic links (mirrors) of other keys in the registry. There's usually little reason to mess with this branch.

In short, everything you'll want to do with the registry can be done in either HKEY_CURRENT_USER or HKEY_LOCAL_MACHINE.

The Meat of the Registry: Values

Values are where registry data is actually stored while keys are simply used to organize values. The registry uses several *types* of values—eight in all—each appropriate to the type of data it is meant to hold. Each type is known by at least two different names, the common name and the symbolic name (shown in parentheses in Table 3-1).

Table 3-1. Value types visible in the Registry Editor

Value type	Icon used in RegEdit	Can be created in RegEdit?
String (REG_SZ)	ab	Yes
Multi-String/string array (REG_MULTI_SZ)	ab	Yes
Expandable string (REG_EXPAND_SZ)	ab	Yes
Binary (REG_BINARY)	011 110	Yes
DWORD 32-Bit (REG_DWORD)	011 110	Yes
QWORD 64-Bit (REG_QWORD)	011 110	Yes
DWORD (REG_DWORD_BIGENDIAN)	011 110	No
Resource List (REG_RESOURCE_LIST, REG_RESOURCE_REQUIRE-MENTS_LIST, or FULL_RESOURCE_DESCRIPTOR)	ab	No

Although the Registry Editor allows you to view and edit all eight types of values, it is only capable of creating the six most common (and not surprisingly, most useful) types. In practice, you'll mostly only create string, binary, and DWORD values.

The Registry

String values

String values contain *strings* of characters, more commonly known as plain text. Most values of interest to you will end up being string values; they're the easiest to edit and are usually in plain English. To edit a string value, just double-click, type a string of text into the text field (Figure 3-3), and click OK when you're done.

In addition to standard strings, there are two far less common string variants, used for special purposes:

- *Multi-String/string array values* contain several strings, concatenated (glued) together and separated by *null* characters. Although the Registry Editor lets you create multistring values, it's impossible to type null characters (character #0 in the ASCII character set) from the keyboard. The only way to place a null character into a registry value is either through a programming environment (see Chapter 9) or via cut-and-paste from another application.

- *Expandable string values* contain special variables, into which Windows substitutes information before delivering to the owning application. For example, an expandable string value intended to point to a sound file may contain `%SystemRoot%\Media\doh.wav`. When Windows reads this value from the registry, it substitutes the full Windows path for the variable, `%SystemRoot%`; the resulting data then becomes (depending on where Windows is installed) `c:\Windows\Media \doh.wav`. This way, the value data is correct regardless of the location of the Windows folder.

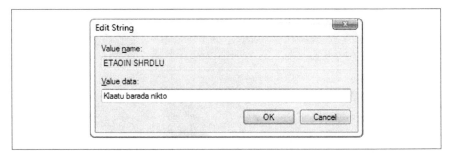

Figure 3-3. Edit a string value by typing text into this box

 If you were to type data intended for an expandable string value into an ordinary string value, the variables wouldn't necessarily be expanded when read by an application. Make sure you select the Multi-String value type when adding values with localized variables (common in file type keys).

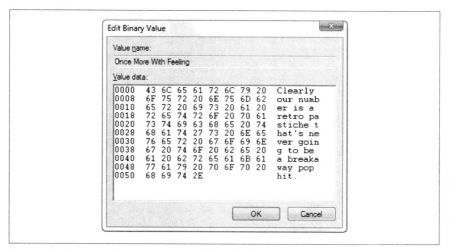

Figure 3-4. Binary values are entered differently from the common string values, but the contents are sometimes nearly as readable

Binary values

Similar to string values, binary values hold strings of characters. The difference is the way the data is viewed and edited. Instead of a standard text box, binary data is entered with hexadecimal codes in an interface commonly known as a *hex editor*. Double-click any binary value to use Registry Editor's standard binary editor, shown in Figure 3-4.

The purpose of binary values is to hold data that can't be easily represented by ordinary string values. As such, binary values are much less likely to contain readable text (despite the example value in Figure 3-4), but rather some form of raw data. Of course, the format and purpose of the data in any given binary value depends entirely on the application that created it.

Each individual character is specified by a two-digit number in base-16, also known as hexadecimal (e.g., 6E is 110 in good-ol' base 10), which allows you to enter characters not available on the keyboard. You can type hex codes on the left side or normal ASCII characters on the right, depending on where you click with the mouse.

Registry Editor also offers an alternative binary viewer (Figure 3-5); just select any value (binary or otherwise) and from the View menu, select View Binary Data. Pity you can't use this window to edit values, as it's wider than the standard binary value edit window and provides four different viewing formats. It's best-suited to investigate nonprintable characters found in non-binary values.

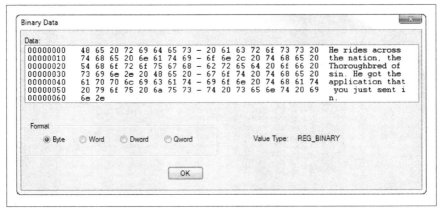

Figure 3-5. View any value in binary mode using the Binary Data window, useful only to programmers and the geekiest of geeks

DWORD values

Essentially, a DWORD is a number. Often, the contents of a DWORD value are easy to understand, such as 0 for no and 1 for yes, or 161 for the number of seconds it took you to solve your best game of Sudoku. A DWORD value is used where only numerical digits are allowed, whereas a string or binary value can contain anything.

In the DWORD value editor (Figure 3-6), you can change the base of the number displayed (think back to your grade-school math). For instance, the number 64 in hexadecimal (also known as base 16) is equal to 100 in decimal (base 10).

 Type the number in the wrong base, and you'll unwittingly be entering the wrong value, although the **Base** option doesn't matter for any value of 0 to 9.

In most cases, you'll want to select **Decimal** (even though Microsoft didn't bother to make it the default), since decimal notation is what most humans use for ordinary counting numbers. Note that if there's already a number in the **Value data** field, switching the **Base** converts the number in real time, which incidentally is a good way to illustrate the difference between the two settings. (You can also use the Windows Calculator, *calc.exe*, to do hex-to-decimal conversions.)

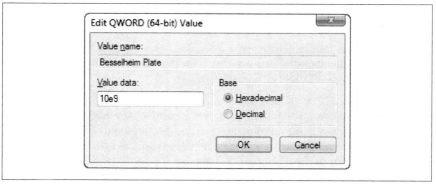

Figure 3-6. DWORD values are just numbers, but they can be represented in decimal or hexadecimal notation

Windows also supports the QWORD value, which is nothing more than a DWORD with a larger storage capacity. See the upcoming sidebar "When Is a Number Not Just a Number?" for details.

The application that creates each value in the registry solely determines the particular type and purpose of the value. In other words, no strict rules limit which types are used in which circumstances or how values are named. A programmer may choose to store, say, the high scores for some game in a binary value called High Scores or in a string value called Lard Lad Donuts. All you have to do in your role as registry hacker is provide the values in the format expected by a given application.

An important thing to notice at this point is the string value named (default) that appears at the top of every key, which is a holdover from early versions of Windows where each key only had a single value. The (default) value cannot be removed or renamed, although its contents can be changed; an empty default value is signified by value not set. The (default) value doesn't necessarily have any special meaning that would differentiate it from any other value, apart from what might have been assigned by the programmer of the particular application that uses the key.

When Is a Number Not Just a Number?

Sometimes the number stored in a DWORD value is actually made up of several components, all glued together with the binary arithmetic we were supposed to have learned in the seventh grade.

The term "DWORD" is an abbreviation for "Double Word," which means that it can store two 16-bit values (known as *words* in geekspeak). A 16-bit value is basically a whole number (integer) that can be stored in 16 *bits*, which means it can be no larger than 2^{16}, or 65,536. So, a DWORD value can be used to store two of these, *or* one 32-bit number (up to 2^{32}, or 4,294,967,296), *or even* thirty-two 1-bit binary numbers (each of which can be 1 or 0).

Windows 7 also supports the 64-bit QWORD value, which is available even if you're using the 32-bit edition. A 64-bit QWORD—a Quadruple Word, equivalent to two DWORDs—can hold sixty-four 1-bit values, four 16-bit values, two 32-bit values, or one 64-bit value (which can be up to 2^{64}, or 18,446,744,073,709,600,000).

So, the question that's probably on your mind is, "Huh? How can this knowledge possibly help me with my love life?"

The answer is that it can't. In fact, it'll probably just make things worse. But it'll be invaluable when you come across a DWORD value that's made up of a bunch of smaller components. For instance, say you flip a switch in some application and you witness a DWORD value change from 16 to 8. What you've uncovered is that the aforementioned switch is stored as the fourth bit (the first being 1, the second being 2, and the third being 4) in this value. (If you're confused, look up "Binary numeral system" in Wikipedia for help with the concept.)

To make things more complicated, there's also the BIGENDIAN variant of the DWORD value (REG_DWORD_BIGENDIAN). This is basically the same as an ordinary 32-bit DWORD, except that the two 16-bit words are stored in the opposite order (the larger one coming first). These are rare, but you might run into trouble if you replace one with an ordinary DWORD value.

The Registry on 64-bit Windows

Windows x64 isn't a purely 64-bit operating system; like Vista x64 and XP x64, it's a *transitional* operating system that—while 64-bit at its core—also includes a 32-bit WOW (Windows-on-Windows) layer that runs your 32-bit applications. (See Chapter 1 for more on 64-bit Windows.)

Problem is, 64-bit applications and software components don't easily mingle with 32-bit ones, which means you've got to have two registries to keep these bits isolated from one another. Now since it would be impractical to have two completely separate registries, only certain keys and branches are kept separate, while others are shared.

For instance, file type associations (covered later in this chapter) are shared between the two layers,* so you can associate your .txt documents with your favorite plain text editor just once, and it'll work whether you double-click readme.txt with the 32-bit edition of Windows Explorer or the 64-bit version.

But at the same time, a 64-bit program can't link with a 32-bit DLL without some clumsy magic. So the portion of the registry that manages shared DLLs and other components is different for each Windows layer. This way, for instance, the 64-bit editions of Windows Explorer and Internet Explorer are never exposed to 32-bit extensions (DLLs) you've installed, and vice versa.

 This separation of registered software classes is why you need to fire up the 32-bit version of Windows Explorer if you want to use 32-bit context menu add-ons, or install only native 64-bit context menu add-ons if you want to use the 64-bit version of Windows Explorer exclusively.

The upshot is that most of the time this partially bifurcated design doesn't matter. Each of your 32-bit applications sees only the registry keys it's supposed to, and for the most part, your 64-bit applications see only the 64-bit registry.

When it does matter are those circumstances where this duality of the registry gets in the way of day-to-day hacking and annoyances removal.

In places where there are two disparate registry branches, Registry Editor includes a special branch named Wow6432Node so you can access 32-bit entries from the same window as the 64-bit ones. There are three such "nodes" by default in Windows 7:

```
HKEY_CLASSES_ROOT\Wow6432Node†
HKEY_CURRENT_USER\Software\Wow6432Node
HKEY_LOCAL_MACHINE\SOFTWARE\Wow6432Node
```

---

* This works much better than the system in Vista and earlier versions, where there were two sets of file types that were *reflected* (synchronized). The biggest problem was that this reflection was incomplete and unreliable; registry permissions, for instance, were not reflected, which led to chaos and mass hysteria.

† HKEY_CLASSES_ROOT\Wow6432Node is a symbolic link of HKEY_LOCAL_MACHINE\SOFTWARE \Wow6432Node\Classes and HKEY_LOCAL_MACHINE\SOFTWARE\Classes\Wow6432Node. See "The Structure of the Registry" on page 123 for more on symbolic links.

So let's say you wanted to change a registry setting for Adobe Photoshop. For the 64-bit edition of Photoshop, you'd navigate to:

```
HKEY_CURRENT_USER\Software\Adobe\Photoshop
```

or for the 32-bit edition, you'd go to:

```
HKEY_CURRENT_USER\Software\Wow6432Node\Adobe\Photoshop
```

Since 32-bit and 64-bit classes (software components) aren't cross-compatible, 64-bit classes are registered here:

```
HKEY_CLASSES_ROOT\CLSID\{class_id}
```

while 32-bit classes can be found here:

```
HKEY_CLASSES_ROOT\Wow6432Node\CLSID\{class_id}
```

Alternatively, you can use the 32-bit version of Registry Editor (*%systemroot%\syswow64\regedit.exe*), although there's not much to be gained by doing so. Include the -m command-line parameter when launching *regedit.exe* to open the 32-bit and 64-bit versions side-by-side.

Registry Tasks and Tools

So, that's it for registry basics. The real fun begins with the various registry tools you can use, and what you can do with them.

Search the Registry

The Registry Editor has a simple (to a fault) Search feature, allowing you to search through all the keys and values for text. Just select **Find** from the Registry Editor's **Edit** menu, type the desired text (Figure 3-7), and click **Find Next**.

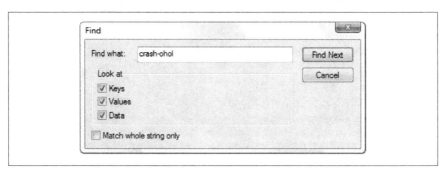

Figure 3-7. Use Registry Editor's Search feature to find text in key names, value names, and value data

The Registry Editor's Search feature is pretty terrible. For one, it's hopelessly slow, and doesn't show a history of past searches. But its biggest drawback is that it only shows one match at a time; you have to click **Find Next** repeatedly to cycle through all the search results, one by one. And if you accidentally double-click **Find Next**, there's no going back. Finally, there's no search-and-replace feature, but more on that later.

Press **Ctrl-F** or select **Edit→Find** to begin a search at the selected key. (Scroll to the top and select **Computer** beforehand to search the entire registry.)

In the Find window, make sure that all three options in the **Look at** section are checked, unless you know specifically that what you're looking for is solely a **Key**, a **Value** (value name), or **Data** (value contents). You'll also usually want the **Match whole string only** option turned off, unless you're searching for text that commonly appears in other words; searching for handle might otherwise trigger entries like PersistentHandler and TeachAndLearn.

The Registry Editor stops once it finds the first match to your search term; just press **F3** to continue searching for the next match. If you want to show all the matches at once, use registry Agent, introduced in the next section.

You may need to employ some tricks to find certain types of things in the registry, such as:

Context menu items

Context menu items are usually stored in the HKEY_CLASSES_ROOT branch (see "File Type Associations" on page 166). When searching for any menu items, keep in mind that most of them have underlined characters to signify keyboard shortcuts, even though, ironically, Windows 7 doesn't display them by default. For instance, the **Datasheet** action associated with Access Form Shortcuts in Microsoft Office 2007 is actually stored as Data&sheet in the registry. This allows it to be displayed as **Datasheet** if you manage to open the menu with the keyboard (an increasingly difficult task in Windows 7). The & character in Data&sheet instructs Windows to underline the character that follows it (the s in this case), and since it's present in the registry value, you'll need to include the & character in your searches; if you don't, the Search tool won't find it.

Text searches are *not* case-sensitive, so you don't have to worry about capitalization when typing your search terms.

File and folder names

Despite the fact that long filenames (those longer than the archaic 8-dot-3 standard left over from the early days of DOS) had been in wide use on the PC platform for well over a decade before Windows 7 was released, short filenames still have a role in modern Windows computing, particularly in the registry. Specifically, a folder path like *C:\Program Files* may be occasionally represented in its short 8.3 form: *C:\PROGRA~1*. (See "Advanced NTFS Settings" on page 320 for more information on short filename generation.)

Why, even Microsoft still uses short filenames; a fresh installation of Office 2007 places a reference in the registry to *C:\PROGRA~1\MICROS~2\Office12\1033\ACCESS12.ACC*.

Unfortunately, this means you need to search for both the long and short versions of a file or folder name if you want to find them all. For example, say you want to move your *Program Files* folder from one drive to another. When you install Windows, any settings pertaining to this folder may be stored in the registry as *C:\Program Files* or *C:\Progra~1*. Make sure you search for both.

 Now, when searching the registry for both Program Files and Progra~1, it may occur to you to just search for progra, which will indeed catch both variations. Because this will stumble upon other instances of the word program, try limiting the results by placing a backslash (\) in front of the text (e.g., \progra) to limit the search to only directory names beginning with those letters. Neato.

DLLs, classes, components, extensions, and CLSIDs

Windows and all your applications are constructed from smaller building blocks, sometimes referred to as classes, extensions, or objects. I'll spare you a tirade on COM components, .NET architecture, and a bunch of other developer jargon (sorry). Suffice it to say, the majority of these building blocks are registered in the HKEY_CLASSES_ROOT\CLSID branch of your registry, and are identified by a 32-digit (16-bit hex) code called a Class ID, or CLSID. CLSIDs are formatted like this:

    {AC0EEBCA-73FA-4EB3-87FF-96E58401FA1F}

Why is this important? It means that you can track down where a class is referenced (in other words, where in Windows it's used) as well as where it's registered, all by searching the registry for the CLSID.

For instance, configuration data for the aforementioned class is located in:

`HKEY_CLASSES_ROOT\CLSID\{AC0EEBCA-73FA-4EB3-87FF-96E58401FA1F}`

If a component isn't working, odds are you can fix the problem, or at least help diagnose it, by fussing with the values in this key. Or, delete the key altogether to effectively unregister the class with Windows. For instance, to turn off Windows' support for "compressed folders" (ZIP files appearing as folders in Windows Explorer), you need to delete two such CLSID branches, as described in Chapter 2.

 Using 64-bit Windows? 64-bit classes are stored in a different location from 32-bit classes; see "The Registry on 64-bit Windows" on page 130 for details.

Register and Unregister Components

Windows comes with a utility, *regsvr32.exe*, that you can use to register or unregister DLL files manually. For instance, you can repair a CLSID branch for a specific component by opening a Command Prompt window in Administrator mode (see Chapter 8) and typing:

```
regsvr32 "c:\program files\my app\some file.dll"
```

and pressing **Enter**. Or, to remove all the entries used by a DLL, type:

```
regsvr32 /u "c:\program files\my app\some file.dll"
```

and press **Enter**.

Find yourself doing this often? Set up two new context-menu actions—one to register and another to unregister—for your *.dll*, *.ax*, and *.ocx* file types. See "File Type Associations" on page 166 for instructions.

See the section "Get Videos to Play" on page 195 for an example of *regsvr32.exe* in action.

If a CLSID is found elsewhere (even within another key under `HKEY_CLASSES_ROOT\CLSID`), it means that the program that owns the key is using the component. Delete the reference, and you break the link without disrupting the core component. See Chapters 6 and 8 for some examples.

Search and Replace Registry Data

The Registry Editor has no search-and-replace feature, seemingly with good reason: a single poorly chosen replace operation could make Windows inoperable. But there are times when you do need to replace all occurrences of, say, a folder name like *C:\Program Files\My Program* with another folder name like *D:\My Folder*. Depending on the number of occurrences, such an operation could take hours.

registry Agent (part of Creative Element Power Tools, available at *http://www.creativelement.com/powertools*) not only gives you a better way to search the registry (search results are shown in a list, instead of one at a time), but supports search-and-replace operations as well. Here's how to move an application from one drive to another without having to reinstall it:

1. Open Creative Element Power Tools Control Panel, and click the **Start Registry Agent now** link.

2. Type text to search (e.g., c:\program files\acme), and click **Find Now**. Note that in order to search for text containing a backslash, you'll need to turn off the **Keys** option, since registry key names cannot contain backslashes.

3. The results are shown in a list (Figure 3-8) with three columns. The left column shows the location (key) where the text was found; you can click it to open the Registry Editor at that location. The middle and righthand columns show the value name and contents, respectively.

4. Choose the **Replace** tab.

Replacing a common word like Microsoft in your registry is a really bad idea. Don't try it at home. I mean it. Ordinary searching with registry Agent is harmless, but the **Replace** feature can be as dangerous as it is handy if you're not careful.

5. Place a checkmark next to the found items you wish to replace. Use the checkmark at the top of the list to check or uncheck all of them.

6. Type the new text—which will replace the old text in each selected item in the search results—in the **With** field (e.g., d:\new acme).

You don't have to replace the same text you used to conduct the search. For instance, you can search for c:\program files \acme, and then do a search-and-replace within these results for anything you like, such as acme by itself, or even portmeirion.

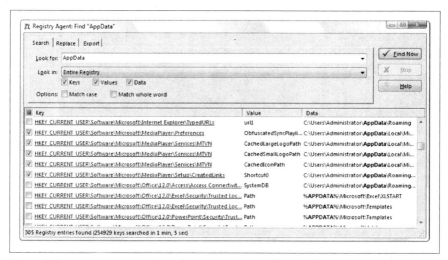

Figure 3-8. Use registry Agent for a faster registry search, as well as for search-and-replace operations

7. Choose which types of text you'd like to replace by checking or unchecking the **Keys**, **Values**, and **Data** options. Note that the **Keys** checkbox is grayed-out (disabled) by default for safety reasons; click **Help** for instructions to lift this restriction.

The Replace tool has no "undo" feature, which means that if you screw up something here, the only way to recover is to restore your registry from a backup. Want a shortcut? Use the **Export** tab to create a registry patch (described later in this chapter) containing the selected values, which can be used as a quick and dirty backup.

8. Click the **Replace** button to perform the search and replace.

Even if you don't use the search-and-replace feature, registry Agent is a pretty slick searching tool, as it overcomes the annoying hunt-and-peck approach of the Registry Editor's Search feature and ends up being much faster, too.

Locate the Registry Key For a Setting

So now you know how to change an item in the registry, but how do you find which item to change?

Sometimes it's obvious. Say you want to reduce the time it takes to load your favorite application, and it occurs to you that perhaps you could disable the program's splash screen (the friendly logo you stare at while the program loads, which takes time to load itself). Sure enough, there's a value called Show SplashScreen in the application's registry key in HKEY_Current_User\Software. Set it to 1 (one) to turn it on, or 0 (zero) to turn it off.

 Zero and one, with regard to registry settings, typically mean *false* and *true* (or *off* and *on*), respectively. However, sometimes the value name negates this—if the value in the example were instead called DontShowSplashScreen, then a 1 (one) would most likely turn *off* the feature.

Other times it's not so easy. You might see a long, seemingly meaningless series of numbers and letters, or perhaps nothing recognizable at all. Although there are no strict rules as to how values and keys are named or how the data therein is arranged, there's a trick you can use to uncover how a particular setting—any setting—is stored in the registry.

What's the point? Once you find the registry value(s) responsible for a particular setting, you can:

Find hidden settings

Not all application settings have tidy little checkboxes in a Preferences dialog window; some things can only be changed in the registry. By finding out where an application saves its settings, you can uncover others nearby and even learn how they work.

Reproduce settings

By finding the registry keys and values responsible for one or more settings, you can consolidate them into a registry patch file (described later in this chapter), and then apply them to any number of other PCs. This is particularly useful for network administrators and software developers.

Enter values not permitted by the software

For instance, say you've configured a virus scanner to scan your system once a week. You'd rather have it perform a scan every 10 days, but the program lets you choose only a multiple of 7. If you find the registry value responsible, you may be able to enter any arbitrary number.

Fix bugs in software

If an application won't save a particular setting properly in the registry, you can fix it by hand if you know where it's stored.

Prevent changes to certain settings

Some programs—including Windows 7 itself—have a habit of "forgetting" certain settings, reverting them to their default values for no apparent reason. Once you know where the setting is stored, you can change the permissions (more on that later) to prevent further changes without your consent.

The idea is to take "snapshots" of your entire registry *before* and *after* you make a change in Windows. By comparing the two snapshots, you can easily see which registry keys and values were affected. Here's how you do it:

1. Close all applications except the one you wish to examine. Any unnecessary running applications—including those in the system tray/notification area—could write to the registry at any time, adding unexpected changes.

2. Open the Registry Editor and select the HKEY_CURRENT_USER root branch.

3. Select **Export** from the **registry** menu. Type User1.reg for the filename, select your desktop or another convenient location to put the file, and click **Save** to export the entire branch to the file.

4. Next, select the HKEY_LOCAL_MACHINE branch and repeat step 3, exporting it instead to *Machine1.reg*.

Although the registry has five main branches, the others are simply "mirrors," or symbolic links of portions of HKEY_CUR RENT_USER and HKEY_LOCAL_MACHINE. See "The Structure of the Registry" on page 123 for details.

5. Now make the change you want to track.

For instance, say you want to find the value responsible for showing hidden files in Windows Explorer. In this case, you'd go to **Control Panel→Folder Options**, choose the **View** tab, and in the **Advanced Settings** list, turn on the **Show hidden file, folders, and drives** option. Click OK when you're done.

6. Immediately—and before doing anything else—switch back to the Registry Editor, and re-export the HKEY_CURRENT_USER and HKEY_LOCAL_MACHINE branches into new files named *User2.reg* and *Machine2.reg*, respectively, as described earlier in steps 2 and 3.

What you now have is a *snapshot* of the entire registry taken before and after the change was made. It's important that the snapshots be taken immediately before and after the change, so that other trivial settings, such as changes in window positions, aren't included with the changes you care about.

7. All that needs to be done now is to distill the *changed* information into a useful format. Windows comes with the command-line utility File Compare (*fc.exe*), which quite handily highlights the differences between the *before* and *after* files.

There are several Windows-based third-party alternatives that are easier to use or offer more features than *fc.exe*, such as UltraEdit (available at *http://www.ultrae dit.com*); even Microsoft Word can do text comparisons (although you'll need to remember to save the results as plain text).

Open a Command Prompt window (type `cmd` in the Start menu **Search** box and press **Enter**), and then at the Command Prompt, use the `cd` command (Chapter 9) to change to the directory containing the registry patches. For instance, if you saved them to your desktop, type:

```
cd %userprofile%\desktop
```

8. To perform the comparison, type the following two lines:

```
fc /u user1.reg user2.reg > user.txt
fc /u machine1.reg machine2.reg > machine.txt
```

At this point, the File Compare utility scans the two pairs of files and spits out *only* the differences between them. The > character redirects the output, which normally would be displayed right in the Command Prompt window, into new text files: *user.txt* for the changes in `HKEY_CUR RENT_USER` and *machine.txt* for the changes in `HKEY_LOCAL_MACHINE`.

9. Examine the results. The *user.txt* file should look something like this:

```
Comparing files user1.reg and USER2.REG

***** user1.reg
[HKEY_CURRENT_USER\Software\Microsoft\Windows\CurrentVersion\
                    Explorer\Advanced]
"Hidden"=dword:00000001
"ShowCompColor"=dword:00000000
***** USER2.REG
[HKEY_CURRENT_USER\Software\Microsoft\Windows\CurrentVersion\
                    Explorer\Advanced]
"Hidden"=dword:00000002
"ShowCompColor"=dword:00000000
*****
```

From this example listing, you can see that the only applicable change was the `Hidden` value, located deep in the `HKEY_CURRENT_USER` branch. (There may be some other entries, but if you inspect them, you'll find that they relate only to MRU lists from RegEdit and can be ignored.)

MRU stands for *Most Recently Used*. Windows stores the most recent filenames typed into file dialog boxes; from this example, you'll notice several references to the filenames you used to save the registry snapshots.

Note that for the particular setting explained in step 5, no changes were recorded in the HKEY_LOCAL_MACHINE branch, so *machine.txt* ends up with only the message, "FC: No differences encountered". This means that the changes were made only to keys in the HKEY_CURRENT_USER branch.

10. The lines immediately preceding and following the line that changed are also included by FC as an aid in locating the lines in the source files. As luck would have it, one of the surrounding lines in this example happens to be the section header (in brackets), which specifies the full path of the registry key in which the value is located.

In this case, the value that changed was located in HKEY_CURRENT_USER\Software\Microsoft\Windows \CurrentVersion\. If you take a peek in that key, you'll find that it contains other settings, some of which aren't included in the Folder Options dialog box. Experiment with some of the more interesting-sounding values, such as CascadePrinters and ShowSuperHidden. Or, search the Web for the value names to see what others have discovered about them.

If you don't see the line in square brackets, you'll have to do a little more reconnaissance. To find out where the value is located, open one of the source files (*User1.reg*, *User2.reg*, *Machine1.reg*, or *Machine2.reg*) and use your text editor's Search tool to find the line highlighted in step 9. For this example, you'd search *User2.reg* for "Hidden"=dword:00000002 and then make note of the line enclosed in square brackets ([...]) most immediately *above* the changed line. This represents the key containing the Hidden value.

Sometimes, changing a setting results in a registry value (or key) being created or deleted, which could mean an entire section may be present in only one of the two snapshots. Depending on the change, you may have to do a little digging, or perhaps try the document comparison feature in your favorite word processor for an easier-to-use comparison summary.

11. This last step is optional. If you want to create a registry patch that activates the registry change, you can either convert FC's output to the correct format (described here), or return to Registry Editor and export the appropriate key, as described in "Export and Import Data with Registry Patches" on page 149.

Because the FC output is originally derived from registry patches, it's already close to the correct format. Start by removing all of the lines from *user.txt*, except the *second* version of the *changed* line—this would be the value in its *after* setting, which presumably is the goal. You'll end up with something like this:

```
"Hidden"=dword:00000002
```

Next, paste in the key (in brackets) immediately above the value. (In the case of our example, it was part of the FC output and can simply be left in.) You should end up with text that looks like this:

```
[HKEY_CURRENT_USER\Software\Microsoft\Windows\CurrentVersion\
                    Explorer\Advanced]
"Hidden"=dword:00000002
```

Finally, add the text Windows Registry Editor Version 5.00 followed by a blank line at the beginning of the file, like this:

```
Windows Registry Editor Version 5.00

[HKEY_CURRENT_USER\Software\Microsoft\Windows\CurrentVersion\
                    Explorer\Advanced]
"Hidden"=dword:00000002
```

When you're done, save this as a new file with the *.reg* filename extension (e.g., *My Neato Setting.reg*).

 If the settings you've changed also resulted in changes in the HKEY_LOCAL_MACHINE branch, simply repeat this step for the *machine.txt* file as well. You can then consolidate both files into one, making sure you have only one instance of the Windows Registry Editor Version 5.00 line.

For some settings (such as the one in this example), you may want to make two patches: one to turn it on, and one to turn it off. Simply double-click the patch corresponding to the setting you desire.

There are some caveats to this approach, mostly in that the File Compare utility will often pull out more differences than are relevant to the change you wish to make. It's important to look closely at each key in the resulting registry patch to see whether it's really applicable and necessary.

See Chapter 9 for a way to use Windows Script Host to automate changes to the registry without using registry patches.

Create an Interface for a Registry Setting

The whole point of messing around in the registry is to view and modify settings that are otherwise inaccessible in Explorer, Control Panel, or the hundreds of dialog boxes scattered throughout the operating system. However, there is a way to patch into the interface and add checkboxes and radio buttons that are linked to whatever registry settings you want.

Why would you want to do this? Perhaps there's a registry setting you change frequently, or maybe you administer a building full of PCs and there's a feature you want to expose to your users without having them mess around with the registry themselves. (Or, conversely, perhaps there's a setting you'd like to hide from your users.)

Start by going to **Control Panel→Folder Options→View tab**. At first glance, the **Advanced settings** list in this dialog box is presented in a somewhat awkward format, apparently to accommodate the large number of options. However, the less-than-ideal presentation is actually designed to allow customization, permitting Microsoft (or you) to easily add or remove items from the list. See Figure 3-9 for an example of a customized version of this window.

You've probably guessed that Microsoft didn't make this list of options customizable just so you can mess with it. Rather, it was designed to accommodate different settings for different editions of Windows (the actual options present on your PC, for instance, depend on your edition of 7). But that doesn't mean you can't change it around to suit your needs.

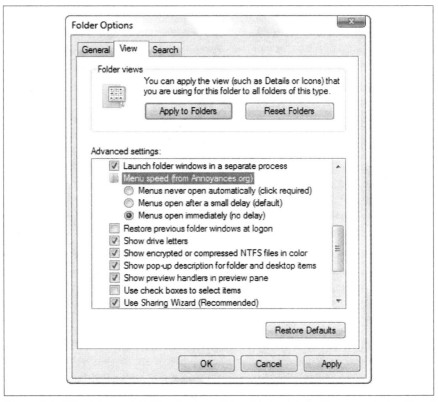

Figure 3-9. The Advanced Folder Options dialog box is a flexible, customizable list of registry settings

The idea is that you link up a checkbox or radio button to a value—any value you choose—in your registry. This would, for example, allow you to make certain registry changes accessible to yourself or others (such as users of other PCs you administer), reducing the need for them to mess around in the registry. Or, if you're a software developer, you can add your own program's options to this window. Or, maybe you just want easier access to a hidden Microsoft setting you find yourself changing often.

The format is actually quite remarkable, because you don't have to be a programmer to utilize this feature. You can add new options to a certain portion of the registry and then tie those options to values you choose anywhere else in the registry. The downside is that it's a little cumbersome to type it all out, and the options are rather limited. Here's how you do it:

1. Open the Registry Editor.

2. Expand the branches to `HKEY_LOCAL_MACHINE\Software\Microsoft\Windows\CurrentVersion\Explorer\Advanced\Folder`.

   Take a look at the keys inside of the `Folder` key. The structure of the hierarchy in the Folder Options window is reproduced here in the registry, although the list items will appear in a different order than their corresponding registry entries. This is because the captions in the Folder Options list aren't necessarily the same as the names of the corresponding registry keys here, yet both collections are sorted alphabetically. For example, the **Remember each folder's view settings** option is represented by the `ClassicViewState` key in the registry.

3. Take this opportunity to back up the entire branch by highlighting the `Folder` key and selecting **Export** from the **File** menu. This way, you'll be able to easily restore the defaults without having to reinstall Windows.

4. At this point, you can remove any unwanted entries by deleting the corresponding keys from this branch; the `Text` value in each key should be enough to explain what each key is for.

5. To add a new item, start by simply creating a new key inside the `Folder` key. Name the key anything you want, as long as it doesn't conflict with an existing key name. Bonus points for a nice, descriptive key name.

> Some settings are divided into groups, such as **Hidden files and folders**, which contains two radio buttons. A group is merely a key, like the existing `Hidden` key in your registry, that holds two or more subkeys. In the group key itself, specify a caption and icon and set `Type` to `group`, as explained next. Then put each entry in the group into a subkey of your new group key. If you get lost, use the `Hidden` key as a template.

6. The values inside each key determine the properties of the corresponding setting. Feel free to fish around the existing keys for examples.

   Start by adding a new string value to your key named `Text`, and then double-click it to enter the caption of the new entry. When you're done, add another string value named `Type`, and type either `group`, `checkbox`, or `radio` as the value's contents. These two values, plus the others that determine how your new setting looks in the Folder Options window, are explained in Table 3-2.

Table 3-2. Visual properties of Folder Options items

Value name	Datatype	Description of value contents
Type	String	This can be set to either group, checkbox, or radio, representing a folder, checkbox, or radio button, respectively. Checkboxes are square options and can be either on or off. Radio buttons are round options that are linked to other radio buttons in the same folder, in that only one at a time can be selected (you can have multiple groups of radio buttons). And folders, of course, are used to organize the various other options. This parameter is required by all items.
Text	String	This is the actual caption of the option as it will appear in the dialog box. This can be as long as you want (better too descriptive than too vague), but the paradigm dictates that only the first word be capitalized and that there be no period. This parameter is required by all items.
Bitmap	String	This specifies the icon, used for folder items only. If omitted, it's a rather ugly bent arrow. The syntax[a] is *filename,index*, where *filename* is the full path and filename of the file containing the icon, and *index* is the icon number (starting with zero), if the file contains more than one icon. To specify the familiar yellow folder, type %SystemRoot%\system32\Shell32.dll,4 here. This parameter is optional for all folders, and has no effect on checkboxes and radio buttons.
HelpID	String	This is the filename and optionally the help context ID, pointing to the documentation for this item. If the user selects the item and presses the F1 key, this specifies the help note that will appear. The syntax is *filename#id*, where *filename* is the name of a .hlp or .chm file, and *id* is the numeric help context id (commonly used by programmers) of the topic you want to display. Omit *id* to simply show the index page of the specified help file. This parameter is optional.

[a] The Bitmap value uses the same syntax as the DefaultIcon property for file types, as documented in "File Type Associations" on page 166.

7. Next, add values—explained in Table 3-3—to your key to specify which registry value Windows should change when you place a checkmark next to your custom setting in the Folder Options window. For radio and checkbox items, you'll need the following values: HKey-Root, RegPath, ValueName, and CheckedValue. (This step isn't necessary if your item is a group.)

Table 3-3. registry-related properties of Folder Options items

Value name	Datatype	Description of value contents
HKeyRoot	DWORD	This is an eight-digit number representing the root of the registry path containing the target registry setting. Use the *hexadecimal* number 80000000 for HKEY_CLASSES_ROOT, 80000001 for HKEY_CURRENT_USER, 80000002 for HKEY_LOCAL_MACHINE, 80000003 for HKEY_USERS, or 80000005 for HKEY_CURRENT_CONFIG. For some reason, it must be separated from the rest of the registry path, specified in RegPath, discussed next. This parameter is required for all checkbox and radio items.
RegPath	String	This is the path specifying the location of the target registry setting, not including the root (see HKeyRoot, earlier). For example, for HKEY_CURRENT_USER\Software\Micro soft\Windows\CurrentVersion, you would only enter Software\Microsoft\Windows\CurrentVersion here. This parameter is required for all checkbox and radio items.
ValueName	String	This is the name of the target registry value. This value is where the setting data is stored when the option is turned on or off in the Folder Options window. The key containing said value is specified by the RegPath and HKeyRoot parameters, listed earlier. This parameter is required by all checkbox and radio items.
CheckedValue	Should match target value datatype	This holds the data to be stored in the target registry value (specified by the RegPath and ValueName parameters earlier), when said option is turned *on*. If you're configuring an option to be used on both Windows 9x/Me and Windows 7/2000 systems, use both the CheckedValueW95 and Checked ValueNT parameters *instead of this value*. This parameter is otherwise required by all checkbox and radio items.
CheckedValueW95	Should match target value datatype	Use this instead of CheckedValue, above, if you're configuring an option to be used on both Windows 9x/Me and Windows 7/2000 systems. This value contains the data that will be applied if the system is running Windows 9x/Me. Used in conjunction with CheckedValueNT, discussed next.
CheckedValueNT	Should match target value datatype	Use this instead of CheckedValue, discussed earlier, if you're configuring an option to be used on both Windows 9x/Me and Windows 7/2000 systems. This value contains the data that will be applied if the system is running Windows 7, 2000, or NT. Used in conjunction with CheckedValueW95, later.
UnCheckedValue	Should match target value datatype	This holds the data to be stored in the target registry value, when said option is turned *off*. This value is optional; if omitted, it is assumed to be 0.

The Registry

Value name	Datatype	Description of value contents
DefaultValue	Should match target value datatype	This is the data Windows sets to your target value if the **Restore Defaults** button is pressed in the Folder Options window. This value is optional; if omitted, it is assumed to be 0.

 The value type (String, Binary, DWORD) of the Checked Value, UnCheckedValue, and DefaultValue parameters all depends on what the target value requires. For example, if the target value you're changing is a DWORD value, then all three of these parameters must also be DWORD values.

For instance, if placing a checkmark next to your custom entry is supposed to change the data from 0 to 1 in the Tree value, located in HKEY_CUR-RENT_USER\Software\Annoyances, then you'd set HKey-Root to 80000001, RegPath to \Software\Annoyances, ValueName to Tree, Checked Value to 1, and UnCheckedValue to 0.

8. After you've created keys and entered the appropriate property values, your registry should look something like Figure 3-10, and the resulting Folder Options dialog box should look like Figure 3-9, shown earlier. If Folder Options is open, you'll have to close it and reopen it for the changes to take effect.

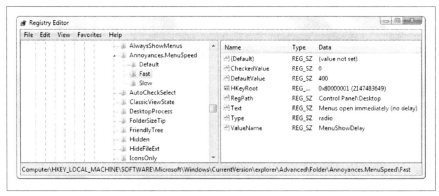

Figure 3-10. Settings that appear in the Advanced Folder Options list are configured in the registry

 If you add a setting and it doesn't show up in the Folder Options window (after closing and reopening it), most likely one or more required values are missing.

9. Close the Registry Editor when you're finished.

The next time you open the Folder Options dialog window, the current data stored in each target value is compared with the corresponding CheckedValue and UnCheckedValue, and the option in the **Advanced settings** list is set accordingly. In other words, if you did everything right, each option in **Advanced settings** should correctly reflect its own current state. Change a setting and click OK, and the corresponding options are written to the registry.

To reproduce a setting elsewhere in the Windows interface or the interface of another application, you'll first need to find the respective registry setting as described in "Locate the Registry Key For a Setting" on page 137.

Export and Import Data with Registry Patches

Typing in registry data gets awfully tedious, particularly if the **N** key is broken on your keyboard. Thankfully, it's not the only way to add keys and values to the registry.

A registry patch is a plain-text file with the *.reg* filename extension that contains one or more registry keys or values. Double-click on a *.reg* file, and Windows runs the Registry Editor, which "applies" the patch to the registry, meaning that its contents are *merged* with the contents of the registry.

Patch files are especially handy for backing up small portions of the registry, distributing registry settings to other PCs, and duplicating keys.

For example, say you spend an hour or so customizing the toolbars in a particular application used by many employees in your office. Since most programs store their toolbar settings in the registry, you can use a registry patch to not only back up the completed toolbar setup—and thus save an hour of reconfiguring should your PC subsequently burst into flames—but to quickly copy the toolbar to all the other PCs in your office.

Or, perhaps you've spent the last six months gradually customizing your file types (covered later in this chapter), only to find that a newly installed application or a Windows upgrade erased all your hard work and reset all your context menus. Provided you had made a registry patch containing all your saved file types (a backup), all you need to do is apply it (restore the backup) should the need arise.

Create a registry patch

1. Open the Registry Editor, and select a branch you wish to export.

 The branch can be anywhere from one of the top-level branches to a branch a dozen layers deep. Registry patches include not only the branch you select, but all of the values and subkeys in the branch. Don't select anything more than what you absolutely need.

2. From the **File** menu, select **Export**, type a filename and choose a destination folder, and click OK. All of the values and subkeys in the selected branch will then be stored in the patch file. Make sure the filename of the new registry patch has the *.reg* extension.

Clearly, there's not much to making registry patches with the Registry Editor. But it gets a little more interesting when you modify them, or even create them from scratch to automate registry changes.

Edit a registry patch

Since a registry patch is just a plain-text file, you can edit it with any decent plain-text editor, or lacking that, Notepad (*notepad.exe*). The contents of the registry patch will look something like the text shown in Example 3-1.

Example 3-1. Contents of a registry patch created from HKEY_CLASSES_ROOT\.txt

```
Windows Registry Editor Version 5.00

[HKEY_CLASSES_ROOT\.txt]
@="txtfile"
"PerceivedType"="text"
"Content Type"="text/plain"

[HKEY_CLASSES_ROOT\.txt\ShellNew]
"ItemName"="@%SystemRoot%\\system32\\notepad.exe,-470"
"NullFile"=""
```

The first line, `Windows Registry Editor Version 5.00`, tells Windows that this file is a valid registry patch; don't remove this line. The rest of the registry patch is a series of key names and values.

Backward Compatibility

Registry patches created in Windows 95, 98, or Me can be imported into the Windows 7 registry without a problem (that is, not taking into account the screwy settings contained therein).

However, the same is not true the other way around. Patch files made in Windows 7, Vista, XP, 2003, and 2000 are encoded with the Unicode character set, and as you've seen, bear a header indicating the 5.0 version number that will choke the older Registry Editor. To use a 7-created *.reg* file in Windows 9x/Me, you'll need to deal with both of these issues.

First, replace the `Windows Registry Editor Version 5.00` header line with `REGEDIT4`. Whew, that was hard.

Next, to convert the Unicode *.reg* file into an ASCII-encoded file those earlier versions of Windows can understand, open the file in Notepad. Then, from the Notepad's **File** menu, select **Save As** and choose a new filename, and from the little **Encoding** drop-down listbox at the bottom of the window, select **ANSI**. Click **Save**, and your patch is now backward-compatible.

The key names appear in brackets ([...]) and specify the full path of the key, thus indicating where the values that follow are to be stored. On each subsequent line until the next key section begins, the name of a value appears first (in quotation marks), followed by an equals sign, and then the data stored in the value (also in quotation marks). A value name of @ tells the Registry Editor to place the value data in the (`Default`) value (as shown in the fourth line of the example).

You can go ahead and make changes to anything in the registry patch file as long as you keep the format intact. Of course, those changes won't take effect in the registry until the registry patch is merged back into the registry, a process described in the next section.

So, why would you want to edit a registry patch file? Modifying a large number of registry values often turns out to be much easier with a text editor than with the Registry Editor, since you don't have to open—and then close—each individual value.

It may be tempting to perform a quick search-and-replace in the text editor, and then apply your changes back to the registry. But be careful, as the effect may not be what you expected. If you replace any text in the *name* of a value (to the left of the equals sign) or even the name of a key (the lines in brackets), Registry Editor will create new values and keys with those names when you apply the patch, *leaving the old values and keys intact.* A better choice is to use a tool like registry Agent, described in the section "Search and Replace Registry Data" on page 136.

There's no requirement that the keys in a registry patch file need to have lived next to one another in the registry, or that they be in any particular order. This means you can combine several separate patch files into one, and use it to restore any number of keys in one step. All it takes is a little copy and paste between side-by-side Notepad windows. The only thing you need to do, besides making sure all the keys and values remain intact, is to remove any extraneous `Windows Registry Editor Version 5.00` header lines.

If you're creating a registry patch to be used on other PCs, make sure you fix any references to absolute pathnames before you distribute the file. If, for example, your patch file references *D:\Windows\notepad.exe*, it'll cause a problem on any PC where *notepad.exe* is located in *C:\Windows*. The best solution is to use expandable string values, as described earlier in this chapter, along with the appropriate system variables, like this: *%SystemRoot%\notepad.exe*. Now, since expandable string values are stored like binary values in registry patch files, such an entry would look like this:

```
"Open"=hex(2):26,00,53,00,79,00,73,00,74,00,65,00,6d,00,52,00,6f,00,6f,\
00,74,00,25,00,5c,00,6e,00,6f,00,74,00,65,00,70,00,61,00,64,00,2e,00,65,00,\
78,00,65,00,00,00
```

Now, you've probably worked out that it's considerably easier to edit expandable string (and binary) values in the Registry Editor than in any text editor, so you'll probably want to make such corrections *before* you export the key to a patch file. If you need to add a binary or expandable string value to a registry patch file you've already started editing, though, all you have to do is return to the Registry Editor, create a temporary key somewhere, and then create your new value. When you're done, just export the key to a new file, delete the key from the registry, and then copy and paste the value to your other registry patch file.

Delete keys and values from a registry patch

Although the Registry Editor won't ever create a patch that *deletes* registry keys or values, it's easy enough to make one by hand. To delete a key with a registry Patch, place a minus sign *before* the key name, like this:

```
-[HKEY_CURRENT_USER\Control Panel\don't load]
```

This patch, when applied, deletes the specified key and all of its values, as well as any subkeys. To delete a single value from a key, place a minus sign *after* the equals sign, like this:

```
[HKEY_CURRENT_USER\Control Panel\don't load]
"desk.cpl"=-
```

Of course, these tricks only work if you have sufficient permission to delete those keys. See "Prevent Changes to a Registry Key" on page 154 for more information.

Apply a registry patch

To copy the stuff from a registry patch file back into your registry, you need to apply it. The easiest way is to double-click the file (it doesn't matter if the Registry Editor is running or not).

If you see a UAC prompt at this point, click **Continue**. Then answer **Yes** when asked whether you're sure you want to add the information in the *.reg* file to the registry, and finally, click OK when you see the "Information in *My-Patch.reg* has been successfully entered into the registry" message. (You can also apply a patch from within the Registry Editor: from the **File** menu, select **Import**, select the patch file to apply, and click OK.)

To apply a registry patch without any other warning messages—except for the UAC prompt; see Chapter 8 to get rid of that—you need to use the command line. Either from an open Command Prompt window or from **Start→Run**, type the following:

```
regedit /s c:\folder\mypatch.reg
```

where `c:\folder\mypatch.reg` is the full path and filename of the patch file to import. Or, if you want to get rid of the confirmation messages any time you double-click a *.reg* file, add the **/s** switch (as shown here) to the *.reg* file type, as described later in this chapter.

If the Registry Editor is already open and one of the keys modified by a patch that was just applied is currently open, RegEdit should refresh the display automatically to reflect the changes. If it doesn't, press the **F5** key or go to **View→Refresh**.

When you apply a registry patch, you *merge* the keys and values stored in a patch file with those in the registry. Any keys and values in the applied patch that don't already exist will be created. If a key or value already exists, only its contents will be changed. It's important to understand that if a key you're updating already contains one or more values, *those values will be left intact* if they're not explicitly modified or deleted by the patch.

 See Chapter 9 for another way to automate changes to the registry from files.

Prevent Changes to a Registry Key

Security has always been one of Microsoft's favorite marketing buzzwords, and never more so than when Windows 7 was introduced. But as it turns out, Windows' security features are quite a bit more useful for protecting your PC from itself than from any alleged intruders.

The permissions system covered in Chapter 8 doesn't just protect files and folders, it restricts who can read and modify registry entries. This feature is tremendously useful, yet most people don't even know it's there. It means you can lock a registry key to prevent employees from installing software on a company PC, or prevent kids from disabling parental controls on a family PC. Permissions also let you lock file type associations (covered later in this chapter), preventing other applications from changing them. And by locking the keys that list programs to load on startup, you can help protect your PC from some kinds of malware.

Here's how you do it:

1. Open the Registry Editor, and navigate to the key you want to protect.

 You can't protect individual values, but rather only the keys that contain them. This means that if you lock a key to protect one of its values, the lock applies to all values in that key.

2. Right-click the key, and select **Permissions**. For details on how to use this window, see Chapter 8.

3. Click **Advanced**, and then click **Add**.

 If the **Add** button is disabled (grayed out), you'll have to take ownership of the key, close the Permissions window, and then reopen it before you can make any changes to the permissions of this object. See Chapter 8 for details.

4. In the **Enter the object names to select** field, type Everyone, and then click OK. (The "Everyone" user encompasses all user accounts, including those used by Windows processes and individual applications when they access the registry.)

5. In the next window, "Permission Entry for...", click the checkbox in the **Deny** column, next to the actions you want to prohibit, as in Figure 3-11 (see upcoming examples).

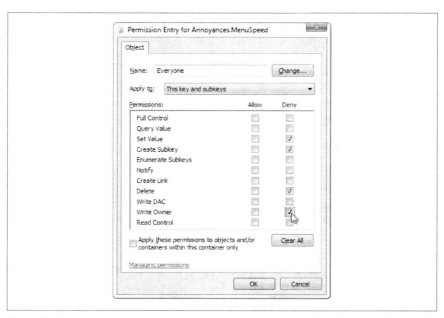

Figure 3-11. Lock a registry key to prevent applications or Windows from modifying it

6. When you're done, click OK in each of the three open dialog windows. The change will take effect immediately.

Now, you may be tempted to remove **Allow** permissions for a particular user (or even all users), rather than add the **Deny** entry shown here. The problem is that doing so wouldn't prevent an application or Windows from taking ownership or adding the necessary permissions and breaking your lock. Furthermore, it would make it much more difficult to restore the old permissions should you need to remove the lock; using this procedure, all you need to do is remove the Deny rule and you're done.

This works because Windows gives Deny rules priority over Allow rules, which means you can lock a key with a single Deny entry even if there's another Allow rule that expressly gives a user permission to modify the item.

So, which keys do you lock, and which actions do you forbid? Here are some examples:

Make a key read-only
> To lock a value yet still allow applications and Windows to read it, place a **Deny** checkbox next to **Set Value**, **Delete**, and **Write Owner**, as in Figure 3-11.

Create a complete lock-out
> To prevent all applications from reading, modifying, or deleting a value, place a **Deny** checkbox next to **Full Control**.

Keep away ShellNew
> To prevent applications from making new keys under the selected key, place a **Deny** checkbox next to **Create Subkey**. For instance, you can do this to file type keys to prevent applications from adding themselves to Windows Explorer's **New** list by creating the ubiquitous ShellNew subkey; see "Customize Windows Explorer's New Menu" on page 187 for instructions.

Enforce security policies on a multiple-user PC
> To prevent another user from modifying a security policy (such as those covered in Chapter 8), use the procedure in "Locate the Registry Key For a Setting" on page 137, to locate the corresponding key in the registry. Then, instead of adding a **Deny** rule to the key as described above, remove any permissions that allow anyone other than an administrator to delete, modify, or add subkeys to the key. Make sure that there's still at least one rule for the Administrators group (or at least your own administrator-level account) that affords **Full Control**.

Lock individual file types
> The File Type Doctor utility mentioned in the section "File Type Associations" on page 166 has a feature that uses permissions to lock file types, thus preventing applications from "stealing" them.

Protect file types from Windows' UserChoice feature

As described in "The Evils of UserChoice Override" on page 178, Windows will ignore your custom file type settings if a certain key is present in the `HKEY_CURRENT_USER\Software\Microsoft\Windows\CurrentVersion\Explorer\FileExts` key. To prevent this from happening ever again, place a **Deny** checkbox next to **Create Subkey**. This will immediately protect all your file types, but you'll need to delete one or more existing entries in the `FileExts` key to restore individual file types. See "File Type Associations" on page 166 for details.

Back Up the Registry

In a way, the Windows registry is a weak link in the operating system's stability and robustness. It's remarkably easy to damage, but very difficult to repair. And unless you go to the trouble of making your own backup copy, it's not necessarily easy to replace it if it's damaged (unlike, say, DLLs, which can be pulled right off the Windows CD). A broken registry—either due to physical corruption or errant data—might cause Windows to behave erratically (or more so than usual) or it may prevent Windows from starting at all.

The System Protection feature (also known as *System Restore*, and discussed further in Chapter 6) is found in **Control Panel→System→System Protection**. Windows automatically creates a *restore point* once a day, plus each time you install an application, device driver, or any update from Windows Update. Restore points contain essential Windows system files and registry settings, although it's not clear how much of the registry is backed up, nor is it possible to restore all or part of the registry alone.

So, what's the big problem? Why not just zip up the registry files or copy them to a CD? Problem is, the files that contain your registry data (called *hives*) are constantly being read from and written to, so Windows locks them to ensure they can't be modified, deleted, or even read directly. (Although you can copy a `HKEY_CURRENT_USER` hive file by logging out and then logging in as a different user.)

This means you have to use a procedure like the following if you want a backup you can create and restore at will. You may want to do this, for instance, just before you install a new program or device driver:

1. Open Registry Editor, and collapse all the branches so only the five main root keys are showing.

2. Highlight `HKEY_CURRENT_USER`.

3. From the **File** menu, select **Export**.

4. From the **Save as type** list, choose **registry Hive Files (*.*)**.

5. Type a filename, and give it the *.hive* filename extension (e.g., *hkcu.hive*). RegEdit won't do this for you, nor will Windows recognize the *.hive* extension by default, but it will make the files much easier for you to identify than if they have no extension, which is the default. See "File Type Associations" on page 166 for how to properly register a new file type.

6. Choose a folder in which to save the backup, and click **Save**.

7. Next, comes `HKEY_LOCAL_MACHINE`. Although Registry Editor won't let you export this entire branch to a hive, you can export individual branches contained therein. Just repeat steps 3–6 for these keys and respective target filenames:

   • `HKEY_LOCAL_MACHINE\HARDWARE` → *hklm_hardware.hive*

   • `HKEY_LOCAL_MACHINE\SAM` → *hklm_sam.hive*

   • `HKEY_LOCAL_MACHINE\SECURITY` → *hklm_security.hive*

   • `HKEY_LOCAL_MACHINE\SOFTWARE` → *hklm_software.hive*

   • `HKEY_LOCAL_MACHINE\SYSTEM` → *hklm_system.hive*

8. To restore either or both of these backups, and replace the current registry with the data in your backup hive files, select **Import** from the Registry Editor's **File** menu. Select **registry Hive Files (*.*)** from the unlabeled listbox next to the **File name** field, select the *.hive* file to import, and click **Open**.

There are two things worth noting about this backup procedure. First, it makes use of registry *hive* files, which are binary files, and the same type of file Windows uses to store the registry it uses day-to-day. If you were to instead export ordinary registry patch files—which is what you'd get if **Registration Files (*.reg)** was selected in step 4—then you'd end up with files that couldn't be easily restored back into the registry. This is because the Registry Editor only *merges* patch files with existing registry data, which can leave errant data intact, as described in the section "Export and Import Data with Registry Patches" on page 149. When the Registry Editor imports hive files, however, it deletes the existing keys from the registry before bringing in the new (backed-up) data.

 Registry patches can be handy for backing up individual keys, as explained in "The Local Backup", the next sidebar.

The Local Backup

The easiest type of registry backup to make is the local backup, akin to the local anesthetic. Rather than backing up the entire registry, you simply back up the portion you'll be working on. If you screw up, you can quickly and easily restore the affected keys without touching anything else.

Say you want to make some changes to the key, `HKEY_CURRENT_USER\Software` `\Microsoft\Windows\CurrentVersion\Run`, which happens to be responsible for running programs when Windows starts. Just open the Registry Editor, navigate to this key, and select **File→Export**. Type a filename and save the registry patch file on your Desktop. (See "Export and Import Data with Registry Patches" on page 149 for more information on this feature.)

Make a mistake and want to restore the backup? Just delete the key you changed, and double-click the registry patch to load it back in. (Deleting the key before loading the patch ensures that no newly-added entries remain.)

Of course, registry patch files can be hard to keep track of, particularly if you change a setting and only discover two weeks later that it's caused a problem. In this case, you can make an easy-to-find backup right in the registry.

Before you make any changes to the registry, make a patch file as just described. Then, rename the key in which you'll be working by adding `.backup` to the end of the key name. For instance, if you want to make a change to this key:

```
HKEY_CURRENT_USER\Software\Microsoft\Windows\CurrentVersion\Run
```

Highlight the `Run` key, press the **F2** key (or right-click and select **Rename**), and change the name to `Run.backup`.

Then, immediately re-import the registry patch you just made and delete the *.reg* patch file. You'll end up with two identical keys right next to each other:

```
HKEY_CURRENT_USER\Software\Microsoft\Windows\CurrentVersion\Run
HKEY_CURRENT_USER\Software\Microsoft\Windows\CurrentVersion\Run.backup
```

At this point, you can go ahead and mess with the `Run` key to your heart's content, and even use the nearby `Run.backup` key as a handy reference. If you ever need to restore your backup—either today or six months from now—just delete the `Run` key and then rename `Run.backup` to `Run`.

See Chapter 2 for a quick way to make a local backup of files you're working on.

Second, notice that only HKEY_CURRENT_USER and HKEY_LOCAL_MACHINE are backed up here, leaving HKEY_CLASSES_ROOT, HKEY_USERS, and HKEY_CURRENT_CON FIG seemingly unprotected. This is done because the data in HKEY_CLASSES_ROOT and HKEY_USERS is duplicated in the first two root keys (HKLM and HKCU, respectively) and HKEY_CURRENT_CONFIG is dynamically generated and not stored on the hard disk at all. See "The Structure of the Registry" on page 123 for details.

Now, other than saving time by not exporting more than you have to, why is it important to know how Windows stores the registry data? Because if you use a slightly more advanced approach when you back up the registry, you'll have a backup you can restore *even if Windows won't start*. Here's how:

1. Open a plain-text editor (e.g., Notepad).

2. Type the following into a blank document:

```
if exist C:\Backups\COMPONENTS.OLD del C:\Backups\COMPONENTS.OLD
if exist C:\Backups\SAM.OLD del C:\Backups\SAM.OLD
if exist C:\Backups\SECURITY.OLD del C:\Backups\SECURITY.OLD
if exist C:\Backups\SOFTWARE.OLD del C:\Backups\SOFTWARE.OLD
if exist C:\Backups\SYSTEM.OLD del C:\Backups\SYSTEM.OLD
if exist C:\Backups\NTUSER.OLD del C:\Backups\NTUSER.OLD

ren C:\Backups\COMPONENTS COMPONENTS.OLD
ren C:\Backups\SAM SAM.OLD
ren C:\Backups\SECURITY SECURITY.OLD
ren C:\Backups\SOFTWARE SOFTWARE.OLD
ren C:\Backups\SYSTEM SYSTEM.OLD
ren C:\Backups\NTUSER.DAT NTUSER.OLD

REG SAVE HKLM\COMPONENTS C:\Backups\COMPONENTS
REG SAVE HKLM\SAM C:\Backups\SAM
REG SAVE HKLM\SECURITY C:\Backups\SECURITY
REG SAVE HKLM\SOFTWARE C:\Backups\SOFTWARE
REG SAVE HKLM\SYSTEM C:\Backups\SYSTEM
REG SAVE HKCU C:\Backups\NTUSER.DAT
```

3. Save the file somewhere convenient, such as your desktop, and give it the *.bat* filename extension (e.g., *back up registry.bat*).

4. Open Windows Explorer, open the *Computer* branch, and select drive *C:*. Create a new folder in *C:* named *Backups*. If you want to store the backup hive files in a different location, replace all 24 instances of *C:\Backups* in the listing in step 2 with the full path of your backup folder.

5. To run the backup, just right-click the *back up registry.bat* file and select **Run as administrator**. (See Chapter 8 for an explanation of why you can't just double-click the file to run it.)

To run this backup automatically every time you start Windows, create a shortcut to the *back up registry.bat* file in your *Startup* folder in your Start menu. Or, if you typically hibernate your PC instead of shutting down, use the Scheduled Tasks feature (Chapter 9) to schedule the backup to run at regular intervals, say, once every three days.

6. At this point, you can be extra compulsive and copy the backed-up hive files to a CD or network drive for safekeeping.

So, what's different about this second procedure? For one, it's automated, using the little-known *REG.exe* command-line registry tool instead of the Registry Editor to create the hive files. (To learn more about *REG.exe*, open a Command Prompt window, type `reg /?` and press **Enter**.) Also, it automatically archives the last backup, thus maintaining *two* sets of backup files at all times, a feat accomplished by some simple batch-file commands (see Chapter 9 for more on batch files).

Most importantly, though, it creates five separate hive files from the HKEY_LOCAL_MACHINE branch—one for each sub-branch except HARDWARE, which is dynamically generated—instead of just one. As a result, the backup files you'll end up with are the same as those Windows normally uses to store the registry on your hard disk.

Windows stores the active hive files—those for HKEY_LOCAL_MACHINE, at least—in the *\Windows\System32\Config* folder. The exception is the HKEY_CURRENT_USER branch, stored in the *NTUSER.DAT* file located in the user's home directory (usually *\Users\{username}*). See Chapter 8 for more on user accounts.

In your snooping, you might discover the *\Windows \System32\config\RegBack* folder. Check the dates of the files in the *RegBack* folder, and sure enough, you'll see that they're recent—perhaps with yesterday's or today's date—backups of your HKEY_LOCAL_MACHINE hive files.

Although Windows does regularly create these backups, they're neither complete (the HKEY_CURRENT_USER branch isn't included) nor as useful as a backup you make yourself. For instance, a problem that prevents Windows from loading is likely to have made its way to the automatic backups, but not necessarily the manual backup you made three days ago, just before you installed an application.

All of this means that you can restore your registry from the backup in a variety of ways. Of course, you can always use **File→Import in Registry Editor**, as described earlier in this section, but that only works if Windows is running.

If Windows won't start, and you suspect a registry glitch, here's how to restore your registry from the six hive backups. (See Chapter 6 for general startup troubleshooting.)

1. Insert your Windows 7 setup disc in your drive, and start your PC.

 See Chapter 1 if your PC doesn't boot off your CD, or if you only have a "recovery disc" provided by your PC manufacturer.

2. Click **Next** on the first Install Windows screen, and then click **Repair your computer** on the second page.

3. On the System Recovery Options window, select **Microsoft Windows 7** in the list and then click **Next**.

4. Click **Command Prompt**.

5. In the Command Prompt window that appears, take this opportunity to back up the current state of the registry, as described earlier in this section. Then, type the following commands to rebuild your registry from your hive files:

```
REG RESTORE HKLM\COMPONENTS C:\Backups\COMPONENTS
REG RESTORE HKLM\SAM C:\Backups\SAM
REG RESTORE HKLM\SECURITY C:\Backups\SECURITY
REG RESTORE HKLM\SOFTWARE C:\Backups\SOFTWARE
REG RESTORE HKLM\SYSTEM C:\Backups\SYSTEM
REG RESTORE HKCU C:\Backups\NTUSER.DAT
```

 You can omit one or more of these lines if you only want to restore part of the registry.

6. When you're done, pop out your 7 setup disc and restart your PC.

With any luck, Windows should start normally. If it doesn't, either your most recent backup is defective, or the problem lies elsewhere. If you suspect that an older backup may work where the newer one failed, add the .*OLD* filename extension to each filename in step 5, like this:

```
REG RESTORE HKLM\COMPONENTS C:\Backups\COMPONENTS.OLD
```

If Windows still won't start at this point, try reinstalling Windows (see Chapter 1).

Now, there's a chance that the *REG.exe* tool won't work, which might happen if your registry is sufficiently corrupted or if the *REG.exe* file itself is damaged. In this case, try replacing the active hive files with your backups, like this:

1. Open the Command Prompt as instructed in steps 1–4 above.
2. Type these commands to copy the files:

   ```
   copy C:\Backups\COMPONENTS C:\Windows\System32\Config
   copy C:\Backups\SAM C:\Windows\System32\Config
   copy C:\Backups\SECURITY C:\Windows\System32\Config
   copy C:\Backups\SOFTWARE C:\Windows\System32\Config
   copy C:\Backups\SYSTEM C:\Windows\System32\Config
   copy C:\Backups\NTUSER.DAT C:\Users\your_user_folder
   ```

   where **your_user_folder** (on the last line) is the name of your user folder, which may or may not be the same as your user name. If you don't know the folder name, type `dir c:\users` to list all the user folders on your PC. If your user folder name has spaces in it, add quotation marks, like this:

   ```
   copy C:\Backups\NTUSER.DAT "C:\Users\Phillip J. Fry"
   ```

3. When you're done, pop out your 7 setup disc and restart your PC.

See Chapter 6 for more information on backup software that copies your full registry along with all of your system files. And check out the "Other Ways Windows Backs Up the Registry" sidebar, next, for some other features in Windows 7.

Other Ways Windows Backs Up the Registry

The aforementioned automatic hive file backups stored in the *Windows\System32\config\RegBack* folder represent just one of several fail-safe systems built in to Windows 7.

There's also a way to undo a bad hardware driver installation without backing up or restoring the registry at all. Just open Device Manager, right-click the cranky device, select **Properties**, choose the **Driver** tab, and click **Roll Back Driver**. If that doesn't work, right-click the device and select **Uninstall**. When prompted, confirm that you want to delete the driver files. Then, disconnect and reconnect the device, or restart Windows if reconnecting isn't practical.

You can remove petulant software with the Programs and Features tool in Control Panel, but only if the program's uninstaller behaves itself. Otherwise, search the Web for the program name and the word "uninstall" to see whether there are any special removal tools or procedures for the program you're trying to remove.

Of course, neither of these tools will do you much good if Windows won't start. There's also an entry called **Last Known Good Configuration** in the 7 startup menu (covered in Chapter 6), typically shown if Windows didn't shut down properly last time, or if you press the **F8** key before Windows starts loading. In theory, this feature starts Windows with an earlier collection of hardware drivers and settings taken from the last successful boot. In practice, however, Windows 7 seems to have a hard time defining "good" (with respect to the *Last Known Good* moniker), and is usually unable to find an earlier configuration that either solves the problem or works at all. It's worth trying if you don't have a valid registry backup, but don't expect miracles.

Edit Another PC's Registry Remotely

You can use Registry Editor to browse the registry of a remote PC, much like you can use Windows Explorer to browse a remote hard disk. Although intended for administering workstations and servers miles away, this feature also particularly useful for affecting repairs on PCs infected with malware that prevent direct access to the registry.

Here's how you do it:

1. On the remote PC—the one you want to connect to—open the Services window; in the Start menu **Search** box, type services.msc and press **Enter**.

2. Select the **Remote Registry** service in the list and click the green **Start** arrow in the toolbar (or right-click the service and select **Start**).

 If you'll be remote-editing this PC's registry often, right-click the **Remote Registry** service, select **Properties**, and from the **Startup type** list, select **Automatic**. That way, it'll start automatically each time Windows starts, and it'll be ready to go at a moment's notice.

3. Repeat steps 1 and 2 for the local PC as well.

4. Start Registry Editor on the local PC, and from the **File** menu, select **Connect Remote Registry**.

5. When the Select Computer window appears, type the name of the remote PC in the **Enter the object name to select** field and click OK.

6. When prompted, type the username and password of an administrator-level account on the remote PC.

7. After a few moments, two branches of the remote registry will appear at the bottom of the tree in Registry Editor, beneath the local registry, as shown in Figure 3-12.

Figure 3-12. Connect to a remote PC's registry, and it'll appear at the bottom of the tree in Registry Editor

 Note that only the `HKEY_LOCAL_MACHINE` and `HKEY_USERS` branches are shown from the remote registry. But since the other root branches—`HKEY_CURRENT_USER` and `HKEY_CLASSES_ROOT`—are only symbolic links of subkeys of the first two, you'll still be able to read the entire registry. For instance, to access the remote `HKEY_CLASSES_ROOT` branch, navigate to `HKEY_LOCAL_MACHINE\Software\Classes`.

8. When you're done, right-click the remote PC name in the tree in Registry Editor and select **Disconnect**.

The most likely snag you'll encounter when accessing a remote registry is an "Access is denied" error, but this can mean different things at different times. If you get the error while logging in, the username or password you typed in step 6 is incorrect (obviously). But once you're logged in, any such errors are caused by restrictive permissions (see "Prevent Changes to a Registry Key" on page 154).

First, the branch you're trying to access must be readable—and writable as well, if that's what you're trying to do—by the user account matching your login (again, step 6).

Second, the specific key HKEY_LOCAL_MACHINE\SYSTEM\CurrentControlSet\Control\SecurePipeServers\winreg must be readable by both the login account (step 6) and by the user account under which the **Remote Registry** service (step 2) is running. By default, the service uses the "Local Service" user account; check this by right-clicking the **Remote Registry** service in the Services window, selecting **Properties**, and choosing the **Log On** tab.

 You can restrict remote registry access for certain users by denying them read access to the aforementioned WinReg key.

File Type Associations

File type associations are the links between your documents and the applications that use them. The most apparent use of this feature is that, for example, Windows knows to open Notepad when you double-click a text document on the desktop or show you an online order form for anatomical enhancement if you click the link in a spam email message.

One might assume that the aforementioned text file somehow knows it's a Notepad document, but that isn't the case. Instead, Windows determines how to handle a file based solely on the filename extension. The extension is the group of letters—usually three—that follow the period in most filenames. For example, the extension of the file *Readme.txt* is *.txt*, signifying a plain-text file. Likewise, the extension of *Resume.docx* is *.docx*, which tells Windows the file is a word processor document in the Microsoft Word file format. See the "Extension Exception Example" sidebar, next, for a little detail on this point.

Extension Exception Example

It may seem that there are exceptions to the file extension rule: files that seem to know what applications created them despite their filename extensions. For instance, open Microsoft Excel and save a worksheet as a **web page** (***.htm;*.html**), and the resulting file will have an Excel icon in Windows Explorer even though the rest of your *.html* files have a icon matching your default web browser. Furthermore, right-click the file and select **Edit**, and the file will open in Excel rather than your default HTML editor.

What's happening isn't an exception to the "extension determines type" rule, but rather a consequence of it. When you install Microsoft Office, the file *msohevi.dll* (among other things) is registered with some of your file types in the registry. From then on, Windows is instructed to look inside each *.html* file for header tags like these:

```
<meta name=ProgId content=Excel.Sheet>
<meta name=Generator content="Microsoft Excel 12">
```

If you were to open the file with Notepad and delete those two lines, you'd break the link: the file would become an ordinary *.html* file, icon and all. Or if you were to change the filename extension to, say, *.txt*, Windows would no longer know to look inside the file; again, it would behave like any other *.txt* file.

Some might argue that it isn't fair for Microsoft to change the rules like this, to create files that don't behave like all the other files of their type. If you're one of them, you could also delete the registry keys pointing to the Office DLL in the *.html* file type, which would not just break the link to Excel, but prevent Windows or Excel from reestablishing it permanently. (See the discussion of IconHandlers later in this section for details.) Although you'd be breaking functionality (gasp!), you'd be restoring consistency, and—more importantly—enforcing your own preferences when Microsoft otherwise chooses to ignore them.

The Registry

Now, it may seem silly that so much of Windows' ability to open files rests on something as easy to break as the filename, but the design does have its advantages. For instance, it's trivially easy to change the program used to open all your digital photos without having to modify every one of your *.jpg* files to do it. And being able to easily predict what happens whenever you double-click a *.tif* file is certainly comforting.

But there are downsides, too. For one, it's easy for a single application to assert itself as the default for any file type on your PC, and instantly hijack a whole group of files. Windows 7 does provide a mechanism to combat this—see "The Evils of UserChoice Override" on page 178—but taking advantage of it can break your custom file types and context menu items.

Another flaw in Windows' file extension system is that Windows Explorer hides filename extensions by default, which is why the file *Invoice.xlsx* appears only as *Invoice*. Fortunately, this is easy enough to change; just open **Folder Options** in Control Panel (or click **Organize→Folder and Search Options** in Windows Explorer). In the Folder Options window, choose the **View** tab, turn off the **Hide extensions for known file types** option, and click OK.

If you have Windows show filename extensions, it's easier to determine what kind of files you're dealing with. Instead of merely a file named *recipe*, you might see *recipe.tif* if it's a scan of a recipe, *recipe.pdf* if it's an Acrobat file with a recipe inside, or *recipe.exe* if it's a Trojan horse you just received via email. Sure, you'll have to open the file to see whether you're making cookies or explosives, but at least you can anticipate which application will appear, and will know whether or not you'll have to convert it to a different format before posting it on your Chocolate Chip Anarchist blog.

 Having extensions visible also means you can change Windows' perception of the type of a file by merely renaming its extension. (Note that changing a file's extension doesn't actually change the contents or the format of the file, only how Windows interacts with it.) Now, Microsoft started hiding filename extensions back in Windows 95 (in a vain attempt to make Windows easier to use), but it wasn't until Windows Vista that Microsoft made a subtle but important (and welcome) change. In Vista and now Windows 7, when you rename a file, Windows Explorer selects the filename only up to the dot, allowing you to easily type a new name without inadvertently changing the extension.

Since only *registered* filename extensions are hidden by default, *recipe.pdf* appears as *recipe.pdf* until you install Adobe Acrobat Reader. Double-click a *.pdf* file without a reader application, and Windows asks you what you want to do, as shown in Figure 3-13. Don't be surprised if you don't get any useful information after clicking **Use the Web service to find the correct program** in the window in Figure 3-13. Some of the better resources for identifying unfamiliar file extensions include *http://wikipedia.org/wiki/list_of_file_formats* and *http://filext.com*.

So, once the Acrobat installer registers the *.pdf* file type, the *.pdf* extensions vanish in Windows Explorer, and the file is shown merely as *recipe*...unless you elect to make file extensions visible as described above. But what does it mean to register a file type?

Figure 3-13. If you see this window, the selected file's filename extension isn't currently registered on your PC

Anatomy of a File Type

A registered file type is constructed out of a handful of keys and values in the registry that Windows Explorer reads in real time to handle your documents appropriately. Register a new file type, and Explorer will know what to do with files of that type right away.

Usually it's an installer or an application that registers new file types, but anyone (or any program, for that matter) can add new ones or modify existing file type associations. Customizing your PC's file types is one of the most effective ways to save time and reduce annoyances in Windows, but Windows 7 doesn't make it easy. So you've got to know what makes them tick if you're going to take matters into your own hands.

It starts with a single key in HKEY_CLASSES_ROOT, named for a filename extension (including the dot). The (Default) value in that key contains the name of another key that has all the file type's meat in it. For instance, open up the Registry Editor and peer into these keys:

```
HKEY_CLASSES_ROOT\.log
HKEY_CLASSES_ROOT\.scp
HKEY_CLASSES_ROOT\.txt
```

Each one has a (Default) value that contains the word txtfile. Thus, each filename extension *points* to the txtfile file type, which is located in HKEY_CLASSES_ROOT\txtfile. And it's the txtfile key that has all the good stuff. See the "Special File Type Keys" sidebar, next, for some catch-all file types.

Special File Type Keys

There are a few special file type keys in the registry, each of which work like standard file types, despite having much greater scope. They are:

HKEY_CLASSES_ROOT*

The asterisk (*) registry key, conveniently placed at the beginning of the HKEY_CLASSES_ROOT branch in the Registry Editor, defines actions and extensions for all files (but not folders or drives). If there's a context menu item you'd like to eliminate, odds are it's in the Shell or ShellEx subkeys of the * key.

By adding a new action key to HKEY_CLASSES_ROOT*\Shell, you can add a context menu item for all the files on your PC. For instance, you could add a key named OpenInNotepad, type Open in Notepad into the key's (Default) value, and then add a command key that points to *notepad.exe*, as described later in this section. When you're done, right-click **any file** and select **Open** in Notepad to view the file in a new Notepad window. See "Customize Context Menus for Files" on page 175 for details.

HKEY_CLASSES_ROOT\AllFilesystemObjects

This branch works similarly to *, above, except that its entries apply to all files, folders, and drives (not just files).

HKEY_CLASSES_ROOT\Unknown

This key is used to define the behavior of all files with unregistered file extensions. By default, there's only one file type here, openas, which is responsible for the dialog window shown in Figure 3-13. You can, of course, add new actions or even change the default action here. For example, you may routinely work with a bunch of different types of documents Windows doesn't recognize, and wish to open them all in your favorite text editor by default without having to register them all first.

The system Windows uses to keep track of its file types has been around for years and has survived a bunch of different Windows versions. As a result, you'll see a lot of inconsistencies. Although most file types do follow the structure laid out on these pages, don't be surprised if you see something that doesn't belong *and* still works.

A typical file type key (e.g., HKEY_CLASSES_ROOT\txtfile) has a few values and subkeys, most of which appear in Figure 3-14.

First, the (Default) value contains the display name of the type, the text that appears in Windows Explorer's **Type** column.

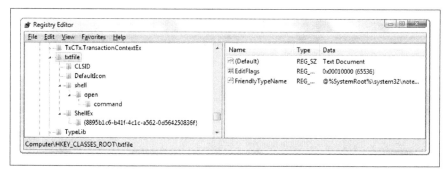

Figure 3-14. A file type key has values and subkeys that determine how associated files behave in Windows Explorer

If a value named `AlwaysShowExt` is present in this key, the extension for this file type will be displayed in Explorer, even if you've elected to hide your filename extensions (a setting explained at the beginning of this section). A related value, `NeverShowExt`, appears in a few file type keys—such as those for Windows Shortcuts (*.lnk* files), Internet Shortcuts (*.url* files), and Explorer Commands (*.scf* files)—and instructs Explorer to always hide the extensions for these files, regardless of your preferences.

You'll also see some other values such as `EditFlags`, `FriendlyTypeName`, and `InfoTip` that are fairly inconsequential, but it's the stuff in the following three subkeys that's responsible for most of the magic:

`DefaultIcon`
> The `(Default)` value in this key contains the full path and filename of the file containing the icon used for all files of this type. See the next section for details.

`Shell`
> Each subkey of `Shell` corresponds to an item (called an *action*) in the file's context menu. See "Customize Context Menus for Files" on page 175 to find out how this branch is structured.

`ShellEx`
> The `ShellEx` branch lists Windows Explorer *extensions*, add-on programs designed to interact with Explorer and add features. This branch is covered in the sidebar "Fix Wonky Shell Extensions" on page 183.

Once you know where all the essential keys are, you can use Registry Editor or one of the other tools mentioned in the upcoming sections to do just about anything you want with 7's file types system. When you have everything the way you want it, don't forget to take some steps to protect your customized file types from overzealous application installers, as described in "Lock Your File Types" on page 184.

Change the Icon for All Files of a Type

Every file type has a default icon, the icon shown for all files with filename extensions linked to that type. Yet Windows 7 offers no way to choose your own icons—apart from editing the registry by hand—despite the fact that you could do this right in Windows Explorer in all versions of Windows prior to Vista.

The (Default) value in the DefaultIcon key mentioned in the previous section contains the full path and filename of the file containing the default icon. Often it points right to the application executable that uses the file (e.g., *excel.exe* for *.xls* files), but sometimes it references a *.dll* or *.ico* file containing a bunch of icons. The filename is then followed by a comma and then a number (called the *index*) that indicates *which* icon to use. For example:

```
C:\Program Files\Photoshop\Photoshop.exe,15
```

points to the file *Photoshop.exe*, located in the *C:\Program Files\Photoshop* folder, and references the 16th icon in that file (0 or no number indicates the first icon, 1 indicates the second, and so on).

Occasionally, you may see something like this in the DefaultIcon key:

```
%SystemRoot%\system32\wmploc.dll,-731
```

Here, %SystemRoot% is a variable that represents the Windows folder (usually *C:\Windows*). When the (Default) value in which this information is stored is an expandable string value (described in "The Meat of the Registry: Values" on page 125), Windows converts the filename to *C:\Windows\System32\wmploc.dll* before retrieving the icon. You may also sometimes find a negative value following the filename (-731, in this case) which represents the *resource ID* of the icon to use—as opposed to a positive value indicating the index (position) of the icon as described earlier.

 A trick you can use for certain image files, like *.ico* icons, is to set the (Default) value in DefaultIcon to simply "%1" (quotes included). This self-referencing variable tells Explorer to use each file's own image as its icon. Although it also works for several other image formats, this feature has mostly been supplanted by IconHandlers, described next.

In most cases, you can specify your own icon for a given file type by placing the full path to an *.exe*, *.dll*, *.ico*, or *.bmp* file in the DefaultIcon key's (Default) value. (Hint: there are some nice "Windowsy" icons in *\Windows \System32\shell32.dll*.) Include a number to indicate which icon to use, or leave out the number to use the first icon in the file. In some cases, Windows

Explorer will recognize the change right away, although due to the way Explorer caches icons, you may need to restart Windows for your change to fully take effect.

 The easiest way to change an icon for a file type is with a third-party tool like File Type Doctor, discussed in the next section.

The only time when Windows won't pay attention to the icon specified in the DefaultIcon key is when an *IconHandler* is defined. IconHandlers generate dynamic icons on the fly (Figure 3-15), typically showing thumbnails of the files' contents in lieu of static icons.

Figure 3-15. If an IconHandler is defined for a file type, Windows generates icons dynamically for each file instead of using the static icon referenced in the DefaultIcon key

An IconHandler is a program—typically a *.dll* file in the program folder of the application with which the file is associated—that understands the file format. For instance, Adobe Acrobat (version 7.0 and later) makes use of this feature to facilitate thumbnail previews for *.pdf* files in Windows Explorer. For the *.pdf* filename extension, Acrobat's IconHandler might be referenced in any of these registry keys:

```
HKEY_CLASSES_ROOT\.pdf\ShellEx\IconHandler
HKEY_CLASSES_ROOT\.pdf\ShellEx\{BB2E617C-0920-11D1-9A0B-00C04FC2D6C1}
HKEY_CLASSES_ROOT\AcroExch.Document.7\ShellEx\IconHandler
HKEY_CLASSES_ROOT\AcroExch.Document.7\ShellEx\{BB2E617C-0920-11D1-9A0B-
    00C04FC2D6C1}
HKEY_CLASSES_ROOT\SystemFileAssociations\.pdf\ShellEx\IconHandler
HKEY_CLASSES_ROOT\SystemFileAssociations\.pdf\ShellEx\{BB2E617C-0920-11D1-
    9A0B-00C04FC2D6C1}
HKEY_CLASSES_ROOT\SystemFileAssociations\image\ShellEx\IconHandler
HKEY_CLASSES_ROOT\SystemFileAssociations\image\ShellEx\{BB2E617C-0920-11D1-
    9A0B-00C04FC2D6C1}
```

As it turns out, Adobe chose the fourth of these keys to register its IconHandler. The (Default) value in that key contains a 38-digit class ID that points to an entry in HKEY_CLASSES_ROOT\CLSID, which in turn contains details about the *.dll* file.

 If the reference to the IconHandler is contained in one of the keys named IconHandler, the *.dll* is responsible for the dynamically generated icon. But newer programs will use the {BB2E617C-0920-11d1-9A0B-00C04FC2D6C1} key to reference the IconHandler, which facilitates image previews for the Preview pane in Windows Explorer as well as dynamic icons. See "Expand the Scope of Your File Types" on page 186 for more information on the SystemFileAssociations key.

Want to replace dynamic icons with static ones? Once you find the reference to the IconHandler, you can delete the key—either the IconHandler key or the {BB2E617C-0920-11d1-9A0B-00C04FC2D6C1} key—to disable the IconHandler and allow Windows Explorer to use the static icon defined in the DefaultIcon key.

But what if you want to fix a broken file type for which icon previews have stopped working? Often it's easier to just reinstall the associated application to repair the IconHandler keys, but if that application is Windows itself, you'll probably want to follow these steps to reinstate icon previews on your PC:

1. Open the Registry Editor.
2. Navigate to the registry key for the filename extension you want to modify. For instance, if you want to enable icon previews for TIFF files, go to HKEY_CLASSES_ROOT\.tif.
3. Look for a PerceivedType value inside the .tif key. If it's not there, select **Edit→New→String Value**, and type PerceivedType for its name.
4. Double-click the PerceivedType value, type image for its contents, and click OK.
5. Next, navigate to HKEY_CLASSES_ROOT\SystemFileAssociations\image. As described in "Expand the Scope of Your File Types" on page 186, this key provides common properties for all image files, such as *.jpg*, *.bmp*, and *.tif* files.
6. Open the ShellEx key, and look for a key named {BB2E617C-0920-11d1-9A 0B-00C04FC2D6C1}. If it's not there, select **Edit→New→ Key**, and type {BB2E617C-0920-11d1-9A0B-00C04FC2D6C1} for the name of the new key.

7. Open the {BB2E617C-0920-11d1-9A0B-00C04FC2D6C1} key, and double-click the (Default) value. Type {3F30C968-480A-4C6C-862D-EFC0897BB84B} for its contents, and click OK when you're done.

 Of the two Class IDs mentioned here, {BB2E617C-0920-1 1d1-9A0B-00C04FC2D6C1} connects the file type to Windows Explorer's Preview pane, and {3F30C968-480A -4C6C-862D-EFC0897BB84B} points to Windows' own *PhotoMetadataHandler.dll*, the *.dll* file responsible for generating icon previews for all supported photo file formats.

8. The change should take effect immediately; if not, restart Windows to see the new icons.

IconHandlers are most likely to be broken by misbehaving installers for graphics applications, so if you don't want to have to repeat these steps later on, use the solution in "Lock Your File Types" on page 184.

Customize Context Menus for Files

A *context menu* (sometimes called a *right-click menu* or a *shortcut menu*) is the little menu that appears when you use the right mouse button to click a file, folder, application title bar, or nearly any other object on the screen. Most of the time, this menu includes a list of *actions* appropriate to the object you've clicked. In other words, the options available depend on the *context*.

The context menu for files, shown in Figure 3-16, is an assortment of standard actions common to all files (e.g., **Copy**, **Paste**, **Delete**, **Rename**, and **Properties**) plus one or more custom actions depending upon the type of file. Each of the custom actions is linked to an application: if you right-click a *.txt* file and select **Open**, Windows launches Notepad (by default) and instructs Notepad to open the selected file. The *default* action—the action carried out when you double-click the file—appears in bold text in the context menu, and the rest of the actions are listed below. Among other things, this means you can have *more than one program* associated with a single file type.

In the case of *.html* files, for example, you could add an **Edit** action to open your favorite web page editor, a **View with Firefox** action, and a **View with Internet Explorer** action—all in addition to the default **Open** action. To see this in action, see the next sidebar, "Copy File Contents to the Clipboard".

Figure 3-16. Right-click a file to show its context menu; Windows 7 doesn't make it easy to customize the items you see here

Copy File Contents to the Clipboard

Here's a walk-through example showing how to add a custom context menu to a file type, one that uses a little-known new toy in Windows 7 called *clip.exe*. Clip is a command-line program that copies text to the clipboard, and as luck would have it, it works nicely with text files.

Open Registry Editor and navigate to `HKEY_CLASSES_ROOT\.txt`. Look at the `(Default)` value in the right pane to get the name of the file type key (it's usually `txtfile`).

Navigate to the file type key (e.g., `HKEY_CLASSES_ROOT\txtfile`) and open the `shell` subkey (`HKEY_CLASSES_ROOT\txtfile\shell`). Create a new key inside `shell` named `copycontents`. Open the new key, click the `(Default)` value, type `Copy Contents to Clipboard` for the value data, and click OK.

Next, create a key named command inside the copycontents key. Open the new command key and set its (Default) value to cmd.exe /c clip < "%1". Click OK and close Registry Editor when you're done.

To test it out, right-click any *.txt* file in Windows Explorer and select **Copy Contents to Clipboard**. (If the new entry isn't there, you may've put your keys in the wrong place in the registry.) Confirm the file's contents have been copied to the clipboard by pasting them into an empty Notepad window.

You can use the Clip utility to copy just about anything to the clipboard. For instance, to copy the name of the selected file, use this for the (Default) value data in the command key:

```
cmd.exe /c echo %1 | clip
```

Or, say you've added the context menu item to the Folder file type; you can copy the contents of any folder with this command:

```
cmd.exe /c dir "%1" /b /o:n | clip
```

Open a Command Prompt window (Chapter 9) and type clip /? for the usage of this tool.

Sounds great, right? Unfortunately, the File Types window—the tool found in earlier versions of Windows that lets you edit context menus from within Windows Explorer—is completely absent in Windows 7. In its place is the extremely dumbed-down Set Associations window shown in Figure 3-17. Here, you can only choose default applications for your various file types, and in doing so, obliterate your applications' defaults or any custom context menus you've built (more on that later).

So, you're left with two options if you want to customize your context menus: either hack the registry or use a third-party program. Given that this is the registry chapter, let's have some fun digging through keys and values.

As described in "Anatomy of a File Type" on page 169, there's a registry key named Shell inside the file type key where all the magic happens. Each subkey of Shell corresponds to a single action in the file's context menu. The text that appears in the context menu is defined in the action key's (Default) value; if the (Default) value is empty, Windows Explorer just uses the name of the key (e.g., **Open**). Unfortunately, Windows 7 has two competing systems that determine the default actions for your file types; for details, see the next sidebar, "The Evils of UserChoice Override".

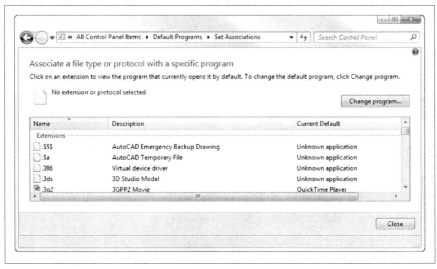

Figure 3-17. The Set Associations window—accessed through Control Panel→ Default Programs→Associate a file type or protocol with a program—just plain sucks

The Evils of UserChoice Override

If you right-click a file, select **Open With**, and then select a default application—or if you use the Set Associations window shown in Figure 3-17—Windows doesn't actually change the file type. Instead, Windows adds a new key for the filename extension in `HKEY_CURRENT_USER\Software\Microsoft\Windows\CurrentVersion\Explorer\FileExts`, and then in that new key, adds a `UserChoice` key with the full path of the program you've chosen, like this:

```
HKEY_CURRENT_USER\Software\Microsoft\Windows\CurrentVersion\Explorer\
                                             FileExts\.wav\UserChoice
```

The point of the `UserChoice` key is to prevent applications from changing your defaults without your permission; as long as that `UserChoice` key exists, Windows ignores all the actions defined in the ordinary file type key. Any custom context menu actions disappear, and even the icon is replaced with the icon of the newly-selected application.

Like so many other patchwork features in Windows, the UserChoice system just doesn't work that well. For one, the UserChoice-infected file types can't have custom context menus or custom icons. And the old trick of reinstalling an application to restore its file types won't work if the `UserChoice` key is present (unless the installer is smart enough to deal with it, which is unlikely). But the worst part is there's no way to defeat the system without digging through the registry.

The solution is to open the Registry Editor, navigate to `HKEY_CURRENT_USER` `\Software\Microsoft\Windows\CurrentVersion\Explorer\FileExts` and delete the extension you want to restore (or delete the `FileExts` key altogether to restore all file extensions). Thereafter, refrain from using the **Open With** menu or Control Panel to modify your file types, and your file associations will continue to behave in their full capacity.

Want to prevent Windows from overriding your file types? See "Prevent Changes to a Registry Key" on page 154 for instructions.

It's worth noting a circumstance where the UserChoice system can actually be of benefit. Traditional file types are stored in the `HKEY_CLASSES_ROOT` key, which is a subset of `HKEY_LOCAL_MACHINE`; this means your file types are the same for all users on your PC. But the `UserChoice` keys are buried in `HKEY_CUR` `RENT_USER` branch, allowing each user to have his or her own set of overrides.

Say you right-click a Microsoft Excel document (*.xlsx* file), and at the top of the menu that appears you see **Open** (in bold), **New**, and **Print**. If you open the registry, you'll see that `HKEY_CLASSES_ROOT\.xlsx` points to `HKEY_CLASSES_ROOT\Excel.Sheet.12`, so you proceed to `HKEY_CLASSES_ROOT` `\Excel.Sheet.12\Shell`. Inside the `Shell` key, you'll see three subkeys named— you guessed it—`New`, `Open`, and `Print`. Add a new subkey to `Shell`, followed by the subkeys described shortly, and you'll get a new entry in the context menu for all files of the selected type.

See a context menu item you want to get rid of? Just delete the corresponding action key (e.g., `New`, `Open`, `Print`), and it'll disappear immediately. Better yet, add a string value named `LegacyDisable` to the key to hide it in Windows Explorer without having to delete anything. If you don't see the key here, it may be listed in one of five other places:

- The `ShellEx\ContextMenuHandlers` branch, discussed later in this section.
- The `*` key covered in the sidebar "Special File Type Keys" on page 170.
- The `SystemFileAssociations` branch explained in "Expand the Scope of Your File Types" on page 186.

The action shown in bold (usually **Open**) is called the *default*, and is the one carried out when you double-click the file. The `(Default)` value in the `Shell` key determines which action is the default; if `(Default)` is empty and there's more than one action, Windows assumes it's the one named `Open`. Otherwise,

Windows just takes its best guess. You can, of course, choose a default by setting the (Default) value to the name of any action key shown here.

Inside each action key is a subkey named command (and sometimes another named ddeexec). Inside the command key is a (Default) value that specifies the full path and filename of the program to run. Right-click an *.xlsx* file and select **Open**, and Windows runs the program listed in HKEY_CLASSES_ROOT \Excel.Sheet.12\shell\Open\command. For example:

```
"C:\Program Files\Microsoft Office\Office12\EXCEL.EXE" /e
```

The quotes around the full path and filename of the application accommodate the spaces, and tell Windows where the filename ends and the command-line options (such as /e, here) begin. Most of the time, though, the command-line contains a placeholder, %1, for the selected filename, like this:

```
"C:\Program Files\UltraEdit\UEDIT32.EXE" "%1"
```

When Windows opens this program, it passes the full path and filename of the selected file to the program by putting it in place of %1, like this:

```
"C:\Program Files\UltraEdit\UEDIT32.EXE" "C:\Users\Asher\Desktop\readme.txt"
```

Now, that little option, %1, is the cause of a lot of problems in Windows' file types system, such as:

Application displays "not found" error
The quotation marks are missing around the "%1" and the document you're trying to open has a space in its file- or pathname. Just add the quotes to the (Default) value and try again.

Older application displays a "bad command line" error or something similar
Not all programs respond well to the quotation marks around the "%1" parameter. Try taking them out if this happens.

Application doesn't open the file at all
The "%1" parameter is missing altogether, or the application requires a different syntax. For instance, the Mozilla SeaMonkey web browser requires the -url parameter in front of %1, like this:

```
C:\Program Files\Mozilla SeaMonkey\seamonkey.exe -url "%1"
```

If you're not sure what your application needs, check the documentation or search Google for the application name and the words "command line."

 In a few cases, you can get help with a program's command-line parameters by running the application from with the /? or -help command-line switches.

Application only opens a document if the application isn't already running

This problem (and the next one) are caused by a background technology called Dynamic Data Exchange, or DDE, that allows Windows programs to communicate with one another. Windows sends a DDE signal to an application that's already running to instruct it to open the document. (If the application isn't already running, Windows launches it just like any other.) The specific DDE commands that the application needs are stored in the ddeexec registry key, alongside the aforementioned command key (shown previously in Figure 3-14). If the ddeexec key is missing, Windows won't send the signal, and the program won't open your document. You can try rebuilding the ddeexec key if you can find documentation, but it's usually easier to just reinstall the application that owns the key. (Not all programs use DDE; don't bother creating the ddeexec key unless you are having this specific problem.)

Application opens the document twice

The ddeexec key just described often causes more problems than it solves. Sometimes Windows sends the aforementioned DDE message *and* launches another copy of the program, which means you get two document windows. If this happens, rename the ddeexec key to ddeexec.backup.

 If an application has stopped responding (in other words, it crashed), it won't respond to Windows' DDE instructions to open your document, nor will Windows open a second copy of the program. To find out if this is happening, right-click an empty portion of your taskbar, select **Start Task Manager**, and click the **Processes** tab. If the program you're troubleshooting is there, highlight it and click **End Process**, and then try opening your document again.

At this point, you're probably thinking, "so, I have to type all these registry keys by hand if I want the least bit of control over my file types?" If so, I laugh at you.

File Type Doctor, part of Creative Element Power Tools (available at *http://www.creativelement.com/powertools/*) and shown in Figure 3-18, lets you customize your context menus, change file type icons, and choose defaults.

In the File Type Doctor window, file types are organized by their names (shown in the righthand column) and by their corresponding filename extensions (shown in the lefthand column); click either column header to sort the list accordingly. Select any file type to show its details on the right side of the window.

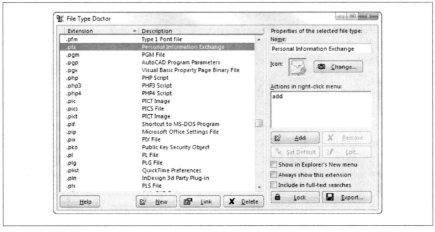

Figure 3-18. File Type Doctor gives you the complete control over your file associations that Windows 7 doesn't

Once you've turned on the **Edit file type associations** option in the Creative Element Power Tools Control Panel, you can also right-click any file in Windows Explorer or on your desktop and select **Edit File Type** to customize the file's context menu in File Type Doctor on the fly.

Edit the name of the type—the text that appears in Windows Explorer's **Type** column and in the file's Properties window—by typing it in the **Name** textbox at the top-right of the window. Click the **Change** button to choose an icon for all files of this type, or open any action from the list underneath and turn on the **Set file type icon to match this action** option to use the icon from that action's application.

File Type Doctor saves changes automatically as you make them. This makes it easy to test your context menus as you go, but it also means that many changes cannot be easily undone.

The **Actions in right-click menu** list on the right side shows all the context menu items registered for the selected file type. Click **Add** to create a new item or click **Edit** (or double-click the item in the list) to modify the associated application and its options.

You can also remove unwanted context menu items by highlighting them here and clicking **Remove**. The list shows everything registered for the selected file type, as well as the *perceived type*, explained in "Expand the Scope of Your File

Types" on page 186. Shell extensions (explained in the upcoming sidebar, "Fix Wonky Shell Extensions") are shown in *italicized* font; these can be removed but not modified in the traditional sense.

Fix Wonky Shell Extensions

Shell extensions are programs—usually *.dll* files—that add features to Windows Explorer. When they work, they're great, but when they falter, they can cause poor performance, crashes, and other problems. You can disable shell extensions by unregistering them (deleting their registry keys) or by simply disconnecting them from their associated file types, as described here.

The `shell` registry key dissected in the section "Customize Context Menus for Files" on page 175, houses the keys responsible for the *static* items in a file's context menu. But context menu shell extensions—ones that can *dyamically* generate context menu items—are located in the `shellex\ContextMenu Handlers` registry key. Each subkey of `ContextMenuHandlers` usually contains nothing more than a cryptic, 38-character code that looks like this:

`{E88DCCE0-B7B3-11d1-A9F0-00AA0060FA31}`

This 32-digit hex code (a.k.a. 16-bit number) is a *Class ID* (or *CLSID* for short) that points to a subkey of the same name in `HKEY_CLASSES_ROOT\CLSID\ {class_id}`. Class IDs are the means by which shell extensions—not to mention components used in all types of software—are registered in Windows and connected to the programs that use them.

In addition to `ContextMenuHandlers`, you'll find these other keys inside the `shellex` key:

`DropHandler`
> Extensions in this branch are activated when you drag files of this type or drop other files *onto* files of this type.

`IconHandler`
> This key points to a program that dynamically generates an icon—usually a preview of the contents of the file—to be used instead of a static icon. See "Change the Icon for All Files of a Type" on page 172 for details.

`PropertySheetHandlers`
> These extensions add extra pages (tabs) to the window that appears when you right-click a file of this type and select **Properties**.

Of course, the keys in the `shellex` branch aren't always so neatly organized; sometimes you'll find keys named for a Class ID, with another Class ID in its `(Default)` value. See "Search the Registry" on page 132 for some tools you can use to track down Class IDs.

File Type Doctor shows context menu shell extensions associated with the selected file type in *italicized* font. Although you can't edit them (you'll need their source code and development software like Visual Studio for that), you can remove their context menus by selecting them and clicking **Remove**. This won't unregister the extension, it'll just disconnect it from the selected file type, and likely fix the problem you're having. (Or, just do it to remove clutter.) You can also right-click a shell extension in File Type Doctor to search the registry or the Web for its Class ID or other related information to learn more about it.

To list all the shell extensions installed on your PC, use ShellExView, available for free at *http://www.nirsoft.net/utils/shexview.html*.

 The only items not shown in the **Actions in right-click menu** list are those actions registered for the * file type discussed in the sidebar "Special File Type Keys" on page 170. If you're trying to remove clutter from your context menus and you don't see an item you're looking for, try selecting the * **(all files)** entry at the very top of the list of file types.

One of the most useful features of File Type Doctor is the **Lock** feature, described next.

Lock Your File Types

Tech companies used to spend millions trying to get you to buy their products (OK, they still do), but now the race is on to be "the default." Microsoft positioned its own Bing web search (formerly Live Search, formerly MSN Search, formerly a sack of bat guano) as the default search tool in Internet Explorer 8, much to the chagrin of competitors like Google.‡ Companies pay PC manufacturers to preinstall trial versions of their software on all their machines so their products appear first when customers unwittingly click their own files. And when you install an application on your PC, the installer invariably makes the new program the default for all the file types it supports.

Why is being the default so important? Because people don't change the defaults.

‡ In 2007, Google even went to far as to sue Microsoft before Windows Vista shipped, to prevent them from forcing their Live Search down the throats of Internet Explorer 7 users. This is why you now have to answer a bunch of questions about your search preferences before you start IE 8 for the first time.

As a result, software companies—Microsoft included—make a habit out of steamrolling over your preferences to promote their own products. Luckily, you have a defense, and it takes place in the registry.

There are basically two approaches to protecting your file types: you can back them up so they can be restored in case they're ever overwritten, and you can "lock" them, preventing such changes in the first place.

 There's actually a third way to protect your file types, by way of 7's UserChoice feature described in the sidebar "The Evils of UserChoice Override" on page 178. It's not without its drawbacks, but it's easy and convenient if you don't use context menus.

The easiest way to back up your file types is to create registry patches as explained in "Export and Import Data with Registry Patches" on page 149. To make the backup effective, you have to include all the keys laid out in "Anatomy of a File Type" on page 169. For instance, if you're backing up the file type for plain-text (*.txt*) files, your registry patch should include all of these keys:

```
HKEY_CLASSES_ROOT\.txt
HKEY_CLASSES_ROOT\txtfile
HKEY_CLASSES_ROOT\SystemFileAssociations\text
```

That last one—the one in the SystemFileAssociations branch—is described in "Expand the Scope of Your File Types" on page 186. And if you want to include other related filename extensions, such as *.log*, *.ini*, and *.csv* (to name a few), you'll want to include those keys as well.

So, if your file type associations for text files ever get wiped out, just double-click your registry patch backup to restore them.

But a slicker solution is to lock your file types by setting restrictive permissions on the aforementioned keys as described in "Prevent Changes to a Registry Key" on page 154. That way, no application, no installer, and not even Windows itself can change them unless you unlock them first.

If you want a shortcut, you can use File Type Doctor, introduced in the previous section. Just highlight the file type you want to lock and click the **Lock** button. File Type Doctor will not only protect the selected filename extension and associated file type with one click, but all linked filename extensions as well.

Most programs and installers won't have a problem with locked file types; they'll likely just ignore the error and move on. But it's not beyond the realm of possibility that an application may crash or refuse to continue until it has all the registry access it needs. (For instance, the Adobe CS4 installer won't complete if any file types used by the included applications are locked.) In this case, you may need to unlock the affected file types first, at which point you'll want to back them up as described previously.

To remove the lock, just select a locked file type (you can click the leftmost column header to group all locked file types together) and click the **Unlock** button.

Expand the Scope of Your File Types

To every rule there's an exception, and in Windows 7, doubly so. In "Anatomy of a File Type" on page 169, the basic file types system is laid out, with a collection of keys named for filename extensions (e.g., HKEY_CLASSES_ROOT \.jpg) and the corresponding file type keys (such as HKEY_CLASSES_ROOT\jpeg file). As it turns out, there's yet another connection in the registry that affects your file types.

Many extension keys—like HKEY_CLASSES_ROOT\.jpg—contain values named PerceivedType, which point to subkeys of HKEY_LOCAL_MACHINE \SOFTWARE\Classes\SystemFileAssociations. The keys therein work like ordinary file type keys, but they're much broader in scope. Instead of being linked to one or two filename extensions, a *perceived type* key could be linked to dozens.

Say you just installed a new image-resizing utility that you'd like to use with a variety of photo formats. But rather than make it the default for those file types, you decide to add a context menu item for each supported file format (e.g., *.jpg*, *.bmp*, *.png*, and so on). Sure, you can do this for each of the 10 or so graphic formats it supports, but it turns out that all you need to do is add it to this key to affect all your image files at once:

```
HKEY_LOCAL_MACHINE\SOFTWARE\Classes\SystemFileAssociations
                    \image\shell\my_new_ program
```

By default, the image key shown here is linked to all filename extensions with a PerceivedType set to image, namely *.bmp*, *.dib*, *.emf*, *.gif*, *.ico*, *.jfif*, *.jpe*, *.jpeg*, *.jpg*, *.png*, *.rle*, *.tif*, *.tiff*, *.wdp*, and *.wmf*.

Windows 7 comes with only five perceived type keys (audio, image, system, text, and video) out of the box, but you can add your own to the SystemFileAssociations branch at any time, provided you then link at least one file extension to it by adding a PerceivedType value pointing to your new key. The benefit is that you can use this key to add a custom context menu item that affects a large number of different file types at once. The drawback is that it's one more place you'll have to look to track down a misbehaving or unwanted context menu item.

To break the connection between a filename extension and a perceived type, just delete the PerceivedType value from the extension key. Or, to link up a file type with an existing PerceivedType, create a new string value named PerceivedType in the extension key (e.g., HKEY_CLASSES_ROOT\.jpg), and set its contents to the name of the matching perceived type key in the SystemFileAssociations branch.

File Type Doctor (see "Customize Context Menus for Files" on page 175) also supports perceived types through its "scope" and "affiliation" features. For instance, if you try to delete a context menu action that's connected through a perceived type, File Type Doctor displays a confirmation box that lists the other filename extensions that will be affected by the change. Likewise, when creating a new action, you can choose the scope; click the **Properties** button next to the **Scope** list to display all the extensions tied to the current selection.

While you're digging around the HKEY_CLASSES_ROOT\SystemFileAssociations branch in the registry, you may find some file extension keys here as well, like HKEY_CLASSES_ROOT\SystemFileAssociations\.png. These look and work just like the extension keys and file type keys in HKEY_CLASSES_ROOT, discussed earlier in this chapter, but they're used primarily to reference the Windows Explorer extensions that were preinstalled with Windows. Why they're here instead of in HKEY_CLASSES_ROOT with the rest of the extensions is not entirely clear, but what is clear is that the SystemFileAssociations branch is yet another place to look for registry keys that affect file types.

Customize Windows Explorer's New Menu

If you right-click an empty area of the desktop or any open folder and select **New**, you'll see special list of registered file types that can be created on the spot. Choose one, and Explorer will create a new (usually empty) file with the appropriate filename extension right there. Not surprisingly, you can edit that list, and even make it do more than just create empty files.

Here's the easiest way to remove unwanted items from Explorer's **New** menu:

1. Install Creative Element Power Tools (introduced earlier in "Customize Context Menus for Files" on page 175), turn on the **Edit file type associations** option in the Creative Elements Power Tools Control Panel, and click **Accept**.

2. Right-click an empty area of your desktop, select **New**, and then select one of the entries you'd like to remove.

3. Right-click the new file and select **Edit File Type**.

4. Remove the checkbox next to the **Show in Explorer's New menu** option.

5. The change will take effect immediately; right-click the desktop again and select **New** to check it out.

If you want to do it by hand, you'll need to look in a few different places in the registry:

1. Open the Registry Editor.

2. Navigate to the key named for the filename extension you'd like to remove from Windows Explorer's **New** menu. For the *.txt* extension, you'd go to HKEY_CLASSES_ROOT\.txt.

3. If you see a subkey here named ShellNew, rename it to Shellnew- (Shell new followed by a hyphen). You can also delete the ShellNew subkey, but this method allows easy retrieval and is recognized by several third-party tools.

4. Next, look at the (Default) value of the extension key, and then look for a subkey therein that matches the contents of the (Default) value. Again, for the *.txt* extension, you'd go to HKEY_CLASSES_ROOT\.txt\txtfile.

5. As in step 3, if you see a subkey here named ShellNew, rename it to Shell new- (Shellnew followed by a hyphen).

6. The change will take effect immediately; right-click the desktop and select **New** to check it out.

As you can see, it's merely the presence of a ShellNew key that determines whether a file type shows up in Windows Explorer's **New** menu. (Actually, it's a little more complicated than that, but more on that subject later.)

To get a list of all the potential entries to appear in the **New** menu, fire up registry Agent (see "Search and Replace Registry Data" on page 136), and search the entire registry for Shell New. (If you want to weed out erroneous matches, turn on the **Keys** option, uncheck the **Values** and **Data** options, and then turn on **Match whole word**.)

Now, there are some nifty hacks you can use on the ShellNew keys you choose to leave intact. A typical ShellNew key has only one value—NullFile, described in the upcoming list—but if you add any of the other following values to the ShellNew key, you'll change how Windows Explorer behaves when you select the corresponding item from the **New** menu. All values are string values unless otherwise specified:

Command

If you include the full path and filename of an executable program (.*exe* file), Explorer will launch the program *instead* of creating a new file. Make sure to include the "%1" parameter (see "Customize Context Menus for Files" on page 175) so the target program knows where to create the new file, like this:

```
c:\windows\system32\notepad.exe "%1"
```

Consult your application's documentation to see whether any other command-line parameters are needed to create the new document; otherwise, the program may just open and complain that it can't find the (as yet nonexistent) file.

Data

Any text stored in this binary value will be placed into the new file. For instance, the Data value for .*rtf* files (in HKEY_CLASSES_ROOT\.rtf\Shell New) contains the text, {\rtf1}, which ensures that the new .*rtf* file is readable by whatever program you use to open it. Explorer ignores the Data value if either FileName or NullFile is present. (Hint: the FileName value, next, is a better way to create nonempty files.)

FileName

This is the full path and filename of a template file—a file to be copied and used for each new document you create—in lieu of creating an empty (zero-byte) file. If you don't include the path, Windows looks in *C:\Users\ {your_user_name}\AppData\Roaming\Microsoft\Templates* as well as *C:\Windows\ShellNew* for the template file.

Handler

The Class ID (e.g., {CEEFEA1B-3E29-4EF1-B34C-FEC79C4F70AF}) of the shell extension used to create the new file. For example, Windows Shortcuts (.*lnk* files) use a handler. (See the sidebar "Fix Wonky Shell Extensions" on page 183 for the scoop on Windows Explorer extensions.)

IconPath

The full path and filename (plus the icon index) of the icon that appears next to the item in Windows Explorer's **New** menu. If you leave this out,

Explorer uses the file type's default icon. See "Change the Icon for All Files of a Type" on page 172 for the syntax.

ItemName

By default, the name of the new file you create is the name of the file type, preceded by the word "New" and followed by the appropriate filename extension; for instance: *New Text Document.txt*. This value determines the name of the new file, but like MenuText, described next, it can't be plain text but must rather point to a text resource in a *.dll* file.

MenuText

Unfortunately, this is not what it looks like. Yes, it determines the text that appears in Explorer's **New** menu, but you can't just type the text here. Instead, it must be a reference to a text resource in a *.dll* file, such as @%systemroot%\system32\mspaint.exe,-59414.

NullFile

This instructs Explorer to create an empty (zero-byte) file. If none of these other values are present, you need to include the NullFile value, or the file type won't show up in Explorer's **New** menu.

So, how do you keep applications from recreating the ShellNew keys and continuously cluttering up Explorer's **New** menu? Adobe Photoshop does this every time it starts, but all it takes is a quick change to the registry to prevent it from happening again:

1. Open the Registry Editor.

2. Navigate to the extension key you want to permanently exclude from the **New** menu. For Photoshop documents, you'd go to HKEY_CLASSES_ROOT\.psd.

3. Delete any ShellNew keys you find here; see the solution spelled out earlier in this section for details.

4. Right-click the extension key (e.g., *.psd*), and select **Permissions**.

5. In the Permissions window, click the **Advanced** button, and then in the Advanced Security Settings window, click **Add**.

6. Next, in the Select User or Group window, type everyone into the **Enter the object name to select** field, and then click OK.

7. Finally, in the Permission Entry window, place a checkmark in the **Deny** column for **Create Subkey**, and then click OK when you're finished.

8. Click OK, then click **Yes** when asked whether you're sure you want to set a "deny permissions entry," and then click OK to close the final window.

9. The change will take effect immediately. Test it out by starting the application; you can press **F5** in the Registry Editor to refresh the view and confirm that no new **ShellNew** subkey has been added.

You can accomplish pretty much the same thing with File Type Doctor's **Lock** feature (covered in "Lock Your File Types" on page 184), but that may be overkill if all you want to do is keep unwanted items out of Explorer's **New** menu. See "Prevent Changes to a Registry Key" on page 154 for other things you can do with registry permissions.

Fix Internet Shortcuts

Customization is fun, but sometimes all you need to do to a file type is fix it when it breaks. Most of the time you can just reinstall the application that originally created it—unless a UserChoice key is in effect, explained in the sidebar "The Evils of UserChoice Override" on page 178—but that doesn't always work.

One file type that's always getting munged is the *.url* (Internet Shortcut) type, and repairing it can be a little tricky. For one, *.url* files don't launch your web browser directly; instead, they activate a Windows *.dll* that does the launching. In essence, it's a two-step process that employs two different file types; the following sequence of registry keys shows how it works.

 The keys discussed in the steps below should all have been locked when Windows 7 was installed, a fact that should've prevented them from being corrupted in the first place. (Alas, such things seem to happen anyway.) If Windows won't let you make changes to any of these keys, you'll need to take ownership of them first, as described in "Prevent Changes to a Registry Key" on page 154, and in Chapter 8.

1. Go to HKEY_CLASSES_ROOT\.url, and confirm that the (Default) value is set to InternetShortcut.

2. Next, go to HKEY_CLASSES_ROOT\InternetShortcut\Shell\Open\Command, and make sure the (Default) value here is set to:

```
rundll32.exe shdocvw.dll,OpenURL %1
```

This command instructs Windows to crack open the selected Internet Shortcut file, read the URL stored inside (which you can also do with Notepad, by the way), and then launch the program appropriate to the variety of URL. Notice that the default web browser (e.g., Internet Explorer, Firefox, etc.) isn't yet part of the equation.

3. Internet shortcuts also use an "icon handler" by default (explained in "Change the Icon for All Files of a Type" on page 172), which chooses an icon for each file depending on the type of URL inside. So, this key:

    HKEY_CLASSES_ROOT\InternetShortcut\ShellEx\IconHandler

should be set to {FBF23B40-E3F0-101B-8488-00AA003E56F8}. Of course, if you want to disable the icon handler and choose your own static icon instead, just rename the IconHandler key to IconHandler.backup, and then specify your icon file in the DefaultIcon key, as described earlier in this chapter.

4. Once Windows has determined what type of URL it's dealing with, it executes the **Open** command in the key named for the protocol being used. For instance, the URL *http://www.annoyances.org/* uses the http:// protocol, so its' default application is stored in this registry key:

    HKEY_CLASSES_ROOT\http\shell\open\command

There are similar keys for the other protocols, like https://, file://, ftp://, news://, nntp://, snews://, telnet://, and mailto:. (In File Type Doctor, the protocol file types are found at the bottom of the list.) These keys aren't just used for Internet Shortcuts; they control Windows' behavior whenever you try to open a web address by clicking a hyperlink in an email message, opening a web link from an installed application, or typing a URL into the Start menu's **Search** box.

5. The (Default) value of the protocol's command key should be set to the full path and filename of your default web browser. The Windows default is, of course, Internet Explorer:

    "C:\Program Files\Internet Explorer\iexplore.exe" -nohome

Or, if you're using Mozilla Firefox:

    C:\Program Files\Mozilla Firefox\firefox.exe %1

Or, if you want Mozilla SeaMonkey to be your default browser, you'd use:

```
C:\Program Files\Mozilla SeaMonkey\seamonkey.exe -url "%1"
```

See "Customize Context Menus for Files" on page 175 for details on the command key, command-line parameters, and the sometimes necessary ddeexec key.

6. The change takes effect immediately. Double-click any applicable Internet Shortcut to try out your new settings.

As you can see, there are a lot of registry keys responsible for something as seemingly simple as opening a web address, and all it takes is one missing key, one misplaced quotation mark, or one mangled class ID to break the whole system. And so it goes with the registry in Windows 7.

CHAPTER 4

Video, Audio, and Media

Working with videos, photos, and music can be a frustrating experience on a Windows machine. That's really a shame seeing as how so many people buy computers specifically for that purpose.

Windows 7 is finally caught up with where it should have been about 10 years ago. It can display thumbnail previews of pictures and videos and it can put to use the embedded EXIF information in photos and embedded tags in music files in ways that XP never could. For years, Windows included Media Player, but didn't provide the necessary drivers to play DVD movies; now Windows can play DVDs (but not many other types of videos). And it's never been easy to add or manage the software required to do so.

Thankfully, many of the buggy media features in Windows Vista—some of which are responsible for the green ribbon of death—have been improved enough to be useful in Windows 7. But Microsoft has a habit of taking a few steps back every time it staggers forward. For instance, Movie Maker, the *Notepad* of video editors included with Windows since XP, is absent in Windows 7, available now only as a download (free at *http://download.live.com/ moviemaker*). The fact that it's not in the box (and that it's no match for Apple's iMovie) is one of many cues that Microsoft still can't grasp what people want out of their computers.

Get Videos to Play

Windows 7 can handle full-screen, high-definition video streamed over the Internet from websites like Hulu without any special software beyond a web browser, the Adobe Flash plugin, and a suitable video driver. But try to play a low-res video file sitting on your hard disk, and it gets complicated.

Unlike most other types of files, the filename extension alone doesn't dictate the encoding scheme of a video. All *.jpg* image files use standard JPEG compression, but a given *.avi* movie file may employ any one of dozens of available compression standards, called *codecs*. Without the proper codec for a video file, you won't be able to play the video or even convert it to a playable format.

A codec (which stands for *compressor/decompressor*) is software installed on your PC, akin to a device driver, with most of the pitfalls and frustrations that implies. Codecs are frequently buggy, and a bad one can cause video playback problems and even application crashes.

Windows 7 only includes codecs for a few common (and aging) standards; need anything else, and you're on your own. And since Windows provides no "Device Manager" or "Windows Update" tool for codecs, there's no easy way to list the codecs installed on your PC, get updates, or install missing ones. (At least not without add-on software.) And don't even get me started on the **More Information** link in Windows Media Player, which doesn't provide anything one would recognize as useful information.

To play a particular video, you need to install the same codec that was used to create (compress) the video in the first place, regardless of the player application you're using. (In other words, a missing codec isn't a deficiency of Windows Media Player, per se, but rather of Windows.). To determine which codec was used for a particular video, you'll need a program like GSpot (*http://www.headbands.com/gspot/*) or AVIcodec (*http://avicodec.duby.info/*), both of which are free. Just drag-drop the video file onto GSpot (Figure 4-1) or AVIcodec, and the program will display the file's video codec, audio codec, and other statistics.

 The codec utility may indicate that the required codec is already installed. As comforting as that may be, you might still need to download and install the latest version of the codec to play the troublesome video. Otherwise, you may not have all the latest bugs...er, fixes.

If one of these tools can't identify the codec, the file might be corrupted or encoded with a nonstandard scheme. This doesn't necessarily mean the video isn't playable, but rather that it might be a bit of a chore to find out how to make it playable.

Provided you're not able to personally ask whoever created the video for details about the software used, the easiest trick is to open the file in a standard text editor and look for the four-digit 4CC code near the beginning. Figure 4-2 shows the code buried in a file, DIVX in this case, which indicates that the DivX decompressor is needed to play this video.

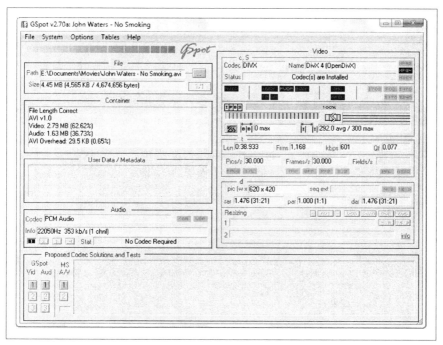

Figure 4-1. Use GSpot to find the software necessary to play a given video clip

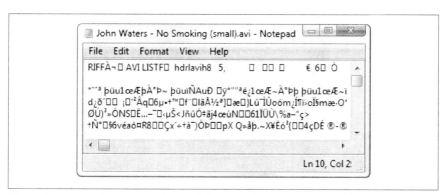

Figure 4-2. A hex editor or text editor will show you the 4CC code embedded in the beginning of most movie files

Armed with the name (or 4CC code) of the codec, go to *http://www.fourcc.org/ fcccodec.htm*, and download the codec installer from the list. If the 4CC code isn't there, a quick Google search (along with the word "codec") should turn up some useful leads. After a bit of searching, you'll probably figure out how widespread this video codec problem really is.

Once you've installed the codec, close any lingering Windows Media Player windows, and then try playing the video again. Keep in mind that there are often multiple versions of a single codec available—sometimes from different vendors—so you may need to install several codecs before you find the one that works.

Some of the more requested codecs include DivX (*http://www.divx.com*), Xvid for MPEG-4 (*http://www.xvid.org/*),Apple Quicktime (*http://www.apple.com/quicktime/*), and and FLV/Flash Video (described in the next section, "Install the FLV Flash Video Codec"). After installing the latest versions of these four codecs, you should be able to play most of the videos you come across.

Some enterprising individuals have created *codec packages*, large installers that include several, if not dozens, of the codecs that people seem to need most. While these packages may seem convenient, there are several problems with this approach. For one, you're installing more software and drivers than you really need. Second, these packages typically do away with the standalone installers, which means updating or removing individual codecs can be a chore. And worst of all, if one or of the installed programs or codecs causes a problem, it's nearly impossible to troubleshoot it. My advice: avoid the packages and install codecs one-by-one as you need them.

If, after installing an individual codec or codec package, some of your videos no longer play (or their thumbnails no longer show up), there's a little trick you can try before you uninstall and give up. The FFDShow Video Decoder Configuration tool, included with many codec packages and shown in Figure 4-3, helps you troubleshoot specific codec problems.

For instance, on one occasion, Windows lost the ability to play back some .*avi* files: Media Player crashed every time it tried to play one, and Windows Explorer displayed an error message whenever it attempted to render thumbnails for the videos. To fix a problem like this, open the FFDShow Video Decoder Configuration tool, select **Codecs** on the left, and in the right pane, find the codec used by the video file that's causing the problem. Then, in the **Decoder** column, use the drop-down listbox to choose a different decoder from the list. Click OK when you're done; the change should take effect immediately.

Another way to manage codecs is with the free CodecInstaller utility (*http://www.jockersoft.com/*). Not only does it list all the codecs installed on your PC —along with their version numbers and filenames—but it can analyze media files to identify required codecs and even download common codec installers.

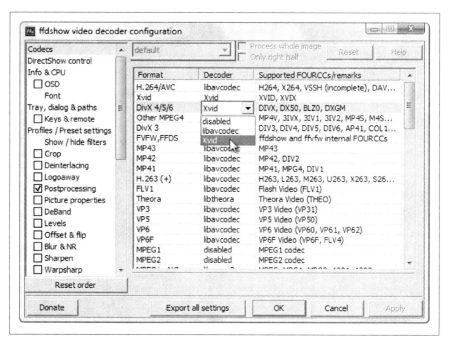

Figure 4-3. When more than one codec is installed for a specific video format, you can choose which one to use with FFDShow Video Decoder Configuration Tool

Install the FLV Flash Video Codec

The FLV codec is the one used to create—and therefore play back—Adobe Flash video, the format used to stream video on many websites (most notably, YouTube). If you have the Adobe Flash authoring software installed, you can play FLV files with Adobe Player; but if you don't have the full Flash package, or you want to play FLV files with Windows Media Player, you'll need to install the standalone codec. Unfortunately, Adobe doesn't provide the codec by itself, so you've got to obtain and register the files manually.

In an attempt to find the right codec to play a video, you might come across a lone *.ax* codec file that doesn't have its own installer (sometimes referred to as a *splitter*). This procedure is an example of how to install such a codec.

First, download the FLV DirectShow Filter (FLV Splitter), which you can get from the Guliverkli2 project (*http://sourceforge.net/projects/guliverkli2/files/*).

To install the codec, just copy the *FLVSplitter.ax* file to your *\Windows\System32* folder.

Video, Audio, and Media

Open a Command Prompt window in Administrator mode (see Chapters 9 and 8, respectively) and type:

```
regsvr32 \Windows\System32\FLVSplitter.ax
```

to register the file. Or, to uninstall, type

```
regsvr32 /u \Windows\System32\FLVSplitter.ax
```

If you see a message like "DLLRegisterServer in C:\Windows\System32\FLVSplitter.ax succeeded," then the new codec is installed and ready to use. Test it out by double-clicking any *.flv* video file.

 Don't want to hassle with the command prompt every time you register an *.ax* or *.dll* file? Try EMSA Register DLL Tool (*http://www.e-systems.ro/register_dll_tool.htm*) or DllRegSvr (*http://chestysoft.com/dllregsvr/*), both free, to do it with the Windows GUI.

To get thumbnail previews of FLV files in Windows Explorer, you'll need to make a connection manually in the registry:

1. Open Registry Editor (see Chapter 3), and navigate to HKEY_CLASSES_ROOT \.flv.

2. Look at the (Default) value and then navigate to the key by that name under HKEY_CLASSES_ROOT. For instance, if (Default) is set to flvfile, then you'd go to HKEY_CLASSES_ROOT\flvfile.

3. Select the ShellEx key here (e.g., HKEY_CLASSES_ROOT\flvfile\ShellEx), and then from the **Edit** menu, select **New** and then **Key**.

4. Name the new key {BB2E617C-0920-11D1-9A0B-00C04FC2D6C1}.

5. Inside the new {BB2E617C-0920-11D1-9A0B-00C04FC2D6C1} key, double-click the (Default) value and type {c5a40261-cd64-4ccf-84cb-c394da41d590} for its contents.

If you don't want to do all this by hand, you can download a registry patch file from *http://annoyances.org/downloads/flvthumbs.reg*. Next, complete steps 1 and 2 above; if the (Default) value is *not* set to flvfile, edit the *flvthumbs.reg* file with Notepad and replace *flvfile* with whatever (Default) is set to. When you're ready, just double-click the file and click **Yes** to merge it with your registry. See "Export and Import Data with Registry Patches" on page 149 for more on *.reg* files.

If you can't get the codec to work, or you'd prefer not to undertake the messy installation, you can get a dedicated *.flv* player like FLV Player (free at *http://www.martijndevisser.com*).

Repair Broken and Incomplete Videos

There are reasons that Windows Media Player might have trouble playing a video *other* than a missing or broken codec—namely, problems with the video file itself. First, make sure your video file is complete; if you downloaded it from the Web, try clearing your browser cache and downloading the file again.

If you're unable to obtain an intact version of the video, you may be able to repair it with the free MPEG Header Corrector, available at *http://www.video help.com/tools/sections/video-repair-fix*, although this typically only works on true *.mpg* files. Need to repair an *.avi* file? Use DivFix (free, *http://divfix.maxe line.com*) instead.

OK, I know I just said that the filename extension doesn't dictate the codec, but it *does* determine how the video data is organized in the file. See the "Does It Have the Right Extension?" sidebar if you suspect a video file has been misnamed.

Does It Have the Right Extension?

There's always a chance someone gave your file the wrong filename extension; before you attempt to repair that video, make sure it has the correct extension. To check whether that *.mpg* file is really an *.mpg* file, open the file in a text or hex editor. The header (before the aforementioned 4CC code) will read `RIFF` if it's an *.avi* file, `RMF` if it's an *.rm* (Real Media) file, `MOOV` if it's a *.mov* (Apple Quicktime) file, `FLV` if it's an *.flv* (Flash Video) file, or `W.M.F.S.D.K` if it's a Microsoft *.asf* or *.wmv* file. If you see no header (only junk), it's likely an *.mpg* file.

See Chapter 3 for more information on file types, and Chapter 2 to find out how to show filename extensions in Windows Explorer. Once extensions are visible, you can change a file's extension merely by renaming the file and typing new letters beyond the final dot.

But what if you're in the middle of downloading a video from the Web? Eventually, it'll be intact and playable, but if you want to start playing it before the download is complete, you'll need to employ a few tricks.

First thing to know: Windows Media Player (and many other players) won't play most kinds of videos while they're *in use*—that is, while they're currently being saved by another program (e.g., your browser). The big exception to this rule is streaming video, commonly found in files with the *.asf* or *.wmv* extension (Quicktime *.mov* files, too); by design, these files can be played even while in use by other applications.

To get around this limitation for non-streaming video formats, open the folder containing the file, and create a duplicate of the partially downloaded file. Using the right mouse button, drag the file to an empty area in the same folder, and select **Copy Here** from the menu that appears. When that's done, you should be able to open the duplicate file with no problems.

 You may have to change the filename extension when playing videos that are in the midst of downloading. For instance, if you're downloading a video with certain types of peer-to-peer clients named *skiing.mpg*, the intermediate filename will be something like *skiing.mpg.downloading*, and thus the filename of the duplicate you create will be *skiing.mpg-Copy.downloading*. Just rename the file to *skiing.mpg-Copy.downloading.mpg* (or simply *skiing.mpg*) and then double-click the file to play it. Of course, some P2P programs download files out of order, so your video will only play the first contiguous block of complete data.

With some video formats, particularly *.avi* files, there's a catch: the *index*, essential information about the sequence of frames in the video, is located at the *end* of the file instead of the beginning. Thus an incomplete *.avi* file won't have an index, and can't be played at all. The solution is to use a rendexing utility to rebuild this data and make the file playable. DivFix, shown in Figure 4-4, does this quite nicely, but only works on true *.avi* files (discussed earlier in this section). If DivFix can't repair your file, the Windows Media Encoder (free, *http://www.microsoft.com/windows/windowsmedia/forpros/encoder/default.mspx*) is capable of indexing video files, albeit requiring a bit more work to navigate the complex interface.

Fix Other Playback Problems

So, what if your video plays, but not well? Problems like stretched or squashed video (too wide or too tall), bad color, and choppy playback can all be caused by buggy, misconfigured, or out-of-date video codecs. Just track down and install the latest version of the codec required by the misbehaving video, as described at the beginning of this chapter, and try again. If that doesn't help, there are some other fixes, as follows:

Change the aspect ratio
    If *all* your videos seem squashed (too narrow) or stretched out (too wide), you may have to correct your display's aspect ratio setting. In Windows Media Player, press the **Alt** key by itself to open the menu, and then from

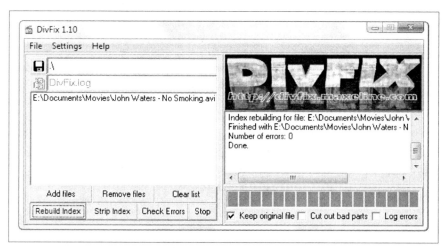

Figure 4-4. Use DivFix to reindex incomplete videos so you can play what you've downloaded so far

the **Tools** menu, select **Options**. Choose the **Devices** tab, highlight **Display** in the list, and then click **Properties**. Move the slider until the oval looks like as close to a true circle as possible, and then click OK.

On the other hand, if only a single video clip has an incorrect aspect ratio, it may've been encoded that way. Sure, you can fix the file with a video-editing program like River Past Video Perspective (*http://chestysoft.com/dllregsvr/*), Open Video Converter (*http://www.009soft.com*), or Adobe Premiere (*http://www.adobe.com*), but that's a lot of trouble for a video you might only watch once. Instead, open the file in Windows Media Center and use the Zoom feature, or watch the video with VLC Media Player (free from *http://www.videolan.org/vlc/*), which lets you change the aspect ratio on the fly.

If you do decide to reencode the video, the hardest part is the math (and it's not that hard). Most video has a 4:3 aspect ratio, which means the width is four-thirds the height. (HD television and some feature films typically have a 16:9 aspect ratio, while wider "anamorphic" feature films have a 2.39:1 aspect ratio.) If your botched video clip has, say, a resolution of 400×400 (giving you a 1:1 aspect ratio and a square video frame), you can either increase the width to 600 (400×4/3) or decrease the height to 300 (400 divided by 4/3). Of the two choices, decreasing the height will usually give you a sharper-looking video, since compressed pixels always look better than stretched pixels.

Synchronize audio and video

If *all* your videos are out of sync, open the Sound page in Control Panel. Choose the **Playback** tab, select your speakers in the list, and then click **Properties**. Choose the **Enhancements** tab, select **Room Correction** from the list, and click the **Settings** button. (If **Room Correction** isn't there, your sound card driver doesn't support the feature.) You'll need a microphone and a few minutes to complete the exercise.

If the Room Correction tool doesn't help, or if it's unavailable, open Windows Media Player and press the **Alt** key by itself to open the menu. From the **Tools** menu, select **Options**, and then choose the **Performance** tab. Turn on the **Drop frames to keep audio and video synchronized** option, and then click OK.

 If the audio is out of sync while playing a DVD, try pausing playback, waiting a few seconds, and then starting up again. Sometimes that's all it takes to get a movie back on track.

If settings alone don't fix the problem, there may be a problem with your hardware drivers. Go ahead and install the latest drivers for your video card and sound card, and then run Windows Update to make sure you have the latest video-related updates.

If the audio and video in only a single clip are out of sync, try watching the video with VLC Media Player (free from *http://www.videolan.org/vlc/*), which lets you fix the sync on the fly. But to repair the file, you'll need a timeline-based video-editing application like Adobe Premiere (*http://www.adobe.com*). (Unfortunately, Windows Live Movie Maker, which comes with Windows 7, won't let you manipulate video and audio streams separately.) Drag your video to the timeline, then drag the audio portion of the clip slightly to the left or right until it's synced up with the video. (Naturally, this takes some trial and error, so I hope it's not a boring clip.)

 The aforementioned dragging method works only if the audio and video are out of sync consistently throughout the video. If the movie starts out in sync but gradually gets out of sync, a little more massaging of the audio track is necessary. Either you have to insert delays or delete tiny bits of silence here and there to straighten everything out, or you have to stretch or shrink the entire audio track by a small amount—a two-second lag on a two-hour movie is just under 0.03%.

When you're done, export the project into a new movie file. Consult the documentation that comes with your video application for details.

Speed it up or slow it down

Is a video playing too fast or too slow? In Windows Media Player, click the **Now Playing** button, select **Enhancements**, and then select **Play Speed Settings** (Figure 4-5). Adjust the slider until the video plays at the correct speed.

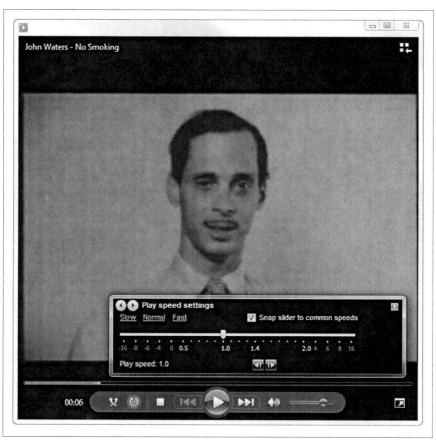

Figure 4-5. Play any video faster or slower with the Play Speed Settings panel in Windows Media Player

Fix bad color

If some of your videos seem to have messed-up color, open Windows Media Player, click the **Now Playing** button, select **Enhancements**, select **Video Settings**, and then click the **Reset** link. Next, click the little arrows until you see **Color Chooser**, and click the **Reset** link here as well. Now, play a video to try it out; if the colors are still off, you may have to play with the **Video Settings** and **Color Chooser** sliders to fine-tune the color.

If that doesn't do the trick, or if you see colored lines running through your videos, you can usually correct the problem by updating your display drivers.

Shed light on blank videos

Ever feel like Sergeant Schultz from *Hogan's Heroes*?* You might hear something, but you definitely *see nothing* when you play most videos. This is often caused by a missing video codec, but might instead point to a video overlay problem.

When you play video, Windows usually paints a special rectangle on your screen, and your video driver is responsible for superimposing the moving video over it. This *overlay* scheme allows your display adapter (video card) to handle the burden of playing the video rather than your CPU, which affords better performance and smoother video. Unfortunately, it can also be the source of problems in some cases, usually manifesting itself as only the black rectangle where video should appear.

First, conduct a little test to see whether you indeed have an overlay problem. Try maximizing or resizing the Windows Media Player window, or cover it with another window and then bring it to the front. If this makes the video play, or if you see pieces of windows left behind in the black rectangle, your video card driver may be to blame. Visit your video card manufacturer's website and download the latest driver. Also, pay a visit to the company's support website and look for recommended BIOS settings (see Appendix A).

Simplify Your Media Players

The Windows Media Player has lots of interesting features and gadgets, most of which just get in the way when all you want to do is play a simple video. Of course, it looks downright minimalistic compared with Real Networks' cumbersome RealPlayer. Fortunately, you have a few choices.

To switch to the simpler Windows Media Player window, just press **Ctrl-2** to switch to Skin Mode. (Or, press **Alt** to show the normally hidden menu, and then select **View→Skin Mode**.) The default skin is "Corporate," but you can choose another skin by clicking **Alt** and selecting **View→Skin Chooser**.

---

* I would've also accepted Sergeant Schulz from Billy Wilder's *Stalag 17* (1953).

Figure 4-6. Media Player Classic is an alternative to the overblown Windows Media Player and messy RealPlayer applications

Alternatively, Media Player Classic - Home Cinema, available for free at *http: //sourceforge.net/projects/mpc-hc/*, can take the place of Windows Media Player, RealPlayer, and QuickTime Player. It has a slimmed-down interface (shown in Figure 4-6), loads more quickly than Windows Media Player, and doesn't need to be installed (it's just a standalone *.exe* file). Best part is that it plays any video format that Windows Media Player can play. (Really, it's just replacement "shell" that ties into the playback engines that come with the aforementioned media players.)

Aside from the streamlined interface and its ability to handle just about any video format, Media Player Classic has several features that make it worth using. For instance, you can play more than one video at once, something Windows Media Player won't let you do. And it's kind enough to show detailed error messages with enough information to solve the problem, such as listing any missing codecs.

Also available is the free VLC Media Player, which, in addition to providing a simple, clean interface, gives you superior control over playback speed, aspect ratio, audio/video sync, color, subtitles, and volume.

Rewind or Fast-Forward Stubborn Video

You've probably encountered a video on the Web that won't let you jump back (without starting over) or skip ahead. It's not such a big deal with a 20-second clip, but when you're watching a half-hour broadcast mostly featuring a talking head, it can be infuriating when you can't just skip ahead to the car chase.

Usually, this is a limitation of the video file (or of the player), and not simply an option that can be turned on or off. A lot of streaming video clips have this problem, particularly *.wmv* and *.asf* videos. To jump to an arbitrary position while watching these videos, they must be indexed, something you can only do if the video file is stored on your hard disk. If there's a web-based video you want to index, you'll need to download it to your hard disk first, as described in "Download Online Video Clips" on page 209.

To index a *.wmv* file, download the free Windows Media Encoder at *http:// www.microsoft.com/windows/windowsmedia/forpros/encoder/default.mspx* (don't worry about the "9 series" moniker; it'll work fine with Windows 7 and Media Player 12. Open the Windows Media File Editor, drag-drop the video onto the Editor window, and from the **File** menu, select **Save and Index**. Thereafter, you'll never have to wait for the car chase again.

Control Video Buffering

Most online video clips are designed to *stream*, allowing you to start watching before your PC has finished downloading. To keep the video playing smoothly, video players often download a few seconds of video ahead of the playback, a technique called *buffering* (or *caching*), and sometimes this means you have to wait. The good news is that you can choose *when* to wait: now, or later.

 The buffering settings discussed here have no effect on video clips stored on your hard disk, nor on video handled by other players (e.g., Flash, Quicktime, and RealOne). To eliminate buffering messages altogether, see the next section, "Download Online Video Clips".

In Windows Media Player, click the **Now Playing** button, select **More Options**, and then choose the **Performance** tab. Select **Buffer [5] seconds of content**, the second option in the **Network buffering** section.

To shorten the lead time so that videos will start playing sooner, enter a small number, say 3. Depending on the speed of your Internet connection and number of visitors the web server is currently juggling, those 3 seconds of content could take anywhere from 2 seconds to 20 minutes to download. (Obviously, upgrading to a faster Internet connection will minimize the waiting most of the time.)

Unfortunately, entering a small number means that Media Player has to stop playback more often to buffer more content. If you find that Media Player frequently stops playing to buffer more data, raise the buffer number to 10 or 20 seconds. You'll get smoother playback, but you'll have to wait longer before your online videos play.

Download Online Video Clips

Most online video publishers don't make it easy to download video files to your hard disk, and for good reason. For one, if you're forced to watch video only on the originating website, the video provider can monetize your visit with ads, cross-promotions, etc.. And of course, nobody wants you to take copyrighted material and upload it to YouTube. That's all well and good, but who's looking out for *your* needs?

What happens when the publisher takes down a video or moves it to a subscription-based archive before you have a chance to watch it? What if the server is too busy, and your PC isn't able to stream it smoothly? What if you want to save the video so you can index it (as described earlier in this section)? What if the video is long, and you want to watch it later on your mobile phone or laptop on the road? What if you just want to needlessly fill up your hard drive?

Straighten Out Browser Video Plug-ins

Odds are you have the most popular video plug-ins already installed in your browser, but if you can't play one or more online videos, make sure you have the latest versions of these four major plug-ins installed in each web browser you use:

Quicktime (http://www.quicktime.com):
    IE plugin(s): *qtplugin.ocx*
    Firefox plugin(s): *npqtplugin.dll, npqtpluginx.dll*

RealPlayer (http://www.real.com):
    IE plugin(s): *oc3260.dll*

    Firefox plugin(s): *nppl3260.dll, nprpjplug.dll*

Shockwave Flash (http://www.adobe.com)
    IE plugin(s): *flash9.ocx*

    Firefox plugin(s): *npswf32.dll*

Windows Media Player (http://www.microsoft.com):
    IE plugin(s): *wmp.dll, msdxm.ocx*

    Firefox plugin(s): *npdsplay.dll, npwmsdrm.dll*

To see a list of plug-ins that are installed in Internet Explorer, open IE, click the **Tools** drop-down, and select **Internet Options**. Choose the **Programs** tab, click **Manage add-ons**, and then from the **Show** drop-down, select **Add-ons that run without requiring permission**. In the **Settings** box, you can also disable any plug-in you suspect might be causing playback problems, or, if you're lucky, you may be able to go to **Control Panel→Programs and Features** to uninstall the plug-in completely.

In Mozilla Firefox (and Mozilla SeaMonkey), just type about:plugins in the address bar and press **Enter** to see a list of installed plug-ins. (Note that plug-ins, used to view embedded content, are indeed different from extensions, which only add features to the browser interface.) Like IE, Mozilla plug-ins can be uninstalled from Control Panel.

It's often tricky to save online video for several reasons, not the least of which is the variety of delivery protocols and anti-downloading mechanisms in use. So before you start mucking around, look for the simplest solution. Some sites, such as Google Video, include a download link right on the page. Or, if the video is presented bare in the middle of the browser window (as opposed to having been embedded in a page), and the URL ends with a filename extension commonly associated with video files (e.g., *.mpg*, *.mov*, *.wmv*), then you can often just save the file by pressing **Ctrl-S**. (Likewise, **Page→Save As** in IE or **File→Save Page As** in Firefox.)

Otherwise, the first step is to find out what kind of video file you're dealing with, and the easiest way to do that is to right-click the center of the video frame in the browser window. The context menu that appears should indicate the plug-in being used: most notably, the **About** entry (if there is one). If you're having trouble playing an embedded video, see the sidebar "Straighten Out Browser Video Plug-ins" on page 209.

How you proceed depends on the plug-in.

Saving Video: Adobe Flash Player/Macromedia Flash Player

Flash-based videos typically come in two parts: the player module and the video file. The Flash plug-in first loads the player module (an *.swf* file), which then downloads and controls the video source (an *.flv* file); the *.flv* file is what you want. (This isn't always the case; sometimes there's no separate *.flv* file, and the video is likely embedded in the main *.swf* file.)

As soon as the player has finished downloading the entire *.flv* file, you can usually find it in your web browser cache, as described in the sidebar "Pull Files Out of Your Browser Cache" on page 212.

 Windows Media Player can't play *.flv* files unless you install a special codec, as described in "Install the FLV Flash Video Codec" on page 199.

Video, Audio, and Media

If you don't feel like digging through your cache folder, you can use one of these handy browser add-ons designed to provide direct links to *.flv* files on the most popular Flash-based video websites:

Bookmarklet (JavaScript button on your Links toolbar):

If you're using Firefox, SeaMonkey, or Opera, go to *http://1024k.de/book marklets/video-bookmarklets.html* and drag the "All-In-One Video Book-marklet" link from the page onto your browser's Links toolbar. Then, navigate to a video page and click the bookmarklet to open a pop-up window with a download link.

Since Internet Explorer doesn't support bookmarklets longer than 2,083 characters, you won't be able to use the aforementioned "All-In-One" link in IE. Instead, use the "old" bookmarklets listed at *http://1024k.de/book marklets/video-bookmarklets.html*; you'll need to install a bookmarklet for each website you use (e.g., YouTube, Google Video, etc.).

Greasemonkey User Script (Firefox/SeaMonkey only):

If you have the Greasemonkey extension (available from *http://greasespot .net*), go to *http://1024k.de/bookmarklets/video-bookmarklets.html*, click the "All-In-One Video Script" link, and then click **Install**. Next, navigate to a video page, and click the yellow bar that appears to display the down-load link.

There are also many Greasemonkey user scripts specialized for individual websites, all available for free from *http://userscripts.org*. For instance, the excellent YousableTubeFix script not only provides convenient FLV and MP4 download links on all YouTube pages, it enlarges the video and reorganizes the page to improve usability.

Firefox Extension (Firefox only):
First, install the VideoDownloader extension from *http://videodownloader .net/*, and then restart Firefox. Next, navigate to a video page, and click the VideoDownloader status bar icon to display a pop-up window with the download link.

Pull Files Out of Your Browser Cache

Web browsers store copies of recently viewed pages and all associated media (images, audio, and video) in a folder on your hard disk, called the *cache*. This improves performance when you're surfing, but also makes it easy to grab copies of media files—such as Flash videos (.*flv* files)—for storage elsewhere.

Internet Explorer's cache folder is *\Users\{username}\AppData\Local\Micro-soft\Windows\Temporary Internet Files*. (In IE, go to **Tools→Internet Options**, click **Settings** in the **Browsing history** section, and then click **View files**.) Sort the list by file type to group all the .*flv* files together, and then drag the file out of the folder or double-click it to play it.

Mozilla Firefox isn't so friendly with its cache; cached files have obfuscated filenames and no extensions, making it difficult to pull individual files its cache (located in the *Cache* subfolder of *\Users\{username}\AppData\Local\Mozilla \Firefox\Profiles*). The solution is to install the CacheViewer extension, available for free from *https://addons.mozilla.org/*.

Also available is VideoCacheView (*http://www.nirsoft.net/*), which is specifically designed to retrieve .*flv* files from the cache of both Internet Explorer and Firefox.

Unfortunately, not every Flash player caches video. In this case, follow the instructions for Windows Media Player later in this section; just substitute the .*flv* filename extension for the Windows Media extensions in the instructions.

Apple QuickTime

QuickTime files are typically the easiest videos to deal with. If the video file is playing by itself in the center of the browser window, select **Page→Save As** in Internet Explorer (or **File→Save As** in any other browser). If the video is playing in a standalone QuickTime window, you can select **File→Save As** and save

---

the file right on the spot, but only if you're using QuickTime Pro (the extra-cost upgrade to the free QuickTime player).

If the video is embedded in a web page, you'll need one of these add-ons to yank it out:

Bookmarklet (Internet Explorer, Firefox, SeaMonkey):
Go to *http://plasmasturm.org/code/bookmarklets/* and drag the "unembed" link from the page onto your browser's Links toolbar. Then, navigate to a video page and click the bookmarklet to download the embedded video.

Greasemonkey User Script (Greasemonkey extension plus Firefox/SeaMonkey).
If you have the Greasemonkey extension (available at *http://greasespot .net*), go to *http://neugierig.org/software/greasemonkey/*, and install the "unembed" user script. This adds a **download** link next to any embedded video; just click the link to download the video file.

Firefox/SeaMonkey Extension (Firefox or SeaMonkey).
Get the AdBlock Plus extension from *http://adblockplus.org/*, and then re-start your browser. Open the Adblock Plus Preferences window, select **Options**, and turn on the **Show tabs on Flash and Java** option. There-after, a small tab will appear just above embedded videos; click the tab to view the URL, highlight the URL text and copy it to the clipboard, and then click **Cancel**. Armed with the URL of the source video file, download the file as described in the sidebar "Download Files Without Viewing Them".

Download Files Without Viewing Them

Type a URL into your browser's address bar and hit **Enter**, and the browser will attempt to display the file in its own window or launch the associated player. Only if the file can't be displayed (such as a *.zip* or *.exe*), will you get a standard **Save As** dialog. But what if you want to save (download) a file the browser wants to open, such as a video?

If you're using Mozilla SeaMonkey, this is easy. Instead of pressing the **En-ter** key in the address bar, press **Shift-Enter** to save the file instead of opening it. This won't work in Internet Explorer or Firefox, though, so you'll need a slightly trickier method for those browsers.

Open Notepad and paste the URL of the file you want to download. In front of the URL, add this text:

```
<a href="
```

and then after the URL, add this:

```
">download</a>
```

Save the file on your desktop as *download.html*, and then double-click the new file to open it in your browser. Right-click the lone **download** link on the page, and select **Save Target As**.

Alternatively, you can use Bulk Downloader, available at *http://www.creati velement.com/powertools/*. Just choose the **List Manually** tab, paste the URL (or URLs) into the box, and then click **Download**.

Helper website (any browser)
   Go to *http://file2hd.com* and paste the URL of the site containing the video into the **URL** field. Check the "Terms of Service" checkbox, select the **Movies** filter, and click **Get Files**.

Saving Video: Real Player

If the video is embedded in a web page (including a small pop-up web page), try right-clicking the video itself. Select **Play in RealPlayer** to open the clip in a standalone window, and then in Real Player, select **File→Clip Properties→View Clip Info**. Armed with the URL of the file, download it as described in the sidebar above.

The file you download likely won't be the video itself, but rather only a *.ram* file, a playlist of sorts that points to one or more videos stored on a server somewhere. Open Notepad and drag the *.ram* file into it to view the URL inside. If the URL begins with http://, you can probably download it normally, again following the routine in the sidebar "Download Files Without Viewing Them". On the other hand, if the URL begins with rtsp:// (which stands for Real Time Streaming Protocol), you'll need a special program capable of downloading the stream to a file.

Copy the URL (highlight and press **Ctrl-C**) and paste it (**Ctrl-V**) into a program like CoCSoft Stream Down (*http://stream-down.cocsoft.com*), shown in Figure 4-7, WMRecorder (*http://www.wmrecorder.com*), or WebVideoCap (*http://www.nirsoft.net/*), and it will stream the file and save it to your hard disk.

Saving Video: Windows Media Player

Windows Media Player videos are a pain in the neck because of the wide variety of tricks publishers must use to get the videos to appear in web pages. If you encounter one of these beasts, first try the bookmarklets and extensions for QuickTime videos, listed earlier in this section. If none of those work, you'll need to do some digging to get the URL of the source file.

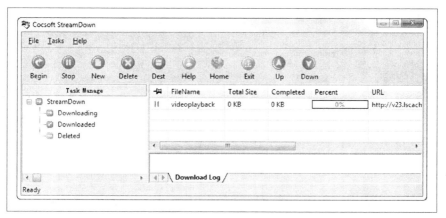

Figure 4-7. *Use a program like CoCSoft Stream Down to download streaming video clips to your hard disk*

If the video is playing in a standalone Windows Media Player window, getting the URL is not too hard: from the **File** menu, select **Properties**, and it will be shown in the **Location** field (see Figure 4-8).

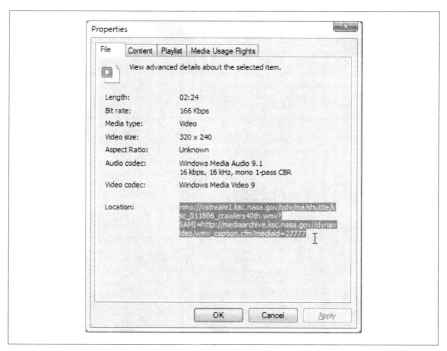

Figure 4-8. *Get the URL of an online Windows Media Player video clip*

If the video is embedded in a web page, getting the URL is a little trickier. If you're using Firefox or SeaMonkey, right-click an empty area of the web page and select **View Page Info**. Click the **Media** tab, and then scroll down the list until you see the URL of the video, which is often the only entry that isn't an image file (*.jpg*, *.gif*, etc.).

 Firefox and SeaMonkey users can also use the AdBlock Plus extension, described in the Apple QuickTime portion of this section, to get the URL of an embedded Media Player video file.

If you're using Internet Explorer, right-click an empty area of the web page and select **View Source** (this works in Firefox and SeaMonkey, too); some familiarity with HTML will make this task much easier. Press **Ctrl-F** and search the code for text that would likely appear in a video clip URL, such as `.asf, .asx, .wmv,` or `rstp:`. Somewhere in the code, you'll hopefully find a full (or partial) URL for the source video clip that looks something like *rstp:// www.some.server/videos/penguin.asx*. If you're lucky enough to find the URL, you can proceed to download it by following the instructions for Real Player, covered earlier in this section.

Saving Video: any source

As a last-ditch solution, you can try a screen recording program such as CamStudio (free from *http://camstudio.org/*), Jing (free from *http://www.jing project.com/*), Webinaria (free from *http://www.webinaria.com/record.php*), Hypercam (free trial at *http://www.hyperionics.com/hc/*), or Camtasia (free trial at *http://www.techsmith.com/camtasia.asp*). You won't get the original video files, but you will get something you can play back at your convenience.

The Trouble with Webcams

Historically, buying a webcam has been an exercise in compromise. Webcams don't have the universal appeal of, say, printers, and as such, don't enjoy an abundance of high-quality choices nor the comfort of well-established industry standards.

For instance, most webcams are cheap and offer horrendous video quality. As a result, many are quickly discontinued, making it extremely difficult to find up-to-date drivers for older models. (A webcam designed for Windows XP isn't likely to work in Windows Vista or 7, and don't even get me started on the search for 64-bit drivers.)

If you're lucky enough to find a webcam that works with Windows 7/Vista, it probably won't do everything you need it to. Of course, the most hyped feature—resolution—is the least important: a 5-megapixel webcam isn't necessarily any better than a 1.3-megapixel model. (How often will you be taking still photos with an eyeball-cam tethered to your laptop?) But the sexier features, like motorized face tracking (enabling video chat without having to sit perfectly still), autofocus, network streaming (for surveillance, baby monitoring, and web publishing), and high frame rate (for smooth, blur-free video) are often mutually exclusive, making compromise inevitable.

If you'd rather do without the compromise, you'll have to narrow the field a bit. Highest priority is UVC (USB Video device Class) compliance: you can plug a UVC webcam into any Windows 7 machine, and it'll work without any special drivers. A UVC webcam won't pose any problem for x64 Windows, nor the next few successors to Windows 7 (not to mention XP, Mac OS X, Linux, etc.).

 You may also run across IIDC (Instrumentation & Industrial Digital Camera), which is an earlier counterpart of UVC, but exclusively for Firewire (IEEE 1394) connections. For instance, the Apple iSight is a IIDC camera, and is automatically recognized in Windows 7 as a "1394 Desktop Video Camera." Alas, Windows 7 has no universal driver for the microphone in IIDC cameras, so it's probably best to avoid IIDC unless you already own one and use a separate audio source.

Also important is the brand name. If you don't want to buy yet another disposable webcam you'll have to replace in six months, avoid the cheap, no-name webcams and stick with Logitech, Creative Labs, or even Microsoft (gasp) to ensure driver availability in the years to come.

 Another way to avoid the "driver trap" is to use an IP camera, one that connects directly to your network (either wirelessly or with a Cat-5 cable). No USB connection means no USB driver is needed. And since most IP cameras with special features like pan-tilt-zoom controls are web-based, all you need is a browser to control it. (For this reason, avoid IP cameras that require proprietary software.) See "Use an IP Webcam for Videoconferencing" on page 218 for more on network cameras.

Finally, read online reviews—not surprisingly, they're plentiful at YouTube—to see how well a particular model actually renders an image. Look for a webcam that performs well in low light and handles motion without blurring. A widescreen aspect ratio (16×9) is a plus, as is a good mounting system (for attaching to laptop and desktop screens, resting on a desktop, or perching on a tripod) and a built-in microphone that reproduces voice clearly.

Once you've got a webcam that works, check out the following sections for ways to use it in Windows 7.

Turn a USB Webcam into an IP Webcam

An IP camera can transmit a video stream over a network connection, allowing you watch video from a remote location and even embed the video in a web page. These are typically standalone devices that either plug into your router or connect wirelessly over WiFi, but you can turn the ordinary USB webcam you already own into an IP camera with a spare laptop and the right software.

webcamXP (which, despite the name, works just fine on Windows 7) is available free for personal use from *http://www.webcamxp.com/*. Once you install and start it up, right-click the video box and select your camera from the list of video sources. Then, from any other computer on your network, type the first PC's IP address in the address field followed by **:8080** (e.g., *http:// 192.168.1.107:8080/*) to view the live video feed right in the browser.

Now, the "video" shown on the webcamXP web page is merely a constantly updating still image, which works on any browser and any platform—it'll even give you live video on an iPhone via Safari. But if you need a true Windows Media stream, fire up the **webcamXP [Windows Media]** link in the Start menu instead. Then go to *mms://192.168.1.107:9001*, and Windows Media Player will open and play your stream.

 Don't want to tether your camera to a laptop? You can turn any composite video source into a wireless IP webcam by connecting it to a "Wireless IP Video Transmitter," a small box with a WiFi antenna. But if you don't already have a camera, you can get an all-in-one wireless webcam for about the same amount of money, and do away with the clutter and fuss of all those wires.

Use an IP Webcam for Videoconferencing

You can turn a common USB webcam into an IP camera (as described in the previous section), so why not the other way around? To use a network camera with programs like Windows Media Encoder, Windows Live Messenger, Yahoo! Live, and Skype, you have several options.

For one, there's Link2Cam (free from *http://sourceforge.net/projects/link2cam/*), which is a DirectShow filter that effectively tricks Windows into thinking your remote camera is just another video source. Link2Cam works with ASF video streams.

If the free software doesn't cut it, there are commercial alternatives. The IP Camera DirectShow Filter from *http://www.webcamxp.com/* supports MPEG, H264, MJPEG, and JPEG streams, and is discussed in the previous section. Also available is Willing Webcam (*http://www.willingsoftware.com/*), which also supports motion detection, live video streaming, and time-lapse photography.

Want to record video from a remote camera? Try Debut Video Capture Software, which is free at *http://www.nchsoftware.com/capture/*.

Sound and Music

Windows 7 has the same audio subsystem as its predecessor, Windows Vista. Microsoft revamped Vista's audio subsystem to solve a series of problems it maintains caused stability and quality shortcomings in earlier versions. If you skipped Vista and upgraded directly from XP, this is why your sound doesn't work.

As a result, manufacturers of sound cards simply discontinued their older products rather than trying to make them compatible with Windows 7 and Vista. This is why you have to throw out your old sound card, and why you shouldn't spend too much on a new one.

Get Sound Where There Is None

Sound in Windows 7 is quite a bit more complicated than it needs to be, so troubleshooting sound problems is a real chore. The best way to fix a PC that won't play sound is with a systematic approach.

Start with the obvious. If you're using external speakers, make sure they're plugged in, turned on, and turned up. Try plugging your speakers into an iPod, home stereo, or other audio source to make sure they're actually working.

Using a laptop with integrated speakers? Most laptops have their own independent volume controls, and some are unlucky enough to have two or three. The first type is the old-school Walkman-esque dial, usually found near the headphone/speaker jack (sometimes these dials only control external audio, but not always). The second type is usually found on the keyboard, accessed by holding the **Fn** key while pressing another key decorated with a speaker icon. The third type is found on newer laptops, in the group of media quick-access buttons. Make your best effort to turn all these controls up.

 Sometimes the push-button volume controls on laptops operate the system volume directly, and sometimes they merely send signals to a Windows application that, in turn, controls the volume. If your laptop's volume controls don't seem to be working, the application with which they communicate may not be installed or running. If there's no Windows 7-compatible media access software on the PC manufacturer's website, then you probably won't be able to use those keys to control your PC's volume.

If hardware volume controls are a dead end, open the Volume Mixer, *sndvol.exe*—not *sndvol32.exe*, as it was on some earlier versions—and click the little down arrow in the **Device** section. If there's more than one device listed, make sure the little dot is next to the one you want to use. Turn up the **Device** volume control as high as it will go. Also check the subordinate volume controls to the right, one for each open sound-enabled application and one for Windows itself, and make sure they're all turned up.

Next, go to **Control Panel→ Sound**, and choose the **Playback** tab (Figure 4-9). If, again, there's more than one device listed here, highlight the one you want to use and click the **Set Default** button; a green checkmark icon marks the default playback device.

 Note that a single hardware device, such as a sound card, may be responsible for multiple sound devices shown in Control Panel. For instance, most higher-end audio cards have both analog (headphone jack) and digital (coax or optical/SPDIF) outputs, so make sure the one you're using is set as the default, and is marked with the little green checkmark.

With the sound device you want to use highlighted in the Playback window, click the **Properties** button, choose the **Levels** tab, and make sure all the volume controls here are turned up, and none are muted. (Muted levels have small red symbols on the blue speaker buttons).

Next, choose the **Advanced** tab. Click **Test** to play three tones in the left channel, followed by three in the right (more if you have a 5.1 or 6.1 setup).

- If you don't hear anything, and you don't see an error message at this point, there's likely a problem with your speaker jack, cable, or speakers.

Figure 4-9. More than one sound device on your PC? If so, you may have been setting the volume on the wrong card all this time

- If you hear only one set of three tones, it means only one stereo channel is working; either the left or right channel (or speaker) is out. The left channel tones decrease in frequency (higher to lower), while the right channel tones increase (lower to higher).

- If you have more than two speakers, but don't hear sound out of all of them, close the Properties window and click **Configure** to show the Speaker Setup page. Follow the prompts to tell Windows how many speakers you have.

- If you hear sound in some applications and not others, it could be the fault of the **Exclusive Mode** options in the Properties window. Try turning off one or both of the options here, click **Apply**, and try again.

- If you hear the tones, but you can't hear music played from an audio CD, the analog audio cable that typically connects CD drives in desktop PCs to sound cards might be missing, or plugged into the wrong connector. (Laptops and newer SATA drives don't usually use these cables.) It's a thin cable with small, plastic, three- or four-conductor plugs, and is found inside your PC case. Unless you're using an add-on sound card, this cable should be plugged into your motherboard; if there's more than one port, try the others until you get sound.

- If you see the message, "Failed to play test tone," it means there's a problem with the driver. Either it's the wrong driver for the device, or the driver (or device) isn't compatible with Windows 7.

 Can't find a Windows 7 driver for your sound card? Try the Windows Vista driver. If there's only a driver for XP, it might be time for a new sound card.

- If you're using your motherboard's built-in sound outputs (all laptops and most modern desktops), and they're not working, check your BIOS settings and make sure the adapter is enabled, as described in Appendix A. If Windows won't support your built-in sound, try an add-on sound card.
- Likewise, if you're using an add-on sound card that won't work with Windows 7, try taking it out and using the sound outputs built into your motherboard.

Still no luck? Time to start digging around in Device Manager (**Control Panel→Device Manager** or run *devmgmt.msc*). Expand the **Sound, video and game controllers** branch; if your device isn't listed, then Windows hasn't detected it, and hasn't loaded a driver for it. If it's listed, but its icon is covered with a red **X**, then it's just disabled; right-click the device and select **Enable**.

If the device icon is covered with a yellow exclamation point, then there's something wrong with the driver or the device. The first course of action is to right-click the device and select **Uninstall**. Check the **Delete the driver software for this device** option, and click **OK**. When the uninstallation is complete, restart Windows, and it should redetect the device and install new drivers by itself when it reboots. If this doesn't work, visit the sound card manufacturer's website and download the latest drivers for your card. (Or, if the problem appeared just after a recent driver update, try using the **Roll Back Driver** feature in Device Manager; see Chapter 6 for more on troubleshooting hardware.)

Get Windows to Listen

Want to transfer those old vinyl LPs to MP3s? Want to use voice dictation software? Want to record video, and need to send the audio track through your sound card? Want to use your PC as a makeshift karaoke machine? Because modern sound devices often have multiple audio inputs, and Windows lets you use only one at a time, you may have to jump through a few hoops to record sound.

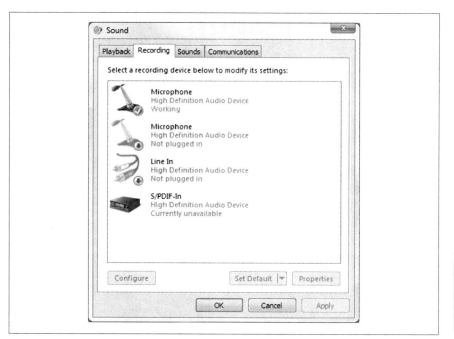

Figure 4-10. Most recording problems are caused by incorrect settings on this Control Panel page

 Want an easy way to record sound? Check out HarddiskOgg, free from *http://www.fridgesoft.de/*, which lets you record any audio your PC can receive (coming in from a microphone or line-in device) or produce (going out from an application or game).

A single audio device may have two or three audio inputs: an analog (mono) microphone input, an analog stereo "line-In" or auxiliary input, and sometimes a digital S/PDIF input. And special devices, like voice dictation headsets and TV tuner cards, have their own inputs. All the inputs for all your audio devices are listed in the **Recording** tab, on the **Sound** page in **Control Panel**, shown in Figure 4-10. (Most desktop sound cards also have internal inputs for CD audio, discussed in the previous section, but these almost never show up in Control Panel.)

To choose the default audio source, highlight the device you want to use and click **Set Default**. Most applications will automatically use the default device to record sound, but some (particularly voice-dictation software) require that you choose a source separately in the application itself.

If you have a USB audio device, such as a voice-dictation headset, Windows may set it as the default recording *and* playback device each time you plug it in. This will make it look like your sound stops working each time you use the headset; of course, all you have to do is change the default playback device, as described in the previous section.

Next, you'll need to set the recording level (volume) of the device; most of the time, the default level is 0 (off), which won't produce any sound at all. With the device highlighted, click **Properties**, choose the **Levels** tab and move the slider to the right until the level is at least 50. (You won't see a **Levels** tab if the status for the device reads "Not plugged in.")

Next, choose the **Listen** tab, and select the **Continue running when on battery power** option. To confirm the microphone, line-in jack, etc. is working, turn on the **Listen to this device** option, choose **Default Playback Device** from the list below, and click **Apply** to start listening. If you hear something through your speakers, the device works; turn off **Listen to this device** and click OK.

If you're setting up a voice-dictation microphone, you may have to complete a separate wizard in the software itself to set the input source and its recording level. For instance, if you're using Windows' built-in speech recognition feature, go to **Control Panel→Ease of Access→Speech Recognition Options→Set up microphone** (or with the device still highlighted in the **Recording** tab, click **Configure**).

 For best results using voice-dictation software or recording voice, use a USB microphone/headset instead of the conventional type that plugs directly into your sound card. Not only will the quality and clarity improve, but you'll effectively bypass the often troublesome sound card drivers in favor of a more direct link.

Fix Garbled Music

Your music not sounding its best? The most likely candidate is an "enhancement" in your music player; sometimes these just don't play nice with Windows' audio drivers.

In Windows Media Player, press Ctrl-**3** to switch to the Now Playing window. Then right-click the center of the player and from the **Enhancements** menu, select **Graphic Equalizer**. (Or, if you're using Skin mode, press the **Alt** key to open the menu, and select **View→Enhancements→Graphic Equalizer**.) In the Enhancements window that appears, click the **Turn off** link that appears (if the link says **Turn On**, the equalizer is already turned off). Next, return to the **Enhancements** menu, select **SRS WOW Effects**, and click the **Turn off** link there as well.

If you're having this problem in iTunes, select **View→Show Equalizer**, and clear the checkbox next to the **On** option. Next, select **Edit→Preferences**, choose the **Playback** tab, and turn off the **Sound Enhancer** option. Click OK when you're done.

Or, in WinAmp, select **Options→ Equalizer**, and if there's a checkbox next to **EQ enabled**, turn it off.

If this doesn't fix the problem, open the Sound page in Control Panel and choose the **Playback** tab. Select your speakers in the list, and then click **Properties**. Choose the **Enhancements** tab, turn on the **Disable all enhancements** option, and click OK.

Whether or not this adjustment fixes the problem, this is not a problem a fully functional sound card should have. Make sure you have the latest drivers, and consider replacing the card if nothing else seems to work.

Crossfade Your Music

Crossfading is a feature present in Windows Media Player and other music players that eliminates the gaps between songs by gradually overlapping adjacent tracks. (Radio DJs do this, but they undoubtedly have better equipment than you do.)

In Windows Media Player, press Ctrl-**3** to switch to the Now Playing window. Then right-click the center of the player and from the **Enhancements** menu, select **Crossfading and Auto Volume Leveling**. (Or, if you're using Skin mode, press the **Alt** key to open the menu, and select **View→Enhancements→Crossfading and Auto Volume Leveling**.) In the Enhancements window that appears, click the **Turn on Crossfading** link (Figure 4-11), and then adjust the amount of overlap to your liking.

Crossfading only works on data files (such as MP3 or WMA), and then only when the two songs are encoded with the same sampling rate (e.g., 192 Kbps or 256 Kbps). Crossfades won't work if you are playing an ordinary audio CD, or, for some reason, a *data* CD that was originally burned with Windows Media Player.

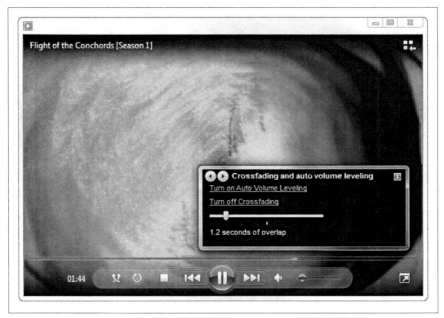

Figure 4-11. Crossfading, which overlaps songs to reduce dead air, works only in certain circumstances

 Now, it's possible that crossfading is actually working, but you can't tell because your music files have more than a few seconds of silence at the beginning or end. To test the feature, try playing a few songs that don't begin or end in a fade. And try increasing the amount of overlap by moving the crossfade slider to the right.

To enable crossfading in iTunes (which, ironically, is not something you can do on an iPod), select **Edit→Preferences**, choose the **Playback** tab, and turn on the **Crossfade playback** option.

 Crossfading is *really* annoying when you're listening to spoken-word tracks or dialog from movie soundtracks. Try it; you'll see what I mean.

Extract Sound from Video

Want to listen to the literal video of Journey's *Separate Ways* without having to literally watch the video?

The Windows Media Stream Editor, a component of the free Windows Media Encoder (available at *http://www.microsoft.com/windows/windowsmedia/for pros/encoder/default.mspx*), can extract the audio from a *.wmv* video file and save it into a standalone Windows Media Audio (*.wma*) file:

1. First, open the Windows Media Stream Editor and click **Add Source**. Locate a *.wmv* or *.asf* file, and click **Open**.

2. Expand the branches by highlighting the file in the list and pressing the asterisk (*) key, place a checkmark next to the **Audio** entry, and then click **Add**.

3. Then, click **Create File**, specify an output filename, and click **Save**.

4. When you're ready, click **Start** to begin the extraction.

When the process is complete, you'll have a standard *.wma* file; see the next section for ways to convert it to MP3 or any other format.

To yank out the audio track from non-Microsoft video formats, you'll need a different program. A full-blown video editing application like Adobe Premiere (*http://www.adobe.com*) can do this handily, as can Blaze Media Pro (*http://www.blazemp.com?*), but if you want to do it for free, try the AoA Audio Extractor (*http://www.aoamedia.com/audioextractor.htm*).

Convert Audio Files

You'd think after all these years, the tech industry would learn its lesson. They put us through the Beta versus VHS battle in the '80s, the Netscape versus Internet Explorer battle in the '90s, and the HD DVD versus Blu-Ray battle in the naughts. On the computer front, the battle of the formats is everywhere, including digital music.

It wasn't always this way. At the beginning of the digital music revolution, it was the compact file size and passably good quality of the MP3 file format that popularized portable digital players like the iPod (not to mention P2P file-sharing and the like, but that's a different story). But now we have Apple's M4A, M4P, and lossless AAC formats; Microsoft's various versions of the WMA format; OGG Vorbis; Sony's bygone ATRAC; and so on. Granted, most of these formats have risen from the need to copy-protect downloadable music, as well as offer audiophiles better fidelity, but the lack of a single standard is nothing more than a pain in the neck to music lovers everywhere.

Protected music purchased from Apple's iTunes music store can only be played by Apple iPods (and some Motorola phones). Very few players are compatible with audio files from Microsoft's URGE music store; even some of Microsoft's own Zune players can't play URGE files! And there's no music player that'll play all the commercially available protected formats.

So, in order to play all the music you have on any particular player, you may have to convert some of it to the proper format, and that's easier said than done.

For one, converting anything other than lossless audio to your desired format will reduce the quality of the music. (Examples of lossless audio include WAV files, Apple's lossless AAC, and, of course, audio CD tracks.) Also, most music purchased online is distributed in protected formats (like iTunes' M4P and Microsoft's protected WMA), although many stores, including iTunes, are selling more unprotected files. And converting protected media isn't exactly encouraged by these large companies.

Windows Media Player doesn't convert audio files at all. But Apple's iTunes software (*http://www.apple.com/itunes/*), which is free even if you don't have an iPod or any intention of buying music from the iTunes Music Store, can convert songs easily and quickly. It supports MP3 (all bitrates), AAC (*.m4p, .m4a,* and *.m4b*), AIFF, lossless AAC, WMA (read-only), and even *.wav* files. Here's how to do it:

1. Start iTunes, and select **Music** from the **Library** section on the left.

2. If all your music isn't already in the iTunes library, drag-drop your music files onto the iTunes window.

 If you move the files into your iTunes music folder *before* dragging them into the iTunes application, iTunes will, by default, organize them into folders based on their embedded tag information. If the files are located elsewhere, they'll be left in their current locations. Of course, if the **Copy files to iTunes Media folder when adding to library** option is turned on, and you drag files from another location, you'll end up with two copies of each file...plus a third after you've converted.

3. Next, select **Edit→ Preferences**, choose the **General** tab, and then click **Import Settings**. Select the file format you want to use from the **Import Using** listbox (e.g., choose MP3 Encoder to convert to the MP3 format), and then select a compression level from the **Setting** listbox. (If you don't know which settings to use, **MP3** at **192kbps** is a good compromise among quality, flexibility, and resulting file size, and the files you create can be played anywhere.) Click OK when you're done.

4. Finally, highlight one or more songs in your music library, right-click, and select **Convert Selection to MP3** (or AAC, or whatever). Shortly thereafter, iTunes will place the newly converted file alongside the original—both in the library and in same folder on your hard disk—while leaving the original file intact.

Of course, neither iTunes nor Windows Media Player will let you convert *protected* files, but they'll both let you burn protected music to an audio CD. Then, all you have to do is rip the CD back into an unprotected format. In fact, NoteBurner (*http://www.noteburner.com*) creates a virtual CD-RW drive on your system specifically for this purpose, allowing you to burn and rip your protected songs without wasting any discs. Unfortunately, the burn-rip process will completely obliterate the embedded tags (meaning that you'll have to retype the track names and other information by hand).

 By default, Windows Media Player adds DRM copy protection to all music files you rip from CDs. To turn this off, open Windows Media Player, press the Alt key to open the menu, select **Tools→ Options**, choose the **Rip Music** tab, and turn off the **Copy protect music** option.

To convert protected files and preserve your tags, you'll need one of the dozens of different DRM removal tools available, such as Tunebite (*http://www.tune bite.com/*) or MyFairTunes (*http://www.hymn-project.org/*).

Of course, no matter how you do it, there will always be a loss in quality when you're converting from one compressed format to another. The exception is when you convert a protected file to an unprotected file of the same format, such as *.m4p* to *.m4a* or protected *.wma* to unprotected *.wma*, provided the software you use supports lossless conversion.

Fix Music Tags

Most music players, including both Windows Media Player and Apple iTunes, pay no attention to the filenames of your music files, but rather read the information (called *tags*) embedded therein. Most audio formats support tags for the artist, track, album, year, genre, and about a hundred other things. To get your music player to display and organize your music properly, the tags in your music files must be correct, and unless all your music came from the same source, some tag cleaning is often in order.

Most music library programs allow you to edit the tags of your music files. Windows Media Player (via the Advanced Tag Editor feature) as well as iTunes (discussed earlier in this chapter) even let you modify the tags of several files at once. You can also edit tags for individual files right in Windows Explorer (see Chapter 2), or multiple files if you install the free AudioShell (*http://soft pointer.com/*) extension.

Also available for free from *http://softpointer.com/* is a plugin for Windows Media Player that adds tag support for M4a, Flac, Ogg, Ape, and Mpc files. To make use of it, you'll also need to install the appropriate DirectShow filters. To play M4a files in Media Player, get the 3ivx filter from *http://www.3ivx .com/*. To play Ogg Vorbis, Speex, Theora, and Flac files in Media Player, use the Xiph filter from *http://www.xiph.org/ dshow/*. And to play Mpc files, use the Radlight filter from *http://www.radlight.com/*.

But what if you have a lot of music files without any tags at all? Try to import those files into a program like iTunes, and you'll just end up with countless tracks labeled "Unknown Artist." The solution is to use the filenames to generate the tags, and for this, you can use Ultra Tag Editor (*http://www.atelio .com/*):

1. Open Ultra Tag Editor, use the tree to navigate to the folder containing your files, and place checkmarks next to the specific files you want to fix.

2. Below, choose the **Ultra Tagger** tab, and then, from the **Action** listbox, select **Generate Tag from Filename** (Figure 4-12).

3. Now, Ultra Tag Editor needs you to tell it where in your songs' filenames to find the artist name, track title, track number, album name, and so on, so you'll need to examine the filename of a typical music file on your hard disk, which might look something like *Artist-Album-Title.mp3*.

Although programs like Ultra Tag Editor are flexible, they do require that your filenames be uniform (e.g., all using the "*Artist-Track.mp3*" format, for instance). Since you likely have a mish-mash of different filenames, you'll need a program like Power Rename (part of Creative Element Power Tools, *http://www.creativelement.com/ powertools/*) to fix up your filenames with ease, without resorting to manually renaming individual files.

First, determine the delimiter used to separate the information in your filenames (a hyphen, -, in this case), and type it into the **Delimiters** field.

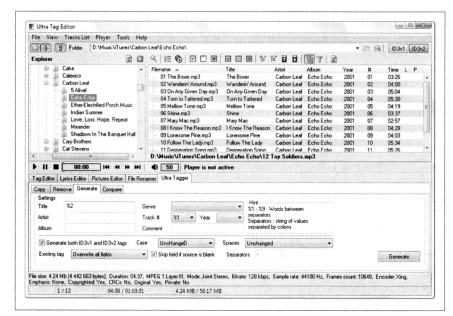

Figure 4-12. Use the Ultra Tag Editor to generate MP3 tags from filenames

Next, type %1 into the field containing the first piece of information (e.g., Artist), %2 into the field containing the second (e.g., Album), %3 for the third (e.g., Title), and so on. (Imagine your files look like %1-%2-%3-%4...mp3).

4. When you're done, click the **Generate** button to preview the new tags, and click **Write Tags** to commit your changes.

Ultra Tag Editor can also go the other direction—that is, to generate filenames based on tags. Better yet, both Windows Media Player and Apple iTunes can organize your music into folders (e.g., *\Music\Artist\Album*) and rename the files based on the embedded tag information.

Another tool that does the same thing as Ultra Tag Editor is Tag&Rename, available at *http://softpointer.com/*.

Photos, Pictures, and Images

Linux-based netbooks have some pretty huge advantages over Windows-based PCs: they're cheaper, faster, lighter, less crash-prone, and safer (no malware threats, yet). But there's no place for your stuff. Aside from some bewildering shortcomings, Windows 7 does a good job of giving you a home for your tens of thousands of photos (not to mention music, video, etc.).

But things could be better. Photo sorting is harder in Windows 7 than in Vista. Windows doesn't support all the file formats it could. And getting decent color takes some work. Here's how to make Windows take better care of your pictures.

Quickly Sort Photos

Windows Vista was a big leap in photo management over its predecessor, XP, and Windows 7 offers a few additional enhancements...with one glaring omission. In Windows Vista, you could view a folder full of photos in the **Large Icons** view, and retain the useful column headers from the **Details** view for quick and easy sorting. Alas, the column headers are gone in Windows 7. Stupid Microsoft.

Things get worse when you drag new photos into a sorted folder. Sometimes the file stays where you put it, and sometimes Windows Explorer moves it after a short delay...and not always to the correctly sorted place. If the column headers were present, you could simply click, say, **Date Modified** (twice), to quickly re-sort the listing. Even if you didn't need to change the sorting of a collection of photos, the column headers would show the current sort order at a glance, something that isn't available anywhere else on the surface of Windows Explorer.

Instead, you've got to right-click an empty area of the folder (be careful not to select a photo), select **Sort By** and then the sorting method you want; that's three clicks plus some careful mousing. To sort an unordered listing, that's at least six clicks.

Alas, there's no quick fix for this one. But there are some workarounds:

Use the keyboard

Press **Alt+V**, then **ON** to sort by name, **OT** to sort by type, and **OS** to sort by size. But since the letter **D** is used to sort *descending* (and **A** to sort *ascending*), the only way to sort by date with a keyboard shortcut is to press **Alt+V**, down arrow, and then **Enter**.

To do this with fewer keystrokes, use a Hotkeys tool (part of Creative Element Power Tools, *http://creativelement.com/powertools/*) to assign the command %(V)O{Down}{Enter} to a short keystroke like **Alt-D**. (See the included help for details on building hotkey strings.)

Use a different program

Few applications provide quick image sorting. DxO Optics Pro (*http://dxo.com/?*), for instance, has a **Sort** drop-down above the file list, right where Windows Explorer should have one. Picasa (free from *http://picasa.google.com*) offers basic sorting through a toolbar drop-down and the **Album** menu. And Adobe Lightroom (*http://www.adobe.com/*) offers sorting through controls at the bottom of the window. But none offer the simple pleasure of single-click sorting we got for free in Windows Vista.

Choose Where to Store Your Pictures

One way Windows helps you organize your files is to direct different kinds of content to different locations. There's a *Music* folder, a *Videos* folder, a *Saved Games* folder, and a *Pictures* folder. Put all your digital pictures in your *Pictures* folder, for example, and that's where most photo applications will prompt you to open and save your files.

 This, of course, is separate from Windows 7's *Pictures* library, which is a database of photos stored in any number of different locations. To change which photo folders are included, right-click the *Pictures* library and select **Properties**. Although some newer applications look in your *Pictures* library by default, many programs still default to the *Pictures* folder discussed in this solution.

Because the pictures folder can grow quite large, it's not unusual to store your photos on a second drive. And if you change the physical location of your *Pictures* folder to that new location, applications will default to that folder when you open and save files. Here's how to tell Windows where your *Pictures* folder ought to be, a task that requires a quick Registry modification:

1. Open the Registry Editor (described in Chapter 3).
2. Expand the branches to `HKEY_CURRENT_USER\Software\Microsoft\Windows\CurrentVersion\Explorer\User Shell Folders`.

 Also in the **Explorer** branch of the Registry is the `Shell Folders` key. According to Microsoft, the key is no longer used in Windows 7, although you should still update it for applications that still read it.

3. Double-click the `My Pictures` value in the right pane, and type (or paste) the full path of the folder you want to use (e.g., `d:\Photos`). (The default here is `%USERPROFILE%\Pictures`, which is an expandable string value that points to the *Pictures* subfolder of your personal profile folder.)
4. Click OK and then close the Registry Editor when you're done.

5. Next, open Windows Explorer, open your profile folder (the one matching your user name at the top of the tree), and select the *Pictures* folder inside.

6. Right-click the *desktop.ini* file and select **Copy**. (This file is hidden; see Chapter 2 for details on configuring Windows Explorer to show hidden files.)

7. Navigate to your new pictures folder (e.g., d:\Photos), right-click an empty area of the folder, and select **Paste**.

The change should take effect immediately, but you may have to restart any open applications before they'll recognize the new location. (Strictly speaking, the copying of *desktop.ini* in steps 5–7 is optional, but it does help Windows Explorer display the folders properly.) To test the change, open Paint (*mspaint.exe*), and select **File→Open**. If the folder that appears is the folder you chose, then you're all done.

 You can change the locations of other "special" folders with the same technique. For instance, put the location of your MP3 collection into the My Music value. Or, put the location of your Media Center recordings into the My Video value.

Generate Thumbnails for RAW Photos

Windows understands a bunch of common image and movie formats out of the box, and can produce thumbnails for your files in **Medium**, **Large**, and **Extra Large Icons** views. To get Windows to recognize a new format, though, you need to install the appropriate Windows Imaging Component (WIC) codec.

If you've set up your digital SLR camera to produce "RAW" images (as opposed to the more common JPEG or TIFF formats), you can install one of these codecs to get Windows to display thumbnails for your files:

Canon CR2
    http://www.usa.canon.com/opd/controller?act=opdsupport7act

Nikon NEF
    http://www.nikonimglib.com/nefcodec/

Olympus ORF
    http://www.olympus.co.jp/en/support/imsg/digicamera/download/soft ware/codec/

Pentax PEF

> *http://www.pentax.jp/english/support/download_digital.html*

Sony SRF

> *http://support.d-imaging.sony.co.jp/www/cyber-shot/download/raw _driver_e/*

If your camera isn't supported, or if the appropriate codec doesn't work, try the free ArcSoft RAW Thumbnail Viewer, available at *http://www.arcsoft.com/ products/rawviewer/*. It adds thumbnail support to Windows for RAW formats from Canon, Hasselblad, Kodak, Leica, Mamiya, Nikon, Olympus, Pentax, Ricoh, Samsung, Sigma, and Sony, and even works with Adobe Digital Negative (DNG) files.

The alternative is to use a separate picture viewer with its own thumbnail display, like Google's free Picasa manager (*http://picasa.google.com/*), or commercial products like Adobe Photoshop Elements (*http://www.adobe.com/*) and DxO Optics Pro (*http://dxo.com/*).

To add thumbnail support for new video formats, just install the latest video codecs, covered earlier in this chapter, and Windows will do the rest.

Tweak the Thumbcache

The Green Ribbon of Death, covered in Chapter 2, is your sign that Windows Explorer is either busy or broken. When it's busy, it's often busy building thumbnail previews of your photos.

In theory, Explorer caches its thumbnails so you don't have to wait so long next time you view a folder. But if the thumbnail cache were seamless, the Green Ribbon of Death would be nothing but folklore; it's not uncommon to be forced to wait while Explorer rebuilds the cache, even for a folder you've viewed recently. What you may not know, however, is that the cache can also be a security or privacy risk.

Windows stores the thumbnail cache in two different places. The main cache is located in six separate *.db* files in this folder:

> *C:\Users\{your user name}\AppData\Local\Microsoft\Windows\Explorer*

which have names like *thumbcache_32.db*, *thumbcache_96.db*, *thumbcache_ 256.db*, and *thumbcache_1024.db* (each representing different thumbnail sizes). But you might also find a file named *thumbs.db*, or perhaps several thousand of them, stored in your individual photo folders.

The *thumbs.db* file was used in Windows XP and previous versions as the sole means of caching thumbnails. So if you've been a Windows user since before Vista, you likely have plenty of these lying around. But Windows 7 uses *thumbs.db* too when browsing network folders; if you've got any on your hard disk, they were likely created by remote users browsing your shared folders. If you don't see them at all, Windows Explorer is probably not set to show "protected operating system files," as described in the section "Customize Windows Explorer" on page 45.

Since most people won't see the *thumbs.db* file, it's hard to make the case that it just adds clutter (although it does, dagnabbit). But since *thumbs.db* is usually readable by anyone, it does mean that anyone rifling through your files may be able to see the thumbnails of your images even if they can't open the images themselves. (See the sidebar "Extract Images From the Thumbnail Cache" on page 239 for details.) What's more, if you zip up a folder of files to send to someone else, any *thumbs.db* files therein will go along for the ride, and you may be sharing more than you meant to.

Disable thumbnail caching

Have the Professional, Ultimate, or Enterprise editions of Windows 7? Open the Local Group Policy Editor (*gpedit.msc*) and expand the branches to *User Configuration\Administrative Templates\Windows Components\Windows Explorer*. In the right pane, double-click the **Turn off caching of thumbnail pictures** entry, select **Enabled**, and then click OK. In the same folder, also double-click the **Turn off the caching of thumbnails in hidden thumbs.db files** entry, select **Enabled**, and then click OK. (To re-enable thumbnail caching later on, set each of these options to **Not Configured**.)

If you have Windows 7 Home Premium edition, you won't have access to the Local Group Policy Editor. Instead, open the Registry Editor (see Chapter 3) and navigate to HKEY_CURRENT_USER\Software\Microsoft\Windows\CurrentVersion\Policies\Explorer. From the **Edit** menu, select **New** and then **DWORD (32-bit) Value**, and then type NoThumbnailCache for the name of the new value (or double-click the NoThumbnailCache value if it's already there). Type 1 for the value data, and click OK. Next, navigate to HKEY_CURRENT_USER\Software\Policies\Microsoft\Windows\Explorer and create a **DWORD (32-bit) Value** named DisableThumbsDBOnNetworkFolders. Likewise, set its value data to 1, and close the Registry Editor when you're finished.

The changes should take effect immediately; the next time you browse a folder full of photos, you'll notice that it takes considerably longer to display the thumbnails. However, any existing cache files will remain on your hard disk indefinitely; read on if you want to delete the lingering cache as well.

Reset the thumbcache

As the thumbnail cache grows, it becomes less efficient. Years of navigating folders—not to mention deleting and moving photos—causes bloat, which slows down the index. As with any cache, all you need to do is delete the cache files, and they'll be recreated as needed (unless, of course, you've disabled the cache).

Your Windows Explorer sluggish when you're browsing photo folders? Try disabling the cache and then reenabling it as described previously; sometimes this is all it takes to speed things up.

Although you can use the Search tool to find and delete all the *thumbs.db* files on your drive, it's quicker to open a Command Prompt window (see Chapter 9), and type this:

```
del /s /q /f /a:h c:\thumbs.db
```

where *c:* can be any valid drive letter containing drive containing *thumbs.db* files to delete. In usually less time than it would take for Search to populate a list of *thumbs.db* files, the del command can wipe them all out in a single shot.

The main cache files are a little trickier, though, since Windows Explorer locks them while it's running. The easiest way to clear them is with the Disk Cleanup utility (*cleanmgr.exe*); just place a checkmark next to **Thumbnails** and click OK.

If Disk Cleanup doesn't do the trick, you can clear the main cache from the Command Prompt window. First, fire up the Windows Task Manager by pressing **Ctrl+Shift+Esc**, choose the **Processes** tab, and close all instances of **explorer.exe**. Then, at the prompt, type del %userprofile%\AppData\Local \Microsoft\Windows\Explorer\thumbcache*.* and press **Enter**. When that's done, switch back to Task Manager, and from the **File** menu, select **New Task (Run)**. Type explorer.exe in the box and click OK to get back your desktop and Start menu.

Open an Explorer window and navigate back to *C:\Users\{your user name} \AppData\Local\Microsoft\Windows\Explorer*. Don't worry that the *.db* files you just deleted are still there; Explorer recreated them when it started back up; confirm this by checking their file sizes and times.

Stop Explorer from resetting the thumbcache

If left unchecked, the thumbnail cache could grow to a gargantuan size. It would be nice if Windows Explorer kept the cache trim by routinely purging infrequently-used thumbnails and checking for deleted photos, but that's ultimately a poor use of system resources. That's why Explorer takes the simple (and dumb) approach of automatically deleting the entire cache once any single *.db* file reaches 500 Mb.

But the consequence of this rapidly revolving cache is that you frequently have to wait while Explorer rebuilds the thumbnails for folders you visited as recently as yesterday.

The good news is that you can stop Explorer from deleting the thumbnail cache, and you'll see improved folder browsing performance as a result. The bad news is that it will grow very quickly, particularly if you have a lot of photos. Here's how to do it:

1. Open Windows Explorer and navigate to *C:\Users\{your user name}\AppData\Local\Microsoft\Windows\Explorer*.
2. Right-click the *Explorer* folder in the tree, select **Properties**, and then choose the **Security** tab.
3. Click the **Advanced** button and then click **Change Permissions**.
4. Click **Add**, type Everyone into the **Enter the object names to select** field, and then click OK.
5. With the new **Everyone** entry highlighted, click **Edit**.
6. In the **Permissions** list, place two checkmarks in the **Deny** column: one next to **Delete subfolders and files** and one next to **Delete**.
7. Click OK in each of the four open windows to return to Explorer.

The change takes effect immediately. To restore the folder to its default permissions, return to the Advanced Security Settings for Explorer window (steps 1–3), highlight the **Everyone** entry, and click **Remove**.

Extract Images From the Thumbnail Cache

Want to see what's in your Thumbnail cache? Open a PowerShell window (see Chapter 9) and issue these five commands:

```
$sql = ("SELECT System.ItemURL, System.DateModified FROM SYSTEMINDEX
                         WHERE System.Kind = 'picture' ")
$adapter = new-object System.Data.OLEDB.OLEDBDataAdapter -ArgumentList $sql,
    "Provider=Search.CollatorDSO;Extended Properties='Application-Windows';"
$dataset = new-object System.Data.Dataset
$adapter.Fill($dataset)
$dataset.Tables[0]
```

and you'll see a list of every photo filename and its modified date in your cache. (You can include any columns you like in place of ItemURL and DateModified on line 1; for a list of properties, see *http://annoyances.org/downloads/shellpro perties.txt*.) You may even notice entries for files that have since been moved, renamed, or deleted.

To pull the actual thumbnail images from your cache, use Thumbnail Database Viewer (free from *http://www.itsamples.com*), dmThumbs (free trial at *http://www.dmthumbs.com/*), or Thumbs.db Viewer (free trial at *http://www .janusware.com/*).

So, what can you do to prevent someone else from reading your thumbnails?

For one, you can encrypt your photo folders, as described in Chapter 8. If you encrypt the folders (as opposed to the individual files), Windows will encrypt newly created *thumbs.db* files as well. You can also encrypt the *C:\Users\[your user name]\AppData\Local\Microsoft\Windows\Explorer* folder, although its contents won't be encrypted until you reset the cache, as described in "Tweak the Thumbcache" on page 235. Of course, encrypting won't protect your data from others who know your login.

You can also delete all the *thumbs.db* files from your hard disk, but that won't stop them from reappearing.

The only sure-fire way to ensure that someone can't see your photo thumbnails is to disable and then reset your thumbcache, as explained in "Tweak the Thumbcache" on page 235.

Video, Audio, and Media

Get Rid of the Windows Photo Gallery

Care to use your own image viewer or editor to manage your photos? Unfortunately, the Windows Photo Gallery application is not easy to get rid of. You can choose any application as the default for opening pictures, and the Windows Photo Gallery will *still* appear when you double-click image files.

If you want to use another image viewer without making any changes to your system, there are ways to open images other than double-clicking. For instance, you can drag-drop an image file onto the window of any viewer to open it, or even right-click an image file and select **Open With** to choose another program.

To choose a different application as the default for photos, you may have to disable the Windows Photo Gallery:

1. Open the Registry Editor (described in Chapter 3).

2. Expand the branches to `HKEY_CLASSES_ROOT\SystemFileAssociations\.ico` `\ShellEx\ContextMenuHandlers\ShellImagePreview`.

3. Highlight the `ShellImagePreview` key, select **File→Export**, type a filename, and click **Save** to back up this Registry key. (See Chapter 3 for details.)

4. Delete the `ShellImagePreview` key and close the Registry Editor when you're done.

If you don't want to mess around in the Registry, you can also do this with File Type Doctor (free trial from *http://www.creativelement.com/powertools/*):

1. Open the Creative Element Power Tools Control Panel, turn on the **Edit file type associations** option, click **Accept**, and then close the Control Panel.

2. Right-click any image file and select **Edit File Type**.

3. On the right side, highlight the **Windows Photo Gallery Viewer Image Verbs** entry.

To back up this setting before you delete, click **Export**, type a filename, and then click **Save**. To subsequently re-enable the Windows Photo Gallery, just double-click the *.reg* file you created here. See Chapter 3 for more information on registry patch files.

4. Click the **Remove** button.

Note that in 2007, Microsoft created a new image file format to coincide with the release of Windows Vista. JPEG XR—formerly known as Windows Media Photo, formerly known as HD Photo—supports better compression and a wider color gamut than the ordinary JPEG format. But since few applications support this format, you may wish to re-enable the Windows Photo Gallery for only files with the *.hdp*, *.jxr*, and *.wdp* filename extensions. To do this, you'll need to manually edit the corresponding file type keys in the Registry Editor, as described in Chapter 3, and add the `ShellImagePreview` key to its `ContextMenuHandlers` key.

Get More Accurate Color

Ever notice that the colors in digital photos you view in Windows don't quite match the real thing, or even the colors on the little screen on the back of your digital camera? Likewise, have you noticed that the colors your printer reproduces don't match those on your monitor?

This is a common problem, and one, unfortunately, without a clear-cut, foolproof solution. The problem is that your monitor, printer, scanner, and digital camera all handle color a little differently, and subtleties like ambient light, paper color, and how much you've had to drink can all affect how an image looks. It's up to you to calibrate Windows so that all of these devices know what adjustments they need to make to preserve your colors without botching your photos too badly.

 Before you proceed, make sure your display adapter (video card) is set to the highest color depth it supports. Right-click an empty portion of the desktop, select **Screen resolution**, click the **Advanced settings** link, and then choose the **Monitor** tab. From the **Colors** drop-down list, select **True Color (32 bit)** and then click OK. If the **Resolution** slider to the left drops when you do this, see Chapter 5.

Calibration hardware

The best way to get accurate color is with dedicated color-calibration hardware. To calibrate your monitor, you place a mouse-like sensor (called a *colorimeter*) on your screen and then run a calibration program. One by one, the software displays known colors on the screen, and the sensor reports back to the software what it "sees." Finally, the software generates a custom color profile and installs it; the whole process takes about 5–10 minutes. Thereafter, your monitor will display all colors more closely to their "true" values. Most modern packages even configure reminders in Windows to recalibrate at regular intervals to accommodate aging displays, changing ambient lighting, and undo inadvertent monitor settings.

If you have two or more monitors, it's not unusual for them to display colors differently, even if they're the same make and model. Color calibration equipment is the only reliable way to adjust your screens so they all display color consistently and accurately. But beware; not all calibration devices support multiple monitor setups. If yours doesn't, you may be able to calibrate your screens individually, changing the default display between each calibration. See Chapter 2 for more multi-monitor tips.

Likewise, you can calibrate a flatbed scanner by scanning a special color key and then having software analyze the scan and produce an appropriate scanner profile. You can calibrate a printer by printing a color key and using a calibration sensor to read it. And you can calibrate your digital camera by shooting photos of a camera-profiling chart and a neutral gray card, and have software analyze the photos.

The Software-Only Approach

While the expense of calibration hardware might be justifiable for professional designers and perfectionist photographers, there are ways of improving the color reproduction of your hardware without spending any money.

If your screen has built-in gamma controls, the simplest method is to go to *http://epaperpress.com/monitorcal/* and adjust your screen by hand. Your goal is to make the individual bars on the *Black Point* and *White Point* test strips distinct and evenly-spaced. Also, the smooth gray patch in the center of the gamma pattern should blend in evenly with the crosshatch pattern when you stand back a few feet.

A better choice, however, is to install gamma-correcting software like Quick-Gamma (Figure 4-13), available for free at *http://quickgamma.de/indexen.html*. (A similar utility also comes with Adobe Photoshop, although the author of QuickGamma claims that QuickGamma is more accurate.) The process essentially involves adjusting a few controls until two different grayish regions appear indistinguishable when you squint. If you have the patience to do so, you can elect to adjust red, green, and blue values independently.

Next, open the Color Management page in Control Panel. Each imaging device on your system should be accompanied by a matching International Color Consortium (ICC) profile, and the Color Management window, shown in Figure 4-14, is where you manage these files.

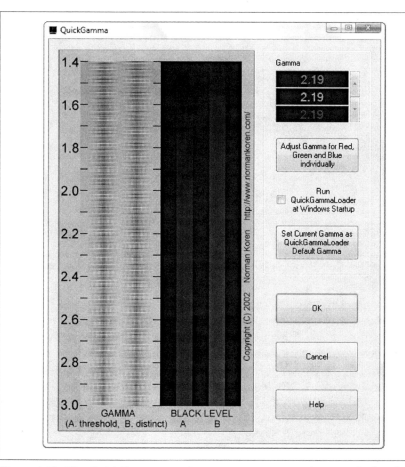

Figure 4-13. Use QuickGamma to adjust your monitor so colors are displayed more accurately

Start with your monitor; select it from the **Device** drop-down list, and then click the **Add** button. If you're lucky, you'll see an appropriate profile (the file having been installed with your driver); otherwise, you'll have to dig up the correct ICC profile from the manufacturer of your monitor and then install it by clicking the **Browse** button.

 If you have trouble finding ICC profiles from the manufacturers of your monitor, scanner, printer, or camera, try a site like Chromix (*http://www.chromix.com*) or IPhotoICC (*http://www.littlecms.com/downloads.htm*). Of course, you can also search Google for your specific product and model, like this: Epson 1520 ICC.

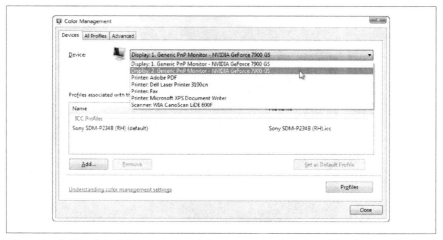

Figure 4-14. The Color Management window is a new, central interface for installing and configuring ICC profiles in Windows 7

In some cases, you may find more than one ICC profile for your device, each differentiated with a numeric code like D93 or 6500K. These numbers indicate the *color temperature*, a number that describes the color of light emitted by the light source, specifically a theoretical object called a *blackbody radiator*. (In the real world, the closest analogy is the sun.) The K numbers indicate temperatures in degrees Kelvin (e.g., 5000K, 6500K, 9300K) while the D numbers indicate standard illuminants (colors of light) corresponding to specific correlated color temperatures (CCT). If in doubt, choose 5000K or D50, both of which correspond to "soft daylight."

When the new ICC profile shows up in the **Profiles associated with this device list**, highlight it and click **Set as Default Profile**.

When you're done with your monitor, repeat the process for your printer(s) and scanner(s). In most cases, you'll want to use the same color temperature (D or K value) for each ICC profile you use.

Now, your digital camera does things a little differently. If it's like most cameras, it should store the appropriate ICC information in the EXIF data (discussed in the next section) embedded into each photo file you shoot. And most high-end applications, such as modern versions of Adobe Photoshop, should be capable of reading these tags and putting them to use. But in the unlikely event that your camera is included in the **Device** list, and you have an ICC profile provided by your camera's manufacturer, then you can go ahead and install it just like the others.

Now, playing with gamma correction and color profiles will only take you so far. Variations in ink or toner, as well as paper, can all affect color reproduction on a printer, and the lighting in your room can affect how color looks on your monitor, so you'll have to employ a little trial and error to get the desired results. If you can't get satisfactory color with free tools, it's time to move up to a colorimeter.

Sort Photos Chronologically

Let me guess. You just had this big party (say, a wedding or commitment ceremony), and you've gotten hundreds of photos from a dozen different people. But when you stick them all in the same folder and sort them by date, they're all out of order.

The **Date Modified** column in Windows Explorer (go to **View→ Details** if you don't see it) probably won't reliably sort your photos. If the photographer did any post-processing (e.g., color correction, cropping, retouching) in a program like Photoshop, file dates will reflect the last time the files were saved, not when the photos were originally shot.

But aren't you lucky you live in an enlightened age of obsessive photographers and feature-laden gadgets? Embedded in each digital photo is a goldmine of information stored by the camera as part of the EXIF (EXchangeable Image File) format used in *.jpg* files, *.tif* files, and raw formats like Nikon's *.nef* files. EXIF data includes the date and time the photo was taken, the camera settings used (f-stop, exposure, metering mode), the photographer's name (sometimes), and the dimensions of the image. If the camera supports it, even GPS data indicating the exact geographical location of the camera when the photo was shot can be included.

To view EXIF data for a single photo, highlight the image file in Windows Explorer, and then stretch the **Details** pane until it looks like Figure 4-15. If you don't see a **Details** pane, click the **Organize** drop-down and select **Layout→Details Pane**.

If you select more than one file, Explorer will only show the data the selected files have in common in the **Details** pane. To view selective EXIF data for a bunch of photos at once, right-click the column header bar in Windows Explorer and select **More**. Place a checkmark next to any new details you'd like to display, and click OK. Unfortunately, the details aren't organized at all here; the EXIF data is mixed in with MP3 tags, and other things like **Search ranking** and **Parental rating reason**. But with a little digging, you should be able to find the relevant bits, like **Dimensions**, **Camera model**, and, thankfully, **Date Picture Taken.**

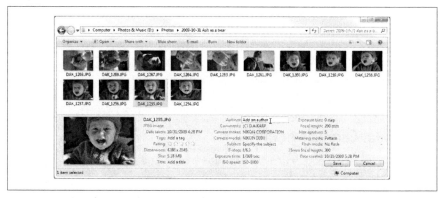

Figure 4-15. Windows Explorer shows all the EXIF information embedded in your digital photos, if you know where to look

 Of course, you won't find EXIF data in scans of film, nor in digital photos that were modified by software that doesn't support the format. For the record, recent versions of Adobe Photoshop and Paint Shop Pro, and even Windows' measly little Paint program, retain all EXIF data in most circumstances, but many older programs and image converters don't. If in doubt, run a test before you modify any precious photos: open a photo in your program and save it to a new filename. If the information shows up in Windows Explorer when you highlight the new file, then your software is safe to use.

Now, sort the photos chronologically by clicking the **Date Picture Taken** column header. Voilà!

But what if you want to make this sorting more permanent? Use the free Stamp utility (*http://www.snapfiles.com/get/stamp.html*) to rename your files with their EXIF dates. After you do this, your photos will appear in chronological order even when sorted *alphabetically*.

What Stamp doesn't do, unfortunately, is allow you to compensate for the differences among the various cameras' internal clocks. The discrepancies might be as small as three or four minutes among your local guests, or several hours for the party guest who last set up his or her camera in a different time zone. As a result, your photos won't sort properly even *after* you use Stamp, a problem requiring the following fix:

1. First, download the free trial of Creative Element Power Tools (available at *http://www.creativelement.com/powertools/*), and turn on the **Change file dates** and **Rename files with ease** options.

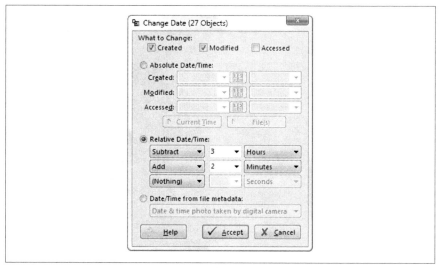

*Figure 4-16. Use the **Change Date** tool to fix discrepancies among the times of different photographers' digital photos*

2. Highlight all the photos you want to fix, right-click, and select **Change Date**.

3. Choose the **Date/Time from file metadata** option, select **Date & time photo taken by digital camera** from the list, and then click **Accept**. This will change all the file dates so they exactly match the dates and times the photos were taken.

4. Next, you'll need to determine the discrepancies among your photographers. Pick one photographer to use as the baseline, and then figure out how far off every other photographer is from that baseline. To do this, you'll need to find common points of reference: one or two representative photos of the same instant by each of your photographers. (The more photos you have, the easier this will be.) After a minute or so of studying, you might find that, say, Kathryn's camera was about 3 hours faster than the baseline, while Henry's camera was 6 minutes, 11 seconds slower. (If you're not as compulsive as I am, you don't necessarily need to get it down to the exact second.)

5. To fix the dates, pick a photographer (other than the baseline you chose in step 4), and highlight all of that person's photos. Right-click the files and select **Change Date**.

6. This time, choose the **Relative Date/Time** option and then make your adjustments with the controls below, like the example in Figure 4-16. Click **Accept** when you're done.

7. Repeat steps 5 and 6 for everyone else's photos. When you're done, the photos should be in perfect order when sorted by **Modified Date** (but not **Date Taken**, at least not yet).

8. [Optional] To update the EXIF data with your new dates, use Attribute-Magic Pro (*http://www.attributemagic.com/*). Select the recently modified files in the main window, use the **Change Dates** feature, and instruct it to set **date taken (exif)** to **modified (file system)**.

> If you don't feel comfortable messing with your photos' valuable EXIF tags, you can alternatively change only the *filenames*, as described next.

At this point, all your photos should appear in chronological order when sorted by modified date *or* date taken, but depending on what you plan to do with your pictures, this may not be enough.

Are you uploading your photos to an online photo sharing/printing service? Or perhaps you're handing them off to someone else to sift through and possibly modify them? If you want to make sure your careful date manipulations remain intact, you may want to tag your filenames as well.

You can do this with Stamp, as described earlier, but only if you've updated the EXIF dates as described in step 8. But if you want to rename your photos *without* changing any EXIF data, you'll need Power Rename (also part of Creative Element Power Tools) to tag the filenames with their *modified dates*. To do this, highlight all the photos, right-click, and select **Power Rename**.

> If you've already renamed the photos with Stamp, place a checkmark next to Power Rename's **Crop** option, select **from beginning**, and type a number representing the amount of text to remove. This will get rid of Stamp's addition to the filename and make room for Power Rename's own **Add stamp** feature.

In Power Rename, place a checkmark next to the **Add stamp** option, select **file date & time**, and then click the **Format** button. From the **Choose a format** list, select **Custom format** and then use the date/time placeholders from the list to assemble a date format conducive to sorting. Your best bet is to start with the year (yy or yyyy), followed by the month, day, hour, minute, and finally, the second, like this:

```
yyyy-mm-dd_hh-mm-ss
```

For example, Power Rename would take a file with the date *August 28, 2005 at 4:53:06 pm* and add this to the beginning of the filename:

    2005-08-28_16-53-06

Click OK and then the **Accept** button to rename the files. With all your photos date- and time-corrected and renamed accordingly, they'll appear in chronological order in almost any circumstance.

Media Center Hacks

Windows Media Center, included with every edition of Windows 7, allows you to use your PC and some sort of TV tuner card as a DVR (Digital Video Recorder). Commonly known as a TiVo (just as a *novelty flying disc* is commonly known as a Frisbee), a DVR lets you pause, rewind, and record live television broadcasts.

> Want to watch your Media Center content remotely, say, on your cell phone? All you need is DLNA-compliant software (or hardware) to interface with Windows Media Player, which is fully DLNA-compliant for the first time in Windows 7. Also available is TVMOBiLi (*http://www.tvmobili.com*), which lets you share any media on your network with other DLNA-equipped devices.

Of course, you don't have to stick with the bundled Windows Media Center (WMC) software. If you don't like the program, if it crashes too often, or if it doesn't like your tuner card or remote control, there are many alternatives. Free DVR software includes GB-PVR (*http://www.gbpvr.com*) and MediaPortal (*http://mediaportal.sourceforge.net*). Commercial products, while not necessarily better than their free counterparts, include SnapStream BeyondTV (*http://www.snapstream.com*) and SageTV (*http://www.sage.tv?*).

Watch TV on Your TV

Unless you enjoy watching television on your tiny laptop screen while Windows hassles you about updates waiting to be installed, you probably want to hook up your Media Center PC to a real television set. Unfortunately, this is not always as easy as it sounds.

An alternative to hooking your PC directly up to a television set is to use a Media Center Extender, a small box that streams recorded video from your PC over your wireless network and connects directly to your TV. Among other things, this means you can put your PC in a different room, and along with it the blinking lights and the whirr of your PC fan that can spoil a good movie. See the section "Add DVDs to Your Movie Library" on page 253 for a way to create a virtual DVD library and use extenders to bring it to every TV in the house.

When you connect a TV to your computer (or is it the other way around?), you should see your entire desktop, Start menu, et al., on the big screen. If you see nothing at all, your video card's TV port may be disabled. If you're using a laptop, you may have to press a special keystroke combination to "activate" the TV-out and external VGA ports. On some Dell laptops, for instance, hold the **Fn** key while pressing **F8** to switch between the internal display, the external display, and both; consult your computer's documentation for details. Press these keys repeatedly until you see a picture.

 If you see everything *except* the video rectangle on the big screen, then you have a video overlay problem. See "Fix Other Playback Problems" on page 202 for details.

Next, make sure you're using the right kind of cable, and with cabling, there's certainly no shortage of possibilities.

The first rule of mating a PC to a TV is to keep it all digital, if you can. If your PC has a DVI or HDMI port (standard on all new desktop PCs and many new laptops) and you have a high-definition television set, you can do precisely that.

If your computer doesn't have a DVI port, you'll need to replace your video card with one that does. If you're using a laptop, you'll need a DVI-equipped video card for your ExpressCard slot (or PC Card, if it's an older model), and these can be *very* spendy.

Now, any modern HD television set will either have a DVI or HDMI plug (tired of acronyms yet?). Depending on what comes out of your PC, you might need a DVI-to-HDMI converter, which sell for a couple of bucks online. (Hint: look on eBay.)

As you're setting up your nifty, all-digital home theater PC system, you may hit a roadblock in the form of HDCP (High-bandwith Digital Content Protection). HDCP is a nasty form of copy protection imposed upon high-definition content, such as that from an HD DVD or Blu-Ray drive, or HD cable signal. If your television or video card is of the older variety, it may be the reason you're getting a black screen instead of the movie you're trying to play. To fix the problem without replacing your equipment, you can either install a "HDCP stripper" or downgrade to an analog signal.

If your TV has no digital video inputs—or if they're already being used—your next best option is to use a DVI-to-component adapter (a.k.a. YPbPr, or Green/Blue/Red). Although your TV's component inputs are analog (not digital), they do support 16:9 wide format and progressive-scan video, which will still look a lot better than S-Video or (gasp) RCA composite connectors.

Many HDTVs have only a single digital (HDMI or DVI) input, which may already be occupied (if you're lucky) by a DVD player with a digital output. If you don't want to settle for an analog connection between your PC and TV, you'll need a HDMI or DVI switch, the best examples of which can be found in newer digital home theater receivers.

If your TV is not high-def, or if for whatever reason digital just isn't going to work, then you've got to go analog.

If your PC has a TV-out port, it might accept a standard S-Video plug, or barring that, an ordinary RCA plug. (If it has a proprietary connector, you may need a special adapter from your PC manufacturer—at extra cost, of course.)

If your computer lacks a dedicated TV-out port, see whether your TV has a 15-pin analog VGA port, in which case you can simply use a VGA-to-VGA cable and connect your TV like a monitor. Otherwise, your PC may support TV-out directly through its VGA port (an admittedly uncommon feature), in which case you can get a VGA-to-RCA or VGA-to-S-Video adapter pretty cheaply online.

So, to sum up, here are the connection methods you can try, in order from best to worst.

Computer side	Television side	Signal	16:9 supported?
DVI	DVI or HDMI	Digital	Yes
DVI	component	Analog	Yes
DVI-A or VGA	VGA	Analog	No
S-Video	S-Video	Analog	No
RCA	RCA/composite	Analog	No

Once you've got the cabling in order, the next step is to set the resolution on your PC to optimize the picture quality. Set it too low, and it'll look fuzzy and pixelated; set it too high, and you might have *overscanning* problems (where the video runs off the screen). If in doubt, try a few standard resolutions until you have one that looks good. For a widescreen TV, use a widescreen resolution like 1280×768 (768p) or 1800×1080 (1080p); for old-style 4:3 screens, 1024×768 usually works pretty well. If you still have trouble, use PowerStrip (*http://entechtaiwan.net/util/ps.shtm*) to find the optimal resolution and timing settings for your TV.

When you have a signal on your TV, open up Media Center and go to **Tasks→Settings→General→Windows Media Center Setup→Configure Your TV or Monitor** and follow the prompts.

Watch Hulu in Media Center

Media Center supports two kinds of streaming video right out of the box: Internet TV and Netflix, in the TV and Movies sections, respectively. (Internet TV is free, while Netflix requires a paid Netflix account.) But neither service offers the breadth of current and classic television shows that you can watch for free at *http://hulu.com*.

Although you can't actually watch Hulu programming from *within* Media Center, you can do the next best thing with the free Hulu Desktop Integration utility (*http://huluwmc.teknowebworks.com/*). Once installed, a Hulu entry appears in Media Center's main menu (see Figure 4-17); select it with your remote control to close Media Center and open Hulu Desktop (also free at *http://www.hulu.com/labs/hulu-desktop*). You can continue to navigate Hulu Desktop with the same remote control; exit Hulu, and Media Center starts back up.

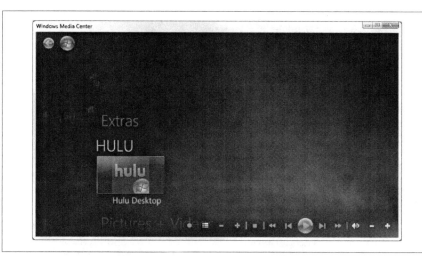

Figure 4-17. Watch Hulu content from Windows Media Center

Of course, it's not as ideal as watching other TV or movies in Media Center (you can't slip back to the Media Center menu while Hulu plays in the background), but it does allow quick switching between the two players without putting down your remote.

 Note that you don't need the Hulu Desktop Integration utility to watch Hulu outside of a browser; your Media Center remote will work with Hulu Desktop regardless. Another way to watch Hulu is with Boxee (http://boxee.tv/), which pulls together your own music and video content, YouTube, and many other online streaming media sources.

Hulu Desktop Integration only works if you install it to the default folder suggested by the installer, although this may be fixed by the time you read this. Also, Hulu Desktop Integration won't send Hulu content to Media Center extenders.

Add DVDs to Your Movie Library

Whether you've connected your PC directly to a TV or you're using an Media Center Extender, it's hard to pass up the opportunity to combine your multi-terabyte hard disk and your vast DVD library. Why mess with a mechanical DVD/Blu-Ray jukebox (or, gasp, have to walk across the room and put discs in the tray by hand), when you can store all your movies on your hard disk and access them with a few clicks of the remote?

If you're going to be storing a bunch of movies on your hard disk, you might get to the point where you care about how much free disk space you have. If you're also recording live TV with Media Center, you may want to limit the disk space it uses by going to **Tasks→Settings→TV→Recorder→Recorder Storage**.

There are a few ways to add movies to your Media Center Library. The most straightforward method involves creating ordinary video files (e.g., *.wmv*, *.mpg*, *.avi*) from DVDs and then accessing them through **Movies→movie library**; unfortunately, movies encoded this way may not work with your Media Center Extender.

A typical DVD rips to a video file of about 800 MB, which means you can store more than 1,200 movies per terabyte of storage. Here's how you do it:

1. Using DVD ripper software, like Handbrake (*http://handbrake.fr/*) or DVDx (*http://sourceforge.net/projects/dvdx/*), save your movies to a folder on your hard disk.
2. In the Media Center menu, select **Tasks→Settings→Media Libraries**.
3. Choose **Movies** and click **Next**.
4. Choose **Add folders to the library** and click **Next**.
5. Choose whether your videos are stored on the local PC or another PC on the network, click **Next**, and then navigate the tree to locate the folder (or folders) containing your videos. Place a checkmark next to each folder you'd like to include, and then click **Next**.
6. Select **Yes**, use these locations and then click **Finish**.

Thereafter, your movies will appear under **Movies→movie library**. Any new movies you add to the folders specified in step 4 will appear in your movie library automatically.

 Alternatively, you can use VideoReDo (*http://www.videoredo.com/*) to convert VIDEO_TS folders from ripped DVDs to .DVR-MS files that Media Center recognizes as recorded TV. This offers many of the advantages of the second solution, next, with the simplicity of the first solution.

There are several drawbacks to compressing your movies into *.avi* or *.mpg* files. For one, you lose the DVD menus, supplemental audio tracks, and special features. Recompressing also takes a lot of time, and if you have a lot of DVDs, that time adds up fast. Finally, most DVD rippers use video codecs not supported by Windows Media Extenders, so you may not be able to play your movies on your TV after all. One way to get the full DVD experience with WMC (admittedly at the expense of considerable amounts of disk space), is to copy the *VIDEO_TS* folders from your DVDs to your hard disk, and then use a transcoder *.dll* and a special plugin to connect them to Media Center. Problem is, there's no readily available transcoder that works with Windows 7 at the time of this writing. So, until one is released, try converting your video to the *.mkv* format; you can use the Haali Media Splitter (*http://www.videohelp.com/tools/Haali_Media_Splitter*) to add *.mkv* playback support to Media Player and Media Center, although your Extender may unfortunately still not be able to play *.mkv* files.

Optical Storage Annoyances

By most reckoning, optical media is dead. Sales of online digital music is growing while CDs are becoming scarce. Movies and TV shows are streamed online, often for free, raising questions about the usefulness of DVD (not to mention its late-to-the-game replacement, Blu-Ray). And why pay several dollars apiece for single-use 8.7GB dual-layer DVDs when you can get 32GB flash memory drives that can be used again and again?

And yet music is frequently less expensive when purchased on CD—particularly used—and DVDs are ubiquitous. There's no better choice right now for archiving lots of data (like thousands of digital photos) for long-term storage. It's typically more convenient to send gigabytes of data on a disc through postal mail than it is to struggle with online file-sharing services. And let's not forget Windows itself, which comes on DVD.

Burning Discs

The first CD burner I ever saw was the size of a small microwave oven. It took 68 minutes to fill a 68-minute CD, and it produced more coasters than Six Flags. Suffice it to say, things have improved, although it's a shame it's taken this long. Windows 7 is the first version of Windows to include disc-burning features in Windows Explorer that actually work. (Show me a CD-R with readable data created by Windows Vista or XP and I'll eat my hat.)

Here's how it works:

1. Open Windows Explorer.
2. Place a blank disc in your burner, and close the drawer.

3. Highlight your CD/DVD drive in the tree, and the Burn a Disc window appears.

4. Name your new disc by typing up to 16 characters in the **Disc title** field [optional].

5. Select **With a CD/DVD player**.

 The first option here, **Like a USB flash drive**, is misleading. This selection instructs Windows to format the disc with the *Live File System*, Microsoft's name for the UDF (Universal Disk Format) "packet writing" filesystem. UDF was invented to address the frustrations of traditional CD burning programs that required you to assemble a list of all the files on a disc before you commence burning. But in Windows 7, you can drag files at your leisure, so it hardly makes a difference. Plus, despite Microsoft's description in this window, UDF discs are *not* reliably readable in Windows XP without additional software; you'll need Vista or later if you want to count on using this disc after you're done with it here. To make a disc readable anywhere, choose the second option, **With a CD/DVD player**.

6. In the empty root folder of your new disc, you should see either "Files Ready to Be Written to the Disc" or "Drag files to this folder to add them to the disc." In either case, you can treat this like any other drive: drag files onto it, create folders, and even delete.

 Windows doesn't actually write any data to your disc until you click **Burn to disc** in the next step. Instead, it stores all dropped files in a temporary folder on your hard disk. You can clear the temporary folder, thereby resetting the disc project, by clicking the **Delete temporary files** button on the task ribbon at the top of Windows Explorer. (You can choose where temporary files are stored by right-clicking your optical drive and selecting Properties and then choosing the **Recording** tab. For this reason, you should never "move" files to a CD or DVD, but rather only copy them. If needed, you can delete the source files after you've burned the disc.

7. When you're done, click the **Burn to disc** button on the task ribbon at the top of Windows Explorer and follow the prompts to complete the burn.

If you're lucky, you'll get a disc with your data on it. Eject it and then pop it back in to confirm your data is there. (If it still says "Files Ready to Be Written to the Disc" or "Drag files to this folder to add them to the disc," click the **Delete temporary files** button; if your data remains, it's on the disc.)

No luck with Windows' built-in burning? Here are some alternatives:

Basic data DVD/CD burning
> Try Express Burn (*http://www.nch.com.au/burn/*), Ashampoo Burning Studio (*http://www.ashampoo.com/*), PowerISO (*http://www.poweriso .com/?*), or Nero Lite (*http://www.nero.com/*).

Audio CD
> Use Windows Media Player or Apple iTunes to create a custom playlist and then burn the playlist to a disc.

DVD Movies
> You can make DVD movies from your TV recordings within Windows Media Center, or burn edited movies from within Windows Live Movie Maker (the latter being a free download from within Windows Update).

ISO Image Files
> Although not available through the Start menu, Windows 7 includes the Windows Disc Image Burner (*isoburn.exe*). Right-click any *.iso* file, select **Open With**, and then pick **Windows Disc Image Burner** from the list.
>
> You can also use ISO Recorder (free; *http://isorecorder.alexfeinman.com*) or PowerISO (*http://www.poweriso.com/*) to burn discs from ISO image files, as well as create ISO files *from* discs.

 Don't want to waste a disc? Try mounting an ISO as a virtual drive instead, and access its files in Windows Explorer as though it were a physical disc. Programs that can do this include Virtual CloneDrive (free, *http://www .slysoft.com/*) and MagicISO (free, *http://www.magiciso .com/*).

With the proper disc burning software, now all that can go wrong is everything else.

Split Huge Files for Storage

So, you've got 11 GB of data you need to fit on a 4.7 GB DVD (or 1 GB to fit on a 700 MB CD). The obvious solution is to zip up the data, but what if your data isn't compressible?

Zip only takes you so far. If you've got gigabytes worth of videos, pictures, or music you want to put on a disc, zipping them up won't help.

The solution is to use the RAR file format, for which you'll need a program like WinRAR (*http://www.rarlab.com/*). RAR works like zip, but it can provide better compression with "solid archives" and can conveniently split large amounts of data into more-manageable chunks.

In WinRAR, navigate to the folder containing the files you want to archive. Click **Add** and then choose an archive filename. Turn on the **Create solid archive** option, and then from the **Split to volumes** list, select either **CD700: 700 mb** or **DVD+R: 4481 mb**. When you're ready, click OK, and WinRAR will get to work.

When it's done, you'll have one or more large files that will fit nicely on one or more discs. Just include a copy of the WinRAR program on one of the discs so you can extract your files easily when you need to.

Stop Windows 7 from Burning Discs

There's no question that having CD/DVD burning built-in to Windows Explorer is convenient, at least when it works. But if you primarily use a third-party burning application, Windows' offers to format a blank disc can be a nuisance. Here's how to disable CD Burning in Windows Explorer:

1. Open the Group Policy Editor (*gpedit.msc*); if you're using Windows Home Premium and you don't have the Group Policy Editor, see below.
2. Expand the branches to `User Configuration\Administrative Templates \Windows Components\Windows Explorer`.
3. In the right pane, double click the **Remove CD Burning features** entry.
4. Click **Enabled** and then click OK.
5. The change should take effect immediately. Open Windows Explorer, right-click your CD/DVD burner, and select **Properties**. Confirm the normally-present **Recording** tab is no longer there.

To re-enable CD/DVD burning, return to the **Remove CD Burning features** window in Group Policy Editor, and select **Not Configured**.

If you don't have Group Policy Editor, open Registry Editor (see Chapter 3) and expand the branches to `HKEY_CURRENT_USER\Software\Microsoft\Windows\CurrentVersion\Policies\Explorer`. Create a new DWORD (32-bit) value named `NoCDBurning` and double-click it to set its value data to 1.

CHAPTER 5

Performance

Windows 7 is, shockingly, the first version of Windows to actually outperform its predecessor. Isn't that one of the signs of the apocalypse?

7 starts faster, opens applications faster, and shuts down faster than Vista ever did. It even outperforms XP on the same hardware.

Traditionally, Microsoft adds more features (and more bloat) to each successive Windows release, betting that the hardware—processors, memory, chipsets—will always improve quickly enough to catch up. But at best, this means that performance is more likely to plateau rather than improve, and that's only if we consumers buy the latest high-end machines each time a new version of Windows comes out.

Perhaps the long delay between the releases of XP and Vista made us all so complacent as to assume that Vista wouldn't be any slower than XP. Perhaps that's why Windows 7 seems so fast by comparison. But try loading Windows 95 on a Windows 7-class PC, and it will make 7 seem like a lumbering ox. Better yet, consider the Google Chrome OS, which is said to boot in under seven seconds.

Some of Windows 7's magic performance reversal is simply sleight of hand. Windows Explorer in 7 loads up more quickly only because it no longer sorts the active folder right away, whereas Vista waited to sort the files before showing you anything. Either way, you're waiting.

But why the wait at all?

The short answer is that Windows 7 has been given more to do. On the surface, there's the Glass interface, covered later, which certainly sucks up a lot of processor cycles. And then there's the improved file copy confirmation windows (covered in Chapter 2) and UAC to review permissions, both of which add to the overhead and bog down file copying in 7. Add to that more robust indexing service, also discussed in Chapter 2, which keeps your hard disk busy much of the time, and all those convenient auto-updaters running in memory checking for big fixes to download.

The solution is to give Windows less to do, and in places where you're not willing to compromise features, give Windows the edge it needs to handle those tasks more quickly. That's what this chapter is about.

Trim the Fat

Surprise: Windows 7 is not configured for optimal performance right out of the box. Rather, it was built to showcase all the features Microsoft included with the product to help sell it.

Fortunately, there are a bunch of things you can do right now to speed things up without spending a dime.

Tame Mindless Animation and Display Effects

Windows 7 animates almost every visual component that makes up its sparkling interface. While these affectations may impress the kids, they create two performance problems. For one, they slow down the motion of visual elements, causing windows, menus, and listboxes to take longer to open and close, all of which makes your PC feel sluggish even when it isn't. Second, they consume CPU cycles that would otherwise be used to open applications, generate icon previews in Windows Explorer, load complex web pages, and handle processor-intensive tasks.

There are settings that affect performance scattered throughout Windows, but the ones that control display effects are the easiest to change, and go the furthest to make Windows feel faster and more responsive.

In Control Panel, open System, and click the **Advanced system settings** link on the left side (or run *SystemPropertiesAdvanced.exe*). In the **Performance** section, click **Settings**. The **Visual Effects** tab, shown in Figure 5-1, contains 20 settings, all explained later.

Unfortunately, the four selections above the list are a bit misleading. For example, the **Let Windows choose what's best for my computer** option

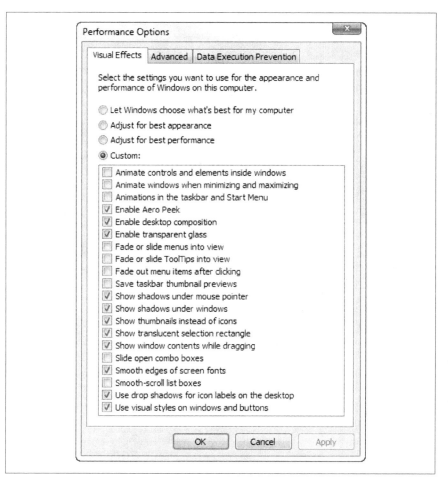

Figure 5-1. The Performance Options window is a good place to start looking for fat to trim

reverts all settings to the defaults chosen by a marketing committee at Microsoft to best showcase Windows' features. The **Adjust for best appearance** option simply enables all features in the list, while the **Adjust for best performance** option just disables them.

Now, depending on the prowess of your video hardware, some of these settings may make more of a difference than others.

Animate controls and elements inside windows

Turn this off to nix the slow-fade effect on buttons and tabs in dialog boxes, the cyclic pulsating effect on the default button, and the fading scrollbar arrows. Buttons will still glow blue as you roll over them with the mouse, but they'll do it sans the delay.

Animate windows when minimizing and maximizing

This controls the squeezing and stretching that happens to windows when you minimize, restore, and maximize them. Leave it on to see where a window went when you minimize it, or turn it off to make windows pop into position when you minimize, maximize, and restore.

 This option also affects the disappearing/reappearing taskbar if you have both the **Auto-hide the taskbar** setting in Taskbar and Start Menu Properties and the **Show window contents while dragging** option (described later) enabled.

Animations in the taskbar and Start Menu

This controls the animated jump lists (see Chapter 2), fading task thumbnail previews, and the sliding taskbar buttons. Turn it off to speed up the taskbar. This setting was named **Slide taskbar buttons** in earlier versions of Windows.

Enable Aero Peek

When you hover your mouse over a taskbar button for a running application, a small preview of the window appears just above the taskbar. If you then hover the mouse over the preview, all the visible windows become translucent except for the one you're previewing. The same thing happens if you press **Alt-Tab** repeatedly and then hesitate on one window.

This also enables or disables the **Preview desktop with Aero Peek** option in the **Taskbar** tab of the Taskbar and Start Menu Properties window, which makes all windows translucent when you hover your mouse over the (blank) **show desktop** button at the far end of the taskbar so you can see the desktop.

Since this feature is only used when you hover in certain places, leaving it enabled shouldn't give you a noticeable performance hit unless you have older video hardware. Turn it off if Windows seems to stumble whenever you use Aero Peek, or if you just find it annoying.

Enable desktop composition

This vaguely named option is one of the more substantial performance drains you can adjust here, but it's required if you want the glass effect (see "Get Glass" on page 286). *Desktop composition* is the behind-the-scenes scheme—run by the Desktop Window Manager (DWM)—that keeps a snapshot of each open window in memory. Turn it off, and Windows draws each window directly to the screen just like XP and earlier versions did. Without it, you can't have the Glass interface or the thumbnail previews on the taskbar and Alt-Tab window, but the Windows interface will feel snappier and more responsive.

Enable transparent glass

One of the few self-explanatory options here, this option is covered in "Get Glass" on page 286.

Fade or slide menus into view / Fade or slide ToolTips into view

Turn these options off to have menus and tooltips "snap" open; leave it on if you prefer to wait for menus to open. See the sidebar "Fade or Slide" if you leave this option enabled and wish to choose whether menus fade or slide into view.

 By default, there is a short delay between the instant you click a menu and the moment the menu actually opens; see "Make Menus More Mindful" on page 269 to adjust this.

Fade or Slide

In previous versions of Windows, you could choose whether animated menus faded or slid open when you clicked them. In Windows 7, the setting is absent from the GUI, with only the **Fade or slide menus into view** and **Fade or slide ToolTips into view** options to turn on or off animation in general.

To choose how menus are animated, open the Registry Editor (see Chapter 3) and navigate to `HKEY_CURRENT_USER\Control Panel\Desktop`. Double-click the `UserPreferencesMask` value, and you'll see a series of eight two-digit numbers. The second number controls this setting:

- Enter `28` for the slide effect
- Enter `3E` for the fade effect
- Enter `32` to disable sliding and fading altogether

Since `UserPreferencesMask` is a binary value, you'll have to be careful to replace the existing number with the new value rather than insert it, shifting all the subsequent values to the right.

When you're done, you'll need to log out and then log back in for this change to take effect.

Fade out menu items after clicking

This imposes less of a performance drain than its companion setting, **Fade or slide menus into view**, but it can slow down windows nonetheless if left enabled.

Show taskbar thumbnail previews

This affects the small previews that appear when you hover your mouse over taskbar buttons for running applications; see **Enable Aero Peek**, earlier, for a related setting.

Show shadows under mouse pointer / Show shadows under windows

These two settings have negligible effect on the performance of most Windows 7-class PCs.

Show thumbnails instead of icons

This one affects performance in Windows Explorer more than any other. It takes a lot of processor power to open all the media files in a folder and generate thumbnail images, so if you turn it off, you'll be able to open folder windows much more quickly. Among other things, thumbnail generation is usually responsible for the slowly moving green progress bar in Windows Explorer's address bar, so you should definitely turn this off if you don't care about thumbnails for your images, videos, and PDF files.

 If an installer window appears briefly or if Windows Explorer crashes each time you view a folder full of video files, it means that one of your video codecs is damaged. Turn off the **Show thumbnails instead of icons** option to bypass the problem, or see the section "Get Videos to Play" on page 195, to fix it.

Show translucent selection rectangle

The translucent selection rectangle—referred to as a "rubber band" in Chapter 2—is what you see when you drag the mouse and make a box to select multiple files in Windows Explorer and on your desktop. It should have no discernable effect on performance, but since it uses alpha channels (an advanced function provided by your display driver), you may want to turn this off if you have an older video card or suspect a buggy display driver.

Show window contents while dragging

Turn off this option to show gray window outlines when moving and resizing windows; consider it a throwback to the early days of Windows. You probably won't notice much of a performance hit with this feature turned on, unless you're using the Glass interface on a PC with a weak graphics engine (display card). In fact, Windows may seem *more* responsive with this feature enabled, since it allows the interface to respond immediately to dragging and resizing.

Slide open combo boxes

This option controls the animation of drop-down listboxes, similar to the **Fade or slide menus** option described earlier. Turn it off to have listboxes pop open.

Smooth edges of screen fonts

Using a process called anti-aliasing, Windows fills in the jagged edges of larger text on the screen with gray pixels, making the edges appear smooth. Turn off this option to slightly improve the speed at which larger fonts are drawn on the screen, although the speed difference shouldn't be noticeable on any modern PC.

If you're using a flat-panel display (laptop or otherwise), you may find text slightly more difficult to read if font smoothing is turned on. But before you simply turn it off, try the alternate anti-aliasing method. Open the Display page in Control Panel and click the **Adjust ClearType text** link on the left to open the ClearType Text Tuner. Place a checkmark next to **Turn on ClearType**, and then click **Next** to find the settings that make text most readable on your display.

Smooth-scroll list boxes

Despite the fact that they don't open or close, ordinary listboxes are animated, too. If you've ever noticed a listbox that scrolls slowly, this option is the reason; turn it off to make listboxes scroll faster.

There's a nearly identical option in Internet Explorer that makes web pages scroll more slowly. In IE, click the **Tools** drop-down, select **Internet Options**, and then choose the **Advanced** tab. At the end of the **Browsing** section, turn off the **Use smooth scrolling** option and click **OK**.

Use drop shadows for icon labels on the desktop

This setting affects more than just the shadows behind icon captions; it makes the text background transparent. If you're using desktop wallpaper (as opposed to a solid color background), and you turn off this option, small swaths of the current solid background color will show through the captions of your desktop icons.

Use visual styles on windows and buttons

Turn off this setting to make Windows 7's interface look more or less like Windows 98/2000. Another way to accomplish this is to open the Personalization page in Control Panel and choose the **Windows Classic** theme.

That's it for this window; click **Apply** to test your changes, and then OK when you're done.

Shrink desktop icons

Next, if you've noticed that Windows has been slow to update desktop icons, and you have a lot of them, there is a setting that may help. Right-click an empty area of the desktop, select **View**, and then select **Small icons**. Your desktop icons will shrink somewhat, returned to the standard 32×32 pixel size used in earlier versions of Windows. When Windows draws larger icons—**Medium Icons**, the default in 7—it has to stretch most application icons to the new size, and this can take a little time on slower PCs. Of course, the icons included with Windows 7 all come in larger sizes and don't need stretching, but that doesn't apply to Internet Shortcuts and the icons for many programs and documents.

Fine-tune video settings

If you're interested in tinkering further with display settings that can affect performance, right-click an empty area of your desktop, select **Screen resolution** and then click the **Advanced settings** link.

 On older PCs, the speed at which a video card can draw to your screen is somewhat dependent on the current color mode and resolution. If your games, or Windows itself, for that matter, are running slowly, try reducing the color depth and resolution. Newer high end video cards will not show any performance hit when run at higher resolutions or color depths.

In the Advanced settings window, choose the **Troubleshoot** tab and click the **Change settings** button to fine tune some of the performance features of your display driver, all of which vary with the make, model, and driver version. If the **Change settings** button is grayed-out, look for extra tabs in this window; any tab to the right of **Color Management** is a special feature of your display driver, and can be used to change video settings.

Now, most high-end video cards allow you to modify or disable certain 3D features, such as 8-bit palletized textures, gamma adjustment, zbuffer, and bilinear filter. In most cases, these settings won't have any effect on Windows outside 3D games, with the possible exception of the Flip 3D application (**Winkey+Tab**). But look for other features you can turn off, such as custom shortcut menus, special effects for your windows, or a virtual desktop feature, all of which may slow down your PC when enabled.

Make Menus More Mindful

Ever noticed the half-second or so delay between the instant you move the mouse over a menu item and the moment the menu is opened? By default, Windows waits 400 milliseconds (just under a half-second) before opening menus, but if you eliminate the delay, menus will open instantaneously, and your PC will feel a little more alert.

1. Open the Registry Editor (see Chapter 3).
2. Expand the branches to HKEY_CURRENT_USER\Control Panel\Desktop.
3. Double-click the MenuShowDelay value. If it's not there, go to **Edit→New→String Value**, and type MenuShowDelay for the name of the new value.
4. The numeric value you enter here is the number of milliseconds (thousandths of a second) Windows will wait before opening a menu. Enter 0 (zero) here to eliminate the delay completely.

 If you ever have trouble holding your mouse perfectly still, you've probably found it frustrating to navigate menus—particularly those in the Start menu—in Windows 7. Try typing a very large value (65534 is the maximum) here to stop menus from automatically opening altogether, which should make them easier to use.

5. Click OK and close the Registry Editor when you're finished. Log off and then log back in or restart Windows for this change to take effect.

Note that another way to navigate touchy menus is to use the keyboard. In any application, press the **Alt** key by itself to jump to the menu bar—or press **Ctrl-Esc** or the Windows logo key to open the Start menu—and then use the arrow keys to navigate. (Or skip navigation altogether and type the first few letters of a program to launch it.)

To make menus open even more quickly, turn off the **Fade or slide menus into view** and **Fade out menu items after clicking** options covered earlier in this chapter.

Start Windows in Less Time

One of the sure signs of a PC that's been used for more than a few weeks is that it takes a lot longer to start up than when it was new. The longer load time isn't fatigue, nor is it a sign that the PC needs a faster processor; it's a casualty of all the junk that Windows accumulates on a day-to-day basis.

One of the best ways to shorten startup times is to not shut down. Rather, if you put your PC to sleep, as described in "Start Windows Instantly (Almost)" on page 274, you can power it back up in just a few seconds.

Several factors can impact the amount of time it takes for your computer to load Windows and display the desktop so you can start working, not the least of which is anything left over from the previous version of Windows. Since Windows 7 can't be installed over any operating system other than Vista—and then only in certain configurations outlined in Chapter 1—this is much less of an issue than with any of its predecessors. That said, even the accumulation of drivers and applications on a one-virgin Windows 7 installation can eventually slow it down.

If you did install Windows 7 as an in-place upgrade from Vista, some of the old operating system files may've been left behind. While they're isolated and shouldn't cause any problems, they may be consuming several gigabytes of disk space. Run the Disk Cleanup tool (*cleanmgr.exe*) and place a checkmark next to **Files discarded by Windows upgrade** to delete them.

Naturally, wiping your hard disk and reinstalling Windows from scratch is a whole lot easier said than done, so here are some other things you can do to reduce Windows' boot time.

Eliminate unnecessary auto-start programs

Probably the most common thing that slows down Windows' loading time is all of the programs that are configured to load at boot time. Not only do they take a while to load, but they commonly eat up processor cycles while they're running, which in turn causes other programs to load more slowly.

Open the Performance Information and Tools page in Control Panel, and click the **Advanced tools** link on the left. If you see an alert that reads, "Startup programs are causing Windows to start slowly," click the link to view details.

The entry corresponds to a single incident in the event log, in which a particular program took longer to boot than usual. But despite the lone alert here, and its **Date reported** indicating that the incident happened months ago, there may be many similar entries in the log, some more recent than others.

Click the **View details in the event log** link to fire up Event Viewer (*eventvwr.msc*), and then click the **Date and Time** column header to sort the list chronologically. Since delays that happened weeks ago aren't of much concern, focus on those from the last few days. If one program stands out as a repeat offender, try the **Level** column header to group the events by severity.

There's more running on your PC than the handful of icons in the notification area (tray) suggests, and there are several places where startup programs are specified in addition to the *Startup* folder in your Start menu. Check out "Manage Startup Programs" on page 362 for all the places to look.

Make more free disk space

You may not have enough free disk space for your virtual memory (swap file) to operate comfortably. Windows uses part of your hard disk to store portions of memory; the more disk space you devote to your swap file, the easier it will be for Windows to store data there. See "Optimize Virtual Memory and Cache Settings" on page 312 for more information.

The easiest way to create more free disk space is to delete the files on your hard disk that you no longer need; see "If in Doubt, Throw It Out" on page 309 for a safe way to do this.

 See also "Optimize Virtual Memory and Cache Settings" on page 312 and "A Defragmentation Crash Course" on page 304, for other things you can do to speed up your hard drive and help Windows load more quickly.

Lastly, a new hard disk—particularly an SATA 3.0 drive with NCQ (Native Command Queuing) and at least a 32 MB cache—will give you dramatically more disk space and can improve boot time considerably. If you're on the fence about replacing that older drive, consider the performance boost as well as the free space you'd get.

Interested in testing the speed of your hard disk? Check out HD Tune, available for free from *http://www.hdtune.com/*. For help interpreting the results, see *http://www.vistaclues.com/ how-to-test-and-understand-hard-disk-drive-performance/*.

Clean out your Temp folder

Sometimes having too many files in Windows' *Temp* folder can not only slow Windows startup, but in extreme cases, can prevent Windows from loading at all. Windows and your applications use this folder to temporarily store data while you're working with documents. When those applications and documents are closed (or when the applications just crash), they often leave the temporary files behind, and they accumulate quickly.

Out of the box, Windows 7 uses up to four *Temp* folders:

C:\Users\{your_user_name}\AppData\Local\Temp
C:\Users\Default\AppData\Local\Temp
C:\Windows\Temp
C:\Windows\winsxs\Temp

although Windows and your applications primarily use only the first one. To clear out your old temporary files, open Windows Explorer, navigate to the *Temp* folder, and delete anything more than a day old. (Windows won't let you delete any files that are still in use.)

Another way to clear out the *Temp* folder is to use the Disk Cleanup tool (*cleanmgr.exe*); after selecting your Windows drive from the **Drives** list (usually *C:*), select **Temporary files** in the **Files to delete** list, and click OK. Or, if you want your *Temp* folder cleaned automatically, use the **Clear out the Temp folder** tool in Creative Element Power Tools (*http://www.creativele ment.com/powertools/*).

You can change the location of your Temp folder, making it easier to locate and clean out by hand. In Control Panel, open System, click the **Advanced system settings** link, and under the **Advanced** tab, click **Environment Variables**. Underneath the *upper* box, click **New**. Type TEMP for the **Variable name**, put the full path of the folder you'd like to use in the **Variable value** field, and click OK. Do the same thing for the TMP variable (no "E" this time), and then click OK when you're done. Restart Windows for the change to take effect.

Tame antivirus software

Antivirus programs (see Chapter 6) are typically set up to not only load automatically whenever you start Windows, but to check for updates, too. For instance, the otherwise excellent (and free) Avast! Home Edition can completely halt a Windows system for 15–20 seconds while it downloads and installs necessary updates.

While you may not want to stop loading your antivirus software automatically, you can delay it by writing a simple startup script (see Chapter 9) that loads the software after waiting, say, 45 seconds. Or, to delay background services, open the Services window (*services.msc*), double-click a service in the list, and set the **Startup type** to **Automatic (Delayed Start)**. This way, you can start working while your antivirus program loads in the background.

Add more memory

Windows 7 needs at least a gigabyte of memory to run, but 3 GB is better for 32-bit Windows, or 4 GB if you have the 64-bit edition.

Memory prices are always dropping, typically making it remarkably inexpensive to add more RAM to your system, and doing so will *significantly* improve performance across the board. See the section "Make Your Hardware Perform" on page 286 for details.

Networking

Windows polls each active *wired* network connection on your system while it boots your system, and then polls your *wireless* adapter (if you have one) for any networks in range. Each of these steps takes time, so if there are any network adapters on your PC you don't use, you can disable them to speed things up. In the Network and Sharing Center in Control Panel, click **Manage network connections**, and then right-click on each network connection you're not using and select **Disable**.

Next, if you have any permanent mapped network drives (see "Access a Shared Folder Remotely" on page 597) you're not using, open Windows Explorer, right-click any unneeded mapped drives, and select **Disconnect**.

Start Windows Instantly (Almost)

You can optimize Windows all you want, possibly shaving 15 or 20 seconds off your boot time (see the previous topic), or you can approach the problem from a different angle.

All modern PCs support a *Standby* mode that allows you to shut down Windows quickly, and more importantly, start it back up in only a few seconds. Standby is a power-saving mode (known as the S3 sleep state) that maintains power to your system memory and a few other components, while cutting power to your hard disk, monitor, network adapters, and most of the rest of the devices in your PC.

While it looks like it's turned off, a PC in Standby mode still uses some electricity. If you remove the battery from your laptop or unplug your desktop PC while it's in S3 Standby mode, the power to your system memory will be cut, and you will likely lose data (just as though you unplugged it while it was still on).

The *Hibernate* mode (the S4 sleep state) solves the power-off problem by storing an image of your RAM on your hard disk and then shutting down *completely*. This means you can cut power to your desktop PC with a separate power strip or remove the battery from your laptop, and still resume your last Windows session in a fraction of the time it would take to start Windows normally. The downside is that Hibernate takes a little longer to shut down and start up than Standby, and you need a lot more free disk space (at least as much as the amount of RAM in your PC). And then there's the small matter of the Hibernate feature being conspicuously absent (or at least hidden) in Windows 7.

 There's potentially a drawback to using any of these sleep states exclusively, as opposed to shutting down formally. Namely, Windows gets cranky when it has had too much sleep: performance worsens, some features stop working properly, and applications are more prone to crashes. (To be fair, this is less of an issue with Windows 7 than previous versions.) The remedy is to shut down and restart Windows periodically, at least once or twice a week (more for heavy use), which, of course, somewhat negates the overall time saved by employing sleep features in the first place. Alternatively, you may choose to avoid sleeping your PC altogether; you'll enjoy a more stable environment, but you'll lose the convenience of the "instant on" feature.

The solicitude of Sleep

Instead, Windows 7 provides only a hybrid of Standby and Hibernate (discussed next) which Microsoft calls *Sleep* mode. Basically, Sleep puts your PC in the S3 power-saving mode just like Standby, but only after saving the stuff in your PC's memory to disk—somewhat like Hibernate—so you won't lose data if you cut power to your PC.

So, Sleep is the best of both worlds, right?

Not so fast. First of all, Sleep doesn't work that well with some older PCs; cut power to your computer, and Windows may lose the saved state from the last session after all, making it no better than Standby. Second, Sleep doesn't completely power off your PC, which means that it's still using more electricity than it would if it were truly powered off. (Although on laptops, Sleep should eventually put the machine in full-fledged hibernate mode, which uses no power.)

If your Windows session doesn't survive a Sleep, you might not have the hybrid sleep feature enabled. Open the Power Options page in Control Panel, click the **Change plan settings** link next to the currently selected plan, and then click the **Change advanced power settings** link. If necessary, click the **Change settings that are currently unavailable** link. Expand the **Sleep** branch, set the **Allow hybrid sleep** option to **On**, and click OK.

Conversely, if you'd prefer the quickest possible startup and shutdown, and you're willing to give up the benefits of hibernation, set the **Allow hybrid sleep** option to **Off**. This effectively gives Windows a bare Standby feature; just don't be surprised when Windows can't resume your previous session because your PC lost power while it was asleep.

Hibernate, for real this time

If you're not happy with 7's Sleep mode, you can instead use the true *Hibernate* feature that's hidden by default in Windows 7.

 Laptop PCs often employ Hibernation to save your state when the battery gets dangerously low (and you're not using AC power); if this applies to you, Hibernation may already be enabled. On the other hand, if your PC crashes when the battery runs out of juice, or simply can't resume once you plug it back in, you'll need to enable Hibernation to fix the problem.

Performance

Open a Command Prompt window in administrator mode: open the Start menu, type command in the **Search** box, right-click the **Command Prompt** icon that appears, and select **Run as administrator**. Then, type:

```
powercfg /hibernate on
```

at the prompt and press **Enter**. If the command returns you to the prompt with no message, the change was successful, and you can type exit or close the Command Prompt window. The change takes effect right away (see the next sidebar "What Is hiberfil.sys?" for evidence), but you'll need to close and reopen any Power Options windows (next) to see the new options.

What Is hiberfil.sys?

To avoid some of the drawbacks of Windows' Sleep power-saving mode, you can hibernate your PC. As described in "Start Windows Instantly (Almost)" on page 274, Hibernate saves a copy of everything in your PC's memory (RAM) onto your hard disk before it shuts down.

Windows uses the file *hiberfil.sys*, stored in the root folder of your hard disk, to hold your hibernation data. Because it must hold everything in memory, its size is the same as the amount of installed system memory. Have 2 GB of RAM? You'll see a 2 GB *hiberfil.sys* file on your hard disk that Windows won't let you delete.

Windows creates the *hiberfil.sys* file automatically when you turn on the Hibernate feature; the only way to delete the file is to turn off Hibernate.

To do this, open a Command Prompt window in administrator mode (see "The solicitude of Sleep" on page 275 for details) and type this command at the prompt:

```
powercfg /hibernate off
```

Then press **Enter**. If the command returns you to the prompt with no message, the change was successful, and *hiberfil.sys* should be gone.

If *hiberfil.sys* is still there, hibernation may've already been turned off, and the file may be left over from an older version of Windows. Another way to delete the file is to use the Disk Cleanup tool (*cleanmgr.exe*); just select the drive containing the file, place a checkmark next to **Hibernation File Cleaner** in the **Files to delete** list, and click OK.

Put your PC to sleep

The key to using Sleep or Hibernate is to set one of them up as the default action to take when your PC would otherwise be shut down.

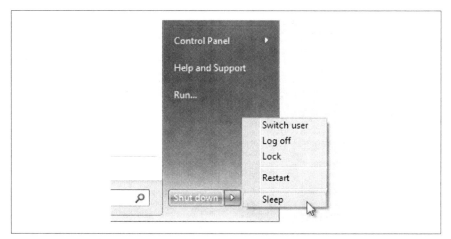

Figure 5-2. Open the Start menu and then click the little arrow to choose how to shut down

Now, regardless of your settings, you can choose to sleep your PC—or for that matter, shut down, restart, or log off—at any time by clicking the tiny arrow next to the **Shut down** button in your Start menu, as shown in Figure 5-2.

You can also change the function of the **Shut down** button itself by right-clicking the button and selecting Properties. From the **Power button action** list, choose either **Switch user**, **Log off**, **Lock**, **Restart**, **Sleep**, or **Shut down**.

But why stop there? You can also change what happens when you press the physical power button on your PC or close the lid. Open the Power Options page in Control Panel, and click the **Change plan settings** link next to the currently selected plan. Next, click the **Change advanced power settings** link to open the Advanced Settings window, and then expand the **Power buttons and lid** branch (Figure 5-3). If necessary, click the **Change settings that are currently unavailable** link (see "Control User Account Control" on page 569 to get rid of this last step).

The options and choices vary depending on your PC's capabilities, but in most cases, you should see at least **Power button action**, which refers to your PC's physical power switch, and **Sleep button action** (whether or not your keyboard or PC has a formal **Sleep** button, which looks like a crescent moon), and **Lid close action** if you're using a laptop.

At most, you'll see four choices under each option: **Do nothing**, **Sleep**, **Hibernate**, and **Shut down**. The **Hibernate** option only appears if hibernation is turned on, as described in the previous section. And if you don't see the **Sleep** option, your BIOS or video driver may not support it. Finally, the **Do nothing** option is particularly useful for those with a tower case on the floor that is frequently visited by a puppy or toddler.

Figure 5-3. Power Options' Advanced settings window lets you choose whether your PC goes to sleep or shuts down when you press the power button or close the lid

Next, scroll up just a bit and expand the **Sleep** branch. Here, you can use the **Sleep after** and **Hibernate after** options to have your PC automatically put itself to sleep after a certain period of inactivity. Think of these settings as a more ecologically friendly—but less entertaining—alternative to the screen saver.

 Want to temporarily override the Sleep setting? Use the Caffeine tool, available at *http://www.zhornsoftware.co.uk/*, to keep your PC awake by simulating a keypress every 59 seconds.

See "Improve Battery Life" on page 296 for a way to automatically change your power button and lid settings when you switch between AC and battery power.

Time to wake up

While in Standby, Sleep, or Hibernate mode, your PC waits for you to hit the power button—or optionally press a key or move the mouse—at which point it powers up and resumes your previous Windows session.

All sorts of devices can be used to wake your PC when it's asleep, such as your keyboard, some kinds of mice, network adapters, and modems. But first, you need to turn on a setting in Windows. Open Device Manager, and expand the branch containing the device (e.g., **Keyboards**). Double-click your device, choose the **Power Management** tab, turn on the **Allow this device to wake the computer** option, and click OK.

Next, put your PC to sleep and test it out. If you've just enabled wake-up for your keyboard, press the Space bar. Or, if you want to wake up the PC with your mouse, give it a nudge.

If that doesn't do it, you'll need to dive into your BIOS setup screen, discussed in Appendix A. Look for a **Power** or **APM Configuration** category, in which you'll find settings like these:

Power Button Mode
> This option lets you choose whether your power switch shuts down your PC or puts it to sleep. Depending on your BIOS, the setting you choose here may or may not be overridden by the similar setting in the Windows Control Panel.

Power On By External Modems
> This is also known as "Wake On Ring" (WOR); if you have an internal modem in a PCI or PCIE slot, you can use this feature to call your PC with a telephone to wake it up. (Despite the name, this feature won't work with serial port or USB modems.)

Power On By PCI/PCIE Devices
> Turn on this option to use the "Wake On LAN" (WOL) feature, which lets you send a wake-up signal to your PC from another PC on your local network. Some motherboards also require that you install a jumper or use a specific type of network card, so check your PC's documentation for details.

Power On By PS/2 Keyboard or Mouse
> Turn this on if you have an old-style keyboard or mouse that has a round connector. Most PCs should wake up from newer USB keyboards or mice regardless of this setting.

Performance

Restore on AC Power Loss

This option lets you decide what happens after you've cut power to your PC. Set this option to **Always On** if you want to turn on your PC with a switch on an external power strip.

As you might've expected, some experimentation may be required at this stage.

When you wake up your PC, Windows may require a password before it resumes your previous session. To turn this off, return to the Advanced Settings window (Figure 5-3), expand the **Additional settings** branch, and set the **Require a password on wakeup** option to **No**.

Sleep and Hibernate troubleshooting

For the Standby, Sleep, or Hibernate modes to work properly in Windows 7, your PC has to cooperate. If it doesn't, you might experience a problem such as:

No sleep
Windows won't go to sleep at all; either nothing happens when you try to stand by, or the system just crashes in the middle of the process.

No wake up
Windows won't wake up after going to sleep, or Windows simply boots normally instead of resuming your previous session.

No more sleep
Windows goes to sleep or hibernates once, but once it wakes up, it won't go back to sleep until you restart it.

Features are unavailable
Some or all of the power management features and settings discussed earlier are grayed-out (disabled) or missing.

Stuff stops working
Some features, like your wireless network, your cordless mouse, or your scanner stop working after waking up, at least until you restart Windows. (Hint: look for new drivers or a firmware update for your device.)

Unfortunately, all of these problems are quite common, mostly because of the inconsistent support for Advanced Configuration and Power Interface (ACPI) in the computer industry. The good news is that there are a few things you can do to help improve your computer's support for APM and ACPI, should you be experiencing any of these problems:

Update your PC's BIOS
Check with the manufacturer of your computer system or motherboard for a BIOS update. 7 requires that your BIOS comply with the ACPI 2.0 specification.

Enable ACPI/APIC

Enter your BIOS setup screen, as described in Appendix A, and make sure the **ACPI APIC support** setting is set to **On** or **Enabled**. If you see a setting referring to **ACPI 2.0** or some later version, try turning it *on* if it's *off*, or vice versa. Reboot your PC when you're done. Depending on how ACPI-compliant your PC is, it may take some trial and error to get 7 to sleep properly.

Fix or disable Hybrid sleep

The second most common cause of sleep and hibernation problems, behind an out-of-date BIOS, is a video card (display adapter) driver that doesn't support Window' *Hybrid Sleep* feature. Check with the manufacturer of your video card for a newer driver, or try turning off Hybrid Sleep, as described in "The solicitude of Sleep" on page 275.

Disable power saving for your wireless adapter

As with the video card, make sure you have the latest driver and firmware for your wireless adapter. Also, try changing the device's power settings: in Device Manager, double-click your wireless network adapter. Choose the **Power Management** tab, and turn off the **Allow the computer to turn off this device to save power** option.

Free up some disk space

As explained earlier, the Hibernate feature creates an image file on your hard disk equal in size to the amount of installed memory. If you have 2 GB of RAM, then Windows will need 2,147,483,648 bytes of free disk space for the *hiberfil.sys* file. If hibernation doesn't work, or if it's exceedingly slow to initiate or recover, try deleting the hibernation file as described in the sidebar "What Is hiberfil.sys?" on page 276. Then, defragment your hard disk, and re-enable hibernation.

Perform a Sleep test

Go to *http://www.passmark.com/products/sleeper.htm* and download the free PassMark Sleeper tool to help test your computer's ability to enter and recover from Sleep, Standby, and Hibernate modes.

Keep in mind that you may never get your system to reliably go to sleep and wake up; but if you are able to get this feature working, it can be very convenient.

Shut Down Windows Quickly

Theoretically, when you shut down Windows, your computer should be powered down in less than 15 seconds. The problem is that all of the cleanup Windows tries to do before it considers it "safe" to power the system down can sometimes cause delays. This includes shutting down your open applications, stopping any running services, and writing any pending cache data to the disk.

 During the course of using your computer, Windows sometimes postpones writing data to the disk to improve performance. This is called *write caching*, and as a consequence, Windows must take a few seconds before you shut down to make sure all data queued to be written is actually, physically written to the disk before power is lost. See "A Quick Performance Hack" on page 303 for a way to disable this feature.

Of course, the most effective way to speed up shutdown is to not shut down at all. Rather, put your PC to sleep, as described in "Start Windows Instantly (Almost)" on page 274. That way, you won't have to close your documents, bookmark open web pages, or even quit your games; they'll all still be where you left them when you wake up and resume your previous session.

Of course, it's good for Windows to shut down completely from time to time. If you sleep your PC exclusively, it may mean you'll be operating under the same Windows session for weeks or even months, and that can cause Windows to slow down and become even more unreliable.

When shutting down, Windows attempts to stop all running tasks. If a task—an application, service, or background program—doesn't respond or refuses to shut down, there's a built-in delay before Windows will force the task to end. This delay is called the *timeout*, and it can be shortened if you're experiencing problems or unreasonable delays every time you shut down your system.

1. Open the Registry Editor (see Chapter 3).

2. Expand the branches to HKEY_CURRENT_USER\Control Panel\Desktop.

3. Double-click the WaitToKillAppTimeout value. (If it's not there, select **Edit→New→DWORD Value (32-bit)** and type WaitToKillAppTimeout for the name of the new value.) This number controls the time to wait, in milliseconds, before unresponsive applications are forced to close. The default is 20000 (20 seconds), but you can type any value here; the

minimum is 1 millisecond, although it's impractical to use any value smaller than about 2000 (2 seconds) here.

4. Also in this key is the HungAppTimeout value, which does pretty much the same thing as WaitToKillAppTimeout; just enter the same number for both values.

5. Next, you can configure 7 to end hung applications automatically and without asking. Select **Edit→New→DWORD Value (32-bit)** and type AutoEndTasks for the name of the new value. Then, double-click AutoEnd Tasks and enter 1 (one) to automatically end tasks or 0 (zero) to prompt before ending tasks (the default).

6. Expand the branches to HKEY_LOCAL_MACHINE\SYSTEM\CurrentControlSet\ Control.

7. Double-click the WaitToKillServiceTimeout value. This works the same as the WaitToKillAppTimeout value described above, except that it applies to services (managed in *services.msc*) instead of applications.

8. Close the Registry Editor when you're done. You'll have to restart Windows for the change to take effect.

These values also affect the timeouts at times other than just shutting down, such as when you click **End Process** or **End Task** in Task Manager. In most cases, however, these values *won't* affect applications that delay shut down merely because they're waiting for you to save an open document.

Start Applications Faster

One of the things we spend most of our time doing at a PC is waiting for applications to start. Larger applications, particularly, can take what seems like an eternity—OK, 5 to 10 seconds on a fast PC—before they're ready to use. And small programs, even though they load quickly, don't always "pop" on screen as quickly as one would like.

Windows has a lot to do when it loads a program. It has to suck the program file data off your hard disk, something that a clean, optimized drive will handle more quickly (discussed later in this chapter). It also has to make room in your PC's system memory (RAM) for the program, which means your virtual memory settings (see the section "Optimize Virtual Memory and Cache Settings" on page 312) play a significant part, and, of course, more RAM definitely helps.

And then there's the program itself, which must read through all your fonts (the fewer the better), load its own add-on components (DLLs, plug-ins, etc.), and allocate its own section of your hard disk to store temporary files.

But there's also something else at work here, something that isn't strictly necessary. Windows 7 includes an "Application Compatibility" system that checks each program you run against a database of known issues, and warns you if there's a potential problem. This takes time and resources, and is really only useful when you're installing or running older programs not specifically designed for Windows 7.

Once you've set up your PC and tested it with most of the software you'll be using on a daily basis, you really don't need the Application Compatibility system any more. Turn it off, and that's one less thing Windows needs to do each and every time you start a program.

If you're using the Professional, Enterprise, or Ultimate edition of Windows 7, open the Start menu, type gpedit.msc into the **Search** box, and press **Enter** to open the Group Policy Object Editor (*gpedit.msc* isn't available in Home Premium). Expand the branches to **Local Computer Policy→Computer Configuration→Administrative Templates→ Windows Components→Application Compatibility**. In the **Application Compatibility** section, double-click the following settings to configure them:

Turn Off Program Compatibility Engine.
> Set this to **Enabled** to turn off the system that checks each program you run, and allow programs to start more quickly.

> The downside is that some of the User Account Control (UAC) features I'll discuss in Chapter 8 may stop working with pre-Windows 7 applications, which may cause those older programs to stop working.

Turn Off Program Compatibility Assistant.
> The *Assistant* is the window that pops up after you install a program or use it for the first time to inform you that it may not have run correctly. Obviously, this is something you're probably able to determine for yourself, so set this option to **Enabled** to get rid of these prompts.

Remove Program Compatibility Property Page.
> This gets rid of the **Compatibility** tab in a program's Properties window. If you're setting the other options here to **Enabled**, you might as well set this to **Enabled**, too.

When you're done, close the Group Policy Object Editor and restart Windows for the change to take effect. If one of your programs stops working, you'll need to come back here to re-enable the Application Compatibility engine.

See the sidebar "Keeping an Eye on Prefetch" on page 309 for another feature that can affect application startup times.

ReadyBoost: Why Not?

Got an extra USB flash drive or digital camera memory card laying around? If you have a slower hard disk, you may be able to improve startup time and overall disk performance by letting Windows use your card to cache its Prefetch files (see the sidebar "Keeping an Eye on Prefetch" on page 309).

Setup is easy. Just right-click the drive in Windows Explorer, select **Properties**, and then choose the **ReadyBoost** tab. Select **Dedicate this device to ReadyBoost** to use the entire drive, or **Use this device** to use only part of the drive. (If selecting the former option, make sure there's nothing on the drive you care about.) Click OK when you're done; the change takes effect immediately.

Now, it's true that a typical flash drive is significantly slower than a hard disk, so how can ReadyBoost help? The idea is to give Windows a place off-disk to store a few cache files so it doesn't have to interrupt your hard disk during heavy activity to access them. Although you probably won't notice any difference with a fast hard disk on a desktop PC, laptop hard disks are notoriously slow, and have the most to gain from ReadyBoost.

The long and the short of it is that ReadyBoost is free, and super-easy to test. And if you need the USB port or memory card slot, you can pull out the flash drive at any time with no ill-effects.

Want to keep ReadyBoost, but don't like Windows Explorer showing a drive you can't use? If you assign a drive letter to your ReadyBoost drive, and it isn't used by any other removable device, you can hide the drive in Explorer with a simple registry hack. Open the Registry Editor (see Chapter 3) and expand the branches to `HKEY_CURRENT_USER\Software\Microsoft\Windows\CurrentVersion\Policies\Explorer`. Double-click the `NoDrives` value, or if it's not there, open the **Edit** menu, select **New** and then **DWORD (32-bit) Value** to create a value by that name. Select the **Decimal** option, and in the **Value data** field, type a binary value representing the drive you want to hide, where *A:* is 1, *B:* is 2, *C:* is 4, *D:* is 8, and so on. For instance, to hide drive *U:*, you'd type `1048576` here. (To hide more than one drive, just add up the numbers and type the sum into the **Value data** field.) The change takes effect when you log out and log back in.

Make Your Hardware Perform

There's no end to the tricks you can employ to squeeze more speed out of your PC, but few—apart from the ones in this chapter, hopefully—will end up making that much of a difference. Probably the most effective steps you can take involve your hard disk, discussed later in this chapter.

Paradoxically, this section's first topic involves the Glass interface, a new feature that indeed makes Windows run more slowly. But making Windows perform isn't always about making it perform *faster*, but rather making it perform *more*.

Boilerplate disclaimer: Keep in mind that there's a certain point beyond which your computer is going to turn into a money and time pit. The older your system is, the less time and energy you'll want to invest in making it run well, and the more you should start looking to replace it. It's easy to calculate the point of diminishing returns: just compare the estimated cost of an upgrade—both the monetary cost and the amount of time you'll have to commit—with the cost of a new system (minus what you might get for selling or donating your old system). I stress this point a great deal, because I've seen it happen time and time again: people end up spending too much and getting too little in return. A simple hardware upgrade ends up taking days of troubleshooting and configuring, only to result in the discovery that yet something *else* needs to be replaced as well. Taking into account that whatever you end up with will still eventually need to be further upgraded to remain current, it is often more cost effective to replace the entire system and either sell or donate the old parts.

That said, the following sections detail some things you can do to make Windows run faster and/or better.

Get Glass

An optimist will tell you the glass is half-full;
the pessimist, half-empty; and the engineer
will tell you the glass is twice the size
it needs to be.

—Anonymous

We're all suckers for a pretty face. You may or may not think Aero Glass, the translucent interface introduced in Vista and refined in Windows 7, is actually *pretty*, but you can't deny that it's a welcome change from the homely, cartoonish look of XP, and a convenient way to see what's behind the window on top, shown in Figure 5-4.

Figure 5-4. Glass—the shiny, translucent interface included with every edition of 7 except Home Basic—is nice to look at, but may be hard to come by on older PCs

Glass also includes some flashy goodies, such as buttons that glow a cool blue when you roll over them with the mouse, live thumbnail previews of running tasks in the taskbar and the **Alt-Tab** window, the Aero Peek window and desktop preview feature, and the silly Flip3D Rolodex-style task switcher (Winkey+**Tab**).

If you got Windows 7 preinstalled on a new PC, you're probably already using the Glass interface. But what if you're using an older PC and you can't get Glass to work?

The problems with 7's Glass feature are twofold. First, Glass has somewhat hefty technical requirements, not the least of which is a *fast* video card with at least 32 Mb of video memory (or more for higher resolutions), a Vista/Windows 7-compatible WDDM video driver, and a 3D gaming feature called *Pixel Shader 2.0* in hardware. And because Aero Glass guzzles CPU cycles, you'll want a fast processor and a fast video card to enjoy it.

Second, it can be a little tricky to get all the pieces in place so that 7 will even give you the *option* of enabling the Glass interface.

So, without further ado, here's a fairly foolproof procedure to get Glass on your PC.

Part 1: Hardware

The number-one ingredient in a good Glass experience is a fast graphics card with sufficient *video* memory onboard.

A faster card, which you can only get by spending money on a replacement and installing it in your PC, will help offload the burden of the Glass interface, so your CPU is free to handle other tasks. (Or, if you have a video card with a graphics chip that can be overclocked, akin to "Overclock Your Processor" on page 300, you can improve performance without spending a dime.) The card must also support a 3D feature called Pixel Shader 2.0 in its hardware (not software), and must be compatible with DirectX 9.

 Modern desktop PCs take PCI-Express (PCIE) cards, and while Glass-capable PCIE cards are common, it can be difficult to find a sufficiently powerful card designed for the AGP slot in an older PC. But if you're not adverse to scrounging on eBay for a used or discontinued card, nVidia's 6800 series of AGP cards are up to the task, and are well-supported by nVidia's frequently updated drivers. If you're looking for top-notch AGP performance, look for a card with the nVidia 6800Ultra chip and 256 Mb of onboard memory.

Video memory may be a different matter. In most cases, video memory is permanently installed on your video card; unlike your PC's system memory, it can't be upgraded unless you replace your card. But if you have a laptop or low-end desktop, your video is likely built into your motherboard, and its video memory is merely a portion of your PC's system memory (which *is* upgradable). This means that it may be possible to allocate more system memory for your video (at the expense of memory Windows can use) by changing a setting or two in your system BIOS. See Appendix A for the appropriate BIOS settings.

So, how much video memory do you need? It depends on your screen's resolution, but a basic rule of thumb is that you need a minimum of about 48 bytes of video memory for each pixel on your screen, as shown in Table 5-1.

Table 5-1. The amount of video memory required to use Glass at common screen resolutions

Resolution	Aspect ratio	# of pixels	Video memory required
800×600	4:3	480,000	32 MB
960×600	16:10	576,000	32 MB
1024×768	4:3	786,432	64 MB
1152×864	4:3	995,328	64 MB
1280×720	16:9	921,600	64 MB
1280×768	5:3	983,040	64 MB
1280×800	16:10	1,024,000	64 MB
1280×960	4:3	1,228,800	64 MB
1280×1024	5:4	1,310,720	64 MB
1360×768	16:9	1,044,480	64 MB
1600×1024	25:16	1,638,400	128 MB
1600×1200	4:3	1,920,000	128 MB
1920×1080	16:9	2,073,600	128 MB
1920×1200	16:10	2,304,000	128 MB
2560×1440	16:9	3,686,400	256 MB
2560×1600	16:10	4,096,000	256 MB
2560×1920	4:3	4,915,200	256 MB

As you can see, it may be possible to get Glass with as little as 32 MB of video memory on some lower resolutions—and there are those who have achieved this—but depending on your card and its driver, your mileage may vary. Also, it's worth pointing out that memory requirements are doubled on a dual-monitor setup: a single video card must have at least 256 MB to drive two screens that would otherwise need 128 MB each.

As for your PC, it's a good idea to have at least 2–3 gigabytes of system memory (RAM). Although you can get away with less—and you may have to if your video memory is being shared with your system memory as described earlier—you may not find the performance acceptable on a PC with merely 1 GB. See the next section, "Maximize the Windows Performance Rating" on page 292, for ways to measure whether your processor and hard disk are also up to running Glass.

Part 2: Software

With the hardware elements in place, the next thing to worry about is your video driver. Although Windows 7 comes with drivers for most common display adapters, the best driver you're likely to get is the one provided by the maker of the chip on your video card.

The most common video chips are nVidia GeForce (*http://www.nvidia.com/*) and ATI Radeon (*http://ati.amd.com/*); if you're not sure who makes the video card in your PC, open Device Manager in Control Panel and expand the **Display adapters** branch. Just make sure the driver supports the Windows Display Driver Model (WDDM); in most cases, the driver must be expressly written for Windows 7 or Vista.

Once you're certain you have the latest video driver, follow these steps to enable Glass:

1. Update your *Windows Experience Index*, as described in "Maximize the Windows Performance Rating" on page 292, so that Windows can reassess your video subsystem's capabilities. You may need to restart Windows if the Performance Information and Tools window doesn't update your score after a reasonable wait. You must have a video score of at least 3.0 to run Glass.

2. In Control Panel, go to the Display page, and click the **Adjust resolution** link.

3. Click the **Advanced settings** link, choose the **Monitor** tab, and from the **Colors** list, select **True Color (32-bit)**.

 If you know how much video memory is installed on your video card, refer to Table 5-1, earlier in this section, to determine the highest screen resolution you can use with Glass. If needed, return to the Screen Resolution page and select a lower set of values from the **Resolution** list.

4. Click OK to return to Control Panel and then switch to the System page.

5. Click the **Advanced system settings** link on the left side (or run *SystemPropertiesAdvanced.exe*), and in the **Performance** section, click the **Settings** button.

6. Turn on the **Enable desktop composition** and **Enable transparent glass** options, and then click OK and then OK again to close the two windows.

7. Back in Control Panel, go to the Personalization page, and select one of the themes in the **Aero Themes** section. After a brief delay, the Glass interface should now be active.

8. If you don't get transparent Glass at this stage, click the **Window Color** link at the bottom of the window, and turn on the **Enable transparency** option. Adjust the **Color intensity** slider to change the transparency level of the window borders: move it further to the right to make windows more opaque. Click **Save changes** when you're done.

9. If Glass still isn't working, open your Start menu, and in the Search box, type Aero. In a moment, several search results will appear; click **Find and fix problems with transparency and other visual effects** and follow the prompts.

If you still don't have Glass at this point, either your video card or your video driver is to blame. See if your video card maker has made a display BIOS upgrade available; for laptops, a system BIOS update should accomplish the same thing.

Part 3: Tweaks

It doesn't take a degree from Art Center to notice that Microsoft took some design cues from the Aqua interface in Mac OS X (not that Apple didn't borrow some of its ideas, too). While Microsoft actually managed to outdo Apple in a few areas—the minimize, maximize, and close buttons spring to mind—the Flip 3D task switcher is no match for Exposé, the Mac's all-at-once task switcher. Luckily, you can mimic Exposé with Switcher, free from *http://insentient.net/*, and shown in Figure 5-5.

If you find the aforementioned title bar buttons—minimize, maximize, and close—too big (or not big enough), you can resize them. Open the Personalization page in Control Panel, click the **Window Color** link at the bottom and then click the **Advanced appearance settings** link. From the **Item** list, select **Active Title Bar** (or just click the little titlebar in the preview pane), and then use the **Size** control to the right to shrink or grow the title bar. (The minimum value is 17 pixels and the maximum is 100.) The preview shows the classic interface only, so take your best guess, and click OK to see how it looks.

See "Improve Battery Life" on page 296 for another tool you can use with Glass.

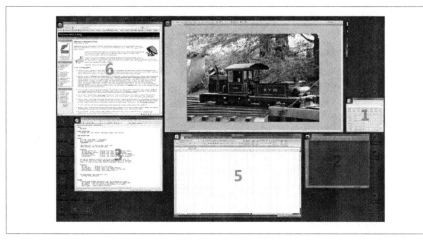

Figure 5-5. Switcher mimics the Exposé all-at-once task switcher from Mac OS X

Maximize the Windows Performance Rating

Ever since the introduction of the Glass interface in Windows Vista (covered in the previous section), Microsoft has started to take display performance seriously in a non-gaming context.

Enter the *Windows Experience Index,* a numeric score that supposedly indicates the baseline performance level of your PC's hardware. To view your PC's current score, open the Performance Information and Tools page in Control Panel (shown in Figure 5-6).

 If you seriously want to benchmark your PC, disregard the Windows Experience Index and instead use a tool like PC Wizard (free, *http://www.cpuid.com/*), HD Tach (free, *http://www.simplisoftware.com/*), or HD Tune (free, *http://www.hdtune.com/*). Among other things, real benchmarking software can compare the speeds of two hard disks, provide accurate results on overclocking, and even help with memory timing.

Here, you'll see the five performance indexes that Windows calculates:

Processor
    This measures your CPU's number-crunching prowess; specifically, how quickly it can compress and decompress data, encrypt and decrypt data, compute a hash, and encode a video stream. For perspective, here are benchmarks from a handful of **Processor** scores culled from the Web.

Processor	Processor subscore	Processor	Processor subscore
Dual Intel Xeon 5160 @3.0Ghz	5.9	AMD Athlon 64 X2 4200+ @2.2Ghz	4.9
Intel Core2 Duo 6600 @2.40GHz	5.4	AMD Athlon 64 X2 3800+ @2GHz	4.8
Intel Core2 Duo 6400 @2.13GHz	5.4	Intel T2500 Core Duo @2GHz	4.8
Intel Core2 Duo T7600 @2.33GHz	5.2	AMD Turion 64 X2 Mobile @1.6Ghz	4.7
AMD Athlon 64 X2 5200+ @2.6Ghz	5.1	Intel Pentium 4 @ 2.80GHz	4.1

Want to raise your Processor score without spending any money? Check out "Overclock Your Processor" on page 300, later in this chapter.

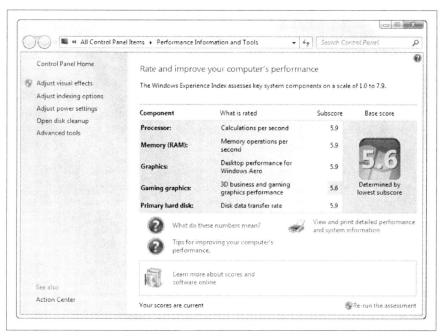

Figure 5-6. The Windows Experience Index is a performance score based on the weakest performer in your PC

 If you're running on battery power, your Processor score may be lower than it would if it were plugged in to AC power. You can change how Windows uses your processor on battery power through the Power Options page in Control Panel.

Memory (RAM)

This measures partly how fast your memory is, but also how much of it your PC has (not including any shared as video memory). Windows actually limits the maximum memory benchmark you can attain, regardless of how fast your RAM is.

Amount of RAM	Max. subscore	Amount of RAM	Max. subscore
Less than 256 MB	1.0	513–704 MB	3.5
257–500 MB	2.0	705–960 MB	3.9
501–512 MB	2.9	961 MB–1.5 GB	4.5

Beyond 1.5 GB, the score is purely speed-based. Want a higher **Memory** score? Add more RAM. (It'll have the meager side effect of making your PC faster, too.)

Graphics

This value is the one most closely tied to your PC's ability to render the Glass interface (see "Get Glass" on page 286), and also indicates your PC's ability to play back video. The score is based on the video bandwidth (the speed at which your video card can move data) as well as the amount of video memory you have.

 A video card that doesn't support DirectX 9 automatically earns a score no higher than 1.0. One for which you don't have a Windows 7/Vista Display Driver Model (WDDM) driver can't receive a score higher than 1.9. To use the Glass interface, you must have a **Graphics** score of at least 2.0. Glass should run beautifully on a system ranked at 5.0 or higher. An updated driver will usually raise your **Graphics** score.

Gaming graphics

This measures your video card's 3D prowess, specifically the frames per second it can attain in certain situations.

 Like the preceding **Graphics** benchmark, there are minimum requirements for certain scores. If your video card doesn't support Direct3D v9, it earns a score no higher than 1.0. If support for Pixel Shader 3.0 is absent, then you won't see a score higher than 4.9, regardless of other factors. If you believe your card is capable of these things, yet your score seems unfairly low, your pesky driver is once again likely to blame.

Primary hard disk

This measures the transfer rate, the speed at which your PC can read and write information to the drive on which Windows is installed. See "Hard Disk" on page 303 for things you can do to increase this score.

Off to the right, you'll see a **Base score** emblazoned on a Windows logo. This score isn't an average of the subscores to the left, but rather an indication of the lowest score—the weakest link in the chain, so to speak.

Don't panic if your **Processor** score is a hair lower than your neighbor's down the street, even though you have a faster CPU. (Because your neighbor is probably worried about your slightly better **Graphics** score, even though her video card cost $40 more than yours.)

Rather, use these scores only to provide quantitative feedback for the upgrades or tweaks you're doing. And keep in mind that these scores, although based on calculations, aren't quite as rigid as they seem. For instance, refresh the index right after booting Windows, and you may see a 0.1 variance from a PC that has been scored after being active all day. Install a new graphics driver, and your **Graphics** subscore may go up a few tenths while **Gaming graphics** dives slightly.

Click the **View and print details** link to shed some more light on exactly how 7 is calculating your PC's score. You can print the results here or, better yet, highlight everything (**Ctrl-A**), copy the text to the clipboard (**Ctrl-C**), and then paste into Notepad (**Ctrl-V**) to save the results to a file.

Update my score

Click the **Re-run the assessment** link at the bottom of the page to rescan your system and perform the benchmarks again. But don't be surprised when you don't see any progress bar or other indication that Windows is testing your system; other than periodic sluggishness in the mouse, occasional screen flashes, or increased hard disk activity, you shouldn't notice much of anything happening.

But don't let that fool you: to maximize your scores, make sure you close any running applications (including background tasks like antivirus programs and anything that uses your network), let go of your mouse, and then go get a cup of tea so you avoid doing anything that may interfere with the scoring. It's not unusual for scoring to take 10–30 minutes, even on a fast PC.

If the reassessment fails, you might be low on free disk space; see "If in Doubt, Throw It Out" on page 309, for some tips. If you see this error or something similar:

Cannot complete the requested operation.

An unknown error has caused WinSAT to fail in an unexpected way.

it either means you clicked the **Re-run the assessment** link while Windows was already reexamining your system, or there's a problem with your video driver that's causing the benchmark system to crash. Update your driver, restart Windows, and try again.

Improve Battery Life

Priorities shift when you're not tethered to an AC outlet. Suddenly, processor speed and the glitzy Glass interface just aren't that important when your laptop battery is going to die in 12 minutes. Now, there are things you can do to reduce your laptop's hunger for power, but the best power-saving features are the ones that engage automatically when you're using the battery, but revert to their high-performance settings whenever you plug in.

Start with the obvious: the Power Options page in Control Panel. Here, you'll find at least three plans: **Balanced** (the default), **High performance**, and **Power saver** (which may be hidden under the **Show additional plans** label). It doesn't really matter which one you choose, because each can be configured any way you like.

Click the **Change plan settings** link next to the currently selected plan and then click the **Change advanced power settings** link to open the Advanced Settings window. If it's there, click the **Change settings that are currently unavailable** link; see "Control User Account Control" on page 569, to get rid of this last step.

The settings here that will have the most bearing on your battery life are:

Hard disk

Being a mechanical device, your hard disk eats up a lot of power (those with solid-state devices have my permission to rejoice at this point). Set the **Turn off hard disk after** option too low, and you'll spend a lot of time waiting for Windows to wake up your hard disk; set it too high, and you're just wasting power. A setting of 10 or 20 minutes is usually a good compromise.

Processor power management

Your processor uses a lot more power than you think. Since it can run at different speeds, it runs fast when needed, but drops down to a slower speed when your PC is idle to save power. The two settings here let you choose the upper and lower bounds of your processor's speed. Unlike with your hard disk, you never have to wait for your processor to be woken up, so there's very little to lose by keeping the **Minimum processor state** setting as low as possible.

 It's worth noting that the **Maximum processor state** is set to only 50% in the **Power saver** plan by default; this means that when this plan is active, your CPU will never run faster than about half its rated speed. Of course, this does save power, but as long as the **Minimum processor state** is set to, say, 5%, it probably doesn't make much sense to limit your CPU in this way. Of course, processors vary, so experiment with this setting to see how well yours manages its own power consumption.

It's also worth noting the System cooling policy, which lets you choose what happens when your processor overheats. Set this to **Passive** to slow your processor before increasing fan speed; both a slower CPU and a slower fan will prolong your battery. On AC power, choose **Active** to prioritize speed and activate the fan before slowing the processor to keep things cool.

Display

Use the **Turn off display after** setting as a battery-friendly alternative to a screensaver. Since it takes very little time to wake up modern laptop displays, set this to a small value like 5 minutes. Next, if your screen has an ambient light sensor, turn on the **Enable adaptive brightness** option to have Windows automatically adjust your screens brightness as needed. (If you know your screen is equipped with a light sensor and you don't see this option, try updating your monitor driver.)

 This setting isn't just for laptops. Microsoft reports that as much as 43% of the total power consumed by a desk-top PC is used for the monitor (and that's for a modern, power-sipping LCD display). Choosing an appropriately small value for **Turn off display after** can save you money and help the environment.

Multimedia settings

In the **Multimedia settings** branch, the **When playing video** setting affects how Windows Media Player renders movies when on battery power. Since this is something you're likely to do, say, while on an airplane, you should select the lowest setting you can get away with and still get acceptable video playback.

Click OK when you're done; the changes take effect immediately.

 In Windows Vista, you could also choose how aggressively the search indexing service ran while on battery power. (Indexing causes heavy disk and processor usage.) Although this setting is absent in the Power Options window in Windows 7, it never provided the option to disable indexing entirely, so it was of limited value. Thus you may want to stop the indexing service manually while using a battery to save as much power as possible.

To switch between power plans, click the battery status icon in your notification area (tray) and then click the one you want. Or, press Winkey+**X** to show the Windows Mobility Center, where you can also choose the plan you want.

Switch plans automatically

On a laptop, you'll see two versions of many settings in the Power Options window: one for running on battery power and one for AC. For instance, you can have Windows hibernate after 20 minutes of inactivity on battery, or after 3 hours when plugged in. But what if you want more control?

Programs like Aerofoil (free from *http://www.silentsoftware.co.uk/*) and Vista Battery Saver (free, *http://www.codeplex.com/vistabattery/*) can switch power plans automatically based on the power source, as well as turn off the power-hungry Glass interface when you switch to battery power.

Find out if your power-saving measures are paying off

Luckily, it's fairly easy to get a quantitative report on how much power your PC is using. That way, you can determine if a particular performance downgrade is getting you any real gains in battery life.

One such tool that will show your battery usage is BatTrack, written by the author of the aforementioned Vista Battery Saver (and also available free at *http://tinyurl.com/battrack*).

But Windows 7 also has a little-known analysis tool of its own, accessible only from the command prompt (see Chapter 9). To use the tool, open a Command Prompt window in Administrator mode (see Chapters 9 and 8, respectively) and then type the following:

```
powercfg -energy -output %userprofile%\desktop\output.html
```

The analysis will take 60 seconds (which you can change with the optional -duration switch), after which powercfg will save its report as an HTML file on your desktop. Just double-click *output.html* to view the report.

Anything in red is an issue that could be wasting power: For instance, you'll find out if any of your USB devices refuse to go to sleep (i.e., "USB Device not Entering Suspend"). Below the red sections are warnings (in yellow), which highlight programs using more than their fair share of CPU cycles (i.e., "Individual process with significant processor utilization"). It's not the friendliest report, but odds are you'll discover something that's causing your PC to use more power than it should.

Disable devices, stop services

Don't need that Ethernet port right now? Not using your DVD drive? Turn 'em off and save some more power.

Open Device Manager, expand the branches to show your "expendable" devices, and then right-click each one and select **Properties**. Choose the **Power Management** tab, turn on the **Allow the computer to turn off this device to save power** option, and click OK. Then, assuming the option was available, right-click the device and select **Disable** (if the option wasn't available, disabling the device won't save any power).

Next, open the Services window (*services.msc*), and stop any unnecessary services (don't touch the ones you don't understand). For instance, if you've installed Apple's iTunes on your PC, you'll see at least two related services here: **Apple Mobile Device** and **iPod Service**. If you have no plans to connect an iPod for the next few hours, right-click each service and select **Stop** to give your PC one less thing to do while you're running on precious battery power.

Cooler or hotter to save power

One of the most significant things you can do to increase battery life is to take your laptop off your lap. Put it on a book, magazine, airline tray table, tennis racket, pasta strainer, or any hard—and preferably ventilated—surface. If the bottom of your laptop is allowed to breathe, it won't get so hot, and the fan won't have to work so hard to keep the processor cool. The harder your fan works—and for that matter, the hotter your CPU gets—the more power is drained from your battery.

If your laptop never seems to get that hot, even when it's on your lap, you may be able to experiment with some more lenient cooling settings. Using your PC's BIOS setup page (see Appendix A) or, optionally, a fan control program like I8kfanGUI (free at *http://www.diefer.de/i8kfan/*), try increasing the allowed temperature of your CPU by a degree or two, and see what happens. With luck, your fan should come on less often and your battery should last a little longer, all without (hopefully) frying your processor.

Manage IRQ Priority

Most components directly attached to your motherboard—including PCI slots, IDE controllers, serial ports, the keyboard port, and even your motherboard's CMOS—have individual IRQs assigned to them. An *interrupt request line*, or *IRQ*, is a numbered hardware line over which a device can interrupt the normal flow of data to the processor, allowing the device to function.

Windows lets you prioritize one or more IRQs (which translate to one or more hardware devices), potentially improving the performance of those devices:

1. Start by opening the System Information utility (*msinfo32.exe*), and navigating to `System Summary\Hardware Resources\IRQs` to view the IRQs in use on your system, and the devices using them.

2. Next, open the Registry Editor (see Chapter 3), and navigate to `HKEY_LOCAL_MACHINE\SYSTEM\CurrentControlSet\Control\PriorityControl`.

3. Create a new DWORD value in this key, and call it `IRQ#Priority`, where # is the IRQ of the device you wish to prioritize (e.g., `IRQ13Priority` for IRQ 13, which is your numeric processor).

4. Double-click the new value, and enter a number for its priority. Enter 1 for top priority, 2 for second, and so on. Make sure not to enter the same priority number for two entries, and keep it simple by experimenting with only one or two values at first.

5. Close the Registry Editor and reboot your computer when you're done.

Some users have gotten good results prioritizing IRQ 8 (for the system CMOS) and the IRQ corresponding to the video card (found in the first step).

Overclock Your Processor

The processor (CPU) is the highest-profile component in your PC, and indeed, it does a lot of the heavy lifting. But processors also become obsolete the fastest, and given how expensive they can be, it's not always a wise place to put your money. That's where overclocking comes in; rather than spending money on a slightly faster chip, you can simply change settings in your PC to squeeze a little extra speed out of the one you currently have. (For a little perspective, see the upcoming sidebar, "How Much the CPU Matters".)

How Much the CPU Matters

A common misconception is that—with all else being equal—a computer with a processor running at, say, 2.8 GHz, will naturally be faster than a 2.2 GHz system—and the company that just sold you that 2.8 GHz PC wouldn't have it any other way. Sure, that new system you're drooling over does seem a whole lot faster than your one-year-old machine when you play with it in the gizmo store, but how much is due merely to the processor's clock speed, and how much is determined by other factors?

Naturally, the increased processor speed is an obvious benefit in some specific circumstances, such as when you're applying lens corrections to a few hundred digital photos, creating a PDF from a 200-page document, or playing a particularly processor-intensive game. But in most cases, a faster processor alone won't get you your email any faster, load a website any sooner, or get your book to the publisher when it's actually due.

If you think about it, your qualitative assessment of your PC's speed is based on its ability to respond immediately to mouse clicks and keystrokes, start applications quickly, open menus and dialog boxes without a delay, start up and shut down Windows quickly, and display graphics and animations smoothly. (After all, your computer spends most of its time waiting for you to do something.) These things mostly depend on the amount of system memory (RAM) your PC has, the speed of your hard drive, and the prowess of your video card as much as—if not more than—the speed of your CPU.

Probably the biggest drag on an older PC's performance, and the main reason it may seem so much slower than a new system—not to mention slower than it might've been only last year—is the glut of applications and drivers that have been installed. Any computer that has been around for a year or more will likely suffer a slowdown, a problem that can either be remedied by some of the tricks in the section "Hard Disk" on page 303, or by a thorough cleansing and complete reinstallation of the operating system (see "Reinstall Windows 7" on page 19).

So, if you're wondering how much faster your PC will be if you replace your 2.2 Ghz chip with a 2.4 Ghz chip, the answer is: don't even bother unless someone else is paying for it.

Overclocking is the process of instructing your processor to run at a higher clock speed (MHz) than its rated speed. For example, you may be able to modestly overclock a 2.40 GHz chip to run at 2.48 GHz, or your motherboard may offer overclocking at up to 30% of the rated speed, which would give you more than 3 GHz on that same old chip.

Supposedly, Intel and other chip makers have taken steps to prevent overclocking (theoretically prompting purchases of faster CPUs instead), but some motherboard manufacturers have found ways to do it anyway.

To overclock your processor (assuming your motherboard supports it), go to your BIOS setup page, as described in Appendix A, and use the controls in the **Overclock Options** category. Make sure you consult the documentation that came with your motherboard or PC for some of the restrictions; for instance, overclocking on your motherboard may be limited by the speed of the installed system memory (RAM).

When you're done, load up Windows and update your *Windows Experience Index*, as described in the section "Maximize the Windows Performance Rating" on page 292. Obviously, the **Processor** score should go up as you dial up the overclocking.

Now, over-overclocking a CPU—overclocking past the point where it's stable—can cause it to overheat and crash frequently, and at the extreme, damage the chip beyond repair. Thus, the most important aspect of overclocking your system involves cooling, so make sure you beef up your computer's internal cooling system before you start messing around with overclocking. (Obviously, your options will be limited here if you're using a laptop.)

 Increase your CPU's speed in stages, if possible; don't start off with the fastest setting, or you may end up with a fried processor and lightly singed eyebrows.

If you feel that your system isn't adequately cooled, don't be afraid to add more fans, but beware: do it wrong, and you could actually make things worse. For instance, you need to consider airflow when installing and orienting fans; if the power supply, for instance, exhausts air through the vent in the back of your PC, it must pull it in through the vent near your processor's heatsink. So, make sure you orient the CPU fan so the airflow is as smooth as possible.

Most fans in modern PCs connect directly to special plugs on your motherboard, and are activated when internal thermometers (thermocouples) detect too high a temperature; these typically do a good job of moderating their cooling duties so that they don't produce too much noise. But you may have to tinker with your BIOS settings to make your PC cooler (which can, by itself, improve performance), even if it means a little more noise from your box.

If you're serious about cooling, there are a number of liquid cooling systems that promise to keep hot systems cool. But they're expensive, they work in large desktop PCs only, and they don't necessarily reduce noise.

Hard Disk

Your hard disk is more than just a storage device; it's a friend. It holds your operating system, keeps your personal data intact, and supplements your system's memory. The speed and health of your hard disk is one of the most important factors in your computer's performance, not to mention its reliability and security. Yet it's also the one component that requires the most attention and often is the most neglected. Awww.

The following topics all deal with different aspects of your hard disk and how you can get Windows to use it most effectively. Later in this section, you'll find tips on upgrading and repartitioning your hard disk, to allow you to keep your disk and its data in tip-top shape.

A Quick Performance Hack

There's a nearly hidden option that's turned off by default in Windows 7. It can increase hard disk performance, but in doing so, may also increase the odds of data loss.

Open Device Manager (*devmgmt.msc*) and expand the **Disk drives** branch. Right-click your hard disk, select **Properties**, and choose the **Policies** tab.

By default, the **Enable write caching on the device** option is turned on. But the other option, **Turn off Windows write-cache buffer flushing on the device**, is unchecked. Why?

Both options here allow Windows to wait until a period of low activity before writing unsaved data to the drive, which improves drive performance considerably. In either case, you can lose data if the power is cut to the drive before that data is written. To help quell data loss, Windows periodically instructs the drive to save queued data whether there's a lull in the activity or not; this is called "write-cache buffer flushing." The second option disables this feature, which can further improve performance, but clearly at some risk.

Microsoft recommends using the **Turn off Windows write-cache buffer flushing on the device** feature only for drives that have separate power supplies. But since separate power supplies will lose power just like the one in

Figure 5-7. File fragmentation on your hard disk can hurt performance and decrease reliability

your PC, that recommendation makes little sense. Instead, you probably should only use the second option if your PC is protected by an uninterruptable power supply (UPS), which can supply power to your PC even after the power goes out or your laptop battery dies.

See the discussion of RAID in Chapter 6 for a way to further protect your data from hard drive outages.

A Defragmentation Crash Course

The best way to ensure maximum performance from your drive is to regularly—weekly or biweekly—defragment it (also called *optimizing*). Figure 5-7 shows how frequent use can cause files to become fragmented (broken up), which can slow access and retrieval of data on the drive, as well as increase the likelihood of lost data. And the fuller the drive, the more serious defragmentation becomes.

 Windows 7 is supposed to defragment your drives automatically; by default, it's scheduled to run at 1:00 a.m. every Wednesday morning from now until the end of time. (Your PC off in the middle of the night? Missed tasks are deferred until the next boot; see Chapter 9 for more on the Task Manager.) Unfortunately, this may never happen until you run the program yourself at least once.

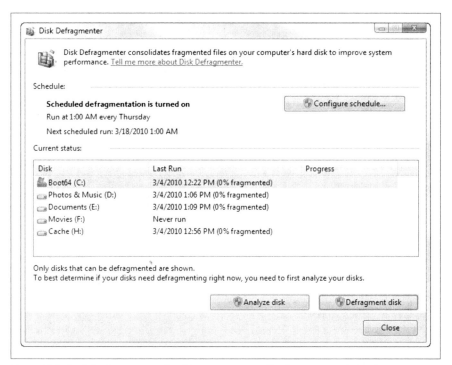

Figure 5-8. Disk Defragmenter should run automatically, but a manual checkup every now and then will make sure it never misses a beat

To start Disk Defragmenter, open Windows Explorer, right-click your hard disk, select **Properties**, choose the **Tools** tab, and click **Defragment Now** (or run *dfrgui.exe*). Click **Defragment disk** (Figure 5-8) to begin the process.

Disk Defragmenter does its job by rearranging the files on your hard disk to make them contiguous (not broken into pieces). It also defragments the free space by consolidating your files as much as it can. When run automatically, it has no interface to speak of, but rather runs invisibly in the background.

Now for the bad news.

From Windows 95 all the way to Vista, Microsoft had a habit of further burying Disk Defragmenter in each successive version. But Windows 7 takes a step in the right direction and actually shows the percentage complete of each drive it's queued to defragment (see Figure 5-8). Unfortunately, the severely minimalist design prevents most advanced defragmenting tasks.

For instance, there's no way to defragment the swap file (virtual memory), the hibernation file (*hiberfil.sys*), the registry, or any other unmovable files. There's no disk map, so there's no visual feedback to tell if there's a large file that won't

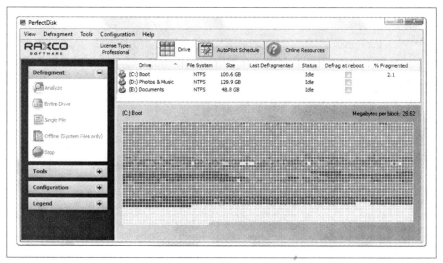

Figure 5-9. PerfectDisk provides the advanced features missing in 7's own Disk Defragmenter

defragment. If you have more than one hard disk (or partition), there's no way to automatically defragment each of your drives in succession; you either do them all at once, or one at a time by hand. And the scheduler is flaky; don't be surprised if it says "Never run" in the **Last Run** column, despite the assurance that "Scheduled defragmentation is turned on" at the top of the window.

Now, to be fair, these are some pretty niche features. If you miss the map, advanced settings, reliable scheduling, or detailed reporting of the old-school defragmenters, check out PerfectDisk (*http://www.perfectdisk.com/*), shown in Figure 5-9). It's not free, but there's a time-limited demo on the website.

There's not a whole lot in the way of free defragmenters, but Auslogics Registry Defrag (*http://www.auslogics.com/?*) promises to improve Windows performance by shrinking and optimizing your Registry.

Command-line defragmenter

As it turns out, Windows 7's Disk Defragmenter isn't quite as feeble as it first appears. Although it doesn't offer anything close to the usability of PerfectDisk, there is a little-known command-line version (*defrag.exe*) that gives you a little more freedom than the one you access through Windows Explorer.

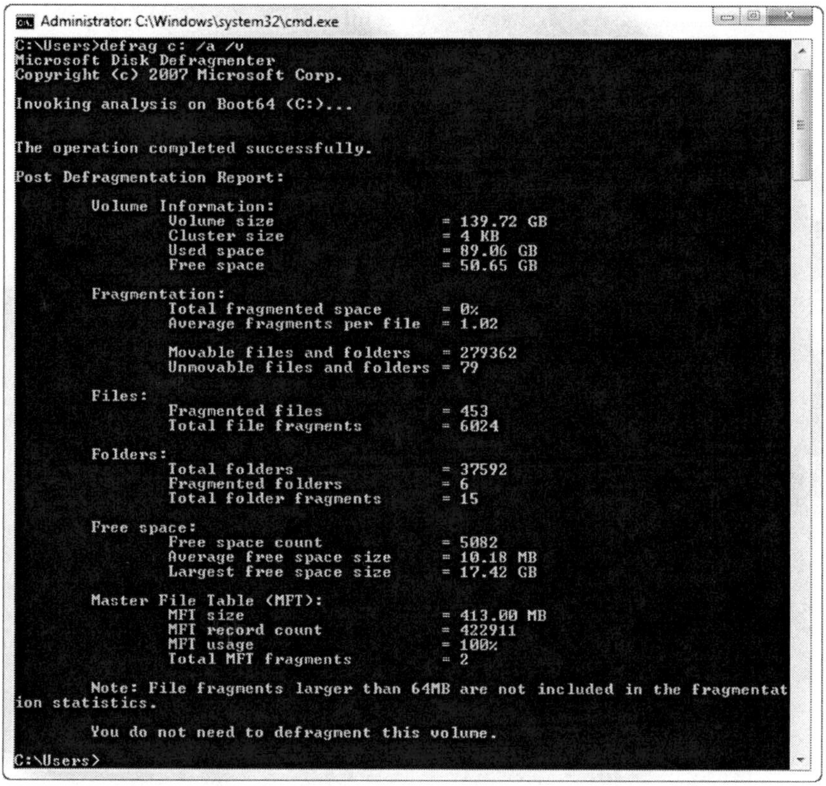

```
 Administrator: C:\Windows\system32\cmd.exe                            _  □  X

C:\Users>defrag c: /a /v
Microsoft Disk Defragmenter
Copyright (c) 2007 Microsoft Corp.

Invoking analysis on Boot64 (C:)...

The operation completed successfully.

Post Defragmentation Report:

        Volume Information:
                Volume size                     = 139.72 GB
                Cluster size                    = 4 KB
                Used space                      = 89.06 GB
                Free space                      = 50.65 GB

        Fragmentation:
                Total fragmented space          = 0%
                Average fragments per file      = 1.02

                Movable files and folders       = 279362
                Unmovable files and folders     = 79

        Files:
                Fragmented files                = 453
                Total file fragments            = 6024

        Folders:
                Total folders                   = 37592
                Fragmented folders              = 6
                Total folder fragments          = 15

        Free space:
                Free space count                = 5082
                Average free space size         = 10.18 MB
                Largest free space size         = 17.42 GB

        Master File Table (MFT):
                MFT size                        = 413.00 MB
                MFT record count                = 422911
                MFT usage                       = 100%
                Total MFT fragments             = 2

        Note: File fragments larger than 64MB are not included in the fragmentat
ion statistics.

        You do not need to defragment this volume.

C:\Users>
```

Figure 5-10. Defrag.exe lets you view reports and schedule more thorough defragmenting than the Windows version

Open a Command Prompt window in administrator mode (right-click the **Command Prompt** icon in the Start menu and select **Run as administrator**), and then type the following at the prompt:

    defrag c: /a /v

and press **Enter** to generate a report like the one in Figure 5-10.

To perform a full defragmentation on a single drive, type:

    defrag c: /u

or to defragment all volumes, type:

    defrag /c /u

The engine used by *defrag.exe* is the same as that used by the GUI version (*dfrgui.exe*). This means that if you start defrag from the command prompt and then press **Ctrl-C**, it'll stop the operation.

For a quick and dirty defragmentation of a drive (wherein it just groups together all the free space), type:

```
defrag c: /x
```

For more options, type `defrag -?` at the prompt and press **Enter**. See the next section for an undocumented defrag option.

Enable automatic boot defragments

Here's a funny little setting in the Registry that seems as though it's supposed to instruct Windows to defragment your hard disk automatically each time it starts:

1. Open the Registry Editor (described in Chapter 3).
2. Expand the branches to `HKEY_LOCAL_MACHINE\SOFTWARE\Microsoft\Dfrg \BootOptimizeFunction`.
3. Double-click the `Enable` value, and type `Y` for its data (or type `N` to disable it).

The funny part is that this setting is probably already enabled on your system (it's enabled by default on most Windows 7 systems). Now, have you ever seen Windows run Disk Defragmenter at startup?

The reason you don't see it is because it isn't a full defragment. Instead, it's only a *boot defragment*, which affects only the files registered with Windows' Prefetch feature (see the upcoming sidebar "Keeping an Eye on Prefetch") and listed in the *Layout.ini* file (not a standard *.ini* file).

You can perform this boot defragment at any time by running the command-line Defrag tool with the undocumented /b option, like this: `defrag c: /b`.

Keeping an Eye on Prefetch

Prefetch is a feature (first introduced in Vista) that stores specific data about the applications you run in order to help them start faster. Prefetch is an algorithm that helps anticipate cache misses (times when Windows requests data that isn't stored in the disk cache), and stores that data on the hard disk for easy retrieval.

This data is located in \Windows\Prefetch, and, as the theory goes, periodically clearing out the data in this folder (say, once a month) will improve performance. As new applications are subsequently started, new Prefetch data will be created, which may mean slightly reduced performance at first. But with older entries gone, there will be less data to parse, and Windows should be able to locate the data it needs more quickly. Any performance gains you may see will be minor (if you see any at all), but those users wishing to squeeze every last CPU cycle out of their computers will want to try this one.

Note that deleting Prefetch data may increase boot time slightly, but only the next time you boot Windows. Each subsequent boot should proceed normally since the Prefetch data will already be present for the programs Windows loads when it boots.

If you want to disable Prefetch, open your Registry Editor (Chapter 3), navigate to `HKEY_LOCAL_MACHINE\SYSTEM\CurrentControlSet\Control\Session Manager\Memory Management\PrefetchParameters`, and change the `EnablePrefetcher` value to `0`. (Other supported values: `1` to Prefetch applications only, `2` to Prefetch boot processes, and `3` to Prefetch both.)

See the sidebar "ReadyBoost: Why Not?" on page 285 for a way to cache your Prefetch files and improve performance.

If in Doubt, Throw It Out

Parkinson's law states that work expands so as to fill the time available for its completion. Along the same lines, it's safe to say that files will quickly expand to fill the amount of available space on your hard drive.

Low disk space doesn't just make it harder to store files; without ample room for virtual memory (discussed later) and temporary files, Windows will slow to a crawl. Less free disk space also increases file fragmentation as Windows scrambles to find places to put data; this in turn lowers performance. Keeping a healthy amount of free disk space is vital to a well-performing system.

Additionally, removing drivers and applications that are no longer used clears more memory and processor cycles for your other applications, which can substantially improve overall system performance.

 If your PC is low on disk space, try NTFS compression. Right-click any folder, select **Properties**, click **Advanced**, and turn on the **Compress contents to save disk space** option. On slower PCs, compression may slightly degrade performance, but on a fast PC with a slow hard disk—your typical laptop—you might actually see performance gains due to the reduced I/O. However, compression has been known to increase fragmentation, so you'd be wise to use it only for data that you don't access or modify often. If you use NTFS compression, you can view the properties of any folder to see how much space it's using, but NTFSRatio (free, *http://www.jam-soft ware.com/*) can show you how much space you're saving overall.

Note that compression is only available on NTFS-formatted drives; see "Choose the Right Filesystem" on page 317 for details. It's also mutually exclusive of the **Encrypt contents to secure data** option discussed in Chapter 8.

Even before you install your first application, your hard disk is littered with files from the Windows installation that you most likely don't need. The standard installation of Windows 7 Ultimate Edition places more than 39,000 files, consuming more than two gigabytes of disk space, on your PC.

Whether you need a particular file can be subjective; some might consider the 24 MB of *.wav* files that 7 puts in your *C:\Windows\Media* folder to be excessive, while others may scoff at the notion of worrying about such a piddly quantity. (To put things in perspective, this is about the same size as three photos from a 10-megapixel digital camera. It's also more than twice the total capacity of my first hard disk back in 1983.)

Naturally, it makes sense to be cautious when removing any files from your system. The removal of certain files can cause some applications, or even Windows itself, to stop functioning. It's always good practice to move any questionable files to a metaphorical purgatory folder before committing to their disposal. And I don't have to tell you that backing up your entire hard disk (Chapter 6) before you clean house is very important and not all that difficult.

The easiest way to delete the stuff Windows considers expendable is to run the super-simple Disk Cleanup tool (*cleanmgr.exe*), and place checkmarks next to all the categories of expendable data. For instance, if you upgraded from Vista, there's likely more than 2 GB of leftover files sitting on your hard disk under the label, **Files discarded by Windows upgrade**. See the sidebar "Disable the Disk Cleanup Nag" if you want Windows to stop bothering you when your disk space gets low.

Disable the Disk Cleanup Nag

When your PC starts running out of disk space, Windows will prompt you to run the Disk Cleanup Wizard, which presents a list of some of the files you can delete to recover free disk space (the solutions in this book are much more comprehensive).

To disable this annoying warning, open the Registry Editor (see Chapter 3) and expand the branches to `HKEY_CURRENT_USER\Software \Microsoft\Windows\CurrentVersion\Policies\Explorer`. If it's not already there, create a new DWORD value (go to **Edit→New→DWORD value**) called `NoLowDiskSpaceChecks`. Double-click the new value and type `1` for its data. Close the Registry Editor when you're done; the change will take effect immediately.

Note that this change only disables the warning; the Disk Cleanup tool will work just fine without it.

 Windows' System Restore feature can consume up to 15% of the total capacity of your hard disk for restore points and shadow copies. To reduce its usage or turn it off entirely, see "Go Back in Time with Restore Points and Shadow Copies" on page 408.

An alternative—or perhaps a supplement—to the Disk Cleanup tool is CCleaner, freely available from *http://www.ccleaner.com/*. CCleaner not only deletes unneeded files, but can also clear your browser cache (IE, Firefox, Chrome, Opera, and Safari), get rid of superfluous registry entries, and wipe out history MRU lists from many popular programs.

Another useful tool is DriveSpacio (free, *http://www.drivespacio.f-sw.com/*), which can help you track down the files using the most disk space.

Unneeded programs

Next, fire up the Programs and Features tool in Control Panel and say bye-bye to the programs you don't need.

While you're there, click the **Turn Windows features on or off** link on the left side, and uncheck any features you don't want. For instance, the **Indexing Service** entry is obsolete (it's not the same one used by Windows 7's Search tool) and **Internet Information Services** (IIS) is only for web servers. Click OK when you're done.

If in doubt

Before you delete any questionable file, there are several things you can do to get a better idea of what the file contains:

Investigate
Right-click the file, and select **Properties**. If the file has a **Version** tab, it's likely an application, driver, DLL, or other support file. Choose the **Version** tab to view the manufacturer, copyright date, and possibly the application it accompanies.

Check the date
Check the file's **Last Accessed** date (right-click it and select **Properties**). The more recent the date, the more likely it's still being used. For information on removing a particular application, contact the manufacturer of that application or refer to the application's documentation.

Hide it first
If you're not sure if something should be deleted but want to try anyway, move it to another directory first to see whether everything works without it for a week or so. If all is clear, toss it.

Why not open it?
Probably the last thing you should do with a suspicious file is to double-click it. Instead, drag it into an open Notepad window to see what's inside without activating any potentially harmful code that might be lurking within. See Chapter 6 for more on malware detectors.

Optimize Virtual Memory and Cache Settings

One of the most frustrating and irritating things about Windows is the way that it can seize up for several seconds with seemingly random, pointless disk activity. One of the causes of this behavior is the way Windows handles disk virtual memory by default.

Normally, Windows loads drivers and applications into memory until it's full, and then starts to use part of your hard disk to "swap" out information, freeing up more memory for higher-priority tasks. The file that Windows uses for this type of "virtual memory" is the paging file (a.k.a. swap file), *pagefile.sys*, and it is stored in the root folder of your Windows drive.

Because your hard disk is so much slower than your physical memory, the more swapping Windows has to do, the slower your computer gets. This is why adding more memory speeds up your PC: it reduces Windows' appetite for virtual memory. But regardless of the amount of installed physical memory in your system, there are always things you can do to improve virtual memory performance.

Windows' defaults here are rather conservative and can fortunately be modified for better performance. It's important to realize, though, that some experimentation may be required to achieve the best configuration for your setup. Different hardware, software, and work habits require different settings; those with ample hard disks, for instance, can afford to devote more disk space to virtual memory, while others may simply wish to use this procedure to place a cap on the disk space Windows is allowed to consume.

Part 1: Virtual memory settings

One of the reasons the default settings yield such poor performance is that the swap file grows and shrinks with use, quickly becoming very fragmented (as illustrated by Figure 5-7, earlier in this chapter). The first step is to eliminate this problem by setting a constant swap-file size.

Note that making the swap file constant will also result in a more constant amount of free disk space. If your hard disk is getting full, consider this solution to restrict Windows from using up every last bit of free space. (Or better yet, upgrade your hard disk.)

1. In Control Panel, open the System page and click the **Advanced system settings** link (or run *SystemPropertiesAdvanced.exe*).

2. Under the **Advanced** tab, click the **Settings** button in the **Performance** section.

3. On the Performance Options page, choose the **Advanced** tab, and then click **Change** to open the Virtual Memory window shown in Figure 5-11.

4. Turn off the **Automatically manage paging file size for all drives** option to enable the rest of the controls in this window.

5. The virtual memory settings are set for each drive in your system independently. If you have only one drive, virtual memory will already be enabled for that drive. If you have more than one drive or partition, virtual memory will be enabled only on the Windows drive by default. Start by selecting the drive that currently holds your paging file (shown in the righthand column) from the **Paging file size for each drive** list.

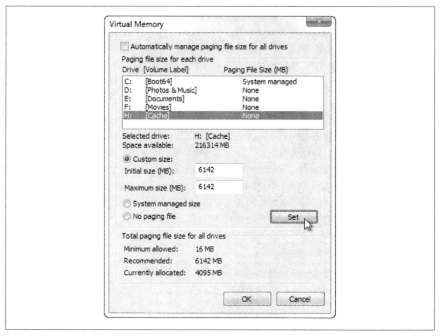

Figure 5-11. Change the way Windows handles virtual memory to improve overall system performance

Another way to stop Windows from using the hard disk so heavily is to disable virtual memory altogether, but the consequence of short-changing Windows of this resource will easily outweigh any performance gains. A better choice is to move the swap file to a different physical drive than the one on which Windows resides; that way, when Windows accesses virtual memory, it won't suck the life out of your primary drive.

6. To set a constant size for your virtual memory, select **Custom size**, and then type the same value for both **Initial size** and **Maximum size**.

   The size, specified in megabytes, is up to you. If you have the space, it's usually a good idea to allocate two to three times the amount of installed RAM (e.g., 4,096–6,144 MB of virtual memory for 2 GB of physical memory), but you may wish to experiment with different sizes for the one that works best for you.

7. *Important:* after you've made a change for any drive, click **Set** to commit the change before moving on to another drive or clicking OK.

8. Press OK on each of the three open dialogs.

If you have only resized your swap file, the change will take effect immediately. But if you've added (or removed) a swap file on any drive, you'll need to restart Windows before it uses your new settings.

Part 2: Defragment the paging file

The steps in the previous section eliminate the possibility of your swap file becoming fragmented, but they won't cure an already fragmented one. You'll need to defragment your virtual memory for the best performance, but the good news is that you need to do it only once if you have a constant-size paging file.

There are several ways to defragment your swap file:

Use PerfectDisk
> Use an advanced defragmenter like PerfectDisk, discussed in "A Defragmentation Crash Course" on page 304. Just instruct it to defragment your system files, and it will schedule a defragmentation for the next time you start Windows.

Use another drive temporarily
> If you have more than one partition or hard disk in your system, start by moving your swap file to a different drive letter, as described in the previous section. Then, open a Command Prompt window (*cmd.exe*) and type:

```
defrag c: /x
```

> to defragment the free space on the drive. See "A Defragmentation Crash Course" on page 304, for more on this tool.

> When it's done, move the swap file to its new home, where it will rest nicely in the newly-allocated contiguous block of free space.

Turn off virtual memory temporarily
> If you don't have a second drive, your other choice is to disable virtual memory altogether by clicking **No paging file** and then **Set** in the Virtual Memory window (see Figure 5-11). After restarting Windows, run Disk Defragmenter as described above to set aside a large chunk of contiguous free space. When you're done, go back to the Virtual Memory window, and re-enable the paging file, making sure to set a constant size.

Clear the paging file automatically
> See "Part 3: Clear the paging file on shutdown", next, for another way to reduce fragmentation in your paging file.

Part 3: Clear the paging file on shutdown

It's possible to have Windows delete your paging file each time you shut down Windows. You may want to do this if you have a multiboot system (see Chapter 1), wherein each operating system on your PC has its own virtual memory settings. If the paging file from one OS is present while the other is running, it may cause a conflict and will certainly waste a lot of disk space.

If your paging file becomes corrupted or highly fragmented, Windows may load more slowly (or not at all). Deleting the paging file automatically forces Windows to recreate it each time it starts, which may alleviate this problem. (Naturally, if you've gone to the steps to defragment your paging file, as described earlier in this topic, you probably won't want to use this feature, lest it become fragmented again when it's recreated.)

1. Open the Local Security Policy console (*secpol.msc*); see Chapter 8 for more information on the settings in this window.

2. Expand the **Local Policies** branch and click the **Security Options** folder.

3. In the right pane, double-click the **Shutdown: Clear virtual memory pagefile**.

4. Select **Enabled** and then click OK. You'll need to restart Windows for the change to take effect.

Part 4: Advanced settings for the adventurous

Like virtual memory settings, disk cache settings in Windows 7 aren't necessarily optimized for the best performance, but rather for the best compromise between performance and compatibility with older PCs.

 You'll probably need to experiment with different values until you find the ones that work best for your system. Since it's possible to render Windows inoperable with incorrect settings here, you'll want to back up your PC before you begin.

Start by opening the Registry Editor (described in Chapter 3), and expanding the branches to HKEY_LOCAL_MACHINE\SYSTEM\CurrentControlSet\Control\Session Manager\Memory Management. Some of the more interesting values in this key include the following:

DisablePagingExecutive
Values: 0 = disabled (default), 1 = enabled.

Enabling this setting will prevent Windows from paging certain system processes to disk, which effectively will keep more of the operating system in the faster physical memory, in turn making Windows much more responsive.

`LargeSystemCache`

Values: `0` = standard (default), `1` = large.

By default, Windows uses only 8 MB of memory for the filesystem cache. Enabling this option will allow Windows to use all but 4 MB of your computer's memory for the filesystem cache. This will improve Windows' performance, but potentially at the expense of the performance of some of your more memory-intensive applications.

Other values in this key include `PagingFiles`, which is more easily set in the Virtual Memory window described in "Part 1: Virtual memory settings" on page 313 and `ClearPageFileAtShutdown`, more easily set in the Local Security Settings console, as described in "Part 3: Clear the paging file on shutdown" on page 316.

Choose the Right Filesystem

The filesystem is the invisible mechanism on your hard disk that is responsible for keeping track of all the data stored on the drive. Think of it as a massive table of contents, matching up each filename with its corresponding data stored somewhere on the disk surface. Windows 7 supports four hard disk filesystem types:

FAT (File Allocation Table, 16-bit)
FAT is used for all drives under 512 MB, such as small flash memory cards and floppy disks. The largest drive supported by the FAT filesystem is 2 GB.

FAT32 (File Allocation Table, 32-bit)
Designed to overcome the 2 GB partition limit with the FAT system, FAT32 is supported by every version of Windows since Windows 95 OSR2. Today, it's used mostly for flash memory cards larger than 2 GB, and on older PCs running Windows 98 and Windows Me. In addition to the support for larger drives, it also supports smaller file clusters (see the upcoming sidebar "Understanding Cluster Sizes" on page 318), so it stores information more efficiently than FAT.

exFAT (a.k.a. FAT64)
The "Extended File Allocation Table" was designed to resolve many of the shortcomings of FAT32 and to be used on drives where NTFS isn't practical, such as flash drives. exFAT is supported in Windows 7, Windows Vista SP1, and earlier versions with a free update.

NTFS (NT Filesystem)

NTFS, designed from the ground up to completely replace FAT/FAT32, is the default filesystem on all Windows 7 PCs. (Specifically, Windows 7, Vista, and XP all support NTFS version 3.1.) It offers security features like encryption and permissions (see Chapter 8), compression, and quotas. It's typically faster and more reliable than FAT/FAT32, and theoretically supports drives up to about 15 exbibytes (2^{64} bytes) in size.

Windows 7 can only be installed on an NTFS drive, but it can read partitions formatted with FAT or FAT32. And you can add support for other filesystems with add-on software; for instance, you can read Mac OS X HFS+ drives with MacDrive (*http://www.mediafour.com/*).

If Windows 7 is the only operating system on your computer, all your drives should be formatted with NTFS. The only compelling reason to use another filesystem is if you have a dual-boot setup with a very old version of Windows, in which case you'd need to choose a filesystem recognized by all operating systems on your computer. Table 5-2 shows which filesystems are supported by all recent versions of Microsoft Windows.

Table 5-2. Filesystems supported by recent versions of Windows

	FAT	FAT32	NTFS
Windows 7	✓ (data only)	✓ (data only)	✓ (v3.1)
Windows Vista	✓ (data only)	✓ (data only)	✓ (v3.1)
Windows XP	✓	✓	✓ (v3.1)
Windows Me, 98, and 95 ORS2	✓	✓	
Windows NT 4.0	✓		✓ (v1.2)
Windows 95	✓		

Understanding Cluster Sizes

Clusters are the smallest units into which a hard disk's space can be divided. A hard disk formatted with the traditional FAT system, found in Windows 95 and an ancient operating system called "DOS," can have no more than 65,536 clusters on each drive or partition. This means that the larger the hard disk, the larger the size of each cluster.

The problem with large clusters is that they result in a lot of wasted disk space. Each cluster can store no more than a single file (or a part of a single file); if a file does not consume an entire cluster, the remaining space is wasted. For example, a 2 GB FAT drive would have a cluster size of 32 KB; a 1 KB file on a disk with a 32 KB cluster size will consume 32 KB of disk space; a 33 KB file on the same drive will consume 64 KB of space, and so on. The extra 31 KB left over from the 33 KB file is called *slack space*, and it can't be used by any other files. With thousands of files (especially those tiny shortcuts littered throughout a Windows installation), the amount of wasted slack space on a sizeable hard disk can add up to hundreds of megabytes of wasted space.

You can see how much space is wasted by any given file by right-clicking on the file icon, selecting **Properties**, and comparing the **Size** value with the **Size on disk** value. The same works for multiple selected files and folders; highlight all the objects in your root directory to see the total amount of wasted space on your drive. To find the current cluster size of your drive, just open the properties sheet for a small file you know will only consume a single cluster (such as a Windows Shortcut); its **Size on disk** will be equal to the size of one cluster.

If you want to reduce the cluster size of a drive, you'll need to reformat it. Right-click a drive in Windows Explorer or Disk Management, select **Format**, and choose the cluster size you want from the **Allocation unit size** list. The smaller **Allocation unit size** you specify, the less space will be wasted. For instance, the NTFS filesystem can handle more than four billion clusters. This means you could choose a cluster size of only 4 kilobytes, and still format a partition of up to 14.9 terabytes (15,259 GB) in total size.

Note that for performance reasons, it's best to stick with the default cluster size unless the slack space turns out to be a significant issue.

Performance

To find out which filesystem is currently being used by a particular drive on your PC, just right-click the drive in Windows Explorer and select **Properties**. Or, open the Disk Management utility (*diskmgmt.msc*) to see an overview of all of your drives.

Convert your drives to NTFS

The easiest way to choose a filesystem for a drive is to format it. But if you need to convert a drive without wiping its data, use the FAT to NTFS Conversion Utility (*convert.exe*). To convert drive *J:*, for example, just open a Command Prompt window (*cmd.exe*) and type:

```
convert j: /fs:ntfs
```

Include the **/v** option to run in "verbose" mode, which provides more information as it does its job. Type convert /? for other, more esoteric options.

Note that this is a one-way conversion, at least when using the software included with Windows 7. If you need to convert an NTFS drive to FAT32 for some reason, you'll need a third-party utility such as Disk Director (*http://www.acronis.com/*).

Advanced NTFS Settings

The extra features of the NTFS filesystem discussed in the previous section come at a price, namely a small amount of disk space and performance overhead. The following settings allow you to fine-tune NTFS to squeeze the most performance out of your NTFS drive; experiment with these settings to find the configuration that works best for you.

Start by opening the Registry Editor (Chapter 3) and expanding the branches to HKEY_LOCAL_MACHINE\SYSTEM\CurrentControlSet\Control\Filesystem.

Double-click any one of the following values to change its data. If the value is missing, create it by going to **Edit→New→DWORD Value**, and then typing the name exactly as shown.

NtfsDisable8dot3NameCreation

> Values: 0 = enabled (default), 1 = disabled, 2 = enable 8.3 naming on a per-volume basis (via *fsutil.exe*), 3 = disabled on all volumes except system volume.
>
> Early versions of Windows and DOS didn't support so-called long filenames, but rather allowed only eight-character filenames followed by three-letter filename extensions. Although Windows 95 and all subsequent versions of Windows more or less eliminated this restriction, an eight-dot-three version of a filename is generated with each file you create to maintain compatibility with older applications. For example, the file *A letter to Mom.wpd* could also be referenced as *alette~1.wpd*. If you don't use older 16-bit programs, you can disable Windows' creation of these 8.3 aliases by changing this value to 1 (the default is zero).

NtfsDisableLastAccessUpdate

> Values: 0 = enabled (default), 1 = disabled.
>
> Windows keeps a record of the time and date every file and folder on your hard disk was created, as well as when it was last modified and last accessed. You can stop Windows from updating the "last accessed" date for folders every time they're opened by changing the value to 1 (the default is zero), which may improve drive performance. This setting has no effect on files.

NtfsMftZoneReservation

> Values: 1 = small (default), 2 = medium, 3 = large, 4 = maximum.
>
> The core of the NTFS filesystem is the master file table (MFT), a comprehensive index of every file on the disk (including the MFT itself). Since disk defragmenters can't defragment the MFT (also known as *$mft*), Windows reserves a certain amount of extra space for it to grow, in an effort

to reduce its eventual fragmentation. The more fragmented the MFT gets, the more it will hamper overall disk performance.

You can determine the current size and fragmentation level of the MFT on any drive by using the command-line Disk Defragmenter tool (*defrag.exe*) along with the -a parameter, as described in "A Defragmentation Crash Course" on page 304. The numbers relating to the MFT are shown at the end of the **Volume Information** report. Probably the most interesting statistic here, though, is **Percent MFT in use**. The higher the number, the less space the MFT has to grow (and it will).

 The NtfsMftZoneReservation setting allows you to increase the space reserved for the MFT. Although the default is 1, values of 2 or 3 are probably better for most systems with large hard disks; the maximum value of 4 is good for very large drives with a lot of small files. Specify too small of a value here, and the MFT will become fragmented more quickly as it grows; too large of a value, and it will consume (waste) too much disk space.

The problem is that changing this setting will not have any effect on your drive's current MFT, but rather only influence its future growth. For this reason, the earlier this value is increased in the life of a disk, the better. To defragment or rebuild the MFT on your Windows drive, you'll need to transfer your operating system to a new drive, as described in the next section.

You'll need to restart Windows for any of these changes to take effect.

Transfer Windows to Another Hard Disk

Each new version of Windows consumes something like four times that of its predecessor. (OK, to be fair, Windows 7 doesn't take up *that* much more room than Vista, but Vista's footprint was many times that of XP.) That kind of bloat would cause an uproar if the sizes of commercially available hard disks weren't growing at an even faster rate.

Luckily, a new drive is an inexpensive way to improve performance as well as get more space for your stuff. And there are basically two approaches:

Add a second drive.
    Hard drive manufacturers sell a lot of external USB drives for this purpose. It's the easiest approach, taking only a few minutes to hook up, but it does very little to improve performance. Why run Windows on an aging 60 GB

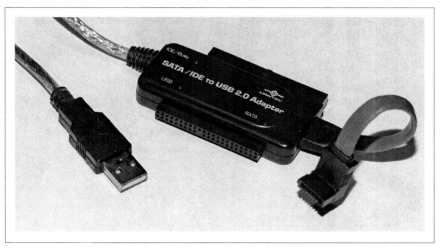

Figure 5-12. Use a handy external USB adapter like this one to hook up your new drive to your PC

drive, while basically static data like photos and music sit happily on a much faster 750 GB drive?

Replace the primary drive.

Use this approach if you want to throw away that old 60 GB drive, and use only the 750 GB drive for Windows *and* all your data. Not only will this give you better performance, you'll have a lot less to worry about if you're running Windows on a new drive rather than one that's seen thousands of hours of use. The downside is that it's more work to completely replace your old drive, and that's what this section is about.

Thanks to improvements in technology, rapidly dropping prices of new hard disks, and a nifty tool in Windows 7, it's easier than ever to replace your old hard disk.

The procedure goes like this: first, connect your new drive to your PC alongside your old drive. Then, create an *image* of your old hard disk—a snapshot of every byte of data on the entire drive—and write the image to your new hard disk. Finally, disconnect the old drive and put the new one in its place.

Start by purchasing an SATA/IDE to USB 2.0 Adapter, like the $20 unit shown in Figure 5-12. Alternatively, you can use an external hard drive enclosure, although a unit like this may be a better investment, as it supports SATA, 3.5 desktop IDE, and 2.5 notebook IDE drives all from the same cable.

Next, plug the drive into the adapter, plug the power supply into the drive, and then plug the adapter into a free USB port on your PC.

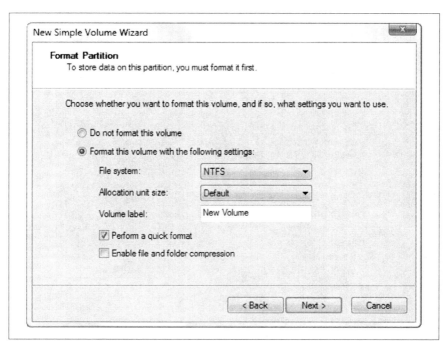

Figure 5-13. Use the Disk Management tool to prepare the new drive

Now, I know what you're thinking: why don't I just plug the drive directly into my SATA or IDE controller? While it's true that you can connect your new drive to your motherboard's controller, there are several reasons to use a USB adapter like this one instead. First, it's quick and easy; you don't need to take your PC apart (yet) and you don't have to leave the new drive dangling from the side of your box while you transfer your data. Second, it's great for laptops that may not have a way to connect two drives at once. Third, it avoids the nasty problems you'd encounter if your PC tried to boot to the wrong drive in the middle of the procedure. And last but not least, when you're done, you can use the adapter to clear off the old drive. A device like this makes things *so* much easier.

When Windows detects and installs the new drive, it'll show up in **Disk Drives** branch in Device Manager (*devmgmt.msc*). (If it doesn't, see Chapter 6.) As soon as Windows finishes installing the necessary drivers, open Disk Management (*diskmgmt.msc*), right-click the new drive in the lower pane, and select **New Simple Volume**, as shown in Figure 5-13.

On the first page of the New Simple Volume Wizard, click **Next**, and then specify the size of the new partition.

You'll need to make two partitions on the new drive: the primary partition to become your new boot drive, and a secondary partition to temporarily hold the backup of your existing data. The *second* partition needs to be no larger than the capacity of your old hard disk, so set the *primary* partition to the total size of the new drive *minus* the total size of the old drive.

 This is where your third-grade math comes in handy, but be prepared for things not to add up. If you're replacing a 60 GB hard disk with a 750 GB hard disk, you'd expect to set the first partition to 690 GB and use the remaining 60 GB for the second partition. But since drive manufacturers exaggerate— read, *lie*—about the capacities of their products, you'll have to determine the actual usable space first. For instance, a typical 750 GB hard disk has roughly 698 GB of actual storage capacity, which means you'd set 638 GB for the size of the first partition to leave 60 GB for the second. (Of course, if the old drive isn't completely full, you can get away with a little less on the second partition.)

So, at the prompt, type a value, in megabytes, for the size of the primary partition (i.e., `690000` for 690 GB) and then click **Next**. Follow the prompts to complete the wizard; make sure to format the drive with the NTFS filesystem, but don't assign a drive letter at this time.

Now, create the second partition in the remaining unused space, and have it consume the rest of the drive. Again, format it as NTFS, but this time, assign a drive letter (your choice).

It's now time to copy your data to the new drive. Luckily, all commercial editions of Windows 7 come with the full version of the Backup and Restore tool. (This is an improvement over Vista, which stingily provided full hard disk backup in only the Business, Ultimate, or Enterprise editions.) Start the Backup and Restore tool either from Control Panel or by running *sdclt.exe*.

On the left side of the window, click the **Create a system image** link. On the first page of the wizard, shown in Figure 5-14, select **On a hard disk**, pick the *second* partition you just created, and click **Next**. Next, select the drives to image; notice your active Windows drive is already checked and grayed out. Click **Next** and then **Start backup** to begin.

When the backup is complete, power down your PC, remove your old drive, connect the new one to your primary controller, and then boot your PC. Follow the instructions in "Recover Your System After a Crash" on page 423 to restore your backup to the primary partition on the new drive.

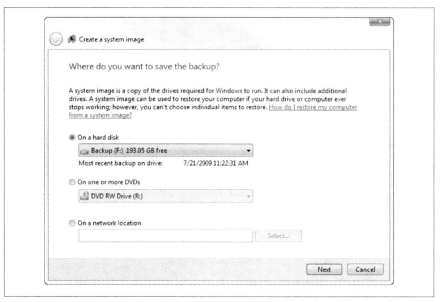

Figure 5-14. The Backup and Restore tool can create disk images on every edition of Windows 7

When that's done, and you're able to boot Windows with the new drive, use the Disk Management tool to delete the secondary partition and extend the primary partition so that it consumes the whole drive, as described in "Work with Partitions" on page 328.

Obviously, this solution requires that you boot off your original Windows disc to initiate the system recovery feature. To do away with this step, use third-party software to image your drive, such as DriveImage XML (free, *http://www.runtime .org*), HDClone Free Edition (free, *http://www.miray.de*), or Acronis True Image Home (commercial, *http://www.acronis .com*). All you do is create an image of your old hard disk and save it to the secondary partition of the new drive. Then use the same software to restore the image to the new drive's primary partition. When that's done, delete the secondary partition and extend the primary partition so that it consumes the whole drive, as described in the section "Work with Partitions" on page 328. Then, right-click the sole remaining partition and select **Mark Partition as Active**. Shut down Windows and then unplug both drives. Set the old drive aside and connect the new drive in its place.

Turn on your PC, and Windows should boot to the new drive. If it doesn't, see "What to Do When Windows Won't Start" on page 355.

What to look for in a new hard disk

The speed of your hard disk is a major factor of your system's overall performance, at least as much as its capacity. After all, the faster it's able to find data and transfer it, the quicker Windows will load, the faster your virtual memory will be, and the less time it will take to start applications and copy files.

Money is usually *the* deciding factor when choosing a drive, but with more money, people usually just opt for more gigabytes. If you want the best performance, though, consider these factors to be at least as important:

RPM (revolutions per minute)
    This is the speed at which the disk spins; higher numbers are faster. Cheap drives spin at 5,400 RPM, but you shouldn't settle for anything less than 7,200 RPM. 10,000 RPM (10k) drives are faster, but more expensive and harder to find. It's also worth noting that a larger-capacity drive can be faster than a smaller drive of the same RPM rating due to the higher data density.

Buffer (measured in megabytes)
    The buffer is memory (RAM) installed in the drive's circuitry that allows it to accept data from your computer faster than it is able to physically write to the disk surface, and to read data from the disk surface faster when your PC isn't necessarily ready for it. A larger buffer is better; don't settle for less than 16–32 megabytes.

MTBF (measured in hours)
    It doesn't matter how fast a drive is if it dies on you. The higher the MTBF—Mean Time Between Failures—the more reliable the drive is supposed to be. Of course, this isn't a guarantee, but rather merely an indicator of the market for which the drive was designed. Hard disks designed for servers tend to have much higher MTBF ratings than the low-end disks available on most computer store shelves.

 If you're buying a drive for use in a DVR (Digital Video Recorder) or HTPC (Home Theater PC), it's also wise to seek out the quietest drive you can find. Some drives offer AAM (Automatic Acoustic Management) features, which let you quiet a drive at the expense of some performance. Although manufacturers typically offer very little in the way of useful, reliable noise data, you can usually cull pretty good feedback from HTPC discussion groups on the Web.

RAID-ready

If you want to set up RAID as explained in Chapter 6, you'll need two or more identical drives. In theory, there are no special requirements, but in practice, it's smart to stick with drives made for this purpose. For instance, Seagate makes two versions of most of their drives: the AS series (consumer grade) and the NS series (server grade). The latter of the two is more expensive, but is designed to cope better with the increased vibrations generated by a RAID array, and typically has a much higher MTBF than the lesser model. Plus, the firmware on these drives is more likely to play nicely with your RAID controller.

Interface

There's rarely any reason to buy anything but a SATA drive these days; if you can, get a drive with SATA3 and NCQ (Native Command Queuing).

PATA (a.k.a. ATA or IDE) is now totally obsolete. Even if your desktop PC has only IDE controllers, it's best to get a SATA drive and a cheap SATA PCI-E/PCI controller to go with it. The only time when you should consider an IDE is if you have an older laptop and you can't upgrade the interface.

Some weirdos may still prefer SCSI or SAS drives, but there are very few cases when that's preferable over SATA anymore. SCSI controllers are unreasonably expensive, as are SCSI drives; consider this option only if you absolutely need a 15k RPM drive.

If you're buying an external drive—which is great for backups, as explained in Chapter 6—you may be tempted to get a USB drive or enclosure. While USB 2.0 is reasonably fast at 480 mbps, and Firewire 800 is slightly faster at 800 mbps, both of these standards will restrict the speed of your drive, and neither can be used to host a primary boot drive. For faster backups and less time spent transferring files, you'd be hard-pressed to beat eSATA (external SATA), which supports speeds up to 2,400 mbps. Most desktop PCs and some higher-end laptops include eSATA ports for this purpose, but if your PC doesn't have one, you can get an internal-to-external (SATA-to-eSATA) adapter cable for just a few dollars, or a standalone eSATA controller for not much more.

Work with Partitions

Most hard disks are known by a single drive letter, usually *C:*. However, any drive can be divided into several *partitions*, each with its own drive letter.

Most PC manufacturers these days ship partitioned hard disks. In fact, your drive may have one primary partition with all your data, plus another, smaller partition containing your PC's recovery data (to restore your hard disk to the state it was in when you bought it), and sometimes a third *EISA Configuration* partition (discussed later in this chapter, and in "Protect Your Data with RAID" on page 420). If you decide to nix the other two partitions, you can combine them and finally start using all the space on your drive.

But you also may want to chop up your drive into smaller partitions. For example, if you have a 500 GB hard disk, you may choose to divide it up into four 125 GB partitions, or perhaps a 300 GB partition and two 100 GB partitions. There are a bunch of reasons why you might want to do this:

Organization
> Use multiple partitions to further organize your files and make your stuff easier to find. For example, put Windows on one drive, work documents on another, games on another, and music and other media on yet another.

Isolation of system and data
> You can use partitions to isolate your programs from your data. For example, place Windows on drive *C:*, your personal documents on drive *D:*, and your virtual memory (swap file) and temporary files on drive *E:*. This setup gives you the distinct advantage of being able to format your operating system partition and reinstall Windows without touching your personal data, and also makes it easier to back up just your data.

Performance
> As illustrated in "A Defragmentation Crash Course" on page 304, the data on your hard drive can become badly fragmented with use, which hurts performance and increases the chances of data corruption. Because files cannot become fragmented across partition boundaries, you can dramatically reduce fragmentation by separating frequently accessed files, like those in the *Windows* and *Program Files* folders, from frequently updated files, like your virtual memory (swap file) and temporary files, as well as infrequently updated files like photos and music. But because fragmentation increases as free space decreases, you'd only get these performance gains with a drive large enough to guarantee sufficient free space on every partition.

Dual-boot

> To set up a dual-boot partition, described in Chapter 1, you'll need to create a separate partition for each operating system you install. (The same is not true for virtual installations, also covered in Chapter 1.)

Server

> If you're setting up a web server (or other type of network file server) or if you're participating in peer-to-peer file sharing, it's a good practice to put the publicly accessible folders on their own partition. This not only helps to secure the operating system from unauthorized access, but allows the OS to be upgraded or replaced without disrupting the shared folders and programs.

Naturally, there's a downside to having multiple partitions. For one, since you have to assign portions of your drive to different tasks ahead of time, multiple partitions use your space less efficiently than one big partition. Next, if you're the indecisive type and find yourself frequently rearranging your files, moving files between partitions takes much longer than moving files between folders on the same partition.

The Disk Management nickel tour

Windows 7 comes with several disk partitioning tools, but the most useful is Disk Management, shown in Figure 5-15. You can use Disk Management to view the partitions of any drive on your system, as well as create, delete, and resize partitions, and even change the drive letters for any drives or partitions on your PC. Open the Start menu, and in the **Search** box, type `diskmgmt.msc` and press **Enter**.

The main Disk Management window is divided into two panes, each of which shows the same information in different ways. (You can change the arrangement of the panes by going to **View→Top** or **View →Bottom**, but Disk Management won't remember any of your settings for next time.)

The **Graphical View**, shown in the lower pane by default, is easily the most useful, and is the subject of most of the rest of this section. The **Volume List**, shown in the upper pane by default, shows only your hard disk drive letters, and is a subset of the drive list in Windows Explorer. And the **Disk List** is merely a list of the physical disk devices in your PC, somewhat like the **Disk Drives** branch in Device Manager.

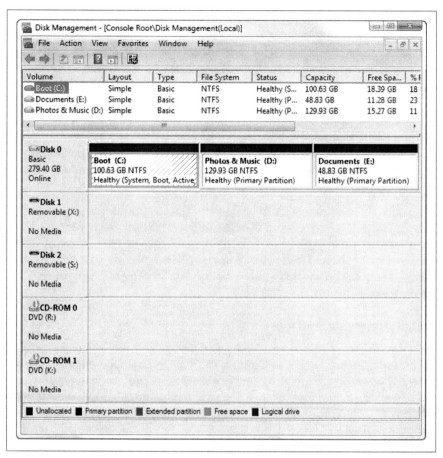

Figure 5-15. Open the Disk Management utility to add or remove partitions, shuffle drive letters, and even change the way volumes are mounted

By default, the boxes in the **Graphical View** representing multiple partitions (volumes) are not displayed proportionally to their size; a 20 GB partition will appear to be roughly the same size as a 100 GB partition. To fix this, go to **View→Settings**, choose the **Scaling** tab, and select the **According to capacity, using linear scaling** option in both sections. You can also customize the program's colors with the **Appearance** tab, but unless you follow the steps in "Save Settings in Disk Management" (the upcoming sidebar), your changes will be lost as soon as you close the window.

Save Settings in Disk Management

The Disk Management tool is actually what Microsoft calls a "snap-in" for the Microsoft Management Console (*mmc.exe*). Other snap-ins include Device Manager, the Services window, and the Group Policy Object Editor.

The *.msc* file you launch to open the Disk Management tool is not actually the program, but rather just a small *console* file, which contains only the settings for the current view. Although you can't save your customizations to *diskmgmt.msc*, you can create a new console file with the snap-ins you need, and customize it to your heart's content:

1. Open the Microsoft Management Console (*mmc.exe*). A new, blank Console Root window will appear in the MMC window.

2. Go to **File→Add/Remove Snap-in**, and then click **Add**.

3. Select **Disk Management** from the **Available Standalone Snap-ins** list, and then click **Add**.

4. From the window that appears, select **This Computer** and then click **Finish**.

5. You can add other snap-ins at this point, or just click OK when you're done.

6. If Disk Management is the only snap-in you selected, highlight the Disk Management entry in the tree on the left to show the tool in the center pane. Then go to **View→Customize**, turn off the **Console tree** and **Action pane** options, and click OK.

7. Now, you can customize Disk Management as you see fit. For instance, to show only the Graphical View, select **View→Top→Graphical View** and then **View→Bottom→ Hidden**.

8. When you're finished customizing, go to **File→Save** to save your custom console view into a new *.msc* file such as *Disk Management.msc*.

The next time you use Disk Management, just open your custom *.msc* file instead of *diskmgmt.msc* to use your customized tool.

Disk Management takes an active role in making drives available in Windows Explorer. Most of the time, as soon as you insert a flash memory card into your card reader or pop in a CD or DVD, the new volume appears in Disk Management and Explorer. But sometimes, Disk Management may fail to acknowledge that you've connected a device (say, an external hard disk), and as a result, its drive letter won't appear in Explorer. To force Windows to recognize your drive changes, press the **F5** key or go to **Action→Rescan Disks**, and in a few seconds, the newly connected drive should appear in all windows.

If it doesn't, open up Device Manager, and from the **Action** menu there, select **Scan for hardware changes**.

In the **Graphical View**, you'll see different kinds of partitions; here are the most common:

Primary partition

Most partitions are of this type. If you have more than one partition, the first usable partition (one that can hold data) is almost always a primary. Primary partitions are marked with a dark blue stripe by default.

The old school approach is to have only one primary partition, followed by an *extended* partition (discussed next). This is no longer needed for NTFS volumes; in fact, if you're setting up a dual-boot system, each OS must have its own *primary* partition.

Extended partition

The extended partition is a holdover from earlier days, and was used when a drive had two or more partitions. It doesn't actually hold data, it merely serves as a container for one or more *logical* drives (discussed next). Extended partitions and logical drives are more or less obsolete today (Disk Management can't even create them), but you may see them on older partitioned drives. The extended partition is, by default, shown as a dark green outline surrounding any logical drives.

Logical drive

If you have a drive with an extended partition, each volume inside is called a logical drive. See the notes for primary and extended partitions, earlier, for details. By default, logical drives are identified in light blue.

EISA Configuration

This is a tiny partition that holds configuration data for the rest of the drive, and it is typically placed at the beginning of the disk. You'll see this on most RAID drives (see Chapter 6) and often on drives installed in mass-produced PCs. Disk Management can't delete EISA Configuration partitions, but Acronis Disk Director (see the section "Resize and move partitions" on page 333) can.

System Reserved

Windows 7 setup creates a 100 MB "System Reserved" partition when you install on a blank hard disk (Professional edition or better). To keep this from happening and use your entire hard disk for the Windows installation, see "Prevent extra partitions during setup" on page 14.

Create and delete partitions

Every hard disk must be partitioned before it can be used, even if that disk only gets a single partition. Here's how to prepare a brand-new hard disk.

First, open Disk Management (*diskmgmt.msc*). If you see the Initialize Disk window at this or any point, select **MBR (Master Boot Record)** and click OK. Next, make sure the **Graphical View**, shown by default in the lower pane, is completely visible. Enlarge the pane and the window if necessary to see all your drives.

To create a new partition, right-click a region of your new disk marked **Unallocated**, and select **New Simple Volume**. The steps in the New Simple Volume Wizard are pretty self-explanatory, and basically involve dialing in a size for the new partition (use the maximum if you want to use the whole drive), choosing a drive letter, and picking a filesystem (choose NTFS, as described in "Choose the Right Filesystem" on page 317).

Or, to delete an existing partition, right-click the partition and select **Delete Volume**.

 If you delete a partition, all the data on that volume will be permanently lost. This happens immediately, and there is no undo. Data on other partitions of the same physical drive won't be affected. If you wish to make a partition smaller or larger *without* erasing the data, see the next section "Resize and move partitions".

In most cases, newly created or deleted partitions will appear (or disappear) in Windows Explorer immediately.

Resize and move partitions

Say you just bought a laptop with an 80 GB hard disk and then discover that Windows Explorer only sees about 70 GB of it. You open Disk Management and discover that there's an extra partition, labeled "Recovery," consuming about 8 GB. How do you get rid of the extra partition and reclaim all that space for your data?

Or, perhaps you've decided to divide a 320 GB hard disk—one that's currently holding an active Windows installation—into two 160 GB partitions. How do you make space for the second partition without deleting the single partition that's currently using the whole disk?

The solution is to resize the partition, which—thanks to some improvements in Disk Manager since Windows XP—is not all that hard to do. And you don't even have to take the data off first. (Of course, despite this confident prose, it's still wise to back up your entire drive before messing with partitions.)

To begin, open Disk Management and expand the Graphical View pane so you can see all your drives.

In the case of the unwanted "Recovery" partition, start by right-clicking it in Disk Management and selecting **Delete Volume**.

 You can't undo **Delete Volume**, so make sure you can live without the "Recovery" partition before you proceed. In most cases, it isn't necessary to keep this volume unless you plan on wiping your hard disk and reinstalling 7 *without* the original installation DVD. If you don't have a disc, check with your PC's manufacturer to see whether they can provide you with one before you proceed.

Once the "Recovery" partition is gone, you'll have a swath of empty space marked **Unallocated** at the end of your drive. (If it's at the beginning, you'll need a tool like Disk Director, discussed in the next section.) Now all you have to do is right-click your primary partition and select **Extend Volume** to resize the remaining partition so that it consumes the unused space.

If you get an error that says "The operation failed to complete because the Disk Management console view is not up-to-date," use DiskPart, described in the sidebar "The DiskPart Command-Line Tool" on page 336, instead.

If you want to do the opposite—that is, make room at the end of the disk for a new partition—just right-click the primary partition and select **Shrink Volume**. After a bit of pondering, Disk Management will show the Shrink dialog (Figure 5-16), which will probably show you less "available shrink space" than you thought you had coming.

Say you have about 150 GB of data on your 500 GB drive, but the Shrink window says you can only reclaim about 75 GB (7,500 MB) of free space. Why so stingy?

It turns out that Windows doesn't necessarily store all your data at the beginning of a partition, but rather scatters it around to help reduce fragmentation. As a result, there may be some data toward the end, serving as a barrier to prevent Disk Management from shrinking your drive past that point.

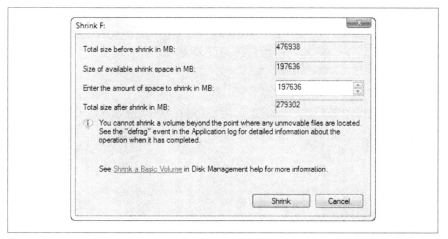

Shrink F:

Total size before shrink in MB: 476938

Size of available shrink space in MB: 197636

Enter the amount of space to shrink in MB: 197636

Total size after shrink in MB: 279302

ⓘ You cannot shrink a volume beyond the point where any unmovable files are located.
    See the "defrag" event in the Application log for detailed information about the
    operation when it has completed.

    See Shrink a Basic Volume in Disk Management help for more information.

                                              Shrink   Cancel

Figure 5-16. Use the Shrink Volume window to make space on your drive for new partitions

The solution is to use the command-line Disk Defragmenter tool (*defrag.exe*) with the /x parameter, as described in "A Defragmentation Crash Course" on page 304. When that's done, return to Disk Management and try **Shrink Volume** once more.

If the **Shrink Volume** feature in Disk Management still won't give you as much space as you need, you'll need a more capable program like Disk Director, covered next.

Alternatives to Disk Management

The Disk Management utility is not your only choice when it comes to repartitioning drives, but as far as the tools included with Windows 7 are concerned, it's the best one.

The other usable alternative is 7's DiskPart utility (*diskpart.exe*), a way of viewing, adding, and removing partitions from the Command Prompt; see the upcoming sidebar "The DiskPart Command-Line Tool" for a walkthrough.

In the good old days—also known simply as the old days—the only way to resize partitions without deleting the data on them was to use a program called PartitionMagic. But since Symantec bought PartitionMagic and ruined it, the best choice now is Acronis Disk Director, available at *http://www.acronis .com/*. If you want a free partition editor, try EASEUS Partition Master Home Edition, available at *http://www.partition-tool.com/*, but keep in mind that it only supports 32-bit Windows (the Professional edition, which costs money, supports x64).

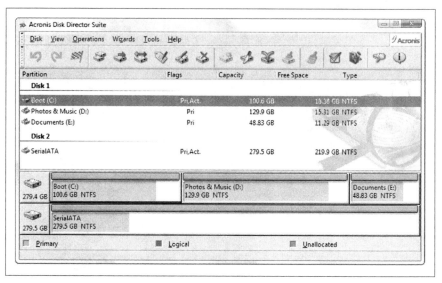

Figure 5-17. To move partitions, delete EISA Configuration volumes, and more, use a partition editor like Acronis Disk Director

The DiskPart Command-Line Tool

DiskPart is essentially the command-line equivalent to the Disk Management tool, and can be useful in certain situations (such as when Windows won't start).

You'll need to run DiskPart in administrator mode (see Chapter 8); one way to do this is to open your Start menu, type `diskpart` in the **Search** box, and then when **diskpart.exe** appears in the search results, right-click it and select **Run as administrator**.

Once it's running, type `help` at any time to see a list of commands. To get started, here's how to extend a volume in DiskPart:

1. At the `DISKPART>` prompt, type:

   ```
   list disk
   ```

   to display all the drives on your computer. Each drive will have a disk number, starting with 0 (zero).

2. Unless you have only one drive, you'll have to tell DiskPart which drive to use, like this:

   ```
   select disk n
   ```

   where *n* represents the number of the disk to modify.

3. Next, at the `DISKPART>` prompt, type:

```
list volume
```

to display all the volumes on the selected disk. Likewise, each volume has a volume number, starting with 0 (zero).

4. Regardless of the number of volumes on the drive, you'll have to tell DiskPart which one to use, like this:

```
select volume 2
```

5. Now that you've selected the partition to expand, go ahead and issue this command:

```
extend
```

to extend the volume. The `extend` command takes no options and displays no warning message or confirmation. The process begins immediately after you press the **Enter** key, and should take only a few seconds.

6. When it's done, type **exit** to quit the DiskPart utility.

See Chapter 9 for more information on the Command Prompt.

Among other things, partition editors like Disk Director and Partition Master let you move partitions, resize from the left (beginning) or right (end), and delete otherwise undeletable partitions, such as the EISA Configuration volumes discussed earlier in this section.

If you're using 64-bit Windows and want a free partition editor, you can use QTParted, the partition editor that comes with Linux. Now, you don't have to install Linux, but rather only boot off a Linux Live CD like the one available at *http://iso.linuxquestions.org/mepis/*. It supports NTFS as well as FAT32, and lets you freely resize partitions without destroying data. Alternatively, Gparted (free from *http://gparted.sourceforge.net/*) comes with its own dedicated Linux Live CD.

Any way you do it, it's always wise to back up before messing with your partitions.

Different ways to mount a volume

As explained earlier in this section, a hard disk can have one partition or many. Other types of storage devices, such as CD and DVD drives, can only have a single partition. These partitions, regardless of the nature of the physical device on which they're located, are all recognized as *volumes* by the Disk Management tool and by Windows Explorer.

Mounting is the method by which a volume is made accessible to Windows Explorer and all your applications. In most cases, each volume has its own drive letter, such as *C:* or *D:*. But a volume can also be accessed through a folder on any other volume, called a *mount point* (available on NTFS drives only). Finally, there can be volumes on your system that aren't mounted at all, such as those with filesystems Windows doesn't support and those you don't want to show up in Windows Explorer.

You can change how any volume is mounted, except for the *system* volume (the one containing your boot files) and the *boot* volume (the one on which Windows is installed)—these are usually one and the same.

To change the drive letter of a hard disk volume, right-click the partition itself in the right side of the Graphical View pane in Disk Management, and select **Change Drive Letter and Paths**.

Or, to change the drive letter of a non-fixed disk, such as your DVD drive or flash card reader, right-click the disk in the narrow lefthand column, and select **Change Drive Letter and Paths**.

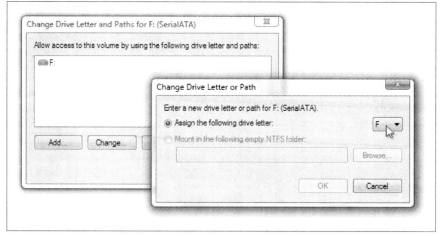

Figure 5-18. You can change the drive letter for any device, as well as mount the volume as a folder on another drive, using the Change Drive Letter and Paths dialog

In either case, you can choose a new drive letter (e.g., *H:*) by clicking the **Change** button, shown in Figure 5-18. Click **Remove** if you don't want the drive to show up in Windows Explorer at all. Or, click **Add** to choose an empty folder as a mount point (or pick a drive letter where there is none).

If you select **Mount in the following empty NTFS folder**, click **Browse** to point to an existing, empty folder on a hard disk that already has a drive letter. If you were to mount the volume in the folder *C:\backdoor*, then the contents of the newly mounted drive would be accessible in *C:\backdoor*. A folder named *some folder* on the new drive would then appear as *D:\backdoor\some folder*. You can view all of the drives mounted in folders by going to **View→Drive Paths**.

Click OK when you're done. For another way to hook up drives and folders, see the sidebar "Force a Login Box for a Remote Folder" on page 602.

CHAPTER 6

Troubleshooting

What's wrong with your PC? I know, stupid question: it's like asking, "how long is a piece of string?" But it's even a harder one to answer than it used to be. While Windows 7 is a big improvement over its predecessor, the list of things that can go wrong grows even longer.

An application won't install? Perhaps the installer is buggy. Or maybe your registry permissions are munged. Or it could be a native 32-bit program that isn't compatible with your 64-bit OS. And then there's User Access Control, which always seems to muck things up.

Does it sometimes seem like your hardware or software "gets tired"? For instance, a device that works normally most of the time may malfunction only when it's used more aggressively, which could point to overheating or a bug in its power saving features. Or Windows works fine until you open multiple applications or use it for more than 20 minutes, which could suggest a faulty power supply or defective RAM.

A message appears to break the bad news: you have a virus. But wait, is that just a browser pop-up? It could be a false-positive from your legit antivirus software...or maybe it's spyware in the guise of an anti-spyware tool.

Your Internet not working? Maybe you flubbed your WiFi passphrase. Or your router has crashed...again. Or the storm knocked out your DSL. Is that smoke coming from your modem?

Of course, this entire book is devoted to problem solving, but this chapter is where you'll want to look when Windows won't start (or shut down), when you have a malware infestation, when you're having trouble with hardware... or when you just want to prevent these things from happening. But if you remember only two pearls of wisdom from this chapter, let them be these:

- 99% of all computer problems are solved by rebooting. (Restart Windows, turn it off and then back on, press your PC's reset button, whatever.)
- Insanity can be defined as repeating the same actions over and over again, expecting different results. (Or, worse: repeating the same actions over and over again, *knowing* that you'll never get different results.)

Naturally, a corollary to these principles is that rebooting repeatedly will get you nowhere. Herein lies the rub: what do you do during that remaining 1% of the time when rebooting the first time doesn't help?

One of the first things you need to do to solve a problem is to find the right words to describe the problem, and those words rarely contain "doesn't" and "work." Instead, consult this short checklist of questions to ask yourself to get you—or rather, your PC—on the road to recovery:

When did the problem start happening?
Sudden changes in your computer's behavior are almost never spontaneous; if something suddenly stops working, you can bet that there's a culprit in a recent change to your system. If the problem surfaced the same day you updated an application, installed a new driver, or added a new toolbar to Internet Explorer, you've got yourself a prime suspect.

Is this an isolated incident, or does this problem occur every time?
Windows 7 may be less crash-prone as a platform than earlier operating systems, but the same can't necessarily be said for Windows Explorer, Microsoft Word, or any other application running on top of it. An isolated incident is often just that, and, if nothing else, is a good reminder to save your work often. On the other hand, if a problem occurs with some regularity and you can manage to connect this incident with other issues, it'll take you a long way towards a fix.

Is the problem with a specific application or hardware device, or is it a conflict?
Don't forget that software products are a lot like pharmaceuticals: interactions can cause problems while the products by themselves are harmless. Got two firewalls running at the same time, and all of a sudden you can't use the Web? Or maybe you've uninstalled one program and now another program from the same publisher won't auto-update?

Conflicts are resolved by the process of elimination. You can rule out a specific application if the problem occurs across several applications. You can rule out individual devices by unplugging them or disabling their drivers in Device Manager. And if you're really motivated, you can install a separate or virtual copy of Windows (see Chapter 1) to rule out your specific Windows installation or try a specific application in an isolated/clean environment.

What's the latest version?

Software and hardware manufacturers frequently release updates and fixes, so it's often desirable to check their respective websites for the latest versions of all applications and drivers. See "Dealing with Drivers and Other Tales of Hardware Troubleshooting" on page 387 for details.

How likely is it that someone else has encountered the same problem?

This is often the most useful question to ask yourself, because the odds are that someone else not only has encountered the same problem (anything from an annoying software quirk to a deafening application crash), but has already discovered a solution and written about it in some online forum. For example, there's a Windows 7 discussion forum at *http://www .annoyances.org* for this specific purpose!

Am I asking the right people?

If you're having trouble connecting to the wireless Internet at the airport, don't call your plumber. On the other hand, the computer store won't be much help with a jammed pressure-balance valve. Again, it comes down to isolating the source of a problem, and this is one of the hardest things to do, particularly when tech support insists that your problem is not *their* problem.

How much is my time worth?

This last tidbit of wisdom comes from years of experience. Some problems require hours and hours of fruitless troubleshooting and needless headaches. In some cases, it makes more sense to replace the product that's giving you trouble than to try to fix it. Keep that in mind when it's four o'clock in the morning and Windows refuses to recognize your $8 flash memory card reader.

Thus endeth the Q&A portion of this evening's programming. Stay tuned for the feature presentation...

Crashes and Error Messages

Once you start peeking under Windows' hood, you'll notice some of the tools that have been included to help the system run smoothly. Some of these tools actually work, but it's important to know which ones to use and which ones are simply gimmicks.

Viruses, Malware, and Spyware

Malware, or *mal*icious soft*ware*, is a class of software designed specifically to wreak havoc on a computer—your computer. Malware includes such nasty entities as viruses, Trojan horses, worms, and spyware. There are actually people who stay up late trying to dream up new ways of screwing up your PC, and apparently, not one of them can spell.

If you're experiencing frequent crashing, nonsensical error messages, pop-up advertisements (other than when surfing the Web), or slower than normal performance, the culprit may be one of the following types of malware (as opposed to a feature authored by Microsoft):

Viruses

A virus is a program or piece of code that "infects" other software by embedding a copy of itself in one or more executable files. When the software runs, so does the embedded virus, thus propagating the infection. Viruses can replicate themselves, and some (known as *polymorphic* viruses) can even change their virus signatures each time to avoid detection by antivirus software. Unlike *worms*, next, viruses can't infect other computers without assistance from people (a.k.a. you), a topic discussed in detail in the next section.

Worms

A worm* is a special type of virus that can infect a computer without any help from its user, typically through a network or Internet connection. Worms can replicate themselves like ordinary viruses, but do not spread by infecting programs or documents. A classic example is the *W32.Blaster.Worm*, which exploited a bug in Windows XP, causing it to restart repeatedly or simply seize up.

---

* The term *worm* is said to have its roots in the writings of J.R.R. Tolkien, who described dragons in Middle Earth that were powerful enough to lay waste to entire regions. Two such dragons (Scatha and Glaurung) were known as "the Great Worms." The *Great Worm*, a virus written by Robert T. Morris in 1988, was particularly devastating, mostly because of a bug in its own code. (*Source: Jargon File 4.2.0.*)

Trojan horses

A *Trojan horse* spreads itself by masquerading as a benign application (as opposed to *infecting* an otherwise valid file), such as a screensaver or even, ironically, a virus removal tool. See the upcoming sidebar "Zombies and Botnets" for one reason people create Trojan horses in the first place, and "How malware spreads" on page 346, for an example.

Rootkits

A rootkit is a form of malware designed to conceal the fact that your computer has been infected. By their very nature, rootkits are particularly difficult to remove, let alone find. To hide its presence, a rootkit must be in memory, so the best means of detection and removal is to access the compromised drive from a different operating system, either using a dual-boot setup (see Chapter 1) or by removing the drive from the PC and plugging it into another PC (see Chapter 5). GMER (free from *http://www .gmer.net/*) can also be used to detect and remove rootkits.

Spyware and adware

Spyware is a little different than the aforementioned viruses and worms, in that its purpose is not necessarily to hobble a computer or destroy data, but rather something much more insidious. Spyware is designed to install itself transparently on your system, spy on you or your employer, and then send the data it collects back to an Internet server. This is sometimes done to collect information about unsuspecting users (automated identity theft), but also can serve as a conduit for pop-up advertisements (a.k.a. adware).

Aside from the ethical implications, spyware can be particularly troublesome because it's so often very poorly written, and as a result, ends up causing error messages, performance slowdowns, and seemingly random crashing. Plus, it uses your computer's CPU cycles and Internet connection bandwidth to accomplish its goals, leaving fewer resources available for the applications you actually want to use.

Zombies and Botnets

Why do people create malware? To turn your PC into a zombie, of course.

Classically, a zombie is a mindless (often deceased) human controlled by a "bokor," or sorcerer. More recently, zombies have been portrayed as autonomous reanimated corpses that feast on the living, but it's the classical definition that's more accurately applied to your computer.

A zombie PC is one infected with malware so that it carries out instructions from a remote server (in essence, a virtual bokor). The goal is usually to send out spam and bypass the IP-blocklist measures in place to stop spam email

---

from known sources, which it does invisibly in the background. Create thousands of zombies around the globe, and you've got a botnet.

If your machine is a zombie, you're paying—with your Internet bandwidth and CPU cycles—to deliver someone else's spam. If that's not enough, this practice can also lead to getting your IP address and email accounts blacklisted so you can't even send legitimate mail.

The best defense is to use the anti-malware software listed in "How to protect and clean your PC" on page 349, but there are other remedies.

For instance, some malware hijacks your email program and uses your preconfigured SMTP server to send infected files to everyone in your address book. In nearly all cases, such malware is designed to work with the email software most people have on their systems, namely Microsoft Outlook and Windows Mail (formerly Outlook Express). If you want to significantly abate your computer's susceptibility to this type of attack, you'd be wise to use *any other* email software, such as Mozilla Thunderbird (*http://www.mozilla .com*) or stick with web-based email like Gmail (*http://www.gmail.com*) or Yahoo! Mail (*http://mail.yahoo.com*).

Also, take time to reconfigure User Account Control (UAC), as described in "Control User Account Control" on page 569, so that unwanted software can't install itself without your permission.

Now, it's often difficult to tell one type of malicious program from another, and in some ways, it doesn't matter. But if you understand how these programs work—how they get into your computer, and what they do once they've taken root—you can eliminate them and keep them from coming back.

How malware spreads

Once they've infected a system, viruses and the like can be very difficult to remove. For that reason, your best defense against them is to prevent them from infecting your computer in the first place.

The most useful tool you can use to keep malware off your computer is your cerebral cortex. Just as malware is written to exploit vulnerabilities in computer systems, the *distribution* of malware exploits the stupidity and carelessness of users.

Malware is typically spread in the following ways:

Email attachments

One of the most common ways viruses make their way into computers is through spam. Attachments are embedded in these junk email messages and sent by the millions to every email address in existence, for unsuspecting recipients to click, open, and execute. But how can people be that dumb, you may ask? Well, consider the filename of a typical Trojan horse:

kittens playing with yarn.jpg .scr

Since Windows 7 has its filename extensions hidden by default (see Chapter 2), this is how the file looks to most PC users:

kittens playing with yarn.jpg

In other words, most people wouldn't recognize that this is an *.scr* (screensaver) file and *not* a photo of kittens. (The long space in the filename ensures that it won't be easy to spot in the Large Icons view, even if extensions are visible.) And since many spam filters and anti-virus programs block *.exe* files, but not *.scr* files—which just happen to be renamed *.exe* files—this innocuous-looking file is more than likely to spawn a nasty virus on someone's computer with nothing more than an innocent double-click.

So, how do you protect yourself from these? First, don't open email attachments you weren't expecting and manually scan everything else with an up-to-date virus scanner (discussed later in this section). Next, employ a good spam filter (see "Stop Spam" on page 537), and employ your ISP to filter out viruses on the server side.

Infected files

Viruses don't just invade your computer and wreak havoc, they replicate themselves and bury copies of themselves in other files. This means that once your computer has been infected, the virus is likely sitting dormant in any of the applications and even personal documents stored on your hard disk. This not only means that you may be spreading the virus each time you email documents to others, but that others may be unwittingly sharing viruses with you.

Peer-to-peer (P2P) file sharing

Napster started the P2P file-sharing craze years ago, but modern file sharing goes far beyond the trading of harmless music files. It's estimated that some 40% of the files available on these P2P networks contain viruses, Trojan horses, and other unwelcome guests. For instance, it's not unusual to find DRM-protected media that prompts Windows Media Player to download malware in the guise of a codec or DRM license.

To protect yourself from malware-infected movies and music, open Windows Media Player. From the **Tools** menu, select **Options** and then choose the **Privacy** tab. Turn off the **Download usage rights automatically when I play or sync a file** option. Next, choose the **Security** tab and turn off all the options in the **Content** section, and click OK when you're done. See also "Lock Down Internet Explorer" on page 514 for more on the security zone settings that can affect Windows Media Player's ability to connect to online content.

But the files you download over P2P aren't necessarily the biggest cause of concern. To facilitate the exchange of files, these P2P programs open network ports (Chapter 7) and create holes in your computer's firewall, any of which can be exploited by a variety of worms and intruders. And since people typically leave these programs running all the time (whether they intend to or not), these security holes are constantly open for business.

But wait...there's more! If the constant threat of viruses and Trojan horses isn't enough, many P2P programs *themselves* come with a broad assortment of spyware and adware, intentionally installed on your system along with the applications themselves. Make sure to do a little research before installing any particular P2P client

Websites and socially engineered malware

It may sound like the rantings of a conspiracy theorist, but even the act of visiting some websites can infect your PC with spyware and adware. Not that it can happen transparently, but many people just don't recognize the red flags even when they're staring them in the face.

For example, the "add-ins" employed by some websites that provide custom cursors, interactive menus, or other eye candy, can be effective Trojan horses. While loading a web page, you may see a message asking if it's OK to install some ActiveX gadget "necessary" to view the page (e.g., Comet Cursor); here, the answer is simple: no.

You may also encounter pop-up browser windows masquerading as legitimate anti-malware tools, presenting messages like "Your computer is infected" (a.k.a., "scareware"). While Internet Explorer has the built-in SmartScreen Filter that's supposed to block content like this, new sites can pop up faster than Microsoft can track them.

Just as many viruses are written to exploit Microsoft Outlook, most spyware and adware targets Microsoft Internet Explorer. By using IE in Protected Mode only, or by switching to browsers incapable of installing system-level software, such as Firefox or Chrome, you can eliminate the threat posed by many of these nasty programs. See the section "Lock Down Internet Explorer" on page 514, for the full story.

Network and Internet connections

Your network connection (both to your LAN and to the Internet) can serve as a conduit for a worm, the special kind of virus that doesn't need your help to infect your system. Obviously, the most effective way to protect your system is to unplug it from the network, but a slightly more realistic solution is to use a firewall. Windows comes with a built-in firewall, although a router provides much better protection. See Chapter 7 for details on both solutions.

USB flash drives

Any storage medium can be a source of malware, and not just because it might contain an unwitting coworker's infected files. There's a scam, for instance, in which a flash drive, adorned with the company logo, is left in that institution's lobby, elevator, or parking lot. An unsuspecting employee grabs the drive and plugs it into a PC to see what's on it, only to have Windows' AutoPlay feature install the malware contained therein in a flash. In no time, the entire company's security has been compromised. At least Windows 7 now prompts before running software on a removable drive, a courtesy Microsoft never gave us in Windows XP and earlier versions.

How to protect and clean your PC

The most popular and typically the most effective way to rid your computer of malware is to use dedicated antivirus, antispyware, and antimalware software. These programs rely on their own internal databases of known viruses, worms, Trojans, spyware, and adware and, as such, must be updated regularly (daily or weekly) to be able to detect and eliminate the latest threats.

Windows 7 includes an antimalware tool, Windows Defender (found in Control Panel and shown in Figure 6-1). It won't catch everything, but left to its own devices, Windows Defender will regularly scan your system and even keep its spyware definitions up to date.

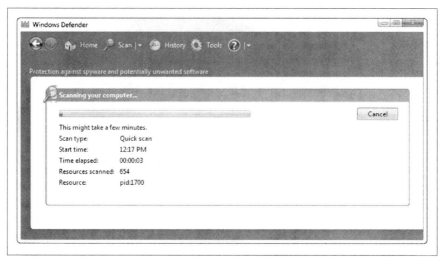

Figure 6-1. Windows Defender is included with Windows 7 to scan for malware, but you should augment it with other tools to fully protect your PC

But after all these years, Windows still doesn't come with an *antivirus* tool, mostly to appease the companies that make money selling aftermarket antivirus software (which is ironic, since the best tools are free). Microsoft even offers a free Antivirus tool (see below), but you have to download and install it separately. The following is a list of the more popular antivirus products.

Avast Home Edition (http://www.avastav.org/)
Freeware, with a slick interface and excellent detection rates.

Avira AntiVir (http://www.avira.com/)
Freeware, with frequent updates, but only average detection rates.

AVG Anti-Virus (http://free.avg.com/?)
Freeware, a popular yet poor-performing antivirus solution.

GMER (http://www.gmer.net/)
A free tool specifically for removing rootkits.

Kaspersky Antivirus Personal (http://www.kaspersky.com/)
Very highly regarded solution with an excellent detection record.

McAfee VirusScan (http://www.mcafee.com/)
Trusted and well-established all-around virus scanner with an intuitive interface and few limitations.

Microsoft Security Essentials (http://www.microsoft.com/security_essentials/)
A new tool, and completely free at that, that is not preinstalled in Windows for all the wrong reasons.

Panda Anti-Virus Titanium & Platinum (http://www.pandasecurity.com/)
Lesser-known but capable antivirus software.

Symantec Norton AntiVirus (http://www.symantec.com/)
Mediocre, slow antivirus software with a well-known name—beware of its expensive subscription plan to keep virus definitions updated.

Antispyware/antimalware software is a more complex field, and as a result, you'll have the best luck using multiple tools in addition to Windows Defender. The top antispyware products include:

Ad-Aware Personal Edition (http://www.adawarepe.com/)
Ad-Aware is one of the oldest antispyware tools around, but its definitions are still updated frequently. The personal edition is free and very slick, although it sometimes isn't as effective at removing infestations as Malwarebytes' Anti-Malware or Spy Sweeper, both discussed next.

 When using Ad-Aware, make sure you click **Check for updates now** before running a scan. Also, to turn off the awful, jarring sound Ad-Aware plays when it has found spyware, click the gear icon to open the Settings window, click the **Tweak** button, open the **Misc Settings** category, and turn off the **Play sound if scan produced a result** option.

Malwarebytes' Anti-Malware (http://www.antimalware.us/)
A relatively new player to the field, MBAM can often eliminate malware that other tools miss (Figure 6-2.) If Windows Defender identifies a threat but can't wipe it from your system, don't be surprised if MBAM cleans your system in minutes. The basic version is free; the paid edition adds real-time protection.

Spy Sweeper (http://www.spysweeper.us/)
This highly regarded antispyware tool, while not free like the first two, is still a welcome addition to any spyware-fighter's toolbox, and can often remove malware that the others miss.

 Once the top of its field, *Spybot: Search and Destroy*, has fallen far behind its competition. Recently, I've seen many PCs riddled with spyware that were supposedly protected by Spybot; these days, other tools (just mentioned) do a better job.

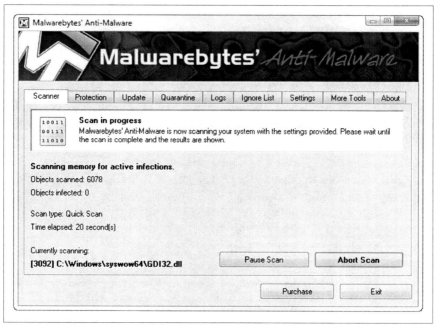

Figure 6-2. Malwarebytes' Anti-Malware is one of several antispyware tools that can be used in conjunction with Windows Defender to help keep your PC malware-free

So, armed with proper antivirus and antispyware software, there are four things you should do to protect your computer from malware:

- Place a router between your computer and your Internet connection, as described in Chapter 7.

- Scan your system for viruses regularly, and don't rely entirely on your antivirus program's auto-protect feature (see the next section). Run a full system scan at least every two weeks.

- Scan your system for spyware regularly, at least once or twice a month. Do it more often if you download and install a lot of software.

- Use your head! See the previous section for ways that malware spreads, and the next section for some of the things you can do to reduce your exposure to viruses, spyware, adware, and other malware.

The perils of auto-protect

Antivirus software is a double-edged sword. Sure, viruses can be a genuine threat, and for many of us, antivirus software is an essential safeguard. But antivirus software can also be a real pain in the neck.

The most basic, innocuous function of an antivirus program is to scan files on demand. When you start a virus scanner and tell it to scan a file or a disk full of files, you're performing a useful task. The problem is that most of us don't remember or want to take the time to routinely perform scans, so we rely on the so-called "auto-protect" feature, where the virus scanner runs all the time. This can cause several problems:

Performance hit
> Loading the auto-protect software at Windows startup can increase boot time; also, because each and every application (and document) you open must first be scanned, load times can increase. Plus, a virus scanner that's always running consumes memory and processor cycles, even though you're not likely to spend most of your time downloading new, potentially hazardous files for it to scan.

Browser and email monitoring
> Some antivirus auto-protect features include web browser and email plug-ins, which scan all files downloaded and received as attachments, respectively. In addition to the performance hit, these plug-ins sometimes don't work properly, inadvertently causing all sorts of problems with the applications you use to open these files.

Annoying and obtrusive messages
> The constant barrage of virus warning messages can be annoying, to say the least. For instance, if your antivirus software automatically scans your incoming email, you may be forced to click through a dozen or so messages warning you of virus-laden attachments, even though your spam filter will likely delete them before you ever see them. And nearly every antivirus program makes a big show each time it receives definition updates; while it's nice to know the software is doing its job, it would also be nice to have it do so *quietly*.

False sense of security
> Most importantly, having the auto-protect feature installed can give you a false sense of security ("Sure, I'll open it—I have antivirus software!"), reducing the chances that you'll take the precautions listed elsewhere in this section and increasing the likelihood that your computer will become infected. Even if you are diligent about scanning files manually, no antivirus program is foolproof, and software is certainly no substitute for common sense.

Now, if you take the proper precautions, your exposure to viruses will be minimal, if not nil, and you'll have very little need for the auto-protect feature of your antivirus software. Naturally, whether you disable your antivirus software's auto-protect feature is up to you. But if you keep the following practices in mind, you should be able to effectively eliminate your computer's susceptibility to viruses and not need the protection in the first place.

If you don't download any documents or applications from the Internet, if you're not connected to a local network, if you have a firewalled connection to the Internet, and the only type of software you install is off-the-shelf commercial products, your odds of getting a virus are pretty much zero.

Viruses can only reside in certain types of files, including application (*.exe* and *.scr*) files, document files made in applications that use macros (such as Microsoft Word), and some types of application support files (*.dll*, *.vbx*, *.vxd*, etc.). And because ZIP files (described in Chapter 2) can contain any of the aforementioned files, they're also susceptible.

 Conventional wisdom holds that plain-text email messages, text files (*.txt*), image files (*.jpg*, *.gif*, *.bmp*, etc.), video clips (*.mpg*, *.avi*, etc.), and most other types of data files are benign in that they simply are not capable of carrying a virus. However, things aren't always as they seem. Case in point: the *Bloodhound.Exploit.13* Trojan horse (discovered in 2004) involved certain *.jpg* files and a flaw in Internet Explorer (and most other Microsoft products). The bug has since been fixed, but it's not likely to be the last. Likewise, a given script file (*.vbs*, discussed in Chapter 9), being merely a plain text file, is unlikely to contain any virus code. But that doesn't mean it can't download and execute malware, which is why it's considered just as hazardous.

You've heard it before, and here it is again: don't open email attachments sent to you from people you don't know, especially if they are Word documents or *.exe* files. If someone sends you an attachment and you're tempted to open it, scan it manually beforehand, and then *refrain from opening it*. Most antivirus software adds a context-menu item to all files, allowing you to scan any given file by right-clicking on it and selecting **Scan** (or something similar).

If you're on a network, your PC is only as secure as the least-secure PC on the network. If it's a home network, make sure everyone who uses machines on that network understands the concepts outlined here. If it's a corporate network, there's no accounting for the stupidity of your coworkers, so you may have no choice but to leave the auto-protect antivirus software in place.

What to Do When Windows Won't Start

Unfortunately, Windows' inability to boot is a common problem, usually occurring without an error message or any obvious way to resolve it. Sometimes you'll just get a black screen after the startup logo, or your computer may even restart itself instead of—or even after—displaying the desktop.

Common causes include incorrect hardware drivers, registry glitches, file corruption, and malware, all of which are discussed elsewhere in this chapter.

But when Windows won't start, how do you implement a fix? There's no Windows Explorer to delete files, no Internet to research solutions, no Device Manager to check and uncheck boxes, and no Solitaire to while away the time while you wait for antimalware downloads to complete. You have only this book and the sound of your breath wafting over your keyboard like an evening breeze over a dead mongoose.

Thankfully, Microsoft has done away with the frustratingly limited *Recovery Console* found in Windows 2000 and XP, replacing it with a full automated (and mostly useless) repair tool, explained next, and a full-featured command-prompt, covered later.

Startup Repair

When assembling the Startup Repair tool for Windows 7, Microsoft employed the Apple Computer approach: dead simple to use, but not quite enough options to make it work in the real world.

By default, Startup Repair is installed in its own partition by Windows 7 setup (described in "Prevent extra partitions during setup" on page 14), but depending on the level of damage, you may not be able to get to it. See "Use the F8 menu" on page 358 for instructions.

If **F8** doesn't work, you'll need to dig out your Windows 7 setup disc, the location of which has probably escaped your mind. (If Windows 7 came preinstalled on your PC and you never got a physical disc, contact your PC manufacturer and request the original Windows setup DVD; after all, you paid for it when you bought the machine.)

Pop the Windows disc in the drive and turn on your computer. (If your PC won't boot off the disc, see the section "Install Windows on an Empty Hard Disk" on page 10.) When you see the "Install Now" page, click the **Repair your computer** link at the bottom. When prompted, select the **Use recovery tools...** option, choose your OS from the list, and click **Next**.

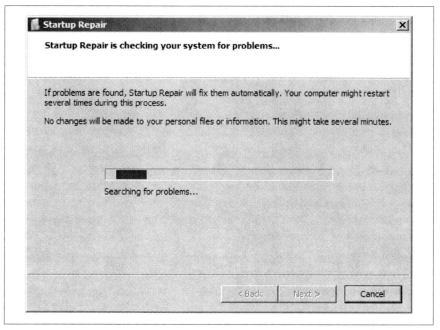

Figure 6-3. The fully-automated Startup Repair tool is bereft of options and utility

The other option here, **Restore your computer using a system image...** is useful only if you used the **Create a system image** tool on the Backup and Restore page in Control Panel, as described in the section "Recover Your System After a Crash" on page 423. Beware of this tool; you will almost certainly lose data if you choose this option.

The good news is that you can kick back in your chair and watch the pulsating indicator shown in Figure 6-3 for up to 20 minutes. The bad news is that you have no other choice.

You may've grown accustomed to the interactive menu of five useful recovery tools found in Vista; don't worry, these are still present in Windows 7, but you've got to wait for them. Windows pretends to investigate the problem without your help for several minutes, only to present you with the option to restore your Windows installation from a backup. (Although some folks have reported success with this tool, it often took several attempts to make Windows bootable again.) Click **Cancel** to continue watching the dancing black stripe; you'll have better restoration options later.

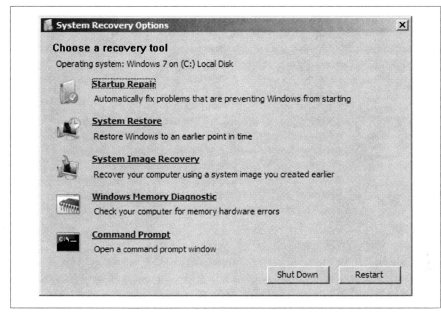

Figure 6-4. When you finally arrive at the System Recovery Options page, you'll have the tools you need to fix a PC that won't boot.

If setup is actually able to fix your problem, consider yourself lucky. Otherwise, you may see the message, "Startup Repair cannot repair this computer automatically," with an option to send a report of the problem to Microsoft; of course, since Windows isn't running, your network connection is likely not active, and such a report will end up in the circular file. Click Cancel to display the long-awaited System Recovery Options page shown in Figure 6-4.

Here's how these options work:

Startup Repair
This takes you back to the previous step; if you got this far, it means this option has already proven itself to be worthless.

System Restore
This reverts your Windows installation to an earlier incarnation, which is useful if a recent driver installation has prevented Windows from booting. Depending on the age of the most recent restore point, this may do nothing, or may go back too far. It's usually worth a try, but don't be surprised if it breaks a recently installed application or driver. See "Go Back in Time with Restore Points and Shadow Copies" on page 408 for details.

System Image Recovery

Use this option to wipe your hard disk clean and restore a backup you made with the **Create a system image** tool on the Backup and Restore page in Control Panel, covered in "Recover Your System After a Crash" on page 423.

 The fact that the Windows Complete PC Restore feature wipes your hard disk clean is a strong case for having your personal data on a separate partition from Windows, as explained in "Work with Partitions" on page 328. That way, a System Image Recovery operation would only overwrite the Windows partition, leaving alone any files modified since your last backup.

Windows Memory Diagnostic

This examines your PC's system memory (RAM) for errors; see "Test for Bad Memory (RAM)" on page 398. Unlike the other tools here, this one makes no changes to your hard disk, so it's safe to use at any time.

Command Prompt

Of all the tools on this page, this is likely to be the one that will save your day. Use this tool to open a Command Prompt window, from which you can copy, delete, or rename files that may be preventing Windows from loading. Also available is the Safe Mode with Command Prompt, discussed later in this section. See Chapter 9 for details on the Command Prompt, including an overview of the commands you can type at the prompt.

 This command prompt is a great tool for making repairs to Windows, particularly if you can't even get to the **F8** menu. But the **Safe Mode with Command Prompt** tool described in the next section provides access to Windows tools—like Device Manager and Registry Editor—that aren't accessible from the System Recovery Options Command Prompt.

Use the F8 menu

Just after you power up your PC (and after it displays its own logo or POST screen), but before you see the Windows logo, press the **F8** key on your keyboard to invoke the **Advanced Boot Options** menu shown in Figure 6-5.

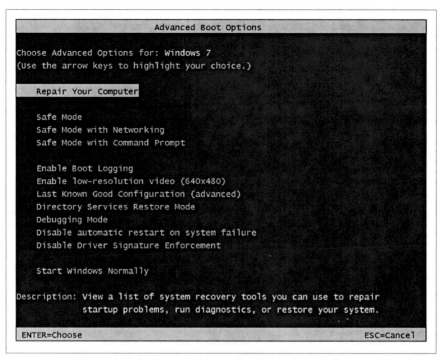

```
                    Advanced Boot Options

Choose Advanced Options for: Windows 7
(Use the arrow keys to highlight your choice.)

    Repair Your Computer

    Safe Mode
    Safe Mode with Networking
    Safe Mode with Command Prompt

    Enable Boot Logging
    Enable low-resolution video (640x480)
    Last Known Good Configuration (advanced)
    Directory Services Restore Mode
    Debugging Mode
    Disable automatic restart on system failure
    Disable Driver Signature Enforcement

    Start Windows Normally

Description: View a list of system recovery tools you can use to repair
            startup problems, run diagnostics, or restore your system.

 ENTER=Choose                                              ESC=Cancel
```

*Figure 6-5. Press **F8** just before you see the Windows logo to display this menu, from which you have access to several tools to help you get into Windows when it won't load normally*

If you can't get to the **F8** menu, then your PC may not be recognizing your Windows installation, and the problem may be bad enough to require the Startup Repair tool on the Windows setup disc, described in the previous section. If those tools don't work, or if you don't have the original 7 disc, then your best bet is to remove your hard disk from your PC and hook it up to another computer using the special USB tool extolled in the section "Transfer Windows to Another Hard Disk" on page 321. There, you should be able to determine the problem, or—worst case scenario—try to recover whatever data you can, as described in "Recover Your System After a Crash" on page 423.

From the **F8** menu, you'll have these choices:

Repair your computer

Choose this option to jump directly to the System Recovery Options page shown in Figure 6-4 and covered in the previous section.

If you don't see the **Repair your computer** option, your hard disk doesn't have the hidden 100 mb "System Reserved" partition described in "Prevent extra partitions during setup" on page 14. Without this partition, you'll need a true Windows 7 setup disc to access these tools.

Safe Mode

This forces Windows to start up in a hobbled, semi-functional mode, useful for troubleshooting or removing software or hardware drivers that otherwise prevent Windows from booting normally. Use the next option, **Safe Mode with Networking**, instead of **Safe Mode**, unless it turns out that your network drivers are the ones responsible for breaking Windows.

Safe Mode with Networking

This is the same as Safe Mode, except that Windows loads your network drivers. This is vitally important if you need Internet access for researching solutions, downloading antimalware tools, or transferring files to or from other PCs on your network.

Safe Mode with Command Prompt

Instead of loading Windows and your desktop, all you'll see is a Command Prompt window, sort of like the one you can get to from the System Recovery Options window (Figure 6-4, earlier).

The **Safe Mode with Command Prompt** option is a good choice if you suspect that a recent driver installation is to blame for Windows' inability to start. Once the Command Prompt appears, type devmgt.msc at the prompt and press **Enter** to start Device Manager. Then, find the driver in the Device Manager window, right-click the entry, and select **Disable**. Close Device Manager and restart Windows when you're done.

To get out of the Command Prompt cleanly and restart Windows, type exit at the prompt and press **Enter**. If typing exit closes the Command Prompt window but leaves Windows running, press **Ctrl-Alt-Del** and then click the tiny arrow next to the red button at the bottom of the screen.

See Chapter 9 for help with the Command Prompt. To fix file errors on your hard disk from the Command Prompt, see "Check Your Drive for Errors" on page 366.

Enable Boot Logging

This starts Windows normally, except that a log of every step is recorded into the *ntbtlog.txt* file, located in your *\Windows* folder. If Windows won't start, all you need to do is attempt to start Windows with the **Enable Boot Logging** option at least once. Then, reboot your PC, press **F8** again, and choose one of the Safe Mode tools above (preferably, **Safe Mode with Networking**). When you're back in Windows, read the log with Notepad; the last entry in the log is most likely the cause of the problem.

Enable low-resolution video (640×480)

This starts Windows normally, but in VGA mode (640×480 resolution at 16 colors). This helps you troubleshoot bad video drivers or incorrect video settings by allowing you to boot Windows with the most compatible (and ugliest) display mode there is.

Last Known Good Configuration (advanced)

This starts Windows with the last set of drivers and Registry settings known to work. Use this if a recent Registry change or hardware installation has caused a problem that prevents Windows from starting. See "Go Back in Time with Restore Points and Shadow Copies" on page 408 for details.

Directory Services Restore Mode

If your PC is a Windows Domain Controller—which, strictly speaking, is not possible in Windows 7—this option takes the Active Directory offline. In other words, you'll never use this entry.

Debugging Mode

This option, typically of no use to end-users, sends debug information to your serial port to be recorded by another computer. Does your PC even have a serial port?

Disable automatic restart on system failure

Unlike the previous eight entries here, this option merely changes a setting so you can determine why Windows won't start. By default, if Windows crashes while it's loading (see "Blue Screen of Death" on page 382), it reboots your PC so fast, you can't read the error message on that infamous blue screen. Choose **Disable automatic restart on system failure** if you want to read the message and then reboot by hand.

Disable Driver Signature Enforcement

By default, the 64-bit edition of Windows 7 won't allow you to install any device drivers that haven't been digitally signed. (Digital signatures are largely a bureaucratic requirement to get the Microsoft certification logo on a product's packaging, but also a means to detect whether or not a file has been compromised.)

In theory, you should be able to choose **Disable Driver Signature Enforcement** to allow your PC to install unsigned drivers, but in practice, this never works. Instead, boot Windows normally, open a Command Prompt window (in administrator mode; see Chapter 8), and type the following:

```
bcdedit.exe -set loadoptions DDISABLE_INTEGRITY_CHECKS
```

Press **Enter** and then close the Command Prompt and restart Windows for the change to take effect. If that doesn't help, you may have to forgo supporting a specific device until the manufacturer makes a signed, native (64-bit) driver available.

Start Windows Normally
Use this self-explanatory option to continue booting Windows normally, as though you'd never invoked the **F8** menu.

With these tools and the referenced sections in this book, you should have everything you need to get Windows running again. At the point you discover the grim fact that your repair mission has turned into a *recovery* mission, see "Recover Your System After a Crash" on page 423.

Manage Startup Programs

The *Startup* folder in the Start menu is where most people go if they want Windows to start an application automatically when it boots. Just drag a shortcut to the program into the folder, and Windows will do the rest. Or, delete an existing shortcut to stop a program from loading at boot time.

Trouble is, there are many ways apart from the *Startup* folder to configure startup programs, and if you're trying to solve a problem or just reduce boot times, you need to look at them all. To see them all in one place, open the System Configuration tool (*msconfig.exe*) and choose the **Startup** tab. Uncheck any programs you'd rather not have running, and click **Apply**. Also available is the free Autoruns tool (*http://technet.microsoft.com/en-us/sysinternals/bb963902.aspx*), which, among other things, has a command-line tool you can use to make changes when Windows won't start.

Here are all the places Windows looks for startup items:

Startup folders
There are actually two of these on your hard disk, but shortcuts in both places show up in the **Startup** menu (under **All Programs** in your Start menu). If you have a lot of cleanup to do, you'll find it's easier to open Windows Explorer than to repeatedly open the Start menu. First, your personal *Startup* folder is located here:

C:\Users\\{username}\AppData\Roaming\Microsoft\Windows\Start Menu\Programs\Startup

and programs listed therein will load automatically when you first log in to your user account. Next, the "All Users" *Startup* folder here:

C:\ProgramData\Microsoft\Windows\Start Menu\Programs\Startup

lists the programs to load automatically when *anyone* logs into your PC.

Registry

There are several places in the registry (see Chapter 3) in which startup programs are specified. Installers add their programs to these keys for several reasons: to prevent tinkering, for more flexibility, or—in the case of viruses, Trojan horses, and spyware—to hide from plain view.

These keys contain startup programs for the current user (er, you):

```
HKEY_CURRENT_USER\SOFTWARE\Microsoft\Windows\CurrentVersion\Run
HKEY_CURRENT_USER\SOFTWARE\Microsoft\Windows\CurrentVersion\RunOnce
```

These keys contain startup programs for all users:

```
HKEY_LOCAL_MACHINE\SOFTWARE\Microsoft\Windows\CurrentVersion\Run
HKEY_LOCAL_MACHINE\SOFTWARE\Microsoft\Windows\CurrentVersion\RunOnce
```

And if you're using 64-bit Windows, there also may be entries here:

```
HKEY_LOCAL_MACHINE\SOFTWARE\Wow6432Node\Microsoft\Windows\
                               CurrentVersion\Run
HKEY_LOCAL_MACHINE\SOFTWARE\Wow6432Node\Microsoft\Windows\
                               CurrentVersion\RunOnce
```

The naming of the keys should be self-explanatory. Programs referenced in either of the Run keys listed previously are run every time Windows starts, and are where you'll find most of your startup programs. An entry referenced in one of the RunOnce keys is run only once and then removed from the key.

Other, less common places for startup programs to hide in your registry include:

```
HKEY_LOCAL_MACHINE\System\CurrentControlSet\Control\
                               Session Manager\BootExecute
HKEY_LOCAL_MACHINE\System\CurrentControlSet\Control\
                               Terminal Server\Wds\rdpwd\StartupPrograms
HKEY_LOCAL_MACHINE\SOFTWARE\Microsoft\Windows NT\
                               CurrentVersion\Winlogon\Shell
HKEY_LOCAL_MACHINE\SOFTWARE\Microsoft\Windows NT\
                               CurrentVersion\Winlogon\Userinit
```

Troubleshooting

Services

The Services window (*services.msc*) lists dozens of programs especially designed to run in the background. The advantage that services have over the other startup methods here is that they remain active even when no user is currently logged in. That way, for example, your web server can continue to serve web pages when the Welcome/Login screen is displayed.

By default, some services are configured to start automatically with Windows and others are not, and this distinction is made in the **Startup Type** column. Double-click any service and change the **Startup type** option to **Automatic** to have it start with Windows, or **Disabled** if you never want it to start automatically. You can even group all the automatic services together by clicking the **Startup Type** column to sort the list.

 Changing the Startup type for a service won't load (start) or unload (stop) the service. Use the **Start** and **Stop** buttons on the toolbar of the Services window, or double-click a service and click **Start** or **Stop**. Unfortunately, there's no way to delete a service from the Services window; for that, see the sidebar "Delete a Service" on page 366.

Scheduled Tasks

A program doesn't have to be launched at boot time to be run automatically. The Scheduled Tasks tool can launch programs at any time. See Chapter 9 for more on Scheduled Tasks, and check out the aforementioned Autoruns tool to see a concise list of all the programs Scheduled Tasks may launch.

Drivers

An oft-neglected category of programs run when Windows starts, device drivers can become infected with viruses just like any other executable. While it's true that the 64-bit edition of Windows 7 won't allow unsigned drivers, and altered code breaks digital signatures, it's also true that an intact driver can launch a separate unsigned, infected program at any time.

Drivers that load with Windows can be found in Device Manager, as well as the **Drivers** tab of aforementioned Autoruns tool.

So, you've decided to scour your system for superfluous or dangerous startup programs, and you've encountered one you don't recognize. Before you pull the plug on a particular entry, follow a few simple steps to find out what it's for.

First, determine the executable file involved. For *Startup* folder items, right-click the shortcut icon and select **Properties** to uncover the program filename.

On the **Shortcut** tab, click **Open File Location** to reveal the location of the file.

If it's a Registry entry, the filename (and usually the full path) is shown in the **Data** column in the Run/RunOnce key. If there's no folder path included, type the filename into Explorer's **Search** box to find the containing folder, and be sure to look beyond the index, as described in Chapter 2.

Or if it's a service, double-click the service and look at the **Path to executable** line under the **General** tab. Once you have the program filename, open Windows Explorer and navigate to the file's location.

 Trying to track down a running program, but don't know where it's loaded? Open Windows Task Manager, choose the **Processes** tab, and click the **Show processes from all running users** button at the bottom. To show file and path names for running processes, open the **View** menu, click **Select Columns**, and turn on the **Image Path Name** option. Note that if the filename is *svchost.exe*, the entry represents a service, as described in the sidebar "What Is Svchost?" on page 376.

Right-click the program executable, select **Properties**, and choose the **Details** tab to see the manufacturer name, product name, version number, etc. If there's no **Details** tab, it means the file has no version information; although this situation is more common with viruses and malware than legitimate applications, it doesn't necessarily point to malware.

If you're still not sure what the program is for, yet antimalware and antivirus scans have declared it clean, fire up a web browser and search Google for the filename. In nearly all cases, you'll find several references to the file's purpose, and in the case of malware, how to remove it. Of course, many types of malware—particularly rootkits—mask their identities by adopting randomly generated filenames, so don't expect helpful results for *AJJDG91.EXE*.

To disable a Startup folder shortcut without deleting it for good, just move it to a different folder. To disable a registry entry, create a Registry patch (see Chapter 3) to back up the key, and then simply delete the offending entry. Or, use the aforementioned System Configuration tool (*msconfig.exe*), which backs up deactivated startup programs for easy reactivation later.

Reboot Windows to test your changes.

Delete a Service

Since a service can be turned off, Microsoft hasn't felt the need to let users delete services outright from the Services window. But services can cause all sorts of problems, whether they're unwanted add-ons to otherwise useful software, left behind by buggy uninstallers, or inserted surreptitiously by malware. So here's how to remove a service once and for all.

Open the Services window (*services.msc*) and double-click the service you want to remove. Highlight the text next to **Service name** (the first entry under the **General** tab) and press Ctrl-C to copy the name to the clipboard.

Next, open a Command Prompt window in Administrator mode (see Chapters 9 and 8, respectively), and type the following at the prompt:

```
sc delete "Rogue Service"
```

where *Rogue Service* (in quotes) is the name of the service you just copied. Press **Enter**, and if the removal was successful, you should see this message:

```
[SC] DeleteService SUCCESS
```

Return to the Services window and press **F5** to refresh the list, and confirm the service is now gone.

Check Your Drive for Errors

The Chkdsk utility—*chkdsk.exe*, pronounced "check disk" for those who enjoy pronouncing program executable filenames out loud—scans your hard disk for errors and optionally fixes any it finds. To run Chkdsk, open a Command Prompt window in Administrator mode (see Chapters 9 and 8, respectively), type chkdsk at the prompt, and press **Enter**.

 File errors—one of the problems Chkdsk can detect and fix— are also capable of preventing Windows from booting. If Windows won't start, fire up the **Safe Mode with Command Prompt** startup option discussed in "What to Do When Windows Won't Start" on page 355, and run Chkdsk from there.

When you run Chkdsk without any options, you'll get a report that looks something like this:

```
The type of the file system is NTFS.
Volume label is SHOEBOX.

WARNING! F parameter not specified.
Running CHKDSK in read-only mode.
```

```
CHKDSK is verifying files (stage 1 of 3)...
  156352 file records processed.
File verification completed.
  433 large file records processed.
  0 bad file records processed.
  2 EA records processed.
  54 reparse records processed.
CHKDSK is verifying indexes (stage 2 of 3)...
  586626 index entries processed.
Index verification completed.
  5 unindexed files processed.
CHKDSK is verifying security descriptors (stage 3 of 3)...
  156352 security descriptors processed.
Security descriptor verification completed.
  18159 data files processed.
CHKDSK is verifying Usn Journal...
  36020056 USN bytes processed.
Usn Journal verification completed.
Windows has checked the file system and found no problems.

  105520148 KB total disk space.
   58674344 KB in 134061 files.
      60396 KB in 18160 indexes.
          0 KB in bad sectors.
     320208 KB in use by the system.
      65536 KB occupied by the log file.
   46465200 KB available on disk.

       4096 bytes in each allocation unit.
   26380037 total allocation units on disk.
   11616300 allocation units available on disk.
```

You can interrupt Chkdsk at any time by pressing **Ctrl-C**.

If Chkdsk finds any errors, it'll say so in its report. However, as suggested by the WARNING! F parameter message in the report, it won't fix any problems it finds unless you specifically instruct it to do so with the /f parameter, like this:

```
chkdsk /f
```

The following terms describe most of the different types of problems that Chkdsk might report:

Lost clusters

These are pieces of data that are no longer associated with any existing files. They just need to be cleaned up.

Bad sectors

Bad sectors are actually physical flaws on the disk surface. Use the /r option, explained shortly, to attempt to recover data stored on bad sectors.

Note that recovery of such data is not guaranteed unless you have a backup somewhere.

 You may have one or more bad sectors if you see gibberish when you view the contents of a directory (with the `dir` command), or if Windows crashes or freezes every time you attempt to access a certain file. Of course, this may also be the work of the "Green Ribbon of Death," covered later in this chapter.

Cross-linked files

If a single piece of data has been claimed by two or more files, those files are said to be *cross-linked*.

Invalid file dates or times

Chkdsk also scans for file dates and times that it considers "invalid," such as missing dates or those before January 1, 1980.

 By default, Chkdsk will only scan the current drive (shown in the prompt—`C:>` for drive C:). To scan a different drive, include the drive letter as one of the command-line options, like this: `chkdsk d: /f`.

The other important options available to Chkdsk are the following:

`/r`

The `/r` parameter is essentially the same as `/f`, except that it also scans for—and recovers data from—bad sectors, as described earlier. This just takes longer, and probably isn't necessary unless `/f` is insufficient.

`/b`

When Chkdsk finds a bad sector (as the result of an `/r` scan), it effectively "fences off" the region so Windows can never store data there again. Use the `/b` parameter to recheck those regions in the hopes that they can be used once again. For obvious reasons, this is usually not a good idea, and is pretty much a big waste of time.

`/x`

Include this option to force Windows to dismount the volume before scanning the drive, a useful step for drives with shared folders (see Chapter 8). If you don't include `/x`, and the drive is in use, Chkdsk usually has to schedule a scan during the next boot. The `/x` parameter implies the `/f` option.

There are also the /i and /c options, which are used only to skip certain checks in order to complete the scan more quickly; there's usually no reason to use them. And the /l option only shows the current size of the NTFS log file, and optionally changes it (e.g., chkdsk /l:128 to make the log file 131,072 bytes in size).

To run Chkdsk from Windows Explorer, right-click any drive, select **Properties**, choose the **Tools** tab, and click **Check Now**. Here, the **Automatically fix file system errors** option corresponds to the /f parameter, and the **Scan for and attempt recovery of bad sectors** option corresponds to the /r parameter. When the scan is complete, you'll get a report akin to the command-line version (in a nice departure from previous versions). Of course, when Windows won't start, the Command Prompt interface to Chkdsk is basically your only choice.

To see the results of any recent Chkdsk scan, open the Event Viewer (*eventvwr.exe*). In the tree on the left, open the **Windows Logs** branch and select **Application**. Click the **Date and Time** column header to sort the list chronologically or the **Source** column header to sort the list by program, and then find the most recent **Information** event with **Chkdsk** in the **Source** column.

Dirty drives and automatic scans

When a volume is marked "dirty," Windows scans it with Chkdsk automatically during the boot process. A drive can become dirty if it's in use when Windows crashes, or Chkdsk schedules a scan when you attempt to check a disk that is in use. Not surprisingly, a drive not considered dirty is marked "clean."

You can use the Fsutil (*Fsutil.exe*) utility to manage dirty drives. Open a Command Prompt window and type fsutil (without any arguments) to display a list of commands that can be used with the tool. As you might have expected, the dirty command is the one that's most relevant here. Here's how it works:

To see whether drive *G:* is currently marked as dirty, type:

```
fsutil dirty query g:
```

To mark drive *H:* as dirty, so it will be scanned by Chkdsk the next time Windows starts, type:

```
fsutil dirty set h:
```

Fsutil has been found to be unreliable when used on FAT or FAT32 drives, so you may wish to use it only on more modern NTFS volumes. (See the section "Choose the Right Filesystem" on page 317.)

Another utility, Chkntfs, is used to choose whether or not Windows runs Chkdsk automatically at Windows startup, regardless of the so-called cleanliness of the drive. (It is not used to check NTFS drives as its name implies, however.) Here's how it works:

To display a dirty/clean report about any drive (say, drive *G:*), type:

```
chkntfs g:
```

To *exclude* drive *H:* from being checked when Windows starts (which is not the default), type:

```
chkntfs /x h:
```

To *include* (un-exclude) drive *H:* in the drives to be checked when Windows starts, type:

```
chkntfs /c h:
```

To force Windows to check drive *H:* the next time Windows starts, type:

```
chkntfs /c h:
fsutil dirty set h:
```

To include all drives on your system, thereby restoring Windows' defaults, type:

```
chkntfs /d
```

Finally, when Windows detects a dirty drive, it starts a timed countdown (10 seconds by default), allowing you to skip Chkdsk by pressing a key. To change the duration of this countdown to, say, five seconds, type:

```
chkntfs /t:5
```

 The Registry location of the timeout setting is stored in the AutoChkTimeOut value in the HKEY_LOCAL_MACHINE\SYSTEM\CurrentControlSet\Control\Session Manager key.

You'll have to restart Windows for any of these changes to take effect.

What to Do When a Program Crashes

Error messages are passé. When a program crashes, Windows doesn't necessarily tell you that it has crashed. Rather, the program simply "stops responding." This means that you can't click any of the controls in its interface, save your open document, nor (most importantly) close and reopen it easily. Sure, Windows usually lets you move it around the screen, and sometimes even click the **Close** button to end the task, but that's about it. But these are also symptoms of an application that's simply busy, caught up in the last task you asked it to perform.

Annoyed that Windows insists on "searching for a solution" after you close a crashed program? Although it's true that Windows finds solutions to some problems you report—if not now, then eventually—it's unlikely that Microsoft will come up with a solution faster than the developer of the crashed application will release an update. To turn off the "searching..." box, making it so you have only one window to close instead of two, open the Action Center in Control Panel. Click the **Change Action Center** settings link on the left and then click the Problem reporting settings link below. Select the **Never check for solutions** option and click OK.

Either way, triggered by your first attempt to use a crashed or busy program, Windows turns the whole window pale while trying to communicate with it. If you want to know whether a program has reached this state *without* triggering it with a click, just try moving the mouse over the edges of the window; if the mouse cursor doesn't change to the familiar "resize" arrows (and given that it's a resizable window), the program has probably stopped responding.

So, how do you tell the difference between a crashed program and a busy one? Well, Windows can't even do that reliably, instead showing you a window that looks like the one in Figure 6-6 when you try to close it. The solution is to be patient and use your best instincts.

But patience only gets you so far. After waiting an intolerable length of time, say, three to four seconds, one has to wonder whether the program will ever start responding. If you're through waiting, you can go ahead and elect to close the program, a strategy that works some of the time.

Troubleshooting

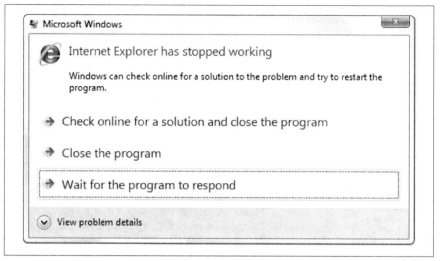

Figure 6-6. When you see this message, it means that Windows doesn't know whether the program you're trying to use has crashed, or is simply busy

 If an application window is visible, it's easy enough to click the small × button on the application title bar to close it. But if it's minimized, or if the main window isn't responding at all, right-click the program's button on the taskbar and select **Close**.

If closing doesn't help, or if, after closing a window, you can't open another one, then it's time to pay a visit to Task Manager, shown in Figure 6-7.

There are three ways to start Task Manager:

Taskbar
    Right-click an empty area of the taskbar (or the clock) and select **Start Task Manager**.

Keyboard
    Press the **Shift-Ctrl-Esc** keys together.

Three-finger salute
    If the taskbar and keyboard methods don't work, then Windows itself is crashed or busy. In this case, press **Ctrl-Alt-Del** to blank the screen and show a special administrative menu, at which point you can click **Start Task Manager** to launch it.

Although the **Applications** tab is inviting and easy to understand, it's not too helpful for this purpose. Choose the **Processes** tab, click the **Show processes**

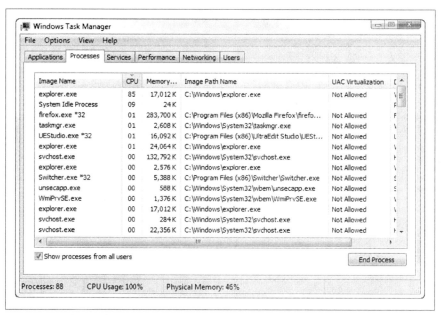

Figure 6-7. Choose the Processes tab in Task Manager to list all the programs running on your PC, a necessary step if one of them has crashed and you need to close it (the hard way)

from all users button at the bottom (present only if UAC is in effect), and then locate the crashed program in the list.

There's a funky bug in Windows 7's Task Manager, but fortunately, it's one that's easy to fix. If your Task Manager appears with no title bar, menu, or tabs, just double-click the thin gray border around the main list to bring them back. If that doesn't help, or if your mouse is unavailable, open the Registry Editor, navigate to HKEY_CURRENT_USER\Software\Mic rosoft\Windows NT\CurrentVersion\TaskManager and delete the TaskManager key.

To find the program to close, sort the list. You can sort the list alphabetically by filename (e.g., *explorer.exe* for Windows Explorer) by clicking the **Image Name** column header. Or, sort by application title by clicking the **Description** header. To show the full path and filenames for each running process, open the **View** menu, click **Select Columns**, and turn on the **Image Path Name** option.

But for most hung applications—also known as "frozen" or "locked up"—it'll be most entertaining to sort by exactly *how* busy the program is. Click the **CPU** column header twice (so its little arrow is pointing down) to sort by processor usage (a percentage from 0 to 99), and the crashed program will usually leap to the top of the list. For instance, if Windows Explorer has crashed—unfortunately, such a common occurrence in Windows 7 and Vista that a new term was invented for it, explained in "Green Ribbon of Death" on page 380—its CPU usage will usually be in the high 80s! (Or, if you have a dual-core processor, the CPU usage for a crashed program will be closer to 50.)

Just highlight the program in the list and click **End Process**. Only after you do this will you be able to reopen the application.

 Windows Vista came with a nifty tool called the Windows Defender Software Explorer, which was unfortunately removed for Windows 7. In its absence, you can use Task Manager to list processes in memory, or System Configuration (*msconfig.exe*) and the free Autoruns tool to list programs that start with Windows, all of which are covered in "Manage Startup Programs" on page 362.

See "Shut Down Windows Quickly" on page 282 to configure how long Windows waits for a busy application to respond before it considers it crashed.

Programs commonly running in the background

Windows is basically just a collection of components, and at any given time, some of those components may be loaded into memory and listed as running processes in Task Manager. In fact, you'll probably see more programs running than you expected, especially after you click the **Show processes from all users** button.

If you see a program you don't recognize, don't panic; it's not necessarily malware, but then again, it's not necessary legitimate. See Table 6-1 for a list of those items commonly found on most Windows 7 systems.

Table 6-1. Processes you should expect to find running on your system

Process	Description
csrss.exe	Called the Client Server Runtime Process, *csrss.exe* is an essential Windows component, as it handles the user-mode portion of the Win32 subsystem. It is also a common target for viruses, so if this process appears to be consuming a lot of CPU cycles on your system, you should update and run your antivirus software.
explorer.exe	This is simply Windows Explorer, which is responsible for your desktop and Start menu. If this program crashes or is closed, Windows will usually start it again automatically. If you see more than one instance of *explorer.exe*, it means that folder windows are being launched as a separate process, as explained in Chapter 2. If Windows Explorer crashes and you have to end the process in Task Manager, select **New Task** from the **File** menu, type `explorer`, and click OK to get your desktop and Start menu back.
lsass.exe	This is the Local Security Authority subsystem, responsible for authenticating users on your system.
rundll32.exe	This program, the purpose of which is to launch a function in a DLL as though it were a separate program, is used for about a million different things in Windows. Since it's simply a loader for other programs, it's neither necessarily harmful nor benign.
services.exe	This is the Windows NT Service Control Manager, and works similarly to *svchost.exe*, described shortly. The difference is that *services.exe* runs services that are standalone processes while *svchost.exe* runs services from DLLs.
smss.exe	Called the Windows NT Session Manager, *smss.exe* is an essential Windows component. Among other things, it runs programs listed in the `HKEY_ LOCAL_MACHINE\SYSTEM\Current ControlSet\Control\Session Manager` key in the Registry.
spoolsv.exe	This handles printing and print spooling (queuing).
svchost.exe	This is the application responsible for launching most services (listed in *services.msc*). See the upcoming sidebar "What Is Svchost?" on page 376 for details. See also *services.exe*.
System	This is the System process (*ntoskrnl.exe*), an essential Windows component.
System Idle Process	The "idle" process is a 16k loop, used to occupy all CPU cycles not consumed by other running processes. The higher the number in the CPU column (99% being the maximum), the less your processor is being used by the currently running programs.
winlogon.exe	This process manages security-related user interactions, such as logon and logoff requests, locking or unlocking the machine, changing the password, and the remote Registry service.
wmiprvse.exe	This is responsible for WMI (Windows Management Instrumentation) support in Windows 7, also known as WBEM. Like *csrss.exe*, above, *wmiprvse.exe* is a common target for viruses, so if this process appears to be consuming a lot of CPU cycles on your system, you should update and run your antivirus software.

Naturally, you shouldn't interfere with the components Windows requires to operate while you're looking for errant programs or programs you can get along without. And just because something isn't listed here doesn't mean it isn't required by your system, so use caution when ending a process with which you're unfamiliar.

What Is Svchost?

Svchost.exe and *services.exe* are responsible for launching the processes associated with the behind-the-scenes programs controlled by the Services window (*services.msc*).

A single instance of *svchost.exe* may be responsible for a single service or several. You should never interfere with any instances of *svchost.exe* or *services.exe* you might see listed in Task Manager. Instead, use the Services window to start or stop a service or choose whether or not a service is started automatically when Windows starts.

Want to know what a specific instance of *Svchost.exe* or *services.exe* is doing? In Task Manager, right-click the entry and select **Go to Services(s)** to jump to the **Services** tab and automatically highlight the related running services.

If you're using the Professional edition of Windows 7 or better, you can also use the TaskList utility (*tasklist.exe*) to see which services are handled by any given instance of *svchost.exe*. Just open a Command Prompt window (*cmd.exe*), and type:

```
tasklist /svc
```

Then, match up the numbers in the **PID** column of TaskList's output with those in the **PID** column of Task Manager's **Processes** tab.

See "Manage Startup Programs" on page 362 for tips on researching and identifying processes and programs you don't recognize.

What to Do When a Program Won't Start

Ever double-click an icon on your desktop, only to see the mouse cursor momentarily turn into the little spinning circle before it reverts to the arrow pointer, with no newly opened application in sight? This is typically what happens when a program won't start, and this is not necessarily Windows' fault.

One of these four things is usually responsible for preventing a program (or software installer) from loading in Windows 7:

User Account Control (UAC)

As explained in Chapter 8, Windows' UAC feature is designed to prevent malicious or poorly written applications from harming your PC. Unfortunately, a program not specifically written for Vista or 7 won't be UAC-aware, and as a result, may close when UAC prevents it from doing something like writing to its own folder in *Program Files*. Assuming there's no update available, you can usually run the program in administrator mode to get it to start; see the section "Control User Account Control" on page 569 for details.

Written for an older version of Windows

Some programs—particularly those that interact with the operating system or rely on features only available in certain versions of Windows—won't load if your version of Windows isn't on their preapproved list. (This also applies to setup programs.) To get around this, right-click any *.exe* file (or a shortcut to any *.exe* file), select **Properties**, and choose the **Compatibility** tab. Turn on the **Run this program in compatibility mode for** option, and from the list immediately underneath, choose a Windows version you know to be supported by your software. Click OK and then try running the program again.

 Just because the program now thinks it's running under, say, Windows XP with Service Pack 2, doesn't mean the program will actually function correctly in Windows 7. But much of the time, a little spoofing is all it takes. If your app only functions properly in Windows XP, you can use the special Windows XP Mode edition of Virtual PC, covered in Chapter 1.

Missing file or setting

Most applications require a laundry list of different support files—not to mention a few dozen Registry settings to be in place—for them to function. If the program worked at one point, but no longer does, it might need nothing more than to be reinstalled. (This is particularly true of programs that were installed on a previous version of Windows, and were simply left intact when you upgraded to Windows 7.)

Software codecs, hardware drivers

Does the application interact with a hardware device? If so, you may need a native Windows 7 or Vista driver before the support application will work. Likewise, if you're having trouble starting a video editing program or movie player, one of your installed codecs (see Chapter 4) may be corrupt or incompatible with Windows 7.

It's a piece of junk

OK, maybe this is too harsh, but don't discount the possibility that there's simply a bug in the software that is preventing it from running. Check the software publisher's website for an update, patch, or other workaround.

Software is an ever-evolving landscape, so don't be surprised if you have to eventually retire an old favorite because it just won't run anymore. Of course, your favorite is likely someone else's, too, so it's worth a quick web search to see whether anyone else has come up with a trick to get your program running.

What to Do When an Application Won't Uninstall

It's not exactly fun when an application won't uninstall, and yet can't be reinstalled because remnants of a previous installation remain on your PC.

The most common problem is a broken link in the Programs and Features page of Control Panel. Each entry here corresponds to a registry subkey of `HKEY_LOCAL_MACHINE\SOFTWARE\Microsoft\Windows\CurrentVersion\Uninstall`. So if all you want to do is remove an entry from the Programs and Features page, just delete the respective subkey in the registry; see Chapter 3 for more on deleting registry keys. But don't delete the key if you actually want to run the uninstaller and remove the software from your PC.

You'll notice a bunch of subkeys at the top of the `Uninstall` key that have names like class IDs (e.g., `{50A0F899-A8B3-42B3-8494-BFD8276C785B}`). If one of these represents the program you want to uninstall, open the Start menu and type this command into the Search box:

```
msiexec /x {50A0F899-A8B3-42B3-8494-BFD8276C785B} /q
```

where `{50A0F899-A8B3-42B3-8494-BFD8276C785B}` is the ID of the program to remove.

If running *msiexec.exe* manually like this doesn't work, the culprit may be a corrupt installation. This is a common enough problem with Microsoft's troublesome Windows Installer service—employed by many application developers including Microsoft—that Microsoft released a tool to fix it.

Start by downloading the Windows Installer CleanUp Utility, which you can download from *http://support.microsoft.com/kb/290301*. Run the program (*msicuu2.exe*), select the application to remove from the list, and click the **Remove** button.

Removing an entry with the Windows Installer CleanUp Utility won't actually remove the software from your PC, but rather only erase the installer data from your registry. To subsequently complete removal of all the unwanted software, you'll need to install it fresh, and then uninstall it immediately thereafter.

If your application doesn't show up in the Windows Installer CleanUp Utility, and its registry key isn't of the form exemplified above, then it uses a third-party or proprietary installer. In this case, you'll need to contact the manufacturer for removal instructions.

Quick Fixes for App Hiccups

Sometimes—and I know it's hard to believe—it's not Microsoft's fault when something goes wrong. It's at those times programs like Enabler and Dud are most useful.

Got an application with a disabled (grayed out) menu item or button that shouldn't be? Just run the free Windows Enabler (*http://www.angelfire.com/falcon/speedload/Enabler.htm*) utility, and then left-click its icon in the notification area (taskbar tray). Thereafter, disabled controls in the active window will become re-enabled, allowing you to click with abandon. Of course, this doesn't always work; some programs are smart (or dumb) enough to forbid the action anyway, but it's often worth a try.

Sometimes, an application insists on running a program even when it doesn't need to. A classic example is the software that comes with Canon flatbed scanners: the program won't let you scan an image into a file unless you specify an application to open it with. The solution is Dud, free from *http://www3 .telus.net/_/dud/*, which does absolutely nothing. Just specify *dud.exe* as the target app, and you'll have trouble-free scanning. You should also be able to replace any existing .*exe* or .*dll* file with *dud.exe*, and it'll run (and exit) instead of the offending program. Note that the author of Dud also has a companion program, Replacer (*http://www3.telus.net/_/replacer/*), which lets you replace an in-use file with *dud.exe*.

Along these lines, it's also worth mentioning ShutDownGuard, which can prevent Windows from shutting down; it's free, and available from *http://code .google.com/p/shutdownguard/*. A similar app, Shut It (free from *http://www .delphiness.com/*), adds monitoring features that can automatically disrupt a shutdown request if a particular program is running. With these apps, you don't have to worry about a rogue auto-updater or even malware rebooting your PC without your approval.

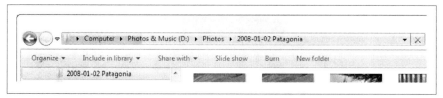

Figure 6-8. The Green Ribbon of Death, the harbinger of a Windows Explorer window that has crashed (or is about to)

Green Ribbon of Death

Don't you just love it when something is so notorious for a particular short-coming that a new term is invented to describe it? It happened with the *Blue Screen of Death*, described in the next section. It happened with the *Spinning Beach Ball of Death* in Mac OS X. And it happened with the *odd-number curse*, referring to every other *Star Trek* film.

It also happened with the *Green Ribbon of Death* (Figure 6-8), which debuted in Vista and lives on in Windows 7.

The green ribbon is basically a progress bar, a screen element Microsoft has otherwise gone to great pains to excise from Windows 7. But this particular progress bar may be the harbinger of death for the active Windows Explorer window, which, unfortunately, is not that uncommon.

The green progress bar inches across Windows Explorer's address bar as Windows attempts to assemble a list of files to show for the current folder. Most of the time, it's only visible for a few seconds, if it shows up at all. The problem occurs when it doesn't go away, at which point Windows Explorer stops co-operating when you try to view another folder or cancel the progress by clicking the little red × button next to the address bar.

What's worse, if you try to open another Windows Explorer window, that one is likely to malfunction, too, *even if you closed the first one*! The solution, tem-porary as it may be, is to close the seized *explorer.exe* process in Task Manager, as described in "What to Do When a Program Crashes" on page 371. But if you want to stop the Green Ribbon of Death from visiting you again, you'll have to take matters into your own hands.

There are basically four things that cause this problem:

Broken thumbnails
> This is the most common cause of this problem, and also the easiest to fix. Each time you view a folder containing photos (JPG, TIF files) or movies (AVI, MPG, WMV files), Windows Explorer opens each one to extract and build thumbnail previews for the file icons. If even one file in

the folder is corrupted, or if one of the files makes use of a corrupted *codec* on your system, Windows Explorer crashes.

To fix this problem, you need to do two things. First, figure out which file is crashing Explorer. Of course, since you can't view the folder in Explorer without it crashing, you'll have to turn off the thumbnails feature first. On the System page in Control Panel, click **Advanced system settings**, and then in the **Performance** box, click **Settings**. Turn off the **Show thumbnails instead of icons** option, and click OK.

 By default, Windows Explorer caches your thumbnail icons; if this cache is defective, Explorer may crash. To fix the problem, see "Disable thumbnail caching" on page 236, delete the *thumbs.db* file, and then try again.

Next, open the folder and then test each of your media files. The video that won't play or the photo that won't display is the likely culprit. Now it's just a matter of figuring out whether the file is corrupt, or the codec needs to be fixed, as described in the beginning of Chapter 4. Either way, move the file to a different folder and try re-enabling the **Show thumbnails instead of icons** option to see if Explorer can now read the folder.

Slow network access

When you open the Network folder to view other PCs on your LAN, Windows Explorer sometimes takes a long time to show them all. See Chapter 7 and Chapter 8 for help troubleshooting network connections and shared folders.

Searching when files are changing

If you're searching a folder, especially if you're using the **Include non-indexed** option as described in Chapter 2, and another program is writing files to that folder, the search results may repeatedly appear and disappear while you stare at the green progress bar. To solve this problem, close the **Search** window (or select a real folder in the tree) while programs are saving files to your hard disk.

Copying files

Windows 7 is hopelessly slow at copying files in certain situations, two in fact. (More on this in Chapter 2.)

First, the UAC feature forces Windows Explorer to evaluate the security impact of each file you copy, and this has far-reaching consequences, particularly when you're copying files over a network. See "Control User Account Control" on page 569 for more information.

And second, Windows 7 notoriously has trouble copying files to and from USB devices. So, if you copy a folder full of images from your USB card reader directly to your external USB hard disk, or move document files from a USB flash drive to a shared network folder, Windows Explorer may crash. There's no easy fix to this one, but you can work around it by copying files to your desktop first.

As explained above, you need to use Task Manager to close a crashed Windows Explorer window. But if you want to be able to close a crashed window and leave any other Explorer windows (and the desktop) intact, you'll need to make a change in Control Panel. Open Folder Options and choose the **View** tab. In the **Advanced settings** list, turn on the **Launch folder windows in a separate process** option, and then click OK. From now on, when you see the Green Ribbon of Death, it'll only mean death for one of your Windows Explorer windows, not all of them.

Blue Screen of Death

The Blue Screen of Death (BSoD) is aptly named. It's blue, it fills the screen, and it means death for whatever you were working on before it appeared. Microsoft refers to BSoD errors as "Stop Messages," a euphemism for the types of crashes that are serious enough to bring down the entire system.

A single error is no cause for concern. Only if a BSoD error happens a few times, or repeatedly, do you need to pursue any of the solutions listed here.

By default, Windows restarts your computer as soon as the BSoD appears, leaving almost no time to read the error message before it vanishes. To change this, open the System page in Control Panel and click the **Advanced system settings** link on the left side. In the **Startup and Recovery** box, click **Settings**, turn off the **Automatically restart** option, and click OK. You can also see your BSoD errors in the Event Viewer (*eventvwr.exe*), provided you can boot Windows.

If Windows won't start, and you need to read the BSoD error message, use the **Disable automatic restart on system failure** option, as described in "What to Do When Windows Won't Start" on page 355.

Alphabetical list of BSoD errors

There are a whole bunch of possible BSoD messages; probably more than a hundred. However, only about 20 happen frequently enough that they might imply that an actual problem exists. More than likely, you've seen at least one of the following stop messages on your own system:

Attempted Write To Readonly Memory (stop code 0X000000BE)
A faulty driver or service is typically responsible for this error, as is outdated firmware. If the name of a file or service is specified, try uninstalling the software (or rolling back the driver if it's an upgrade). Check with the manufacturer for firmware and driver updates.

Bad Pool Caller (stop code 0X000000C2)
Causes and remedies are similar to "Attempted Write To Readonly Memory." Additionally, this error might also be the result of a defective hardware device.

If you encounter this message while upgrading to Windows 7 (see Chapter 1), it may mean that one or more devices in your system are not compatible with the new OS. Try disconnecting unnecessary devices, or at least look for updated drivers and firmware. Also, disable any antivirus software you may have running.

Data Bus Error (stop code 0X0000002E)
This can be caused by defective memory (see "Test for Bad Memory (RAM)" on page 398), including system RAM, the Level 2 cache, or even the memory on your video card. Other causes of this error include serious hard disk corruption, buggy hardware drivers, or physical damage to the motherboard. See "What to Do When Windows Won't Start" on page 355 for one way to test your PC's memory.

Driver IRQL Not Less Or Equal (stop code 0X000000D1)
Drivers programmed to access improper hardware addresses typically cause this error. Causes and remedies are similar to "Attempted Write To Readonly Memory (stop code 0X000000BE)," earlier in this list.

Driver Power State Failure (stop code 0X0000009F)
This error is caused by an incompatibility between your computer's power management and one or more installed drivers or services, typically when the computer enters the Hibernate state (discussed at length in Chapter 5). If the name of a file or service is specified, try uninstalling the software (or rolling back the driver if it's an upgrade). Or, try disabling Windows' support for Hibernation altogether. See Appendix A for BIOS settings that may affect your PC's support for power management features.

Driver Unloaded Without Cancelling Pending Operations (stop code 0X000000CE)

Causes and remedies are similar to "Attempted Write To Readonly Memory (stop code 0X000000BE)," earlier in this section.

Driver Used Excessive PTEs (stop code 0X000000D8)

Causes and remedies are similar to "No More System PTEs (stop code 0X0000003F)," later in this section.

Hardware Interrupt Storm (stop code 0X000000F2)

This error occurs when a hardware device (such as a USB or SCSI controller) fails to release an IRQ, a condition typically caused by a buggy driver or firmware. This error can also appear if two devices are incorrectly assigned the same IRQ (discussed later in this chapter). Sometimes just moving an expansion card (desktop PCs only) from one slot to another can fix this problem.

Inaccessible Boot Device (stop code 0X0000007B)

You may see this error during Windows startup if Windows cannot read data from the system or boot partitions (described in Chapter 1). Faulty disk controller drivers are often to blame, but this problem can also be caused by hard disk errors.

If you have a multiboot system, a corrupt Boot Manager configuration may cause this problem; see "Modify the Boot Manager configuration" on page 27 for details. If all is well with your drivers and your drive, and you haven't been messing with the Boot Manager, check your system BIOS settings (described in Appendix A).

If you encounter this message while upgrading to Windows 7 (see Chapter 1), it may mean that one or more devices in your system are not compatible with the new OS. Try disconnecting unnecessary devices, or at least look for updated drivers and firmware. Also, disable or update any antivirus software you may have running.

Kernel Data Inpage Error (stop code 0X0000007A)

This error implies a problem with virtual memory (discussed in Chapter 5), most often in the case that Windows wasn't able to read data from—or write data to—the swap file. Possible causes include bad sectors, a virus, bad memory, or physical damage to the motherboard or disk controller.

Kernel Stack Inpage Error (stop code 0X00000077)

Causes and remedies are similar to the previous entry, "Kernel Data Inpage Error (stop code 0X0000007A)."

Kmode Exception Not Handled (stop code 0X0000001E)

A faulty driver or service is sometimes responsible for this error, as are memory and IRQ conflicts, and faulty firmware. If the name of a file or service is specified, try uninstalling the software (or rolling back the driver if it's an upgrade).

If the *Win32k.sys* file is mentioned in the message, the cause may be third-party remote control software (discussed in Chapter 7).

This error can also be caused if you run out of disk space while installing an application or if you run out of memory while using a buggy application with a memory leak.

No More System PTEs (stop code 0X0000003F)
Page Table Entries (PTEs) are used to map RAM as it is divided into page frames by the Virtual Memory Manager (VMM). This error usually means that Windows has run out of PTEs.

Aside from the usual assortment of faulty drivers and services that can cause all sorts of problems, this error can also occur if you're using multiple monitors.

NTFS File System (stop code 0X00000024)
This is caused by a problem with *Ntfs.sys*, the driver responsible for reading and writing NTFS volumes (see Chapter 5). If you're using the FAT32 filesystem, you may see a similar message (with stop code 0X00000023).

Causes include a faulty IDE or SCSI controller, improper SCSI termination, an overly aggressive virus scanner, or errors on the disk; try testing your drive with Chkdsk, as described earlier in this chapter.

To investigate further, open the Event Viewer (*eventvwr.msc*), and look for error messages related to **SCSI** or **FASTFAT** (in the **System** category), or **Autochk** (in the **Application** category).

Page Fault In Nonpaged Area (stop code 0X00000050)
Causes and remedies are similar to "Attempted Write To Readonly Memory (stop code 0X000000BE)," earlier in this list.

Status Image Checksum Mismatch (stop code 0Xc0000221)
Possible causes for this error include a damaged swap file (see the discussion of virtual memory in "Optimize Virtual Memory and Cache Settings" on page 312), or a corrupted driver. See "Attempted Write To Readonly Memory (stop code 0X000000BE)," earlier in this section, for additional causes and remedies.

Status System Process Terminated (stop code 0Xc000021A)
This error indicates a problem with either *Winlogon.exe* or the Client Server Runtime Subsystem (CSRSS). It can also be caused if a user with administrator privileges has modified the permissions (see Chapter 8) of certain system files such that Windows cannot read them. To fix the problem, you'll have to install a second copy of Windows 7 (see "Set Up

a Dual-Boot System" on page 26), and then repair the file permissions from there.

Thread Stuck In Device Driver (stop code 0X000000EA)

Also known as the infamous "infinite loop" problem, this nasty bug has about a hundred different causes. What's actually happening is that your video driver has essentially entered an infinite loop because your video adapter has locked up. Microsoft has posted a solution on its website that involves disabling certain aspects of video acceleration, but I've never encountered an instance where this worked. Instead, try the following:

- If you're using a desktop PC, try upgrading your computer's power supply. A power supply of poor quality or insufficient wattage will be unable to provide adequate power to all your computer's components, and may result in a "brown out" of sorts in your system. Note that newer, more power-hungry video adapters are *more* susceptible to this problem. See "Don't Overlook the Power Supply" on page 401.

- Make sure you have the latest driver for your video card. If you older driver to see whether that solves the problem.

- Make sure you have the latest driver for your sound card, if applicable. Also, make sure your sound card is not in a slot immediately adjacent to your video card (desktop PCs only), lest the resulting interference or heat disrupt the operation of either card.

- Inspect your video card and motherboard for physical damage.

- For desktop PCs only: make sure your video card is properly seated in its PCI-E, AGP, or PCI slot. If applicable, try moving it to a different slot. Next, try messing with some of your system's BIOS settings, especially those concerning your video card slot or video subsystem, as described in Appendix A. For example, if your AGP slot is set to 8x mode, and your video adapter only supports 1x AGP mode, then you'll want to change the setting accordingly.

- Make sure your computer and your video card are adequately cooled. Overheating can cause your video card's chipset to lock up.

- Check with the manufacturer of your motherboard for newer drivers for your motherboard chipset.

  For example, the "infinite loop" problem is common among motherboards with VIA chipsets and nVidia-based video cards. Visit the VIA website (*http://www.viaarena.com/?pageid=64*) for updated drivers and additional solutions.

- Try replacing your system's driver for the Processor-to-AGP Controller. Open Device Manager (*devmgmt.msc*), expand the **System**

devices branch, and double-click the entry corresponding to your Processor-to-AGP Controller. Choose the **Driver** tab, and click **Update Driver** to choose a new driver. Unless you can get a newer driver from the manufacturer of your motherboard chipset, try installing the generic "PCI standard PCI-to-PCI bridge" driver shown in the Hardware Update Wizard.

- If your motherboard has an on-board Ethernet adapter, try disabling the **PXE Resume/Remote Wake Up** option in your system BIOS (see Appendix A).

Unexpected Kernel Mode Trap (stop code 0X0000007F)

Typical causes of this error include defective memory, physical damage to the motherboard, and excessive processor heat due to overclocking (running the CPU faster than its specified clock speed).

Unmountable Boot Volume (stop code 0X000000ED)

This means that Windows was unable to mount the boot volume, which, if you have more than one drive, is the drive containing Windows (see Chapter 1 for more information on the boot and system volumes). This can be caused by using the wrong cable with a high-throughput IDE controller (more than 33 MB/second); try an 80-pin cable instead of the standard 40-pin cable. See also "Inaccessible Boot Device (stop code 0X0000007B)," earlier in this list.

Stop code 0x0000008E

This error, which typically has no title, is often caused by bad memory. But it could also be the result of a rootkit infestation, described in "Viruses, Malware, and Spyware" on page 344.

If you get repeated BSoD errors, and the previous remedies don't work, try installing a second copy of Windows on your PC, as described in "Set Up a Dual-Boot System" on page 26. If the second copy of Windows exhibits the same problem, then the cause is your hardware. But if the second copy runs well, then your best bet is to copy your data over to the new installation, and abandon the old OS.

Dealing with Drivers and Other Tales of Hardware Troubleshooting

A driver is the software that allows Windows and all of your applications to work with a hardware device, such as a printer or video card. That way, for example, your word processor doesn't need to be preprogrammed with the details of all available printers (as in the early days of PCs). Instead, Windows manages a central database of drivers, silently directing the communication among all your applications and whatever drivers are required to complete the task at hand.

Problems arise when a driver is buggy or outdated, or one of the files that comprise a driver is missing or corrupted. Outdated drivers designed either for a previous version of Windows or a previous version of the device can create problems. Additionally, manufacturers must continually update their drivers to fix incompatibilities and bugs that surface after the product is released. It's usually a good idea to make sure you have the latest drivers installed in your system when troubleshooting a problem. Furthermore, newer drivers sometimes offer improved performance, added features and settings, better stability and reliability, and better compatibility with other software and drivers installed in your system.

The other thing to be aware of is that some drivers may just not be the correct ones for your system. For example, when installing Windows, Setup may have incorrectly detected your video card or monitor and hence installed the wrong driver (or even a *generic* driver). A common symptom for this is if Windows does not allow you to display as many colors or use as high a resolution as the card supports. Make sure that Device Manager (*devmgmt.msc*) lists the actual devices, by name, that you have installed in your system.

Device drivers worth investigating include those for your video card, monitor, motherboard chipset, network adapter, and any USB devices you may have. If you're not sure of the exact manufacturer or model number of a device installed inside your computer, take off the cover of your computer and look, or refer to the invoice or documentation that came with your system.

How to Add Hardware

Windows 7 comes with a huge assortment of drivers for hardware available at the time of its release, but as time passes, more third-party devices are released, requiring drivers of their own. The first rule is to never use the disc that comes with a device, but rather go straight to the manufacturer's website for the latest version. That said, hardware installation in Windows 7 is pretty straightforward...that is, when it works. When it doesn't, Windows is no help.

Now, you've probably discovered the **Add a device** link in the Devices and Printers page in Control Panel, and while it seems inviting enough, it's not what you need. Any modern hardware that's working properly will identify itself to Windows as soon as you connect it—or in some cases, as soon as you boot Windows—at which point Windows will do the rest. Never try to do it the other way around; it will always end in tears.

But what happens if Windows doesn't detect your new device? First, open the Troubleshooting page in Control Panel, click **Hardware and Sound**, and then click the **Hardware and Devices** entry to open the Hardware and Devices troubleshooter. Click the **Advanced** link, turn off the **Apply repairs automatically** option, and then click **Next**.

After a brief interlude, Windows will prompt you to "Select the repairs you want to apply," followed by a list. Unless one of the entries precisely matches your problem, turn off all repairs except **Scan for recent hardware changes**, and then click **Next**.

 If you want to do this more quickly, open Device Manager (*devmgmt.msc*, also in Control Panel) and select the first entry (the name of your PC). From the Action menu, select **Scan for hardware changes** and wait to see what appears.

If Windows doesn't detect your newly-connected hardware, it's likely that it's not connected all that well. For instance, if it's a USB device, your USB port may be disconnected or malfunctioning; try a different port if possible. Also check your BIOS settings (see Appendix A) and make sure all your ports are enabled.

Update a driver

In nearly all cases, Device Manager will show an entry for the device you're installing, whether it's working or not. If the device isn't working, either its parent branch will pop open automatically with a teensy, yellow exclamation point over its icon, or the device will appear in the **Unknown Devices** branch, as shown in Figure 6-9.

These are often symptoms of a driver problem, and this can be fixed. (Of course, it may also be an errant BIOS setting, as described in Appendix A, or a problem with the hardware itself...but usually, it's the driver.)

To see what driver a device is currently using, double-click the device in Device Manager and choose the **Driver** tab. An easy (but certainly not foolproof) way to tell whether you're using the driver that came with Windows 7 is to look at the driver date—it should be July 13, 2009 (for the initial release, that is)—and its version number should be `6.1.7600.xxxxx`. If not, it probably came from another source, such as from a driver disk, from the Web, from Windows Update, or from a previous installation of Windows. Drivers with newer dates are usually—but not always—more recent, but the date alone is not a reliable indicator.

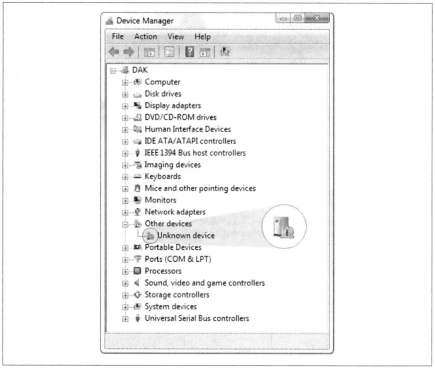

Figure 6-9. Here are two signs that Windows isn't loading the driver for your device

Click the **Driver Details** button to view the files in use by the driver. Sometimes a driver won't load merely because one of the files listed here is missing or broken—a problem updating the driver, discussed next, doesn't always fix. Instead, uninstall and reinstall the device, as described later in this chapter.

Recently updated a driver? In Device Manager, use the **Roll Back Driver** button to undo the latest update. For even better protection, use Double Driver, free from *http://www.boozet .org/dd.htm*, to maintain an archive of drivers for your hardware, and never let another errant driver update ruin your day. Also available is DriverMax (free, *http://www.innovative-sol .com/drivermax/*), which also makes it easy to copy driver files from one PC to another—useful for when you can no longer find the installer.

To install a new driver for a device, right-click the device in Device Manager and select **Update Driver Software**. When prompted, point to the folder containing the latest and greatest driver you've just obtained from the manufacturer's website and, if necessary, extracted from a Zip file.

Or, to start over, right-click the device and select **Uninstall**. Then, from the **Action** menu, select **Scan for hardware changes**.

When troubleshooting a device, don't forget to update the firmware, as explained in "Firmware: Software for Your Hardware", the next sidebar.

Firmware: Software for Your Hardware

User-upgradable firmware is a feature found in many modern devices, including hard disks, printers, video cards, and, of course, your PC's motherboard. Firmware is software stored in the device itself, used to control most hardware functions. Although it's not possible to, say, increase a hard disk's capacity by upgrading its firmware, it is possible to improve performance and fix bugs in devices like wireless routers, DVD recorders, motherboards, and even digital cameras.

The beauty of firmware is that if you purchase a peripheral and the manufacturer subsequently improves the product, you can usually update the firmware to upgrade the product.

When a device isn't working or a driver won't install, go to the hardware manufacturer's website and look for a firmware update. Since there's no standard method of upgrading firmware, be sure to get the firmware upgrade utility and installation instructions from the website as well.

What to do when Windows can't find a common driver

There's a bug in Windows 7 that makes it seem like it has amnesia. You plug in a device—even one you've used before—and after quite a long time of thinking about it, Windows complains that it can't find the driver. This is particularly disconcerting when it's a common device like a hard disk or a USB card reader. Fortunately, it's fairly easy to fix.

The problem is that Windows maintains a cache of its driver locations, and for reasons that aren't entirely clear, Windows won't abandon the cache when it becomes corrupted. Such is the case here.

To clear the driver cache, open Windows Explorer, and navigate to the C: \Windows\inf folder. If you see a file named *INFCACHE.1*, delete it immediately. If Windows won't let you delete the file, see the section "Delete In-Use Files" on page 104.

When you've excised the file, try uninstalling and then reinstalling the misbehaving device to reinstall the driver. For real this time.

What to do when Windows can't find an obscure driver

Trying to get Windows 7 to recognize an old piece of hardware is like trying to reason with a toddler: it's usually not worth the trouble, but that doesn't stop us from trying.

The first task is to identify the device. If it's an external unit, this is usually as easy as reading the label on the back. But for internal devices and generic hardware, sometimes a little detective work is in order. Open Device Manager (*devmgmt.msc*), double-click the driverless device in question, and choose the **Details** tab. From the **Property** list, select the **Device Instance Path**, and you'll see something like this:

```
USB\VID_04A9&PID_2224\5&10EF021E&0&2
```

Here, VID represents the vendor ID (manufacturer) and PID is the product ID (model number). Armed with this new information, a few creative Google searches should turn up an appropriate driver.

So what happens when you find a driver, but it won't install, citing an incompatibility with your version of Windows? In some cases, you can extract the driver files and install them manually, like this:

1. Run the setup program to begin installation.

2. When the first dialog window appears, leave it open and fire up a Windows Explorer window.

3. Navigate to your *Temp* folder (see "Start Windows in Less Time" on page 270) and look for an *.msi* file, either in the main *Temp* folder or one of its subfolders.

4. Copy (but don't move) the *.msi* file to a new folder.

5. Go back to the setup wizard from step 2, and click **Cancel**.

6. Open a Command Prompt window in Administrator mode (see Chapter 8), and use the CD command (Chapter 9) to change the working directory to the folder containing the *.msi* file (from step 4).

7. Type this command to extract the files to the current folder:

```
msiexec /a "setup.msi" /qb targetdir=.
```

where *setup.msi* is the filename of the *.msi* file. Close the Command Prompt window when you're done.

8. Return to Device Manager, right-click the device in question, and select **Update Driver Software**.

9. On the page that appears, click **Browse my computer for driver software**, and then click **Browse** to locate the folder containing the extracted files.

These steps will give your device the best chance at working, but don't be surprised if the driver—even after being successfully installed—still doesn't work with Windows 7.

Install a 32-bit driver on 64-bit Windows

Some drivers have no binary files (e.g., *.dll*, *.sys*, *.exe*), and instead are nothing but *.inf* files that contain information about the device. (Monitor drivers are an example of such a device.) Even so, the 64-bit edition of Windows 7 won't even attempt to install a *.inf* file intended for 32-bit Windows.

To force 64-bit Windows to accept the driver, just open the *.inf* file in a text editor like Notepad, and look for the [Manufacturer] section, like this:

```
[Manufacturer]
%SONY%=SONY
```

add a comma and then the text NTamd64 to the end, like this:

```
[Manufacturer]
%SONY%=SONY,NTamd64
```

Next, find a section that matches the manufacturer (in this case, [Sony]):

```
[SONY]
%SDM-P234%=SDM-P234.Install, Monitor\SNY03D0
%SDM-P234D%=SDM-P234D.Install, Monitor\SNY02D0
```

Highlight this section, press **Ctrl-C** to copy, and then paste (**Ctrl-V**) a second copy of the text immediately following the first. Then, add a period and then the text NTamd64 to the end of the new section, like this:

```
[SONY]
%SDM-P234%=SDM-P234.Install, Monitor\SNY03D0
%SDM-P234D%=SDM-P234D.Install, Monitor\SNY02D0

[SONY.NTamd64]
%SDM-P234%=SDM-P234.Install, Monitor\SNY03D0
%SDM-P234D%=SDM-P234D.Install, Monitor\SNY02D0
```

When you're done, save the file and try installing again.

Stop Plug and Play from detecting devices

One of the problems with Plug and Play (PnP) is its tendency to detect and load drivers for devices you don't want to use. Although there is no way to prevent the Windows PnP feature from detecting and installing drivers for some devices, you can disable most devices that may be causing conflicts.

To disable a device and prevent Windows from detecting it again, right-click it in Device Manager (*devmgmt.msc*), and select **Disable**. A red × then appears over the device's icon to signify that it has been disabled. You can later re-enable the device by right-clicking and selecting **Enable**.

Uninstall drivers for devices you no longer use

By default, Device Manager doesn't show devices that are no longer connected to your computer, even if the drivers for those devices are still installed and taking up space on your drive. This makes it terribly difficult to remove those drivers without either reattaching the device or showing "hidden" devices.

In Device Manager, you can select **Show hidden devices** from the **View** menu, but all this will add to the listing are non-PnP devices. To have Device Manager show *all* hidden devices, including drivers for long-forgotten hardware, follow these steps:

1. Open the System page in Control Panel, and then click the **Advanced system settings** link on the left.
2. Click the **Environment Variables** button.
3. In the lower **System variables** section, click **New**.
4. Type devmgr_show_nonpresent_devices for the **Variable name**, and enter 1 for the **Variable value**. Click OK when you're done, and click OK to close the System Properties window.
5. If Device Manager is open, close and reopen it.
6. In Device Manager, select **Show hidden devices** from the **View** menu.

Hidden devices (sometimes called *ghosted* devices) now appear in Device Manager with grayed-out icons. Other than the fact that they represent non-present hardware, these hidden entries should behave normally, in that you can uninstall them or change their properties like those for any other devices.

Interpret Device Manager Errors

From time to time, Device Manager will report a problem with one of your devices by marking it with a yellow exclamation mark (**!**) or a red ×. Here are the common error messages you'll see when you double-click entries for malfunctioning devices, along with their respective remedies:

This device is not configured correctly (Code 1).
    This is a driver problem; click **Update Driver** to install a new driver.

Windows could not load the driver for this device... (Code 2).
    Again, try installing a new driver. If that doesn't work, contact the manufacturer of your motherboard for a BIOS update.

The driver for this device may be bad, or your system may be running low on memory or other resources (Code 3).

Try removing the device (right-click and select **Uninstall**), restarting Windows, and then reinstalling the driver.

This device is not working properly because one of its drivers may be bad, or your registry may be bad (Code 4).

Of course, try updating the drivers. (Laughably, Microsoft may suggest running *Scanregw.exe*, a program designed for Windows Me and not included in Windows 7, to fix this error.) If a new driver doesn't fix the problem, try the solution for Code 3, just discussed.

The driver for this device requested a resource that Windows does not know how to handle (Code 5).

Remove the device (right-click and select **Uninstall**), disconnect it, and then plug it back in and wait while Windows rediscovers and installs the device.

Another device is using the resources this device needs (Code 6).

You'll see this error if you've installed a device that doesn't support PnP. Tsk tsk.

The drivers for this device need to be reinstalled (Code 7).

Click **Update Driver** to reinstall the drivers. Duh.

This device is not working properly because Windows cannot load... (Code 8).

This may indicate a missing or damaged *.inf* file, located in the *Windows* *INF* folder, which may make it difficult to reinstall the driver for this device. If the **Reinstall Device** button doesn't work or is absent, and installing drivers provided by the manufacturer fails, see "What to do when Windows can't find a common driver" on page 391. If that doesn't work, contact the manufacturer for manual driver removal instructions.

This device is not working properly because the BIOS in your computer is reporting the resources for the device incorrectly (Code 9).

This indicates a problem with your motherboard's support for ACPI power management (discussed in Chapter 5). Check with the manufacturer of your motherboard for a BIOS update. Next, try removing the device (right-click and select **Uninstall**) and then restarting Windows.

This device is either not present, not working properly, or does not have all the drivers installed (Code 10).

If the device is a PCI or ISA card inserted in your computer (desktop PCs only), make sure it's firmly seated in its slot. Otherwise, make sure it's plugged in and powered up. If it's an external device, try turning it off and then on again. Then, of course, try removing the drivers (right-click and select **Uninstall**) and then run reconnect to reinstall.

Windows stopped responding while attempting to start this device, and therefore will never attempt to start this device again (Code 11).

Windows may disable devices that prevent it from loading. To re-enable this device, right-click the device name and select **Uninstall**, and then restart Windows.

This device cannot find any free {type} resources to use (Code 12).

See the solution for error code 6.

This device is either not present, not working properly, or does not have all the drivers installed (Code 13).

See the solution for error code 10.

This device cannot work properly until you restart your computer (Code 14).

Do I really need to tell you what to do here?

This device is causing a resource conflict (Code 15).

See the solution for error code 10.

Windows could not identify all the resources this device uses (Code 16).

Right-click the device, select **Properties**, and then choose the **Resources** tab. You may have to fill in some information provided by your hardware documentation. See also the solution for error code 10.

The driver information file {name} is telling this child device to use a resource that the parent device does not have or recognize (Code 17).

You'll need to obtain and install newer drivers for this device.

The drivers for this device need to be reinstalled (Code 18).

See the solution for error code 7.

Your registry may be bad (Code 19).

This extremely helpful message will appear if there is any corrupt data in your Registry pertaining to this device. Note that if you restart Windows, it may revert to an earlier copy of your Registry, which you may nor may not want to happen. See Chapter 3 for help with backing up your Registry before you do anything else. Uninstalling and then reinstalling the driver may help here.

Windows could not load one of the drivers for this device (Code 20).

The driver you're using is likely designed for an earlier version of Windows; contact the manufacturer of the device for a driver written explicitly for Windows 7.

Windows is removing this device (Code 21).

This temporary message will appear immediately after you've attempted to uninstall a device. Close the Properties window, wait a minute or two, and then try again. If it doesn't go away, try restarting Windows.

This device is disabled (Code 22, version 1).

This means you've manually disabled the device by right-clicking and selecting **Disable**. Click **Enable Device** to re-enable the device. If you can't enable the device, try removing it (right-click and select **Uninstall**) and then restarting Windows.

This device is not started (Code 22, version 2).

Some devices can be stopped, either manually or via their drivers. Click **Start Device** to re-enable the device. If this persists, look for updated drivers, and see whether the device has any power management features you can disable.

This display adapter is functioning correctly (Code 23).

Despite the fact that the message states the device is functioning correctly, there's obviously a problem. This typically occurs in systems with two display adapters (video cards), wherein one doesn't fully support being installed in a system with two display adapters (desktop PCs only). Try updating the drivers for both cards, and look for an updated BIOS for either card. You can also try physically swapping the two cards.

This device is either not present, not working properly, or does not have all the drivers installed (Code 24).

See the solution for error code 10.

Windows is in the process of setting up this device (Code 25 and Code 26).

You'll see this if Windows is waiting until the next time it starts to complete the installation of the drivers for this device. Restart Windows to use the device. Note that you may have to restart twice. If that doesn't help, remove the device (right-click and select **Uninstall**), restart Windows one more time, and then try again.

Windows can't specify the resources for this device (Code 27).

See the solution for error code 16.

The drivers for this device are not installed (Code 28).

Click **Reinstall Driver** to install the drivers currently on your system, or obtain new drivers from the manufacturer of the device.

This device is disabled because the BIOS for the device did not give it any resources (Code 29).

This message appears for devices on your motherboard—such as on-board hard disk controllers, network adapters, or video adapters—that have been disabled in your computer's BIOS setup. See Appendix A for more information. (Note that this error may also appear for devices not on your motherboard, in which case you'd need to change the settings in the device firmware to fix the problem.)

This device is using an Interrupt Request (IRQ) resource that is in use by another device and cannot be shared (Code 30).

See the solution for error code 10.

This device is not working properly because {device} is not working properly (Code 31).

This means that the device is dependent on another device (or driver). For instance, this message may appear for a joystick (game) port that is physically installed on a sound card that's having problems. To fix this error, troubleshoot the hardware on which this device is dependent.

Windows cannot install the drivers for this device because it cannot access the drive or network location that has the setup files on it (Code 32).

First, restart your computer. If that doesn't fix the problem, manually copy said drivers directly to a new folder on your hard disk, and try installing them from their new location.

This device isn't responding to its driver (Code 33).

This may indicate a problem with the hardware, or simply a bad driver. Start by removing the device (right-click and select **Uninstall**), restarting Windows, and then reinstalling the drivers. If that doesn't help, you may have a dead device on your hands.

Currently, this hardware device is not connected to the computer (Code 45).

This message will appear for any hidden or ghosted device, shown when you select **View→Show Hidden Devices** in Device Manager. This means the driver is installed, but the hardware has been physically disconnected or removed (or at least Windows thinks it has).

Test for Bad Memory (RAM)

Bad memory can manifest itself in anything from frequent error messages and crashes to your system simply not starting. Errors in your computer's memory (RAM) aren't always consistent, either; they can be intermittent and can get worse over time.

Problems due to using the wrong kind of memory are not uncommon; odds are your friend's old memory modules not only won't work in your system, but they're probably responsible for that burning smell, too. See the sidebar "How to Buy Memory" on page 400 for details.

Not sure what kind of memory is in your PC? Download the free SIW utility from *http://www.gtopala.com/siw-download .html*. Run the program and choose the **Memory** item in the **Hardware** tree to see the manufacturer, capacity, speed, form factor and other vital details of your installed RAM modules.

So, you suspect a memory problem? The first thing to do is pull out each memory module and make sure there isn't any dust or other obstruction between the pins and your motherboard (use a microfiber cloth or lens-cleaning paper; don't use any liquids or solvents). Look for broken or bent sockets, metal filings or other obstructions, and, of course, any smoke or burn marks. Make sure all your modules are seated properly; they should snap into place and should be level and firm (don't break them testing their firmness, of course).

If all that is in order, there are two ways to determine whether your RAM is actually faulty: test it or swap it out.

The easiest and least-effective memory test is the one your PC does for you; see Appendix A for the BIOS setting that disables "quick start," which is necessary to perform a full memory test each time you boot your PC.

For a more thorough test, use the **Windows Memory Diagnostic Tool**, mentioned in "What to Do When Windows Won't Start" on page 355.

For best results, use Memtest86+, available free from *http://www.memtest .org/*. (Avoid releases of Memtest86 earlier than version 4.0—those without the plus + moniker—as they have trouble with some multicore CPUs and more than 4GB of RAM.) To use the program, download the latest ISO file and burn it to a CD (see Chapter 4). Then, boot your PC with the CD, as described in Chapter 1.

If testing has revealed a problem, it's time for a trip to your local computer store or web store to spend some money. It may only be necessary to buy a single additional module (assuming you've already got more than one), because most likely only one module in your system is actually faulty. Next, systematically replace each module in your computer with the one you've just acquired, and test the system by turning it on. If the problem seems to be resolved, you've most likely found the culprit—throw it out immediately. If the system still crashes, try replacing the *next* module with the new one, and repeat the process. If you replace all the memory in your system and the problem persists, there may be more than one faulty memory module, or the problem may lie elsewhere, such as a bad CPU or motherboard (or you may even find that you're not using the correct memory in the first place).

You can, of course, also take this opportunity to add more memory to your system (possibly replacing all your existing modules). Adding memory is one of the best ways to improve overall system performance; see the sidebar "How to Buy Memory" for more information.

How to Buy Memory

There are no two ways about it: the more memory, the better (at least up to a point). Adding more memory to a computer will almost always result in better performance, and will help reduce crashes as well. Windows loads drivers, applications, and documents into memory until it's full; once there's no more memory available, Windows starts pulling large chunks of information out of memory and storing them on your hard disk to make room for the applications that need memory more urgently. Because your hard disk is substantially slower than memory, this "swapping" noticeably slows down your system. The more memory you have, the less frequently Windows will use your hard disk in this way, and the faster your system will be. (See "Optimize Virtual Memory and Cache Settings" on page 312 for more information on this mechanism.)

The nice thing about memory is that it's a cheap and easy way to improve performance. When Windows 3.x was in wide use, 32 MB of RAM cost around a thousand dollars. Modules 32 times that size today cost less than a ticket to the movies.

The type of memory you should get depends solely on what your motherboard demands. To find out which type of memory you should use, try to get recommendations for specific brands and part numbers from your motherboard/PC manufacturer. You can also visit a reputable memory manufacturer's website and get recommendations for your specific PC or motherboard; one of the best such sites is *http://crucial.com*.

That simply leaves one thing to think about: quantity. In short, get as much memory as you can afford. Like everything else, though, there is a point of diminishing returns. 1 GB (1,024 MB) is the absolute lowest amount you should tolerate on a Windows 7 system, but 3-4 GB is better. As described in Chapter 1, though, you'll need the 64-bit edition of Windows 7 if you want to make use of 4 or more GB of RAM.

How to handle too much memory

There is one situation in which the right kind of memory may still not work properly in a PC, even when there's nothing technically wrong with it. Despite what your computer's marketing literature may promise, you may encounter problems if you install too much memory in your PC. (It's worth mentioning that this problem is more typical of desktop PCs, as laptops rarely have more than one or two memory slots.)

 The 32-bit edition of Windows 7—or rather any 32-bit operating system—has a limitation on the amount of memory it will recognize. As explained in Chapter 1, you'll need the 64-bit edition of Windows 7 if you want to make use of 4 GB or more of RAM. The most 32-bit Windows can use is about 3 GB.

Say your motherboard has four slots for RAM, each of which (the manual states) supports memory modules of up to 8 GB. This means, at least in theory, that you could install 32 GB of memory in your PC. So why won't Windows boot when you fill all four slots?

Imagine a pickup truck; you pick the color. The manufacturer says it has a towing capacity (how heavy a trailer it can pull) of 6,000 pounds. But when you're towing 6,000 pounds, you can't necessarily go 65 mph on the freeway without scaring a whole lot of other drivers. Perhaps 35 mph on a side road makes more sense.

Computer memory works the same way. You may be able to run 4 or even 8 GB of RAM without a problem, but fill all those slots, and something else has to give.

Turns out, the compromise you'll need to make is the memory speed. In order to fill up your motherboard, you'll probably need to slow down your memory, which, unfortunately, negates some of the speed gains that much memory might otherwise provide. The specific memory times you'll need vary widely among memory types and motherboard manufacturers, but it's a common enough problem that a quick search online may reveal some memory timings known to work. The manufacturer of your memory will probably also have some recommendations.

To change the timing for your memory, you'll need to dive into your PC's BIOS setup, covered in Appendix A. Unfortunately, some trial and error is inevitable with something like memory timing; expect to restart your PC a dozen or so times until you find values that work.

Don't Overlook the Power Supply

Every time I encounter a problem that seems to have no reasonable explanation (on a desktop PC, that is), the culprit has been the power supply. I'm beginning to think it's a conspiracy.

Troubleshooting

Say, all of a sudden, one of your storage devices (hard disk, tape drive, etc.) starts malfunctioning, either sporadically or completely. You try removing and reinstalling the drivers (if any), you replace all the cables, and you take out all the other devices. You may even completely replace the device with a brand-new one—and it still doesn't work. Odds are your power supply needs to be replaced.

Your computer's power supply powers all of your internal devices, as well as some of your external ones (i.e., the keyboard, the mouse, and most USB devices). If your power supply isn't able to provide adequate power to all your hardware, one or more of those devices will suffer.

The power supplies found in most computers are extremely cheap, a fact that ends up being the cause of most power supply problems. This means that it doesn't make too much sense to replace one cheap unit with another cheap unit, even if the replacement has a higher wattage rating.

Power supplies are rated by the amount of power they can provide (in watts); most computers come with 200–300W supplies, but many power users end up needing 350–400W. The problem with power ratings, however, is that most of those cheap power supplies don't hold up under the load. A cheap 400W unit may drop under 300W when you start connecting devices, but better supplies can supply more than enough power for even the most demanding systems, and will continue to provide reliable operations for years to come. A well-made power supply will also be heavy and have multiple fans, as well as being a bit more expensive than the landfill fodder lining most store shelves.

Possible exceptions are portable computers, which usually don't have user-replaceable power supplies. However, the need for increased power is generally only applicable to a desktop system that can accommodate several additional internal devices, so the matter is pretty much moot on a laptop.

Fix USB Power Management Issues

Power management is a common cause of USB problems; if Windows is able to shut down your USB controller to save power, it sometimes won't be able to power it back up again, which will prevent some USB devices (especially scanners) from working.

To prevent Windows from "managing" power to your USB controller or devices, follow these steps:

1. Open Device Manager (*devmgmt.msc*).
2. Expand the **Universal Serial Bus controllers** branch.

3. Double-click the **USB Root Hub** device, and choose the **Power Management** tab. (If there's more than one **USB Root Hub** device, repeat these steps for each one.)

4. Turn off the **Allow the computer to turn off this device to save power** option, and click OK when you're done.

See "Start Windows Instantly (Almost)" on page 274 for other power management issues.

Fix Printer Problems

What was once a source of lots of frustration in Windows computing—installing a printer—is now a fairly simple task. Gone are the awful parallel cables; in their place are reliable USB cables and built-in wireless network connections. But there are two quirks in Windows 7 that can cause printing headaches, even with the latest printers and the friendliest plug-and-play drivers you ever did see.

The first hurdle, one you'll likely have to jump as well if you're trying to get a printer to work, is to clear the print queue. The queue is the collection of documents waiting to be printed by a particular printer. For years, the print queue has been a lousy tool in Windows, and Windows 7 doesn't make things any better. Try to delete (cancel) one or more documents queued to be printed by a malfunctioning printer, for instance, and you'll wait an eternity before Windows actually removes the entry from the list.

The solution is to forcibly clear the print queue. First, open the Services window (*services.msc*), right-click the **Print Spooler** service, and select **Stop** to halt the service. Next, open Windows Explorer, navigate to the *Windows\System32\spool\printers* folder, and delete all the files therein. When the printers folder is empty, return to the Services window, right-click the **Print Spooler** service, and select **Start** to start the service once again.

The next problem with Windows 7 is that there's no obvious way to uninstall a printer driver, which is the #1 ingredient in the *fix-my-printer* soufflé. Sure, you can delete any printer by right-clicking its icon in the Devices and Printers page of Control Panel and selecting **Remove device**. But this won't remove the driver software from your PC, only the device instance from Control Panel. And the next thing you know, the device will reappear, thanks to plug-and-play, with the same buggy driver that prompted you to remove it in the first place.

To fix the problem, open the Print Server Properties window. Assuming at least one printer currently appears in your Devices and Printers list, select it and then click the **Print server properties** button in the ribbon across the top of the window. (If the button isn't there, open your Start menu, and in the **Search** box, type printui /s /t2 and press **Enter**.)

 You can't remove a printer driver if there's a printer still using it. Make sure you delete the printer instance from the Devices and Printers window before you proceed.

Next, choose the **Drivers** tab, select the driver to uninstall, and click **Remove**. On the Remove Driver and Package window, select **Remove driver and driver package**, and then click OK. Click **Yes** to indicate that you're absolutely, positively certain you want to delete this crappy driver, and then click **Delete** on the next window to actually go through with it. Whew!

When you're done, restart Windows and then try connecting your printer again; this time, it'll prompt you for a driver, at which point you can install something that works.

Preventative Maintenance and Data Recovery

Face it: some sort of data loss is inevitable. Whether it's a single lost file or a dead hard disk—whether it's tomorrow or 12 years from now—it will happen. On that happy note, there is plenty you can do about it.

First and foremost, there's no better method of disaster recovery than having a good backup copy of all your data. Any stolen or damaged hardware is easily replaced, but the data stored on your hard disk is not. Unfortunately, hindsight is 20/20, and if you didn't back up, there's not much you can do about it after the fact; even if your computer equipment is insured with Lloyd's of London, once your data is gone, it's gone. Thus, a little preventative maintenance is in order.

Manage Windows Updates

If software manufacturers waited until their products were completely bug-free before releasing them, then this book would've been called Typewriter Annoyances.

Windows 7 has a fairly automated update system, wherein patches to the operating system that Microsoft considers important are made available on its website, and, by default, automatically downloaded and installed on your PC.

Just open Windows Update in Control Panel, and click the **Check for updates** link on the left to compile a list of the updates you haven't yet installed. This is a fairly straightforward procedure, but largely unnecessary because Windows does it for you. Or is it necessary after all?

Right out of the box, Windows asks you how you'd like to handle updates. Microsoft recommends the **Install updates automatically** option, and even goes so far as to alert you through Security Center (see Chapter 7) if you've selected any other option (or none at all). But if you go this route, you're setting yourself up to have your PC indiscriminately hijacked by Microsoft whenever it needs to install an update. That means annoying pop-up reminders to restart Windows while you're trying to get your work done, or worse: a long delay when you need to shut down in a hurry.

Of course, the other end of the spectrum is **Never check for updates**, which some Windows users swear by. Sure, you never get the frequent bug fixes for Internet Explorer, but that's not such a big deal if you're a Firefox user.

But the **Download updates but let me choose whether to install them** option is the best of both worlds. This way, you can pick and choose your updates, and more importantly, install them only when it's convenient for you.

The hardware drivers delivered along with the other Windows updates are a mixed bag, at best. Sometimes the driver install fails, and other times, it succeeds and then breaks the device. Update a driver only when you're already using a Microsoft driver (see "How to Add Hardware" on page 388); otherwise, use the manufacturer-supplied driver. Fortunately, drivers installed through Windows Update can be "rolled back," but who wants to roll back drivers when you don't have to?

If, for some reason, you need to uninstall an update, you can do so most of the time. In Control Panel, open Programs and Features, and then click the **View installed updates** link on the left. Highlight any update in the list and click **Uninstall** to get rid of it.

If you're using Microsoft Office or another high-profile Microsoft product, you can download updates for those products along with those for Windows. To do this, open Windows Update, turn on the **Give me updates for Microsoft products** link, and then click OK.

Silence the restart nag

Some updates can only be applied while Windows isn't running, which is why Windows Update sometimes prompts you to restart Windows to complete installation. What? You're busy? Sure, you can decline to reboot, but Windows will hassle you again just 5 short minutes later.

At this point, you can postpone the reboot for up to 4 hours, but unfortunately, there's no "stop bothering me" button. To get rid of the nag window, at least until the next reboot, open the Services window (*services.msc*), highlight the Windows Update service, and click the square **Stop** button on the toolbar. Don't worry; Windows will restart the service when you finally get around to restarting.

Here's how to turn off the restart nag altogether:

1. Open the Registry Editor (see Chapter 3) and navigate to `HKEY_LOCAL_MACHINE\SOFTWARE\Policies\Microsoft\Windows`.
2. Inside the `Windows` key, create a new key and name it `WindowsUpdate`.
3. Then inside the `WindowsUpdate` key, create a new key and name it `AU`.
4. Next, in the new `AU` key, create a new DWORD (32-bit) value and type `NoAutoRebootWithLoggedOnUsers` for its name.
5. Double-click the new `NoAutoRebootWithLoggedOnUsers` value, type `1` in the Value data field, and click OK.
6. Restart Windows just this once for the change to take effect.

   To undo the change, just delete the `NoAutoRebootWithLoggedOnUsers` value.

Force a failed update to install

So, what do you do when Windows reports that an update has failed? Microsoft never provides a useful explanation nor any means of solving the problem: your only recourse is to keep trying until you lose interest.

The first step is to figure out which update won't install. Open the Windows Updates page in Control Panel and then click the **View update history** link on the left. Locate the update that reads "Failed" in the **Status** column, and then make sure the update wasn't subsequently installed successfully.

Next, right-click the update, select **View details**, and click the web link under the **More information** heading. If the link takes you to a generic page that explains how updates work (typical with definition updates for Windows Defender), this is a dead end. But if instead you get a numbered bulletin that is specific to the update in question (e.g., "Microsoft Security Bulletin MS09-035 – Critical"), then you're on the right track.

Read the summary and see if this update applies to you; if it fixes a problem with a component you never use, you may be able to abandon the update and save yourself some time. Otherwise, scroll down the page and look for prerequisites. Some updates require certain software (or certain installation features) to be present; without them, the update won't install.

 One common prerequisite is the version of the Windows Installer engine currently on your PC. To determine the version number, open Windows Explorer and navigate to the \Windows\System32 folder. Right-click the *msi.dll* file, select **Properties**, and choose the **Details** tab. The **Product version** is the magic number; Windows 7 ships with MSI 5.0.7600.

Next, look for a standalone installer. Sometimes you can download the update in a packaged *.exe* or *.msi* file, and these installers sometimes succeed where the automated updates fail. But more importantly, standalone updaters usually display a log of their progress (or lack thereof), which you can use to determine the precise problem.

Can't find a download link? Just open Internet Explorer (not Firefox) and navigate to *http://catalog.update.microsoft.com/v7/site/Home.aspx* to view the Windows Update Catalog. In the **Search** box, type the knowledge base number (e.g., KB971091), not the bulletin number (e.g., MS09-035), which you can get from the update history.

When the update appears in the catalog search results, click the **Add** button. Then, click the **view basket** link at the top of the page and click the **Download** button. When prompted, click **Browse** to choose a destination folder and then click **Continue** to initiate the download.

When the download is complete, you may've gotten an *.exe* file or an *.msi* file. (See Chapter 2 if you can't see your filename extensions.)

If the update was delivered in an *.exe* file, just double-click the file to launch the interactive installer. If the install fails, click the **View the log file** button on the last page of the wizard; scroll down until you see a line in red explaining the error.

If instead you have an .msi file, you'll need to take a few extra steps to get an install log. First, open a Command Prompt window in administrator mode (see Chapter 9 and Chapter 8, respectively). Use the CD command to change the active directory to the folder in which you saved the .msi file, like this:

```
cd "c:\users\{your user name}\Desktop\my failed update"
```

Troubleshooting

and then run the update with the `/qf /Le` command-line switches, like this:

```
msiexec /i msifilename.msi /qf /Le .\log.txt
```

where *msifilename.msi* is the filename of your *.msi* file. When the update concludes, open the *log.txt* file for clues as to why it failed.

Once you know the problem—often an issue with registry or file permissions—you should be able to fix it easily and try again.

Go Back in Time with Restore Points and Shadow Copies

The System Restore service runs invisibly in the background, routinely backing up drivers, important system files, and certain Registry settings so that at some point, you can roll back some or all of your computer's configuration to an earlier time. Windows extends this feature to include your personal documents as well, forming what are called *shadow copies*. (In Vista, shadow copies were only available to those with high-end Windows editions; in Windows 7, everyone gets 'em!)

 Windows maintains your PC's restore points somewhat like the Recycle Bin; old data is deleted invisibly in the background to make room for new restore points. For this reason, never rely solely on restore points to provide backups of your documents.

There are several different ways to access restore points, each with its own purpose and scope:

Roll Back Driver

In Device Manager (*devmgmt.msc*, also in Control Panel), expand a category, right-click a device, and select **Properties**. Choose the **Driver** tab, and then click **Roll Back Driver** to replace the current driver with an earlier version. If the **Roll Back Driver** button is grayed out, then either you've loaded no earlier version of this driver, or the System Restore feature isn't operational (discussed later in this section). What's nice about this feature is that the scope of the change is crystal clear; when you click **Roll Back Driver**, only the driver files and settings for that very device are affected.

System Restore

To open the System Restore wizard, open the Start menu, type `rstrui` into the **Search** box and press **Enter**. Click **Next** on the first page to show a list of the recent restore points, and then select an entry and click **Next** to revert your PC's system files and configuration to an earlier state. (If you don't see any restore points, read on to see how to enable this feature.)

It's best to think of this feature as neither an uninstall tool nor a time machine, but rather something in between. Windows makes a restore point when you install hardware drivers, when you install software (most of the time), and occasionally at regular intervals. (You can also create restore points manually in the System Protection window, described later in this section.) But it's never made clear what exactly changes when you restore a restore point, making this a potentially dangerous tool. The good news is that you can return to the System Restore wizard and undo your last change should something go wrong (assuming you can boot Windows thereafter).

If all you're trying to do is uninstall software, you should do so through the Programs and Features page in Control Panel. Likewise, to uninstall a hardware driver, open Device Manager (*devmgmt.msc*), right-click the device, and select **Uninstall**. With these features, at least the scope of your change will be easily predictable.

Last Known Good Configuration

If a recent driver or software installation has prevented Windows from loading, press **F8** just after your PC powers up (see "What to Do When Windows Won't Start" on page 355), and from the Advanced Boot Options menu that appears, select **Last Known Good Configuration (advanced)**.

If you're lucky, the effect is more or less the same as choosing a recent restore point in the System Restore wizard, allowing you to subsequently start Windows. But in practice, this feature often has no effect, either because the scope of the change isn't great enough to fix whatever problem you're having, or because Windows wasn't set up to create restore points in the first place (more on that shortly).

Previous Versions

Right-click a document you've been working on recently, select **Properties**, and choose the **Previous Versions** tab. What you see in the **File versions** list here depends on several factors.

First, if you've used the Back up now tool on the Backup and Restore page in Control Panel described later in this chapter, and the backup included the file you right-clicked, at least one entry should appear indicated by

Backup in the **Location** column. (Thus the usefulness of this feature relies heavily on the scheduled backup feature that comes with Windows 7.)

Next, if the file is on a drive protected by System Restore, you should see at least one entry marked **Restore point** in the **Location** column.

 The Previous Versions feature relies on administrative (hidden) shares of your drives; if you've disabled them as described in the section "Turn Off Administrative Shares" on page 605, the **File Versions** list won't appear. Furthermore, Windows will never save previous versions of encrypted files (also covered in Chapter 8).

To roll back a file to an earlier version, select the backup or shadow copy you want, and click **Restore**. But beware: this will overwrite the newer file with the older version, which may not be what you want. To restore the backup to a new location, click **Copy** instead. You can also retrieve shadow copies with ShadowExplorer, free from *http://www.shado wexplorer.com*.

The biggest problem with the System Restore and Previous Versions features is that they often don't work. If they're not properly set up, the restore points on which they rely don't get made. To get restore points to work on your PC, follow these steps:

1. Start by opening the System Protection window; in the Start menu **Search** box, type SystemPropertiesProtection, and press **Enter**. (Or, open the System page in Control Panel, click the **Advanced system settings** link on the left, and choose the **System Protection** tab.)

2. Here, highlight drive C: and then click **Configure**.

3. Select one of the first two options here, either **Restore system settings and previous versions of files** or **Only restore previous versions of files**. Then, make sure **Max Usage** is set to a reasonably large value (several gigabytes, if you can afford it) and click OK.

 To completely deactivate System Restore, select the **Turn off system protection** option for each of your drives and then click OK.

4. Repeat steps 2 and 3 for any other drives for which you want to create restore points.

5. If any drives weren't previously protected, take this opportunity to save a restore point by clicking **Create**.

6. Click OK when you're done.

7. Next, open the Services window (*services.msc*), and find the **Volume Shadow Copy** entry in the list. If it doesn't say **Started** in the **Status** column, double-click the entry, and from the **Startup type** list, select **Automatic**. Click **Start** to get the service running, and then click OK.

8. Repeat step 7 for the **Microsoft Software Shadow Copy Provider** service as well.

If shadow copies still don't appear to be working, check your PC for utilities that may not be fully compatible with Windows 7's restore points. For instance, some Registry "cleaners," like TuneUp Utilities and CCleaner, have been known to interfere with restore points (among other things). And Diskeeper 2007 (defragmenter software) and earlier versions were known to erase shadow copy data (Diskeeper 2008 fixes this problem). If you're having trouble getting shadow copies to work, try disabling any "fix-it" utilities on your PC until you track down the culprit.

Manage disk space used by shadow copies and restore points

By default, restore points are allowed to consume as much as 15% of your hard disk's total capacity; on a 320 GB drive, that means up to 48 GB can be sucked up by previous versions of your files, hardware drivers, and other detritus. Of course, if you're an avid user of shadow copies, and you've got a sufficiently large drive, then you might prefer this value to be even higher.

To find out how much space restore points are currently taking up, open a Command Prompt window in administrator mode (see Chapter 8), type this command:

```
vssadmin list shadowstorage
```

and press **Enter** to produce a report that looks like this:

```
vssadmin 1.1 - Volume Shadow Copy Service administrative command-line tool
(C) Copyright 2001-2005 Microsoft Corp.

Shadow Copy Storage association
   For volume: (C:)\\?\Volume{3b5ab54e-c86b-11cb-a2d6-306f6f6e7963}\
   Shadow Copy Storage volume: (C:)\\?\Volume{3b5ab54e-c86b-11cb-a2d6-
                                                      306f6f6e7963}\
   Used Shadow Copy Storage space: 14.126 GB (10%)
   Allocated Shadow Copy Storage space: 14.425 GB (10%)
   Maximum Shadow Copy Storage space: 20.959 GB (15%)
```

Here, restore points and shadow copies consume a little more than 14 GB. The files themselves are stored in the *\System Volume Information* folder, which is hidden in Windows Explorer unless you turn off the **Hide protected operating system files** option covered in Chapter 2. (Regardless of the setting, Windows will never let you view the files therein directly.)

To allocate more or less space for shadow copies, open the System Protection window; in the Start menu **Search** box, type SystemPropertiesProtection, and press **Enter**. (Or, open the System page in Control Panel, click the **Advanced system settings** link on the left, and choose the **System Protection** tab.) Highlight the drive you want to manage, click **Configure**, and adjust the Max Usage slider accordingly. To eliminate the storage limit, move the slider all the way to the right and set it to 100%.

 Need disk space fast? Click the **Delete** button here to delete all your shadow copies and restore points without changing any settings, and get back 10%–15% of your hard disk capacity on the spot. Of course, you'll lose your previous versions, so you may want to back up your hard disk first, as described later in this chapter.

For you typing fans, you can also manage shadow copy storage by typing this command in a command prompt window (again, in Administrator mode):

```
vssadmin resize shadowstorage /for=C: /on=C: /maxsize=5GB
```

(Replace *C:* with the drive you want to adjust, and *5GB* with the actual amount of space you wish to allocate.) You may have noticed that you need to indicate the drive letter twice. This permits a nifty little hack: it turns out you can allocate space on one drive to hold the shadow data from another drive. For instance, type:

```
vssadmin add shadowstorage /for=C: /on=D:
```

to have the shadow data for drive *C:* stored on drive *D:*. (If *C:* is your primary Windows drive, putting your shadow data on *D:* should improve system performance, provided *D:* is a real hard disk.) To rescind this order, delete the shadow storage "association" with this command:

```
vssadmin delete shadowstorage /for=C: /on=D:
```

You can also delete shadow copy data without changing the associations, akin to the aforementioned **Delete** button:

```
vssadmin delete shadows /for=C: /all
```

Or, if you have a lot of drives and you want to clear the shadow data for all of them at once, use this WSH script (see Chapter 9):

```
Set oWMI=GetObject("winmgmts:{impersonationLevel=impersonate}!\\.\root\
    cimv2")
Set cVolumes = oWMI.ExecQuery("Select * From Win32_ShadowCopy")
For Each oVolume in cVolumes
    oVolume.Delete
Next
```

See "Quick, On-the-Fly Backups" on page 414, for a quick and dirty alternative to shadow copies.

Choose a schedule for shadow copy creation

The usefulness of shadow copies, and the Previous Versions feature in particular, depends heavily on how often Windows creates those backups. Shadow copies are created on a schedule: by default, this happens every day at midnight—but only if your PC is on and idle—and 30 minutes after each time you start Windows.

But there are conditions that must be met. For one, the process only begins if your computer has been idle for at least 10 minutes, so don't expect any backups to occur while you're working. Next, to extend the life of your laptop battery, backups are only made when you're on AC power, so don't expect any backups at the coffee shop. Finally, if the backup fails for some reason, Windows won't try again until the next scheduled backup. If you rely on the Previous Versions feature, you'll probably want to adjust the schedule so backups can occur more reliably.

Start by opening the Task Scheduler (*taskschd.msc*), and in the right pane, navigate to `Task Scheduler Library\Microsoft\Windows\SystemRestore`. Right-click the **SR** entry in the middle pane, select **Properties**, and choose the **History** tab to see how often Windows has been making your shadow copies.

To change the schedule, choose the **Triggers** tab. Unless you've already made a change here, you'll see two entries in the list: **Daily** and **At startup**. Highlight a trigger and click **Edit** to make a change.

 There's a limit of 64 shadow copies for each volume (drive letter), so if you think it might be wise to create backups every hour on the hour, keep in mind that this means you'll have a maximum of only 2 days and 16 hours worth of shadow copies at your fingertips. And this doesn't take into account any hard disk space limitations you may've imposed in Control Panel (covered earlier in this section).

When you're done changing settings in the Edit Trigger window, make sure the **Enabled** option is checked, and click OK.

Next, choose the **Conditions** tab. You may wish to turn off the **Start the task only if the computer is idle for** option if your PC is frequently busy, or else the shadow copies may be forever postponed. Or leave it on to improve performance elsewhere. Likewise, turn off the **Start the task only if the computer is on AC power** option if your laptop is frequently untethered, or leave it on to improve battery life.

Finally, flip over to the **Settings** tab, and make sure the **Run task as soon as possible after a scheduled start is missed** option is checked. Click OK to commit your changes.

See the sidebar "Quick, On-the-Fly Backups" for a more reliable, but less automated way to backup up previous versions of files, or the next section for a foolproof full system backup. See Chapter 9 for more on the Task Scheduler.

Quick, On-the-Fly Backups

Backups can take a long time, and even if you complete one every day, you can still lose up to a day's work with quick slip, power outage, or application crash. Since a backup is not much more than a simple copy of your data, why not do a quick and dirty backup several times a day when you're working with particularly important data? No special software or hardware is required, and, best of all, it takes only a few seconds.

Solution 1: Simple copy

The next time you've put a few hours into a document, open the folder in Explorer, and make a duplicate of the file: drag it to another part of the same folder with the right mouse button and select **Copy Here**. Then, when you need it, you'll have a fresh backup right in the same folder. Of course, you can also place your quick backup on a USB flash drive, online backup server, or another PC on your network.

Solution 2: Simple Zip

To make a quick and dirty backup of an entire folder, just right-click the folder, select **Send To** and then **Compressed (zipped) Folder**. A new *.zip* file containing compressed versions of all of its contents will appear next to the folder in a few seconds. If you then need to retrieve a file from the backed-up folder, just double-click the new *.zip* file, and drag the files you need back into the source folder. See "Zip It Up" on page 107, for the scoop on this ubiquitous format.

Solution 3: Previous Versions

Right-click a document, select **Properties**, and then choose the **Previous Versions** tab to see any automated backups Windows has made for you. Unless you want to overwrite the newer version with the backup, click

---

the **Copy** button to retrieve a backed-up version of the file. Windows makes its backups on its own schedule, if at all, so there's no guarantee that the file you need has been recently protected. But it's automatic, provided you can get it to work, and that counts for a lot. For complete control of this feature, see "Go Back in Time with Restore Points and Shadow Copies" on page 408.

Solution 4: Add-on software

If you're not averse to add-on tools, Microsoft's own SyncToy is free and actually quite excellent; get version 2.1 or later from *http://www.microsoft .com/downloads/*. In short, SyncToy is designed to synchronize two or more folders and keep their contents identical, but you can use it to maintain an instant, up-to-date backup of any folder. (Hint: use it over a network or on a flash drive for extra protection.) Think of SyncToy like RAID 1 for individual folders; see "Protect Your Data with RAID" on page 420. Also available is Second Copy (free trial at *http:// www.secondcopy.com/*), which offers additional features.

Back Up Your Entire System

There are more ways to back up your data than to store it in the first place. The sole purpose of a backup is to have a duplicate of every single piece of data on your hard disk that can be easily retrieved in the event of a catastrophe (or even just an accidental deletion). Imagine if your computer were stolen or suddenly burst into flames and you had to restore a backup to a brand-new computer. Could you do it? If the answer is no, you're not backed up.

You need to be able to complete a backup easily and often, to store the backup in a safe place (away from the computer), and to retrieve all your data at any time without incident. If it's too difficult or time-consuming, odds are you won't do it—so make it easy for yourself.

A bare minimum backup could be little more than a single CD or USB memory key with your last three or four dozen important documents on it. It's better than nothing, and it does protect your most recent work, but what about your email, your web browser bookmarks, your digital photos, and the thousands of documents you've written over the past six years?

Ideally, you should be able to back up your entire hard disk on a single piece of media. We won't even entertain the idea of CDs—you'd need 625 of them to back up a full 500 GB hard disk—nor DVDs (you'd need 58 dual-layer discs). ZIP drives are a joke, and USB memory keys are too slow and too small. Tapes are so far beyond passé, Windows 7 doesn't even include drivers for tape drives.

The only practical choice for completely backing up a modern PC is a removable hard disk. Shortly after the initial release of Windows 7, a 1.5 TB 3.5-inch hard disk cost less than US$100, with a decent external enclosure adding only about 30% more.

 Another option is to use an online backup service. Although they typically require recurring/monthly fees to store your data, they offer the significant advantage of an completely off-site backup. Such services are best for your personal files (provided there's nothing too sensitive to share with a 5-dollar service); even if you decide to back up your entire drive remotely, it would take an awfully long time to download it all again in the event of a hard disk crash. But if you value your data, an online backup is a great supplement to an easily-restored removable hard disk. Some of the more well-regarded services include MozyHome (*http://mozy.com/home*) and Carbonite (*http://www.carbonite.com/*).

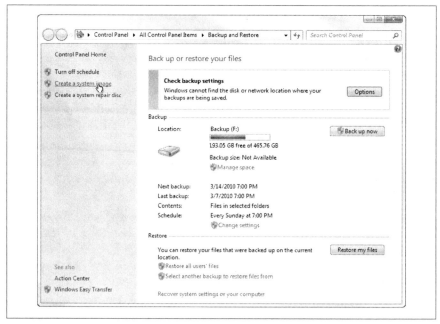

Figure 6-10. The Backup and Restore page in Control Panel allows you to back up your personal files and create a system image with backups of every file on your hard disk

There are basically three software-based backup technologies included with Windows 7:

Back up or restore your files

The *Back up your files* tool makes it pretty easy to back up your personal data onto any drive—removable or otherwise—and restore individual files as needed. Just open the Backup and Restore page in Control Panel (Figure 6-10) and click the **Back up now** button.

 If the **Back up now** button is grayed out, it means your backup hasn't been set up yet or your backup drive is unavailable (disconnected). Click the **Change settings** link below to choose the details of your backup and re-enable the **Back up now** feature.

To restore one or more backed-up files, click the **Restore my files** button and then use the **Search**, **Browse for files**, and **Browse for folders** buttons to select files to restore. None of the file selection windows show a folder tree, so it's a little cumbersome to restore more than a handful of files or folders at a time, but it's serviceable.

Files backed up with this tool are stored in individual Zip files (see Chapter 2) of up to about 200 Mb each, which means you can retrieve your backed-up files on any computer using any operating system, merely by opening the individual Zip files and dragging files out.

The automatic backup provided by the Back Up Files wizard is also an ingredient to the *Previous Versions* feature discussed in "Go Back in Time with Restore Points and Shadow Copies" on page 408. This means that you can right-click a file on your hard disk, select **Properties**, and then choose the **Previous Versions** tab to access any earlier copies of the file backed up with the *Back up your files* tool.

The *Back up your files* tool is infinitely more useful than Vista's *Back Up Files* wizard—particularly with so many ways to restore your files—but it still falls short when compared to the other backup tool on the same page of Control Panel, **Create a system image** (next). For one, it's intolerably slow, taking about 3–4 times as long to back up data as a system image. And it doesn't necessarily back up all your files unless you explicitly tell it to do so. But most importantly, it doesn't let you easily restore your PC entirely from a backup, as described in "Recover Your System After a Crash" on page 423.

Create a system image

A system image is a snapshot of every last byte on your hard disk, stored in a single file on the destination of your choice. This is the easiest way to restore your PC entirely in the event of a hard disk crash or other catastrophe. Just open the Backup and Restore Center (Figure 6-10), click the **Create a system image** link on the left, and follow the prompts to create image files of each of your hard disks. (This tool is the latest incarnation of what was known as *Complete PC Backup* in Vista.)

But as though Microsoft had plotted some cruel joke, you can't restore individual files from system image backups, at least not without a little hack demonstrated later in this section. Rather, system images are only intended for tasks like restoring a complete system after a crash (discussed later in this chapter) and replacing your hard disk (covered in Chapter 5).

 Unfortunately, system images don't play with the Previous Versions feature (discussed earlier in this chapter), so unless you want to use both the *Back up your files* tool and system images, you'll have to rely entirely on restore points for your Previous Versions.

The other problem with system images is that you can't schedule a system image backup, at least not without third party software. About the closest you can come is to create an entry in Task Manager (see Chapter 9) that runs this command line:

```
sdclt.exe /blbbackupwizard
```

which just starts the *Create a system image* wizard. The only way to automate the entire system image backup process past this point is to use a program that can send keystrokes to the wizard, such as the free AutoHotKey tool (*http://www.autohotkey.com/*).

Shadow Copies/Previous Versions

The *Shadow Copies* feature, also known as *Previous Versions*, is an extension of the System Restore tool, which stores older versions of system files and hardware drivers in case Windows won't start as the result of a recent change. See "Go Back in Time with Restore Points and Shadow Copies" on page 408 for ways you can use the feature as an on-the-fly backup and restore tool.

See also "Protect Your Data with RAID" on page 420 for another means of automated backup.

Restore a system image

Restoring a Complete PC Backup involves erasing your hard disk and replacing all your data with the data in the backup. This means any data on your hard disk created or modified since your last backup will be sucked into oblivion, so you'll likely only want to use this feature if your hard disk crashes. If you're restoring from within Windows, consider making another, newer backup on different media before you restore the older archive.

There are two ways to restore a backup from a system image. The first method, useful when you're rebuilding your PC with a new hard disk or when Windows won't start, is outlined in the section "Recover Your System After a Crash" on page 423. The other method—the one Windows doesn't support out of the box—is explained next.

Restore individual files from a system image

The most frustrating limitation of the **Create a system image** tool is that Microsoft made no straightforward provision for restoring individual files from image files. You shouldn't have to back up your data with both backup tools in order to have complete protection *and* the convenience of individual file recovery.

System images are virtual hard disk image (*.vhd*) files, the very same files used by Microsoft Virtual PC and Virtual Server to store data for virtual machines. Not only does this allow Windows 7 to rebuild a hard disk from a backup, but it also means that you can open a window to the past, so to speak, and operate a Virtual PC session off your backup, described in Chapter 1. (If you have the Enterprise or Ultimate edition, you can even boot off a virtual hard disk.) It also means you can restore individual files...if you know where to look.

The easiest way to mount a *.vhd* file is to open the Disk Management tool (*diskmgmt.msc*), covered in "Work with Partitions" on page 328. From the **Action** menu, select **Attach VHD**, and then click **Browse** to locate your backup *.vhd* file (see Figure 6-11). Open your backup drive and navigate to \WindowsImageBackup\{computername}\Backup {date}, where {computername} is the name of your PC and {date} is the date of your last backup.

Figure 6-11. To restore individual files from a disk image, mount the backup VHD in Disk Management

Back on the Attach Virtual Hard Disk window (Figure 6-11), turn on the **Read-only** option to prevent changes to your backup, or leave it unchecked if you want to alter your backup files. Click OK, and in a few moments, Disk Management will mount your *.vhd* file and assign it a drive letter. It'll also appear in the list of drives in the main Disk Management window, more or less indistinguishable from your physical disks except for its blue drive icon.

 You can unmount the virtual drive by right-clicking the disk in the leftmost column and selecting **Detach VHD**. To change the drive letter, right-click the volume in the graphical view (lower pane) and select **Change Drive Letter and Paths**.

Once mounted, the new drive will appear in the Computer branch in Windows Explorer, from which you can restore any individual files from your backup by dragging and dropping.

If you find yourself mounting and unmounting *.vhd* files frequently, you can use the VHDMount command-line utility, which comes with Virtual Server 2005, freely available at *http://www.microsoft.com/virtualserver/*. (Nevermind the version number; the latest release at the time of this writing, R2 SP1, works just fine with Windows 7.) Then download the *vhdmount.reg* Registry patch file from *http://annoyances.org/downloads/vhdmount.reg*, and double-click *vhdmount.reg* to add Windows Explorer integration. (If your *Program Files* folder is on a different drive than *C:*, edit the *vhdmount.reg* file and change both occurrences of the *VHDMount* folder path to the correct location.) Thereafter, you can right-click a *.vhd* file and select **Mount**. (A Command Prompt window will appear briefly with a message; leave it alone while it does its job.) When you're done with the backup, return to the folder containing your *.vhd* files, right-click the one you've mounted, and select **Unmount (discard changes)**. (Only use the other option, **commit changes**, if you made changes to the virtual drive that you want to keep.) The drive should disappear from Windows Explorer immediately.

Protect Your Data with RAID

RAID, or *Redundant Array of Inexpensive Disks*, is a collection of two or more hard drives that your PC (and Windows) treats as a single volume. Save your data once, and it's invisibly stored on two different physical disks simultaneously. If one of your drives fails, just swap it out for a new one and keep working while your RAID subsystem rebuilds the new drive in the background.

RAID comes in several varieties, but not all offer this vital redundancy. *Raid 1* is the most common, safeguarding your PC by "mirroring" your data on your multiple drives. *Raid 0*, on the other hand, spreads your data across multiple drives to improve performance (called *striping*), yet offers no data redundancy. *Raid 5* works similarly to Raid 0, but adds a "parity" mechanism to safeguard your data, and requires at least three drives. Finally, *Raid 10* offers true mirroring (like Raid 1) and striping (like Raid 0)—the best of both worlds—but requires four drives for the full effect. Raid 1 is the easiest to implement and is the least expensive way to get data protection from RAID.

The first ingredient you need is a SATA RAID controller, one either built in to your motherboard, or, barring that, an add-on RAID card. Next, you need two SATA hard disks of the same capacity, preferably the same brand and model, too.

Not all drives play nicely with RAID, dropping out of the array randomly or causing other problems. Before settling on a specific model, read some online reviews and see if others have had trouble getting the drive to behave in a RAID setup. In some cases, such as the well-known Seagate 1.5 TB unit, a drive can be made more RAID-friendly with a firmware update.

To get started, plug your drives into ports 0 and 1, respectively, unless your documentation says otherwise. (Some controllers have dedicated RAID plugs.) To make room, you may need to relegate any other SATA devices, such as DVD drives, to higher-numbered ports.

To set up the drives, enter your PC's BIOS setup screen (see Appendix A), and make sure all of the SATA ports you're using are enabled. Next, disable any unused SATA ports (some RAID controllers mistake unused ports for missing drives), and then turn on the RAID feature if it's not already on. Save your settings and reboot when you're done.

After the BIOS setup prompt but before Windows begins to load, look for a boot message from your RAID controller, and then press the required keystroke (e.g., **Ctrl-I** for the Intel Matrix Storage Manager) to enter your RAID configuration utility. Use this screen to select drives and build your array. If given the chance to name your new array, make sure to include the word RAID or Array, as these names will later show up in Device Manager.

Joining a drive to a RAID is likely to erase any data on the drive, so make sure back up anything you care about before you proceed.

When you're done, Windows will see the array as a single drive. Thereafter, you can install Windows (see Chapter 1) fresh on the new array or restore your backup, if applicable. Once you're back in Windows, install the RAID management software so you can easily monitor the health of your array.

Drawbacks of RAID

RAID sounds great on paper: an instant, transparent backup of every byte written to your drive in real time. But this also means an instant backup of every malware infestation, every deleted file, and every corrupt Registry entry. Thus RAID is not so much of a backup as a simple safeguard against mechanical failure; to fully protect your data, you'll still need to conduct separate, regular backups, as described earlier in this chapter.

RAID also consumes more power, generates more heat and noise, and costs at least twice as much as a lone drive. But probably the biggest problem is vibration. Two drives vibrate in your PC chassis much more than one, and those vibrations can lead to premature drive failure: an irony not to be taken lightly.

 The best way to deal with the vibrations is to install each drive in an isolated, vibration-dampening chassis. Some drive manufacturers also sell upgraded drives that are less susceptible to the effects of vibration (e.g., Seagate's NS series). Also make sure your array has plenty of ventilation and active cooling.

One of the benefits of RAID is that it actively monitors the health of your drives and data; aside from the hardware redundancy, this is one of the reasons most people use RAID. But this monitoring has costs, too. For instance, if you encounter a Blue Screen of Death of other fatal crash that prevents Windows from shutting down properly, your RAID will check your array for errors the next time you start your PC. Since this means reading every byte on every drive in your array, you can expect poor overall performance until it's finished (often 4–5 hours, depending on the size and speed of the drives).

Department of Redundancy Department

If a drive fails, your RAID controller will remove it from the array, and the remaining drive(s) will continue to function as though nothing happened. The faster you can replace the dead drive, the sooner your RAID will be protecting your data once again.

Typically, high-demand servers have slide-out racks to make drive changes painlessly quick; you don't even need to open the case to swap out a drive.

And due to the design of SATA connectors, some racks even let you slide in and out bare SATA drives, so you don't have to fuss with screws or a slide-out drive holder. But these racks also tend to stack drives close together, which can cause overheating and increased vibration: two things that can negate the benefits of an array.

But for PCs that don't need to be pumping out data 24 hours a day, a slide-out rack can be a very convenient addition to a RAID system. At the end of the day, when you've shut down Windows and turned off your computer, slide out just one of your RAID drives and bring it home with you. Presto: an instant, up-to-date, offsite backup of every single byte of data. The next day, bring it back and slide it in its slot before powering your PC back on.

 If you boot up your PC before reinserting the take-home drive, Windows will load normally on the now compromised array. But doing so will instantly obsolete the missing drive, so that when you finally do plug it in, your RAID controller will insist on erasing it and populating it with data from the other active drives. The whole process should be seamless, but you'll experience decreased system performance and a lack of data redundancy until it's finished rebuilding your array. You can avoid this by diligently inserting your take-home drive *before* pressing your PC's power switch.

If you'll be regularly removing one of the drives in your array, consider employing at least three drives, so that you'll have data redundancy even without the take-home drive.

Given the ease at which drives can be removed from slide-out racks, it's a good idea to employ drive encryption to protect your data from spying eyes, as described in Chapter 8.

Recover Your System After a Crash

The purpose of backing up is to give you the opportunity to restore your system to its original state if something nasty should happen to your hard disk, whether it be theft, fire, malfunction, termites, tornado, the inevitable alien attack, or sabotage by your evil twin. But you'd be surprised at how many people back up their systems without having any idea how to restore it later should the need arise. The backup doesn't do you any good if you can't get at your files later, so it's important to take steps to make sure you can restore your system *from scratch* if necessary.

So, assume your hard disk is completely dead, totally empty, or missing, and you now need to restore your PC onto an empty volume. How you proceed depends on the type of backup you made.

 What if your hard disk isn't empty? Say Windows got hosed and won't start, or perhaps you just lost half your data files. Unless your backup is from this morning, you won't necessarily want to erase all your remaining files and replace them with whatever is in your backup archive. In this case, you can install a new, empty drive, restore your system image onto it, and then hook up your old drive and copy your recent data onto it. This has the advantage of allowing you to format or discard the damaged drive, something you couldn't do if you were still using it for your primary Windows partition.

Restoring from a system image

If the target drive is empty, you'll need your original Windows setup disc, system repair disc, or recovery partition (the latter two supplied by your PC manufacturer). Boot up off the disc (see Chapter 1 for tips), and on the Install Now page, click the **Repair your computer** link at the bottom. When prompted, select **Restore your computer using a system image...** and follow the prompts to complete restoration.

 Restoring from a system image will erase the target drive. If you need to restore individual files, see the previous section.

If the target drive has a nonfunctional Windows installation, press the **F8** key to get to the **Advanced Boot Options** menu, as shown in Figure 6-5, earlier in this chapter. Use the up and down arrow keys to highlight **Repair your computer** and then press **Enter**. When prompted, choose a keyboard layout and then type your username and password. On the System Recovery Options page (Figure 6-4), select **System Image Recovery** and then follow the prompts to restore your hard disk from the backup.

In the unlikely event you can boot into Windows, and you still prefer to erase your hard disk and restore a system image—perhaps to cleanse your drive of a vast malware infestation—open the Recovery page in Control Panel. Click the **Advanced Recovery Methods** link and on the next page, click **Use a system image you created earlier to recover your computer**.

Restoring from backed up files

If your only backup is one made with the *Back up your files* tool, you'll need to install a fresh copy of Windows 7 on the drive before you can do anything else. Once you boot into the new Windows installation, open the Backup and Restore page in Control Panel, connect your backup drive, and click the **Restore all users' files** link. (The more obvious **Restore my files** button offers less of a guarantee that you'll get everything you backed up.)

Troubleshooting

CHAPTER 7

Networking and Internet

Pop quiz: how do you compromise your PC's security, stability, and performance in about 10 seconds, without installing any new software? If you guessed "sledgehammer," you're wrong—that takes only two seconds.

Of course, the correct answer is "connect it to a network." You get bonus points if you added, "leave Windows 7's security settings intact."

It's fair to say that Windows 7 is more secure than any previous (network-capable) version of Windows, but unfortunately, that's not all that reassuring. Sure, the Windows Firewall isn't booby-trapped to prevent file sharing or time synchronization like it was in XP, but the defaults can still leave your PC vulnerable to anyone who knows where to look.

Use this chapter and Chapter 8 to connect your PC to a local network and the Internet without having to worry that Windows isn't doing its job of keeping your data safe. Certain aspects of networking, such as homegroups, file and printer sharing, and security, are covered exclusively in Chapter 8.

Build Your Network

Firewalls notwithstanding, your connection to the Internet is not much different than your connection to other PCs in your home or office. It's this fact that makes Windows all at once easy to network and frustrating to troubleshoot and secure.

Terminology Primer

To start building a network, you should understand a few basic networking concepts:

The distinction between local and remote resources

A *local resource* is an object—a folder on your hard disk or a printer physically connected to your PC—that's accessible without a network connection. A *remote resource* is one that resides on another computer to which yours is connected over a network. For example, a web page at *http://www.annoyances.org* is a remote file, but an HTML file on your own hard disk is a local file, even though they may appear indistinguishable in a browser. Microsoft tries to blur the line, a strategy that sometimes works and other times backfires: for instance, Windows applies different security restrictions and drag-drop rules to remote files than to local ones, and that subtlety can be a pain in the keester.

LAN versus WAN

LAN is shorthand for *Local Area Network*, a small assemblage of PCs in a home or small office connected with cables or wireless signals. Likewise, WAN stands for *Wide Area Network*, or a network formed by connecting computers over large distances (e.g., the Internet).

Ethernet

Ethernet is the wired technology upon which the vast majority of non-wireless local area networks is built. Any PC capable of handling Windows 7 is likely to have a built-in Ethernet adapter (also called a NIC, or Network Interface Card).

 A standard Ethernet connection is capable of moving data up to 10 megabits per second (Mbps; see "Bandwidth," later in this list), a Fast Ethernet connection (sometimes marked "10/100") can move data at 100 Mbps, and a Gigabit connection can move data at up to 1000 Mbps.

WiFi

WiFi is a trendy shorthand term for wireless networking based on the 802.11x standards. The early favorite was 802.11b, but with a leisurely maximum speed of only 11 Mbps, it was quickly obsoleted by 802.11g (54 Mbps). Further tweaking has given us multichannel 802.11g and 802.11n standards, both of which promise even faster speeds and greater range. Of course, all of these advertised specs assume laboratory-perfect conditions, so unless you're interested in building a vacuum chamber for your wireless equipment, you'll likely get about a third of the quoted speed of your equipment (and less, the poorer the reception gets).

A further caveat is that you need matched equipment to get the best performance: your laptop must have an 'n' radio to get the most out of an 'n' network. Luckily, each of these standards (with the exception of 802.11a) is backward-compatible with earlier incarnations, so an older 'g' laptop will still work on a newer 'n' network, albeit at the slower 'g' speed. Of course, with typical DSL and cable Internet speeds at only 1–3 Mbps, a faster WiFi signal will do nothing to get you your email any faster.

Bluetooth

Bluetooth is a wireless networking "standard" (the term must be used loosely here). Bluetooth will never supplant WiFi, nor is it meant to. Rather, it's an inexpensive, low-power technology and is commonly used in high-end cell phones, handheld PDAs, and some laptops. Most people get their first taste of Bluetooth with wireless cell phone headsets or cordless mice and keyboards, but it does much more than that (at least in theory). See "Get Bluetooth to Work" on page 465, if you feel like wasting an afternoon installing and reinstalling Bluetooth drivers.

Bandwidth

Bandwidth is the capacity of a network connection to move information (the size of the tube, so to speak). Bandwidth is measured in Kbps (kilobits per second) for slow connections, Mbps (megabits per second) for faster connections such as DSL, cable, or Ethernet LAN connections, and Gbps (gigabits per second) for the kinds of connections used by huge corporations and Internet providers.

Bandwidth is a shared resource. If a network connection is capable of transferring data at, say, 1.5 Mbps, and two users simultaneously download large files, each will only have roughly 0.75 Mbps (or 768 Kbps) of bandwidth at their disposal.

Ethernet-based local networks can transfer data at up to 1,000 Mbps. High-speed broadband (DSL and cable modem) connections typically transfer data up to 1.0 to 8.0 Mbps, while the fastest analog modems (remember those?) communicate at a glacial 56 Kbps, or 0.056 Mbps. Wireless 3G connections, due to varying reception, also offer varying performance as high as 1 Mbps (if you're lucky) to about 100 Kbps (if you're in a tunnel).

To translate a bandwidth measurement into more practical terms, you'll need to convert bits to bytes. There are 8 bits to a byte, so you can determine the theoretical maximum data transfer rate of a connection by simply dividing by 8. For example, a 384 Kbps connection transfers 384/8 = 48 kilobytes of data per second, which should allow you to transfer a 1 megabyte file in a little more than 20 seconds. However, there is more going on than just data transfer—such as error correction and bags of inefficiency—so actual performance will always be slower than the theoretical maximum.

TCP/IP

TCP/IP is a protocol (language), or more accurately, a collection of protocols, used in all Internet communications and by most modern LANs. For those of you excited by acronyms, the TCP/IP specification includes TCP (Transmission Control Protocol), IP (Internet Protocol), UDP (User Datagram Protocol), and ICMP (Internet Control Message Protocol).

The amazing thing about TCP/IP, and the reason that it serves as the foundation of every connection to the Internet, is that data is broken up into *packets* before it's sent on its way. The packets then travel to their destinations independently, possibly arriving in a different order than they were originally sent. The receiving computer then reassembles the packets (in the correct order) back into data.

Among the aforementioned protocols, IP (or rather, IPv4) is expected to be obsolete sometime in 2011, due to *IPv4 address exhaustion*. Not unlike the need to abandon 32-bit Windows in favor of the 64-bit edition to support 4+ GB of RAM, IPv4 is in the process of being replaced by IPv6 to accommodate the need for more IP addresses around the globe. Whereas IPv4—a 32-bit standard—offers a maximum of 4.3 billion addresses (covered next), IPv6—a 128-bit standard—gives us all a little more room with 3.4×10^{38} unique addresses.

IP addresses

An *IPv4* IP address is a set of four numbers (e.g., `207.238.132.130`) that corresponds to a single computer or device on a TCP/IP-based network. Each element of the address can range from 0 to 255, providing 256^4 or nearly 4.3 billion possible combinations. The newer standard, IPv6, with 128-bit addressing, employs addresses four times as long.

On the Internet, dedicated machines called *domain name servers* are used to translate named hosts, such as *http://www.annoyances.org*, to their respective numerical IP addresses and back again.

No two computers on a single network can have the same IP address, but a single computer can have multiple IP addresses. A router, discussed later in this chapter, uses Network Address Translation (NAT) to allow multiple PCs to share a single Internet connection, and thus a single IP address.

To connect two different networks to each other, while still maintaining two separate sets of IP addresses, you'll need either a *bridge* or a *router*. Provided that you install two network adapters in your PC, Windows can act as an impromptu bridge; just highlight two connections in your Network Connections window (discussed later in this chapter), right-click, and select **Bridge Connections**. A router, of course, is a better choice because it works even if your PC is off, and includes firewall protection to boot.

TCP Ports

TCP/IP data moves in and out of your PC through *ports*, virtual doors opened by the software that uses your network connection. For example, your email program uses port 25 to send email (using the SMTP protocol) and port 110 to retrieve email (using the POP3 protocol), while your web browser downloads pages through port 80 (using the HTTP protocol). Other commonly used ports are listed in Appendix B.

 Windows and some applications typically leave more ports open than you probably need, potentially making your PC vulnerable to spyware, pop ups, viruses, intruders, and other annoyances. See "Secure Your Networked PC" on page 498 for the solution.

Firewalls, and why you need one

A firewall can be used to restrict unauthorized access to your system by intruders, close backdoors opened by viruses and other malicious applications, and eliminate wasted bandwidth by blocking certain types of network traffic.

A firewall is a layer of protection that permits or denies network communication based on a predefined set of rules. These rules are typically based on the TCP port through which the data is sent, the IP address from which the data originated, and the IP address to which the data is destined.

The problem is that an improperly configured firewall can cause more problems than it ends up preventing. Windows includes a rudimentary

Networking and Internet

firewall feature, described later in this chapter, but software-based firewalls simply don't work as well as hardware firewalls like those found in routers.

Switches, access points, and routers

A *switch* allows you to connect more than two computers together—using cables—to form a local network (see Figure 7-1). (Note that a *hub* does pretty much the same thing as a switch, but much less efficiently.) Without a hub or switch, the best you could do is connect two computers to each other with a *crossover* cable (discussed later in this chapter).

A wireless access point is essentially a switch (or a hub) for a wireless network, allowing you to connect multiple computers wirelessly. Without an access point, you could only connect two computers wirelessly in "ad hoc" mode (more on that later, too).

Finally, a *router* is a device that connects two networks, and *routes* traffic between them. For example, a router can connect a peer-to-peer workgroup to the Internet, allowing you to share a single Internet connection with all the computers in your office (see "Share an Internet Connection" on page 478 for details). Most routers also double as switches, just as *wireless routers* double as wireless access points. Plus, any modern router (wireless or otherwise) will have a built-in firewall (typically superior to a software firewall that runs on your computer), so you can basically get everything you need in one inexpensive package.

The good news is that Windows 7 comes with everything you need to take advantage of all of these standards, and use them to access the Internet or share files and devices with other PCs on your network. The bad news is that it's almost never as easy to get it working properly as the industry would lead you to believe.

To Wire or Not to Wire

Wiring is a pain, but it works. Wireless is convenient, but flaky. Luckily, you don't have to just stick with one system, nor have it all planned out ahead of time.

For best results, wire your non-portable desktop system to your router/switch/hub when it's nearby. Cables aren't affected by poor reception, security codes, or interference, and they provide full speed all the time.

Plug one end of an Ethernet cable into your router or DSL/cable modem, and the other end into your PC, and you're done; Windows will set up the connection and get you on the 'Net in less than two seconds, no questions asked.

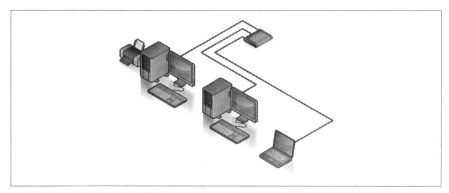

Figure 7-1. An example of a wired peer-to-peer network (LAN) comprised of three computers connected with a switch; the printer is connected to one of the PCs, which shares it with the others

And unless a small rodent chews its way through said cable, it'll keep working until you unplug it.

 If you see a prompt that entices you to **Connect to a net-work**, resist the urge if you're using cables; even though it doesn't explicitly say it, the window that appears when you click this link is only for connecting to wireless networks.

Wiring can vary in complexity and cost, depending on your needs, budget, and office layout. (See the upcoming sidebar "Cabling Tips" on page 434 for additional help.) For example, if you have two or more desktop computers in the same room, wiring is a simple matter of adding a switch and one category-5 *patch* cable for each machine, as shown in Figure 7-1. More PCs require a switch with more ports, or possibly multiple switches connected together, and of course, more cables.

If you only have two computers, you can eliminate the switch and simply connect them with an inexpensive category-5 *crossover* cable, as shown in Figure 7-2. Total cost: $3.99.

Most of the time, it doesn't make sense to use cables to connect a laptop to your network unless its wireless doesn't work. (Of course, if you're using a docking station, plugging in is more practical, but that's up to you.) Wireless, of course, is slicker than using cables, and works anywhere within range of the router; no drilling holes in walls so you can feed cables to all parts of your home or office. Figure 7-3 shows a typical wireless network with four computers (three PCs and one PDA).

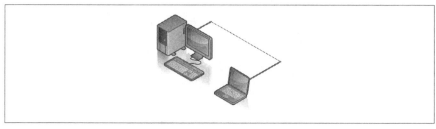

Figure 7-2. A quick and dirty switchless workgroup; given its limitations, however, it's best suited as a very temporary solution

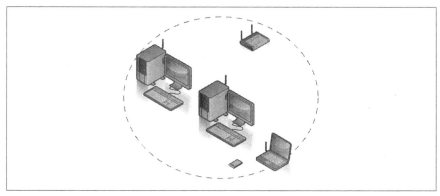

Figure 7-3. A wireless router acts as both a wireless access point and a switch, allowing you to connect any number of computers—and even WiFi-enabled PDAs—to form a wireless LAN (WiFi antennas are shown exaggerated for cuteness)

Cabling Tips

Within a second or two of connecting both ends of a network cable, the corresponding lights on your hardware should light up. Lights should be visible right on the network adapter, whether it's in the back of your desktop computer or in the side of your laptop. (Note that some devices use multicolor LEDs that appear green if the connection is correct and red if it's wrong.) Quickly flashing lights usually indicate data being transferred; slowly blinking lights often indicates a problem somewhere.

Connect all your cables while your switch and any other equipment are turned on and while Windows is running. That way, you'll see the corresponding lights go on, indicating that the switch, router, or NIC has detected the new connection. Note that the lights only confirm that the cabling is correct; they won't tell you whether your drivers and software are correctly set up.

Use only category-5 (cat-5) *patch* cables, except for a few very specific situations that require cat-5 *crossover* cables. Use a crossover cable to connect two computers directly (without a hub, switch, or router) or to connect two switches. In some cases where a DSL/cable modem connects directly to a computer with a patch cable, a crossover cable may be required to connect either of these devices to a hub or switch (naturally, consult the documentation to be sure). Either way, if the lights go on, you're using the right kind of cable.

(It's worth mentioning that a lot of new hardware—switches, routers, etc.—can auto-detect the type of cable you're using and work accordingly.)

When measuring for cables, always add several extra feet to each cable; too long is better than too short. Also, bad cables are not uncommon, so have a few extras around in case any of those lights don't light up.

Wireless needs more setup than cables and tends to be less reliable. Windows needs at least 5–10 seconds to connect to a previously configured wireless network (more for the first time), and may drop your connection if you switch rooms, receive a phone call, or sneeze.

Speed may or may not be a factor in your decision. WiFi is not nearly as fast as wired Ethernet; common 802.11g wireless connections (rated at 54 Mbps) transfer data at about 20–30 Mbps, and this speed drops rapidly as reception worsens. The fastest gigabit Ethernet connections move data at 600–700 Mbps, reception notwithstanding. Of course, the speed discrepancy is moot if you're only doing Internet (typical broadband is only about 1–6 Mbps), but if you need to transfer files between PCs in your workgroup, wired Ethernet will do it in a fraction of the time. (Wireless connections can also add latency—delays before data begins to flow—although this is typically not noticeable on small, home networks.)

So, what if you want the convenience of wireless, but the speed and reliability of cables? The short answer is to wait about five years for the technology to improve, and then pick up the latest Annoyances book to learn why you'll need to wait another five years. The even shorter answer is to simply connect your WiFi-equipped laptop to your network with a cable when your wireless gets cranky or you need to transfer a lot of files. Luckily, a properly configured network should have no trouble handling both wired and wireless PCs. Figure 7-4 shows a common peer-to-peer network setup with two wired desktop computers and a wireless connection to a laptop.

There's one crucial aspect of wireless networking that simply doesn't exist on a wired network: intruders. By default, most wireless routers have no security features enabled, meaning that any WiFi-enabled computer within range can

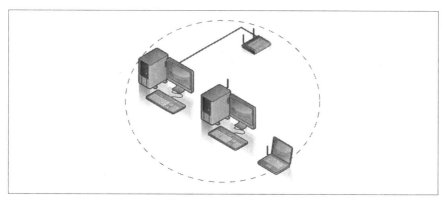

Figure 7-4. You can mix and match wired and wireless devices with a wireless router; these three computers are on the same network, despite the different means of connection

connect to your workgroup and use your Internet connection. See "Set Up a Wireless Router", next, and "Sniff Out WiFi Hotspots" on page 446, for help securing your wireless network and connecting to someone else's unsecured wireless network, respectively.

Set Up a Wireless Router

If you've read other solutions in this chapter, you've probably seen routers mentioned several times (if not, drop back to the section "Terminology Primer" on page 428 to read up).

A router allows you to connect your computer (or your workgroup) to the Internet, while simultaneously protecting you with its built-in firewall. A *wireless* router does the same thing, but also adds a wireless *access point*, which allows you to connect WiFi-equipped devices to each other and to the Internet.

A typical WiFi setup was shown in Figure 7-3 (see, no wires), but you'll probably want something closer to the setup shown later in Figure 7-20, in which a wireless router provides Internet access to all your computers. Here's how to set this up and configure the security measures that *should've* been enabled out of the box:

1. Plug your DSL or cable modem (or whatever broadband connection you're using) into your router's WAN or Internet port.

2. Use an Ethernet cable to connect at least one PC to one of the numbered ports on your router, even if you eventually want to use that PC wirelessly.

3. Dispense with the software that comes with your router; it usually just makes things worse. Instead, open a web browser on the wired PC and type the IP address of your router into the address bar. In most cases, this

is `192.168.1.1`, but your router may be different; refer to your router's documentation for details. (You may also need to log in with a username and password at this point, also listed in said documentation, at least in theory.) If you can't connect to your router, and you're sure your PC's network card is working, see "Can't Connect to Your Router?".

Can't Connect to Your Router?

If you can't load your router's setup page, and you're certain you're using the correct IP address, the most likely cause is that your PC and your router are not on the same *subnet*. The subnet is the range of addresses governed by the first three components of the IP address, and Windows likes the default `192.168.1.x` subnet.

This means that the first three groups of numbers (called *octets*) of your computer's IP address needs to match the first three numbers of your router's IP address, while the fourth number must be different. For instance, if your router's address is `192.168.0.1`, then you might not be able to connect to it until you either change your PC's address to `192.168.0.x` (where *x* is any number larger than zero) *or* change your router's address to `192.168.1.1` to connect to the router.

Now, in theory, Windows should do all of this for you when you use the **Obtain an IP address automatically** option described later in this chapter, but this is notorious for not working when the subnets don't match. If you suspect this is the problem, try setting a static IP address on your PC, at least temporarily, until you can connect to your router and reconfigure it to use the `192.168.1.x` subnet.

---

4. Once you get your connection to your router working, you'll see your router's setup page, which should look vaguely like the one in Figure 7-5. Of course, your router's setup page will almost certainly look different, but most of the same settings will still be there.

5. Choose your connection type from the list. If your Internet connection requires a username and password, select **PPPoE**. If your ISP has bespoken a unique IP address for your connection, select **Static IP**. Otherwise, choose **Automatic Configuration - DHCP**.

6. If you've selected **PPPoE** or **Static IP** in the previous step, you'll probably need to enter the IP addresses of your ISP's DNS servers (your ISP should provide these numbers for you).

7. Click **Apply** or **Save Settings** at the bottom of the page when you're done.

Figure 7-5. Most routers use a web-based setup, meaning that you can configure your router from any computer, running on any platform, as long as it has a web browser

8. At this point, you should have Internet access; go ahead and test it by opening a second browser window (**Ctrl-N**) and visiting any website.

9. Once you have Internet, take this opportunity to update the firmware of your router, as described in "Upgrade Your Router" on page 443.

10. Next, go to your router's *wireless* setup page, like the one shown in Figure 7-6—you can get there with either a link in the main menu or a tab across the top of the page—and choose a new name (SSID) for your wireless network. (Note that the SSID should not be confused with the Windows network name used in Chapter 8.)

    The only way Windows distinguishes one configured network from another is the SSID, so choose a *unique* name for your network. If you were to use a generic name like "wireless" or leave the default name (e.g., "linksys") intact, you might have problems later on. For instance, if a neighbor has a WiFi network with the same name, you might have trouble connecting to your own network. Or, if your home network has the same name as the one at work, yet both have different encryption settings (set later in this section), Windows may not recognize both networks as unique without a lot of hassle.

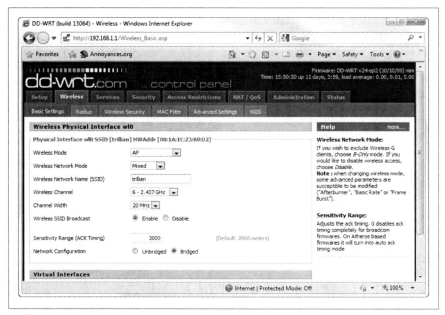

Figure 7-6. Use your router's wireless setup page to configure the security settings for your wireless network

When choosing an SSID, you should also avoid names that give away your location, such as your street address, your last name, or the name of your business. An intruder—or WiFi leech, for that matter—might exploit that extra information to break into your network.

11. Next, check to see whether the **Wireless SSID Broadcast** option is turned on or off, and make sure it's set the way you want it.

 Opinions differ on whether turning off SSID broadcast is a good or bad idea. Your SSID is a backdoor to your wireless network; if you broadcast your SSID, you expose one more piece of information someone could use to connect to your network. If it's hidden (and you've chosen a unique name), you make it that much harder for someone to break in. On the other hand, a hidden SSID doesn't necessarily guarantee an invisible network; in fact, certain settings in Windows can be exploited to expose your hidden SSID, as described in "Sniff Out WiFi Hotspots" on page 446. So, don't rely solely on a hidden SSID to protect your wireless network.

12. When you're done here, click **Apply Settings** or **Save**.

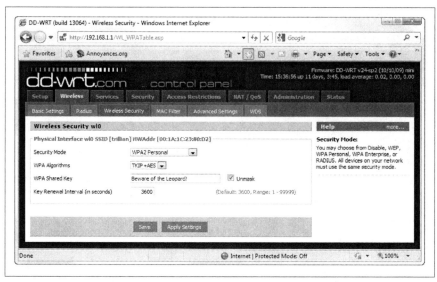

Figure 7-7. Configure your wireless router's encryption settings to prevent intruders from connecting to your wireless network

13. Next, you'll want to set up your router's encryption feature for the best wireless security. You can typically get to this setting by clicking a button on the wireless page named **Encryption, WEP**, or—in the case of the example in Figure 7-6—a separate tab named **Wireless Security**. Figure 7-7 shows a typical wireless encryption setup page.

Now, Windows understands several different types of wireless encryption, all used to prevent intruders from connecting to or spying on your wireless network unless they have your secret encryption key. Of course, some are better than others; see the upcoming sidebar "Choosing the Right Encryption Scheme: WEP, WPA, or WPA2?" for details.

Choosing the Right Encryption Scheme: WEP, WPA, or WPA2?

Encrypting your wireless network accomplishes two things: it helps keep out leeches who would otherwise use your WiFi for free Internet, and it helps prevent intruders from breaking into your system to snoop around your PCs.

Of course, most wireless routers have encryption turned off by default, so any choice you make is better than none at all. The three prevailing standards for wireless encryption—all supported by Windows out of the box—are:

WEP

   Wired Equivalent Privacy (or Wireless Encryption Protocol) is the original protection scheme included with early wireless routers, and it is also

---

the weakest. With the right software, an intruder can easily break into a WEP-protected network in a few minutes using the *Related-key attack*. Use WEP only if you have older PCs or devices that don't support *WPA*, described next.

WPA

WiFi Protected Access was established as a stopgap measure to remedy the vulnerabilities in WEP. If you have any Windows XP machines on your network, they'll need Service Pack 2 to connect to a WPA-encrypted network.

WPA2 or PSK (use this one!)

Also known as 802.11i or PSK for *Pre-Shared Key*, WPA2 is the completed form of WPA, and is considered the strongest nonproprietary encryption scheme for 802.11x wireless networks. Any wireless products certified after March 2006 are supposed to fully support WPA2. WPA2 is supported under Windows XP if the WPA2/WPS IE update (available at *http://support.microsoft.com/kb/893357*) is installed. Macs will need AirPort 4.2 or later to use WPA. See "Upgrade Your Router" on page 443 if your router doesn't fully support WPA2.

Those using WPA or WPA2 will have a choice between the *Personal* and *Enterprise* varieties. As enticing as Enterprise may sound, it requires a RADIUS server typically used only in large companies, making Personal the proper choice for most home and small-business networks.

Next, your router may support the *AES* (*Advanced Encryption Standard*) or *TKIP* (*Temporal Key Integrity Protocol*) encryption algorithms, or both. Of the two, AES is stronger, but it is supported only by WPA2. If you experience connection problems with AES, wherein certain websites won't load, try switching to TKIP (or vice versa). If your router allows it, select both AES + TKIP to make troubleshooting easier, and then choose one algorithm or the other in Windows.

So, for best wireless security, choose WPA2-Personal with AES + TKIP.

14. Once you've enabled wireless encryption, you'll need to choose a *key* or *passphrase*.

With WPA or WPA2, you type a word or a phrase into your router's setup page, and then type the *same* word or phrase into Windows to connect, as described in "Sniff Out WiFi Hotspots" on page 446. (In Figure 7-7, I chose "Beware of the Leopard!" as my passphrase.) The stronger the passphrase you enter, the more secure your wireless network will be. A WPA passphrase can be 8–63 characters (bytes) long, but the 802.11i standard recommends a passphrase at least 20 characters long to deter practical attacks.

With WEP, your router may have you type a passphrase, but it's only used to generate a *key*. WEP keys are hexadecimal strings of numbers (0–9) and letters (A–F), and are either 10 or 26 digits long (for 64- or 128-bit security, respectively). You then type the hex key—not the passphrase—into Windows to connect.

 Before you save your changes here, make things easy on yourself and take this opportunity to record your passphrase or key. Highlight the key (if there's more than one, use the first key, **Key 1**) and press **Ctrl-C** to copy it to the clipboard. Then, open your favorite text editor (e.g., Notepad), and press **Ctrl-V** to paste it into a new, empty document. Save the file on your desktop (or a USB memory key to set up other PCs); this will allow you to easily paste it into various dialog boxes later on, which is easier than having to type it.

15. Click **Apply Settings** or **Save** at the bottom of the page when you're done.

16. Unplug the cable connecting your PC to your router, and then attempt a wireless connection, as described in the upcoming section, "Sniff Out WiFi Hotspots" on page 446. See the next sidebar, "Router Placement 101" for ways to improve reception, and thus the performance of your wireless network.

Router Placement 101

The tiny WiFi transceiver in your laptop should be capable of picking up any wireless network within about 100 feet, perhaps a little more if you have newer equipment. If indoors, this typically includes no more than about two or three walls, and perhaps one floor or ceiling. But the placement of your wireless router and the arrangement of natural obstacles near it will have a significant effect on the strength and range of your WiFi signal.

Assuming you're using a setup like the one pictured later in Figure 7-20, your router will need to be within spitting distance of your DSL or cable modem. But provided that the cable from your modem to your router is long enough, you should have a little leeway there.

Your router should be out in the open; don't put it under your desk, in a drawer, behind a metal file cabinet, or at the bottom of a jar of Indian Head pennies. If you're feeding more than one computer, it should be placed in a central location, if possible. Use the signal strength indicator (Figure 7-10) to test various configurations. Consider cabling stationary computers so that you can optimize the placement of the router for your portable ones.

The 802.11b, g, and n standards operate over the 2.4 Ghz band, which is also inhabited by cordless phones and microwave ovens. (802.11n routers also support the interference-free 5Ghz band, but unless you use exclusively 802.11n devices or you have a dual-band/dual-radio router, you'll still be operating at 2.4 Ghz.) This means that you'll get better results if you move the router away from any cordless-phone base stations, Bluetooth devices, televisions, radios, or TV dinners.

If, after adjusting the placement of your router, you still need more range than it seems to be able to provide, consider either a repeater (range extender) or an aftermarket antenna for your router. There are even a number of do-it-yourself antenna projects for both the router and client (e.g., laptop), including the creative use of a Pringles™ can.

Note that replacing the antenna alone will only make the signal more or less directional, and only affects the signal leaving the device to which it's connected.

 If you employ encryption using these settings, but you subsequently can't connect to it wirelessly, it most likely means that you've entered the encryption key incorrectly on your PC. To fix the problem, you'll have to reconnect your PC to your router with a cable and modify the settings as described here. If that doesn't help, make sure you've installed the latest firmware on your router (see "Upgrade Your Router" on page 443) and the latest wireless drivers on your PC. As a final resort, reset the router as described in your router's documentation, and start over.

While it's important to employ as many security features on your wireless network as you can, you shouldn't rely entirely on them to protect your sensitive data. When you're done here, make sure you set a password for your Windows user account, and keep a watchful eye on precisely what resources you're sharing, both as described in Chapter 8.

Upgrade Your Router

The software—a.k.a. firmware—in most routers is lousy, mostly because it doesn't need to be any better. But you may not realize how lousy yours is until you replace it.

Most manufacturers equip their routers, wireless and otherwise, with user-upgradable firmware. Just log into your router's configuration page via a web browser (covered in the previous section) and somewhere on the main page or status page, you'll see the current firmware version. Then head on over to the manufacturer's website to see if there's a newer version available for your model. (It would be a no-brainer to include an automatic firmware updating feature, but nobody seems compelled to add this convenience to their devices at the moment.) If there's an update, download the file to your desktop and, if necessary, unzip it. Through your router's interface, upload the file and wait a few minutes for your router to complete the update (a process called "flashing" the firmware).

Of course, since router manufacturers would rather you buy new equipment than get new features on your old equipment for free, firmware updates rarely do more than fix bugs and occasionally add support for newer encryption protocols like WPA2 (discussed earlier). If you're lucky, though, your router manufacturer's offering isn't your only choice.

DD-WRT is a free, open source, Linux-based alternative firmware upgrade that improves performance and reliability and adds features over the stock firmware shipped with routers from nearly 70 companies. The upgrading process takes no longer than it does to update the stock firmware to a newer version (roughly 5 minutes), but this is time much better spent.

 See the upcoming sidebar "Life with DD-WRT" for anecdotal experiences after upgrading a particular Linksys router. A less commercial—but also less-polished—alternative to DD-WRT is the OpenWRT project (*http://openwrt.org/*). OpenWRT is a modular system, and requires that you also install an interface package like X-Wrt (*http://x-wrt.org/*) if you want a graphical web interface like DD-WRT or your router's stock firmware.

Life with DD-WRT

I had a troublesome 2-year old Linksys WRT150N router that was just begging to be put out to pasture. Wireless transfer speeds were disappointing and wireless connections were unreliable. But worst of all, the router would crash during heavy activity, requiring a reboot at least 1–2 times a day. Some speculated that overheating was the cause, while others blamed flaky hardware.

After a quick and painless (not to mention free) DD-WRT upgrade, the problems stopped; no more crashes, no more flaky connections. Typical wireless transfers (reported by WinSCP) were a lethargic 600–700 KB per second before the upgrade, but nearly tripled to 1700-1800 KBps with DD-WRT. And not a single reboot was needed in six months.

The DD-WRT interface is better than the stock Linksys one as well, as shown in Figures 7-5, 7-6, and 7-7. A DHCP client list, showing connected devices and their automatically-assigned IP addresses, is shown on the main page instead of buried 4 levels deep. The controls to adjust the access restrictions, firewall, and port forwarding are easier to understand and use. There's now more control over the UPnP service, useful for any Macs and iPhones on the network and the PCs that connect to them. And the upgrade added some cool features, like the ability to set up a wireless hotspot in case I decided to open a café in my garage.

In short, the DD-WRT firmware turned a lousy router into a better product for free.

To get started, go to *http://www.dd-wrt.com/* and browse the **Router Database** for your router's model number. If your model appears in the list, click the link to view the available downloads for your router, and you'll see 5–10 different downloads. For first-time flashing, DD-WRT recommends using the **Mini** or **Mini Generic** flavor. You'll get a file with the *.bin* filename extension; just save the file to your desktop.

 While the upgrade is taking place, you won't have an Internet connection (unless you bypass the router). So make sure you have all the files, documentation, and stock firmware (just in case) before you begin. Furthermore, some routers require "activation," which is free for personal use, so, if needed, go ahead create an account at *http://www.dd-wrt.com/* and visit the **Activation Center** before you begin as well.

When you're ready, upload the DD-WRT *.bin* file as you would any standard firmware update; consult your router documentation or manufacturer website for specific instructions.

The first time you log into a newly-upgraded DD-WRT router, you'll be asked for a username and password: enter `root` and `admin`, respectively. (You can change the password later on the **Administration** tab.) Then set up your Internet connection, wireless SSID, and wireless security, as described in the previous section, "Set Up a Wireless Router" on page 436.

Figure 7-8. The "Connect to a network" window in Windows 7 lets you sniff out and connect to WiFi hotspots in range

Sniff Out WiFi Hotspots

The centerpiece of Windows' built-in wireless networking is the "Connect to a network" pop-up window shown in Figure 7-8, which basically serves as a WiFi *sniffer*. To see networks in range, click the tiny 5-bar signal strength meter in your notification area (taskbar tray), or open your Start menu and select **Connect To**. A little yellow star over the taskbar icon means you're not connected; one or more white bars indicates an active connection.

To display the "Connect to a network" window, open the Start menu and click **Connect To** (if it's there). Or, click the network icon to the right of the notification area (tray) and then click the **Connect to a network** link. Or, if you're in Control Panel, open the **Network and Sharing Center**, and click the **Connect to a network** link on the Tasks pane on the left side. (Note that this window is not needed at all if you're connecting your PC to a network with a cable.)

A WiFi sniffer is a program (or device) that scans for and lists the WiFi networks within range. This is where the SSID Broadcast setting in "Set Up a Wireless Router" on page 436, comes into play: as long as your router is broadcasting your SSID, any sniffer within range will see it.

Just highlight an entry in the list and click **Connect**. Now, if a network is identified as a **Security-enabled network**, you'll need its encryption passphrase or key to connect to it. Provided it's your own network, you can just paste the passphrase from step 14 of "Set Up a Wireless Router" on page 436; otherwise, you'll have to get it from the administrator of that particular hotspot.

 If you turn on the **Connect automatically** option when connecting to a network, Windows will save the SSID and passphrase so it can connect without your help next time it sees the hotspot in range. To see a list of saved networks, open the Manage Wireless Networks window, discussed in "Troubleshoot Wireless Networks" on page 451.

Things are a little different if you've disabled your router's SSID broadcast option. For one, your WiFi network will either show up as **Unnamed Network** in the sniffer window, or it won't show up at all. But more importantly, you may have to go a different route to connect to your hidden network (particularly if there's more than one "unnamed" network in range).

On the "Connect to a network" pop-up, click the **Open Network and Sharing Center** link on the bottom and then on the Network and Sharing Center page, click the **Set up a new connection or network** link. From the list, select **Manually connect to a wireless network** and click **Next** to open the page shown in Figure 7-9.

In the **Network name** field, type the SSID exactly as it appears in your router setup page, and then choose the **Security type** (e.g., WEP, WPA2) that matches the one used by your router.

Next comes the encryption key or passphrase. Now, despite the fact that it clearly says **Security Key** here, Windows 7 only expects a "key" if you're using the older WEP encryption; for WPA or WPA2, enter the passphrase from step 14 of "Set Up a Wireless Router" on page 436. (Capitalization, punctuation, and spacing all count.) Turn off the **Hide characters** option so you can see what you're doing, and then paste (**Ctrl-V**) the key.

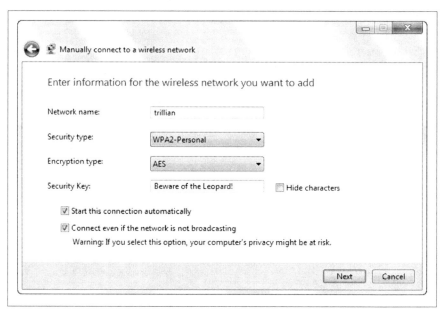

Figure 7-9. To connect to a wireless network that isn't broadcasting its SSID, go to this page to hand-enter the SSID and encryption passphrase

Below, turn on the **Start this connection automatically** option, and then pause while you try to figure out what Microsoft means when it warns you that "Your computer's privacy might be at risk" if you turn on the **Connect even if the network is not broadcasting** option.

Give up? It turns out that Microsoft's stated position—one not explained anywhere on this window, but rather only published online at *http://technet.mi crosoft.com/en-us/library/bb726942.aspx*—is that if you turn off your router's SSID broadcast feature, bad things can happen.

It works like this: when connecting to a normal, broadcasting network, Windows waits until it sees a network you've already set up before it attempts to connect. But when you turn *off* SSID broadcast to hide your wireless network, Windows *continually* sends out a signal with the hidden SSID until it finds your network. And as you may have guessed, some clown wrote a program that "listens" for a PC that's trying to connect to a hidden network and records any SSIDs it encounters.

Now, in order for someone to discover your network's hidden SSID, the hacker must be within range of your PC when it's on, and listening at the moment it attempts to connect to your wireless network. If you're already connected at home or if you're surfing the Web at the coffee shop down the street, Windows won't send out any signals. But more importantly, if someone discovers your

SSID, she still won't be able to connect to your network as long as you've enabled encryption. As it is, a hidden SSID won't adequately protect your network if it's the sole security measure, and that's what Microsoft means by its vague warning.

 The aforementioned **Connect even if the network is not broadcasting** option was first introduced in Windows Vista. If you have any older PCs on your network running, say, Windows XP, there is no such option unless you install the Wireless Client Update at *http://support.microsoft.com/?kbid =917021.*

So, to connect to your home network with a hidden SSID, you have four choices:

Take Microsoft's advice and configure your wireless router to broadcast its SSID
Instead, rely on encryption, explained in the section "Set Up a Wireless Router" on page 436, and authentication, described in Chapter 8, to protect your privacy. Then, connect to your network as described earlier in this section.

Turn off your router's SSID Broadcast setting...
...and enable the **Connect even if the network is not broadcasting** option. This way, your PC will automatically connect to your hidden network whenever it's in range, but you'll run the risk of exposing your "secret" SSID. If you do this, make sure you encrypt your network and that you employ authentication (Chapter 8) in full force.

Turn off your router's SSID Broadcast setting...
...but don't use the **Connect even if the network is not broadcasting** option. But beware: it's a trap!

Here's the problem: since your network is not broadcasting, Windows won't ever connect to it automatically. So, you need to connect by hand, but how?

When you click **Next** on this page, Windows saves the network you've just set up in the Manage Wireless Networks window (discussed in the next section), but there's no **Connect** button there. Don't try using the "Manually connect to a wireless network" window either, as it'll just ask you to set up another new network. And since your network isn't broadcasting, it won't show up in the "Connect to a network" window, at least not yet.

The solution is to wait. *Eventually*, the "Connect to a network" window will list your hidden network, assuming it's in range. (It knows when it's in range, by the way, because it continually polls the airwaves for the network, using the process described earlier in this section that supposedly compromises your privacy.) If you don't see your new network entry after a few minutes, close all open network windows and then reopen the "Connect to a network" window; if that doesn't help, restart Windows and try again.

If your hidden network entry never shows up, you'll need to either turn on the **SSID Broadcast** option in your router, taking Microsoft's advice, or use the **Connect even if the network is not broadcasting** option, while leaving your SSID hidden.

Abandon wireless altogether and use a cable

Yes, cables are a pain, but intruders won't be able to break into your wireless-less network without cables of their own. And that's about as secure as it gets.

Back on Earth, or more specifically, the "Manually connect to a wireless network" window, click **Next** when you're done toiling with these settings. If you see a message at this point that reads, "A network called *xxx* already exists," see "Troubleshoot Network Connections" on page 469. Otherwise, Windows should tell you that it has "successfully added" your network.

If you used the **Start this connection automatically** option on the last page, Windows should be connecting as you read these words, and you can just click **Close** here. Otherwise, click **Connect to** to return to the "Connect to a network" window, select your new network, and click **Connect**. Of course, if it's a hidden network as described earlier, it won't show up there, so you'll have to click **Change connection settings** and then turn on the **Connect even if the network is not broadcasting** option in order to connect.

If Windows won't connect, see the section "Troubleshoot Wireless Networks" on page 451. See the upcoming sidebar "Quick and Dirty WiFi Piggyback" for another way to connect to a wireless network.

Quick and Dirty WiFi Piggyback

Say you and a partner are staying in a hotel, and each of you has a laptop. The hotel, of course, charges for wireless, and you don't feel like ponying up the extra dough for two connections, nor do you feel like taking turns.

Or, perhaps a friend visits your home or office and wants to check her email with her laptop. What if you don't want to share your wireless encryption passphrase with any passerby who asks for it? Or, what if the laptop doesn't have wireless?

Assume you have a sample wireless network like the one illustrated in Figures 7-3 or 7-4. You can, of course, plug any PC (provided that it has an Ethernet port) directly into your wireless router with an ordinary category-5 patch cable, and give it instant access to the Internet. But what if the router isn't in a convenient location?

Fortunately, any Windows PC can act as a gateway, funneling Internet access to any computer to which it is physically connected, using Windows' built-in Internet Connection Sharing feature (discussed later in this chapter). All you need to do is connect this new laptop directly to your own desktop or laptop PC, and this typically requires only a single cable.

If the visitor's laptop has an Ethernet port, and the connected PC has an unused Ethernet port (likely if it's on a *wireless* network), just connect the two computers with a category-5 *crossover* cable, and you've got yourself something like the wired network shown later in Figure 7-19. Just activate Internet Connection Sharing on your PC, and the guest PC will have Internet access.

You wouldn't want to use this as a long-term solution, but it works well enough for a quick email download, takes only a few minutes and a $4 cable, and doesn't compromise your network's security (much).

Troubleshoot Wireless Networks

WiFi tends to be temperamental, not to mention annoying and tear-your-hair-out frustrating. So, what do you do when you can't connect to a wireless network you've just set up?

Your instinct might be to attempt to connect again through the "Connect to a network" window. Or, if you're connecting to a network with a hidden SSID (described in the previous section), you may click the **Set up a connection or network** link to attempt to enter all the information about your network *again*. Of course, Windows will either let you complete setting up this network only to have it not work, or complain that a network by that name already exists. Arrgghhh.

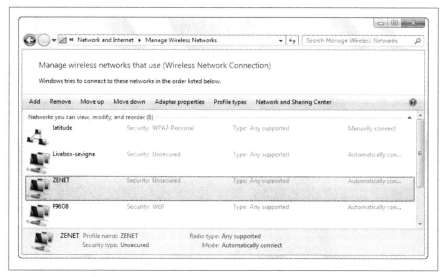

Figure 7-10. Use the Manage Wireless Networks window to fix broken wireless connections or delete wireless networks you no longer use

Instead, you should go directly to the little-known Manage Wireless Networks window (Figure 7-10) via a tiny link by the same name on the left of the Network and Sharing Center window.

Here, you'll see all the wireless networks you've ever saved or set up manually, whether they're in range or not. Double-click a network in the list to show the Wireless Network Properties window (Figure 7-11). All the options here are described in "Sniff Out WiFi Hotspots" on page 446.

Here's how to solve some of the more common wireless connection problems:

Windows cannot connect to xxx.

This can be caused by a variety of problems, but Windows won't tell you which one. The most likely cause, at least when you're connecting to an encrypted network, is that you entered the wrong encryption passphrase/ key. If the network is hidden, you may have typed the wrong SSID (or if there's more than one hidden network in range, you may have selected the wrong one).

If you ask Windows to diagnose the problem, it'll probably suggest a weak signal, but that's unlikely if the network is showing up in your list with at least two signal strength bars. More likely, it's not a real network (perhaps someone else's laptop errantly set to accept incoming connections), or it's using MAC address filtering, as described in "Lock Out Unauthorized PCs" on page 457.

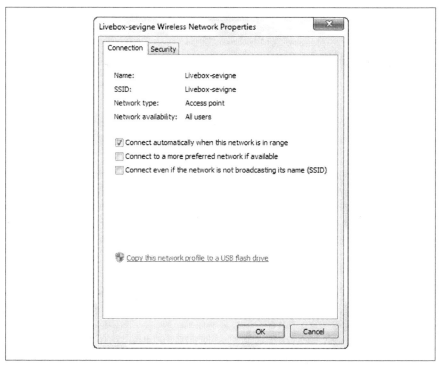

Figure 7-11. Open the Properties window for a wireless network you've saved to change the connection options or modify the encryption passphrase/key

Non-broadcasting network won't show up.

If you see an entry named **Unnamed Network**, don't try to connect to it if you've previously set up the hidden network manually, as described in "Sniff Out WiFi Hotspots" on page 446. You either set it up incorrectly or that's someone else's hidden network; either way, trying to connect to this **Unnamed Network** won't help. Use the Manage Wireless Networks window, described earlier in this section, to remove the network and then try adding it manually again.

Broadcasting (non-hidden) network won't show up.

This may be caused by mixing old and new wireless equipment. For instance, most 802.11n routers have a setting that controls whether earlier, slower equipment (g- and b-class routers) can connect. If you change the setting so that only n-class devices can connect, then no laptop with an older g- or b-class radio will be able to join the network wirelessly.

If you have an 802.11n router, you might choose to permit only n-class devices so that the router can operate exclusively on the 5 Ghz band. Unless you have a dual-band/dual-radio router, connecting older 802.11g devices will force it to drop to the more crowded 2.4 Ghz band, making it more susceptible to interference.

Also, make sure both your router and your other equipment are communicating on the same channel (channel 6, 2.437 Ghz, is the typical default).

Windows tries to connect to the neighbor's network first.

Open the Manage Wireless Networks window and delete the entry for your neighbor's network if it's there. Next, double-click the entry for your own network to show the Properties window, turn on the **Connect automatically when this network is in range** option and turn *off* the **Connect to a more preferred network if available** option (unless it's grayed out). Click OK, and then drag your network to the top of the list (or use the **Move up** button just above the list).

At this point, if your network isn't showing up in the list of hotspots in range, then you haven't set it up yet. Close the Manage Wireless Networks window, and then follow the instructions in "Sniff Out WiFi Hotspots" on page 446 to connect to it, and be sure to use the **Save this network** option when you're done.

After disconnecting, Windows immediately tries to reconnect.

Just click **Disconnect** again; Windows rarely does this more than two or three times. If the problem persists, open the Manage Wireless Networks window and delete the entry for this network.

A network called xxx already exists.

You'll see this error if you try to set up a new wireless network with the same SSID as one already saved on your PC. If they're one and the same hotspot, open the Manage Wireless Networks window and double-click the network to modify that entry's settings. However, if you're trying to set up two different hotspots that just happen to have the same SSID and different encryption, see the next section.

Handle two networks with the same SSID.

Windows distinguishes one network from another by its SSID; in other words, its name. Say you've named your home network *wirelessnetwork*, and it works. (Yay!) Then, you take your PC to work and learn that your employer's SSID is also *wirelessnetwork*. When Windows sees *wirelessnetwork*, it tries to connect with the encryption passphrase it already knows, and not surprisingly, fails.

The best solution to this problem is to rename your home network to something more unique, but this won't help if both networks are administrated by other people. In this case, you have to make some changes. First, open the Manage Wireless Networks window, right-click the network you have saved, and click **Rename**; this changes the superficial title of the network entry while leaving the SSID intact. Next, double-click the saved network, turn off the **Connect automatically when this network is in range** option, and click OK. With that out of the way, you should be able to connect to the new network by the same name *and* save its encryption settings for next time.

 If you frequently connect to different wireless networks, use the Network and Sharing Center (shown in Figure 7-12 and discussed in Chapter 8) to quickly switch between *Public* and *Home* modes.

Windows loses its wireless connection when the phone rings.

If you have a cordless telephone on your land line, it's likely the older 2.4 Ghz variety. 802.11b/g/n wireless networks operate on the same frequency, so move the cordless base station away from the router. For best results, replace your old phone with a new WiFi-friendly 5.8 Ghz model; or, if it's your neighbor's phone that causing the interference, consider splurging on an early Arbor Day gift.

Alternatively, you can switch your router and all your wireless equipment to the newer 802.11n standard, which operates in the 5 Ghz band. If you still have g-class wireless devices (like iPhones and PDAs), make sure you use a dual-band/dual-radio router so connecting a single 802.11g device doesn't force the entire network onto the 2.5 Ghz band.

Windows connects to WiFi, but the Internet doesn't work.

If you seem to be getting a solid wireless connection, but you can't load any web pages or check your email, open the Network and Sharing Center, shown in Figure 7-12. Now, this window is mostly a "home base" of sorts that provides links to the other networking tools discussed in this chapter and the sharing tools discussed in Chapter 8, but the **View your active networks** section right in the middle of the window is a quick way to diagnose this particular problem.

If there's no active network connection—no LAN and no Internet—it'll simply say **You are currently not connected to any networks** here. If you're using a wired connection, the cable could be disconnected, your router or switch could be turned off, or your network adapter could be disabled or malfunctioning. If you're using a wireless connection, you'll need to connect to a hotspot, as described earlier in this chapter.

If there's any active network connection at all, this block will be divided in two. On the left, you'll see how Windows categorizes this network (**Home network**, **Work network**, or **Public network**), which influences only file and printer sharing (see Chapter 8). On the right, you'll see which physical network adapter is in use, and the **Access type** field will indicate the status of the connection. **Access type** should be **Internet**; if this is the case and you still can't surf, try restarting your PC and temporarily disabling any firewall software that may be interfering.

 If you're on a public network (e.g., coffee shop, hotel, airport), you might need to sign in or pay a subscription fee for full Internet services, a fact that might be clear from the first page your browser loads or perhaps suggested by the SSID.

If **Access type** says **No Internet**, then it could be an issue with your router or broadband modem; try rebooting both devices and trying again. If you connect with PPPoE (discussed later in this chapter) then there might be a problem with your login credentials. If this is a new wireless network, make sure you're connecting to a true access point (router) and not someone else's dormant ad-hoc (PC-to-PC) network. If all else fails, you may need to mess around with your PC's TCP/IP settings as described in "Troubleshoot Network Connections" on page 469.

Everything works until you enable encryption.

Make sure your router has the latest router firmware; see "Upgrade Your Router" on page 443 for details, plus an alternative that may fix the problem.

If that doesn't help, it's likely that either your router or your wireless adapter in your PC is not fully 802.11i-compliant. This means you'll have to either downgrade your encryption to one of the weaker standards explained in the "Choosing the Right Encryption Scheme: WEP, WPA, or WPA2?" on page 440 sidebar, earlier in this chapter, or upgrade your router.

Beyond SSIDs and encryption, a wireless connection is not much different than a wired connection. See "Troubleshoot Network Connections" on page 469 for help fine-tuning TCP/IP addresses, a particularly useful tool when you have a mix of different computers and devices on your network.

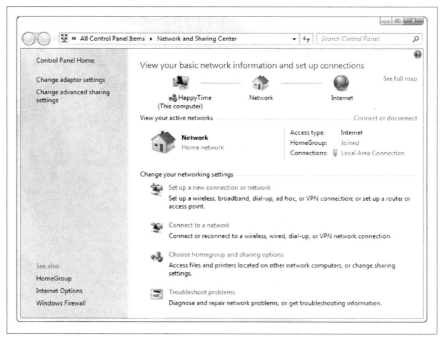

Figure 7-12. The Network and Sharing Center shows the status of your LAN connection, your Internet connection, and your sharing options, and provides links to most of Windows' networking tools

Lock Out Unauthorized PCs

You've got encryption. You've got a hidden SSID. You've set up passwords and restrictive permissions on all your shared folders (see Chapter 8). You're probably thinking that your biggest problem is that nobody seems capable of remembering any of their passwords, but it may be quite the opposite.

All of these security schemes rely on *preshared* information: anyone with your WPA2 passphrase, your SSID, and your Windows password can connect to your wireless network and possibly even read the files on your hard disk. The system is built upon secrecy, and all it takes is a breach of that secrecy for the whole system to break down.

For example, say you've got a small business with 20 employees, and someone gets fired. Or, perhaps you live in an apartment building with shared wireless, and someone moves out. Either way, the person who has left the system may still have the wireless passphrase (and, in the case of the small business, a common Windows password), and may still be able to get into your network.

What do you do? For one, you can change the password and then update the remaining PCs and have everyone try to remember the new password. But the ex-employee, ex-tenant, or ex-boyfriend might get the new password from a friend or during a subsequent visit, and then you're back where you started. In short, a network that relies *only* on passwords to keep out intruders is still vulnerable.

One solution for home networks and small businesses—any outfit without the means to install an authentication server typically available only to large companies—is to use *MAC address filtering.*

A MAC (Media Access Control) address is a (more or less) unique ID for each network adapter on your PC, or—from the point of view of your router—a unique ID for each connection on your network. You can configure your router to allow only specific MAC addresses to connect to your network, and in so doing, turn away anyone else whether he or she knows your WPA2 passphrase or not.

A typical Wireless MAC Filter page is shown in Figure 7-13. (If your router doesn't have this feature, see "Upgrade Your Router" on page 443.) Here, turn on the **Permit only PCs listed to access the wireless network** option, and then type or paste the MAC address of your PCs' wireless adapters into the boxes. Click **Save Settings** when you're done.

To get your PC's MAC address—which has nothing to do with Macintosh computers, by the way—open the Network and Sharing Center in Control Panel, and then click the link named for the active network adapter (under **View your active networks**, next to **Connections**). Finally, click the **Details** button to open the Network Connection Details window shown in Figure 7-14; the six-segment **Physical Address** is the MAC address for this adapter.

 To show the MAC addresses for all the network adapters on your PC at once, open a Command Prompt window and type ipconfig /all. Or, for a more abbreviated view, type getmac at the prompt. (Note that only the MAC address of your wireless adapter matters here.)

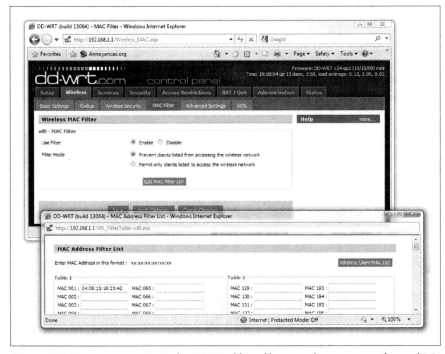

Figure 7-13. Use your router's wireless MAC address filtering to keep out unauthorized PCs

You'll need to enter the MAC address of each and every PC that connects to your network wirelessly; leave one off, and it won't be able to connect (and the person using the PC won't know why). Don't worry about any PCs connected to your network with cables; they won't be affected.

Now, MAC address filtering is a useful solution, but it's not foolproof. For one, anyone with access to your router setup page can make changes to the approved list, so you'll want to change your router's administrative password if you haven't done so already; you're asking for trouble if you leave the default password in place. Next, turn *off* your router's **Remote Administration** option to ensure that only those connected to your private network have access. Finally, consider the potential weakness in MAC address filtering explained in "Why MAC Address Filtering Is Not Foolproof", the next sidebar.

Why MAC Address Filtering Is Not Foolproof

MAC addresses—which are different for each device on your network—may seem to be the perfect way to keep out intruders, but there's a catch. Since you can change the MAC address on most modern hardware, someone could theoretically connect to a filtered network by spoofing the MAC address. This makes the MAC address somewhat like a password, right?

Not exactly. First, no two devices on a network can have the same MAC address, so if your PC is connected, and someone else tries to break in by spoofing your MAC address, the attempt will fail. Second, each PC has its own MAC address and its own entry on your router's MAC address filter page; this means that an administrator can remove a compromised entry without affecting any other PCs. (This is in contrast to the single WPA-Personal passphrase or WEP encryption key that everyone on the network shares.)

The real problem is that, like the hidden SSID dilemma explained in "Sniff Out WiFi Hotspots" on page 446, a savvy intruder can use monitoring software to grab MAC addresses out of the air and use them to connect.

Think it's difficult to change your PC's MAC address? Think again. You can use Mac Makeup, free from *http://www.gorlani.com/publicprj/macmakeup/*, MadMACs, free from *http://www.irongeek.com/i.php?page=security/madmacs -mac-spoofer*, or Technitium MAC Address Changer (*http://www.technitium .com/tmac/*) to change your wireless adapter's MAC address in a few moments.

You can also change your MAC address—without any special software—by editing the Registry. Open Registry Editor (Chapter 3) and expand the branches to `HKEY_LOCAL_MACHINE\SYSTEM\CurrentControlSet\Control \Class\{4D36E972-E325-11CE-BFC1-08002BE10318}`. Press **Ctrl-F**, type `Driver Desc` in the box, and click **Find Next**. Press **F3** to cycle through the subkeys here (e.g., 0001, 0002, etc.) until you hit the one where the `DriverDesc` value matches the name of your wireless adapter. Once you stumble upon the correct key, select **Edit→New→String Value**, and name the value `NetworkAd dress`. Double-click the new value, type the MAC address you want to use in the **Value data** field (without any hyphens, like this: `040815162342`), and click OK. To put the new address into effect, use the Network Connections window to disable and then re-enable your network adapter (or restart Windows).

Of course, there are plenty of legitimate reasons to change one's MAC address, such as troubleshooting or conflict management. Even your router probably has a way to change its MAC address—via the **MAC Address Clone** feature— to match your PC's address so remote servers that have been configured to permit access from your PC won't reject your router.

All this means that there's no such thing as an impenetrable wireless network. If you really care about security, abandon wireless and stick with cables.

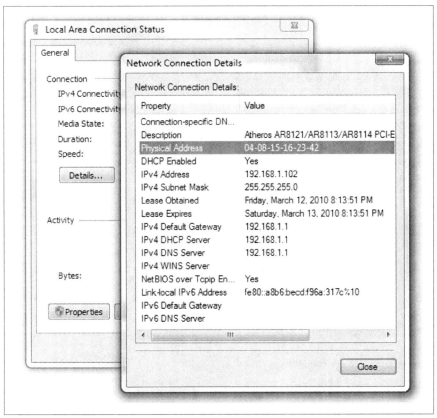

Figure 7-14. The MAC address of your wireless is adapter is the "Physical Address" listed in the Network Connection Details window

With MAC address filtering in place, all you have to do is create a new entry for each new PC you want to allow to connect wirelessly. And of course, you'll need to remove entries for PCs you want to deauthorize. For this reason, it's useful to keep a record of the MAC addresses of all the PCs on your network in say, a text file, somewhere safe.

If you're worried about others on your local network breaking into your PC and reading your files, see "Turn Off Administrative Shares" on page 605 for another backdoor you can close.

Connect to a Public Wireless Network

The point of wireless networking is not necessarily to do away with a few feet of cables, but to make a network do things it could never do before. For instance, if you have a portable computer equipped with wireless, you should be able to walk into any airport, coffee shop, hotel, or college dormitory and connect to the Internet in a matter of seconds. In more populated areas, it's not uncommon to walk down the street and have your pick of unsecured WiFi networks; do it in a moving vehicle, and all of a sudden, you're *wardriving*.

As described in "Sniff Out WiFi Hotspots" on page 446, you can connect to any unsecured wireless network that Windows' built-in WiFi sniffer is able to detect. (The exceptions, of course, are those networks requiring a paid subscription or account access, but that's a different story.) This applies to networks you'll encounter while you're on the road, as well as those that are in range of your home or office.

The problem is that by connecting to these networks, you're exposing your computer to the full array of viruses, hackers, and other dangers present on any network. (Thus the motivation for securing your own WiFi network becomes more urgent.) The solution is to take steps to protect your computer (or workgroup), and the steps necessary depend on the scenario.

Scenario 1: Single-serving Internet

Say you've just sat yourself down at a sidewalk café, airport, or hotel lobby and pulled out your laptop. You boot up Windows, open the "Connect to a network" window as described in "Sniff Out WiFi Hotspots" on page 446, find a local network, and connect for 20 minutes or so to check your email. When you're done, you'll likely never use this network again.

Now, if you typically use your laptop when connected to your own private network, protected by your wireless router's firewall, you'll want to take some extra steps to secure your PC *before* you connect elsewhere. Since you won't have your router with you on the road, and thus won't have any dedicated firewall hardware, you'll want to employ the built-in Windows Firewall software (or a third-party firewall solution), as described later in this chapter. (The Windows Firewall is put in full force automatically if you choose **Public network** when first connecting to a new network or through the Networking and Sharing Center.) This will provide basic protection, but certainly nothing you'd want to live with for the long haul.

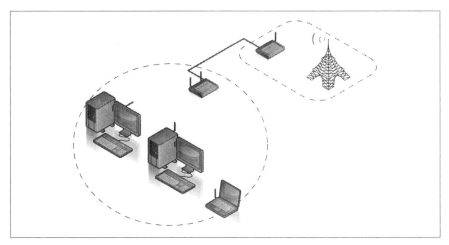

Figure 7-15. Use a wireless bridge in conjunction with a wireless router to protect your workgroup when connecting to a public Internet connection

Scenario 2: The long haul

Say your apartment complex, office building, or city provides free wireless Internet. Naturally, you would never want to connect your computer or workgroup to this wireless free-for-all without some sort of reliable, long-term firewall protecting you from the rest of the riff-raff (and vice versa). Now, since this is not your own private Internet connection, you can't just plug in a router to facilitate your firewall. But you can add another device, a *wireless bridge*, in order to build an "island" of sorts, in a sea otherwise filled with carnivorous phytoplankton.

 If you're connecting to a wireless 3G network, versus a more local WiFi hotspot, a wireless bridge won't do the trick. Instead, you'll need a 3G broadband router, or at least one that supports USB-based WAN adapters.

A bridge connects two networks; in this case, you're bridging the public network to your private, secure network, as shown in Figure 7-15. Between them is the wireless bridge and your router (which protects your private network with its built-in firewall). The two dotted areas represent the scope of the two different WiFi networks in effect: your own private, encrypted wireless network is shown on the left, and the public network is illustrated on the right. (Your bridge and router actually form a tiny, third network, complete with its own IP space separate from those in either of the two wireless networks.)

Here's how you set it up:

1. Use the "Connect to a network" window as described in "Sniff Out WiFi Hotspots" on page 446, to find the name (SSID) of the public wireless network to which you'd like to connect. Connect to the network temporarily to confirm that it actually works.

2. Obtain a wireless bridge, and follow the procedure laid out in its documentation to set it up with the public wireless network you want to use, a process that typically involves plugging the bridge directly into your PC with an Ethernet cable.

3. While the bridge is still connected to your PC, obtain the *local* IP address of your bridge; it'll be something like 192.168.1.1 or 192.168.0.1. (You won't need the bridge's *remote* IP address assigned to it by the public network.)

4. When you're done setting up the bridge, unplug it from your PC and connect it directly to the WAN port of your wireless router. (This is the port into which you'd normally plug a DSL or cable modem.)

5. Connect your PC to your router and use a web browser to open up your router's setup page, as described in the section "Set Up a Wireless Router" on page 436.

6. Configure your wireless router so that it has a **Connection Type** of **Static IP**. (Refer to your router's documentation for the specific details on this and the next few settings.)

7. In the router setup, set the **Gateway** address to the IP address of your bridge that you obtained in step 3.

8. Then, still on the router setup page, set the static IP address of the Internet connection (as the router sees it) to a fictitious IP address in the same *subnet* as your bridge. This means that the *first three numbers* of both IP addresses should be the same, but the fourth should be different. That is, if your bridge's address is 192.168.1.1, then you could set the IP address of your Internet connection to something like 192.168.1.2 or 192.168.1.73.

 Don't confuse these addresses with the IP addresses used on your private network. The local IP address of your bridge and the IP address for your Internet connection that you enter here form the tiny, third network mentioned at the beginning of this section. Alternatively, you could set your router to obtain its IP address automatically (back in step 6), a strategy that may or may not work depending on how cooperative your bridge is.

9. Finally, set the DNS server addresses in your router setup to the IP addresses of your Internet Service Provider's DNS servers.

   If you don't know which ISP is responsible for the public network you're trying to connect to, try connecting directly with your PC once more. Open a web browser, type *http://www.annoyances.org/ip* in the address bar, and press **Enter**; this will show the true IP address of your Internet connection. Then, open a Command Prompt window and type `nslookup ip_address`, where `ip_address` is the set of four numbers reported by *http://www.an noyances.org*. This gives you the name of your ISP, plus some extra stuff. So, you might see something like `dsl456.eastcoast.superisp.net`, which means your ISP is `superisp.net`. Then, it's only a matter of visiting the ISP's website (e.g., *http://www.superisp.net/*) and determining its DNS server addresses from its online documentation. Alternatively, you can use Google's free public DNS servers (`8.8.8.8` and `8.8.4.4`) or those provided by OpenDNS (*http://www.opendns.com/*).

10. Complete the setup of your router as explained in "Set Up a Wireless Router" on page 436, and make sure to enable wireless encryption and any other security settings at your disposal.

This should do it. The bridge will funnel the public Internet connection into your router, and your router will funnel it to the computers in your workgroup. The router acts like a firewall, provided that you connect all your computers directly to your own, personal WiFi network, and not the public, unsecured one.

Among other things, your bridge/router combination will serve as a repeater (a.k.a. range extender), and should boost the signal strength and might even improve performance over connecting your PCs directly to the public network.

Get Bluetooth to Work

Bluetooth holds a lot of promise. For one, you can do things like connect a laptop wirelessly to a Bluetooth GPS receiver for portable navigation, or to a cell phone for cordless address-book synchronization. With your Bluetooth-equipped PC, you can use a Bluetooth cell phone as a portable wireless modem, handheld wireless presentation remote control, or wireless data storage drive for your files.

The problem is that Bluetooth standards are poorly implemented in most devices; don't be surprised if you can't exchange a simple address book entry between your Bluetooth-capable PDA and your cell phone, even if they're the same brand. Even Windows 7's built-in Bluetooth stack only works with certain types of Bluetooth transceivers, and then only on Tuesday. When the moon is full. But usually the biggest stumbling block is getting Windows to recognize and use the Bluetooth transceiver in your PC. Only after Windows fully supports your Bluetooth adapter can you easily pair Bluetooth cell phones, PDAs, cordless mice and keyboards, presentation remotes, headsets, GPS receivers, and other devices with Windows.

 You can tell whether Windows is aware of—and has loaded a proper driver for—your Bluetooth hardware if there's a **Bluetooth Devices** icon in your notification area (taskbar tray). Don't go looking for the **Bluetooth Devices** icon in Control Panel, found in earlier versions of Windows; it's gone in Windows 7, replaced by a hidden subpage of the Devices and Printers page in Control Panel. But more on that later.

Most PC-based Bluetooth adapters are either tiny cards wired inside some laptops or lipstick-sized USB dongles that plug in to the back of your PC. But just because the manufacturer of that adapter claims compatibility with Windows 7 doesn't mean you'll see the Bluetooth icon in your taskbar. The problem is that only some Bluetooth adapters use Microsoft's *Bluetooth stack*, the set of drivers and utilities that allows your programs to talk to your Bluetooth devices. Many adapters instead use either the Toshiba Bluetooth stack or the Broadcom Bluetooth stack; good luck trying to find out which stack your adapter uses simply by reading the packaging.

To determine the missing pieces on your PC, open Device Manager in Control Panel. If all is well, you'll see a **Bluetooth Radios** category, under which you'll find an entry for your adapter and another for **Microsoft Bluetooth Enumerator**. If you don't see the Microsoft driver, or if your adapter appears in the **Unknown Devices** category, you have three choices: hunt down a native Windows 7 or Vista driver, be content with your device's proprietary software (if it works), or discard your adapter and spend $20 on a newer one.

 Don't bother trying to brute-force install a driver right here in Device Manager. If you manage to install the proper software, Device Manager will identify your Bluetooth adapter and install the driver automatically. Otherwise, the best you'll get with a manually loaded driver is an icon in the **Bluetooth Radios** category covered by a yellow exclamation mark and the error "Device cannot start." Before you try to install one of the Bluetooth stacks listed here, unload any drivers already on your PC by right-clicking the entry for your Bluetooth radio in Device Manager and clicking **Delete**. See Chapter 6 for more on installing drivers.

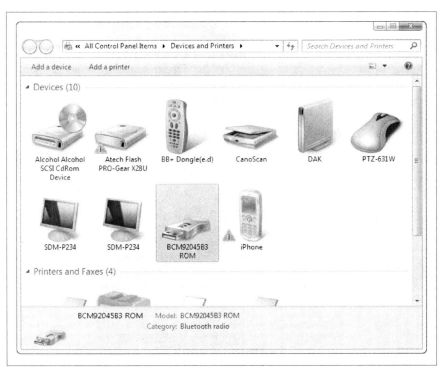

Figure 7-16. Your Bluetooth adapter and any Bluetooth devices you've paired with Windows will all appear in the Devices and Printers page in Control Panel

Inspect the software that comes with your Bluetooth adapter (even if it won't install on Windows 7), or check the manufacturer's website to find out what kind of chip your adapter uses. If you have a Toshiba Bluetooth adapter, you can get the Toshiba stack at:

http://aps2.toshiba-tro.de/Bluetooth/?page=download

Or if you have an adapter that uses a Broadcom or Widcomm Bluetooth chip, you can get the Broadcom stack at:

http://www.broadcom.com/support/bluetooth/update.php

If the proper drivers are installed, your Bluetooth adapter will show up in the Devices and Printers page in Control Panel, as shown in Figure 7-16. (Don't be surprised if the name of your adapter is something unfriendly like *BCM92045B3 ROM*.)

To pair a new device, click **Add a device**, and then while Windows waits, make your device "discoverable."

As soon as Windows sees the device, highlight it and click **Next**. If prompted to select a pairing option, choose **Pair without using a code** for simple devices like mice and keyboards. For devices that have their own codes (refer to the device's documentation), select **Enter the device's pairing code** and then enter the code, which is often 0000. And for smart phones and other devices with a screen and means of entry, click **Create a pairing code for me** and then enter the code shown into your device. Note that Bluetooth devices time out quickly, so don't dawdle when entering pairing codes.

When you've successfully paired the device, an icon for it will appear in the Devices and Printers window, like the iPhone shown in Figure 7-16.

 To show *only* paired Bluetooth devices—but not your Bluetooth adapter—open your Start menu, type bthprops.cpl in the Search box, and press **Enter**. The Bluetooth Devices page doesn't add any features over the main Devices and Printers page in Control Panel, but it does conveniently filter out all non-Bluetooth devices for easier setup and troubleshooting.

But to make your PC discoverable to other devices, to configure COM ports, or to change other settings, right-click your Bluetooth adapter and select **Bluetooth settings** to show the Bluetooth Settings window in 7-17.

Most PC software communicates over Bluetooth airwaves via virtual COM ports that Windows opens on your PC (just like the ones you plugged your mouse into in the 1980s, except invisible). Click the **COM Ports** tab to see which ports have been claimed by the devices listed in the Devices and Printers window. Some applications that communicate with Bluetooth devices auto-detect the COM port(s) being used, but you may have to inspect this list to determine which ports your device is using. If you don't see at least one COM port associated with your device—and you know there should be at least one here—return to the Devices and Printers page in Control Panel, right-click the device, click **Properties**, and choose the **Services** tab to see what the device is capable of.

 There's no **Edit** or **Properties** button on the COM ports page, so you'll need to open Device Manager if you want to change any settings, like the COM port number or baud rate. In Device Manager, expand the **Ports (COM & LPT)** category, and then double-click a **Standard Serial over Bluetooth link** entry and select the **Port Settings** tab to configure it.

Figure 7-17. Use the Bluetooth Settings window to make your PC discoverable, set up virtual serial ports, or choose whether or not to show the Bluetooth icon on the taskbar

Don't be surprised if you can successfully pair a device with Windows, but Windows can't actually make use of the device. In most cases, you'll need to get software specifically designed to work with Bluetooth to use the device wirelessly. For instance, get MeHere, free from *http://mehere.glenmurphy .com/*, to use your Bluetooth GPS to navigate a live Google Maps window.

Troubleshoot Network Connections

Whether you're connected wirelessly or with a cable, Windows needs certain numeric details to be squared away, or nothing will work right. With that in mind, you should get to know the Network Connections window: on the Network and Sharing page in Control Panel, click **Change adapter settings** to open the folder shown in Figure 7-18. If you haven't done so already, open the **Views** drop-down and select **Details** to show the pertinent information.

Figure 7-18. Use Network Connections to manage the hardware that connects your PC to your network

Here you'll see the status of all your network adapters—both wireless and wired—at a glance. The **Status** column tells you which connections, if any, are connected, albeit with some inconsistencies. Wireless and Bluetooth adapters that are not in use say **Not connected**, but Ethernet (wired) adapters say **Network cable unplugged**. In either case, any adapter currently in use (connected) is marked only the current *network name*.

 Don't let the *network name* throw you. It's not the SSID of the wireless network you're using (see "Sniff Out WiFi Hotspots" on page 446), nor is it the workgroup name used for sharing folders and printers (explained in Chapter 8), nor does it have anything to do with your Internet connection. Rather, it's a superficial title you can enter by clicking the **Customize** link in the Network and Sharing center, used to make it easy to switch between public and private networks; see Chapter 8 for details.

Also important is the **Connectivity** column, which shows exactly what each adapter is providing (e.g., **to Internet Access**); see the previous section for more on this indicator.

To see the IP address and other TCP/IP settings are currently being used by a connection, double-click the connection to view the Status window and then click the **Details** button. If a connection is connected but isn't delivering any data, an incorrectly assigned IP address may be to blame.

But the main reason to use this window is to *change* TCP/IP settings. Right-click the connection you need to fix and select **Properties**. Then, select **Internet Protocol Version 4 (TCP/IPv4)** from the list and click the **Properties** button to open the Properties window shown in Figure 7-19.

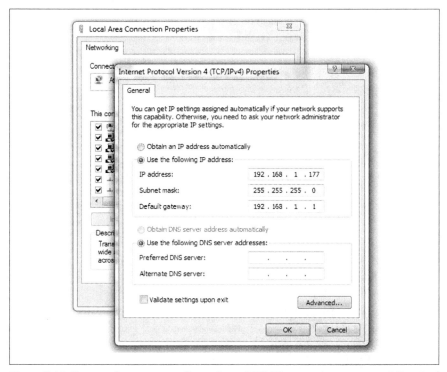

Figure 7-19. You may have to manually configure TCP/IP properties to get your PC noticed on your network

In most cases, selecting the defaults—**Obtain an IP address automatically** and **Obtain DNS server address automatically**—will suffice. This works because your router, if you have one, automatically assigns a unique IP address to each new PC it sees using Dynamic Host Configuration Protocol (DHCP).

But sometimes DHCP doesn't cooperate as well as it should; either a PC is given the wrong IP address or no address at all. To get around this problem, try pulling your PC out of the DHCP arena and assigning it a *static* (non-changing) IP address:

1. If you have a router, open its configuration page in a web browser (usually *http://192.168.1.1* or *http://192.168.0.1*), and navigate to the DHCP client table. This shows all the PCs connected to your network (both wired and wireless) controlled by DHCP, along with their dynamically assigned IP addresses. (In most cases, PCs with static addresses will be absent from this list.)

While you're here, check also the DHCP settings and determine the range of IP addresses your router is allowed to use for automatic assignments. For instance, if the **Start IP Address** is set to 192.168.1.100 and **Maximum DHCP Users** is set to 50, then the addresses from 192.168.1.100 to 192.168.1.149 are fair game for DHCP and should be avoided by you.

2. Open the Internet Protocol Version 4 (TCP/IPv4) Properties window as described at the beginning of this section, and choose the **Alternate Configuration** tab.

 The settings in the **Alternate Configuration** tab, as opposed to the **General** tab, allows you to choose a static IP address for only the current network, a useful strategy for portable computers that may connect to other networks. If you're not using a portable PC, the **General** tab works just as well.

3. Select **User configured** (or, if on the **General** tab, select **Use the following IP address**).

4. Pick an IP address (e.g., 192.168.1.177) not claimed by the DHCP (see step 1) and then type it into the **IP address** field. The first three numbers of the address you use must be the same as the rest of your network (e.g., 192.168.1.*xxx*).

5. For the **Subnet mask**, type 255.255.255.0.

6. For the **Default gateway**, type the IP address of your router (again, usually 192.168.1.1 or 192.168.0.1).

7. For the **Preferred DNS server** and the **Alternate DNS server**, type the IP addresses of your ISP's DNS servers.

8. Click OK in both boxes when you're done. The change should take effect immediately.

9. Return to the Network Connections window when you're done, and look at the **Status** column entry for the connection you've just modified. If it says **Acquiring network address**, it means Windows is in the process of establishing a connection; if you see this for more than, say, 10 seconds, you've probably done something wrong. If the status is **Limited or no connectivity**, it means that a connection has been established, but your IP address is incorrect.

In a perfect world, you'd never have to issue static IP addresses to your PCs, but doing so may help them cooperate with other cranky computers on your network.

Static IP addresses are sometimes also necessary to simplify port forwarding (IP routing), wherein your router redirects incoming traffic on a certain port to a specific IP address you specify. See "Control a PC Remotely" on page 488 for an example.

If, at this point, your network appears to be functioning, you can proceed to set up the various services you need, such as file and printer sharing (described in Chapter 8) and Internet Connection Sharing (described later in this chapter). Otherwise, look through the following checklist for possible solutions:

Restart
Heed the advice at the beginning of Chapter 6: restarting your computer will fix 99% of all problems. This is never truer than when diagnosing a networking problem.

Firmware
Nearly all network hardware (adapters, routers, print servers, etc.) has user-upgradable firmware. Check the device manufacturers' websites for the latest firmware if you're experiencing any network problems. It may also be worth looking for a router firmware update or replacement to eliminate the need for static IP addresses, as described in "Upgrade Your Router" on page 443.

Bad cables
Make sure the green light is on next to each cable you've plugged in. If not, try replacing one or more of the cables, especially if they're old or their connectors are worn.

Blinkenlights
When you transfer data across a network connection, each network adapter, your router/switch/hub, and even your broadband modem, should all have "activity" lights that flash. Some devices have separate lights for receiving and transmitting data, while others have only a single light for all incoming and outgoing traffic. Activity lights tend to flash intermittently and irregularly; if they pulsate regularly and slowly, it may indicate a problem with the device or connection.

No dupes
Make sure no two computers on your network are attempting to use the same IP address (see Step 4 earlier in this section) or computer name (see the sidebar "What's My PC's Name?" on page 594).

Drivers
Make sure you have the latest drivers for each network adapter on your PC, and remove any proprietary software that may have come with your

network hardware. See Chapter 6 for more on updating and trouble-shooting stubborn drivers.

Some problems are caused by improper hardware settings, usually attributed to the network adapter itself. Open Device Manager and double-click the icon for your troublesome adapter (or right-click it in the Network Connections window, select **Properties**, and then click **Configure**). Choose the **Advanced** tab, and thumb through the **Property** list on the left, looking for possible problems. If you don't understand a particular setting, look it up in the documentation or on Google.

Can't see another PC

This is a nasty problem, one with several different causes and often no clear-cut solution. First, open the Services window (*services.msc*), find the **Computer Browser** service, and make sure its **Status** is **Started** and its **Startup Type** is **Automatic** (if it isn't, double-click the service to change its settings). Next, try the Ping utility, described in "Test an IP Address" on page 475, to determine whether your PC can actually see another PC on your network. If the Ping test fails, try pinging your router (if you have one) from each computer to see which PC's connection isn't working. If Ping is successful, proceed to Chapter 8 for help with file sharing.

Add new network connections

You may have noticed that there's no obvious way to add a new connection to the Network Connections window. By default, the Network Connections window only shows your installed hardware, which means you can add a new network adapter, and it will show up in this list.

But the Network Connections window also supports *virtual* connections, such as dial-up (analog modem) connections and broadband (PPPoE) connections. To add one of these, open the Network and Sharing Center and click the **Set up a connection or network** link, as described in "Internet Me" on page 476. Of course, you'll have to return to the Network Connections window if you want to modify or delete one of these virtual connections.

Prioritize multiple, simultaneous network connections

If you ever use more than one network connection simultaneously, there's a little known setting you can play with that may solve some problems. Say you connect wirelessly at home most of the time, but when you transfer a lot of files from one PC to another, you prefer to use a cable for greater speed.

Except in specific cases, Windows will only use one network adapter at a time. So, if you're connected wirelessly *and* with a cable, you'll want to choose which connection Windows prioritizes. In the Network Connections window, press the **Alt** key to temporarily show the menu, and then from the **Advanced** menu, select **Advanced Settings**. Pick the fastest connection, and use the up arrow to move it to the top of the list.

While you're here, choose the **Provider Order** tab, and make sure the **Microsoft Windows Network** entry appears at the top of the list.

Click OK when you're done; the change will take effect immediately.

Test an IP Address

Once you know the IP address of a PC or device—whether it's dynamically assigned or static—you can easily check if that machine is running and visible to other machines on the network. The Ping utility sends small packets of information to another computer on your network and reports on its success (if any).

Open the Start menu, type cmd, and press **Enter** to open the Command Prompt. At the prompt, type ping *address*, where *address* is the IP address of another computer or perhaps your router. For example, to ping the computer at 192.168.1.102 from any other PC, you'd type:

```
ping 192.168.1.102
```

If the connection is working, the Ping transaction will be successful, and you'll get a result that looks like this:

```
Pinging 192.168.0.1 with 32 bytes of data:
Reply from 192.168.0.1: bytes=32 time=24ms TTL=53
Reply from 192.168.0.1: bytes=32 time=16ms TTL=53
```

To be fair, this test only works if *both* connections are working, and if the network is functional. If you get this result:

```
Pinging 192.168.0.1 with 32 bytes of data:
Request timed out.
Request timed out.
```

it means that Ping never got a response from the other computer. A failed Ping can mean that the adapter on your local PC is misconfigured, or that the target machine isn't up and running. (There's also a small chance that the target machine has a firewall blocking Ping.)

You can also test your Internet connection by pinging a host on the Internet (outside your local subnet), like this one:

```
ping 64.233.187.99
```

Now, if you get a reply from 64.233.187.99, but *no reply* when you ping a host name, like this:

```
ping google.com
```

it means that your DNS nameservers—the machines at your ISP that translate host names to their IP addresses and back—are misconfigured or possibly down. In this case, follow the steps in "Troubleshoot Network Connections" on page 469, to enter the correct DNS addresses.

Internet Me

Connecting to the Web is much easier than it used to be, so much so that Windows basically takes this for granted. In fact, I'm going to make this really easy for you: if you have broadband (typically via DSL or cable), and you're not using a router, get one right now and hook it up. Once you set up your router (see "Set Up a Wireless Router" on page 436), connect your PC to the router either wirelessly or with a cable, and you're online. That's it.

Now, if you have broadband but you can't use a router for some reason, or if you're (gasp) still using dial-up, then you need to configure Windows to connect to the Internet for you. Of course, the procedure depends on the type of connection you're setting up:

Broadband with a static IP address
Follow the steps in "Troubleshoot Network Connections" on page 469, to set up your Ethernet adapter to use your Internet connection's static IP address. But do this only if you have no router, which means you also have no protection.

Broadband with a username and password (PPPoE)
Point-to-Point Protocol over Ethernet (PPPoE) is used to establish temporary, dynamic IP connections over broadband. If your Internet connection has a dynamic IP address, it means your ISP assigns you a different IP address every time you connect to the Internet. The PPPoE protocol facilitates this connection by sending your username and password to your provider. Again, follow these steps only if you have no router to do this for you.

Never use the proprietary software provided by your ISP to connect via PPPoE; use the procedure explained here instead for best results.

To set up a PPPoE connection, open the Network and Sharing Center, and click the **Set up a connection or network link** on the bottom. Select **Connect to the Internet**, and click **Next**. Click **Broadband (PPPoE)**, type the **User name** and **Password** provided by your ISP, and turn on the **Remember this password** option. Type a name for the connection (anything you like) and then click **Connect**.

You can subsequently connect with the Connect to a network pop-up window or modify your connection from the Network Connections window, both of which are covered earlier in this chapter.

Dial-up (analog modem) connection

Sure it's obsolete, but it's cheap, and if there's no broadband around, it may be your only choice. To set it up, open the Network and Sharing Center and click the **Set up a connection or network link** on the bottom. Select **Set up a dial-up connection**, and click **Next**. Type the **Dial-up phone number** and **User name** and **Password** provided by your ISP, and turn on the **Remember this password** option. Type a name for the connection (anything you like), and click **Create**. To connect, click the **Manage network connections** link, and then double-click your new connection.

See the "Live with PPPoE" sidebar, next, for tips that also apply to dial-up connections.

Live with PPPoE

PPPoE can be a pain on a day-to-day basis, mostly because Windows is responsible for the dialing. Here are some ways to make it a little more seamless:

Connect on demand

To have Windows connect automatically whenever the connection is needed, open the Network Connections window, right-click the connection icon and select **Set as Default Connection**. Then, go to **Control Panel→Internet Options**, choose the **Connections** tab, and select the **Always dial my default connection** option.

Connect automatically

To have Windows connect automatically when you first start your computer, drag the connection from the Network Connections window to your *Startup* folder.

Connect without asking

To skip the Connect dialog that asks for your username and password each time, open the Network Connections window, right-click the connection, and select **Properties** (or click the **Properties** in the Connect window itself). Choose the **Options** tab, turn off the **Prompt for name and password, certificate, etc.** option, and click OK.

Share a PPPoE connection

If you're using PPPoE in conjunction with Internet Connection Sharing, discussed later in this chapter, and you've found that some web pages won't load on the client computers, see the sidebar "Change the MTU" on page 482.

Of course, the best way to live with PPPoE is to get a router and let it handle the connection. It'll do a much better job than Windows will, plus it provides a superb firewall and a very convenient means of sharing an Internet connection among several PCs.

Share an Internet Connection

When including an Internet connection, you have several choices. The old school approach, shown in Figure 7-20, involves a single computer connected directly to the Internet (via broadband, dial-up, or whatever). That PC then serves as a *gateway* (thanks to Internet Connection Sharing, discussed shortly) and shares the Internet connection with the other computers on the LAN.

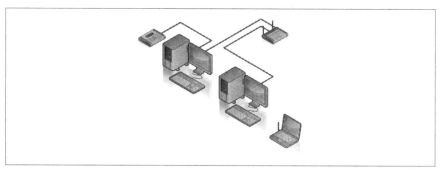

Figure 7-20. A simple workgroup with three computers, one of which has a shared Internet connection

There are several downsides to Internet connection sharing. For one, it can be temperamental and frustrating to set up. Performance and security leave a lot to be desired, and it tends to be slow. Also, one computer (the gateway) must always be on for the others to have Internet access, and that computer must have two network adapters.

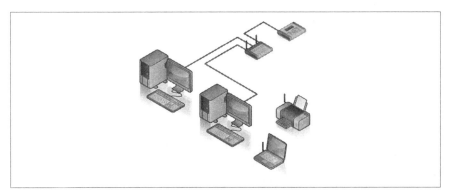

Figure 7-21. A wireless router not only makes it easy to share an Internet connection, it offers better security and more flexibility than the old-school approach shown in Figure 7-20; all of these computers, wired and wireless, have equal access to the Internet—note the wireless print server

The preferred method is to use a wireless router, forming the setup shown in Figure 7-21.

The router is a sole unit (the little box with two antennas in Figure 7-21) that plays a whole bunch of valuable roles on your network:

- A switch, which connects all the PCs on your network to one another.

- A wireless access point, which serves as a base station for your wireless PCs and devices, and connects them to the rest of your network.

- A router, which *bridges* your local network to the Internet and provides Internet access to all computers on your LAN. Plus, if you use a broadband connection that requires a username and password (e.g., PPPoE), the router automatically logs in for you, and keeps you logged in.

- A DHCP server, which automatically assigns IP addresses to computers in your local network (typically starting with 192.168.1.100, where 192.168.1.1 is the router itself), allowing them to coexist peacefully on your network. (See "Troubleshoot Network Connections" on page 469 when this doesn't work.)

- A firewall, preventing any and all communication from the outside world, except that which you specifically allow (facilitated by your router's port-forwarding feature).

You'll see routers discussed throughout this chapter. If you don't yet have one, do yourself a favor and pick one up. They're cheap, and as shown here, do quite a lot. Even if you only have a single PC (no local network to speak of), the firewall feature of a router provides excellent security, and far better protection than Windows' built-in firewall.

Now, if you don't have a router, or you want to follow the steps in the sidebar "Quick and Dirty WiFi Piggyback" on page 451, you can use the Internet Connection Sharing (ICS) feature built into Windows, along with at least one cable. To get ICS to work, you'll need the following:

- At least two computers, each with a network adapter properly installed and functioning. ICS can be used with both conventional and wireless networks.

- One PC must have an Internet connection properly set up, as described in "Internet Me" on page 476.

- If you're sharing a broadband (DSL or cable) connection, the PC with the Internet connection must have *two* network adapters installed: two Ethernet cards, or one wireless adapter plus one Ethernet card. See Figure 7-20, earlier, for a diagram of this setup.

 If your Internet connection is accessed through a router or you've allocated multiple IP addresses, you don't need ICS.

The first step in setting up ICS is to configure the host, the computer with the Internet connection that will be shared:

1. In the Network and Sharing Center, click the **Change adapter settings** link to open the Network Connections window. If you haven't already done so, open the **Views** drop-down and select **Details**.

2. Here, you should have at least two connections listed: one providing your Internet, and the other providing access to your LAN. If they're not there, your network is not ready. (For clarity, rename the two connections to "Internet Connection" and "Local Area Connection," respectively.)

3. Right-click the connection providing your Internet, and select **Properties**. This is either an Ethernet adapter plugged into your DSL or cable modem, or—if you're using PPPoE—your broadband connection.

4. This step is optional, but may be required if there are any PCs on your network running Windows 98 or older versions: follow the steps in "Troubleshoot Network Connections" on page 469, to set the IP address of the host PC to 192.168.0.1.

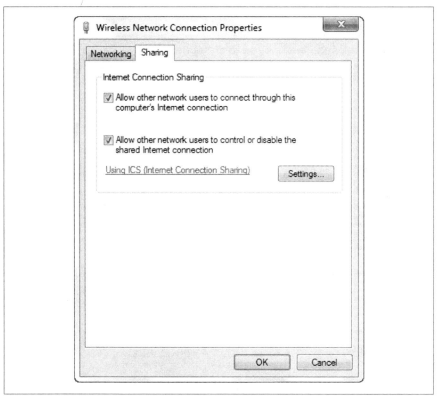

Figure 7-22. Any Internet connection can be shared with other computers in your workgroup

5. Choose the **Sharing** tab, and turn on the **Allow other network users to connect through this computer's Internet connection** option, as shown in Figure 7-22. (The **Sharing** tab will be absent if there's only one network adapter.)

6. Click OK when you're done. Verify that Internet Connection Sharing is enabled; among other things, it should say **Shared** in the **Status** column of the Network Connections window.

That's it! The change will take effect immediately, and you won't have to do anything special on the client PCs. Verify that the Internet connection still works on the host by attempting to open a web page, and then try it on each of the clients.

Change the MTU

The MTU, or Maximum Transmission Unit, is the largest chunk of data that can be passed through a network interface. The MTU in Windows 7 is fixed, but there are times you may want to change it, such as when client computers have trouble downloading data through a shared Internet connection facilitated by PPPoE.

To find a suitable MTU, sit down in front of one of your client machines, and type:

```
ping -f -l 1500 192.168.0.1
```

where `192.168.0.1` is the address of the host computer (or router) and `1500` is the MTU to test. If, at this point, you get an error message at this point about fragmentation, try the Ping command again with a lower value, say, `1492` in lieu of `1500`. Keep trying with lower values (`1492`, `1480`, `1454`, etc., down to as low as `1400`) until the ping is successful.

Once you've found an MTU that works for you, open a Command Prompt window in Administrator mode (see Chapters 9 and 8, respectively), and type:

```
netsh interface ipv4 show subinterfaces
```

to list the network connections on your PC.

```
netsh interface ipv4 set subinterface "Local Network Connection"
                        mtu=1454 store=persistent
```

where `Local Network Connection` is the name of the connection to modify (in quotes), and `1454` is the MTU value you've settled upon. Restart Windows for the change to take effect.

Test Your Throughput

Throughput is the practical measurement of bandwidth: the quantity of data you can transmit over a connection in a given period of time.

The simplest way to measure your throughput is to visit one of the many bandwidth-measuring websites, such as *http://www.broadbandreports.com/*, *http://www.dslreports.com/stest/*, or Bandwidth Place (*http://bandwidthplace.com/*).

For the most accurate results, make sure you close all superfluous programs before running the test. In addition to calculating your bandwidth and reporting the results, these services typically ask for your postal (zip) code and connection type to compile statistics on typical connection speeds in your area. The results should look something like Figure 7-23.

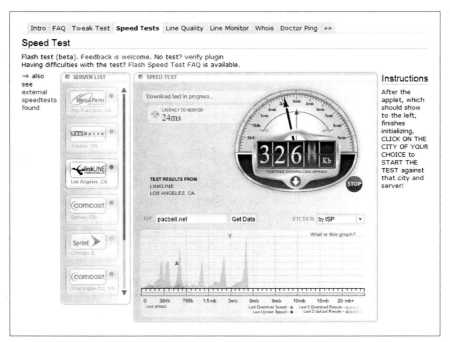

Figure 7-23. Use a free online speed test page to measure the speed of your Internet connection

Now, according to the results in Figure 7-23, the download speed is a fair 3,268 Kbps, which means, hypothetically, it should take about 6.5 seconds to download a 1 MB file.

So, what do you do if your connection seems too slow? First, close all open windows, turn off all background programs (see Chapter 6), and shut down any other PCs and devices that share your Internet. Next, examine the lights on your router or broadband modem; if they're flashing, it means that some program is still running on your PC, possibly consuming bandwidth. There's a chance that the unexplained traffic is the result of malware (covered in Chapter 6) that has made its way onto your PC.

Since your connection speed (or lack thereof) is most noticeable during file downloads (compared with web surfing or emailing), you can overcome some of these conditions by using a download manager, as described in "Do Download Accelerators Really Work?", the next sidebar.

Do Download Accelerators Really Work?

There are a number of "download accelerator" software products available, all of which promise to speed up the transfer of files downloaded to your computer. As you might've guessed, none of them are actually capable of increasing the bandwidth or throughput of your Internet connection. Rather, they employ *download managers* that compensate for inefficiencies in the download process.

These programs work by downloading a file in pieces, via multiple concurrent download streams (not unlike the TCP/IP protocol itself). While two concurrent downloads would each be allotted half the bandwidth normally consumed by a single download, this boundary only applies when your Internet connection is the bottleneck. In practice, download managers do use a larger percentage of your available bandwidth, and as a result, do tend to shorten download times, particularly for large files.

The problem is that any speed advantage you notice may be offset by the annoying and cumbersome interfaces these programs add to the mix: numerous dialog boxes and unnecessary prompts, not to mention bloated manager applications that take too long to load before they even get started. But in the end, the convenience afforded by some of these programs' extra features may make them worth the hassle.

Some of the better download managers available, all free, include Download Express (*http://www.metaproducts.com/*) and Free Download Manager (*http://www.freedownloadmanager.org/*).

The real advantage of products like these is not so much in the speed increase, but in the perks. Some programs also can resume aborted downloads, find alternative servers from which to download your files, and schedule downloads for off-peak times.

Do-it-yourself bandwidth test

One of the simplest ways to measure the throughput is to transfer a precompressed binary file (such as a *.jpg* or *.zip* file) from your computer to another location and then back again, recording the time it takes to complete the transfer each way. Just divide the file size by the transfer time to get the throughput, typically in kilobytes or megabytes per second.

When testing the speed between two PCs on your local network (for instance, when comparing the speed of your wireless network with that of cables), you might be inclined to drag and drop the files in Windows Explorer, a process discussed at length in Chapter 8. Sure, it's a good real-world test, but Windows 7 adds a lot of overhead to this process, so it won't be a true test of raw throughput. If you're feeling adventurous, try using SCP or FTP: just set up an FTP server on one PC, either using Windows' built-in IIS service or a third-party freeware alternative, and then connect to that PC with a basic SCP client like WinSCP (*http://winscp.net/*).

A slightly more scientific approach is to use the Performance Monitor (*perfmon.msc*). When it opens, highlight **Performance Monitor** from the **Monitoring Tools** branch in tree. Right-click the chart, select **Add Counters**, and then click the tiny arrow next to **Network Interface** in the list. Highlight both **Bytes Received/sec** and **Bytes Sent/sec** (use the **Ctrl** key to select multiple entries) and below, highlight your network adapter. Click **Add >>** and then click OK. (Forget the **Current Bandwidth** entry here, which shows the theoretical maximum bandwidth of your network adapter, not that of your actual connection.)

Performance Monitor than starts ticking away, recording incoming and outgoing traffic and displaying the results in the chart. Now, transfer a large file and watch what happens. At the bottom, highlight either **Bytes Received/sec** or **Bytes Sent/sec** to see the **Average** and **Maximum** data throughput that results.

Set Up Virtual Private Networking

Virtual Private Networking (VPN) allows you to construct a private workgroup of two or more computers across a standard Internet connection. With a VPN, you can accomplish tasks previously available only over a LAN, such as file and printer sharing, user authentication, and even networked games. Figure 7-24 illustrates a typical scenario with a tunnel connecting a single computer to a remote workgroup.

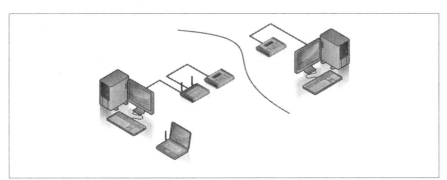

Figure 7-24. Form a virtual private workgroup through a tunnel across the Internet

Need privacy on a public wireless network? Set up a VPN to transfer data between PCs securely. For another way to get privacy on a public network, see "Connect to a Public Wireless Network" on page 462.

Before you can set up VPN, you need a *tunnel server*. If you're connecting to a large company, the VPN administrator will provide the necessary settings (and software, if necessary) to establish a connection. Otherwise, you can use a Windows 7 PC as a tunnel server by following these instructions.

Part 1: Set up the tunnel server

Despite the fact that Microsoft markets its server-class operating system for this purpose, Windows 7 can indeed serve as a VPN server without any extra software.

Here's how you do it:

1. Open the Network and Sharing Center, and click the **Change adapter settings** link on the left to open the Network Connections window.

2. Press the **Alt** key to show the menu, and then from the **File** menu, select **New Incoming Connection**.

3. On the "Who may connect to this computer?" page shown in Figure 7-25, place a checkmark next to each user account you wish to use as a login for VPN clients. Unless you're using this VPN connection yourself, you'll probably want to click **Add someone** to create a separate user account for others to use. Otherwise, you'll have to share your own username and password with those who will be connecting. Click **Next** when you're done.

4. On the next page, turn on the **Through the Internet** option, and then click **Next**.

5. Highlight **Internet Protocol Version 4 (TCP/IPv4)** and click **Properties**. Turn on the **Allow callers to access my local area network** option, and then specify how you'd like to assign IP addresses to incoming connections; you can optionally assign a range of addresses here.

6. Click OK and then **Next** when you're done, and then click **Allow access** to complete the wizard.

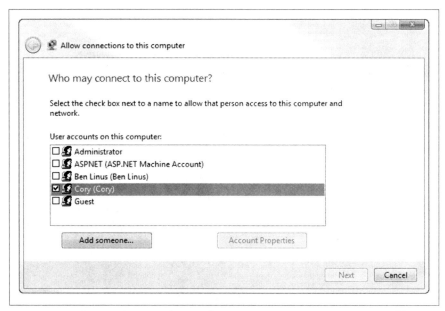

*Figure 7-25. This page lets you choose who can join the VPN connection hosted by your Windows 7 PC; click **Add someone** to create a new account on the fly*

7. If you're using a router on the server end, you'll need to set up Port Forwarding to route VPN traffic to the IP address for your tunnel server. VPN over PPTP uses port 1723, and IPSec uses 500, 50, and 51. See "Control a PC Remotely" on page 488 for details, and see Appendix B for more information on TCP/IP Ports.

Next, set up at least one other PC as a VPN client to connect the two.

Part 2: Set up the VPN client

Although there only needs to be one VPN tunnel server, you can have as many clients as you like (that is, until you reach the limit specified in the tunnel server's configuration). Here's how to connect a Windows 7 PC to an existing VPN network:

1. Open the Network and Sharing Center, and click the **Set up a connection or network link** on the bottom.

2. Select **Connect to a workplace** from the list and then click **Next**.

3. Click **Use my Internet connection (VPN)**.

4. In the **Internet address** field, type the IP address (157.54.0.1) or the host name (sally.mydomain.net) of the tunnel server.

Networking and Internet

5. Next, choose a title for the new connection (it can be anything you want), type it into the **Destination name** field, and click **Next**.

6. On the next page, type your user name and password on the tunnel server; this is either the login for a valid Windows user account on that PC (see Step 3 in Part 1, earlier) or a login provided by the tunnel server's administrator.

7. Turn on the **Remember this password** option, and click **Connect** (or **Create**, if you opted not to connect on the previous page).

 As soon as you're connected, you should have access to the additional resources shared on the remote network; see Chapter 8 for details on accessing shared folders and printers. Later on, you can connect by double-clicking the VPN connection in the "Connect to a network" popup window.

8. If you connect to the Internet through a router, you'll most likely need to turn on the IPSec option in your router's setup to get VPN to work. See "Set Up a Wireless Router" on page 436, or refer to your router's documentation, for details.

For additional tips on working with VPN connections, such as how to bypass the Connect dialog, see the sidebar "Live with PPPoE" on page 477.

Control a PC Remotely

With virtualization, covered in Chapter 1, running an operating system in a window is commonplace, not to mention very cheap. But virtualization is no substitute for a real, live PC, particularly when that PC is miles away and is more than just a bare-bones Windows box.

Got important data on a remote machine? Sure, Windows Explorer does let you transfer files to and from other computers by dragging and dropping (see Chapter 8), and even over long distances with the help of VPN, but you can't run programs or use your hardware merely through Explorer.

Enter the Remote Desktop feature, included with the Professional and Ultimate editions of Windows 7 (lesser editions can only use the feeble Remote Assistance feature described later in this section). Remote Desktop lets you view and interact with the desktop of a PC in a window, as though you were sitting in front of it.

Remote computing is great for travelling, as it allows you to leave the lion's share of your data and processing power at home, and lug around nothing more than an ultra-lightweight netbook. It's also useful for commuters, who need to access work documents and programs from home, or vice versa.

Of course, the concept of remote assistance—fixing someone else's PC from afar—is so valuable that many paid help websites now employ some form of remote control. And anyone administrating PCs in other rooms or other buildings will likely need remote control on a regular basis.

 You can access Device Manager, Registry Editor, the Disk Management tool, the Services window, and any administrative tools remotely without initiating a Remote Control session. From the Files menu in Registry Editor, for instance, select Connect Network Registry and then type the name of the remote PC to browse the registry of that computer. Just make sure Administrative Shares are enabled, as described in Chapter 8.

Of course, there are drawbacks to remote control as well. For one, you'll need a relatively fast connection to use any remote control software like Remote Desktop, since a lot of data is transferred to update the screen image. For example, a direct Ethernet (LAN) connection will provide nearly instantaneous responsiveness, while a DSL or cable connection will be more sluggish. And network setup, particularly if you're connecting through a router, can be a chore.

Finally, while just about any computer—even a Mac—can connect to a Remote Desktop PC, only the higher-end editions of Windows 7 (plus Vista, XP, and 2000) can host a Remote Desktop session and be controlled remotely. Of course, the alternatives described later in this section overcome this limitation, but that's just more software to install.

Follow the following procedure to set up Remote Desktop on both the host and client PCs.

Part 1: Enable the Remote Desktop host

Allowing others to connect to a computer with Remote Desktop is relatively easy. Open the System page in Control Panel and click the **Remote settings** link on the left side.

Windows offers two levels of security. If you know you'll be using another Windows 7 or Vista machine to access this PC, select **Allow connections only from computers running Remote Desktop with Network Level Authentication**. Or, if you'll need to access this PC from an older Windows 2000 or XP machine, use the **Allow connections from computers running any version of Remote Desktop** option.

Network Level Authentication (NLA) is also known as Terminal Services Client 6.0. To use NLA with Windows XP or Windows Server 2003, install the update available at *http:// support.microsoft.com/kb/925876*.

By default, all active administrator-level users can connect to your PC when Remote Desktop is enabled. If you wish to grant access to a lesser user account, click **Select Users**. (See Chapter 8 for more information on user accounts.) Click OK when you're done; the change will take effect immediately.

Next, if you're using a router, you'll have to set up your router's *port forwarding* feature to permit the incoming connection. (This step, of course, is not necessary if you're connecting from another PC from within your local network or VPN workgroup.)

The simplest way to make your PC work with your router's port forwarding feature is to assign a static IP address to your PC, as described in the section "Troubleshoot Network Connections" on page 469. See also the section "Upgrade Your Router" on page 443 for an upgrade that may make a static IP unnecessary.

Open your router's setup page as described in "Set Up a Wireless Router" on page 436, and navigate to the Port Range Forwarding page, which should look something like the one in Figure 7-26. Here, fill out the first blank line as follows:

Application

This is just a description; type Remote Desktop here.

Start, End

Type 3389, the TCP port number used by Remote Desktop, into both the **Start** and **End** fields. (See Appendix B for more information on TCP/IP Ports.) If you have more than one PC, you can specify additional ports (3390, 3391, etc.) here and then customize them in Remote Desktop on each PC.

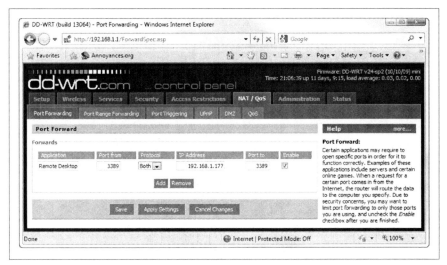

Figure 7-26. To control a PC across an Internet connection, you'll need to permit the incoming signal by going to your router's Port Range Forwarding page

Protocol
Choose **TCP**.

IP Address
Enter the static IP address you chose for your PC.

Enable
Place a checkmark in this box to permit this service.

Click **Save Settings** when you're done.

To connect from another PC elsewhere on the Internet, you'll need the IP address of the host PC on the Internet (not the address in your workgroup). Just open a web browser, navigate to *http://annoyances.org/ip/*, and record the number displayed.

If you'll only be connecting to this PC from another PC on your network, you can skip the port forwarding and external IP address and instead use the computer name of the host to connect. You can find the computer name on the System page in Control Panel, next to **Computer name** in the middle of the page. Click the **Change settings** link and then click the **Change** button to choose a new name for the PC.

Part 2: Connect to a remote computer

Once you've set up a host to accept remote connections, jump over to another PC and run `mstsc.exe` to open Remote Desktop Connection.

 If you're using an older Windows PC without Remote Desktop, you can get the RDP software for free from *http://www .microsoft.com/windowsxp/downloads/tools/RDCLIENTDL .mspx*. RDP for the Mac is available at *http://www.microsoft .com/mac/products/remote-desktop/*. For Linux, use rdesktop (*http://www.rdesktop.org/*), or for iPhone, get Remote Desktop (*http://www.mochasoft.dk/*), WinAdmin (*http://iphonewi nadmin.com/*), or Gooer (*http://www.gooer.com/iphone/*).

The default Remote Desktop Connection dialog is very simple, with only a single field. Click **Options** to display the full dialog, shown in Figure 7-27.

If you're connecting to another computer in your workgroup, type the name of the computer in the **Computer** field, or, if you're connecting to another computer on the Internet, type its IP address here. Next, type the **User name** of a valid Administrator-level user account on the remote computer; you'll be prompted for a password later.

The rest of the options in this dialog are optional. The settings in the **Display** and **Experience** tabs deal with performance issues, and the **Programs** tab lets you start programs on the remote computer automatically when you connect. The **Local Resources** tab has similar options, plus a **Local devices** section, which lets you share remote drives and printers.

 If you plan on reconnecting to the remote computer at a later time, click **Save As** to create an *.rdp* file with all the information in this dialog. You can subsequently double-click the file to initiate a connection, or right-click and select **Edit** to change its settings. Of course, if the remote PC you're connecting to has a dynamic IP address, it won't do much good to save the connection settings. See the upcoming section "Tips for Remote Desktop" on page 493 for workarounds if you need to access this PC consistently.

Click **Connect** to initiate a connection to the remote computer. If all is well, a window will appear with an image of the desktop of the remote computer. You can interact with this desktop by pointing, clicking, and dragging, just as though you are sitting in front of it.

Figure 7-27. Use Remote Desktop Connection to initiate a connection to another computer and view and interact with its desktop as though you're sitting in front of it

Simply close the window or open the remote Start menu and select **Disconnect** to close the connection. Or, for better security and to relinquish control to someone sitting at the remote PC, select **Log Off** instead.

Tips for Remote Desktop

Here are some ways to improve your experience with Remote Desktop:

Shut down remotely.
    You'll see in the remote Start menu that the **Shut down** button is gone, with **Disconnect** in its place. This is obviously on purpose, since a shut-down computer can't accept remote connections. But it does make it more difficult to actually shut down or restart a remote PC. To shut down a remote computer, click an empty area of the desktop and press **Alt-F4**. Or, open a Command Prompt window and type:

    ```
    shutdown -s -t 5
    ```

    where 5 is the number of seconds to wait before shutting down; specify 0 here to shut down immediately.

Want an audience?

When you connect to a remote PC, anyone currently logged into that computer will be unceremoniously logged out to make way for your remote connection. This poses a problem if you wish to use the remote PC while its owner watches. The Remote Assistance feature, described in the next sidebar "Using Remote Assistance", as well as VNC, both overcome this limitation.

Using Remote Assistance

The Remote Assistance feature is optional, but can make it easier for less-experienced users to transmit the required information to the person who will be accessing her computer remotely, including the IP address and user account.

On the PC to be controlled (the host), open the System page in Control Panel and click the **Remote settings** link on the left side. Turn on the **Allow Remote Assistance invitations to be sent from this computer** option, and then click the **Remote Assistance** link in this window to open the Remote Assistance dialog (or launch `rcimlby -launchra`).

Here, you have the option of using Windows Messenger (Microsoft Live/Passport account required) or your default email program (set in the **Programs** tab of Internet Options) to send the invitation. When asked to type a personal message, just leave it blank. You can also choose a special password for the person connecting to your computer, which is useful if you don't want to give the remote user your normal password.

Since an open invitation can be a security hazard, there are two safeguards in place to automatically disable the feature after a specified amount of time. In the **Remote** tab of the System Properties window, click **Advanced** to disable the feature completely after a few days. Plus, when sending an invitation, you can configure it only to expire an hour or two after being sent.

Keep it windowed

While you can have your Remote Desktop session fill your screen, it makes things simpler to have it in a window you move around. To do this, set the resolution of the remote desktop lower than the resolution of the *local* desktop. For example, if you're using a computer with a display resolution of 1280 × 1024, use the **Display** tab of the Remote Desktop Connection Properties window to set the remote desktop to no more than 1024×768. (Note that this setting will have no effect on the remote computer's normal desktop size once you log out.)

Share files, too

As nice as it would be to drag files into (and out of) the Remote Desktop window to transfer them (rather like Windows Virtual PC), this isn't a reality (yet). Instead, you can use traditional file sharing over your local network connection, as described in Chapter 8. Or, if you're connecting across the Internet, you can use the Remote Desktop's built-in file transfer feature. On the Remote Desktop Connection window, click **Options**, choose the **Local Resources** tab, and then click **More**. Expand the Drives branch and place a checkmark next to any drive on the local PC you'd like to share with the remote host. Then, after you connect, those drives will appear in Windows Explorer inside the Remote Desktop session.

Control a Windows 7 Home edition PC, as well as Macs, Linux, etc.

The Remote Desktop Protocol (RDP) is not your only choice when it comes to controlling a computer remotely. Although there are several commercial alternatives available, one of the most widely-supported is VNC, of which there are tons of derivatives. One of the best is UltraVNC (*http://www.uvnc.com/*), which happily supports Windows 7.

Among other things, VNC has the advantage of a very small "viewer" executable that doesn't even need to be installed on the client PC, and there's a version available for almost every platform on Earth (remember Palm OS?). It also lets both the person sitting in front of the PC and the person controlling it remotely view the desktop and even interact simultaneously.

 If given the choice, run the VNC server application as a "service" (controlled through *services.msc*), which is much more reliable than a mere icon in the Start menu's *Startup* folder.

The downside is that VNC doesn't use Windows resources as efficiently as Remote Desktop, so performance may suffer over slower connections.

Punch through any firewall

If you run into a problem getting Remote Desktop or VNC working through a firewall, proxy, or router, or you simply need to get a connection up and running fast, try GoToMyPC (*http://www.gotomypc.com/*). It's a web-based service that tends to work when the others fail, and doesn't require any special software apart from a web browser. Short sessions are free; longer sessions require a paid subscription.

Manage the Name Server (DNS) Cache

As mentioned a few times elsewhere in this chapter, a name server (or DNS) is a machine that translates IP addresses to domain names and back again. For example, when you type *http://www.oreilly.com* into your web browser's address bar, Windows sends a request to your service provider's name server, and the name server responds with something like 209.204.146.22, allowing your browser to contact the web server and download the requested page.

Each time such a DNS (Domain Naming System) lookup is performed, the information is stored in the DNS cache so Windows doesn't have to query the name server over and over again. The DNS cache is emptied when you shut down Windows, which is why it can take a little longer to find websites just after you've booted up.

The following two solutions allow you to change the way Windows interacts with its DNS cache, and will affect all applications that access the Internet (not just your web browser).

Part 1: Increase the size of the DNS cache

A larger DNS cache will mean fewer trips to the name server and faster overall performance. Start by opening the Registry Editor (see Chapter 3) and expanding the branches to HKEY_LOCAL_MACHINE\SYSTEM\CurrentControlSet\Services\Dnscache\Parameters.

Add the following four DWORD values by going to **Edit→New→DWORD Value**. Then, enter the numeric data specified by double-clicking and selecting the **Decimal** option:

- CacheHashTableBucketSize, set to 1
- CacheHashTableSize, set tot 384
- MaxCacheEntryTtlLimit, set to 64000
- MaxSOACacheEntryTtlLimit, set to 301

Remember, these are **Decimal** values (not **Hexadecimal** values). Close the Registry Editor when you're done. You'll have to restart Windows for this change to take effect.

Part 2: Add a permanent entry to the DNS cache

Adding a permanent entry to the DNS cache always overrides the information provided by the name server. There are several reasons you might want to do this, including temporarily working around a genuine DNS problem; if a name server gives the wrong address for a server, a permanent entry may restore access.

But you can also add intentionally incorrect information to block requests sent by some spyware and stop some pop-up ads when you visit web pages. Go to *http://www.mvps.org/winhelp2002/hosts.htm* for a list of known tracking hosts, or better yet, install a browser add-on like Adblock Plus (*http://adblockplus .org/*) for Firefox or Adblock (*http://chromeadblock.com/*) for Chrome.

The other advantage to permanent entries in the DNS cache is improved lookup performance. If you frequently access a particular server, and you know its IP address isn't likely to change anytime soon, you can add a permanent entry to eliminate the initial delay as Windows looks it up. For example, add an entry for your mail server to decrease the time it takes to check for mail.

Providing incorrect information here can prevent you from accessing certain remote servers, which is a tactic used by some malware. Use care when modifying the permanent DNS entry table; although it's not too difficult to fix later on, it may be *very* difficult to remember what you did.

To create and modify the list of permanent DNS entries, open Windows Explorer and navigate to the *C:\Windows\System32\Drivers\etc* folder. Look for a file called *hosts* (no filename extension). If it's not there, create a new, empty text file and typing `hosts` (with no extension) for the filename. Fire up your favorite text editor (or Notepad) in Administrator mode—right-click and select **Run as Administrator**—and then open the *hosts* file.

A standard entry looks like this:

```
207.46.230.218 www.microsoft.com
```

The first part is the IP address, and the second part (separated by a tab or several spaces) is the domain name. Keep in mind that variations like *http:// www.microsoft.com* and *http://microsoft.com* aren't necessarily the same server and may represent different DNS entries. You'll need to add a separate *hosts* entry for each variation if you want to access them all, like this:

```
207.46.230.218 www.microsoft.com
207.46.230.218 microsoft.com
```

Using this syntax, add an entry for each domain you wish to hardcode into Windows' DNS table. Note that these addresses affect your machine only; other machines, such as those in your workgroup or (obviously) others on the Internet, won't be affected.

If you already have a *hosts* file, you may also see some lines that begin with the # character; these are comments, and they are ignored by Windows. It's good practice to add a comment with each new entry, explaining the reason for the entry and the date and time it was made. You can also deactivate entries without deleting them by adding a # character to the beginning of the line.

Save the *hosts* file when you're done. The change should take effect immediately, although you may have to flush the DNS cache, next, before you can use this information.

Part 3: Flush the DNS cache

If the IP address of an Internet server ever changes during a Windows session, it'll look like the server is down until you reboot. To "flush" the cache, open a Command Prompt in Administrator mode (see Chapters 9 and 8 respectively). At the prompt, type:

```
ipconfig /flushdns
```

and press **Enter**. If all goes well, you'll see:

```
Successfully flushed the DNS Resolver Cache
```

and you can resume surfing and be sure you're only getting fresh DNS information.

But if you still have problems contacting a server, your ISP's DNS servers may still be sending you a stale address. To test this, open a Command Prompt window and type:

```
nslookup www.servername.net
```

where *www.servername.net* is the host name you're trying to connect to. Then, open a web browser and look up the host at *http://www.kloth.net/services/ nslookup.php*, *http://www.zoneedit.com/lookup.html*, or *http://network-tools .com/nslook/*. If the IP address these services report matches the one you get from the nslookup command, it's probably correct, and the server may either be down or blocked by a firewall.

Secure Your Networked PC

Some people spend their whole lives working to improve security for individuals and corporations alike, and they spend much of that time patching holes in Windows. Windows is the main conduit for malware that creates zombies

---

(bots), explained in Chapter 6, and that's just the tip of the iceberg. To be fair, the overwhelming popularity of Windows is largely to blame, but there are enough holes in Windows 7 to make you wonder whether anyone in Redmond, WA, is taking this seriously.

There are three basic categories of security threats. First, there's the deliberate, targeted attack by a human being trying to break into your computer over a network connection. Then there's the targeted attack by a human sitting at your keyboard. And finally, there's the automated attack perpetrated by a worm or other kind of malware.

Windows 7, and Vista before it, includes User Account Control to help stem the tide of unintentional and unwanted software installations—this is covered in Chapter 8, along with passwords and encryption—but your network connection is where most of this stuff comes from in the first place, so it's a good place to start securing your PC.

Windows 7 includes several features that will enable you to implement a reasonable level of security without purchasing additional software or hardware. Unfortunately, few of these features are in effect by default. The following are backdoors that you shouldn't overlook:

UPnP bad

Another feature, called Universal Plug-and-Play (UPnP), can open additional vulnerabilities on your network. UPnP could more aptly be called *Network Plug and Play*, since it only deals with network devices. UPnP is a collection of standards that allow newly connected devices to announce their presence to UPnP servers on your network, much in the same way as USB devices announce their presence to Windows' own plug-and-play system.

On the surface, UPnP sounds like a good idea. But in practice, the lack of authentication in the UPnP standard and the ease at which malware can use UPnP to punch holes in your firewall and create port forwarding rules in your router, make UPnP nothing but trouble. Now, UPnP is used by some games, most media extenders, instant messaging, Remote Assistance, and the like, which is why it's turned on by default in Windows 7 and many network devices. But if you don't need it, you can turn it off.

 If you choose **Public network** when first connecting to a new network or through the Networking and Sharing Center, UPnP is disabled by default.

To disable UPnP, open the Services window (*services.msc*). Find the **SSDP Discovery Service** in the list and then click the square **Stop** button on the toolbar to stop the service. Doing so should also stop the **UPnP Device Host** service; if not, stop it as well. Now test any applications or devices you suspect might use network discovery, like media servers or extenders. If you don't have any such products, you can permanently turn off UPnP by double-clicking each service, and from the **Startup type** list, select **Disabled**. Otherwise, the services will start back up the next time you boot Windows.

Next, open your router's configuration page (described earlier in this chapter) and turn off the UPnP service to prevent applications from automatically setting up new port forwarding rules. If your router doesn't give you control over UPnP, consider updating the firmware as explained in "Upgrade Your Router" on page 443.

Open ports bad

Look for vulnerabilities in your system by scanning for open ports, as discussed later in this chapter.

Remote Desktop good, but only when you need it

The Remote Desktop feature, described in the section "Control a PC Remotely" on page 488, is enabled by default in the Windows 7 Professional and Ultimate editions. Unless you specifically need this feature, it should be disabled. In Control Panel, open System and then click the **Remote settings** link on the left. In the **Remote** tab of the System Properties window, turn off the **Allow Remote Assistance connections to this computer** option, and select the **Don't allow connections to this computer** option, beneath it.

Passwords good

In theory, file sharing doesn't work for accounts that have no password, which is the default when you create a new user account. But a password-less account offers no protection from someone sitting at your keyboard, and if it's an administrator-level account, can open the door to every other account on the machine. Again, see Chapter 8 for user accounts and passwords.

Homegroups and file sharing good, usually

Every shared folder is potentially an open door, so share only the folders you need to share, and be mindful of the permissions on the files and the sharing permissions, which, in Windows 7, are two different things. See Chapter 8.

Sharing Wizard bad

One of the main reasons to set up a workgroup is to share files and printers with other computers. But it's wise to share only those folders that need to be shared, and disable sharing for all others. A feature called **Use Sharing Wizard**, introduced in Chapter 2 and examined in Chapter 8, doesn't give you full control over who can view and modify your files.

Administrative shares bad

Administrative shares, also covered in Chapter 8, shares every drive on your PC whether you explicitly share folders on those drives or not.

Firewall good

Set up a firewall, covered next, to strictly control network traffic into and out of your computer, but don't expect the included Windows Firewall software to be all the protection you need.

The Action Center good, until you stop listening

The Action Center, shown in Figure 7-28, is a central page in Control Panel used to keep tabs on the Windows Firewall, Windows Defender, User Account Control, and automatic updating. It also monitors your antivirus software, but for purely political reasons, Windows 7 includes no antivirus functionality of its own.

Above all, the Action Center is a monitoring tool. If it sees that a particular security measure is turned on—whether or not that tool is actively doing its job—the Action Center is happy, and you won't see any messages to the contrary.

 Tired of Action Center messages? Click the **Change Action Center settings** link to the left to choose which issues are worth reporting and which are worth ignoring. Although you can effectively disable the Action Center messages by turning off all the options on this page, you'll need to open the Services window (*services.msc*) and disable the **Action Center** services in the list to deactivate the feature altogether. Of course, doing so won't actually disable the firewall, antivirus, or automatic update features you may be using, only the monitoring of these tools and the messages that go along with them.

But you can't actually change firewall or antimalware settings in the Action Center; instead, return to Control Panel and open the respective tool there.

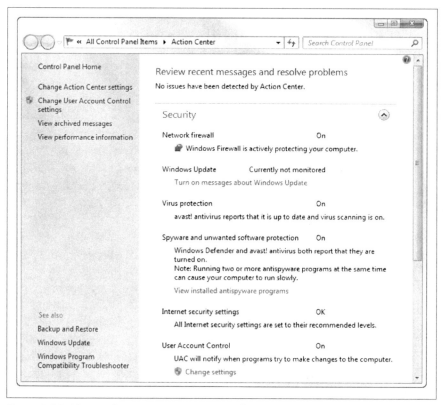

Figure 7-28. The Windows Action Center goes a long way to make Windows appear safer

Put Up a Firewall

A firewall is a layer of protection that permits or denies network communication based on a predefined set of rules. These rules restrict communication so that only certain applications are permitted to use your network connection. This effectively closes some backdoors to your computer that otherwise might be exploited by hackers, certain types of viruses, and other malicious applications.

For the most part, you can leave Windows Firewall alone and never touch it. Unlike the early firewall debacle that came with Windows XP, the one in Windows 7 is not booby-trapped to prevent file sharing or the Internet time feature. In fact, it's pretty unobtrusive, bothering you only if it detects a program it hasn't seen before.

The biggest problem with Windows Firewall is that it can be so easily defeated by software. While Windows does prompt you when a program tries to initiate a blocked connection, smart installers and applications can create new rules in the firewall without your approval. Of course, routers can be compromised by software as well, but not as easily, particularly if you've turned off your router's support for UPnP (discussed in the previous section).

One of the main reasons a router is so effective is that it provides a layer of abstraction between your network and the outside world. Consider a single packet of incoming data: if your PC is connected directly to the source of the threat (no router), all that packet has to do is sneak in through one of Windows Firewall's exceptions (explained later), and it's home free. But with a router, that incoming packet hits a wall once it reaches your network; unless you enable the *port forwarding* feature described in "Control a PC Remotely" on page 488, that packet will have nowhere to go. This means of security through obscurity. (See also *"UPnP bad,"* which can create port forwarding rules without user intervention.)

To illustrate another difference between the security offered by the Windows Firewall versus that afforded by a router, consider Figure 7-29. The larger dotted rectangle shows what's protected by your router's firewall, and the smaller rectangle shows what's protected by Windows. The difference in scope allows you to safely transfer files between PCs in your LAN without sharing them with the rest of the world.

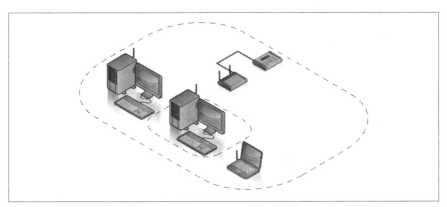

Figure 7-29. The larger dotted box shows the scope of protection offered by a router; the smaller box shows the scope of the Windows Firewall

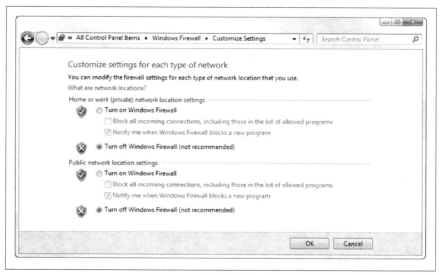

Figure 7-30. Turn off Windows Firewall temporarily to see whether it is indeed causing the problem

Now, assuming you've bought the previous argument, you might think that more firewall is better—that using Windows Firewall along with a router will protect your system better than a router alone. The problem with this approach is that, again referring to Figure 7-29, Windows Firewall somewhat isolates your PC from the other computers in your workgroup. This can be good, in that viruses and other spyware on other PCs on your network will have a harder time infecting your PC (a particularly useful feature when you're surfing on a public network), or it can be bad, in that the Windows Firewall can break features you use every day.

 If you're on the road, and not behind the protective veil of your router's firewall, you should always use Windows Firewall or some other software-based firewall to help protect your PC from other riff-raff lurking on public networks you use.

Unlike previous versions of Windows, the Windows 7 Firewall isn't enabled or disabled for individual network connections, but rather for each generalization—Home, Work, Public—found in the Network and Sharing Center. On the Windows Firewall page in Control Panel, click the **Turn Windows Firewall on or off** link on the left to choose what sort of protection you want for Home and Public locations, as shown in Figure 7-30.

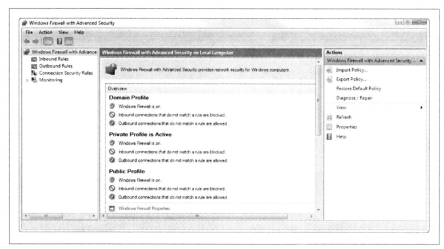

Figure 7-31. The secret Windows Firewall with Advanced Security window lets you fine-tune inbound rules, enable outbound rules, and even log firewall activity

If you suspect that Windows Firewall is preventing an application from working, try turning it off temporarily. If that fixes the problem, it's time to create a new rule.

Poke holes in the firewall

The real control over the Firewall isn't in Control Panel; to open the "Windows Firewall with Advanced Security" window shown in Figure 7-31, click the **Advanced settings** link on the Windows Firewall page (or run *wf.msc*).

On a day-to-day basis, the Windows Firewall creates new rules on the fly as it needs them. When it detects that a program it hasn't seen before wants to open a port, it'll ask your permission. Whether you choose to grant or deny the request, Windows Firewall makes a new rule, and that rule remains in effect indefinitely, or until you change it.

 Application installers can create new Firewall rules, too, so it's a good idea to periodically check the Windows Firewall with Advanced Security window for rules currently in effect.

Here's how to create a new Firewall rule manually. Click the **Inbound Rules** category in the left pane, and then click **New Rule** in the right pane to show the New Inbound Rule Wizard (Figure 7-32).

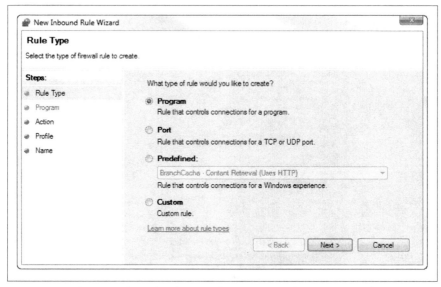

Figure 7-32. The New Inbound Rule Wizard gives you much more control than the feeble Windows Firewall window in Control Panel

For the **Rule Type**, choose one of the following:

Program

Use this to give a specific application free reign over your Internet connection. This is the easiest way to fix an application that has been broken by Windows Firewall's restrictions, but it can be risky if you're not exactly sure how that application will use its new freedom.

Port

This option exposes a TCP/IP port (see Appendix B) that can be used (read *exploited*) by any application.

Predefined

Choose this if you want to create a rule for a built-in Windows service. Note that this selection doesn't start or stop the service, it only instructs Windows Firewall to permit or block it; use the Services window (*services.msc*) to enable or disable Windows services.

Custom

Use **Custom** if you want to make a rule that involves both a specific application and a specific port simultaneously, something you can't do with the Windows Firewall window in Control Panel.

Click **Next** when you're done; what happens next depends on the type of rule you're creating:

- If you chose **Program** or **Custom**, the subsequent **Program** step lets you associate the rule with all programs, or a specific *.exe* file.

- If you chose **Port** or **Custom**, the subsequent **Protocol and Ports** step asks you to specify a port number. Most of the time, you'll want to select **TCP** from the **Protocol type** list and **Specific Ports** from the **Local port** list. Below **Local port**, type one or more port numbers used by the connection to be governed by your new rule; see Appendix B for more information on TCP/IP ports.

Next, the **Scope** step gives you the opportunity to fine-tune the rule by providing the IP addresses of the PCs involved in the connection. The local IP address (the top box) is basically your PC, so in most cases, you'll want to leave the **Any IP address** default selected. But below, you can select **These IP addresses** and then add the addresses of specific remote PCs; that way, you can be extra careful and, say, open a port only when a trusted PC wants to connect.

The **Action** step is more or less self-explanatory. By default, Windows Firewall blocks all inbound data except when a rule instructs it to let the data through, so typically you'll want to choose **Allow the connection** here.

The **Profile** step lets you choose when this rule is in effect; this is covered in more detail shortly.

Finally, use the **Name** and **Description** fields to label your new rule so you can find it easily in the list later on, and then click **Finish** when you're done. The new exception will take effect immediately, at which point you can test the new exception. You may have to experiment with different firewall rules until your software or service works properly.

In most of the pages in the Windows Firewall with Advanced Security window, settings are divided into three "profiles," used at different times depending on the type of network Windows thinks you're using at the moment:

Private Profile
> The settings in this profile are automatically put into effect when you choose **Home** or **Work** when Windows asks you to select a network location. This is typical of a home or small-office network, protected by a router, and with folder and printer sharing (explained in Chapter 8) in effect.

Public Profile
> This is the profile used when you choose **Public location**, such as when you connect wirelessly to a public hotspot.

*Figure 7-33. Click the **Windows Firewall Properties** link to choose whether or not to block Inbound and Outbound connections, change notification options, and enable logging*

Domain Profile

This firewall profile is active when your PC is part of a corporate network with a domain controller.

By default, the assortment of settings in each of these profiles is more or less the same, but the inbound and outbound rules are typically different. To change the settings shown on the summary page in Figure 7-31, click the **Windows Firewall Properties** link, and choose the tab corresponding to the profile you want to configure, as shown in Figure 7-33.

Here, you can make a pretty substantive change: from the **Outbound connections** list, select **Block** to give Windows Firewall control over data flowing in both directions (rather than just inbound data). This option won't necessarily be trouble-free until you take the time to customize the outbound rules in the main window. But it can, for instance, let you contain a virus outbreak on a PC without completely severing the network connection you may need in order to make repairs.

Click the **Customize** button in the **Logging** section to have Windows Firewall keep a log of data it blocks in a text file you choose. Although logging enables you to see exactly what the firewall is doing behind the scenes, the real value is in troubleshooting. For instance, if you know Windows Firewall is interfering with a specific application, but you want to know exactly what the application is trying to do before you grant it permission, check the log. To use your router for logging, see "Scan Your System for Open Ports" on page 509.

Alternatives to Windows Firewall

The Firewall that comes with Windows 7 is better than its predecessors, but it still may not provide the ease-of-use or flexibility of a third-party program. Here are some alternative solutions:

- Agnitum Outpost (*http://www.agnitum.com*)
- Kerio Personal Firewall (*http://www.kerio.com*)
- 7 Firewall Control (*http://www.sphinx-soft.com*)

 Be careful, however, when installing and configuring a third-party firewall solution, including the ones discussed here. Overly strict firewall rules may break some software on your system. Worse yet, overly lenient rules may not protect your computer adequately and only give you a false sense of security. Check out the PC Flank Leaktest at *http://www.pcflank.com/* if you want to test your firewall.

No matter which firewall solution you choose, however, you'll most likely still need to take the time to configure custom rules using a similar procedure to the one described earlier in this section.

Scan Your System for Open Ports

Each open network port on your computer is a potential security vulnerability, and while Windows has a tendency to leave more ports open than it needs, the real concern is any ports left open by applications or malware. Fortunately, there's a way to scan your computer for open ports so you know which holes to patch.

Start by opening a Command Prompt window (*cmd.exe*). Then, run the Active Connections utility by typing:

```
netstat /a /o
```

The /a option tells `netstat` to show all applications listening for inbound connections; without it, only ports participating in active connections would appear. And the /o option shows the owning process of each port (explained shortly). The report will be displayed in the Command Prompt window, and will look something like this:

```
Active Connections
Proto  Local Address      Foreign Address            State          PID
TCP    annoy:pop3         localhost:4219             TIME_WAIT        0
TCP    annoy:3613         javascript-of-unknown:0    LISTENING     1100
TCP    annoy:3613         localhost:3614             ESTABLISHED   1100
TCP    annoy:3614         localhost:3613             ESTABLISHED   1100
UDP    annoy:1035         *:*                                      1588
UDP    annoy:1036         *:*                                      1588
UDP    annoy:1037         *:*                                      1588
UDP    annoy:1038         *:*                                      1588
UDP    annoy:1039         *:*                                      1588
```

 The width of the Command Prompt window is typically limited to 80 characters, causing some pretty ugly word-wrapping. To send the report to a text file (say, *report.txt*) for easier viewing in Notepad, type `netstat /a /o > report.txt` at the prompt.

The Active Connections utility displays its information in these five columns:

Proto

This will either be TCP or UDP, representing the protocol being used (see Appendix B).

Local Address

This column has two components, separated by a colon. The first part is the computer name, which will typically be the name of your computer. The second part will either be a port number or the name of a service. See Appendix B for help deciphering the port numbers that appear here and in the `Foreign Address` column, detailed next.

Foreign Address

For active connections, this will be the name or IP address of the remote machine, followed by a colon, and then the port number being used. For inactive connections (showing only the open ports), you'll typically see only *:*.

State

This shows the state of the connection (TCP ports only). For example, for server processes, you'll usually see LISTENING here, signifying that the process has opened the port and is waiting for an incoming connection.

For connections originating from your computer, such as a web browser downloading a page or an active Telnet session, you'll see ESTABLISHED here.

PID

This is the Process Identifier of the application or service that is responsible for opening the port.

To find out more about a particular PID, open Task Manager (launch *taskmgr.exe* or right-click an empty area of your taskbar and select **Task Manager**), and choose the **Processes** tab. If you don't see a column labeled **PID**, go to **View→Select Columns**, turn on the **PID (Process Identifier)** option, and click OK. Finally, turn on the **Show processes from all users** option at the bottom of the Windows Task Manager window. You can then sort the listing by PID by clicking the **PID** column header. The corresponding program filename is shown in the **Image Name** column.

Next, open the Resource Monitor shown in Figure 7-34, by opening the Performance Monitor and then clicking the **Open Resource Monitor** link (or run perfmon.exe /res). Choose the **Network** tab to view a live list of applications using your network connection, complete with the aforementioned PID, bytes sent and received, and even the foreign address to which they're connected. You can even sort by network usage and find the processes most responsible for hogging your connection.

This means that you can use the Active Connections Utility in conjunction with the Windows Task Manager, as described here, to look up the program responsible for opening any network port on your computer.

 Don't be alarmed if you see a lot of open ports. Just make sure you track down each one, making sure it doesn't pose a security threat.

You may see *svchost.exe* listed in the Windows Task Manager, and reported by the Active Connections utility as being responsible for one or more open ports. This program is merely used to start the services listed in the Services window (*services.msc*). For an example of a service 7 runs by default, but shouldn't for security reasons, see the discussion of Universal Plug-and-Play in "*UPnP bad*," earlier in this chapter.

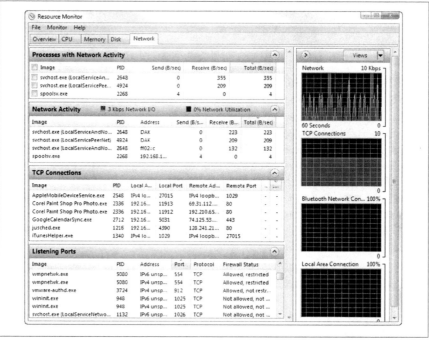

*Figure 7-34. The **Network** tab of the Resource Monitor lists all of the programs using your network connection*

Use an external port scanner

If you're using a firewall, such as the Windows Firewall feature built in to Windows, it should block communication to most of the currently open ports, even though they're listed by the Active Connections utility.

For this reason, you may prefer to use an external port scanner, a program that can connect to your computer through an Internet connection to check for all open ports, and do it more aggressively than the Active Connections utility. Here are some example utilities that you can run from your own computer:

- Nmap Security Scanner (*http://nmap.org/*)
- AATools Port Scanner (*http://www.glocksoft.com/port_scanner.htm*)

Or, using one of these websites will allow you to perform port scans right from your web browser:

- PC Flank Advanced Port Scanner (*http://www.pcflank.com/*)
- Open Ports Tool (*http://www.yougetsignal.com/tools/open-ports/*)
- Microsoft Baseline Security Analyzer (*http://www.microsoft.com/mbsa*)

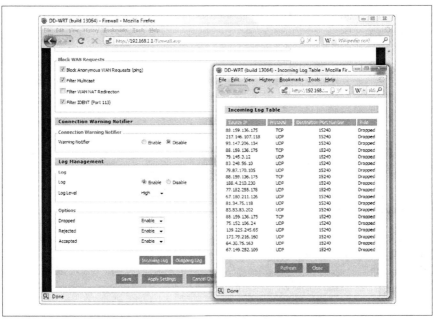

Figure 7-35. Use incoming and outgoing router logs to see what your firewall catches and what it lets through

Among other things, you can use these services to test the effectiveness of your firewall. If a port scanner cannot detect any open ports, cannot determine your computer name, and cannot detect any running services, then you're in good shape!

Use your router log

A port scanner can only find holes it's designed to look for. If you're still seeing flashing activity lights on your router even after everything has supposedly been locked down, the next step is to enable your router's incoming and outgoing logs to see what's actually happening.

Logging is typically disabled by default, so pay a visit to your router's setup page and enable logging, as shown in Figure 7-35. If your router doesn't support logging, see "Upgrade Your Router" on page 443 .

In the example shown in Figure 7-35, you can choose whether to log **Dropped** (blocked) packets, **Rejected** (blocked with a reply) packets, and **Accepted** (passed through) packets. Set the **Log** option to **Enable** and choose how verbose you'd like your log to be (**Log Level**). Make sure you close any applications and turn off or disconnect any devices that use your Internet connection, and then click **Apply Settings** to begin logging.

If there is genuine activity, it should take only a few seconds for new entries to show up in the log. Click **Outgoing log** to see the activity initiated by your PC, or **Incoming log** to see attempted connections from the outside world. The log should show the IP address, port number, and whether the data was blocked or permitted. If you see any suspicious activity, check Appendix B to look up the ports involved, and the `nslookup` tool (via the Command Prompt) to see who's on the other end.

Don't be surprised if you see a lot of unsolicited activity in these logs. Although a lot of it is malicious, it doesn't necessarily mean you're vulnerable: remember, the log shows attempted connections, even those that failed.

Web and Email

The Web makes our world simultaneously bigger and smaller; it's hard to imagine computing—or even a meal—without a web browser within reach. It's also hard to forget everything that comes along for the ride, such as pop ups, spam, and the constant reminders that "your privacy may be at risk."

Lock Down Internet Explorer

Over the years, Microsoft has fixed hundreds of security holes in Internet Explorer, and if you've been using the Windows Update feature regularly, you already have the benefit of all their sweat and tears sitting on your hard disk. But the larger issue is IE's underlying design—and its cozy connection with the underlying operating system—that has caused so much trouble all these years.

The premise is that a web page can contain code that instructs Internet Explorer to install software on your PC. In the early days, web designers used this capability sparingly, mostly to install widgets and small helper programs to add trivial features to their pages. But it didn't take long for unscrupulous hackers and greedy corporate executives to learn how to exploit Internet Explorer's open-door nature, which is why we now have spyware, adware, browser hijackers, rootkits, and other nasty surprises.

Microsoft finally addressed many of Internet Explorer's unfortunate short-comings in IE8, which comes with Windows 7, and not a moment too soon. But just because IE now looks for signed code and has a list of malicious websites at its disposal, doesn't mean it can't still be a conduit for malicious software. Thanks to the *strategy tax* explained in the preface, you have two choices: hobble Internet Explorer by turning off the most dangerous features, use a different browser, or both.

If you're using Mozilla Firefox, discussed later, avoid the *Microsoft .NET Framework Assistant (ClickOnce)* add-on like the plague. It adds to Firefox the same core vulnerability of Internet Explorer, namely the ability for websites to easily and quietly install software on your PC, and is installed surreptitiously with several Windows updates. Since this design flaw is one of the reasons you may've originally switched to Firefox in the first place, you'd be wise to remove it. If you find the **Uninstall** button grayed out in Firefox, see *http://www.annoy ances.org/exec/show/article08-600* for removal instructions.

If you want to stick with Internet Explorer for now, open the Internet Options window in Control Panel (or from the **Tools** drop-down in IE, select **Internet Options**). Choose the **Security** tab, and turn on the **Enable Protected Mode** option if it's not already enabled. Then select the **Internet** "zone" icon at the top (the globe), and then click **Custom Level** below to open the Security Settings dialog box shown in Figure 7-36.

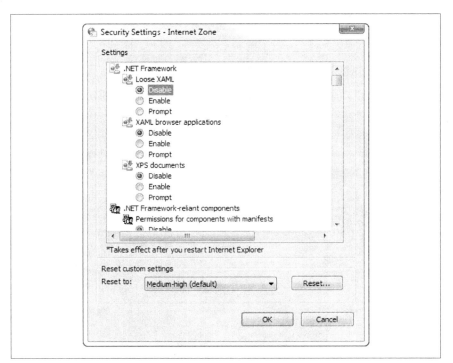

Figure 7-36. Use the Security Settings window to turn off some of the more dangerous Internet Explorer features

Next, go down the list, and set the options as follows. (Note that your list may differ slightly as the result of recent updates from Microsoft.)

Option	Set to...
.NET Framework→	
Loose XAML	Disable
XAML browser applications	Disable (!)
XPS documents	Disable
.NET Framework-reliant components→	
Permissions for components with manifests	Disable (!)
Run components not signed with Authenticode	Disable (!)
Run components signed with Authenticode	Disable
ActiveX controls and plug-ins→	
Allow previously unused ActiveX controls to run without prompt	Disable (!)
Allow Scriptlets	Disable
Automatic prompting for ActiveX controls	Disable
Binary and script behaviors	Administrator approved
Display video and animation on a web page that does not use external media player	Disable
Download signed ActiveX controls	Disable (!)
Download unsigned ActiveX controls	Disable (!)
Initialize and script ActiveX controls not marked as safe for scripting	Disable (!)
Only allow approved domains to use ActiveX without prompt	Enable
Run ActiveX controls and plug-ins	Administrator approved
Script ActiveX controls marked safe for scripting	Disable
Downloads→	
Automatic prompting for file downloads	Disable
File download	Enable
Font download	Prompt or Disable
Enable .NET Framework setup	Disable
Miscellaneous→	
Access data sources across domains	Disable
Allow META REFRESH	Enable
Allow scripting of Internet Explorer Web browser control	Disable
Allow script-initiated windows without size or position constraints	Disable
Allow web pages to use restricted protocols for active content	Disable

Option	Set to...
Allow websites to open windows without address or status bars	Disable
Display mixed content	Prompt
Don't prompt for client certificate selection...	Disable
Drag-and-drop or copy and paste files	Enable
Include local directory path when uploading files to a server	Disable (!)
Installation of desktop items	Disable (!)
Launching applications and unsafe files	Disable (!)
Launching programs and files in an IFRAME	Disable (!)
Navigate subframes across different domains	Prompt
Open files based on content, not file extension	Enable
Submit non-encrypted form data	Enable
Use Pop-up Blocker	Enable (!)
Use SmartScreen Filter	Enable (!)
Userdata persistence	Enable
Websites in less privileged web content zone can navigate...	Enable
Scripting→	
Active Scripting	Prompt
Allow Programmatic clipboard access	Disable (!)
Allow status bar updates via script	Disable (!)
Allow websites to prompt for information using scripted windows	Disable
Enable XSS filter	Enable
Scripting of Java applets	Enable
User Authentication→	
Logon	Anonymous logon

Click OK when you're done changing security settings.

 Setting the **Launching applications and unsafe files** option may have consequences even if you use Mozilla Firefox to download files. If Firefox tells you that a "download has been blocked by your Security Zone Policy," try changing this option to **Prompt** instead of **Disable**.

Next, click the **Trusted sites** (green checkmark) icon, click the **Sites** button, and turn off the **Require server verification (https:) for all sites in this zone** option. Type the following URLs into the **Add this Web site to the zone** field, clicking the **Add** button after each one:

```
http://*.update.microsoft.com
https://*.update.microsoft.com
http://*.windowsupdate.com
http://*.windowsupdate.microsoft.com
```

These four URLs permit the Windows Update feature to continue working unencumbered by your new security settings. The asterisks are wildcards allowing these rules to apply to variants, such as *http://download.windowsupdate.com*. Feel free to add the domains for other websites you trust, and then click OK when you're done.

Now that you see what's required to make Internet Explorer safer (albeit not bulletproof), you might be tempted to dump IE entirely in favor of a design that doesn't put your PC quite so much at risk:

Mozilla Firefox

Available for free from *http://www.mozilla.com/*, Firefox is an open source, standards-compliant web browser that is safer and more feature-rich than Internet Explorer. It does a better job of blocking pop ups, has a more customizable interface than IE, and can be enhanced with powerful extensions (see "Improve Any Website" on page 526 for an example).

Google Chrome

Chrome, also free (*http://chrome.google.com/*), is the minimalist's browser. It's very fast, has support for extensions, and, like Firefox, there's no worry about drive-by installations or system-level access from the browser. On the downside, extensions support is in its infancy (compared with Firefox), as is its customizability.

Once you have another browser installed, you can disable IE altogether, as described in the "Turn Off Internet Explorer" sidebar.

Turn Off Internet Explorer

Thanks to a court settlement in the late 1990s, you can completely block Internet Explorer on your PC, a particularly effective tactic if you're setting up a PC for someone else and you don't want to have to come back six months later to cleanse it of spyware.

On the Default Programs page in Control Panel, click **Set program access and computer defaults**. In the window that appears, select **Custom**, and then click the little double-arrow icon on the right side to expand the category. In the **Choose a default Web browser** section, make sure your favorite web

---

browser is selected, and then next to the Internet Explorer entry, turn off the **Enable access to this program**.

When you're done, click **OK**; the change will take effect immediately. The IE icons will disappear, and you'll get an error if you try to launch *iexplore.exe*.

Want another, possibly more satisfying way to remove IE8? Open the Programs and Features page in Control Panel, and click the **Turn Windows features on or off** link on the left. On the Windows Features window that appears, clear the checkmark next to **Internet Explorer 8**, click OK, and then reboot Windows when prompted.

Note that some websites require Internet Explorer for full functionality, although such sites are dwindling rapidly with the rise of Firefox and Chrome.

Change Internet Shortcut Icons

Drag the bookmark icon from the Address Bar in your browser to your desktop, and you'll get an Internet Shortcut file you can use to open the site later on. If the shortcut is going to live on your desktop for a while, you may want to choose what it looks like.

Turns out the icon used for any given Internet Shortcut depends on a number of factors. The generic Internet Shortcut icon is a tiny white piece of paper emblazoned with the logo of your default browser (Internet Explorer, Firefox, Chrome, etc.). To change the generic, default icon, you'll need this Registry hack:

1. Open the Registry Editor (see Chapter 3) and expand the branches to `HKEY_CLASSES_ROOT\http\DefaultIcon`.

2. This key may be locked by default, so before you can make any changes, you'll probably need to unlock it. Right-click the `DefaultIcon` key and select **Permissions**. Click **Advanced**, and then choose the **Owner** tab. From the **Change owner to** list, select your username (or select **Administrators**) and turn on the **Replace owner on subcontainers and objects** option. Click OK and then OK again to close both windows.

   Right-click the `DefaultIcon` key *again* and select **Permissions**. From the **Group or user names** list, select your username (or, again, select **Administrators**), place a checkmark in the **Allow** column next to **Full Control**, and then click OK.

Networking and Internet

3. Inside the DefaultIcon key, double-click the (Default) value in the right pane, and type (or paste) the full path and filename of the icon you want to use, followed by a comma and a zero:

```
c:\icons\maeby.ico,0
```

4. Click OK and then close the Registry Editor. If the change doesn't take effect immediately, restart Windows.

5. To prevent Windows from undoing this change during the next Internet Explorer update, lock the DefaultIcon key, as described in "Prevent Changes to a Registry Key" on page 154.

If an originating website has a *favicon*—a custom shortcut icon—the Internet Shortcut file you create will inherit the site's icon rather than the generic one. Unfortunately, this only works in Internet Explorer; both Firefox and Chrome ignore favicons when creating Internet Shortcut files.

 Want to add a favicon to a Firefox-generated Internet Shortcut? Start by installing the getFavicon add-on for Firefox (free from *https://addons.mozilla.org/en-US/firefox/addon/9548*). Then, navigate to the site in question, click the getFavicon icon on the your Address Bar, and save the icon file to a folder on your hard disk. When that's done, right-click the Internet Shortcut you want to customize, select **Properties**, click **Change Icon**, and locate the icon file you just saved.

Fix broken Internet Shortcut icons

Windows 7 finally fixes a longstanding problem that caused many Internet Shortcuts to be created incorrectly, resulting in broken or blank icons, or shortcuts that won't open the originating sites. If you have any of these Shortcuts left over from earlier versions of Windows, here's how to fix them.

First, drag the Internet Shortcut onto any plain text editor like Notepad. The simplest Internet Shortcut (*.url* file) looks like this:

```
[InternetShortcut]
URL=http://annoyances.org/
```

If you've chosen a custom icon by right-clicking and selecting **Properties**, then you'll also see an IconFile entry, like this:

```
IconFile=C:\icons\toad.ico
IconIndex=0
```

Problem is that a particularly long URL may fall victim to a line-length limit that causes the URL to wrap to the next line and disrupt any subsequent entries, like this:

```
[InternetShortcut]
URL=http://www.evilleagueofevil.org/members/badhorse/Thoroughbred_of_Sin/
file_downloads/new_member_application.pdf
IconFile=C:\icons\toad.ico
IconIndex=0
```

To fix the shortcut, put the URL all on one line, and then for good measure, move the URL entry to the end of the file. Save the file when you're done; you may have to log out and then log back in for Windows Explorer to recognize the change.

 You can also try the AM-free DeadLink tool (*http://www .aignes.com/deadlink.htm*), which can download favicons and scan your existing bookmarks, favorites, and shortcuts for dead links.

It's worth noting that Internet Shortcuts created by Internet Explorer 8 look like this:

```
[{000214A0-0000-0000-C000-000000000046}]
Prop3=19,2
[InternetShortcut]
URL=http://annoyances.org/
```

The first two lines allow the file to work with Windows 7's icon handler (covered in Chapter 3), which retrieves the favicon stored elsewhere and uses it for the file icon. To fix this type of icon, it's easiest to simply delete and recreate it.

Live with Firefox in an IE World

Ever found a website that won't let you in because you're using Firefox or some other browser instead of Internet Explorer? The problem is the *user agent* string, a text "signature" your browser sends to every website you visit that identifies the browser name and version, and even the operating system version you're using. For example, the user agent string for Internet Explorer 8.0 on the Windows 7 Ultimate edition looks like this:

```
Mozilla/4.0 (compatible; MSIE 8.0; Windows NT 6.1; WOW64;
Trident/4.0; SLCC2; .NET CLR 2.0.50727; .NET CLR 3.5.30729;
.NET CLR 3.0.30729; Media Center PC 6.0)
```

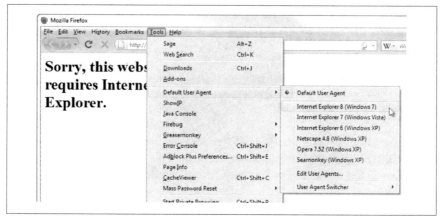

Figure 7-37. The User Agent Switcher can masquerade as IE to gain entry to sites that don't expressly support Firefox

On the other hand, Firefox 3.x looks like this to websites you visit:

```
Mozilla/5.0 (Windows; U; Windows NT 6.1; en-US; rv:1.9.2)
Gecko/20100115 Firefox/3.6
```

If you use Firefox (or any non-IE browser, for that matter), you'll occasionally encounter a website that won't cooperate. The problem is usually caused either by lazy developers who haven't made their websites standards-compliant, or corporate licensing restrictions that forbid developers from supporting any non-Microsoft products. The good news is, you can fool 'em all!

The User Agent Switcher Firefox add-on, available for free from *http://chrispe derick.com/work/useragentswitcher/*, allows Mozilla browsers to masquerade as any other browser, including Internet Explorer, good ol' Netscape 4, and even Opera. When you stumble upon an IE-only website, just go to **Tools→User Agent Switcher** and pick a browser, as shown in Figure 7-37.

Click **Options** to edit the browser list; you can even type in a custom user agent string and spoof a different version of Windows. What fun!

Of course, dressing up your browser as Internet Explorer doesn't necessarily mean the site will work like it's supposed to. Often, these sites require Internet Explorer because they employ proprietary IE features, such as the ActiveX add-ons that can open the door to spyware (see "Lock Down Internet Explorer" on page 514). In these cases, you must either view the page in IE or abandon the site. If you take the former course of action, you'll appreciate the IE View Firefox add-on, freely available from *http://ieview.mozdev.org/*. When you encounter a site that won't work properly in Firefox, just right-click an empty area of the page and select **View This Page in IE** or right-click any link on the page and select **Open Link Target in IE**.

Make Firefox more like IE

Firefox has a lot of advantages over Internet Explorer, but there are a few areas where Firefox is still playing catch-up. Fortunately, Mozilla's add-on catalog allows Firefox to do everything IE can do, and more.

To have Firefox use Windows 7's taskbar jump lists, just like Internet Explorer and Windows Explorer, install Winfox, free from *http://www.compugeeksoft ware.com/software/winfox.aspx*. Thereafter launch Firefox using the Winfox icon to add support for frequently used websites, window stacking, and download progress right in the taskbar icon.

Install the Grab and Drag extension, free from *https://addons.mozilla.org/en -US/firefox/addon/1250*, to make it possible to scroll any web page by clicking right on the page and dragging, much like the hand tool in Internet Explorer 8. With adjustable momentum, flick gestures, and other options, Grab and Drag is far more customizable than IE's version.

The Find dialog, allowing you to find text on the current page when you press **Ctrl-F**, is stuck at the bottom of the Firefox window, where it's hard to see and can be easily obscured by the Windows taskbar. To move it to the top of the Firefox window, install the free Find Toolbar Tweaks extension (*https: //addons.mozilla.org/en-US/firefox/addon/2585*). Then, from the list of Extensions on the Add-ons window, highlight **Find Toolbar Tweaks**, click **Options**, choose the **Advanced** tab, and turn on the **Move toolbar to upper area** option.

Lastly, Firefox came out with tabbed browser windows years before IE (although NetCaptor predated them both). Yet, only IE lets you easily disable tabbed browsing; in Firefox, you must install a free extension to get rid of tabs, as described next.

Opt Out of Tabbed Browsing

Some people like tabs because they can be used to reduce screen clutter, but if you don't specifically want to use them (for instance, if you like to view pages side-by-side), tabs are just a nuisance.

Fortunately, it's easy to do away with tabs in Internet Explorer. Just open the **Tools** drop-down, select **Internet Options**, and choose the **General** tab. In the **Tabs** section, click **Settings**, and turn off the **Enable Tabbed Browsing** option. Click OK and then OK again, and then close any open Internet Explorer windows for the change to take effect.

If you're using Firefox, turning off tabbed browsing is a little more involved. To disable all tabs in Firefox permanently, install the free Tab Killer extension available at *http://piro.sakura.ne.jp/xul/_tabkiller.html.en*, and then restart Firefox. Next, from Firefox's **Tools** menu, select **Add-ons**, highlight **Tab Killer**, and click **Options**. Choose **Ignore the request** to have new-tab links open in the same window, or **Open new window instead of new tab** to fill up your taskbar fast.

On the other side of the fence are those who despise the pile-up of windows, and are happy to put up with tabs to keep the browser window tidy. If you fall into this category (and you're a Firefox user), open the **Tools** menu, select **Options**, and in the **Tabs** category, turn on the **Open new windows in a new tab instead** option. For more control, install the Switch Windows Mode extension, free from *https://addons.mozilla.org/addon/3881*, or any of a thousand other tab-tweaking extensions on the Mozilla website.

If you don't want to turn off tabbed browsing or mess with add-ons, you can use keystrokes to control what happens when you click links:

Internet Explorer
> Hold **Ctrl** when clicking a link to open it in a new tab, or **Shift** to open it in a separate window. If you have IE's pop up blocker set to the highest filter level, you can also press **Ctrl-Alt** to temporarily allow pop ups from the site.

Firefox
> Like IE, hold **Ctrl** when clicking a link to open it in a new tab, or **Shift** to open it in a separate window. You can also hold **Alt** to save the link target on your hard disk.

Fix Symbols in Web Pages

Ever view a page with strange symbols in the text, particularly where you'd expect to see hyphens or apostrophes? Though it may look like a font or language problem, it's more likely that you just have the wrong code page selected.

The code page is the mapping of characters your browser uses to render text, and it must match the code page that was used to create the site. Usually your browser picks the correct one automatically, but if you've previously changed the code page (or if another website switched code pages on you), or if the website doesn't specify the correct code page, the site won't display properly.

In Internet Explorer, open the **Page** drop-down, and select **Encoding→Auto-Select**. If there's already a checkmark next to **Auto-Select**, or if that doesn't help, go to **Encoding→ More**, and choose the nationality that best matches the document you're viewing. The default code page for sites in English is **Western European (Windows)**.

In Firefox, go to **View→Character Encoding**, and select **Western (ISO-8859-1)** for sites in English, or another nationalization that more closely matches the site you're viewing. If you find yourself returning to this menu often, go to **View→Character Encoding→ Customize** to choose which code pages are displayed in the top-level menu. With either browser, some trial and error may be necessary before the site displays correctly.

Fix Broken Pictures in Web Pages

There are a bunch of things that can cause this problem, not the least of which is a web server that's down or a page that's out of date. But if several different sites are missing photos, try the following fixes.

First, clear your browser cache to remove any corrupt data that your browser might be using to display pages. In Internet Explorer, open the **Tools** drop-down, select **Internet Options**, and in the **Browsing history** section, click **Delete**. Check the **Temporary Internet files** box and click **Delete**. Or in Firefox, go to **Tools→Options**, choose the **Advanced** category, then the **Network** sub-tab, and click the **Clear Now** button.

Some improperly configured firewall software, particularly Norton Internet Security and Norton Personal Firewall, can interfere with images in some websites. Temporarily disable your firewall; if that helps, consult the firewall's documentation (specifically relating to the anti-hotlinking features) to help fix the problem. (Note that neither Windows Firewall nor most firewall-equipped routers typically exhibit this problem.)

Ad-blockers may also be suppressing content you want to see. By design, ad-blockers block images, animations, inline frames, and other content served up by certain sites, but your ad-blocker might be blocking more than just the ads. Many sites also pull non-ad content from these same servers, sometimes for economic or technical reasons, but primarily in an attempt to thwart ad-blockers. Either way, turn off your ad-blocking software to see whether that solves the problem.

Finally, bad proxy settings can break all sorts of things in websites. If you're surfing from work, your employer may require you to go through a proxy server; turn it off and see whether the problem stops. Likewise, if you're surfing from home and you're using a proxy server (as described in "Surf Anonymously" on page 531), you may have to turn it off to view sites reliably. In Internet Explorer, open the **Tools** drop-down, select **Internet Options**, choose the **Connections** tab, and click the **LAN Settings** button to configure your proxy server. In Firefox, go to **Tools→ Options**, choose the **Advanced** category, then the **Network** sub-tab, and click **Settings**.

Improve Any Website

Websites aren't as untouchable as they may seem. In the early days of the Web, if you frequented a website with some annoying quirks or features that didn't quite work right, you just had to grit your teeth and live with it. But Greasemonkey has changed all that.

Greasemonkey is a free extension (available at *http://www.greasespot.net/*) for the Firefox web browser that lets you add custom JavaScript code to any web page. The code then runs automatically as though it were part of the page itself and alters its appearance or changes its behavior accordingly.

 If you're using Chrome, get Greasemetal from *http://greaseme tal.31tools.com/*. For Safari, get Greasekit at *http://8-p.info/ greasekit/*. Or for Internet Explorer, try Trixie from *http://www .bhelpuri.net/trixie*. Keep in mind that most Greasemonkey user scripts are written for—and tested with—Greasemonkey on Firefox, so there's no guarantee that they'll work as well (or at all) with other setups.

By itself, Greasemonkey doesn't do much of anything. To bring it to life, you must install *user scripts* that you download or write yourself. Most user scripts are designed to add features to individual websites, but some are written to fix bugs or remove clutter. Visit *http://userscripts.org/*, and you'll find enough gems to keep you entertained for some time.

The easiest way to find a user script is to search *http://userscripts.org/* for the site you want to grease up. For instance, there were 151 scripts for Google Maps at the time of this writing, including one that changes the input field to a multiline textbox, making it easier to copy and paste street addresses, and another that lets you quickly zoom to a specific region on the map by drawing a rectangle right on the page.

Or, in the eBay section, you'll find a script that makes it easy to show only the complaints in an eBay member's feedback profile (Figure 7-38), something eBay won't let you do. (See my book, *eBay Hacks*, Second Edition—also from O'Reilly—for more tricks like this.)

When you've found a user script you want, right-click the link to the script and select **Install User Script**. Or, click the link to display and examine the script in the browser, and if you like what you see, go to **Tools→Install User Script**. The script will be active immediately, but you'll have to reload any applicable pages to see the results.

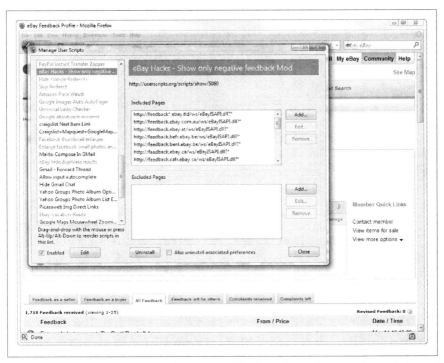

Figure 7-38. Greasemonkey is also responsible for adding the Complaints Left and Complaints Received tabs to this eBay page

Not all scripts are site specific. The "Linkifier" script turns anything that looks like a URL—on any page—into an active link you can click. Similar scripts do the same thing for email addresses and even UPS and FedEx tracking numbers. The best part, though, is that with some knowledge of JavaScript, you can write your own user scripts and customize the Web to your heart's content! To get started authoring user scripts, visit *http://diveintogreasemonkey.org/* and pick up a copy of O'Reilly's *Greasemonkey Hacks* by Mark Pilgrim.

Put an End to Pop Ups

Pop-up ads are everywhere, but alas, I suspect anti-pop-up laws would be about as effective as anti-spam laws. But that doesn't mean you can't take matters into your own hands and stop the madness (more or less). In the old days, all you'd have to do is install a third-party pop-up blocker, and you'd be set. Today, all major browsers come with built-in pop-up blockers, though some are better than others. The problem is that pop ups are no longer limited to websites, which means your anti-pop-up arsenal must grow to keep up.

Although web-based pop ups are blocked by default in Internet Explorer, you may want to make it more aggressive to block more pop ups. Open the **Tools** drop-down, and select **Pop-up Blocker→Pop-up Blocker Settings**. From the **Blocking level** list, select **High: Block all pop-ups**, and then click OK.

Of course, some sites use pop-up windows for legitimate purposes, so you may decide to exclude sites from the blocker from time to time to allow their pop ups to work. Return to the Pop-up Blocker Settings window, type (or paste) the URL of the site into the **Address of Web site to allow** box, click **Add**, and click OK.

 You can also allow pop ups on a case-by-case basis by clicking the yellow information bar when it appears. And if you've selected the **High: Block all pop-ups** filter level as described above, you can also press **Ctrl-Alt** when clicking links to temporarily allow pop ups.

Firefox also blocks pop ups by default. To permit pop ups from certain sites, go to **Tools→ Options**, choose the **Content** category, and click the **Exceptions** button next to **Block pop-up windows**.

Firefox also give you more control than IE over JavaScript, the programming language used to facilitate most pop ups and add some other annoying traits to websites. In Firefox, go to **Tools→Options**, choose the **Content** category, and click the **Exceptions** button next to **Enable JavaScript**. You can prevent sites from moving or resizing windows, changing the text in the status bar, and more, by simply turning off the respective options.

 If you want even more control over JavaScript, get the free NoScript Firefox add-on from *https://addons.mozilla.org/en -US/firefox/addon/722*, and allow scripts only from sites you trust. See "Improve Any Website" on page 526 for other ways to make sites less annoying.

So, now you're blocking pop ups, but ad windows are still showing up? If you see pop ups when you're not surfing the Web, your PC may be infected with spyware, software designed to display advertisements and sometimes even monitor your surfing habits. (Of course, the software you're using, such as Windows Live Messenger, may be showing you its own ads, but that's a different problem.) Spyware, adware, and other types of malware (malicious software) come from some websites (see the section "Lock Down Internet Explorer" on page 514) and also piggyback on some downloadable applications, commonly P2P file-sharing programs and, strangely, many weather-forecast desktop applications. See Chapter 6 for various malware removal techniques.

Solve the Blank Form Mystery

When was the last time you filled out a form on a web page and clicked **Submit**, only to be told there's something wrong with what you've entered? You do as you're told and click the **Back** button to return to the previous page, but now the form is completely empty. Then, you click **Forward**, and your browser insists on resending submitted content to the server instead of just displaying the page sitting in the browser cache.

This is usually caused by a bug in your web browser rather than the website. All versions of Internet Explorer exhibit this bug. While browsers based on the Mozilla engine, such as Firefox, are better at saving form information than IE, they still fail with disappointing regularity.

To date, no browser handles form data in previously visited pages perfectly, but there are a few workarounds.

For one, most website designers are aware of the bug, and have built their websites accordingly. So, if you submit a form, and need to go back and change what you've typed, don't press your browser's **Back** button. Rather, look for a **Back** button or **Edit** button *right on the page*, and click it to safely modify your text.

Next, make a habit of performing an impromptu backup *before* you submit any form. For instance, if you've written a long message, click in the text box, press **Ctrl-A** to highlight all the text, press **Ctrl-C** to copy it, open Notepad, and press **Ctrl-V** to paste. (Repeat these steps for each long field in the form.) If you're later returned to an empty form, simply paste your text back into the fields and try again.

Stop Annoying Animations

It seems like everywhere you go on the Web, something is pulsating, flying across the screen, or playing music. So, how do you make this online circus stop?

In most cases, pressing the **Esc** key stops the animations, but this is temporary and only works with animated *.gif* image files. If you want to permanently disable *.gif* animations altogether in Internet Explorer, open the **Tools** dropdown, select **Internet Options**, choose the **Advanced** tab, and in the **Multimedia** section, turn off **Play animations in web pages**. You can also turn off

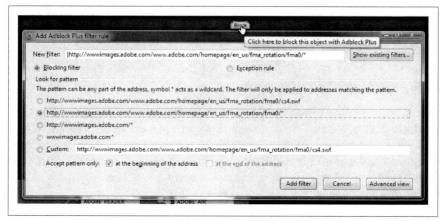

Figure 7-39. The tabs feature in AdBlock Plus is a quick way to get the address of an embedded web object, as well as a means of eliminating annoying animations from a web page

sounds and videos with similar settings in the same section. Click OK when you're done.

In Firefox, type about:config into the address bar to show the staggering list of all available fine-tuning options for these browsers. Find **image.animation_mode** in the list (type something like anim in the **Filter** field to locate it quickly), double-click the option, and type none in the **Enter String Value** box. If you don't want to completely disable animations, you can type once here instead (normal is the default) to let sites play all animations only once, but never repeat (loop) them. Click OK when you're done.

Other types of animations require different strategies. To turn off Flash animations in Internet Explorer, you must uninstall the Flash player using Macromedia's elusive uninstaller tool, available at *http://www.macromedia .com/support/flashplayer/* (search the knowledgebase for "uninstall"). Of course, this means that you'll lose all Flash content henceforth, so you may not want to take this step.

In Mozilla Firefox, you can use the powerful Adblock Plus extension, available for free at *http://adblockplus.org/*, to selectively hide animations *without* disabling Flash altogether. Once installed, restart your browser, and then go to **Tools→Adblock Plus**. Open the **Options** menu, and if the **Show tabs on Flash and Java** entry doesn't have a checkmark next to it, select it and then click OK. Thereafter, a little tab labeled **Block** will protrude from any Flash animation on a page (see Figure 7-39); just click the **Block** tab to show the address of the ad, and then click OK to begin blocking that particular Flash animation.

JavaScript, not to be confused with Java, is often used to create flyovers (where a button or icon changes when you move the mouse over it) as well as cursor trails (the flying bits that follow your mouse pointer). Now, because so many sites rely heavily on JavaScript, it isn't a good idea to turn it off just to purge these sorts of animations. In most cases, you can curb annoying JavaScript behavior with an appropriate *user script*, as described in "Improve Any Website" on page 526. If you're using Firefox, the NoScript extension, introduced in the previous section, can easily block one or more of a specific site's JavaScript source files.

Surf Anonymously

Websites you visit know more about you than you probably realize. Along with the browser signature (see "Live with Firefox in an IE World" on page 521), your browser sends your PC's Internet IP address to every website it visits, and from that, a website can extract some pretty interesting things. (See the upcoming sidebar "What Can They Find Out About You?" for the nitty gritty.)

What Can They Find Out About You?

Your IP address is sent to every website you visit. While no one can determine your exact street address and shoe size directly from your IP address, it's a trivial matter to get your rough geographic location. (For an example, check out *http://www.yougetsignal.com/* or *http://www.geobytes.com/ipLocator .htm.*)

Of course, there's no shortage of elaborate tracking schemes that effectively turn your IP address into a serial number, a unique identifier some websites can use to identify you when you visit. For instance, let's say you make a purchase from an online store that sells toasters. As soon as you pay for that fancy new four-slicer, the store records your name, street address, credit card information, *and your IP address.* Provided the toaster store keeps your private information private, you've got nothing to worry about. But can you say the same thing for the other site you just used to sign up for a free plasma TV?

This is where advertising comes in. Most ads on many websites originate from only a handful of companies, and those companies track who's looking at their ads, even when you don't click them. If you view a page at a news website that displays a banner ad hosted by, say, *http://adknowledge.com* or *http:// targetnet.com*, and then you sign up to win a free TV on another site that has another ad from the *same agency*, that ad server knows you've visited both sites. What's more, if the ad agency is in cahoots with the contest website, they have your email address, street address, favorite episode of *Battlestar Galactica*, and anything else you typed into the sweepstakes sign-up page.

Now, most folks have dynamic IP addresses, which change every time they start a connection, but a single IP can remain active all day—or with a router, for weeks at a time—which means your IP address can be used to track quite a bit of your online activity. What's more, many unscrupulous sites use so-called tracking cookies to do the same thing—namely, tag your PC with a unique serial number that can be read as you visit many different sites.

So, how can you stop the snooping? Most antispyware software (see Chapter 6) is designed to look for and delete tracking cookies, but you may want to take it one step further and configure your browser to block all cookies from sites like those listed at *http://www3.ca.com/securityadvisor/pest/browse .aspx?cat=tracking%20cookie*. To block cookies in Internet Explorer, go to **Tools→ Internet Options**, choose the **Privacy** tab, and click **Sites**. In Firefox, go to **Tools→Options**, choose the **Privacy** category, and in the **Cookies** section, click **Exceptions**.

Also useful is Internet Explorer's *InPrivate Filtering* feature—oddly named in that it has little to do with the *InPrivate Browsing* tool that turns off the collecting of cookies and history entries while you surf on your lunch break. From the **Safety** drop-down, select **InPrivate Filtering** to break one of the primary conduits tracking websites use to keep track of you: namely, the embedding of content from one website into another website for the purposes of recording your visit.

Or, if you're using Firefox, install ad-blocking software such as the Adblock extension described in "Stop Annoying Animations" on page 529.

Use a proxy server to mask your IP address from the websites you visit. As the name implies, a proxy server stands between your browser and the sites you surf, in effect hiding you from prying sites. Once you set up a proxy server, all information you send and receive with your browser goes through that server (email and other programs must be configured separately to use the proxy). Most large companies use their own proxy servers to help protect the data on company PCs from prying eyes, but you don't have to work at a big company to get the same protection.

Start by visiting *http://annoyances.org/ip* to view your IP address as websites see it. Then browse a list of free IP:Port proxy servers, like the one at *http:// www.hidemyass.com/proxy-list/* or *http://www.xroxy.com/proxylist.htm*. Highlight its IP address and press **Ctrl-C** to copy it to the clipboard; also note the **Port** shown in the adjacent column. Next, configure your browser to use that proxy server.

Wondering whether you can trust the proxy service not to use your IP and other info for nefarious purposes? The truth is that there's no reason to trust an anonymous proxy any more than the sites from which you're hiding. For practical purposes, you should only use one of these proxies when you specifically need to surf anonymously, and avoid logging in to your bank's website while connected to a proxy. Furthermore, many proxies pass through your original IP address in the HTTP headers, so you're not quite as anonymous as you may think.

If you're using Internet Explorer, open the **Tools** drop-down, select **Internet Options**, choose the **Connections** tab, and click **LAN Settings**. Turn on the **Use a proxy server for your LAN** option, and then paste (press **Ctrl-V**) the IP address you got at *http://proxy4free.com* into the **Address** field. Type the port number (usually **80** or **8080**) into the **Port** field, and click OK when you're done.

If you find yourself using proxies often, you may want to reduce the number of trips you make to Internet Explorer's LAN Settings window. Click the **Advanced** button, and in the **Exceptions** box, type the addresses of websites you want to connect to directly (no proxy). If you're using Firefox, check out the free FoxyProxy add-on (*http://foxyproxy.mozdev .org/*). Among other things, FoxyProxy makes to easy to switch between proxy servers (or none at all), and even lets you set up rules (called patterns) to automatically enable a specific proxy when you visit certain websites.

Settings made in the Internet Options window affect Internet Explorer only, so you'll have to use a slightly different procedure for other browsers. If you're using Firefox, go to **Tools→Options**, choose the **General** category, choose the **Connection Settings** tab, and select **Manual proxy configuration**.

Now, go back to *http://annoyances.org/ip* and notice that your IP has changed! (If you can't load the page, the proxy server is down; just choose another proxy server and try again.) From here on, every site you visit will see your proxy server's IP address instead of yours until you disable the proxy.

Every byte of data you send and receive with your web browser will be sent through the proxy server. Unless you know—and trust—whoever is hosting that server, you should always disable the proxy before sending sensitive information (e.g., your home address, credit cards, etc.).

If you don't want to go to the trouble of setting up a proxy server whenever you visit sketchy websites, there are alternatives. One solution is to use a free, single-serving proxy website, many of which are listed and ranked at *http://www.proxy4free.com/*. Browse the proxy list and look for servers marked **HiAnon**; for best results, sort the list by **Rating**, descending, or **Access Time**, ascending.

Here, you'll find sites—like Free Proxy Server (*http://www.freeproxyserver.net/*), Proxify (*http://proxify.com/*), remainhidden.com (*https://remainhidden.com/*), Vtunnel (*http://vtunnel.com/*), and The Cloak (*http://www.the-cloak.com/*)—where you can type or paste the URL of the site you want to visit into the text box and press **Enter**. The proxy site will load up the page, allowing you to surf anonymously for this session. Click the links in the page to continue surfing anonymously, or use your browser's address bar, bookmarks, or Internet Shortcuts to return to the normal, non-proxy surfing.

If you want more flexibility than web-based proxies can offer, and don't mind paying for it, try Anonymizer's Anonymous Surfing tool (*http://www.anonymizer.com/*), the Anonymous Browsing Toolbar (*http://www.amplusnet.com/*), or Hide the IP (*http://www.hide-the-ip.com/*). These products, in the form of software you install on your PC, perform pretty much the same function as the web-based proxies mentioned above, albeit with more features and speed. All things considered, these software-based proxies are probably marginally safer than anonymous proxies, and less of a hassle than web-based proxies.

Now, you might be thinking, why not just use a router? Well, routers—discussed in Chapter 6—offer terrific firewall production and indeed act as a layer between your PC and the rest of the Web. But when you surf from behind a router, websites still see your *router's* IP address, and thus are still able to collect all the same information about you and your geographical location.

See "Lock Out Unauthorized PCs" on page 457 for a way to spoof the MAC address of your PC (or your router).

Change the Default Email Program

Just because email is ubiquitous doesn't mean it's irrelevant which email software you use. Sure, Microsoft would love it if you used exclusively the Live Mail application or website, not to mention Microsoft Office and Internet Explorer instead of OpenOffice and Firefox. If Microsoft had its way, you'd be brushing your teeth with Microsoft toothpaste. Good thing you don't care what Microsoft wants.

The *default* email program, the one that opens when you send a file from an application or click a *mailto:* link in a web page. On the Default Programs page in Control Panel, open, click **Set program access and computer defaults**. Choose the **Custom** option, click the little double-arrow on the right side to expand the category, and in the **Choose a default e-mail program** section, select your favorite email client.

 If your program doesn't appear in the Set Program Access and Computer Defaults window, but the **Use my current e-mail program** entry is selected, your favorite email program may already be set as the default, despite the fact that it isn't mentioned by name here. To test it, open the Start menu, and in the **Search** box, type `mailto:test` and see what happens.

If your favorite email reader isn't showing up in either of the aforementioned lists, it doesn't mean that Microsoft specifically excluded it. (Of course, neither did Microsoft make it easy to browse for a new entry, but that's a different story.) Rather, it simply means that your application or website isn't properly registered with Windows. The easy way to fix the problem is to check the software publisher's website for an update and get it if there is one, and then reinstall your email application.

If that doesn't help, or if the email program you want to use is actually a website, you can edit the list by hand, which, of course, requires a visit to the Windows Registry.

Open the Registry Editor (see Chapter 3), and expand the branches to `HKEY_LOCAL_MACHINE\SOFTWARE\Clients\Mail`. Here, you'll find a separate subkey for each program currently registered on your PC; to remove an entry from the list, just delete the corresponding key here.

Adding entries is a little more involved. Rather than filling out everything by hand, get the template from *http://www.annoyances.org/downloads/gmail.reg* and save it to your desktop. Double-click the *gmail.reg* patch file to merge it with your Registry, and then return to the Registry Editor to have a look at the new entry, located at `HKEY_LOCAL_MACHINE\SOFTWARE\Clients\Mail\Gmail`.

You can rename the `Gmail` key to whatever you like, but to change the title that appears in the Windows list of registered email programs, double-click the `(Default)` value inside.

Next, go to `HKEY_LOCAL_MACHINE\SOFTWARE\Clients\Mail\Gmail\shell\open\command`, and double-click the (`Default`) value there to change the address of the program. If it's an application on your hard disk, type (or paste) the full path and filename of the program's *.exe* file (i.e., *C:\Program Files\AcmeMail\acme.exe*). Or, if it's a website, type the *.exe* filename of your browser followed by the appropriate parameter and then the URL of your site, like this:

```
iexplore.exe -nohome http://gmail.com
```

or, for Mozilla Firefox, type:

```
c:\program files\firefox\firefox.exe http://gmail.com
```

You're not done yet; to set up your new Registry entry to respond correctly to `mailto:` links you click in web pages, navigate to `HKEY_LOCAL_MACHINE\SOFTWARE\Clients\Mail\Gmail\Protocols\mailto\shell\open\command`, and double-click the (`Default`) value to the right.

Just like the `command` key you set earlier, type the path of the application or the path of your browser plus the website address. But this time, also include the `%1` parameter so that Windows can pass the email address you clicked to your email program. You'll need to check the documentation for your program or website for the correct command-line syntax, but for programs it should look something like this:

```
c:\Program Files\Eudora\Eudora.exe /m %1
```

or for a website (like Gmail), type:

```
iexplore.exe -nohome
           https://mail.google.com/mail/?view=cm&tearoff=1&fs=1&to=%1
```

or

```
c:\program files\firefox\firefox.exe
           https://mail.google.com/mail/?view=cm&tearoff=1&fs=1&to=%1
```

It's worth noting that the only difference between this and the syntax in the previous step is the URL to use, which now includes `&to=%1`, among other things. If your website doesn't provide the necessary URL, just search Google for the word `mailto` and the name of your website (or application), and you should get the information you need.

 If you don't want to change your PC's default email program, but you'd like to redirect *mailto:* links to a web-based email client, use GreaseMonkey and the appropriate user script, as described in "Improve Any Website" on page 526.

When you're done, test your changes by clicking the **Email** entry in your Start menu, and then follow-up by clicking a *mailto:* link in any web page.

Stop Spam

Of the 873 messages in your inbox this morning, I bet only about 5 were actually for you (thinning hair and waning sex drive notwithstanding). So, how do you do away with the other 868 messages that are sure to be delivered again tomorrow?

Unfortunately, there is no perfect solution. Either you live with some junk mail in your inbox, or you employ a spam filter that occasionally deletes valid messages. But there are things you can do to mitigate the problem and reduce your exposure to spam.

First, don't post your email address on websites, public forums, or in the backs of computer books. If you've already done this, you're already on every spam list on the planet. Also, be wary of phishing emails (see the upcoming sidebar, "Don't Phall for Phishing"), another source (and scourge) of spam.

Don't Phall for Phishing

"Hmmm, a talking moose wants my credit card number. Sounds fair..."

—Homer J. Simpson

So, you get this message from eBay telling you that your account will be suspended if you don't update your information, and then you get a nearly identical message from Wells Fargo. I'm sure the urgent tone of the messages might be more disconcerting if you actually had accounts at those institutions.

Of course, those messages aren't from eBay or Wells Fargo; they're spam. But unlike come-ons for weight loss and real estate schemes, this spam tries to trick you into revealing personal information through a practice called *phishing* (not to be confused with the musical group Phish).

Phishing messages have become such a problem that *even Microsoft* has snapped into action and designed the SmartScreen filter in Internet Explorer 8 to also look for phishing sites. (Firefox has a similar feature.) The filter, which is enabled by default, warns you if you visit a site it suspects to be fraudulent, and even lets you report a phishing website so others can be warned. (From the **Tools** drop-down in IE, select **Phishing Filter** for options.) But for the IE's Phishing Filter to be effective, you need to have automatic updates enabled, as described in Chapter 6.

But no filter is foolproof. To avoid this trap, you need to recognize the red flags. First, no reputable company will ever ask you to verify your information, and while many sites ask you to log in to access your account, never do so

---

after following a link in an email. Instead, use a trusted bookmark or just type the URL into your browser's address bar by hand. If you're not comfortable simply discarding the message, contact the company and ask whether the email is legitimate.

Second, inspect any URLs in the message. Pass your mouse pointer over the link and the address should pop up (assuming your email program supports this). Odds are, you won't see something like *http://www.ebay.com*, but rather a long arcane URL with lots of symbols or a numeric web address like *http:// 168.143.113.54*. This is a sure sign the link points to a fake website.

Next, if you've configured your browser to save your login information, you'll know you're not looking at the real site if your browser does fill out the form for you; browsers save passwords for specific URLs, and your PC can tell the real thing even if you can't.

To further scrutinize a suspicious email, right-click the message body and select **View Source** to view the HTML source code of the message. Search for http and you'll find the real URLs tied to the links in the message.

Now, some email messages have embedded pictures (as opposed to attachments); when you view one of these messages, your email program fetches the picture from the server, and that server records the event. (And voilà, the sender has confirmed that you've read the message.) If you turn off image fetching, those servers are never notified, and you'll find yourself on fewer spam lists:

Microsoft Outlook
> Go to **Tools→Trust Center**, choose the **Automatic Download** category on the left, and then in the right pane, turn on the **Don't download pictures automatically in HTML e-mail messages or RSS items** option. (It's now Outlook's default, but it's worth checking nonetheless.)

Mozilla Thunderbird
> Go to **Tools→Options**, choose the **Advanced Privacy** category, and select the **Block loading of remote images in mail messages** option.

Eudora
> Go to **Tools→Options**, choose the **Display** category on the left, and then turn off the **Automatically download HTML graphics** option.

Gmail
> By default, inline images aren't displayed in Gmail messages. Instead, you'll see a green stripe at the top of the message; just click the **Display images below** link if you need to see them, or the **Always display images** link if you trust the sender. Now, if you click the **Always display**

images link by accident, you can rescind your permission by clicking **Show details** and then **Don't display from now on**.

Windows Live Mail (a.k.a. MSN Hotmail)

At the top of any Live Mail page, click **Options**. Choose the **Mail** category on the left, click **Mail Display Settings**, and then under **Display Internet content**, select **Automatically suppress Internet content in messages**.

Next, install an independent, passive spam filter—one that marks potential spam instead of deleting it—like SpamPal (free, *http://sourceforge.net/projects/ spampal/*). Then configure your email program's filter to send all email containing the text **Spam** in the subject line to the **Junk** or **Trash** mailbox. That way, you can get the spam out of your face, but later peruse your junk mail for valid messages before it's gone for good. Now, most email programs (e.g., Outlook, Thunderbird, and Eudora) have built-in spam filters that can likewise route spam into the trash. But programs like SpamPal are more configurable and update their spam lists and definitions frequently.

 SpamPal works with any POP3- or IMAP4-based email program, which means it won't work with AOL, or web-based mail systems like Gmail.

All spam filters rely on up-to-date lists and definitions to block spam effectively, so make sure they are kept up-to-date. If you're using Outlook, you can get spam filter updates with Microsoft Update: open Windows Update in Control Panel, click **Settings**, and turn on the **Use Microsoft Update** option. (For older versions of Office, you can get updates manually at *http://office.mi crosoft.com/en-us/officeupdate/*.)

If your spam situation is particularly bad, and passive spam filters aren't cutting it, there are more drastic options. First, contact your ISP and request that it employ a server-based spam filter such as Postini (*http://www.google.com/ postini/*). Server-side filters delete spam en route to your inbox, so you don't even have to download it. The downside: some valid mail may never make it to your inbox.

You can also employ a more aggressive interactive spam filter, such as Cloudmark Desktop (*http://www.cloudmark.com/*), which won't allow any email to reach your inbox unless the sender is on an approved-senders list. (Many ISPs and some web-based email providers offer this type of service to their customers as well.) If a non-approved sender tries to send you a message, the program sends back an email requesting that the sender fill out a web form. This not only trips up spam (which is sent by machines), it lets you reject humans with whom you'd rather not correspond as well. Of course, you can also easily add any sender to your approved list, but that in itself introduces extra work. This approach can turn a flood of spam into a trickle, but it won't ever let valid automated messages through, such as newsletters, registration codes you paid for, or order confirmation emails from online merchants. And spoofed messages, wherein the sender is made to look like someone likely to be on your approved list (such as other people in your domain), won't be stopped by these types of filters.

If you're running an online business, think twice before you deploy one of these aggressive spam filters. The last thing you want is a spam filter deleting your customers' emails! And eBay users take note: spam filters are the number-one cause of negative feedback for both buyers and sellers, so if your spam filter is on the aggressive side, look at eBay's My Messages page for missed correspondence.

If you're already getting tons of spam, perhaps now is the time to change your email address. Get your own domain name and create a bunch of different addresses for different purposes, such as *shopping@mydomain.com* for online shopping, *auctions@mydomain.com* for buying and selling on eBay, *subscriptions@mydomain.com* for newsletters, and *personal@mydomain.com* for correspondence with friends and family, and have them all go to the same inbox. That way, if one of your addresses makes its way onto a spam list, you can take down the address without disrupting the email to your other accounts. Better yet, create a new email address for every site you visit, such as *amazon@mydomain.com*, *ebay@mydomain.com*, *nytimes@mydomain.com*, and *annoyances@mydomain.com*; if an address starts getting spam, you'll know who sold you out.

Do you receive email at more than one address? Use your email program's **Filters** feature to sort through your incoming mail and even mark individual messages so that when you can reply, the correct return address is automatically used.

Send Large Files

Clogging a friend's inbox with 20 megabytes of email attachments is a great way to get your friend to configure a spam filter that automatically dumps all your email in the trash.

If all you need to send is a few photos, emailing them is fine…as long you shrink them down first. Your 12-megapixel digital camera creates 8 Mb files, but your friends don't need full-resolution photos unless they're going to print them. So, use any photo editor to make them all smaller before you email them; the total size of all the files you send should never be more than 400–500 Kb.

 To shrink a bunch of photos in one step, try the free Photo Resizer plugin for Creative Element Power Tools, available at *http://creativelement.com/powertools/*.

Need your recipients to be able to print the photos? There's a plethora of free photo-sharing websites designed for this purpose, but few let visitors download high-resolution pictures. The better ones that do include Picasa (*http://picasa.google.com/*), PhotoBucket (*http://photobucket.com/*), ImageShack (*http://imageshack.us/*), and Flickr (*http://www.flickr.com/*). Just upload your photos to the site and then send the URL the site provides to as many recipients as you like, without fear of email attachment clog.

To send other types of files, such as documents or ZIP files, you need a slightly different tack. Since photo-sharing websites can make money when visitors order prints, they're only too happy to host your photos, but few sites will be interested in hosting that 50 Mb database file you need to send to a colleague.

Now, if you have your own web space (often provided free by your ISP), you can FTP your files to the server, and then send your friends an address like this:

http://www.{my-isp.net}/~{myusername}/{quarterlyanalysis.zip}

where *{my-isp.net}* is your ISP's website, *{myusername}* is your user account, and *{quarterlyanalysis.zip}* is the name of a file you want to share.

Unfortunately, your ISP probably isn't interested in helping you host—and have all your friends download—gigabytes of your data. If you don't have web space, or if your ISP restricts the types or size of files you can upload to it, try a site like YouSendIt (*http://www.yousendit.com/*), DropSend (*http://www.dropsend.com/*), or SendSpace (*http://www.sendspace.com/*). These services accept very large files—up to 300Mb or even 1Gb in some cases—and then permit a limited number of downloads.

Email Long URLs

Ahh, the evils of word wrap. The basic terminal display used to read early email messages was only 80 characters wide, and while few people still use terminals to read email, the standard lives on. Today, if you send someone a message with a long URL, it might be broken apart by his email program to conform to that 40-year-old standard.

Since some email vendors have yet to fix this glitch, and your recipients will likely have no idea what to do when they receive your message with pieces of a URL spanning several lines, shrink the URL before you send it. For example, TinyURL (*http://tinyurl.com/*), can take any horrendously long URL, such as:

http://maps.google.com/maps?ll=37.826870,-122.422682&spn=0.007197 ,0.009112&t=k&hl=en

and turn it into a tidy, easy-to-email URL like this:

http://tinyurl.com/cfpmc

TinyURL is fast and free, and the URLs it makes never expire. Also available is SnipURL (*http://www.snipurl.com*), which does pretty much the same thing, but adds tracking features.

Find yourself making TinyURLs often? Just go to *http://tinyurl.com/#toolbar*, and drag the **TinyURL!** link onto any browser's **Links** toolbar. Thereafter, just click the button to create a TinyURL from the current page.

If you use Firefox, try TinyURL Creator (*https://addons.mozilla.org/en-us/fire fox/addon/126?id=126*, or better yet, *http://tinyurl.com/574q9*). To use the tool, right-click an empty area of the current page and select **Create Tiny URL for this Page**. A shortened URL is created on the spot and copied to your clipboard for your immediate use. A similar tool, Maxthon (free from *http:// www.maxthon.com*), works with Internet Explorer and SnipURL.

 Also available for Firefox and the GreaseMonkey add-on (see "Improve Any Website" on page 526) are user scripts that will expand shortened URLs automatically. That way, you can see where a link will actually take you before you click.

So, what do you do when someone sends you a long URL? Well, you can highlight it, copy it to the clipboard (**Ctrl-C**), and then paste it into Notepad (**Ctrl-V**), where you can then proceed to carefully reassemble the URL onto one line. (Take care to remove extraneous characters, such as spaces and punctuation, while leaving intact the codes that belongs.) Then, copy it again and paste it back into your web browser's address bar. But if you're using Firefox, you can streamline this process with the free Open Long URL extension (*https://addons.mozilla.org/addon/132*). Install the extension, restart your browser, and then select **File→Open Long URL**. Paste the long, broken URL into the box, click OK, and the extension will reassemble the URL for you and open the page. See? Much easier than fixing everyone's email software.

CHAPTER 8

Users and Security

There's no such thing as a totally secure system. Even if you never share files over a network nor let anyone else sit down at your keyboard, Windows is designed to function in a multiuser world. Because of the nature of the beast, you sometimes have to make concessions when trying to balance security and day-to-day convenience. Windows doesn't always make this balance easy, but where's there's a will, there's a hack.

For instance, you'll need to choose a password for your account to share files, but that means typing your password every time you power on your PC. But a hidden dialog—uncovered in this chapter—allows you to log in automatically and still protect your account with a password.

And separate user accounts are great for sharing a PC with family members or coworkers, but that requires being mindful of file permissions and encryption if anyone cares about his or her privacy. But if you do it right, you can use a set-it-and-forget-it approach with file security.

Next, Windows 7's new Homegroups feature aims to make at least file sharing easier. But easier isn't always better: with Homegroups, you have less control over precisely what you share and with whom, and if you're not careful, you may give away the farm. So Homegroups doesn't make traditional file-sharing obsolete just yet.

But probably the biggest concession is to live with User Account Control (UAC). In the past, the purpose of having separate accounts was to make it easy for more than one person to use a single PC: each user got his or her own desktop, documents, settings, and even a password to keep private things private. But UAC employs user accounts to help your PC protect itself from... well, *you*.

UAC, the obnoxious system responsible for the "Windows needs your permission to continue" messages, forces you to work in a restricted environment most of the time, elevating you to "Administrator" status only when you need to install software, make changes in Control Panel, or access certain folders. This helps protects your PC from malware, not to mention a few stupid mistakes, but some of Microsoft's choices in this area leave a lot to be desired. Example: you get a UAC prompt when renaming certain desktop and Start menu icons, but well-crafted programs can make changes to your PC without your knowledge.

Manage User Accounts

User Accounts are the primary means of protecting your data, even if you're the only person who uses your PC. The user accounts system allows you to encrypt your files so they can't be read by someone who doesn't know your password, and it makes it possible to securely share your files with those on your network who do. And it means you can share your PC with your kids without being greeted by their "Astronaut on a Surfboard" wallpaper each time you log in.

There are actually four different User Accounts dialogs in Windows 7, each with a completely different design and "intended audience," so to speak. The problem is that each tool has a few options not found in the other, so no single window can be used exclusively to handle all your tasks.

User Accounts

> The User Accounts page in Control Panel (Figure 8-1) is the one most users see. It's large, friendly, and unfortunately, somewhat cumbersome.
>
> Adding, customizing, and removing user accounts is extremely easy, and for the most part, self-explanatory in this window. That's admirable. But sometimes you'll need one of the alternate dialogs, listed next, to accomplish more advanced tasks, such as managing groups and configuring Windows to log in a password-protected account automatically.

 The standard User Accounts window is the only place you can choose a user's picture, shown in both the login dialog and at the top of the Start menu (see "Prune the Start Menu" on page 68). It's also the only place you can choose between the Welcome screen and the standard Login screen, as discussed in "Hide the List of User Accounts" on page 578.

Figure 8-1. You can add, delete, or modify user accounts in the User Accounts dialog, but not much else

User Accounts 2

Some additional settings, discussed later in this chapter, can be changed only with the alternate User Accounts window, which is essentially a holdover from Windows 2000. To open the old-style User Accounts dialog (Figure 8-2), open the Start menu, and in the Search box, type:

```
%SystemRoot%\system32\control userpasswords2
```

followed by **Enter**.

Like the primary User Accounts window, you can add new users, as well as rename or remove existing accounts. But here, you have more control over a user's permissions and restrictions. You can access accounts that would otherwise be hidden in the User Accounts window, such as the Administrator account (see the section "Log In As the Administrator" on page 584) and the IUSR account used by the IIS web server. See "Hide the List of User Accounts" on page 578 for another use of this dialog.

Find yourself opening the User Accounts 2 window often? To add an icon to Control Panel for this useful tool, download the free User Accounts 2 Control Panel add-on from *http://annoyances.org/downloads/useraccounts2 .zip*. Open the zip, double-click the *install.reg* file, and click **Yes** to import the registry patch. Close and reopen Control Panel to use the new icon.

Figure 8-2. The "other" User Accounts dialog can do many things that are otherwise impossible in the standard User Accounts window

Local Users and Groups

The third way to manage user accounts in Windows is to use the Local Users and Groups policy editor, shown in Figure 8-3; open the Start menu, type lusrmgr.msc in the **Search** box, and press **Enter**. Or right-click Computer in the Start menu, select **Manage**, and select **Local Users and Groups** from the tree.

 Use the Local Users and Groups window and the aforementioned alternate User Accounts dialog with caution, as both allow you to disable all accounts with administrator privileges. If this happens, the computer will be completely inaccessible by any administrator, and you'll probably have to reinstall just to log in.

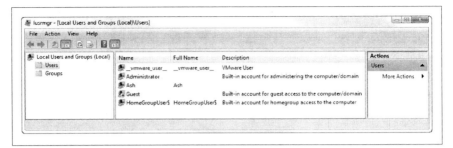

Figure 8-3. The Local Users and Groups window gives you the most control over user accounts, but at the expense of a rather sparse and intimidating Registry Editor-like interface

The Local Users and Groups window (LUaG) is actually a Microsoft Management Console (*mmc.exe*) snap-in, like the Disk Management utility (see Chapter 5) and the Windows Firewall with Advanced Security window (Chapter 7), and therefore can be accessed remotely if necessary. Figure 8-3 shows the LUaG dialog in all its glory.

LUaG is where you manage groups, set the automatic expiration of passwords, and change the location of a user's home directory. Just double-click any entry in the **Users** or **Groups** categories to change their properties. Or, right-click in an empty area of the right pane to add a new user or group.

A *group* is a collection of user accounts that can be referenced with a single name. Groups can be useful when you wish to make a folder accessible to several users (as described later in this chapter); instead of having to specify each one individually, all you would need to do is specify the group name. Note that once the group has been set up here, you can use the aforementioned User Accounts 2 dialog to assign new or existing members to that group.

Credential Manager

The Credential Manager page in Control Panel (Figure 8-21) lets you view, change, and most importantly, add saved passwords for user accounts on other PCs. Although this window doesn't work with accounts on the local PC, it's essential for accessing shared folders on other PCs; see "Access a Shared Folder Remotely" on page 597 for a walkthrough.

What can be confusing is finding the right place to accomplish a specific task regarding user accounts. Table 8-1 shows a bunch of different tasks and where to go to accomplish them.

Table 8-1. *The various places user-account tasks can be performed*

Task	User Accounts	User Accounts 2	LUaG
Add groups			✓
Add users	✓	✓	✓
Assign a user to a group		✓	✓
Assign a user to multiple groups			✓
Change a user's account name	✓		
Change a user's description		✓	✓
Change a user's home profile folder			✓
Change a user's password	✓	✓	
Change a user's password on another PC			✓
Change a user's picture	✓		
Choose a logon script			✓
Copy a user's profile folder	✓		
Disable a user or group account without removing it			✓
Export a list of users/groups to a text file			✓
Find Administrator accounts without passwords	✓		
Manage network user names and passwords	✓	✓	
Modify groups			✓
Password reset disk	✓		
Prevent forgotten passwords	✓		
Remove almost any user	✓	✓	✓
Remove any user		✓	✓
Rename certain users	✓	✓	✓
Remove a user's password	✓		
Require **Ctrl-Alt-Del** to log on		✓	
Set password expiration			✓
Turn on/off Administrator account			✓
Turn on/off Guest account	✓		✓
Turn on/off login window		✓	
Turn on/off User Account Control (UAC)	✓		
Turn on/off Welcome screen	✓		
Use Fast User Switching	✓		
View members of groups			✓

For the most part, adding, removing, and modifying user accounts is a fairly self-explanatory process, so I won't go into every excruciating detail here.

Security Identifiers (SIDs)

Every user on your machine has a unique Security Identifier, which is used in conjunction with most of the features discussed in this chapter, such as permissions and encryption, as well as some of the solutions in other chapters in this book. For example, your personal settings in the registry (see Chapter 3) are stored in a branch that looks something like this:

```
HKEY_USERS\S-1-5-21-1727987266-1036259444-725315541-500
```

The numeric portion is your SID, and is composed of the following elements:

```
S-r-i-sa-xxxxxxxxxx-yyyyyyyyyy-zzzzzzzzz-uid
```

where S stands for security identifier, *r* is the revision level and is always set to 1, *i* is the identifier authority, and *sa-xxxxxxxxxx-yyyyyyyyyy-zzzzzzzzz* is the sub-authority. Finally, *uid* is the user id.

For example, the identifier authority (*i*) can tell you something about the type of user to which an SID corresponds:

- S-1-0...is an unknown group or a group with no members.
- S-1-1...is the "world" group that includes all users.
- S-1-2...is a local user logged into "terminal."
- S-1-3...is the creator of an object (file, folder, etc.).
- S-1-4...is a non-unique user identifier.
- S-1-5...is a standard user account.

Apart from the topics in this book that use them, SIDs can be an issue if you clone your machine, a process described in Chapter 6. After a successful cloning, you may need to use Microsoft's System Preparation Tool (SysPrep) to change your SID.

Permissions and Security

Setting the permissions for a file or folder allows you to permit some users to read or change your files while restricting access to others. Problem is, if you rely on Windows 7's defaults, *anyone* will be able to read your files and *no one* will be able to change them.

Note that permissions can only be used on files and folders stored on NTFS volumes (explained in Chapter 5). Other filesystems, typically used these days on USB flash drives, camera memory cards, CDs and DVDs, and older external hard disks, have no intrinsic security features.

Set Permissions for a File or Folder

Shockingly, Microsoft actually took default permissions seriously when designing Windows 7. In Windows XP and earlier versions, everyone with an account on your PC had access to every file on your hard disk by default; if you wanted to protect your private data, you had to take matters into your own hands. In Windows 7, defaults are set to protect your private data from other users, and to protect Windows operating system files from everybody.

 Of course, no progress is without its price. Some of Windows 7's defaults are so restrictive that they can break certain software not expressly written for Windows 7 or Vista, as described in "Control User Account Control" on page 569.

To give someone access to your files, or to further restrict access, you'll need to mess with his or her permissions. Of course, it gets a little confusing when you realize that there are two different Permissions windows for any given object (file, folder, printer, etc.).

Object permissions
> Right-click any file, folder, drive, registry key, or printer, select **Properties**, and choose the **Security** tab to view or change the permissions for the selected object(s). These settings affect how the object is accessed by users on your machine (including you).

Share permissions
> Right-click any file, folder, drive, or printer, select **Properties**, choose the **Sharing** tab, click **Advanced Sharing**, and then click the **Permissions** button to view or change the share permissions for the selected object(s). These settings affect whether users on other PCs on your network can read or write to your shared files or print to your shared printers.

What's more is that both types of permissions must agree for a user—any user—to access a resource. Fortunately, all Permissions windows look and work the same; the only difference is their scope. Figure 8-4 shows a typical Permissions window.

Typically, a single entry, *Everyone*, will appear at the top of the list. In the example in Figure 8-4, only five single users are shown. Any user not in the list will not be allowed to view or modify the object.

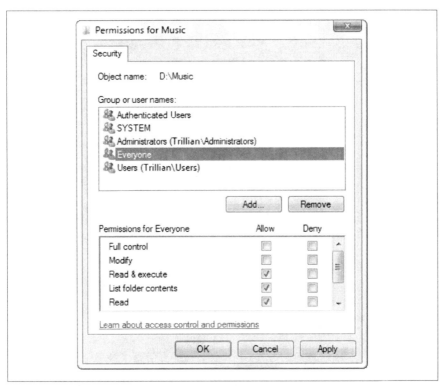

Figure 8-4. The standard Permissions window allows you to permit or deny access to other users on your computer or in your workgroup

 Permissions protect files only from those logged into other user accounts. If you walk away from your PC while you're logged in, for example, someone else sitting down at your keyboard will have full access to all your files, regardless of permissions or even encryption. This is why—when your PC is in a public place, anyway—it's a good idea to use the **On resume, display logon screen** option in the Screen Saver Settings window.

Select any user in the list, and then use the checkboxes in the list below to modify the permissions for that user. In this example, members of the *Everyone* group are allowed to read the selected file, but not allowed to write to it. Although this window shows only the permissions for one user or group at a time, you can click **Advanced** to see a better overview, as shown in Figure 8-5.

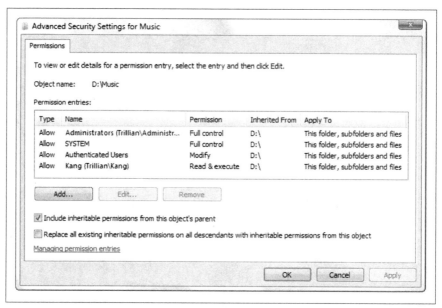

Figure 8-5. Open the Advanced Security Settings window to see all users and permissions for an object at once

In some cases, when you attempt to remove or modify permissions in the standard Permissions window (Figure 8-4), Windows will complain about the fact that the object is *inheriting* permissions. The reason is the **Inherit from parent** option in the Advanced Security Settings dialog shown in Figure 8-5.

Inheritance and ownership

Inheritance can be confusing at first, but it does save time in the long run. Essentially, if you set the permissions of a folder, those permissions will propagate to all of the files and subfolders contained therein (although Windows will usually ask you whether or not you want this to happen). When the permissions for a "parent" folder trickle down to a "child" folder or file, that child object is said to "inherit" the permissions of its parent folder. Furthermore, the child's inherited permissions are locked, at least until you turn off the aforementioned **Inherit from parent** option.

The **Auditing** tab in the Advanced Security Settings window allows you to log access activity relating to the selected object. Before auditing will work, you'll need to set up an auditing policy by opening the Group Policy window (*gpedit.msc*). Then, navigate to `Computer Configuration\Windows Settings \Security Settings\Local Policies\Audit Policy`, and double-click any entry in the right pane (such as **Audit logon events** or **Audit privilege use**) to instruct Windows to start keeping track of those events. Later on, open the Event Viewer (*eventvwr.msc*) to view the corresponding logs. Note that settings in the **Auditing** tab also obey the inheritance scheme just discussed.

Next, the **Effective Permissions** tab is a troubleshooting tool that lets you view the selected object's permissions as they pertain to a single user. This is most useful when dealing with groups of users.

Take ownership

Finally, use the **Owner** tab to assume *ownership* of one or more objects. Object ownership can be the source of a lot of frustration when wrestling with permissions in Windows, but it's one of the means by which Windows 7 maintains its lock on important operating system files and registry keys.

By default, all system-level objects are owned by a user named "Creator Owner." (See the upcoming sidebar "What's the Creator Owner Account?" for details.) To make any changes to these objects, you must first assume ownership by selecting your own name in the list, turning on the **Replace owner on subcontainers and objects** option, and clicking OK in all open Permissions windows. Only then can you reopen the main Permissions window to set the appropriate permissions, after which you can make your changes; there are several examples of this procedure throughout this book, particularly in Chapters 3 and 7.

What's the Creator Owner Account?

From time to time, you'll see a reference to *Creator Owner* in the Permissions window, but if you try to find the account by that name in one of the user account tools described at the beginning of this chapter, you'll come up empty handed.

Why? Because *Creator Owner* is not an account.

Rather, it's a generic moniker that protects an object by ensuring that only the object's owner can modify it.

Say a user on your PC creates an Excel spreadsheet and puts it in a shared folder. Then, someone else logs in to a different user account on the same PC and opens the document. In some cases, and depending on the file's permissions, the second user won't be able to make changes and save the file until she assumes ownership of it.

The subtleties of this scheme can be complex and rather confusing, but luckily, they aren't particularly important. When that second user clicks the **Owner** tab in the Advanced Security Settings window, the **Current owner** may be *Creator Owner* rather than the actual username of the person who created the file. No matter; the new user just selects his own username from the list and clicks OK.

Probably the most you'll see of the *Creator Owner* entry is when you try to modify a registry key and Windows won't let you until you assume ownership, close all the Permissions windows, and then reopen them to give yourself permission to make the change. See "Prevent Changes to a Registry Key" on page 154 for one such example.

While you're fishing around file permissions, you may also run across the related *TrustedInstaller* account. If you ever need to reinstate rights for this account, you can do so by typing `NT SERVICE\TrustedInstaller` into the **Enter the object name to select** field.

Another time when you'd use the **Owner** tab is when you need to share documents between two Windows installations on the same PC (see "Set Up a Dual-Boot System" on page 26); in most cases, Windows won't let you access such files until you "take ownership" using the **Owner** tab of this window.

As you can see, Microsoft doesn't make it easy to take ownership of a file, but it's not unusual to need to do it several times a day, particularly on a multiuser system. Now, Windows includes some tools—the `takeown` and `cacls` commands—that you can use in a Command Prompt window, as explained in the upcoming sidebar "Take Ownership from the Command Line" on page 555.

But if you want quick access to these tools from within Windows Explorer, download the free Take Ownership context menu add-on from *http://annoyances.org/downloads/takeownership.zip*. Open the zip, double-click the *install.reg* file, and click **Yes** to import the registry patch. Thereafter, you can right-click any file or folder and select **Take Ownership** to quickly become the owner of the selected item.

Take Ownership from the Command Line

It's a real pain to dig down through all those windows to take ownership of a file, only to have to close them all, and then reopen them to subsequently change the permissions. If you're comfortable with the Command Prompt or you need a way to take ownership from script (see Chapter 9), there are a few useful tools included with Windows 7 for this purpose.

To assume ownership of a file or folder, use the `takeown` command. Open a Command Prompt window in Administrator mode (see Chapter 9), and at the prompt, type:

```
takeown /f "c:\full_path\myfile.ext"
```

where `c:\full_path\myfile.ext` is the full path and filename to take ownership of. Add the `/r` option—only if you're specifying a folder name—to also take ownership of all the folders and files contained therein. Type `take own /?` for more options.

Next, to set Full Access permissions on the file or folder, use the `cacls` command, like this:

```
cacls "c:\full_path\myfile.ext" /G your_username:F
```

where *your_username* is, obviously, your username.

And for those familiar with Unix, there's a `chown` (change ownership) command-line utility (written for NT but works in Windows 7) available for free at *http://wwwthep.physik.uni-mainz.de/~frink/nt.html*.

Add new users to the Permissions window

Typically, a single entry, *Everyone*, will appear at the top of the **Group or user names** list in the Permissions window. (Here, *Everyone* literally means all users and groups in perpetuity.) More than likely, though, you'll want to eliminate the *Everyone* entry and add only those users (such as yourself) whom you need to specifically grant access to your stuff.

Start by deleting any unwanted users by selecting them and clicking **Remove**. Then, click **Add** to open the Select Users or Groups window, shown in Figure 8-6.

The first time you use this tool, you'll probably expect to see a list of all the users on your PC; unfortunately, Microsoft in its infinite wisdom decided it would be easier for you to type each user's account name by hand. To add a user, type one or more names in the **Enter the object names to select** field; separate multiple names with semicolons.

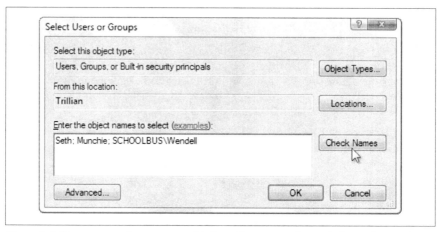

Figure 8-6. New users and groups are added to a Permissions list with this rather confusing dialog

In the example in Figure 8-6, notice that the third entry, *SCHOOLBUS\Wendell*, is unlike the others. While *Seth* and *Munchie* are users on the PC (or in the corporate domain to which this computer belongs), this third entry shows how you'd specify a user account on a different machine; in this case, the user *Wendell* on the computer *SCHOOLBUS* is to be added. The only time you'd likely need to do this is if *Wendell* needed to access your shared files remotely (discussed later in this chapter) and you didn't want to create an account for *Wendell* on the local PC.

So, why, in the Select User or Groups window, can you not actually *select* a user or group? Why aren't all the user and group names on your PC listed in here? Why all the typing? The reason is that this window was originally designed to accommodate a company-wide network with thousands of users, and since Microsoft hasn't made a single change to this interface in over a decade, you'll need to go elsewhere to get a list of users. To see the users on your own PC, open the User Accounts window in Control Panel or use one of the other tools explained at the beginning of this chapter. Or, if you're part of a corporate domain, you can click **Advanced** to search for users on your network.

When you click OK, Windows will verify the user and group names you've entered, and if all is well, will add them to the Permissions window. Mistype a name, and you won't be allowed to leave. (To verify your entries without closing the window, click **Check Names**.)

When you've added a new user to the Permissions window (shown previously in Figure 8-4), highlight the user, and selectively click the checkmarks in the **Allow** or **Deny** columns.

 Deny entries take precedence over any **Allow** entries. Say a user named *Surly* is part of a group named *Duff*. If you deny read access to the *Duff* group, and then allow read access to the *Surly* account, *Surly* still won't be able to read the files.

Depending on the type of object you've selected, you may see any number of different types of entries here, such as **Full Control**, **Read**, **Write** and **Modify**. After playing with the checkmarks, you'll notice that there is quite a bit of redundancy in this list; for example, **Modify** is an umbrella term that includes **Read & Execute**, **Read**, and **Write**.

For more control over permissions, click **Advanced** to show the Advanced Security Settings window (shown earlier in Figure 8-5), select the user with whom you want to work, and click **Edit**. The Permission Entry window shown in Figure 8-7 allows you to fine-tune permissions and allow only those permissions that are absolutely necessary for the object. For most day-to-day permission setting, you won't ever need to use this tool.

When you're done choosing permissions, click OK. If you're modifying the permissions for a folder, Windows may or may not prompt you to have your changes propagated to all subfolders and files.

How permissions affect software

In most cases, you'll want to set permissions to protect your files and folders from unauthorized access. But some permissions are necessary to get certain programs to work.

For example, Windows 7 uses this scheme as part of the UAC feature discussed in "Control User Account Control" on page 569, which is why software not written especially for Windows 7 or Vista won't know that it's not allowed to write files to your PC's *Program Files* folder.

Of course, you can also use overly restrictive permissions to your advantage and prevent changes to certain registry keys, as described in "Lock Your File Types" on page 184.

Users and Security

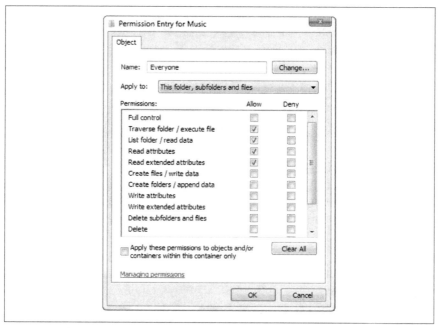

Figure 8-7. The Permission Entry window lets you fine-tune permissions

Protect Your Files with Encryption

Encryption effectively adds another layer of protection for your especially sensitive data, ensuring that a file can only be viewed by its creator (well, sort of). If any other user—even someone with administrator privileges—attempts to view the file, he will see only gibberish or nothing at all. In other words, your encrypted data is unreadable unless Windows is running and logged into your account.

When a file is marked for encryption, the encryption and decryption of the file are handled by Windows invisibly in the background when its creator writes and views the file, respectively. The problem is that Windows 7's on-the-fly encryption can be somewhat unpredictable, and security is one place where you don't want there to be any guesswork.

Encryption is a feature of the NTFS filesystem (discussed in "Choose the Right Filesystem" on page 317) and is not available with any other filesystem. This means that if you copy an encrypted file onto, say, a memory card, USB key, or CD, the file will become unencrypted, since none of those drives support NTFS.

Encrypt an Entire Drive with BitLocker

Windows 7's file and folder encryption is a handy way to protect sensitive data, but mixing encrypted and unencrypted data on the same drive can lead to unpredictable results, as described in "Protect Your Files with Encryption" on page 558. But if you have the Ultimate or Enterprise edition of Windows 7, you'll have the luxury of using the BitLocker drive encryption feature.

BitLocker works by placing all the data on your drive into a single, enormous archive file, and then accesses the file invisibly like a virtual hard disk. You can access the files on a BitLocker-encrypted drive through Windows Explorer as though it were any other drive, while Windows handles the encryption and decryption in the background. The BitLocker approach has the significant advantage of encrypting Windows and all your system files, which makes it more difficult for a hacker to crack your password and break into your account, thus rendering your individual file encryption worthless.

To get started, open the BitLocker Drive Encryption page in Control Panel. If you see a "TPM was not found" error, see whether there's a BIOS update available for your PC (as described in Appendix A) that supports TPM.

TPM, or *Trusted Platform Module*, is a chip on your motherboard that's used to store the BitLocker encryption key, allowing you to boot off an encrypted drive. If your BIOS doesn't support TPM, you can use an ordinary removable USB flash drive for this purpose. Open the Group Policy Object Editor (click **Start** and type gpedit.msc), and then expand the branches to Computer Configuration\Administrative Templates\Windows Components\BitLocker Drive Encryption. On the right, double-click the **Control Panel Setup: Enable advanced startup options** entry, click **Enabled**, turn on the **Allow BitLocker without a compatible TPM** option, and then click OK.

In order for you to use BitLocker, your hard disk must have at least two partitions (see Chapter 5): one for your operating system, and another "active" partition—of at least 1.5 Gb in size—used to boot your PC. If your drive isn't currently set up this way, start the BitLocker Drive Preparation Tool (*BdeHdCfg.exe*) and follow the prompts. When your drive is ready, open the BitLocker Drive Encryption page in Control Panel and click **Turn on BitLocker.**

Hint: if you don't have Windows 7 Ultimate, you can do pretty much the same thing with either FreeOTFE (*http://www.freeotfe.org/*) or TrueCrypt (*http://www.truecrypt.org/*), both of which are free and compatible with all editions of Windows 7.

Need to read a BitLocker-encrypted drive using Windows Vista or XP? Use Microsoft's BitLocker To Go Reader, free from *http://windows.microsoft.com/en-US/windows7/what-is-the-bitlocker-to-go-reader*.

Here's how to encrypt a file:

1. Right-click one or more files in Windows Explorer and select **Properties**.
2. Under the **General** tab, click the **Advanced** button.
3. Turn on the **Encrypt contents to secure data** option, click OK, and click OK again.

After a file has been encrypted, you can continue to use it normally. You'll never have to manually decrypt an encrypted file in order to view it. See "Add Encrypt/Decrypt commands to context menus" on page 566 for a quicker way to encrypt and decrypt files.

You should keep the following caveats in mind when encrypting your files:

Encrypt folder contents?
> If you encrypt a folder that contains files or other folders, Windows will ask you whether or not you want those contents to be encrypted as well. In most cases, you'll want to answer **Yes**. If you decline, the folder's current contents will remain unencrypted, and only newly created files will be encrypted. See "The ins and outs of folder encryption" on page 564 for details.

Encrypted forever?
> When you encrypt a file, there's no guarantee that it'll remain encrypted forever. For example, some applications, when editing and saving files, delete the original file and then recreate it in the same place. If the application is unaware of encryption, the protection will be lost. The workaround is to encrypt the folder containing the file rather than the file itself.

Encrypted for other users?
> If you change the ownership of a file (as described in "Set Permissions for a File or Folder" on page 550) and the file is encrypted, the encryption will remain active for the *original* owner and creator of the file, even though that user no longer technically "owns" the file. In certain cases, this means that nobody will be able to read the file.

Encrypt system files?
> Since all users need to access files in certain folders, such as the \Windows and \Windows\System folders, Windows won't let you encrypt files and system folders or the root directories of any drives. Thus the only way to encrypt these folders as well is to use drive encryption, as described in the sidebar "Encrypt an Entire Drive with BitLocker" on page 559.

Encryption and compression?
> Compression, another feature of the NTFS filesystem, reduces the amount of space consumed by a file or folder. The rules that apply to compression

are more or less the same as those that apply to encryption. But you cannot simultaneously use encryption and compression on any object; turn on one option in the Properties window, and Windows will turn the other off.

Highlight encrypted files in Windows Explorer

By default, Windows Explorer visually differentiates encrypted files, which can be a very handy way to keep track of the scope of your encryption. In Control Panel, open Folder Options, choose **View** tab, and turn on the **Show encrypted or compressed NTFS files in color** option to use this feature, or turn it off if you want all your filenames to be displayed in black text. Click OK when you're done.

By default, the names of encrypted files appear in green, while those of compressed files appear in blue (except for icons on the desktop). Note that files can't be simultaneously compressed and encrypted (as mentioned in the previous section), so you'll never see any turquoise, teal, or aquamarine filenames.

Actually, that's not *entirely* true. You *can* customize the color Windows uses to highlight encrypted filenames by editing the registry (see Chapter 3).

Open the Registry Editor and expand the branches to HKEY_CURRENT_USER\Software\Microsoft\Windows\CurrentVersion\Explorer. Create a new binary value by going to **Edit→New→Binary Value**, and type AltEncryptionColor for the name of the new value. Then double-click the new AltEncryptionColor value and type a code to indicate the color you'd like to use, following this pattern:

```
RR GG BB 00
```

The RGB hex code used here follows the same scheme as RGB codes in HTML web pages (except for the two trailing zeros), which means you can use any common color mixer to generate the hex codes for you. For an excellent, free web-based color mixer, go to *http://colormixers.com/mixers/cmr*. Or, if you have Adobe Photoshop, you can match an existing color with the eyedropper tool and grab the code from the # field in the color mixer window.

For example, to get a nice aquamarine color, you'd type this:

```
00 B4 C5 00
```

Here, the first 00 indicates no red, the B4 is the hex code for 180 (out of 255; roughly 70% green), the C5 is the hex code for 197 (about 77% blue), and then the last two zeros are for good measure. Or, to get the default green color, type:

```
00 80 40 00
```

By the way, don't type the spaces; Registry Editor will do it for you.

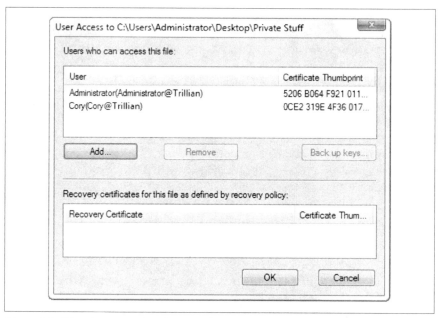

Figure 8-8. This elusive window lets you share an encrypted file with another user while keeping your password secret and the file's encryption intact

Likewise, you can customize the color used for compressed filenames by creating a new binary value named `AltColor` in this same key, and filling its value data with whatever RGB code you like.

Close the Registry Editor when you're done. The change will take effect the next time you log in.

Allow others to access your encrypted files

By default, only you can read your own encrypted files. But what if you want someone else to have access to a file, yet keep your password to yourself and maintain the file's encrypted state?

Right-click a file or folder you've already encrypted, select **Properties**, and under the **General** tab, click the **Advanced** button. Click the **Details** button to open the User Access window shown in Figure 8-8.

If the **Details** button is grayed out (disabled) in the Advanced Attributes window, it means that encryption isn't yet active for the selected file or folder. If you just turned on the **Encrypt contents to secure data** option, you need to click OK twice to close both the Advanced Attributes window and the Properties window. Then return to the Advanced Attributes window and try again.

If the **Details** button is *still* grayed out, and you've right-clicked a folder, try opening the folder and right-clicking one of the files therein.

To permit another user to access your files, click **Add** to show the Encrypting File System window. Here, you won't necessarily see all the user accounts on your PC, only those that already have security certificates. If you don't see the account you want to include here, you'll need to log in to that account and encrypt at least one file or folder.

If the user doesn't have an account on your PC, you can either create one, or you can install the user's own certificate on your PC by hand. To do this, ask the user to send you the certificate from her PC. On her PC, she'd open the User Accounts window in Control Panel, click **Manage your file encryption certificates**, and follow the prompts. (See "Back up your encryption certificates" on page 566 for more on this.)

To import her certificate, fire up the Certificates tool (*certmgr.msc*) and expand the **Personal** branch and select the **Certificates** folder. From the **Action** menu, select **All Tasks** and then **Import**, and then complete the Certificate Import Wizard by following the prompts.

To use a smart card to transfer your credentials to another PC, use the Credential Manager instead of the Certificate Manager to grant access, as described in "Force a Login Box for a Remote Folder" on page 602.

Note that the **Expiration Date** shown here represents the date the user's security certificate expires, and has nothing to do with the permissions you're setting up. No hurry, though; you've got at least 100 years.

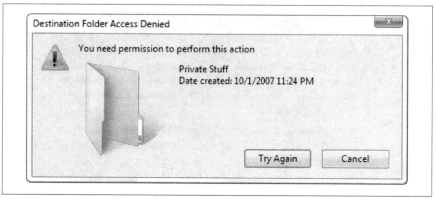

Figure 8-9. Try to access someone else's encrypted file, and you'll get this error

View someone else's encrypted files

So, how do you access someone else's encrypted files *without* that person's permission? (This is an important question to ask if you care about the security of your own data.) If you try to view someone's encrypted files, you'll get an "Access is Denied" error message like the one shown in Figure 8-9.

Not even administrators can view files encrypted by other users. However, any administrator can change any other user's password, and then subsequently log in to that user's account and view (or unencrypt) any protected files. This means that your files won't be totally secure unless you're the only administrator on the machine.

There is a little-known side effect to this fact: if the owner of encrypted files deletes his or her encryption keys, neither the user nor any administrator will be able to read the encrypted files until the key is reinstalled. See "Back up your encryption certificates" on page 566 for more information.

The ins and outs of folder encryption

You can also encrypt a folder and all of its contents using the procedure for files shown earlier. It gets a little more complicated, though, when you mix and match encrypted and unencrypted files and folders, and it can be difficult to predict what happens to the folders' contents.

Now, if a file in an encrypted folder is moved into an *unencrypted* folder, the file becomes unencrypted. The exception is when you've specifically encrypted the file itself; in this case, the file remains encrypted, no matter where you put it. Whenever you try to encrypt a file located in an unencrypted folder, Windows warns you and gives you the option to encrypt the folder as well (shown in Figure 8-10).

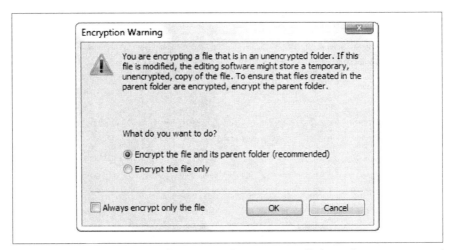

Figure 8-10. Windows displays this warning if you encrypt a file located in an unencrypted folder

Be especially careful here, as the default is to encrypt the containing (parent) folder in addition to the selected file, which can be counterintuitive if you're accustomed to warnings that only deal with child objects. Check the **Always encrypt only the file** option if you never want to see this warning again.

If you ever inadvertently encrypt your desktop (by encrypting an item on your desktop, and then accepting the default in this box), the only way to unencrypt it is to open Windows Explorer, and unencrypt the source desktop folder (usually *\Users\{your username}\Desktop*).

If an unencrypted file is placed in an encrypted folder, the file will become encrypted, too. The catch is when one user encrypts a folder and *another user* places a file in that folder; in this case, the file is encrypted for the *creator of the file*, which means that the owner of the folder, the one who originally implemented the encryption, will not be able to read the file.

On the other hand, if the user places a file in a folder, and a different user comes along and subsequently encrypts the folder, only the user who implemented the encryption will be able to read the file, even though the file is officially "owned" by that first user. So timing is as vital to encryption as it is to comedy.

Add Encrypt/Decrypt commands to context menus

If you find yourself frequently encrypting and decrypting files, having to repeatedly open the Properties window can be a pain. Instead, follow these steps to add **Encrypt** and **Decrypt** commands to the context menus for every file and folder:

1. Open the Registry Editor (see Chapter 3).
2. Expand the branches to `HKEY_LOCAL_MACHINE\SOFTWARE\Microsoft\Windows\CurrentVersion\Explorer\Advanced`.
3. Create a new DWORD value by going to **Edit→New→DWORD (32-bit) Value**, and type `EncryptionContextMenu` for the name of the new value.
4. Double-click the new `EncryptionContextMenu` value, enter 1 for the **Value data**, and click OK.
5. Close the Registry Editor when you're done. The change will take effect immediately.

To use this new trick, right-click any unencrypted file in Explorer or on your desktop, and select **Encrypt**. Or, right-click an already encrypted file, and select **Decrypt**.

If at least one of the selected items is a folder, you'll have the option of encrypting only the folder or all the folders contained therein. If encrypting any individual files, you'll also be asked if you wish to encrypt only the file or the parent folder as well.

Back up your encryption certificates

Think of your encryption certificate as the combination to a safe. Forget the combination, and you can't open the safe. Likewise, lose your certificate, and you won't be able to open your encrypted files.

 Windows 7's encryption system employs symmetric key cryptography, which uses the same key to encrypt and decrypt data. Windows generates a unique key for each user, so that no user can decrypt another user's data. The classic example of cryptographic keys is how Julius Caesar encoded messages to his allies. Each letter in the message was shifted by three: A became D, B became E, C became F, and so on. Only someone who knew to shift the letters *back* by three could decode the messages. Cryptographic keys work the same way, except they're slightly more complicated.

Figure 8-11. The first time you use encryption on your PC, you'll be prompted to back up your encryption certificate (key) so you can access your protected files even if you reinstall Windows

The first time you use encryption on your PC, Windows 7 creates a new encryption certificate for you (if you don't already have one) and prompts you to back up your certificate with the window shown in Figure 8-11.

Whether or not you take Windows up on its offer, you can use one of the three included tools to manage your encryption certificates:

Control Panel
On the User Accounts page in Control Panel, click the **Manage your file encryption certificates** link on the left, and then click **Next**. Select **Use this certificate**, and click **Next**. Select **Back up the certificate and key now**, click **Browse** to choose a filename, and type your password twice. The tool will create your *.pfx* backup file as soon as you click **Next**.

On the next page, you'll be asked to update your previously encrypted files. This ensures that the certificate you're backing up today can be used in the future to restore your data; otherwise, any files encrypted with an older certificate may remain inaccessible if you should lose that certificate. Close the wizard when you're done.

Certificate Manager

Open your Start menu, type `certmgr.msc`, and press **Enter** to fire up the Certificate Manager. Expand the **Personal** branch and select the **Certificates** folder to view the certificates installed on your PC. The one used for NTFS encryption is labeled **Encrypting File System** in the **Intended Purposes** column. View any certificate by double-clicking it.

You can back up a certificate by highlighting it and then selecting **All Tasks→Export** from the **Action** menu. Just save the file to a USB memory key or CD so it's safe in the event that your hard disk crashes and you need to install a second copy of Windows to access your data. (This is the same thing that happens if you click **Back up now (recommended)** when you see the prompt in Figure 8-11.)

If you need to, you can install a backed-up encryption certificate on any PC—and thus read the files encrypted with it—by importing it as described in "Allow others to access your encrypted files" on page 562.

NTFS Encryption Utility

The NTFS Encryption Utility (*cipher.exe*) lets you encrypt or decrypt files and manage certificates from the Command Prompt, but it's not included with all editions of Windows. It does have the added benefit of being able to perform some tricks that the Certificate Manager cannot.

Open a Command Prompt window (*cmd.exe*) in Administrator mode and type `cipher` without any arguments to display the encryption status for all the files in the current folder. (Use the `cd` command discussed in Chapter 9 to change to a different working folder.) Encrypted files will be marked with an E; all others will marked with a U.

To encrypt a file, type `cipher /e `*filename*, where *filename* is the name of the file or folder (include the full path if it's in a different folder). Likewise, type `cipher /d `*filename* to turn off encryption for the item.

To back up your certificate, type `cipher /r:`*filename* at the prompt, where *filename* is the prefix of the output filename (without an extension). Cipher asks for a password, and then generates two separate files based on the specified filename. For example, if you type `cipher /r:julius`, you'll end up with two files: *julius.pfx*, which contains the Encrypting File System (EFS) recovery agent key and certificate, and *julius.cer*, which contains the EFS recovery agent certificate only (without the key). Double-click either file in Windows Explorer to import the certificate or key, or use the Certificate Manager.

Worried that your key got in the wrong hands? You can generate a new key at any time by typing `cipher /k` (without any other options). Then, type `cipher /u` to update the encrypted files on your system with the new key.

Secure your drive's free space

Normally, when you delete a file, only the file's entry in the filesystem table is deleted; the actual data contained in the file remains in the folder until it is overwritten with another file.

Cipher, discussed in the previous section, allows you to *wipe* a folder, which only means that it goes black and cleans out any recently deleted files, overwriting the leftover data with random bits. This effectively makes it impossible to subsequently recover deleted data with an "undelete" utility. Think of the wipe feature as a virtual paper shredder.

To wipe a folder, open a Command Prompt window and type `cipher /w:foldername`, where *foldername* is the full path of any folder on the drive to wipe. Although Cipher requires the path of a folder, it actually wipes all the free space on the drive. This means that the commands `cipher /w:c:\Romulus` and `cipher /w:c:\Remus` have exactly the same result.

 Set up Cipher to wipe folders containing sensitive data at regular intervals (or when Windows starts) to automatically protect deleted data. See Chapter 9 for information on the Scheduled Tasks feature and WSH scripts, both of which can be used to automate Cipher.

Note that Cipher's `/w` option does not harm existing data, nor does it affect any files currently stored in the Recycle Bin. It also works on unencrypted folders and encrypted folders alike.

Control User Account Control

For years, Windows-based PCs have been under siege by viruses, spyware, and adware, concepts explored in Chapter 6. User Account Control, or UAC, is Microsoft's response to this scourge.

It works like this: Windows 7, like its predecessors, supports different levels of user accounts, some with administrator rights—necessary to install software and configure the system—and others with lesser privileges. But Windows 7 doesn't give administrators carte blanche like Windows XP and 2000. Instead,

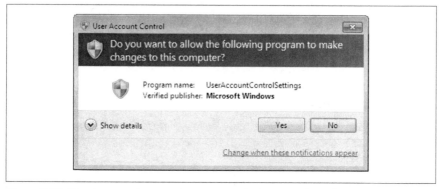

Figure 8-12. Nearly every time you (or a program) tries to make a change to your system, Windows shows you this annoying prompt

an administrator (you, for instance) operates in a more restrictive *standard* user account mode most of the time. Only when you make a change that supposedly affects other users on your PC (whether there are any or not), like installing a new hardware driver or changing Windows Firewall settings, does Windows 7 request your permission with the UAC prompt like the one in Figure 8-12.

If you click **Continue**, Windows permits the action, and thereafter, it's smooth sailing (at least until the next prompt). Or, click **Cancel**, and Windows forbids the request. As with any preventative measure, there are costs and benefits to Windows 7's UAC.

First, the good:

It can make Windows safer
> In theory, nothing bad can happen to your PC without your approval. This means so-called *drive-by installations* from nasty websites you view in Internet Explorer, the source of some spyware and adware, are a thing of the past (in theory). (Of course, you can also deal with this by changing a few settings, as described in "Lock Down Internet Explorer" on page 514.)

It can make Windows more stable
> Provided you take a few extra steps, UAC makes it harder for incompetent users to damage a PC by deleting or replacing files, making unauthorized changes to the registry, and screwing up network settings.

It can make Windows easier to administer
> It's possible to require a password at each UAC prompt, meaning a PC's administrator doesn't have to create a separate account to make changes. The PC's day-to-day user doesn't know the password and can't make changes, but the administrator can sit down and fix a problem in minutes, without even logging out.

Now for the bad:

It breaks some programs

UAC may break software not expressly written for Windows 7 or Vista. For instance, any program that attempts to write files to the *Program Files* folder (even its own application folder) will be denied access; this is why lots of older applications can't save their settings on Windows 7, and some programs can't start up or even be installed. And unless the software is UAC-aware, it won't attempt to "elevate" itself to the administrator level, and you'll never see the UAC prompt; Windows just denies it. In short, you won't know why the program doesn't work.

It's annoying

(OK, this one should be first, but that just seemed a bit self-serving.) How many times today have you sat and watched your screen go black while you waited...and waited...for the UAC prompt to appear? And have you noticed that some features require *two* UAC prompts: one that warns you that you're about to be asked for your permission, and the other that actually makes the request? Couldn't Microsoft have found a less cumbersome way to do this, such as a single window that elevates the current session to administrator status for, say, the next 20 minutes?

It's easily defeated

The UAC feature can be completely disabled with a single setting in Control Panel, but what is more worrisome is the fact that UAC doesn't need to be disabled to be defeated. Any program that already has administrator-level access, such as an installer, can make any changes to your PC without showing any additional UAC prompts. And if you install software that registers a driver or Windows service (managed with *services.msc*), that service could be used to carry out administrator-level requests by any program at any time, even one run under the lowly *standard* user account.

Nobody reads prompts anyway

It's only a matter of time before an average PC user becomes accustomed to the prompt and gets into the habit of clicking **Continue** without reading the message. Even if it were an otherwise flawless system, there's no system in place to make sure the user knows what he is doing.

When designing Windows 7, Microsoft tried to please everybody by making UAC strict enough to prevent certain mischief, yet lenient enough that it wouldn't be such a nuisance that you'd want to turn it off. Of course, the result is a system that is either too much or not enough for most people. The solution, of course, is to customize it.

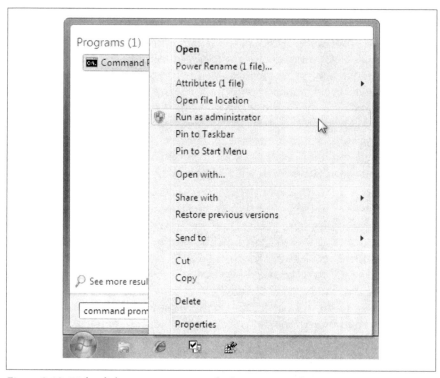

*Figure 8-13. Right-click a program icon and select **Run as administrator** to temporarily elevate a program so it's no longer restricted by Windows 7's security*

Fix a program broken by UAC

So, you've got a program that won't install on Windows 7, can't save its settings, or doesn't run. The problem is likely that UAC is preventing the application (or the installer) from doing what it was designed to do. And since the application isn't UAC-aware, it doesn't request elevation, the step necessary to tell Windows that it's time for the UAC prompt. The result? Windows 7 prevents the change and keeps its mouth shut, and the application doesn't work.

The solution is to elevate the application yourself. You can't do this while it's running, but, as shown in Figure 8-13, you can do it when you start the application. Just right-click the application's icon on your desktop or Start menu (or the program's *.exe* file), and select **Run as administrator**.

This time, you'll see the UAC prompt, and assuming you click **Continue**, Windows will elevate the application and it should work as designed. See the upcoming sidebar, "Command Prompt As Administrator" on page 573, for notes for running programs from the command line.

If you don't see the **Run as administrator** option, it means that the icon you've clicked isn't a standard executable or Windows shortcut. In this case, just open Windows Explorer, navigate to the program's application folder (usually found under *C:\Program Files*), and right-click the main *.exe* file.

This trick also works for application installers, but beware: if the installer needs this workaround, the application is likely to need it, too. Before you install, check the software publisher's website for an update or a new version that's compatible with Windows 7.

If the program won't function unless you use the **Run as administrator** feature, make the change permanent: right-click the program icon (or *.exe* file), select **Properties**, and choose the **Compatibility** tab. In the **Privilege Level** box, turn on the **Run this program as an administrator** option, and click OK.

 Although Windows won't show the **Run as administrator** option when you right-click documents, if you use the **Compatibility** tab as instructed here, the associated application will always run in administrator mode.

Command Prompt As Administrator

The Command Prompt, detailed in Chapter 9, is a special case when it comes to User Account Control. Although obviously designed for Windows 7, the Command Prompt application (*cmd.exe*) does not elevate itself automatically to administrator mode when needed like other Windows components do.

For instance, if you open a Command Prompt with the Start menu icon or by launching *cmd.exe* directly, and then try using netsh, sc, or many of the other commands outlined in the hacks in this book, it won't work because UAC gets in the way. To get around the roadblock, you've got to close the Command Prompt and then open it again by right-clicking and selecting **Run as administrator**.

That's a lot of extra clicking if you're opening Command Prompt windows with any regularity. Unfortunately, if you right-click the *cmd.exe* file—or even a shortcut to *cmd.exe*—and try to turn on the **Run this program as an administrator** option under the **Compatibility** tab, you'll see this message:

Compatibility modes cannot be set on this program because it is part of this version of Windows.

In usual Microsoft fashion, this statement makes some sort of perverted sense, but is absolutely no help. To work around this, just make a copy of *cmd.exe* (it's in *\Windows\System32*) and put it in any other folder. Then, right-click the copy of *cmd.exe*, choose the **Compatibility** tab, and turn on the **Run this program as an administrator** option.

You can also install Creative Element Power Tools (*http://creativelement.com/powertools/*) and in the Creative Element Power Tools Control Panel, enable the **Open a Command Prompt in any folder** tool. Click **Select Command Prompt**, turn on the **Open Command Prompt as Administrator** option, and click **Accept**. Thereafter, you can right-click any folder (or the Desktop) and select **Open Command Prompt here** to open the command prompt, rooted in that folder, with full administrator access.

Alternatively, you can use a program like Start++ (free from *http://brandontools.com/*), which adds a sudo command to the Command Prompt. Like the Unix/Linux command of the same name, sudo lets you run a single command as the administrator without having to open a Command Prompt in Administrator mode. And doing so may keep you from inadvertently causing any damage by providing administrator-level access to only those commands that need it.

Turn off User Account Control

The easiest way to turn off UAC is through the User Accounts page in Control Panel. On the "Make changes to your user account" page, click the **Change User Account Control settings** link, and then drag the slider all the way to bottom to set it to **Never notify**.

The **Never notify** setting here is a bit misleading. The wording suggests that you won't be bothered by another "Windows needs your permission to continue" message, and while this is true, what it doesn't say is that programs previously run under the restricted "standard" user account will now be run in full administrator mode. There is no setting on this page that allows you leave UAC enabled while quietly blocking programs that try to make changes to your PC. However, the second option from the bottom, **Notify me only when programs try to make changes to my computer**, is close in that it turns off the dimming of the desktop when a UAC prompt appears.

Of course, turning off UAC altogether isn't necessarily the best choice if you just want to get rid of the incessant UAC prompts. If you're using the

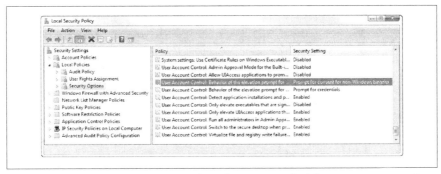

Figure 8-14. Use the Local Security Policy editor to get rid of the UAC prompts without disabling UAC altogether

Professional or Ultimate editions of Windows 7, open the Start menu, and in the **Search** box, type secpol.msc and press **Enter** to bring up the Local Security Policy editor shown in Figure 8-14. If you have Windows 7 Home Premium, see the sidebar "Security Policies in Home Premium" on page 579, which explains the ConsentPromptBehaviorAdmin notes that follow.

Expand the **Local Policies** branch and select the **Security Options** folder. In the right pane, double-click the **User Account Control: Behavior of the elevation prompt for administrators in Admin Approval Mode** setting. Here you have six choices:

Elevate without prompting

This is the best choice if you want to skip the UAC window altogether. Even though this option gets rid of the UAC prompts, it does not disable UAC. This means that applications that aren't UAC-aware won't request elevation, and thus Windows 7 will still block any changes it considers dangerous.

Home Premium users: set ConsentPromptBehaviorAdmin to 0.

Prompt for credentials

Use this to toughen security on your PC by requiring a password each time the UAC prompt appears; a user can't click **Continue** without entering the password.

Home Premium users: set ConsentPromptBehaviorAdmin to 3.

 If you're an administrator who's setting up this PC for someone else to use, your best course of action is to give that person a *standard* account. Then, in the Local Security Policy editor, set the **User Account Control: Behavior of the elevation prompt for standard users** option to **Prompt for credentials**.

Prompt for consent

The UAC prompt appears every time an application requests administrator-level access, but all you have to do is click **Continue**—or in some cases, **Permit**—to allow the action.

Home Premium users: set `ConsentPromptBehaviorAdmin` to 4.

Prompt for credentials / consent on the secure desktop

This is the same as **Prompt for credentials** and **Prompt for consent**, respectively, except that Windows also dims the desktop to bring attention to the UAC prompt.

Home Premium users: set `ConsentPromptBehaviorAdmin` to 1 for **credentials**, 2 for **consent**.

Prompt for consent for non-Windows binaries

This is the default in Windows 7. It's the same as **Prompt for consent**, but only for programs that didn't come with Windows. For an example of a Windows binary, see the sidebar "Command Prompt As Administrator" on page 573.

Home Premium users: set `ConsentPromptBehaviorAdmin` to 5.

As you've probably noticed, there are at least nine other policy settings for UAC in the Local Security Policy window, and while most are fairly self-explanatory, there are a few that deserve special attention.

If you're using the built-in Administrator account described in "Log In As the Administrator" on page 584, then you won't ever see UAC prompts by default. You can change this with the **User Account Control: Admin Approval Mode for the Built-in Administrator account** setting.

Windows 7 tries to automatically elevate most software installers to administrator-level, which may not be such a great idea if you want to cut your odds of a malware infestation on your PC. For a little more security, set the **User Account Control: Detect application installations and prompt for elevation** option to **Disabled**. Thereafter, you may need to right-click older installers and select **Run as administrator** to proceed; newer installers should elevate themselves as needed.

Another way to strengthen UAC is to set the **User Account Control: Only elevate executables that are signed and validated** option to **Enabled**, which will block unsigned applications from running in administrator mode.

Finally, see the "File and Registry Virtualization Explained" sidebar, next, for details on the **User Account Control: Virtualizes file and registry write failures to per-user locations** setting, and an explanation of something else that can break UAC-unaware programs.

File and Registry Virtualization Explained

As described in "Control User Account Control" on page 569, Windows 7's UAC feature is designed to prevent changes to operating system folders like *Program Files*, as well as protected areas of the registry. If a program wasn't designed with UAC in mind, it won't request elevation to administrator-level access, and its attempt to, say, write to its own application folder in *Program Files* will fail. Microsoft had to come up with a compromise that would allow some of these older programs to work.

That compromise is *virtualization*, a system that redirects older (*legacy*, as Microsoft puts it) applications to special, protected areas of your hard disk and registry. So, if a program with an auto-update feature tries to write files to *C:\Program Files\Acme Update\newversion.dll*, Windows will instead send it to *C:\Users\[your_username]\AppData\Local\VirtualStore\Program Files \Acme Update\newversion.dll*.

Likewise, if a program tries to make a change to the registry, in the `HKEY_LOCAL_MACHINE\Software\Acme` key, the change will be made instead to the `HKEY_CURRENT_USER\Software\Classes\VirtualStore\MACHINE\Software\Acme` key.

By default, your *Program Files* and *Windows* folders, and most of their subfolders, are protected, as well as almost all of the `HKEY_LOCAL_MACHINE\Software` branch in the registry. UAC does not protect a user's own folder *C:\Users \[your_username]*, nor does it lock out changes to the `HKEY_CURRENT_USER \Software` branch of the registry.

To turn virtualization off, set the **User Account Control: Virtualizes file and registry write failures to per-user locations** option in the Local Security Policy editor to **Disabled**. But keep in mind that turning off virtualization won't, in itself, permit older applications to write in these protected areas; instead, it will simply cause more of your older programs to stop functioning, since Windows will no longer give them a safe place to play.

To see which of your running programs are subject to virtualization, right-click an empty area of your taskbar and select **Task Manager**. Choose the **Processes** tab, and then from the **View** menu, click **Select Columns**. Turn on the **User Account Control (UAC) Virtualization** column, and then click OK. Now, in the **Processes** list, you'll see that some programs—particularly older ones—have virtualization set to **Enabled**, as do *explorer.exe* and *iexplore.exe* (because of the danger of add-ons). UAC-aware programs will have virtualization set to **Disabled**, and programs already running as the administrator will have it set to **Not Allowed**.

Logon and Profile Options

Here's the dilemma: you've set up multiple user accounts on a machine, and you've gone the extra mile to ensure that your data is properly protected by configuring permissions and employing encryption. Now you find Windows so locked down that you can't do anything without having to enter a password first. Fortunately, you can streamline the logon process to suit your needs and tolerance for cumbersome logon procedures, or use some lesser known features to lock it down even further.

Hide the List of User Accounts

The friendly Welcome screen is the default interface you see when you log on to Windows 7.

Back in the old days, we didn't have any fancy pictures to click; we actually had to type our usernames *and* passwords to log on. In the snow. Uphill, both ways.

If you long for those simpler times, or perhaps if you just realize that it's wise *not* to show a list of all the user accounts on a PC, you can opt for a more retrostyle login box.

Unfortunately, Microsoft removed the bare-bones, "classic" Windows NT-style logon window that was present even in Windows XP, but there is an alternative. To get a login screen with both username and password fields, albeit with a look reminiscent of Windows 7's Welcome screen, follow these steps:

1. Open the Start menu **Search** box, type `secpol.msc`, and press **Enter** to display the Local Security Policy editor.

    The Local Security Policy tool is only available in the Windows 7 Professional and Ultimate editions; for Home Premium, see the upcoming sidebar "Security Policies in Home Premium" on page 579.

2. Expand the **Local Policies** branch and click the **Security Options** folder.

3. In the right pane, double-click the **Interactive logon: Do not display last user name** option, select **Enabled**, and click OK.

4. Close the Local Security Policy window when you're done; the change will take effect the next time you log in.

Keep in mind that if your goal is to hide the list of user accounts from everyone but you, then this is only part of the solution. Sure, this hides the user list from passersby, but anyone with an administrator account on the PC could log in and open the User Accounts page in Control Panel to view—and modify—other users on the system. (Of course, any administrator could also re-enable the Welcome screen, or even create new accounts.) So, to keep your user list hidden, use standard user accounts for all other users.

Security Policies in Home Premium

Several hacks in this book make use of the Local Security Policy tool (*secpol.msc*), which comes only with the Professional, Ultimate, and Enterprise editions of Windows 7. But what if you want to make these changes under the Home Premium version?

The good news is that *secpol.msc* doesn't actually add any features to Windows; rather, it's merely a tool of convenience, providing a slightly friendlier interface to some specific registry entries. Most changes are made to the values in this key and its subkeys:

    HKEY_LOCAL_MACHINE\SOFTWARE\Microsoft\Windows\CurrentVersion\Policies

For instance, the **User Account Control: Behavior of the elevation prompt for administrators in Admin Approval Mode** setting discussed in "Control User Account Control" on page 569 affects a DWORD value named `Consent PromptBehaviorAdmin`, located in the `System` subkey of `Policies`. Just double-click the `ConsentPromptBehaviorAdmin` value (or create it if doesn't exist) and type the number indicated.

In "Hide the List of User Accounts" on page 578, the setting alters the `dont displaylastusername` DWORD value. Like most policies that are a simple **Enable / Disable** switch, set it to `1` to enable the policy, or `0` to disable it.

Note that some policies specifically control or limit features found only in the Professional or Ultimate editions of Windows 7, and changing them through the registry won't necessarily enable those features in lesser editions.

See Chapter 3 for more on the registry.

Users and Security

Log In Automatically

If you assign a password to your account or if you add a second user account in Control Panel, Windows 7 will show you the Welcome screen every time Windows starts. What a pain.

But it's never a good idea to have any accounts, particularly those for administrators, on your PC without passwords to protect them. Apart from a password-less account being a rather large security hole, passwords are necessary to get file sharing to work. To password-protect your computer on the network and skip the Welcome screen, just open the alternate User Accounts window (described at the beginning of this chapter); open the Start menu, and in the **Search** box, type:

```
%SystemRoot%\system32\control userpasswords2
```

and then press **Enter**. Select from the list the username you'd like to be your primary login, turn off the **Users must enter a username and password to use this computer** option, and click OK.

When the "Automatically Log On" window appears, type and confirm the password for the selected user, and click OK when you're done. The change will take effect the next time you start your PC.

Note that this change won't affect your ability to log out and then log in to another user account. Furthermore, logging out and logging back in won't negate this setting; the next time you start Windows, you'll be logged in automatically once again. See the next topic if you don't want this setting to last forever.

Limit automatic logins

It's possible to limit the automatic login feature, so that the Log On dialog (or Welcome screen) reappears after a specified number of boots:

1. Open the Registry Editor (discussed in Chapter 3).
2. Expand the branches to HKEY_LOCAL_MACHINE\SOFTWARE\Microsoft\Windows NT\CurrentVersion\Winlogon. (Note the Windows NT branch here, as opposed to the more commonly-used Windows branch.)
3. Create a new DWORD value here by going to **Edit→New→DWORD (32-bit) Value**, and type AutoLogonCount for the name of the new value.
4. Double-click the new AutoLogonCount value, select **Decimal**, and type the number of system boots for which you'd like the automatic login to remain active.
5. Click OK when you're done.

Every successive time Windows starts, it will decrease this value by one. When the value is zero, Windows forgets the username and password you entered at the beginning of this topic, and the AutoLogonCount value is removed.

Prevent users from bypassing the automatic login

Automatic logins are particularly useful for machines you wish to use in public environments: typically called a "kiosk" or "doorstop." But you'll want to take steps to ensure that a visitor can't log in to a more privileged account during a typical session. There are two ways for a user to skip the automatic login and log in to another user account:

- Hold the **Shift** key while Windows is logging in.
- Once Windows has logged in, log out by selecting **Log Off** from the Start menu or pressing **Ctrl-Alt-Del** and selecting **Log Off**.

To eliminate both of these backdoors, follow these steps:

1. Open the Registry Editor (discussed in Chapter 3).

2. Expand the branches to HKEY_LOCAL_MACHINE\SOFTWARE\Microsoft\Windows NT\CurrentVersion\Winlogon. (Note the Windows NT branch here, as opposed to the more commonly-used Windows branch.)

3. Create a new string value here by going to **Edit→New→String Value**, and name the new value IgnoreShiftOverride. Double-click the new value, type 1 for its value data, and click OK. (This disables the **Shift** key during the automatic login.)

4. Next, create a new DWORD value in this same key by going to **Edit→New→DWORD (32-bit) Value**, and name the new value ForceAutoLogon. Double-click the new value, type 1 for its value data, and click OK. (This automatically logs back in if the user tries to log out.)

5. Close the Registry Editor when you're done. The change will take effect immediately.

To remove either or both of these restrictions, just delete the corresponding registry values.

Force passwords to expire

> *Treat your password like your toothbrush.*
> *Don't let anybody else use it, and get a new*
> *one every six months.*
>
> —Clifford Stoll

If you have the Professional or Ultimate edition of Windows 7, you can have Windows force you to routinely change your password. Open the Local Users and Groups manager (in the Start menu **Search** box, type lusrmgr.msc), and then open the **Users** folder. Double-click your username, turn off the **Password never expires** option, and click OK. (Do the same for any other accounts here, if needed.) When you're done, close the Local Users and Groups manager.

Next, open the Local Security Policy editor (in the Start menu, type secpol.msc) and expand the branches to Account Policies\Password Policy. On the right, double-click **Maximum password age** and enter the amount of time before Windows expires your password. (To take Cliff Stoll's advice, enter 182 days.) Close the Local Security Policy editor; the change takes effect the next time you log in.

Reset a Forgotten Administrator Password

Forgot your password? No problem. There are two ways to get into your PC: the easy way and the hard way.

If there are any other administrator-level accounts on your PC, the easy way is to log in to one of those accounts, open the User Accounts page in Control Panel, and change your password there.

If yours is the only administrator-level account, you'll have to reset your password the hard way. (This won't work if your drive is protected by BitLocker Drive Encryption, described earlier in this chapter.) Start by downloading the free Trinity Rescue Kit from *http://trinityhome.org/Home/index.php?wpid=1&front_id=12*, and burn the ISO image to a blank CD. (Also available is the free Offline NT Password & Registry Editor from *http://pogostick.net/~pnh/ntpasswd/*.)

 If you use a boot disc password recovery tool like Trinity or Offline, any encrypted files on your PC will be unreadable unless you can subsequently recover your original password or restore a backed-up encryption certificate, as described in "Protect Your Files with Encryption" on page 558.

Next, boot your PC with the Trinity Rescue Kit disc, which is essentially a bootable Linux CD. At the prompt, type

```
winpass -u username
```

where *username* is your login name. The software will then search your hard disk for Windows installations, display a list of any it finds, and ask you to choose one.

At this point you'll be asked to either provide a new password or type merely * (asterisk) to choose a blank password (no password). Confirm that you wish to change the password, and you'll be sent back to the terminal prompt when it's done.

Now, restart your PC to log in to your newly unlocked Windows account.

Prevent Users from Shutting Down

Among the restrictions you may want to impose on others who use your computer is that of shutting down Windows. For instance, if you're logging in from another machine, as described in "Control a PC Remotely" on page 488, you'll want to make sure that your PC is always on. Or, if you're setting up a system to be used by the public, you won't want to allow anyone to shut down or reboot the system in an effort to compromise it. Here's how to do it:

1. Open the Registry Editor (discussed in Chapter 3).
2. Expand the branches to HKEY_CURRENT_USER\Software\Microsoft\Windows \CurrentVersion\Policies\Explorer.
3. Create a new DWORD value by going to **Edit→New→DWORD (32-bit) Value**, and type NoClose for its name.
4. Double-click the new NoClose value and type 1 for its data.
5. Close the Registry Editor when you're done. You'll need to restart Windows for this change to take effect.

Keep in mind that this isn't a bulletproof solution, as it only removes the **Shut down** entry from the Start menu. Anyone who knows better will be able to shut down Windows by pressing **Ctrl-Alt-Del** and clicking **Shut Down** there.

Want something stronger? If you have the Professional or Ultimate editions of Windows 7, you can choose which specific users are allowed to shut down the PC and which aren't:

1. Open the Local Security Policy window (*secpol.msc*).
2. Expand the branches to **Local Policies→User Rights Assignment**.
3. Double-click the **Shut down the system** entry in the right pane.

4. The list shows who can currently shut down this PC. Click **Add User or Group** to add someone else to the list, or select a user or group name and click **Remove** to revoke the ability to shut down.

Of course, someone with a twitchy finger and ready access to your computer's on/off switch, reset button, Sleep button, power cord, or fuse box will be able to circumvent this restriction. At the very least, though, these software-based tweaks will provide some reasonable assurance that your PC will remain powered on while you're away.

Log In As the Administrator

When you first install Windows 7, Setup walks you through the process of setting up a user account for yourself by asking for your name and then having you choose a picture. One of the requirements of the username is that it not be "Administrator."

The account named *Administrator* is a built-in account, mostly as a holdover from earlier versions of Windows. For more intents and purposes, it's pretty much the same as any other administrator-level account, except that it *can* have the name "Administrator." So, what's the point?

Truth is, there's not much point for most users. But if you have a network with PCs running older versions of Windows, like XP or 2000, and any of them are using the Administrator account, you may need enable the Administrator account on your own PC to overcome a peculiarity in the way that Windows handles usernames and passwords for folders shared over a network.

Or, maybe you just like the name.

Either way, here's how you do it:

1. Open the Start menu, type `lusrmgr.msc` in the **Search** box, and press **Enter** to start the Local Users and Groups tool described at the beginning of this chapter.
2. In the left pane, select **Users**.
3. In the middle pane, double-click **Administrator**.
4. Turn off the **Account is disabled** option, and click OK.
5. Again in the middle pane, right-click **Administrator** and select **Set Password**.
6. Choose a password for the new account, type it into both boxes, and click OK.
7. Close the Local Users and Groups window when you're done.

8. Log out of your current session, and then log in as Administrator. If the Administrator account doesn't show up on the Welcome screen, you may need to follow the steps in "Hide the List of User Accounts" on page 578 to show the old-fashioned logon box. But once you log in as Administrator at least once, it should start appearing on the standard Welcome screen.

 You can also do this from the command line. Open a Command Prompt window in Administrator mode, as explained earlier in this chapter, and then type net user Administrator/ active:yes and press **Enter**. Close the Command Prompt window and follow step 8, above, to complete the process.

Despite the fact that the Administrator account is turned off by default, it's perfectly acceptable to use it as your primary login. You may wish to do this for no other reason than you've simply gotten tired of seeing your name in huge, blazing letters in the Start menu.

 Three caveats: first, in each successive version of Windows since Windows 2000, Microsoft has gone to greater lengths to discourage use of the Administrator account, which may complicate your efforts to upgrade to Windows 7's successor. Second, one of the reasons Microsoft has tried to get rid of the Administrator account is that having a common username (and Administrator would be the most common) might be seen as a security risk, and it could make it easier for someone to break in to your PC. And third, User Account Control (UAC) doesn't show prompts for the Administrator account by default.

If you've already started using the Administrator account, and you want to change the name of your account without creating and breaking in to a brand-new account, then you can rename it. If you're using Windows 7 Professional or Ultimate, open the Local Security Policy window (*secpol.msc*), go to **Local Policies→Security Options**, and double-click the **Accounts: Rename administrator account** entry in the right pane.

If all you want is a more generic-sounding username, see "Rename Your Profile Folder" on page 590.

Customize the Welcome Screen Background

Unless you've opted to log in automatically (described earlier), you'll see the Welcome screen every time you turn on your PC, not to mention every time you shut down. Why not dress it up a bit with some custom wallpaper?

Fortunately, changing the Welcome screen wallpaper is much easier than it was in earlier versions of Windows; previously, you had to edit the *image-res.dll* file, something still required to choose a startup sound, as described in the next section. Now it's just a quick registry hack and a particular folder to hold your custom image.

To get started, open the Registry Editor (see Chapter 3) and expand the branches to `HKEY_LOCAL_MACHINE\SOFTWARE\Microsoft\Windows\CurrentVersion\Authentication\LogonUI\Background`. Double-click the `OEMBackground` value, type 1 in the **Value data** field, and click OK. (If the value isn't there, create it by right-clicking the key, selecting **New** and then **DWORD (32-bit) Value**, and typing `OEMBackground` for its name.) Close the Registry Editor when you're done.

Next, determine your screen resolution in pixels. If you don't know the current resolution, right-click an empty area of your desktop and select **Screen resolution**.

Then find a photo you'd like to be your new Welcome screen wallpaper and use your favorite image editor to resize and crop the photo so its pixel dimensions (not its print size) is the same as your screen resolution.

 If you've opened the image in Adobe Photoshop, select the Crop tool, and on the **Options** palette, type your target dimensions into the **Width** and **Height** fields. For example, to fit a 1920×1200 screen, you'd type 1920 and 1200, respectively. Draw a box to frame your image, click the Crop tool again, and then click **Crop** to crop and resize.

Save the file as *backgroundDefault.jpg* to the *\Windows\System32\oobe \info\backgrounds* folder. Then, in Windows Explorer, open the *\Windows \System32\oobe\info\backgrounds* folder and check the size of the file you just created. If it's more than 256 Kb, open it up once more in your image editor and either increase the compression ratio or decrease the quality setting. (In Photoshop, a quality setting of 7 works nicely.)

Back in Windows Explorer, make a copy of the *backgroundDefault.jpg* file, naming the new file background followed by the pixel dimensions, like this:

- *background1024x768.jpg*
- *background1280x1024.jpg*
- *background1280x768.jpg*
- *background1280x960.jpg*
- *background1360x768.jpg*
- *background1440x900.jpg*
- *background1600x1200.jpg*
- *background1920x1200.jpg*

When you're done, you'll have at least two identical files here: one *backgroundDefault.jpg* (used when Windows can't load your preferred resolution), and one named for your preferred resolution.

The change takes effect immediately; you'll see it the next time you log off or shut down, and most importantly, the next time you boot Windows, as shown in Figure 8-15.

Figure 8-15. With a simple registry hack and a carefully-placed .jpg file, you can easily customize the Windows 7 Welcome screen

Set the Mood with a Custom Startup Sound

You've got to give props to Microsoft for choosing the great and mysterious Robert Fripp to compose Windows 7's startup sound. Fripp—founder and guitarist of King Crimson, music producer, and, along with crossword-mainstay Brian Eno, inventor of something called *Frippertronics*—created a 5-second sound clip reminiscent of winged faeries dancing on the keys of a Mellotron.

Clearly, Microsoft had their agenda—to make you feel that something wonderful was about to happen—when selecting this sound to greet users of Windows 7, so no slight to Robert if you don't like it. But what if you'd prefer something from Fripp's earlier catalog, like the last 25 seconds to his 1974 masterpiece, *Starless*?

If you open the Sound window in Control Panel and choose the **Sounds** tab, you can only turn on or off the **Play Windows Startup sound** option; unlike the rest of Windows sounds, you can't select a different *.wav* or *.mp3* file to play when Windows first starts.

Turns out the stock startup sound is embedded in the *imageres.dll* file. To replace the sound, open Windows Explorer and navigate to your *Windows* *System32* folder. Take ownership of *imageres.dll*, as described in "Inheritance and ownership" on page 552, and then set the permissions to **Full Control** for your user account. When that's done, create two copies of the file in the *Windows\System32* folder, naming them *imageres-new.dll* and *imageres-old. dll*.

Next, download and install Restorator from *http://www.bome.com/*; it's commercial software, but they offer a free 30-day trial.

 There are other freeware resource editors, such as XN Resource Editor (*http://www.wilsonc.demon.co.uk/d10resourcee ditor.htm*) and Resource Hacker (*http://angusj.com/resource hacker/*), but these tools haven't been updated in years. Plus, if you have the 64-bit edition of Windows 7, you'll need a resource editor—like Restorator—capable of working with 64-bit DLLs.

From Restorator's **File** menu, select **Open**, find *imageres-new.dll*, and open the file. On the left, you'll see the various graphical and user-interface resources in the file organized into a collapsible **Resource Tree**. Expand the **WAVE** branch in the **Resource Tree** pane, and select the sole entry here, **5080**, which contains the startup sound.

It's a 16-bit, stereo (2-channel), 44,100 Hz sound clip in the Microsoft wave format, and is 884,136 bytes in size and 4.975 seconds long. These details are important, because the new sound clip you choose must have the same characteristics. If it doesn't, you'll need to convert your clip using a sound editing program like Audacity (free from *http://audacity.sourceforge.net/*) or Power Sound Editor Free (*http://www.free-sound-editor.com/*).

Microsoft wave files are uncompressed, so any two files of precisely the same length and same characteristics (samples per second, number of channels, etc.) will have the same file size. Since your new file must be 884,136 bytes in size, the easiest way to do this is to export the original sound from Restorator and save it as *5080.wav*. Then open it in your favorite sound editor and paste your new sound data on top of the old waveform. (Make sure your software is set to paste-to-overwrite, not paste-to-insert.)

Once you've prepared a suitable replacement sound, copy it to the clipboard. Back in Restorator, right-click the **5080** resource in the tree and select **Paste** to replace the selected clip with your version. Confirm that the new clip has the same specs as the old one by right-clicking the **5080** resource once again and selecting **Properties**. Save the file and close Restorator when you're done.

The last step is to replace the *imageres.dll* file with the one you've modified, but since it's in use, Windows won't let you touch it. To get around this, restart Windows, press **F8** to show the Advanced Boot Options menu (as described in "What to Do When Windows Won't Start" on page 355), and select **Safe Mode with Command Prompt**. When the Command Prompt appears, click inside the window and type:

```
copy imageres-new.dll imageres.dll
```

When prompted, answer **Y** to confirm that you'd like to replace the file. Then type exit to close the Command Prompt. If Windows doesn't restart at this point, press **Ctrl-Alt-Del**, click the arrow next to the red button on the bottom-right of the screen, and select **Restart**.

If all is well, you'll hear your custom startup as soon as Windows loads. If Windows won't start, or if you don't hear your custom sound, you can restore the original file by returning to the Safe Mode with Command Prompt, as just described, and typing copy imageres-old.dll imageres.dll.

Users and Security

Customize the Default Profile for New Users

Have a lot of user accounts to create, and don't want to waste hours customizing each one? Here's a simple way to customize a single account and then use it as the default for all new user accounts on your PC:

1. From an administrator-level account, use the User Accounts window in Control Panel to create a new account on your PC.

2. Log off and then log on to the new account.

3. Make all the changes you like. See Chapter 2 for some Windows Explorer settings that might be useful in this situation.

4. When you're done, log off and then log back in to your normal, administrator-level account.

5. If you haven't done so already, use the Folder Options window in Control Panel to show hidden files and folders in Windows Explorer, as explained in Chapter 2.

6. Next, open the System window in Control Panel and click the **Advanced system settings** link on the left side.

7. Under the **Advanced** tab, in the **User Profiles** section, click **Settings**.

8. Highlight the user account you just created and customized, and click **Copy To**.

9. In the Copy To window, click **Browse**, select the *C:\Users\Default User* folder, and click OK.

10. Click OK and then answer **Yes** to initiate the copy. Windows will delete the contents of the *Default User* folder, replacing them with the ones you've just customized.

When it's done, the new settings you've created will be in place to be used as the template for new user accounts. If you like, you can go ahead and delete the temporary account you created in the first step.

Rename Your Profile Folder

If you've ever uploaded a file to a website or used a P2P file sharing program (see Chapter 6), you've probably noticed that it's possible in some circumstances for others to see the full path of the files you're sharing. (This doesn't apply to the file sharing system discussed later in this chapter, thankfully.)

This means that if you upload the file *personal.doc* to a website, the website might be able to record that the full path of the file is actually:

C:\Users\Guy Q. Incognito\Documents\Some stuff of mine\personal.doc

And there it is: your full name.

Now, you can rename your account on the User Accounts page in Control Panel, but this won't change the folder name. But you can change the location of your profile folder *without* renaming your account, like this:

1. Open Windows Explorer, and navigate to *C:\Users*. Create a new, empty folder here. This will be your new home folder, so name it whatever you like.

2. Next, use the User Accounts window in Control Panel to create a new, temporary, administrator account on your PC.

3. Log off and then log on to the new account.

4. Open the System window in Control Panel and click the **Advanced system settings** link on the left side.

5. Under the **Advanced** tab, in the **User Profiles** section, click **Settings**.

6. Highlight your user account (the old one you want to move) and click **Copy To**.

7. In the Copy To window, click **Browse**, select the folder in *C:\Users* you created in the first step, and click OK.

8. Click OK again and then answer **Yes** to initiate the copy.

9. Now, use the Folder Options window in Control Panel to show hidden files and folders in Windows Explorer, as explained in Chapter 2.

10. Open Windows Explorer, and navigate to your old home folder (e.g., *C:\Users\Guy Q. Incognito*).

11. Press **Ctrl-A** to select everything in your home folder, and then, holding the **Ctrl** button, drag the selected files into the new location. When Windows asks whether you want to replace a file that already exists, turn on the **Do this for the next** *x* **conflicts** option, and then click **Don't copy**.

12. When it's done, open the Start menu, type lusrmgr.msc in the **Search** box, and press **Enter** to start the Local Users and Groups tool described at the beginning of this chapter.

13. In the left pane, select **Users**.

14. In the middle pane, double-click your username, and then choose the **Profile** tab.

15. In the **Home folder** section, select **Local path**, and in the **Local path** field, type or paste the full path of the new folder you created in step 2. (Ignore the **User profile** section at the top of this window.)

16. Click OK and then close the Local Users and Groups window when you're done.

17. Log out of the temporary account and log back in to your real account.

18. Once you've confirmed everything is working, open Windows Explorer again and delete the old home folder from *C:\Users*.

Share Files and Printers

There are so many things you can do with even a basic network; just a few of them are described in Chapter 7. But one of the best uses for the connection between the PCs in your office or home is to exchange data.

In Windows 7, traditional file sharing is a two-step process. First, you share a folder on one PC, and then someone on another PC reads or even modifies the files in that shared folder. Windows uses the user account system discussed throughout this Chapter to protect your shared data from prying eyes, and the permission system to give you the power to determine exactly what others can and can't do with your shared files. Civilized, isn't it?

Sharing folders is for more than just sending stuff from one PC to another, too. Multiple users can collaborate on a project by working on the same files, and avoid having several versions of each document floating around. (There are limits, of course; for instance, you can't modify a Word document if someone else currently has it open. But database programs like Microsoft Access let multiple users read and write to the same file simultaneously under certain circumstances.)

Naturally the PC hosting the shared folder must be powered on for others to be able to access the folder, but the person who shared the files doesn't necessarily have to be logged in.

But here's the rub: the defaults in Windows 7 could allow anyone on your network to read your files, yet permit nobody to modify them. It's just a matter of knowing where the vulnerabilities are and which buttons to click.

 Whenever you share a folder, you are essentially opening a backdoor to your computer, potentially allowing access to sensitive data. It's important to keep security in mind at all times, especially if you're connected to the Internet. Otherwise, you may be unwittingly exposing your personal data to intruders looking for anything they can use and abuse. Furthermore, an insecure system is more vulnerable to viruses, Trojan horses, and other malware. This doesn't mean that you shouldn't use file sharing, just that you'll want to use some common sense when you do.

Share a Folder

Sharing resources is pretty straightforward, but you'll need to take care of a few things first. (For even easier sharing, see "Going Home-groups" on page 609.)

Before you share any resources on your PC, your account must have a password. If you haven't done so already, open the User Accounts page in Control Panel and click **Create a password**.

 To have Windows enforce passwords for your administrator-level accounts, open the Parental Controls page in Control Panel. If you see a yellow box that says **One or more administrator accounts do not have a password**, click the box. On the Ensure Administrator Passwords page, turn on the **Force all administrator accounts to set a password at logon** option, and then click OK.

Next, open the Network and Sharing Center in Control Panel. If it says **Public network** underneath the name of your network in the **View your active networks** section, click the **Public network** link and choose either **Home network** or **Work network** here. (If the **Public network** caption is not clickable, then your network isn't fully functional; see Chapter 7 for troubleshooting tips.)

Next, open the HomeGroup page in Control Panel and click the **Change advanced sharing settings** link at the bottom to open the page shown in Figure 8-16.

On the "Advanced sharing settings" page, make sure the **Home or Work (current profile)** section is expanded, and then select these options:

- **Turn on network discovery**
- **Turn on file and printer sharing**
- **Use 128-bit encryption to help protect file sharing connections**
- **Turn on password protected sharing**

and click **Save changes** when you're done. Note the 128-bit encryption may cause problems if you're sharing files with Macs or older PCs; disable it if that's the case.

Finally, if you don't already know it, determine the name of your PC, as described in the upcoming "What's My PC's Name?" sidebar.

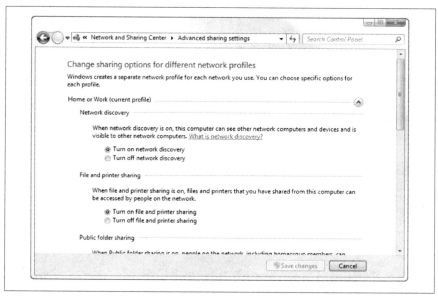

Figure 8-16. The nearly-hidden "Advanced sharing settings" page is where you'll find the setting to enable traditional file and printer sharing

What's My PC's Name?

Your PC's name is the name others see when they access your shared folders over the network, so make it a good one.

In Control Panel, open System, click the **Advanced system settings** link on the left, and then choose the **Computer Name** tab. Ignore the **Computer description** field and instead look at the **Full computer name** entry immediately beneath it: this is your PC's name.

Or, open a Command Prompt window (see Chapter 9), type hostname at the prompt, and press **Enter**.

Each computer on your local network must have a different name, but they should all have the same **Workgroup** name. If you need to rename your PC or modify the Workgroup name, click the **Change** button (don't use the **Network ID** button).

When you're done, you may have to restart Windows for any changes to take effect.

Now you're ready to share.

Windows 7 has three different ways to share a folder: the Sharing Wizard (not really a wizard), the Advanced Sharing window, and Homegroups.

Figure 8-17. The **Share with** *menu is convenient, but has some big security holes*

Sharing Wizard

This isn't actually a wizard, but that's what it's called in the **View** tab of the Folder Options widow in Control Panel (covered in Chapter 2). If you haven't turned off the **Use Sharing Wizard** option, you can highlight any files or folders in Windows Explorer and open the **Share with** drop-down on the toolbar, shown in Figure 8-17. (Or, you can right-click them and select **Share with**.) Here, you'll have four fairly self-explanatory options: **Nobody**, **Homegroup (Read)**, **Homegroup (Read/Write)**, and **Specific people**.

 Unfortunately, Windows won't tell you here if the folder is already shared, or with whom. Furthermore, the **Nobody** option is a lie, plain and simple. If any parent folder of the selected item is shared, then the selected item will remain accessible on the network even if you select **Nobody** from the **Share with** menu. To avoid this trap, use the Properties window, described next. Note also that your entire drive may be shared without your knowledge, as explained in "Turn Off Administrative Shares" on page 605.

Advanced Sharing

Right-click any folder, select **Properties**, and choose the **Sharing** tab to see if the selected item—or one of its parent folders—is already shared, as shown in Figure 8-18.

Users and Security

If the selected folder is already shared though a parent folder, nothing you do in this window will change whether others can access these files through the parent share. To adjust that share, close this window, right-click the parent folder being shared, select **Properties**, and then choose the **Sharing** tab.

Click the **Advanced Sharing** button to open the Advanced Sharing window shown in Figure 8-19. Turn on the **Share this folder** option to start sharing the selected folder and all of its contents. Type a **Share name**—the name under which the folder is accessed from other computers—or leave the default intact if you want the share name to be the same as the name of the source folder.

But wait! You're not done yet. Click the **Permissions** button to open the Permissions window shown in Figure 8-20. As described in "Set Permissions for a File or Folder" on page 550, share permissions are different from file permissions, yet both must agree for sharing to work.

Here, notice that the *Everyone* group (which is indeed everyone) has **Read** access, yet nobody has **Change** or **Full Control** access. This is probably not what you want, so highlight the **Everyone** entry in the **Group or user names** box and click **Remove**. Then, click **Add**, type your own username in the **Enter the object names to select** box, and click OK. Next, highlight the name you just added in the **Group or user names** box, and below, click the checkbox in the **Allow** column for each right you'd like to grant. If you want a remote user to be able to read, write, and delete files in the folder, click the **Allow** checkbox next to **Full Control**.

 Want to share files with someone without sharing your username and password? Create a user account for the person and then explicitly grant sharing rights to that user in the Permissions window in Figure 8-20. Or, if you don't care about security, use a homegroup, next.

Homegroup

If you join a homegroup, described later in this chapter, every file and folder in every library you choose to share will become readable *and writable* by every other member of the homegroup. It's a poor choice if you have any sensitive data on your PC, but it's quick and easy, and may be perfectly adequate for family photos and your music collection.

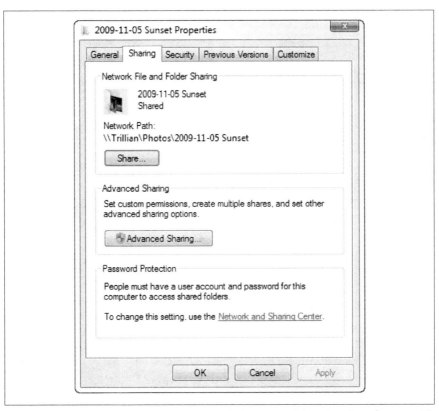

*Figure 8-18. The first section of the **Sharing** tab shows you if the selected item is accessible on the network, even if it hasn't been explicitly shared*

Once you've enabled sharing for a folder or library, Windows provides no visual indication that the folder is shared. (In previous versions of Windows, a tiny two-person insignia appeared on the folder's icon to indicate that the data inside might not be private, but apparently, that sort of information just isn't important to Windows 7 users.) To see a list of most of your shared folders, open your PC's folder in the Network folder in Windows Explorer. Or to see a comprehensive list of shared folders, including hidden shares you might not know about, see "Turn Off Administrative Shares" on page 605.

Access a Shared Folder Remotely

As soon as a folder or drive has been shared, it can be accessed from another PC on your local network. Just open Windows Explorer and navigate to the *Network* folder in the tree.

Figure 8-19. Use the Advanced Sharing window to safely share your folders and allow other users to modify the files therein (at your discretion)

The *Network* folder shows all the PCs (discoverable PCs, that is) on your local network. If it doesn't, press **F5** to refresh the window; if you see the green progress bar moving slowly from left to right at the top of the window, be patient: your files will appear in another hour or two.

Or not. If the PC you want isn't in the list, you don't have to sit around and wait for it to spontaneously show itself. Just click the address bar, erase the text that's there, type two backslashes (\\) followed by the PC's name (as in Figure 8-21), and press **Enter**.

 One reason why another PC may not show up in the *Network* folder is if it's not in the same *Workgroup* as your PC; see the sidebar "What's My PC's Name?" on page 594, for details. Of course, there are other reasons why a PC may not show up; it may not be turned on, it may not be connected to the network, it may not be discoverable (see the previous section), or your network may be down. See Chapter 7 for network troubleshooting topics.

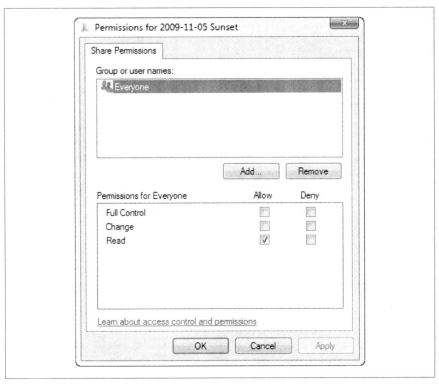

Figure 8-20. To protect your data, you should set the permissions for every folder you share

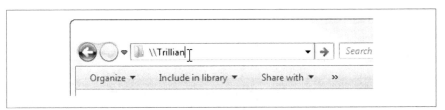

Figure 8-21. If a remote PC doesn't show up in your Network folder, type two backslashes in Windows Explorer's address bar, followed by the remote PC's name

Once you see the remote PC in the *Network* folder, double-click it to see its shared resources. Here, you should see an entry for each shared folder and printer on that PC; just open the resource to see what's inside, and then access those files as though they were on your own hard disk.

Access Shared Folders on Non-Windows PCs

In most cases, you should be able to see folders shared on non-Windows PCs right in Windows Explorer.

Windows uses the SMB (Server Message Block) protocol, which is supported on many platforms, including Mac OS X and nearly all Unix and Linux distributions.

In Mac OS X, open **System Preferences** from the Apple menu, and click the **Sharing** icon. Turn on the **File Sharing** service, and then with the **File Sharing** entry highlighted, click the **Options** button. Turn on the **Share files and folders using SMB** option, place a checkmark next to every user account that's allowed to access files on this Mac, and click **Done**. Next, use the controls back on the Sharing page to add one or more shared folders and set their permissions as you see fit. Your changes will take effect immediately, and your Mac should appear in the *Network* folder in Windows Explorer momentarily, at which point you can browse the Mac's shared folders as though it were just another Windows machine.

If you're using Linux or Unix with the Samba package installed, you'll need to edit *smb.conf* and specify at least one shared folder on that machine; see the Samba documentation for details. (Or, if you've installed the SWAT package, you can configure Samba from any web browser by going to *http://servername:901/*, where *servername* is the IP address or computer name of the Unix machine.) Once Samba is set up, start the smbd daemon. Thereafter, you should see the Unix machine and all its shared folders right in the *Network* folder in Windows Explorer.

To browse the files on an iPhone from Windows Explorer (effectively turning it into a wireless flash drive), get an app called Files (or its free version, Files Lite) from *http://www.olivetoast.com/*. Or, use an online file sync service like Dropbox (*https://www.dropbox.com/iphoneapp*).

If you don't see the remote computer in Windows Explorer, see Chapter 7 for network troubleshooting and tips. If you see the computer but can't connect, turn off the **Use 128-bit encryption to help protect file sharing connections** option discussed earlier in this chapter.

See "Force a Login Box for a Remote Folder" on page 602 if you experience login problems when connecting to computer running another OS. See the sidebar "Access Windows Shares from Non-Windows PCs" on page 602 for a related topic.

Remember remote shared folders

It's not uncommon to return to the same remote folder again and again. So, why navigate manually through the slow-as-molasses *Network* folder each time?

A remote folder has a path just like a folder on your hard disk; it follows the UNC naming convention, which looks like this:

\\Xander\Desktop

This path points to a folder named *Desktop* on the *Xander* PC (presumably Xander's desktop). It's important to note that the local path on the Xander PC—namely, *C:\Users\Alexander\Desktop*—is not part of the UNC path; all you see is the name of the PC and the share name, set in "Share a Folder" on page 593.

Open the *Zeppo* folder on Xander's desktop, and the path changes to:

\\Xander\Desktop\Zeppo

Not only does this mean that you can quickly get to a remote path by typing, but it means that you can create ordinary Windows Shortcuts to remote paths to get back even quicker. Just drag the icon on the left side of Windows Explorer's address bar onto your desktop to create the shortcut.

Of course, if Xander ever renames his PC, or if he ever stops sharing the *Desktop* folder, then the shortcut will stop working. Alternatively, you can access a remote PC with its IP address, like this:

\\192.168.1.107\Desktop\Zeppo

But with the DHCP (Dynamic Host Configuration Protocol) employed by your typical router, any given PC's IP address is much more likely to change than its name.

Got a non-Windows PC on your network? See the sidebar below, "Access Windows Shares from Non-Windows PCs" for help sharing files across platforms.

Users
and Security

Access Windows Shares from Non-Windows PCs

Once a folder is shared on a Windows PC, you can access its contents from just about any other computer or device, regardless of the operating system.

Windows uses the SMB (Server Message Block) protocol, which is supported on many platforms, including Mac OS X and nearly all Unix and Linux distributions.

In Mac OS X, open a new Finder window. If you don't see a globe icon with the question mark on the toolbar, open the **View** menu and select **Customize Toolbar**. Drag the globe icon onto the toolbar and click **Done**. Then click the globe icon, and in the Server Address field, type the `smb://` prefix followed by the name of the Windows PC, like this:

```
smb://totoro
```

and then click **Connect**. You'll then be asked to Select the volumes to mount, at which point you can highlight as many individual shares as you like. Click OK, and the PC will appear in the **Shared** section of all open Finder windows, with the shares you selected off to the right.

From Unix/Linux, you'll likely have the Samba package already installed; if not, you can get it from *http://www.samba.org/*. To list the shares on a Windows PC, type:

```
smbclient -L totoro
```

or to connect, type:

```
smbclient //totoro/desktop
```

where *totoro* is the name of the Windows PC, and *desktop* is the name of the shared folder.

To connect to a Windows share from an iPhone, you'll need an app called NetPortal (or its free version, NetPortalLite) from *http://www.stratospherix .com/products/netportal/*. Or, to connect from an Android phone, use File Explorer from *http://www.estrongs.com/*.

See the sidebar "Access Shared Folders on Non-Windows PCs" on page 600 for a related topic.

Force a Login Box for a Remote Folder

If there's an account on a remote machine with the same username as the one you're using on the local PC, Windows 7 may not give you the opportunity to log in as a different user, even if it's necessary to access the resource.

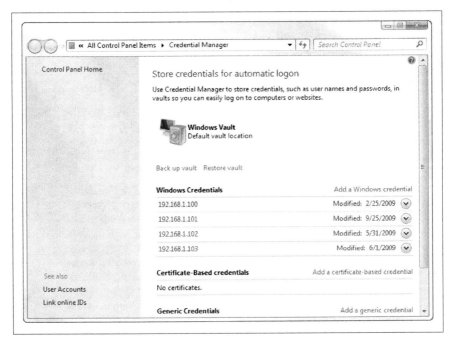

Figure 8-22. Use the Credential Manager to troubleshoot access to remote shared folders and work around the same-username bug that has plagued Windows for years

For instance, say your username is Ned, and you access a remote folder on another PC that also has a Ned account. If both Neds have the same password, and the files you're after belong to Ned, then you'll have no problem. Or, if there's no Ned account on the remote machine, then Windows will ask you to log in. But if the two Neds have different passwords, or if the shared files can only be read by Chuck, Windows could deny you access with no chance to log in as Chuck or anyone else. Worse yet, Windows won't tell you why it's locking you out.

The solution is to use the Credential Manager page in Control Panel, shown in Figure 8-22, to set up your access rights before you even try to access another PC.

First, you'll see a list of **Windows Credentials**, previously saved usernames and passwords you typed when accessing remote folders, organized by PC name. They're all stored in the **Windows Vault**, which, if you're familiar with Mac OS X, is a lot like a Mac keychain.

Click an entry to view or edit the credential. Or, if you're having trouble accessing a folder on a remote PC, and that PC name shows up here, delete the credential by clicking **Remote from vault**.

To set up a credential for a remote PC, click **Add a Windows Credential**. In the **Internet or network address** field, type the name of the PC, followed by the **User name** and **Password**. Click OK to save the credential and then try accessing the shared folder again.

You can skip the login box and enter your credentials quickly from the Command Prompt (see Chapter 9). Type net use \\computer /user:username password and press **Enter**. When you navigate to a shared folder on \\computer in Windows Explorer, you'll find that you're already logged in.

Another way to display a login box is to right-click the shared folder in Windows Explorer and select **Map Network Drive**. Turn on the **Connect using different credentials** option and then click **Finish**, and you'll be prompted for a user name and password. Unfortunately, this won't fix the access problem like a new entry in the Credential Manager would, but you do get a new drive letter in Windows Explorer with which you can access the remote folder. This is particularly useful for providing network access to older applications that don't understand UNC paths.

The Credential Manager serves one other important function with regards to shared folders. If the remote folder is encrypted, as described earlier in this chapter, and the folder's owner doesn't want to give you her username and password, she can share her encryption certificate on a smart card. Provided you have her smart card, plus a smart card reader connected to your PC, just click **Add a certificate-based credential** and then click **Select certificate**. If you're not using smart cards, you'll need to exchange certificates with the Certificate Manager instead, as described in "Allow others to access your encrypted files" on page 562.

While accessing a remote PC, if you get an error to the effect that "Credentials supplied conflict with an existing set of credentials," and you can't resolve the problem with Credential Manager, try opening a Command Prompt window in Administrator mode as explained earlier in this chapter, and typing this command:

```
net use * /delete
```

and pressing **Enter**. This will deactivate all current shares, freeing you up to initiate a new connection. Rest assured, the change is only temporary; when you restart Windows, all your previously configured shares will be active once again.

Turn Off Administrative Shares

In a world where we must concern ourselves with spyware, phishing emails, and clowns trying to break in to our wireless networks, it's almost reassuring when Windows itself is the security threat. Well, not so much reassuring as *infuriating*.

It turns out that every copy of Windows 7 has a backdoor that could permit someone else to read any file on your PC, and that vulnerability exists on Windows 2000, XP, and Vista PCs, too.

By default, every hard disk on your PC is shared. That's right, the whole thing.

What's worse is that the shares are hidden, which means they don't show up in the *Network* folder in Windows Explorer, and thus most users don't know their data is vulnerable to snooping.

You can hide any shared folder by adding the $ character to the end of the share name—as in Desktop$—while creating the share. Then, to access the folder, type the UNC path into Windows Explorer's address bar (e.g., \\Xander \Desktop$) and press **Enter** to open it.

To test your PC, open Windows Explorer on your PC—or better yet, on another PC on your network—and type the name of your own PC into the address bar, followed by the administrative share name for drive C:, like this:

\\your_pc_name\c$

and then press **Enter**. If you see the contents of your hard disk, then administrative shares are enabled on your PC. (You can get a list of all your shared folders—hidden and otherwise—with the Computer Management tool described in the steps that follow.)

 In Windows 7, the default settings are supposed to prevent administrative shares from being accessed over a network. If you can view the *c$* share from your own PC but *not* from another PC on your LAN, then your administrative shares don't post a security threat. But don't be surprised if this is not the case on your own Windows 7 machine. Go ahead and try accessing the *c$* share from another PC; odds are that your whole hard disk is indeed accessible over the network, despite Microsoft's insistence that this hole has been plugged. See the next section if you want to keep administrative shares, but don't want them visible to remote PCs.

Unfortunately, turning off administrative shares is not just a matter of un-sharing the drives; you've got to disable the mechanism that shares them automatically each time your PC starts. If administrative shares are enabled on your PC, here's how to turn them off:

1. Open the Registry Editor (see Chapter 3).

2. Expand the branches to HKEY_LOCAL_MACHINE\SYSTEM\CurrentControlSet \Services\lanmanserver\parameters.

3. In the right pane, double-click the AutoShareServer value, type 0 in the **Value data** field, and click OK. (If AutoShareServer isn't there, go to **Edit→New→DWORD (32-bit) Value** to create a new DWORD value by that name.)

4. Next, double-click the AutoShareWks value, type 0 in the **Value data** field, and click OK. (Again, create the DWORD value if it's not there.)

5. Close the Registry Editor when you're done.

6. Next, open the Start menu, type compmgmt.msc into the **Search** box and press **Enter** to fire up the Computer Management tool. (Or right-click **Computer** in your Start menu and select **Manage**.)

7. Expand the **System Tools** branch on the left, then expand **Shared Folders** underneath that, and then click the **Shares** folder.

 Here, you'll see a list of all the shared folders on your PC, whether they're hidden or not. Even if you're not hunting down administrative shares, this is a handy tool to keep tabs on your shared resources. By the way, you can also list existing shares from the Command Prompt by typing net view /all \\localhost. To then remove a share, type net use /delete *resource*, where *resource* is the name of the share you want to stop sharing.

8. To manually remove the administrative shares, right-click each one (e.g., **C$, D$, E$**) and select **Stop Sharing**. Answer **Yes** to both prompts.

Go ahead and remove any hidden share you want (anything with a dollar-sign suffix in the name), with the following three possible exceptions:

- **IPC$**, which stands for Inter-Process Communication, is used for re-mote administration of your computer, something few people need outside of a corporate environment. Although it has been proven that the *IPC$* share can be exploited, the only way to disable it permanently is to turn off file sharing altogether. You can stop sharing IPC$ tem-porarily, but Windows will recreate the share the next time you restart.

- **print$** is used to exchange printer driver files when you share a printer. Although this shared folder could theoretically be compromised with malware, you're probably save leaving this share intact if you're sharing any printers on your PC.

- **wwwroot$** will be present if Microsoft's Internet Information Server (IIS) software is installed. Leave this share intact if you want to use your computer as a web server or a web software development platform.

9. When you're done, restart Windows. Reopen the Computer Management tool to make sure the administrative shares are gone for good.

The preceding solution is sometimes met with skepticism among those who don't see administrative shares as a security threat. After all, these hidden shares are there for legitimate reasons; namely, to allow network administrators to install software, run Disk Defragmenter, access the registry, or perform other maintenance on a PC remotely. But ask yourself, do you ever do any of those things?

Administrative shares are also required for the Previous Versions feature to work, as described in "Go Back in Time with Restore Points and Shadow Copies" on page 408. Turn off Administrative Shares, and the **Previous Versions** tab of any file's Properties window will be empty. Read on if you want to plug the whole while keeping the Previous Versions functional.

If you're on the fence, consider that Windows passwords can be cracked with a variety of methods, and you'll see the problem. Unless your PC is in a corporate environment and you're required to use remote administration, you have nothing to gain by leaving this backdoor open—and everything to lose.

Manage network access to administrative shares

As stated earlier in this section, Windows 7 is supposed to block network access to your administrative shares. But this isn't the case on many Windows 7 PCs for reasons unknown.

To keep administrative shares intact, yet block access to them from other PCs on your network, follow these steps:

1. Open the Registry Editor (see Chapter 3).
2. Expand the branches to `HKEY_LOCAL_MACHINE\Software\Microsoft\Windows\CurrentVersion\Policies\System`.

3. In the right pane, double-click the `LocalAccountTokenFilterPolicy` value, type 0 in the **Value data** field, and click **OK**. (If `LocalAccountTokenFilter Policy` isn't there, go to **Edit→New→DWORD (32-bit) Value** to create a new DWORD value by that name.)

4. When you're finished, close the Registry Editor and restart Windows. Test the change by navigating to the administrative share from another PC on your network.

Now, if you'd like to *unblock* administrative shares, making them visible to other PCs on your network, just double-click the aforementioned `LocalAccountTokenFilterPolicy` value and set its value data to 1. Close the Registry Editor and restart Windows for the change to take effect.

Hide Your PC from the Network Folder

One of the more common problems with file sharing is that you don't see the remote PC in Windows Explorer's Network folder. The solution, explained earlier in this chapter, is to type two backslashes (\\) followed by the PC's name into the address bar and press **Enter**.

But if you have the opposite problem and don't want your PC to show up on other computers, you can hide it. It won't stop someone from typing the name into the address bar, but it will make it harder to find.

First, open a Command Prompt window in Administrator mode, as explained earlier in this chapter. At the prompt, type:

```
Net config server /hidden:yes
```

and press **Enter**. If it says The command completed successfully, check your work by typing:

```
Net Config Server
```

and pressing **Enter**. In the report, you'll see Server hidden, followed by Yes if it's hidden or No if it's still visible. To unhide your PC,

```
Net config server /hidden:no
```

The change won't take effect until you restart Windows. To confirm your PC is hidden, sit down at another PC on your network and open the *Network* folder in Windows Explorer.

Going Homegroups

Homegroups is Microsoft's latest answer to the years we've all spent toiling with workgroups and traditional file sharing. It's not a new technology, but rather good ol' file sharing in a new guise.

 Never join a homegroup on a PC with any sensitive data on it. When you join a homegroup, Windows changes the share permissions on all the files and folders in your libraries so that the *Everyone* group—and yes, that's everyone—has full read and write access to all your shared files. Even if you later leave the homegroup, those lax permissions remain in effect until you manually revoke access to *Everyone* through the Advanced Sharing window covered earlier in this chapter. See the next topic for more on this.

The idea is that creating or joining a homegroup with which you share everything is much easier than sharing individual folders. And easier it is, but secure it ain't.

Homegroups is more or less an extension of the media sharing feature found in the last few versions of Windows Media Player; but instead of sharing just your music library, a homegroup shares all of your Windows 7 libraries. This includes (at your option) your *Pictures*, *Music*, *Videos*, and *Documents* libraries, plus any custom libraries you've created, plus all your printers. Once you're part of a homegroup, you can then selectively revoke access to specific folders, which is in contrast to the old school—and far more secure—approach of sharing only those folders you want made public.

 Although versions of Windows prior to 7 don't explicitly support Homegroups, any operating system (Windows and otherwise) can access your HomeGroup folders through traditional means, as described earlier in this chapter.

To get started, open the HomeGroup page in Control Panel. If there are no other PCs on your local network that already belong to a homegroup, you'll see "There is currently no homegroup on the network" at the top of the page. Click **Create a homegroup** and then select the libraries you want to share. Click **Next**, ignore the password Microsoft gives you, and then click **Finish**.

Rather than use the cryptic 10-digit password Windows generates for you when you create a homegroup, why not choose something easy to remember and easy to type? If you do it now, it'll be easier than after other PCs have joined. Back on the main HomeGroup page in Control Panel, click **Change the password**, and then click **Change the password** on the first wizard page. In the box, type the password you'd like to use, click **Next** and then **Finish**.

If any another Windows 7 PC on your local network already belongs to a homegroup, it'll say "You have been invited to join a homegroup" or "Mei on Totoro has created a homegroup on the network" at the top of the page. Click **Join now**, and when prompted, choose the libraries to share and type the homegroup password.

When your homegroup has been established, the HomeGroup page in Control Panel should look like the one in Figure 8-23. If you have trouble creating or joining a homegroup, see the next topic.

Once you've joined a homegroup, each other PC in the homegroup should appear in the *Homegroup* folder at the top of the tree in Windows Explorer.

Make your Homegroup more secure

If you read the Windows help pages on Homegroups, you may've noticed that Microsoft suggests that you can stop sharing individual files and folders in an otherwise shared library. This is a boldfaced lie. If you use the **Share with** menu as instructed to unshare a folder in one of your libraries, precisely nothing will happen. Other members will continue to have access to all the files and folders in your shared libraries. The problem with sharing everything is how Windows sets permissions for homegroup shares.

Let's run an experiment, shall we? Create or join a homegroup, as described in the previous section, and when prompted, share only your *Videos* library. By default, the *Videos* library sources its files from the *My Videos* folder, so open Windows Explorer and navigate to *My Videos* (the folder in \Users\[your username]\, not the library). Right-click *My Videos*, select **Properties**, and choose the **Security** tab.

In the **Group or user names** list, select *HomeUsers*, and look in the **Permissions for HomeUsers** box below. You'll see that the *HomeUsers* group has read access on this folder. (To learn more about the *HomeUsers* group, use the Local Users and Groups tool described at the beginning of this chapter.)

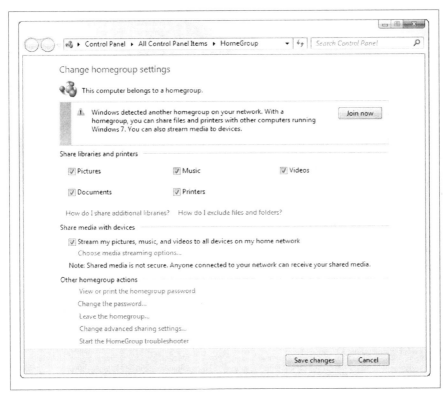

Figure 8-23. Setting up a Homegroup is easy on this page in Control Panel, but be prepared to dig a bit if it doesn't work

Next, choose the **Sharing** tab. In the Network File and Folder Sharing box, you'll see that your *My Videos* folder is currently being shared as *\\pc_name \Videos*. Then click **Advanced Sharing**, followed by **Permissions**, and you'll see that the *Everyone* group now has **Full Control** (**Read + Change**) over your *My Videos* folder.

What does this all mean? First, other users who access your shared libraries through the *Homegroup* folder have read access only, which makes sense. But what Microsoft doesn't tell you is that sharing a library with your homegroup automatically shares all the folders referenced in your libraries and sets their share permissions to that *Everyone* has read and write access. As a result, those same users can stroll on over to the *Network* folder in Windows Explorer, and change your files there.

Next experiment: stop sharing the *Videos* library in your homegroup, or better yet, leave the homegroup entirely. Now, return to the Properties window for your *My Videos* folder; you'll see that the *HomeUsers* group still has read access, and the *Everyone* group still has read and write access, and the folder is still shared! As far as you know, you've unshared this folder, but others on your network can still see and change your files.

 Now, if this PC has nothing on it but family photos and Hanukkah songs, then do really care about lax permissions? Even if there's no sensitive data on your PC, files in your shared folders are still vulnerable to inadvertent tampering: a family member moves instead of copies a photo, deletes a song accidentally, or makes changes to one of your documents rather than saving to a new file.

So how to you make your homegroup more secure?

Prune your libraries

Since libraries gather files from lots of sources, it's easy to share something you don't want to be sharing. In the *Libraries* folder in Windows Explorer, right-click one of the libraries you're sharing and select **Properties**. In the **Library locations** list, remove any folders you'd rather not share. To prune even further without hobbling your libraries, create custom libraries, next.

Make custom libraries

Only the libraries you choose to share with the homegroup are readable by *Everyone*. To limit what you share, open the *Libraries* folder in Windows Explorer and click **New Library** on the toolbar. Open *New Library* and click the **Include a folder** button to add folders you'd like to share.

Although custom libraries won't appear on the HomeGroup page in Control Panel, you can share them with your homegroup via Windows Explorer. Return to the *Libraries* folder, highlight your new library, and from the toolbar, select **Share with** and then either **Homegroup (Read)** or **Homegroup (Read/Write)**.

 If you don't see the **Share with** button on the toolbar after selecting the custom library, open the Folder Options window in Control Panel and choose the **View** tab. Turn on the **Use Sharing Wizard** option and click OK.

Change file permissions

As described in "Set Permissions for a File or Folder" on page 550, share permissions are different from file permissions, yet both must agree for sharing to work. Although Windows sets share permissions automatically when you share a library on a homegroup, there's nothing stopping you from going back and revoking sharing rights for *Everyone* via the **Sharing** tab. Better yet, add some *Deny* rules to the file permissions (**Security** tab), which are not only less likely to be disrupted by Windows' tampering, but will supersede any *Allow* rules Windows adds to the permissions. See "Permissions and Security" on page 549 for complete instructions.

Stop using Homegroups

If you're not a member of a homegroup, you won't have to worry about Windows being careless with your data security. But keep in mind that once you leave the homegroup, you'll have to remove the lax permissions added to your previously shared folders, and they'll remain open to snooping.

This is probably the best option if you have a portable computer. The last thing you want is to join a homegroup at home, and then take your laptop to work or an Internet café, and have all your data accessible to anyone within range. Sure, you can change your network location to **Work network** or **Public network** (see Chapter 7), if you remember, but why take the chance?

One final note about Homegroups versus traditional file sharing. If you belong to a homegroup, anyone can sit down at your PC and click **View or print the homegroup password** to gain access to your PC, and you'd never know it. At least with traditional file sharing, which relies on your user account password, someone can't get your current password quite so easily.

Troubleshoot your homegroup

Having trouble creating or joining a homegroup? Use this prerequisite checklist to make sure everything is in order:

Your network location must be Home network

Open the Network and Sharing Center page in Control Panel. If you see Work network or **Public network** under **View your active networks**, click said link and then select **Home network**. If you see more than one network here, Homegroups won't work. See Chapter 7 for more on this.

Turn on Network Discovery

On the Network and Sharing Center page in Control Panel, click **Choose homegroup and sharing options**, and then click **Change advanced sharing settings**. Place a checkmark next to **Turn on Network Discovery** and **Turn on file and printer sharing**, and then click **Save changes**. More on this page in "Share a Folder" on page 593.

While you're here, make sure the HomeGroup connections setting is the same for each PC in your homegroup.

Internet Protocol Version 6 required

The Homegroup service relies on IPv6 to function. On the Network and Sharing Center page in Control Panel, click the **Change adapter settings** link. Then right-click the network adapter you're using to connect to your home network, select Properties, and turn on the **Internet Protocol Version 6 (TCP/IPv6)** option.

Also, your router must support IPv6. If it doesn't, see "Upgrade Your Router" on page 443.

Homegroup services must be running

Open the services window (*services.msc*) and make sure each of these services are running:

- DNS Client
- Function Discovery Provider Host
- Function Discovery Resource Publication
- HomeGroup Listener
- HomeGroup Provider
- Peer Networking Grouping
- Peer Networking Identity Manager
- SSDP Discovery
- UPnP Device Host

See Chapter 6 for more on managing services, and Chapter 7 for more on technologies like UPnP, SSDP, and DNS.

Clocks must be in sync

The clock on each PC must be set to the correct time and their time zones must match. Use the Internet time feature to keep all your PCs clocks correct.

Still can't join or create a homegroup? Try these fixes to common homegroup problems:

Can't create a homegroup?

You can't create a homegroup as long as there's at least one other PC on your network that belongs to a homegroup. If you don't want to join that PC's homegroup, you'll need to put it to sleep temporarily or disconnect it from the network before you can create a new homegroup.

Can't join a homegroup?

You'll only be able to join a homegroup if another PC on your local network has created one or has previously joined one. Of course, at least one other PC must also be powered on and connected to the same network you are. If you're not sure both PCs are on the same network, see the sidebar "What's My PC's Name?" on page 594.

 If everything is in order and you still don't see the homegroup you're sure exists on your local network, open the Network and Sharing Center page in Control Panel. Click **Change adapter settings** and then disable every adapter except the one you use to connect to your LAN. If you're connected with more than one adapter—say, wired and wireless—Homegroups won't work.

Firewall software (other than the Windows Firewall) can disrupt homegroups. Try disabling any third-party firewall on your PC and the remote PC, and then try again.

The password is incorrect?

Well, duh. But if you can't manage to type the 10-digit mess Windows generates for new homegroups, create your own easy-to-type password, as explained in the beginning of this section.

Another PC isn't showing up?

The other PC must be joined to the same homegroup as your PC and must have at least one library shared to appear in the *Homegroup* folder on your PC. If you're not sure both PCs are connected to the same homegroup, open the HomeGroup page in Control Panel, click **Leave the homegroup**, and then click **Leave the homegroup** again to confirm. Once you've left, try rejoining the homegroup.

PC shows up, but you can't open any of its libraries?

This is a common problem, and is easily solved; just leave and rejoin the homegroup, as described previously. If that doesn't work, open a Command Prompt window in Administrator mode and type net use *remo tepc* where *remotepc* is the name of the PC that isn't showing up.

Homegroup works, but you can't access/change files?

This is a permissions problem. As described in "Set Permissions for a File or Folder" on page 550, share permissions are different from file permissions, yet both must agree for sharing to work.

Which homegroup am I joining?

If there are three or more PCs on a network, and among them, at least two different homegroups, you won't know which one Windows has invited you to join until it's time to enter a password.

 Windows can only connect to one homegroup at a time. But you can have multiple Homegroups on a single local network simultaneously. That way, for instance, your kids can have their own homegroup separate from yours and your partner's. Just disconnect or sleep the PCs you don't want to connect to until after you've joined or created a homegroup.

HomeGroup is currently sharing libraries on this computer?

This isn't an error, but it is misleading. By "sharing," Windows means "setting up sharing." Just wait a few minutes for Windows to set the appropriate permissions, and this error will go away.

Can't see a shared printer in the Homegroup folder?

When you first join a homegroup with shared printers, or someone else with shared printers joins your homegroup, Windows will prompt you to set up those remote printers. Thereafter, shared printers won't ever appear in the *Homegroup* folder, even if the Printers library is shared on that PC. To connect to a remote printer, see the next section.

Got a weird error code that begins with PEER or 0x?

See *http://msdn.microsoft.com/en-us/library/dd433181(VS.85).aspx* for a list of error codes and their explanations.

Don't like the Homegroup folder in Windows Explorer?

Unfortunately, you can't remove it entirely without disabling the Homegroups service. But you can "demote" it so that it appears inside the Desktop branch, as explained in "Clean Up the Navigation Pane" on page 53.

Can't leave a homegroup?

If you get the message, "Windows couldn't remove your computer from the homegroup," it means one or more the services responsible for the Homegroups feature has stopped responding. Just fire up the Services window (*services.msc*) and stop both the **HomeGroup Listener** and **HomeGroup Provider** services. Then try leaving the homegroup again. If that doesn't work, start both services up again and try leaving the homegroup once more.

Share a Printer

As soon as you share a printer, anyone on your local network can print to it. (Network printers, discussed in the next section, don't need to be shared.)

Sharing a printer is, for the most part, just like sharing a folder. The difference is that security and permissions aren't particularly important, unless toner theft is a problem in your workplace. It's understandable, then, that Windows offers to share any newly offered printers, and even (sometimes) connects automatically to remotely shared printers.

To share a printer, open the Devices and Printers page in Control Panel. Right-click the printer you want to share and select **Printer Properties** (but not **Properties**). Choose the **Sharing** tab, turn on the **Share this printer** option (see Figure 8-24), and click OK.

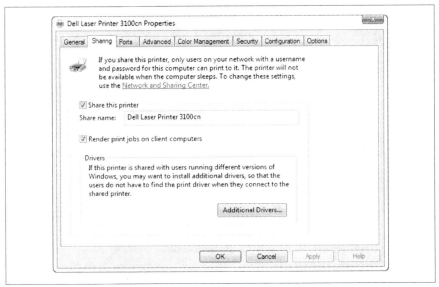

Figure 8-24. You can share a printer in much the same way as sharing a folder

If you're using a HomeGroup, discussed in the previous section, you can share your printers through the HomeGroup page in Control Panel. (It's an all or none proposition here.) But your printer won't show up in the *Homegroup* folder on other PCs; it'll only incite a balloon to appear when the shared printer is first detected. Thereafter, the method to connect to a HomeGroup-shared printer is the same as with a traditionally shared printer.

Connect to a shared printer

Before other PCs on your network can print, they must be set up. Again, Windows 7 sometimes does this automatically, but if not, you can do it by hand by opening Windows Explorer and navigating to the *Network* folder.

Double-click the PC to which the printer is physically connected. (If the printer is a network printer and not connected to any PC, see "Connect to a Networked Printer or Print Server" on page 619, next.) You'll see any shared printers right in the top-level folder (not a *Printers* folder, as in previous versions of Windows).

Then, just double-click the printer icon to install the driver on your PC. When that's done, open the *Printers* folder in Control Panel to see whether the new printer has shown up. Right-click the printer, select **Properties**, and under the **General** tab, click **Print Test Page** to try it out.

If you have a lot of PCs on your network and you don't want to have to dig through each one looking for shared printers, open the Devices and Printers page in Control Panel and click the **Add a printer** button on the toolbar.

In the Add Printer window, click **Add a network, wireless or Bluetooth printer**. Wait while Windows searches for "available printers." Ignore any printers connected to your own PC, which, for some reason, Windows includes in this list. When the printer you want appears in the list, highlight it, click **Next**, and then follow the prompts to complete the wizard.

 If your printer never shows up, click **The printer that I want isn't listed**. On this next page, click **Select a shared printer by name** and then type the UNC path by hand, as described in the previous section. If you select **Browse for a printer** or click the **Browse** button, you'll be sent back to the Network folder in Windows Explorer, as described previously. See the next topic for details on the third option here, **Add a printer using a TCP/IP address or hostname**.

If the printer still doesn't show up, go back to the PC to which it's connected and troubleshoot the problem there. Of course, the PC hosting the shared printer must be turned on and connected to the network, or you'll never see any of its printers. If this limitation turns out to be a deal breaker on a day-by-day basis, you can replace your printer with a network-ready model, or use a standalone print server to connect older printers directly to your network. The next section deals with these types of devices.

Note that some printers can't be shared over a network, which is usually a limitation of the printer's driver, and an intentional one at that. Many virtual printers, like the Windows Fax service and Microsoft XPS Document Writer, can't be shared over a network, but strangely, Adobe's PDF writer *can*. And then there are the bargain-basement "disposable" printers that are deliberately hobbled to not function on a network so you'd be compelled to buy the more expensive model.

Connect to a Networked Printer or Print Server

A print server lets you plug a printer directly into your network so you don't need a PC to host it. Many newer printers come with print servers built in, and for those that don't, you can get a standalone print server.

Print servers gets you three things. First, anyone on your network can print without requiring that a specific PC be turned on and connected. Next, a printer on your wireless network means that no PC needs to be tethered. And third, adding a print server—or even better, a wireless print server—means you can put the printer anywhere; it no longer has to be right next to a PC.

Problem is, most print servers come with software you're supposed to install on every PC, and the software is often buggy, making the printer seem temperamental. The good news is that you can usually dispense with the proprietary software to make your networked printer more reliable, provided you do the setup by hand:

1. First, connect your network printer to your network. Or, if you have a standalone print server, connect it to your network and then plug your printer into the server. If it's a wireless network printer or print server, you'll probably need to temporarily hook it up to a PC to enter the SSID and encryption information, as described in Chapter 7.

2. Next, determine your print server's current IP address. The address might be a static default address, which should be mentioned in the documentation, or an address automatically assigned by your router's DHCP system.

 If it's the latter—a dynamic address—open your router setup page and view the DHCP Client Table, as described in "Troubleshoot Network Connections" on page 469. Here, you'll see the IP address your print server is currently using.

3. Open a web browser, type the print server's IP address into the address bar, and press **Enter**.

4. On the print server setup page, turn off DHCP and specify a static IP address. It can be anything on your subnet range (e.g., 192.168.1.2 to 192.168.1.254) as long as it's not currently being used by another PC or device. For convenience, pick a number not likely to be assigned by your router's DHCP feature: if your PCs usually live at 192.168.1.101 and 192.168.1.102, choose something out-of-the-way like 192.168.1.200. Enter the numbers into your printer's setup page and then save the settings; check the print server's documentation if you need further help with this step.

 One of the most common problems with the day-to-day use of networked printers is that DHCP keeps changing their IP addresses, and the printer driver has a hard time keeping up. You can often dramatically increase the reliability of your networked printer by assigning it a static address.

5. Next, open the Devices and Printers page in Control Panel and click the **Add a printer** button on the toolbar.

6. On the first page of the Add Printer wizard, click **Add a network, wireless or Bluetooth printer**.

7. Don't wait for Windows to search for available printers; instead, click **The printer that I want isn't listed** right away.

8. On the next page, select **Add a printer using a TCP/IP address or hostname** and click **Next**.

9. From the **Device type** list, select **TCP/IP Device**.

10. In the **Hostname or IP address** field, type the static IP address of your print server you chose in step 4. Windows fills in the **Port name** automatically as you type; click **Next** when you're done.

11. If you see the **Additional Port Information Required** page, it means Windows can't connect to your printer or is having a hard time detecting your printer's settings. In the **Device Type** section, select **Standard**, select **Generic Network Card** from the list, and then click **Next**.

12. Next, Windows will attempt to talk to the printer, but it will likely need your help in choosing the manufacturer and model. Unless your printer is in the list of installed drivers, click **Have Disk** and point to the folder containing your printer driver.

 See Chapter 6 for printer troubleshooting, including tips on removing a broken printer driver in case you don't get the printer to work the first time.

13. When you've selected the driver, click **Next**.

14. You'll then be prompted for a name for the printer, followed by sharing options. Since this is a network printer, select **Don't share this printer**.

15. Complete the wizard and then try printing a test page.

Nearly all print servers work this way, but you may find that some units (likely the one you just bought) have trouble remembering their settings. Obviously, a print server that forgets its static IP address won't be much use with an operating system like Windows 7 that requires a consistent IP address for reliable printing. If this happens to you, check the manufacturer's website for a firmware upgrade that may fix the problem, and then try again.

CHAPTER 9

Command Prompt and Automation

Many seasoned computer users find it a comfort and a relief to abandon the GUI in favor of a good ol' command prompt. This isn't nostalgia, but merely an admission that the Windows GUI doesn't solve all our problems. After all these years, it's still faster and easier to rename groups of files with the ren command than by pointing and clicking.

The Command Prompt in Windows 7 is loosely based on MS-DOS (Microsoft Disk Operating System), the operating system used by the first PCs and the basis for many versions of Windows, including 95 and 98, up to Windows Me. Although Windows 7 is long since divorced from its arcane C-prompt ancestry, you'll find many hacks in this book that rely on tools only accessible via the little blinking cursor in the plain black box.

Windows 7 also comes with PowerShell—also known as MSH, or the Monad Shell—which is more or less a geek-centric replacement for the Command Prompt.

But where command-line interfaces shine is their ability to play back sequences of commands called scripts. One of the carry-overs from DOS is the lowly batch file, a rudimentary means of scripting DOS commands. Windows 7 also includes the Windows Script Host (WSH), which can run simple programs written in VBScript or Jscript, or with add-ons, many other languages. (WSH scripts are beyond the scope of this book.) Not to be left out, PowerShell scripts are more powerful than batch files; in some cases, even a single line entered by hand at the PowerShell prompt can do more than a complex batch file or WSH script.

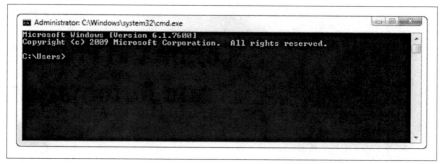

Figure 9-1. The Command Prompt is the old-school way to get things done

Of course, you're not limited to the scripting services offered by Windows. Perl (*http://www.perl.com*) is powerful and flexible, and can even hook into the Windows Script Host if you want easy access to the registry, Windows services, or simple Windows dialog windows. Of course, there's also Ruby (*http://www.ruby-lang.org*) and Python (*http://www.python.org*); check out ActiveState Community Edition (*http://www.activestate.com/*) for free Windows-based Perl and Ruby engines.

Command Prompt

You can open the **Command Prompt** by clicking its icon in the **All Programs** portion of your Start menu, or by typing cmd into the Start menu **Search** box and pressing **Enter**. When you open a Command Prompt window, you'll see a window that looks like the one shown in Figure 9-1. The cursor indicates the command line (where commands are typed), and the prompt usually shows the current working directory (here, *C:\Users\Cory\AppData\Local*), followed by a caret (>).

To run a program or execute a command, just type the name of the program or command at the command line (also called the "C" prompt because it usually looks like **C:\>**), and press **Enter**.

Some Command Prompt applications simply display information and then exit immediately. For example, Figure 9-3 shows some output from the Active Connections utility (*netstat.exe*) discussed in "Scan Your System for Open Ports" on page 509.

DOS Commands

You should know the following basic DOS commands to be able to complete some of the solutions in this book and get by in the world of Windows.

The commands shown here are in `constant width`, and any parameters (the information you supply to the command) are in `constant width italic`. Optional parameters are shown in [square brackets]. It doesn't matter which case you use when you type them in the Command Prompt (DOS, like Windows, is not case-sensitive). If there is more than one parameter, each is separated by a space.

attrib `attributes filename`

Changes the attributes of a file or folder. The four attributes are R for *read only*, S for *system*, A for *archive*, and H for *hidden*.

In Explorer, you can right-click a file or group of files and select **Properties** to change the attributes; **attrib** is the DOS counterpart to this functionality. In addition, **attrib** lets you change the S (system) attribute, something Explorer doesn't let you do.

The **Change file attributes** tool in Creative Element Power Tools (*http://www.creativelement.com/powertools/*) lets you quickly add or remove any of the four standard attributes by right-clicking files in Windows Explorer.

Here's how to change file attributes from the command prompt:

attrib `+h myfile.txt`

This turns *on* the H parameter for the file *myfile.txt*, making the file hidden.

attrib `-r "another file.doc"`

This turns *off* the R (read-only) parameter for the file *another file.doc* (note the use of quotation marks because of the space in the filename).

Type `attrib /?` for additional options.

cd `foldername`

Changes the working directory to *foldername*. If the prompt indicates you are in *C:\Windows* and you want to enter the *C:\Windows\System32* folder, type `cd system32`. You can also switch to any folder on your hard disk by including the full path of the folder. Type `cd ..` to go to the parent folder. Type `cd` by itself to display the current directory.

To switch to another drive, just type the drive letter, followed by a colon (:). For example, type `a:` to switch to the floppy drive.

cls

Clear the display and empty the buffer (the history of output accessible with the scroll bar).

copy *filename destination*

Copies a file to another directory or drive, specified by *destination*. This is the same as dragging and dropping files in Explorer, except that you use the keyboard instead of the mouse. For example, to copy the file *myfile.txt* (located in the current working directory) to another drive, type `copy myfile.txt g:\`. Type `copy /?` for additional options.

del *filename*

Deletes a file. For example, to delete the file *myfile.txt*, type `del myfile.txt`. This is not exactly the same as deleting a file in Windows, because the file will *not* be stored in the Recycle Bin. The advantage of the DOS variant is that you can more easily and quickly delete a group of files, such as all the files with the *.tmp* extension: `del *.tmp`. Type `del /?` for additional options.

dir *name*

Displays a listing of all the files and directories in the current working directory. Use `cd` to change to a different directory, or type `dir c:\files` to display the contents of *C:\Files* without having to first use the `cd` command. Type `dir /p` to pause the display after each page, useful for very long listings (or just enlarge the window). You can also specify wildcards to filter the results; type `dir *.tmp` to display only files with the *.tmp* filename extension. Type `dir /?` for additional options.

echo *text*

Displays the text, *text*, on the screen. See "Variables and the Environment" on page 630.

exit

Closes the Command Prompt window. In most situations, you can just click the close button × on the upper-right corner of the window, but the `exit` command works just as well.

fsutil hardlink create *linkfilename realfilename*

Creates a symbolic link, *linkfilename*, which points to an existing file, *realfilename*.

A *symbolic link*, to borrow the age-old term from the Unix world, is a reference to a file stored elsewhere. The symbolic link looks and acts exactly as though it were a copy of the original file—Windows Explorer even reports the same file size—but the file is physically stored only once on your drive. Change the contents of the original, and the contents of the link changes simultaneously. Windows Shortcuts accomplish something similar, but are only useful for GUI manipulation (double-clicking and drag-dropping); symbolic links can masquerade as any file, and Windows won't see any difference.

Type `fsutil hardlink list` *filename*, where *filename* is the name of either an existing original file or existing symbolic link, to see display other files linked to *filename*.

 Strictly speaking, `fsutil` is a program, not a DOS command. But since it's only usable on the command line (there's no Windows Explorer equivalent), it is included here. See "Add DVDs to Your Movie Library" on page 253 for an example of how symbolic links are used.

md *foldername*
This command creates a new directory (md=make directory) with the name *foldername*. The command will have no effect if there's already a directory or file with the same name.

move *filename destination*
Is the same as `copy`, except that the file is moved instead of copied. Type `move /?` for additional options. (Unlike dragging and dropping in Windows Explorer, this command moves files unconditionally.)

rd *foldername*
This command deletes an empty directory (rd=remove directory) with the name *foldername*. The command will have no effect if the directory is not empty.

ren *oldfilename newfilename*
Renames a file to *newfilename*. This is especially useful, because you can use the `ren` command to rename more than one file at once—something Explorer doesn't let you do. For example, to rename *hisfile.txt* to *her-file.txt*, type `ren hisfile.txt herfile.txt`. To change the extensions of all the files in the current working directory from *.txt* to *.doc*, type `ren *.txt *.doc`. Type `ren /?` for additional options.

set [*variable* =[*string*]]
When used without any arguments, displays a list of active environment variables (described in "Variables and the Environment" on page 630). The `set` command is also used to assign data to environment variables.

type *filename*
Displays the contents of a text file. Type `type` *filename* `| more` to display the file and pause between each page of information rather than displaying the whole file at once.

Filenames with Spaces on the Command Prompt

Need to reference a file or folder name with spaces on the command line? Say you wish to rename a file named *my stuff.txt* to *her stuff.doc*. Instinctively, you might type:

```
ren my stuff.txt her stuff.doc
```

However, this won't work, since the `ren` command sees only that you've typed *four* parameters: `my`, `stuff.txt`, `her`, and `stuff.doc`. Instead, you'll need to use quotation marks, like this:

```
ren "my stuff.txt" "her stuff.doc"
```

Now, this isn't always the case. For example, say you want to use the `cd` command to change the current working directory to *Program Files*, like this:

```
cd Program Files
```

Here, the `cd` command expects only one parameter and is smart enough to interpret this correctly, and no quotation marks are needed.

Tip for you lazy types: you can often leave off the final quote, and it'll still work.

Batch Files

When it comes to quick and dirty scripting, it's hard to beat DOS batch files. Batch files are just plain-text files with the *.bat* or *.cmd* filename extension. However, rather than relying on a complex, unfamiliar scripting language, batch files simply consist of one or more DOS commands (from the previous section), typed one after another.

One of the problems with Windows-based scripting is that it tries to control a graphical environment with a command-based language. Because DOS is a command-based interface, DOS-based scripting (batch files) is a natural extension of the environment.

Consider the following four DOS commands:

```
c:
cd \windows\temp
attrib -r *.tmp
del *.tmp
```

If you type these commands into a plain-text editor, such as Notepad, save them into a *.cmd* file, and then execute the batch file by double-clicking or typing its name at the Command Prompt, it will have the same effect as if the commands were manually typed consecutively at the prompt. Obviously, this can be a tremendous timesaver if you find yourself entering the same commands repeatedly.

 When you run a batch file, each command in the file will be displayed (echoed) on the screen before it's executed, which can be unsightly for the more compulsive among us. To turn off the echoing of any given command, precede it with the @ character. To turn off the printing of all commands in a batch file, place the command @echo off at the beginning of the batch file.

To run a batch file, double-click its icon in Explorer or, if it's in the current working directory (folder), you can type its name at the Command Prompt. You'll want to put more frequently used, general purpose batch files in a folder specified in the system path (see the upcoming sidebar, "The Path Less Travelled" on page 631), so that they can be executed regardless of the current working directory.

In addition to the standard DOS commands, most of which are documented earlier, batch files use a couple of extra statements to fill the holes. Variables, conditional statements, and for...next loops are all implemented with statements that are ordinarily not much use outside of batch files.

The next few sections cover the concepts used to turn a task or a string of DOS commands into a capable batch file.

Quickly Build a Single-Use Batch File

Batch files can be used for rudimentary programming, as described in the next few sections, but one of their most useful roles is to quickly automating a single task. For this exercise, you'll need a spreadsheet (e.g., Excel) and Notepad.

Say you have 150 photos, all with filenames like *DSC_7809.JPG*, that you'd like to give more descriptive names. Now, you could rename the files one-by-one, but that wouldn't be much fun. Instead, select all the files and use a tool like Copy Filenames (*http://www.extrabit.com/copyfilenames/*) or Creative Element Power Tools (*http://creativelement.com/powertools/*) to copy all the filenames to the clipboard.

Next, open a blank worksheet and paste the filenames into column **B**. Then, in cell **A1**, type the ren command, followed by a quotation mark, like this:

```
ren "
```

Copy cell **A1** all the way down column **A** so there's an instance of ren "
adjacent to each filename.

Next, in cell **C1**, type another (closing) quotation mark, followed by a space
and then yet another quotation mark, like this:

```
"  "
```

Once again, copy cell **C1** all the way down column **C** so there's one for each
filename.

Now type all the new filenames in column **D**, one for each filename. (This
method is a particular timesaver if you have your filenames already typed out,
in which case you can just paste the list into cell **D1**.)

If necessary, include the filename extension (e.g., *.jpg*) in cell **E1** and copy that
all the way down. (You can include a final closing quotation mark here if you
like.)

When you're done, highlight the whole worksheet (**Ctrl-A**), copy to the clipboard (**Ctrl-C**), and then paste the text into Notepad (**Ctrl-V**).

Next, in Notepad, you'll notice that there's a tab space between each cell, like
this:

```
ren "   DSC_7809.JPG    " "   Asher playing on the slide    .jpg"
```

Just highlight the first tab space and press **Ctrl-C** to copy. Press **Ctrl-H** to
open the Replace window, and in the **Find what** field, press **Ctrl-V** to paste
the tab character. Leave the **Replace with** field blank, and then click **Replace
All**. When you're done, that spaced-out line should look like this:

```
ren "DSC_7809.JPG" "Asher playing on the slide.jpg"
```

Now save the file, choose a filename, and include the *.cmd* extension at the end.

Double-click the *.cmd* file to run it and rename your photo files, and then delete
the batch file when it's done.

Variables and the Environment

The use of variables in batch files can be somewhat confusing. All variables
used in a batch file (with the exception of command-line parameters) are stored
in the *environment*—an area of memory that is created when you first boot
and kept around until the computer is turned off. The environment variable
space is discussed in more detail in the "The Path Less Travelled" sidebar.

The Path Less Travelled

Although it isn't really emphasized as much as it was in the heyday of DOS and Windows 3.x, the system path is still an important setting in Windows 7. It can be helpful as well as detrimental, depending on how it's used.

The system path is simply a list of folder names kept in memory during an entire Windows session. If a folder name is listed in your system path, you'll be able to run a program contained in that folder *without* having to specify its location. The path is one of several *environment variables* that are kept in memory from Windows startup until you shut down. In early versions of Windows, the path was set with a line in the now-obsolete *Autoexec.bat* file. Now, all environment variables are set in Control Panel; just run *systempropertiesadvanced.exe* and click **Environment Variables**.

By default, the `Path` system variable (shown in the lower box), contains the following folders:

```
%SystemRoot%
%SystemRoot%\system32
%SystemRoot%\system32\Wbem
```

and likely many others. The `%SystemRoot%` element represents the Windows folder (usually *C:\Windows*); see the discussion of expanded string variables in Chapter 3 for details.

To view the contents of the environment, type `set` without any arguments. To set a variable to a particular value, type this command:

```
set VariableName=Some Data
```

The **set** command is required and no quotation marks are used when setting the value of a variable. To remove the variable from memory, you set its value to nothing, like this:

```
set VariableName=
```

To then display the contents of the variable, use the `echo` command, as follows:

```
echo %VariableName%
```

Here, the percent signs (%) on both ends of the variable name are mandatory; otherwise, the `echo` command would take the argument literally and display the name of the variable rather than the data it contains. What's confusing is that in some cases, variables need no percent signs; sometimes they need one, two at the beginning, or one on each end. More on this later.

Note that the **set** command only changes environment variables for the current session; close the Command Prompt window and reopen it, and your custom variables will be gone. To set environment variables on a more permanent basis, use Control Panel as described in "The Path Less Travelled" on page 631.

Flow Control

Batch files have a very rudimentary, but easy-to-understand flow-control structure. The following example exhibits the use of the goto command:

```
@echo off
echo Griff
echo Asa
goto LaterOn
echo 0x
:LaterOn
echo Etch
```

 Running this script from Windows Explorer? Add the pause command to the end of the script so you can see the output before the window closes.

The :LaterOn line (note the mandatory colon prefix) is called a label, which is used as a target for the goto command. If you follow the flow of the script, you should expect the following output:

```
Griff
Asa
Etch
```

because the goto command has caused the printing of 0x to be skipped. The label can appear before or after the goto line in a batch file, and you can have multiple goto commands and multiple labels.

Command-Line Parameters

Suppose you executed a batch file called *Demo.cmd* by typing the following at the Command Prompt:

```
Demo file1.txt file2.txt
```

Both file1.txt and file2.txt are command-line parameters and are automatically stored in two variables, %1 and %2, respectively, when the batch file is run. The implication is that you could run a batch file that would then act with the filenames or options that have been passed to it.

The following two-line example uses command-line parameters and the FC utility to compare two text files:

```
fc %1 %2 >c:\windows\temp\output.txt
notepad c:\windows\temp\output.txt
```

Save this batch file as *compare.cmd*, and execute it like this:

```
compare c:\windows\tips.txt c:\windows\faq.txt
```

which will compare the two files, *tips.txt* and *faq.txt* (both located in your Windows folder), save the output to a temporary file, and then display the output by opening the file in Notepad. Note that the > character on the first line *redirects* the output of the FC program so that it's saved in the *output.txt* file, which would otherwise be displayed on the screen. The second line then opens *output.txt* in Notepad for easy viewing.

There are ways, other than typing, to take advantage of command-line parameters. If you place a shortcut to a batch file (say, *Demo.cmd*) in your *SendTo* folder, then right-click on a file in Explorer, select **Send To** and then **Demo**, the *Demo.cmd* batch file will be executed with the file you've selected as the first command-line parameter. Likewise, if you drag-drop any file onto the batch-file icon in Explorer, the dropped file will be used as the command-line parameter.[*]

Batch files have a limit of nine command-line parameters (%1 through %9), although there's a way to have more if you need them. Say you need to accept 12 parameters at the command line; your batch file should start by acting on the first parameter. Then, you would issue the shift command, which eliminates the first parameter, putting the second in its place. %2 becomes %1, %3 becomes %2, and so on. Just repeat the process until there are no parameters left. Here's an example of this process:

```
:StartOfLoop
if "%1"=="" exit
del %1
shift
goto StartOfLoop
```

Save these commands into *MultiDel.cmd*. Now, this simple batch file deletes one or more filenames with a single command; it's used like this:

```
MultiDel file1.txt another.doc third.log
```

by cycling through the command-line parameters one by one using shift. It repeats the same two lines (del %1 and shift) until the %1 variable is empty (see "Conditional Statements", next, for the use of the if statement), at which point the batch file ends (using the exit command).

---

[*] If you drop more than one file on a batch-file icon, their order as arguments will be seemingly random, theoretically mirroring their ordering in your hard disk's file table.

Conditional Statements

There are three versions of the `if` statement, which allow you to compare values and check the existence of files. The first version, which is usually used to test the value of a variable, is used as follows:

```
if "%1"=="help" goto SkipIt
```

Note the use of quotation marks around the variable name and the `help` text, as well as the double equals signs, all of which are necessary here. Notice also there's no **then** keyword, which those of you who are familiar with VBScript might expect. If the batch file finds that the two sides are equal, it executes everything on the right side of the statement; in this case, it issues the `goto` command.

The second use of the `IF` command is to test the existence of a file:

```
if exist c:\windows\tips.txt goto SkipIt
```

If the file *C:\Windows\tips.txt* exists, the `goto` command will be executed. Similarly, you can you can test for the absence of a file, as follows:

```
if not exist c:\test.gif goto SkipIt
```

The third use of the `if` command is to test the outcome of the previous command, as follows:

```
if errorlevel 0 goto SkipIt
```

If there was any problem with the statement immediately before this line, the `errorlevel` (which is similar to a system-defined variable) will be set to some nonzero number. The `if` statement shown here tests for any `errorlevel` that is greater than zero; if there was no error, execution will simply continue to the next command.

Here's a revised version of the file-compare example first shown in "Command-Line Parameters" on page 632:

```
if "%1"=="" goto problem
if "%2"=="" goto problem
if not exist %1 goto problem
if not exist %2 goto problem
fc %1 %2 >c:\windows\temp\output.txt
if errorlevel 0 goto problem
if not exist c:\windows\temp\output.txt goto problem
notepad c:\windows\temp\output.txt
exit
:problem
echo "There's a problem; deal with it."
```

This batch file is essentially the same as the original two-line example shown earlier, except that some error-checking if statements have been added to make the batch file a little more robust. If you neglect to enter one or both command-line parameters, or if the files you specify as command-line parameters don't exist, the batch file will display the error message. An even more useful version might have multiple error messages that more accurately describe the specific problem that was encountered.

Loops

Batch files have a very simple looping mechanism, based loosely on the for...next loop used in other programming languages. The main difference is that the batch file for loop doesn't increment a variable regularly, but rather cycles it through a list of values. Its syntax is as follows:

```
for %%i in ("Abe","Monty","Jasper") do echo %%i
```

Here, the variable syntax gets even more confusing; the reference to the i variable when used in conjunction with the for...in...do statement gets two percent signs in front of the variable name and none after. Note also that only single-letter variables can be used here.

If you execute this batch file, you'll get the following output:

```
Abe
Monty
Jasper
```

Note also the use of the quotation marks; although they aren't strictly necessary, they're helpful if one or more of the values in the list has a comma in it.

To simulate a more traditional For...Next statement in a batch file, type the following:

```
for %%i in (1,2,3,4,5) do echo %%i
```

Simulating Subroutines

Batch files have no support for named subroutines. However, you can simulate subroutines by creating several batch files: one *main* file and one or more *subordinate* files (each of which can accept command-line parameters). You probably wouldn't want to use this if performance is an issue.

This is useful in cases like the for...in...do statement (described in the preceding section), which can loop only a single command.

In one batch file, called *WriteIt.cmd*, type:

```
if "%1"=="" exit
if exist %1.txt del %1.txt
echo This is a text > %1.txt
```

Then, in another batch file, called *Main.cmd*, type the following:

```
for %%i in ("Kang","Kodos","Serak") do call WriteIt.cmd %%i
```

The single-line *Main.cmd* batch file uses the `call` command to run the other batch file, *WriteIt.cmd*, three times. You could omit the `call` command, but doing so would cause the whole process to end after the subordinate batch file was run the first time. Don't ask me why.

When this pair of batch files is run, you should end up with three files, *Kang.txt*, *Kodos.txt*, and *Serak.txt*, all containing the text, "This is a text." The `if` statement and the `for...in...do` loop are explained in earlier sections.

Get to the Command Prompt Quickly

If you find yourself using the Command Prompt frequently, you'll probably benefit from the following solution. Instead of having to use the `cd` command to change to a given folder, you can simply open a Command Prompt window on the fly in Explorer, already rooted in the selected folder.

1. Open the Registry Editor (see Chapter 3).
2. Expand the branches to `HKEY_CLASSES_ROOT\Directory\shell`. (See "File Type Associations" on page 166 for details on the structure of this branch.)
3. Create a new key by going to **Edit→ New→Key**, and type cmd for the name of this new key.
4. Double-click the (`default`) value in the new cmd key, and type the following for its contents:

   ```
   Open Command &Prompt Here
   ```

5. Next, create a new key here by going to **Edit→New→Key**, and type command for the name of the new key.
6. Double-click the (`default`) value in the new command key, and type the following for its contents:

   ```
   cmd.exe /k "cd %1 && ver"
   ```

This line launches the *cmd.exe* application, and then, using the /k parameter, instructs it to carry out these two commands:

```
cd %1
ver
```

which change the working directory to the folder that has been right-clicked, and then displays the Windows version, respectively.

7. Close the Registry Editor when you're done; the change will take effect immediately. Just right-click any folder and select **Open Command Prompt Here** to open a Command Prompt window at the selected folder.

A simpler and somewhat slicker solution is to use Creative Element Power Tools (*http://www.creativelement.com/powertools/*). Once you turn on the **Open a Command Prompt in any folder** option, you can right-click any folder icon or the background of any open folder window (or the desktop), and select **Command Prompt** to open a new Command Prompt window rooted at the selected folder. The tool supports Administrator mode (for UAC) and can also be configured to open the Windows PowerShell (covered next) or any third-party Command Prompt application.

Windows PowerShell

Windows PowerShell, known prior to its official release as the Monad[†] Shell (MSH), is an advanced replacement for the good ol' Command Prompt. Although it uses many familiar DOS commands (sort of), it introduces some Unix-like functionality to the Windows platform while borrowing some of the Windows-aware features found in WSH scripts, like printing, security, and process control.

 Windows PowerShell 2.0 is installed along with Windows 7; in earlier versions of Windows, you had to download PowerShell separately from *http://www.microsoft.com/powershell/*.

---

† "Monad" literally means "one" or "single," but was likely chosen by Microsoft as the codename for PowerShell to evoke *monadism*, Gottfried Leibniz's philosophy that the physical and metaphysical universe exists because of a divine "harmony" between fundamental elements he called *monads*. To say the comparison is presumptuous on Microsoft's part is an understatement, but a noble goal nonetheless.

Figure 9-2. Microsoft PowerShell, a free, powerful alternative to the Command Prompt, also supports scripting

At first glance, PowerShell (Figure 9-2) looks like an ordinary Command Prompt window, with the main distinguishing feature being the text PS preceding the prompt (and the blue background color). As you may have guessed, you type a command at the prompt and press **Enter** to execute the command. But the commands you can type—and how they interact with each other—are what really set PowerShell apart.

CmdLets and Aliases

PowerShell's built-in commands are called *CmdLets* for reasons that aren't entirely clear, and the CmdLets all have long, rather inconvenient names like Copy-Item, ConvertFrom-SecureString, and Invoke-Expression. The good news is that most of the commands have short versions, called *aliases*, that just happen to coincide with familiar DOS and Unix command names. For instance, instead of typing Copy-Item, you can type copy (as in DOS) or cp (à la Unix) to copy files from one place to another; if nothing else, this dualism is an important advantage over the conventional Command Prompt.

Table 9-1 shows a list of common, basic PowerShell commands, and their DOS and Unix counterparts.

Table 9-1. Common DOS and Unix commands and their PowerShell equivalents

DOS	Unix	PowerShell	Description
cd	cd	Set-Location	Change the working directory (folder)
cls	clear	Clear-Host	Clear the screen
copy	cp	Copy-Item	Copy a file or object from one place to another
del, rd	rm, rmdir	Remove-Item	Delete a file, directory (folder), or object
dir	ls	Get-ChildItem	Display the contents of the current directory or object

DOS	Unix	PowerShell	Description
help	man	Get-Help	Display a list of commands or details about the specified command
md	mkdir	New-Item	Create a directory (folder) or object
move	mv	Move-Item	Move a file, directory (folder), or object to a new location
ren	mv	Rename-Item	Change the name of a file or object
type	cat	Get-Content	Display the contents of a file or object

What's more enticing is that you can make your own aliases. For example, if you find yourself frequently using the Get-Culture command (which retrieves the language in use by Windows), you could shorten it like this:

```
Set-Alias -Name lang -Value Get-Culture
```

so that you could thereafter type only lang to display the current language. The Set-Alias command also lets you overwrite any of the built-in aliases.

 The Set-Alias command only creates aliases for bare commands; you can't bury your favorite command-line parameters in an alias. To replace a complex, multipart command with a single word you can type at the prompt, use PowerShell variables, discussed later.

Of course, once you close the current PowerShell window, your custom alias will be forgotten. So, to save your custom aliases from session to session, add your Set-Alias commands to your PowerShell profile file. Of course, you probably don't have a profile yet, so type:

```
New-Item -type file -force $profile
```

to create one. Then type:

```
notepad $profile
```

to open the newly created profile for editing.

Most PowerShell commands are documented in a series of text files located in the *C:\Windows\System32\WindowsPowerShell\v1.0* folder (yes, that's the *v1.0* folder even for PowerShell 2.0). There's also a simple online help system, via the help command, that displays a list of available commands (in a not-so-helpful format), or if invoked with the name of a command, displays the syntax and explanation of the command. To see all the available information about a command, include the -full parameter, like this:

```
help Get-Item -full
```

While using the online help, you'll soon discover the needlessly complex SYN-TAX section, which lists all the parameters supported by a single command. For instance, the syntax line for the `Copy-Item` command (copy to you and me) consumes four lines, and is about as easy to read as the computer output in the *Matrix* movies.‡ But rest assured, it's more or less the same as its DOS counterpart; in other words, this command:

```
copy c:\stuff\myfile.txt d:\misc
```

still works as you'd expect.

Pipelines

So, if PowerShell looks like the Command Prompt, and most of the commands you know and love work the same, then what's the point?

Without drowning you in technical jargon, what sets PowerShell Cmdlets apart from their Command Prompt counterparts is that they work better with *piping*, a means of redirecting the output of one command so that it's used as the input for another. For example, this two-part command:

```
get-process m* | stop-process
```

works because the `get-process` Cmdlet sends (through the *pipe*) its output—a list of running processes starting with the letter m—as a *structured object*. In turn, the `stop-process` Cmdlet receives this object and uses it as a list of processes to stop. In lesser Command Prompts, this information is passed between commands (piped) as plain text, which means you need to use a variety of tools (like grep in Unix) to format the output so the receiving command can process it. (Imagine what this would all sound like if I had left in the jargon.)

Unfortunately, this particular aspect of PowerShell is a little more hype than dope. For one, the example command above (taken from Microsoft's own documentation) is pointless, since the following simpler command works just as well:

```
stop-process m*
```

Of course, the downside of this object-oriented model is that the various data is all *typed*, and can't be easily converted from one type to another. That is, you can't easily pipe output to a command that hasn't been specifically designed to receive it. In good ol' Unix and DOS, you can pipe anything to anything. For instance, this PowerShell command:

```
help | help
```

‡ Too geeky? Naaah...

which I expected would send a list of Cmdlets generated by help *back to* help, which in turn would spit out a detailed explanation of each Cmdlet, did not work at all. Perhaps this is a silly example, but it sure would've made my job easier.

What does work well is the passing of filenames from one Cmdlet to another. Here's a sophisticated series of commands that illustrates this:

```
Get-ChildItem 'H:\MediaCenterPC\My Music' -rec | where { -not $_.
    PSIsContainer -and $_.Extension -match "wma|mp3" } | Measure-Object
    -property length -sum -min -max -ave
```

This amalgam of three Cmdlets (entered all on one line) does the following:

- Retrieves a list of filenames in the *H:\MediaCenterPC\My Music* folder and all its subfolders (thanks to the -rec option), and passes the list to...
- the where (Where-Object) Cmdlet, which filters out any files that don't have the *.wma* or *.mp3* filename extensions, and then passes the modified list to...
- the Measure-Object Cmdlet, which outputs detailed information about the music files in the list.

And you could keep going like this, including a command that take the output from Measure-Object to process, store, or display it in some fashion. The syntax may look a little messy to the uninitiated, but it would be much more difficult to do this sort of thing in WSH and totally impossible in a batch file.

PowerShell Variables

PowerShell variables work much like variables in other scripting languages: they hold data. A variable name starts with a dollar sign and what follows can be any string of characters. But what makes variables in PowerShell particularly useful is that they can capture the output of Cmdlets, and then be put in place of static information in subsequent Cmdlets, like this:

```
$url = "http://www.nytimes.com/services/xml/rss/nyt/Science.xml"
$content = [xml](new-object System.Net.WebClient).DownloadString($url)
$content.rss.channel.item | select title -first 8
```

The first line fills the $url variable with the address of a website (specifically, an RSS feed for the purposes of this example). The next line downloads the file at the $url address and sends it to the $content variable. And the last line uses a pipe (discussed earlier) to first process the news feed and then show only the first eight headlines.

You can also assign a variable to a command, like this:

```
$showtemp = Get-ChildItem 'C:\Users\Administrator\AppData\Local\Temp' -rec
```

then, to execute the command (complete with all the juicy command-line parameters), just type:

```
$showtemp
```

and (in this case), you'll see a listing of all the files in your *Temp* folder.

Variables can also be used with object references, like this one:

```
$WshShell = New-Object -ComObject WScript.Shell
```

This means you can use this object to do things like access the Registry or create shortcuts. For instance, once the $WshShell object has been initialized, try this:

```
$lnk = $WshShell.CreateShortcut("$Home\Desktop\Solitaire.lnk")
$lnk.TargetPath = "%ProgramFiles%\Microsoft Games\Solitaire\Solitaire.exe"
$lnk.Save()
```

which creates another object reference, $lnk, applies characteristics to it, and then saves it to a file. Note some subtleties:

- The preset $Home variable conveniently contains the full path of the current user's home folder.

- The quotation marks are significant in that if you were to substitute the "double" quotes with 'single' quotes, PowerShell would not interpret your variables, but rather leave them literally as you've typed them.

- The %ProgramFiles% *environment* variable—a separate entity from Power-Shell variables—is explained in "Variables and the Environment" on page 630.

See the PowerShell documentation for more ins and outs of variables and object references.

PowerShell Scripts

Like DOS batch files or WSH scripts, a PowerShell script is just a text file with a list of commands. The PowerShell Integrated Scripting Environment (*PowerShell_ISE.exe*) is an all-in-one editor that lets you build and test your scripts.

Unfortunately, you can't run PowerShell scripts outside of the ISE until you jump through a few hoops to disable some of the security safeguards. The first step is to check the execution policy by opening a PowerShell window and typing:

```
Get-ExecutionPolicy
```

If the reply you get is Restricted (the default), then you need to type this command to allow script execution:

```
Set-ExecutionPolicy RemoteSigned
```

To run a script from an open PowerShell window, type the name of the script file, complete with its path and filename extension, like this:

```
$home\Desktop\MakeShortcut.ps1
```

Unlike the Command Prompt, you can't leave off the path if the script is in the same folder as the working folder. For instance, this doesn't work:

```
MakeShortcut.ps1
```

but this does:

```
.\MakeShortcut.ps1
```

The single dot (.) represents the current folder, and is necessary when launching scripts from the PowerShell command line.

Also, and presumably for security reasons, you can't run PowerShell scripts by double-clicking them until you make a change to your system. To enable script launching, right-click a *.ps1* file, select **Open With→Choose Default Program**, click **Select a program from a list of installed programs**, and then click OK. Click **Browse**, locate the PowerShell executable (usually *C:\Windows\System32\WindowsPowerShell\v1.0\powershell.exe*), and click OK.

 By default, the PowerShell window closes when it's done executing a script, but you can change this by modifying the file type (see Chapter 3) and adding the -NoExit option to the *powershell.exe* command line.

Thereafter, you can double-click any *.ps1* file to run the script.

Run Scripts Automatically

It's sometimes hard to escape feeling like an automaton—an extension of your computer, rather than the other way around. What percentage of the time you spend at your PC is used carrying out repetitive, mundane tasks? Your motor memory has likely enabled you to do things like rename multiple files quickly by hand, or open your database application, email client, and web browser each morning when you sit down at your desk—pretty quickly, and all without thinking about it. But if you do stop and think, your PC, not you, should be handling all this nonsense, leaving you to handle the creative end.

That's why we have the scripting technologies covered at the beginning of this chapter. But why stop there? Use features built into Windows to run these scripts automatically so you don't have to. Whether you need to back up important files once a week, generate custom web pages every three seconds, or close errant processes only occasionally, there's almost certainly a better and faster way to do it than the way you're doing it now.

Automate Scripts with the Task Scheduler

Windows 7's Task Scheduler is fairly simple, allowing you to schedule any program or—more importantly in the context of this chapter—any script to run at a specific time or regular intervals.

To open Task Scheduler, open your Start menu, type `taskschd.msc /s` in the **Search** box, and press **Enter**. (Omit the `/s` parameter to jump to the Task Scheduler Library instead of showing the summary page by default.) The Task Scheduler tool in Windows 7 (Figure 9-3) is complex and somewhat unfriendly, which is surprising since it replaces the simpler (and more feeble) *Scheduled Tasks* folder in earlier versions of Windows.

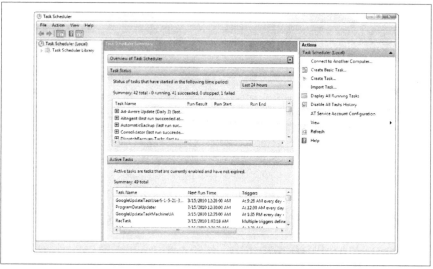

Figure 9-3. Use Task Scheduler to run programs or scripts at certain times or regular intervals, or to change schedules other programs may have set up without your knowledge

What's nice about Task Scheduler is that it's actually a technology that is somewhat well integrated into the operating system. Any application can create a schedule for itself, and you can plainly see those that are in effect simply by opening Task Scheduler and selecting the Task Scheduler Library folder. For the more forgetful among us, you can use it to schedule backups once a week, remind you to stand up and stretch once an hour, or even fire up Media Center when your favorite TV show is about to air.

To create a new schedule, click the **Create Basic Task** link in the **Actions** pane to your right, and then answer the questions as follows:

Create a Basic Task
> Type the name of the task to appear in your task library; the description is optional.

Trigger
> Choose when to run the task: **Daily**, **Weekly**, **Monthly**, **One time**, **When the computer starts**, **When I log on**, or **When a specific event is logged**.

Daily, Weekly, etc.
> Specify your criteria for the trigger you chose. For instance, if you selected **Daily**, you'll be asked what time of day to carry out the task, and for how many days in a row.

Action
> Here's where you specify what to do. If you want Task Scheduler to run a script, select **Start a program**, click **Next**, and then specify the full path and filename of the script to run.

Finish
> This one speaks for itself.

Or, if you don't like wizards, you can click the **Create Task** link instead to jump right to the Properties window shown in Figure 9-4. Here, only two pieces of information are required: the **Name** (under the **General** tab) and at least one action (under the **Actions** tab). But if you want Task Scheduler to ever run your task, you need to add your criteria (**Daily**, **Weekly**, etc.) under the **Triggers** tab. (Here you can also run scripts based on Windows events, like 'disk full' messages; you can even create new tasks directly from Event Viewer.) Click OK when you're done.

The Task Scheduler Library is a little confusing, especially if you're used to the *Scheduled Tasks* folder in earlier versions of Windows. Only on the Summary page—select **Task Scheduler (Local)** in the folder pane on the left—are all your active tasks shown in one place, and it's at the bottom of the window.

Command Prompt

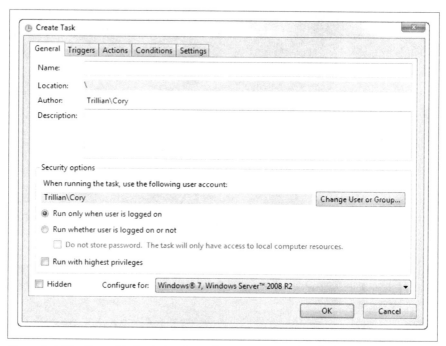

Figure 9-4. The Create Task window is another way to enter the scheduling details of a task, particularly useful if you're not fond of step-by-step wizards

In the **Actions** pane on the right, click the **View** link and then select **Show Hidden Tasks** to make sure you're seeing everything Task Scheduler is doing.

In the Active Tasks pane, you can double-click any task to jump to its entry in the hierarchical library, or click the tiny arrow next to the **Task Scheduler Library** folder on your left to expand the branches and browse the categories. Once you're in the library, highlight a task to view its details in the pane below, or double-click it to edit its properties.

You can also create a new task on the fly from the Command Prompt (or the Address Bar, for that matter). Use the at command, like this:

```
at 11:15 /interactive c:\scripts\myscript.vbs
```

Naturally, you'll want to replace *11:15* with the time you actually want the task to run, and replace *c:\scripts\myscript.vbs* with the full path and filename of the application or script you wish to schedule. You can also use the /every option to specify a repeating day or date, or the /next option to specify only a single day:

```
at 15:45 /interactive /every:tuesday,thursday c:\scripts\myscript.vbs
at 15:45 /interactive /next:saturday c:\scripts\myscript.vbs
```

The /interactive switch allows Task Scheduler to interact with the desktop of the user who is logged on at the time the job runs. Type at /? at the Command Prompt for more options.

To specify which user account is responsible for running tasks created with the at command, open Task Scheduler, click **Task Scheduler (Local)** on the left, and then click the **AT Service Account Configuration** link in the Actions pane to your right.

Task Scheduler does have its pitfalls. For one, it's a rather passive service, and while that's an aspect I like, at least ideologically, it means that tasks can very easily be missed. Your scheduled tasks will not be performed if your computer is turned off, if Windows isn't running (or has crashed), or if the Task Scheduler service isn't running for some reason. (Although it can optionally wake a sleeping PC.) Also, some tasks will only run if you're logged in, and then only if you're running on AC power (not on a battery), although these defaults can be overridden. These may be obvious, but they can be easy to forget, and Windows won't necessarily tell you whether it missed any tasks; for this, you'll need to check the event log or create custom tasks to check for the completion of other tasks.

 If you're using a laptop, and are worried that some of your tasks aren't being performed when you're running off a battery, you can change this on a task-by-task basis. First, edit a task by double-clicking it, and then choose the **Conditions** tab. Turn off the **Start the task only if the computer is on AC power** option to run it regardless of the power source. If you put your PC to sleep frequently, you may also want to turn on the **Wake the computer to run this task** option. (Naturally, use these options only for vital tasks to prevent needlessly draining your battery.) Click OK when you're done.

The use of a scheduler opens up some interesting possibilities. Scheduling helps with repetitive chores, such as running Disk Defragmenter or synchronizing network files; it also helps by taking care of things you may not remember to do yourself, such as backing up or checking the amount of disk space and sending you a text message on your cell phone when it drops below a certain point. And on the flip side of the coin, Task Scheduler is likely doing some things you don't want or need it to do; it's wise to periodically check this tool and disable tasks that might be degrading performance or compromising your PC's security.

Make a Startup Script

The process of making a startup script—a script that is executed automatically when Windows starts—is quite simple. Essentially, you create an ordinary PowerShell Script, batch file, or any other type of script and then take steps to have it executed when Windows starts. There are a few different ways to do this:

Use the Startup folder

Put a shortcut to the script in your *Startup* folder (usually *C:\Users\ {username}\AppData\Roaming\Microsoft\Windows\Start Menu\Programs\ Startup*). This is by far the easiest to implement, but also the most fragile, because it's equally easy to disable.

 If there is more than one user account on a computer, and you want the script to be executed regardless of the currently logged-in user, you can use the "All Users" *Startup* folder (usually *C:\Users\All Users\Microsoft\Windows\Start Menu\Programs\Startup*) instead.

Use the Registry

Open the Registry Editor (discussed in Chapter 3) and expand the branches to HKEY_CURRENT_USER\Software\Microsoft\Windows\CurrentVer sion\Run. Select **New** and then **String Value** from the **Edit** menu, and type startup script. Double-click the new Startup Script value, type the name of your script (e.g., c:\scripts\myscript.vbs), and click OK. Although it's a bit harder to implement, this setup is a little more buried, and thus more difficult for unwitting users to mess up than items placed in the *Startup* folder.

 Many viruses and spyware install themselves in this Registry key precisely because it's so transparent. See Chapter 6 for tips on how to remove malware from this key.

Likewise, you can implement this solution for all users rather than just the current user by adding the Registry value to HKEY_LOCAL_MACHINE\Software \Microsoft\Windows\CurrentVersion\Run instead.

Use the Group Policy Editor

This is probably the coolest solution, as it gives you the most control over precisely when the script is run, and it's the only way to facilitate a shutdown or logoff script as well. Open the Group Policy Editor (*gpedit.msc*), and expand the branches to Computer Configuration\Windows Settings\ Scripts (Startup/Shutdown). Double-click the **Startup** entry on the right side, and then click **Add**. Click **Browse** to locate a script file, and click **OK** when you're done. The script will be run every time you start your computer, but before the logon or Welcome screen appears (and before scripts specified in the Registry or Start menu are ever run).

Likewise, double-click the **Shutdown** entry to specify a script to be run every time your computer shuts down.

Now, there's a similar setting called Scripts (Logon/Logoff), located in the User Configuration branch. Like everything in the User Configuration branch, these settings apply only to the currently logged-on user (as opposed to all users). If you specify your startup script here (under Logon), instead of under Computer Configuration, the script will run *after* you log in. And, of course, a script specified under Logoff will be run when you log off, whether or not you actually shut down the computer.

A startup script can contain a list of programs that you want to run in a specific order when Windows starts, such as connecting to the Internet and then checking your email. (Neither Explorer's *Startup* folder nor the Registry allow you to choose the order in which programs are run.) But there are other, less apparent uses for a startup script, such as for security or remote administration.

For example, say you've discovered malware that has infected some or all of the computers on a network. By writing a script that eliminates the malware by deleting key files or running a removal utility and setting it up as a startup script, you can effectively eliminate it from each computer.

But with scripts, you can take it even further: utilize a single script stored on a single computer that is run, over the network, on all computers. This way, you can make changes to the script once and have those changes propagated to all computers effortlessly. So, if you place the script *Startup.vbs* on a machine called *Server* in a folder called *C:\scripts* (drive C: would be shared as "C"), then each client machine should be configured to automatically execute *\\server\c\scripts\startup.vbs* (using one of the previous methods). The beauty of this is that when you don't want the script to do anything, you can simply leave it intact yet empty. If you find that you need to, say, make a Registry change or copy a group of files onto each computer, just type the appropriate commands into the script and turn on (or reboot) all the client computers. This can turn some administration tasks into very short work.

Command Prompt

BIOS Settings

The BIOS, or Basic Input-Output System, is the software—stored in a chip on your motherboard—responsible for booting your computer and starting your operating system. It also handles the flow of data between the operating system and your peripherals (USB devices, PCI/PCIE slots, hard disk controller, video adapter, etc.), manages your PC's power management features, and cooperates with the Windows plug-and-play subsystem. Incorrect settings in your PC's BIOS can prevent Windows from booting, limit performance, and cause all sorts of hardware and driver problems.

 You change BIOS settings in the BIOS setup screen, which you can usually access by pressing a key—such as **Del**, **F2**, or **Esc**—immediately after powering on your system and before the initial beep. The normal boot screen that appears before the Windows logo often identifies the key you need to press; consult your computer's manual if you need further help.

The settings available in a computer's BIOS setup screen vary from one system to another, but there are many settings that are common among them all. Unfortunately, motherboard and computer manufacturers are notorious for poorly documenting BIOS settings, so it can be difficult to determine what the settings mean, let alone how they should be set. For instance, look up *Microcode Updation* in an ASUS motherboard manual, and here's the entire explanation of the entry for that setting:

Microcode Updation [Enabled]

Allows you to enable or disable the microcode updation.

Configuration options: [Disabled] [Enabled]

Thus, the need for this appendix becomes obvious.

When changing BIOS settings, keep the following in mind:

Change one at a time.

If you're trying to fix a problem, don't change more than one BIOS setting at a time. Although it may take longer, it means you can determine which setting is responsible for fixing the problem (or causing a new one).

Check for updates.

The BIOS is typically stored on a flash chip, which means it can be updated with newer versions. Check with your motherboard manufacturer to see whether a newer BIOS is available for your system. In most cases, BIOS updates only fix bugs, but they occasionally can improve performance or add support for new hardware. If you're unable to install Windows (or its successor) on your system, an outdated BIOS may be to blame.

 Flashing (updating) a BIOS can be a risky procedure. If something goes wrong (e.g., the power goes out, or the BIOS turns out to be corrupted or the wrong version), your computer will probably not boot. Now, such occurrences aren't common, but if you encounter a problem after upgrading your BIOS, check with the manufacturer for a "BIOS recovery" method. For obvious reasons, it's wise to familiarize yourself with the procedure *before* you attempt to update your BIOS.

Names may vary.

The names of BIOS settings listed here may vary, and one appendix can't possibly accommodate them all. For example, a setting named **Event Log** on one system might be called **System Event Log** on another. If you can't find a particular setting, try looking through the list for variations.

Take snapshots.

One of the problems with the BIOS setup screen is that you can't access it from within Windows, which means you can't look up settings on the Web, you can't take screenshots, and you can't take notes without using a pen and paper. However, a digital camera can be very handy in this situation; just take one or more photos of your screen (with the flash turned off, of course) to quickly record all your BIOS settings.

Table A-1 lists many common BIOS settings, along with brief explanations and some tips. For more extensive BIOS setting information and advice, check out the "The Definitive BIOS Optimization Guide" at *http://www.techarp.com/freebog.aspx.*

Setting	Description
AC Power Recovery	Determines whether or not the computer turns on automatically when power is applied (such as from a power loss or external power switch). Note that many PCs don't reliably start when AC power is restored, even if you set this option to **Always On**. See "Start Windows Instantly (Almost)" on page 274, for the Windows settings necessary to prevent data loss when you use an external switch to cut power to your PC.
ACPI 2.0 Support	This enables or disables your motherboard's support for ACPI (Advanced Configuration and Power Interface), a power management feature. In most cases, this should be set to **Enabled**, but if you change this setting after Windows has been installed, you'll get a Blue Screen of Death the next time you boot. If you enable ACPI, you'll need to reinstall Windows (see Chapter 1).
ACPI APIC Support	This enables or disables the APIC (Advanced Programmable Interrupt Controller), which should be enabled, particularly if you have a multicore processor. Like "ACPI 2.0 Support," you may need to reinstall Windows after changing this setting.
ACPI Aware O/S	Set this to **Yes**; see "Power Management" for details.
AddOn ROM Display Mode	Choose whether the startup screen is handled by the primary BIOS or a secondary "add-on" BIOS. Disable this option unless you have a specific need for it.
Address Range Shadowing	Various hardware address ranges can be "shadowed," which means that pieces of faster system RAM are substituted for them. It's best to disable shadowing for all address ranges; this feature is typically not available on newer PCs.
AGP 2X/4X Mode	The AGP 2X and 4X modes double and quadruple the bandwidth to your AGP video card, respectively, but can only be used if your video card supports 2X or 4X. Not applicable on motherboards with PCI-Express slots.
AGP Aperture/ Device Address Space Size	This sets the amount of system memory used to store textures for 3D graphics. The more video memory you have, the lower this setting should be. Many video problems are caused by this value being set too high, but the Glass interface won't work if it's not set at least as high as indicated in "Get Glass" on page 286.
AHCI settings	See "SATA Configuration."
AI Overclocking	See "Overclocking."
AI Quiet	See "Digital Home Mode."
ALPE and ASP	Enables or disables the Aggressive Link Power Management (ALPE) and Aggressive Slumber/Partial (ASP) power management features for SATA drives. **Disabled/ Off** is usually the default; enable this setting if you need advanced features like AHCI Port 3 Interlock Switch or Staggered Spinup Support.
AMD Cool 'n' Quiet/ Power-Now!	See "Intel SpeedStep."
Anti-Virus Protection	Actively scans your hard disk for boot sector viruses. Despite the apparent usefulness of a feature like this, you should always disable it, as it typically interferes with Windows and causes all sorts of problems.

Setting	Description
APM settings	See "Power Management."
Assign IRQ For USB	See "Legacy USB Support."
Assign IRQ For VGA/ Allocate IRQ to PCI VGA	This should be enabled unless your video card does not need its own IRQ *and* you need an extra IRQ for another device.
Auto Power On	See "AC Power Recovery."
Boot Device Priority/Boot Sequence	Specifies the order among the various drives in your system that your computer looks for a drive with a bootable operating system. For example, if your CD/DVD drive has a higher boot priority than your hard drive, then your PC will look for a bootable CD or DVD before it attempts to boot off the hard disk. If the CD/DVD drive has a *lower* boot priority, and Windows has already been installed, your PC will ignore bootable CDs. Put your hard disk at the top of the list for faster booting, or promote your CD/DVD drive if you're installing Windows (see Chapter 1).
Boot Graphic Adapter Priority	If you have more than one video card, use this setting to choose which one is the primary video adapter. Change this setting if you get no video when you boot, but use the settings in Windows Control Panel if you want to configure multiple monitors.
Boot Other Device	If an operating system isn't found on the first boot drive (see "Boot Device Priority/ Boot Sequence") and this setting is enabled, your computer will attempt to boot off of other drives.
Boot Sector Virus Protection	See "Anti-Virus Protection."
Boot to OS/2	Changes how memory above 64 MB is handled for compatibility with IBM's defunct OS/2 operating system. For obvious reasons, this option should be disabled.
Bootup Numlock Status	See "Numlock State."
C000/C400/C800/CC00 16k Shadow	See "Address Range Shadowing."
Chassis Fan	This shows the RPM of the fan connected to the "Chassis Fan" connector on your motherboard. This is typically a read-only display, not a setting you can change.
CPU Current Temperature	This shows the measured temperature of your processor. For dual-processor systems, you'll see two such settings. This is typically a read-only display, not a setting you can change.
CPU Fan	This shows the RPM of the fan connected to the "CPU Fan" connector on your motherboard. For dual-processor systems, you'll see two such settings. This is typically a read-only setting.
CPU Level 1 Cache/ Level 2 Cache	These settings allow you to disable your processor's primary (level 1) and secondary (level 2) cache, respectively. These settings should always be enabled.
CPU to PCI Write Buffer	Enables or disables the buffer used for data sent to the PCI bus by the processor. This should be enabled.
D000/D400/D800/DC00 16k Shadow	See "Address Range Shadowing."

Setting	Description
Delayed Transaction	See "PCI 2.1 Compliance."
Diskette	See all "Floppy" entries.
DRAM CAS Latency	In theory, set this to **CAS2** if your system memory (RAM) is rated at CAS Latency 2; otherwise, use **CAS3**. Interestingly, you should be able to use the faster **CAS2** setting regardless of the type of installed memory; use **CAS3** only if instability results.
DRAM Data Integrity/ ECC Mode	If your system memory (RAM) has the ECC (Error Checking and Correction) feature, set this to **ECC**. Otherwise, choose **Non-ECC**.
DRAM Timing by SPD	Enable this option to have the BIOS set memory timing options automatically according to (Serial Presence Detect).
EHCI Hand-Off	This is a USB 2.0 feature and should be enabled unless you're having USB problems.
Event Log	Your motherboard can log errors (such as BIOS problems and hard disk boot problems) it encounters during startup. Settings in this section allow you to enable or disable logging, view the log, erase the log, etc.
Fast Boot	See "Quick Boot."
First Boot Device	See "Boot Device Priority/Boot Sequence."
Flash BIOS Protection	This prevents the BIOS from being overwritten or updated. You'll need to disable this to update your BIOS, as explained at the beginning of this appendix. Otherwise, leave this enabled to protect against viruses that attack BIOSes.
Floppy Drive A/B	Use these settings to define the floppy diskette drives you have connected to your computer; set to **Disabled** if you have no floppy drive.
Floppy Drive Seek	When enabled, this option will send a signal to your floppy drive(s) to help detect certain drive characteristics. Leave this off for a quicker boot.
Floppy Write Protect	This prevents anyone from writing data to a diskette in your floppy drive, which is useful if the computer is in a public place and you don't want people copying data to floppies.
Front Panel Support Type	Set this to match the audio connectors on the front of your PC, if applicable; choose between the older AC97 and newer high-definition standards.
Full Screen Logo	Show your PC or motherboard's corporate logo on screen instead of the POST (Power On Self Test) messages.
GART W2K Miniport Driver	The GART (Graphics Address Remapping Table) is part of the AGP subsystem. In most cases, you want to disable this option.
Green PC Monitor Power State	If you're using an APM (advanced power management)-compliant "Green PC" monitor, this setting allows you to automatically shut it off after a certain period of inactivity, in lieu of a screensaver. With these types of settings, it's best to let Windows control how and when devices are shut off.
Hard Disk Power Down Mode	Windows can shut down your hard disk to save power after a certain period of inactivity. With these types of settings, it's best to let Windows control how and when devices are shut off.

Setting	Description
Hard Disk Write Protect	This option write-protects your hard disk so data can't be written to it. You won't want to use this on a Windows PC.
Hard-Disk Drive Sequence	If you have more than one hard disk drive, this option allows you to choose the order in which your computer looks for bootable drives. Used in conjunction with "Boot Device Priority/Boot Sequence."
Hardware Reset Protect	Prevent the computer from being restarted with the **Reset** button on the front of your PC's case (helpful if you have a dog who likes to wag his/her tail while standing next to your computer).
HD Audio	Enable the high-definition audio subsystem on your motherboard. Disable this only if it interferes with a separate audio card.
HDD S.M.A.R.T. Capability	Enables the S.M.A.R.T. (Self Monitoring Analysis and Reporting Technology) feature supported by IDE (parallel ATA) hard disks, that helps predict potential problems before they happen. Most users don't need it, and are probably better off disabling this feature.
Hit DEL Message Display	Turns on or off the message on the POST (Power On Self Test) screen that says "Press DEL to enter Setup."
Hyper Path 3	Set to **Enabled** or **Auto** to shorten latency time during data transfers.
IDE BusMaster	Enables or disables bus mastering for the IDE controller, which helps reduce load on the processor when data is transferred to and from IDE devices. Disable if you're using older drives that don't support bus mastering.
IDE Controller	Despite the name, this feature can apply to both IDE (Parallel ATA) and SATA (Serial ATA) controllers; use this feature to enable or disable said controllers on the motherboard. You can shorten boot times and free IRQs by disabling controllers you don't need. However, on older IDE/PATA systems, you can marginally improve performance by enabling all your IDE controllers and then distributing your hard disks and CD drives so you don't ever have two devices sharing the same controller.
IDE Detect Time Out	Choose how long your PC waits for IDE devices to respond before giving up.
IDE HDD Block Mode	This option should not be used with Windows 7.
Intel SpeedStep/AMD Cool 'n' Quiet/PowerNow!	These are power-management features that allow processors to run at lower speeds and use less power. Enable the feature to allow Windows to control your processor speed.
Internal Cache	See "CPU Level 1 Cache/Level 2 Cache."
Interrupt 19 Capture	Enable this feature if you need to boot off a hard disk connected to a separate (add-on) hard disk controller, like a RAID or SCSI controller. Otherwise, disable it.
IRQ3, IRQ4, IRQ5, etc.	There are two different settings named for IRQs. One, used with power management, determines whether or not your computer monitors a given IRQ for activity (used to "wake up" the system). The other, typically found in the PCI section, allows you to "reserve" an IRQ and prevent the Plug-and-Play system from automatically assigning it to a device.

Setting	Description
JMicron SATA/PATA Controller	This controls the additional (optional) RAID controller on some motherboards. Turn it on only if you have a RAID system connected to this controller.
Legacy USB Support	Enable this option if you're using a USB keyboard or USB mouse and you want to use them in the BIOS setup screen, DOS, or some other environment outside of Windows.
Master/Slave Drive Ultra-DMA	This should be enabled for IDE (Parallel ATA) drives that support UltraDMA, and disabled otherwise. In most cases, it should be set to **Auto**.
Memory Hole at 15M-16M	Enable this option to reserve this segment of your computer's memory for use by some older ISA cards. Unless you specifically need it, this option should be disabled.
Memory Write Posting	This option may improve performance on older systems, but will likely degrade performance—and even cause video corruption—on newer systems. Disable this option unless you're willing to experiment with it.
Microcode Updation	This permits BIOS updates from the manufacturer to also update certain code in your processor. Set this to **Enabled** if you want all the latest fixes and bugs.
MPS Version Control	This allows you to choose the multiprocessor specification version supported by your operating system. Windows 7 supports version 1.4, although some other operating systems do not.
Numlock State	Turn this on if you want the **Num Lock** keyboard light turned on when the system starts. Turn this off if you typically use the numeric keypad to move your cursor, instead of the "inverted T" cursor keys.
Onboard FDD Controller	This enables or disables the floppy diskette drive controller on your motherboard.
Onboard IR Function	This enables or disables the infrared port on your motherboard.
Onboard SCSI	This enables or disables the SCSI controller on your motherboard. Note that SCSI settings will typically be set with a separate SCSI BIOS utility (e.g., **Ctrl-A** for Adaptec controllers).
Overclocking	See "Overclock Your Processor" on page 300.
Overheat Warning Temperature	This sets the temperature above which the overheat warning is triggered. See "System Overheat Warning" for more information.
Palette Snooping/ VGA Palette Snoop	Enable this only if you're using an MPEG-2 decoder add-on card that connects to the "Feature Connector" found on older video cards, and then only if the device specifically requires this setting.
Parallel Port	This enables or disables the parallel (printer) port on your motherboard. Disable the parallel port—if your PC even has one—if you have a USB printer.
Parallel Port Mode	Use this to choose among the various parallel (printer) port modes: **ECP**, **EPP**, **ECP +EPP**, **Normal (SPP)**. In most cases, you'll want **ECP**; only choose one of the lesser options if you run into a compatibility problem. Note that such problems are more commonly caused by incorrect or faulty printer cables.
PEG Buffer Length	This sets the size of the packets sent to your PCI-Express graphics (PEG) card; in most cases, this should be set to **Auto**.

Setting	Description
PEG Force X1	Disable this in most cases. Enable this only if you've inserted a PCI-Express X1 card into your PCI-Express X16 slot, the slot normally used for a X16 video card.
PEG Link Latency	Set this to **Normal** or **Auto**; see "PEG Link Mode" for more information.
PEG Link Mode	Used to overclock your PCI-Express video card. Set to **Auto** to be on the safe side, or set to **Faster** for better performance at the risk of frying your video card.
PCI 2.1 Compliance	This should be enabled unless you have one or more PCI cards that are not compatible with the PCI 2.1 specification. Not applicable for PCI-Express slots.
PCI IDE BusMaster	See "IDE BusMaster."
PCI IRQ Assignment	This setting (usually a group of settings) allows you to assign IRQs to specific PCI slots.
PCI Latency Timer	This sets the number of cycles during which a single PCI device can monopolize the PCI bus. Increase this value for better performance, or decrease it if you run into problems. The default is typically 32 cycles, but you may have success with 64 or 128 cycles.
PCI Pipelining	Enable this to improve performance with your video adapter. Not applicable for PCI-Express slots.
Plug and Play OS/ PnP OS Installed	Enable this feature to have Windows manage your Plug-and-Play (PnP) devices, or disable it to have the BIOS manage PnP. This should be enabled.
PME Resume	See "Remote Wake Up."
Power Button Mode	This allows you to choose whether your computer's power button shuts off the computer (after holding it for four seconds) or forces your computer to enter a hibernate state. See "Start Windows Instantly (Almost)" on page 274, for related settings.
Power Lost Control	See "AC Power Recovery."
Power Management	This allows your operating system's APM (Advanced Power Management) feature to turn off the various devices in your system to save power. Enable this option for Windows 7.
Power On By...	See "Start Windows Instantly (Almost)" on page 274, for ways to use these settings to power on your PC.
Primary Display	Allows you to choose whether your PCI or AGP adapter is used as your primary display when using multiple video cards. Not applicable on systems with PCI-Express slots.
Primary IDE Master/Slave	Specify the type of drive connected to your primary IDE (Parallel ATA) controller, and set either as the "master" or "slave" (typically with a jumper). Sometimes this option also applies to SATA controllers.
Processor Serial Number	Enable this only if you want your operating system to be able to read the serial number of your processor. Since this can cause substantial security and privacy problems, this option should be disabled unless you specifically need it.

Setting	Description
Processor Speed	This is typically a read-only setting that shows the speed of your processor (in Mhz or Ghz). Some motherboards allow you to "overclock" your processor, forcing it to run faster than its rated speed.
Processor Type	This read-only setting tells you what type of processor is currently installed.
PS/2 Mouse Support	Use this to enable or disable your PS/2 mouse port. Disable this if you're using a USB mouse, and wish to free up IRQ 12 for another device.
PXE Resume	See "Remote Wake Up."
Quick Boot	Turn this on to skip the thorough, slow memory test performed when the computer is first turned on, allowing a faster boot. It's a good idea to disable this option and sit through the test when first installing new RAM, but once the memory has been tested, it's fine to set this option to **Enabled** to skip it.
Quiet Boot	A "quiet" boot is one where your motherboard manufacturer's logo is displayed on the screen instead of the details, such as the amount of memory, detected disks, and BIOS revision date. Disable this option (or press **Esc** while looking at the logo) to show this information.
Ratio	See "Overclocking."
Read-Around-Write	When this setting is enabled, your processor can read directly from the cache, without waiting for it to be written to memory first. Enable this feature for better performance.
Remote Wake Up	This feature allows your computer to be turned on a signal from another computer on your network. Disable this feature unless you specifically need this functionality. See "Start Windows Instantly (Almost)" on page 274, for details.
Repost Video on S3 Resume	When you wake your PC from the S3 Sleep state (see "Start Windows Instantly (Almost)" on page 274), your video card will be put through its self test if this option is enabled.
Reset Config Data	If enabled, the PnP subsystem will reset and reconfigure all of your PnP devices every time your system starts. Use this only if one or more devices needs to be reset to function.
Restore on AC Power Loss	See "AC Power Recovery."
SATA Configuration	If you're using SATA drives, then all your SATA settings should be enabled. But be careful adjusting these settings after you've installed Windows.
	For instance, the AHCI (Advanced Host Controller Interface) subsystem allows Windows to take advantage of the higher speeds and hot-plug features of SATA hard drives. In theory, you'll want to enable ACPI 2.0 support, but if you change this setting after installing Windows, you'll get a Blue Screen of Death (`INAC CESSABLE_BOOT_DEVICE`) the next time you boot. Microsoft offers a solution in KB article 922976, but it doesn't work. Instead, you'll need to reinstall Windows (see Chapter 1) if you change this setting.
SDRAM settings	See "DRAM settings."
Second Boot Device	See "Boot Device Priority/Boot Sequence."

Setting	Description
Secondary IDE Master/Slave	See "Primary IDE Master/Slave."
Serial Port 1/2 Serial Port A/B	The numbers (or letters) have no correlation to the well-known COM1/COM2 designations, but rather to each of the two physical ports on your motherboard. Set the ports as follows: "3F8/IRQ4" to assign the port to COM1, "2F8/IRQ3" for COM2, "3E8/IRQ4" for COM3, or "2E8/IRQ3 to make it COM4. Disable any port you're not using so it won't consume any resources you can use for other devices. Make sure the two ports don't conflict with each other, or any other devices in your system (such as your modem).
Slot Power	This allows your PC to provide your PCI-Express video card with the power it needs; in most cases, just set this to **Auto**.
Supervisor Password	This setting allows you to password-protect your BIOS setup. Note that if you forget the password (or simply wish to bypass such a restriction), just reset the BIOS configuration; this is typically done with a jumper, but can also be accomplished by disconnecting the motherboard battery for about 20 minutes.
Suspend Mode	Choose whether the computer is placed in Suspend or Hibernate power-saving modes; set to **Auto** if available. In most cases, you should use the settings in the Windows Control Panel instead.
Suspend Timeout	Specifies the number of minutes of inactivity before the system is placed in Suspend power-saving mode. In most cases, you should use the settings in the Windows Control Panel instead.
System BIOS Cacheable	This is similar to "Address Range Shadowing," except that it works with your motherboard's BIOS. Disable this option for best performance.
System Date/Time	Sets your computer's internal clock. This can also be changed in the Windows Control Panel.
System Keyboard	Disable this option if there's no keyboard attached.
System Memory	In most computers, this will be a read-only setting that displays the amount of installed RAM. However, as a holdover from older computers, you may have to enter the BIOS setup screen and then exit for the computer to recognize newly installed memory, even though you won't be able to directly modify this setting.
System Overheat Warning	Enable this to sound an alarm or flash a light if your computer's internal temperature exceeds the value set with the "Overheat Warning Temperature."
Third Boot Device	See "Boot Device Priority/Boot Sequence."
Typematic Rate/Delay	Faster settings will make your keyboard more responsive outside of Windows, but within Windows, these settings are overridden by those found in the Windows Control Panel.
USB Function	This enables or disables the USB ports on your motherboard. Since it's unlikely they'd conflict with anything else, you'll probably want to leave them all enabled. See "Legacy USB Support" for related settings.
VCORE Voltage	This is a read-only display indicating the output of your motherboard's voltage regulators.

Setting	Description
Video BIOS Shadow/Video BIOS Cacheable	This is similar to "Address Range Shadowing," except that it works with the BIOS of your video adapter. This is a holdover from early video cards, and should be disabled in any modern system.
Video Power Down	If enabled, your computer will be able to shut down your video card and monitor to save power. Typically, it's best to use the settings in the Windows Control Panel instead.
Video RAM Cacheable	This is similar to "Address Range Shadowing," except that it works with the memory installed on your video card. This option should always be disabled.
Virtualization Technology	This is a set of Intel extensions for hardware-assisted virtual machine management, used to improve performance for Virtual PC software.
Virus Warning	See "Anti-Virus Protection."
Wait for F1 if Error	If this option is disabled, your computer will continue to boot even if an error is found; otherwise, you'll have to press **F1** before the system will start. Such errors include a missing keyboard, a missing video adapter, and an unexpected quantity of installed memory. Enable this option if you want to know about every problem, or disable it if you want the PC to start without interruption (essential for servers).
Write combining	Enable this option for better video performance, but disable it if you encounter video corruption or system crashes.

TCP/IP Ports

When your web browser or email program connects to another computer on the Internet, it does so through a TCP/IP port. If you have a web server or FTP server running on your PC, it opens a port through which other computers can connect to those services. Port numbers are used to distinguish one network service from another.

Mostly, this is done behind the scenes. However, knowing which programs use a specific port number becomes important when you starting considering security. A firewall uses ports to form its rules about which types of network traffic to allow, and which to prohibit. And the Active Connections utility (*netstat.exe*), used to determine which ports are currently in use, allows you to uncover vulnerabilities in your system using ports. Ports, firewalls, and the Active Connections utility are all discussed in Chapter 7.

Some firewalls make a distinction between TCP (Transmission Control Protocol) and UDP (User Datagram Protocol) ports, which is typically unnecessary. In most cases, programs that use the more common TCP protocol will use the same port numbers as their counterparts that use the less-reliable UDP protocol.

Ports are divided into three ranges:

Well-known ports: 0-1023
Registered ports: 1024-49151
Dynamic and/or private ports: 49152-65535

Since a complete listing of known ports would consume about a hundred pages of this book, only the most commonly used ports are listed here. For a more complete listing, see any of these resources:

http://www.iana.org/assignments/port-numbers
http://www.faqs.org/rfcs/rfc1700.html
http://en.wikipedia.org/wiki/list_of_tcp_and_udp_port_numbers

Table B-1 lists the more commonly used TCP/IP ports.

 Those ports marked with an *X* in Table B-1 are commonly exploited by worms and other types of remote attacks. Unless you specifically need them, you should block them in your firewall or router.

Table B-1. Commonly used TCP/IP ports and how they're used

Port number	Description
20–21	FTP (File Transfer Protocol)
22	SSH (Secure Shell)
23	Telnet
25	SMTP (Simple Mail Transfer Protocol), used for sending email
42	WINS (Windows Internet Name Service)
43	WhoIs
50–51	IPSec (PPTP Passthrough for VPN, Virtual Private Networking)
53	DNS (Domain Name Server), used for looking up domain names
67	DHCP (Dynamic Host Configuration Protocol)
69 *X*	TFTP
70	Gopher
79	Finger
80	HTTP (Hyper Text Transfer Protocol), used by web browsers to download standard web pages
110	POP3 (Post Office Protocol, version 3), used for retrieving email
119	NNTP (Network News Transfer Protocol), used for newsgroups
123	NTP (Network Time Protocol), used for Windows' Internet Time feature
135 *X*	RPC (Microsoft Windows Remote Procedure Call)
137–139 *X*	NETBIOS Services
143	IMAP4 (Internet Mail Access Protocol version 4)
161–162	SNMP (Simple Network Management Protocol)
194	IRC (Internet Relay Chat)

Port number	Description
220	IMAP3 (Internet Mail Access Protocol version 3)
443	HTTPS (HTTP over TLS/SSL), used by web browsers to download secure web pages
445 *X*	Active Directory, file sharing for Microsoft Windows networks (445 UDP used for SMB/Samba)
500	IPSec (PPTP Passthrough for VPN, Virtual Private Networking)
514	RSH (Remote Shell)
531	AOL Instant Messenger (AIM)
554	RTSP (Real Time Streaming Protocol), used for streaming audio and video
563	NNTPS (Network News Transfer Protocol over SSL), used for secure newsgroups
593 *X*	RPC (Microsoft Windows Remote Procedure Call) over HTTP
691	Microsoft Exchange Routing
750	Kerberos IV email authenticating agent
989–990	FTP over SSL (secure File Transfer Protocol)
992	Telnet over SSL (secure Telnet)
993	IMAP4 over SSL (secure Internet Mail Access Protocol version 4)
995	POP3 over SSL (secure Post Office Protocol, version 3)
1026 *X*	Windows Messenger—pop ups (spam)
1194	OpenVPN
1214 *X*	Kazaa peer-to-peer file sharing
1270	Microsoft Operations Manager 2005 agent (MOM 2005)
1352	Lotus Notes/Domino mail routing
1433–1434	Microsoft SQL database system, monitor
1503	Windows Messenger—application sharing and whiteboard
1512	WINS (Windows Internet Name Service)
1701	VPN (Virtual Private Networking) over L2TP
1723	VPN (Virtual Private Networking) over PPTP
1755	MMS (Microsoft Media Services) for Windows Media Player
1812–1813	RADIUS authentication protocol
1863	Windows Live Messenger—instant messaging
1900	Microsoft SSDP Enables discovery of UPnP devices
3074	Xbox Live (Microsoft gaming console)
3306	MySQL database
3389	Remote Desktop Sharing (Microsoft Terminal Services), used for remote control
4444 *X*	W32.BLASTER.WORM virus

Port number	Description
5004 and up	Windows Messenger—audio and video conferencing (port is chosen dynamically)
5010	Yahoo! Messenger
5190	AOL Instant Messenger
5631, 5632	pcAnywhere, used for remote control
5800, 5801 5900, 5901	VNC (Virtual Network Computing), used for remote control
6699	Peer-to-peer file sharing, used by Napster-like programs
6891–6901	Windows Live Messenger—file transfer, voice
6881–6999	BitTorrent peer-to-peer file transfer clients

Index

We'd like to hear your suggestions for improving our indexes. Send email to *index@oreilly.com.*

About the Author

David A. Karp is the author of 12 power-user books, including the bestselling Windows Annoyances series of books and O'Reilly's *eBay Hacks*. David's books are available in 10 languages, and can be found under the short legs of tables around the world.

David is the founder of Annoyances.org, one of the most respected and popular computer help sites on the Interwebs. He writes for *PC Magazine*, but it's curiously reluctant to publish photos of his bicycle. Notable recognition has come from *PC Computing*, *Windows Magazine*, the *San Francisco Examiner*, and the *New York Times*.

He scored 30.96647% on the Geek Test (*http://www.innergeek.us/*), earning a rating of "Total Geek." He hopes future revisions of the test reward publishing his score in the backs of computer books. David spends nearly every spare moment with his son.

Colophon

The animal on the cover of *Windows 7 Annoyances* is the Central American turkey (*Meleagris ocellata*), known today as an ocellated turkey. The spots on its tail feathers, similar to those of a peacock, give the bird its name (from the Latin *oculus* for eye). The range of the ocellated turkey is limited; about 50,000 square miles in Mexico's Yucatan Peninsula, Guatemala, and Belize.

The coloring of the ocellated turkey is extremely vivid. The bird has a blue head with prominent orange or red warts. The body plumage is an iridescent mixture of bronze and green, with copper and white barring on the wings. Their tail feathers are bluish-gray, with blue copper-tipped eyespots. The legs are bright red. This species is smaller than North American turkeys—males weigh 10–12 pounds and females 6–7 pounds.

The ocellated turkey has a wide diet of grasses, leaves, seeds, berries, nuts, and insects. They typically roost in trees at night, but spend the rest of their time on the ground. The bird requires a mixture of forest and grassy clearings for its habitat. The clearings are particularly important during mating season, when the male turkeys will strut, gobble, display their tail feathers, and walk circles around females in the hope of breeding. The chicks that hatch 28 days later are precocial, able to leave the nest and hunt insects within one day.

The cover image is from *Riverside Natural History*. The cover font is Adobe ITC Garamond. The text font is Linotype Birka; the heading font is Adobe Myriad Condensed; and the code font is LucasFont's TheSansMono Condensed.

Buy this book and get access to the online edition for 45 days—for free!

Tips, Secrets, and Hacks for the Cranky Consumer

Windows 7 Annoyances

O'REILLY®

David A. Karp

Windows 7 Annoyances

By David A. Karp
April 2010, $39.99
ISBN 9780596157623

With Safari Books Online, you can:

Access the contents of thousands of technology and business books

- Quickly search over 7000 books and certification guides
- Download whole books or chapters in PDF format, at no extra cost, to print or read on the go
- Copy and paste code
- Save up to 35% on O'Reilly print books
- **New!** Access mobile-friendly books directly from cell phones and mobile devices

Stay up-to-date on emerging topics before the books are published

- Get on-demand access to evolving manuscripts.
- Interact directly with authors of upcoming books

Explore thousands of hours of video on technology and design topics

- Learn from expert video tutorials
- Watch and replay recorded conference sessions

To try out Safari and the online edition of this book FREE for 45 days,
go to *www.oreilly.com/go/safarienabled* and enter the coupon code SHRTOXA.
To see the complete Safari Library, visit safari.oreilly.com.

O'REILLY®

Spreading the knowledge of innovators   safari.oreilly.com

CPSIA information can be obtained at www.ICGtesting.com
Printed in the USA
265869BV00011B/23/P